D1740846

CYCLEWAY
COMPANION

EDITORS
TIM STILWELL, MARTIN DOWLING

STILWELL

Publishing Ltd

Distributed in Great Britain, Europe & the Commonwealth by Orca Book Services, Stanley House, 3 Fleets Lane, Poole, Dorset BH15 3AJ (Tel: 01202 665432) and available from all good bookshops. Distributed in North America by Seven Hills Book Distributors, 1531 Tremont Street, Cincinatti, OH 45214, USA (Tel: 513 471 4311).

ISBN 1-900861-18-6.

Published by Stilwell Publishing Ltd,
59 Charlotte Road, Shoreditch, London, EC2A 3QW.
Tel: 020-7739 7179. Fax: 020-7739 7191. E-mail: tim@stilwell.co.uk

© Stilwell Publishing Ltd, March 2000 (unless otherwise stated).

All maps in this book have been copied from pre-1948 mapping showing the National Grid.

All rights reserved. No part of this publication may be reproduced, stored in a retrieval system, or transmitted in any form or by any means - electronic, mechanical, photocopying, or otherwise - unless the written permission of the Publisher has been given beforehand.

Stilwell Publishing Ltd:
Editor: Tim Stilwell
Assistant Editor: Martin Dowling

Design and Maps: Nigel Simpson

Printed in the Channel Islands by the Guernsey Press Company, Guernsey, Channel Islands.

All the information in this directory is published in good faith on the basis of details provided to Stilwell Publishing Ltd by the owners of the premises listed. Stilwell Publishing Ltd accepts no responsibility for any consequences arising from any errors, omissions or misrepresentations from information so provided. Any liability for loss or damage caused by information so provided, or in the event of cessation of trade of any company, individual or firm mentioned, is hereby excluded.

Key to Entries

🐎 Children welcome (from age shown in brackets, if specified)

🅿 Off-street car parking (number of places shown in brackets)

⚊ No smoking

📺 Television (either in every room or in a TV lounge)

🐕 Pets accepted (by prior arrangement)

✗ Evening meal available (by prior arrangement)

Ⓥ Special diets catered for (by prior arrangement - please check with owner to see if your particular requirements are catered for)

▦ Central heating throughout

♿ Suitable for disabled people (please check with owner to see what level of disability is provided for)

❄ Christmas breaks a speciality

☕ Coffee/tea making facilities

▲ Youth Hostel

⌂ Camping Barn

🍴 Packed lunches available

∥ Drying facilities for wet clothes and boots

🚲 Safe cycle storage

The location heading - every hamlet, village, town and city mentioned in this directory is represented on the path map within each section.

Use the National Grid reference with Ordnance Survey maps and atlases. The letter(s) refer to a 100 kilometre grid square. The first two numbers refer to a North/South grid line and the last two numbers refer to an East/West grid line. The grid reference indicates their intersection point.

Penny Hassett   12

National Grid Ref: PH2096.

🍴 🍺 Cat & Fiddle, The Bull

These are the names of nearby pubs and restaurants that serve food in the evening, as suggested by local B&Bs.

The Old Rectory, Main Street, Penny Hassett, Borchester, Borsetshire, BC2 3QT.
C18th former rectory, lovely garden.
Grades: ETC 3 Diamond
Tel: **01048 598464** Mrs Smythe.
D: £18.00-£22.00 **S:** £20.00-£27.50
Open: All Year
Beds: 1F 1D 1T
Baths: 1 Pr 2 Sh
🐎(4) 🅿(2) ⚊ 📺 🐕 ✗ ▦ Ⓥ ♿ ❄ ☕ 🚲

D = Price range per person sharing in a double room

S = Price range for a single person in a room

Bedrooms
F = Family
D = Double
T = Twin
S = Single

Bathrooms
En = Ensuite
Pr = Private
Sh = Shared

Grades - The English Tourism Council (**ETC**) grades B&Bs for quality in Diamonds (1 Diamond to 5 Diamond, highest) and hotels in Stars (1 Star to 5 Star). Bord Failte (**BF**, the Irish Tourist Board) grades guest houses in Stars (1 Star to 4 Star); the Northern Ireland Tourist Board (**NITB**) rates them as Grade A (higher) or B. Both grade hotels in Stars (1 Star to 5 Star). Both Tourist Boards for Ireland inspect B&B accommodation annually - such premises are entitled to show that they have been approved (**Approv**). Scottish and Welsh Tourist Board (**STB** and **WTB**) grades have two parts: the Star rating is for quality (1 Star to 5 Star, highest), the other part designates the type of establishment, e.g. B&B, Guest House (**GH**), Country House (**CH**) etc. Ask at Tourist Information Centres for further information on these systems. The Automobile Association (**AA**) and Royal Automobile Club (**RAC**) both use, throughout the British-Irish Isles, the same system of Diamonds and Stars as the English Tourism Council.

Contents

Introduction   vi-ix

Path Locations & Map   x-xi

SUSTRANS NATIONAL CYCLE NETWORK ROUTES

Carlisle to Inverness   .   2-26

Clyde to Forth   28-37

Devon Coast to Coast   38-47

Hull to Harwich   48-63

Kingfisher Cycle Trail   64-69

Lon Las Cymru   70-89

Sea to Sea (C2C)   90-102

Severn & Thames   104-112

West Country Way   114-129

White Rose Cycle Route   130-139

REGIONAL ROUTES

Round Berkshire Cycle Route   140-145

Cheshire Cycleway   146-150

Cumbria Cycleway   152-163

Essex Cycle Route   164-171

Icknield Way   172-176

Lancashire Cycleway   178-185

Leicestershire County Cycle Route   186-192

Oxfordshire Cycleway   194-205

Reivers Cycle Route   206-213

South Downs Way   214-223

Surrey Cycleway   224-229

Wiltshire Cycleway   230-237

Yorkshire Dales Cycleway   238-246

Introduction

Several years ago, my wife and I set out to walk one of Britain's National Trails, the North Downs Way over several weekends. Neither of us are born to camping, nor could we afford to stay in expensive hotels. We decided on B&Bs and found a problem straightaway. One could not find good value bed and breakfast accommodation along the route without going to a lot of trouble. Local libraries, directory enquiries, six different Tourist Information Centres and a large pile of brochures yielded nothing but a hotchpotch of B&B addresses, most of them miles out of our way. We abandoned the research and did the walk in one-day stretches, high-tailing it back to our London home each evening on the train.

The point is that we didn't really want to take the train back, especially when the time spent in waiting and travelling matched the time spent walking. A good weekend's walk would have been ideal, but we didn't know where to stay. The Law of Sod dictates that wherever you choose to finish your day's walking, there is either nothing in sight or a large country house hotel charging £100 for a one night stay. The train proved the logical option.

We therefore went on to create and publish a book called the *National Trail Companion* which publishes accommodation details for footpaths in the order that they appear along a path. Three years later, in 1998, the *Cycleway Companion* was launched, arranged along similar lines – for cyclists travelling along recognised cycle routes.

Long distance cycleways have become very popular over the last decade or so. County councils in particular have seen cycleways as a means of promoting tourism in the further-flung parts of their county. The Sustrans initiative has used the leisure-based cycle route as a flagship for their more wide-reaching campaign for sustainable transport. The travel pages of our weekend newspapers regularly feature cycle breaks at home and abroad. The popularity of mountain biking and off-road cycling is clear; they even have their own specialist magazines. All in all, there are three times as many people cycling for their holiday than there were 20 years ago.

So when a man from Cornwall telephoned us in 1997 to ask us whether we could bring out an accommodation book that catered for cyclists rather than for walkers, we finally jumped at the challenge. He had been the umpteenth person to ask us such a question that year. Here is the result, now in its second edition. 23 long distance cycle routes are featured in this book. They fall into two categories. The county cycleways are way-marked routes set up by the relevant county council. Only 9 counties and one National Park so far have had the imagination to set up their own cycleways. These routes are all waymarked except for those in Leicestershire (devised before the split with Rutland) and Essex.

The Sustrans routes are part of the widely-publicised National Cycle Network, supported by the Bristol-based Sustrans organisation. The National Cycle Network was one of the first projects to win financial backing from the Millennium Commission – a cool £42,500,000 up to the year 2000. Sustrans' objective is principally environmental: to create 7,000 miles of cycle routes with common standards in partnership with local government. The Sustrans routes shown here are conceived as leisure routes. In fact, Sustrans is at pains to point out that cycling is not just a leisure activity. It is a sustainable means of transport which does not rely on a finite resource – oil – and which produces no air pollution, no traffic jams, no billion-pound road schemes and no scrap disposal problems. In every sense, cycling costs less than motoring. Sustrans therefore has a loftier aim than happier holiday-making: it is to get us all out of automobiles and onto bicycles. This will not happen if there are no safe places to cycle – hence Sustrans' far-sighted and dedicated work in devising these routes. Sustrans also advise on and initiate civil engineering projects with local government to smooth the way further for the bicycle.

The *Cycleway Companion* does not attempt to tell the reader where to turn left or right, how far it is to the next stop or the steepness of the hills. This we leave to the admirable maps and guides already on the market (each chapter introduction tells you where to get hold of these). Instead, this book offers logistical help – where to stay and where to find pubs that serve evening meals along each route. It's my contention that once you've done one long distance cycle route, you want to do another, perhaps over a series of weekends rather than in one fell swoop. Planning and plotting the accommodation for such a journey is usually a long-winded affair. You have to ring Tourist Information Centres, wait for their literature, and then match unknown place-names to your mapped route. With this *Cycleway Companion* you can happily work out where to stay without the hassle, leaving you longer to devise a more extensive itinerary en route.

All information published in these pages has been collected over one year and provided by the owners themselves. The vast majority offer bed and breakfast at well under £27.50 per person per night, which we consider near the limit a cyclist would wish to pay. The pink highlight boxes are advertisements. Once again, we should make it clear that inclusion in these pages does not imply personal recommendation – we have not visited them all, merely written to them or phoned them. A simple glance over the salient details on any page, however, and the reader will be his or her own guide.

Owners were asked to provide their range of rates per person per night for the year in question. The rates are thus forecasts and are in any case always subject to fluctuation in demand. Of course, some information may already be out of date. Grades may go up or down, or be removed altogether. British Telecom may alter exchange numbers. Proprietors may decide on a whim to move out of the business altogether. That is why the *Cycleway Companion* has to be a yearbook; in general, though, the information published here will be accurate, pertinent and useful for a long time to come.

One of the most important considerations for any cyclist planning a night's rest at a hostel or B&B is 'how far off the route is it?' Our concern has been, of course, to research Youth Hostels and B&Bs that are at least close to a given route; the reader can gauge at a glance how far one village is from the route compared with another. The accommodation lists are published in the order in which they appear along the path. We have numbered the locations to make cross-referencing easier.

We have also included pubs and inns that serve food in the evenings. For many cyclists, the promise of an evening meal will be of prime importance in deciding where to stay. These pubs have been suggested as decent places to eat by the B&B owners themselves – we publish them here so that you know you'll have something to fall back on if that B&B doesn't serve dinner itself. The direction in which the locations are listed is determined by popular choice and not by personal preference. If you wish to cycle the C2C from East to West or the Lon Las Cymru from Holyhead to Cardiff, then you will simply have to flick backwards through the chapter's pages rather than forwards. As far as mapping is concerned, I have omitted giving Landranger map numbers, except in the introduction to each path. The Ordnance Survey's national grid references are more important; to this end we have indicated grid labels and lines at the edge of each map.

Throughout the book you will find boxes offering advice to cyclists staying at B&Bs. Some of you may think these a waste of time and in fact, they are partly a publishing trick. They fill space and tidy the page up. But we really have heard horror stories about all sorts of guests from B&B owners, mainly concerning disregard for other people's property. Much of this is done through thoughtlessness and not by intent. If a few words can remind someone of his or her obligations, then these boxes, however self-important, will have done the trick.

Tim Stilwell
Stoke Newington, March 2000

Cycleway Locations

SUSTRANS NATIONAL CYCLE NETWORK ROUTES

Carlisle to Inverness   1

Clyde to Forth   2

Devon Coast to Coast   3

Hull to Harwich   4

Kingfisher Cycle Trail   5

Lon Las Cymru   6

Sea to Sea (C2C)   7

Severn & Thames   8

West Country Way   9

White Rose Cycle Route   10

REGIONAL ROUTES

Round Berkshire Cycle Route   11

Cheshire Cycleway   12

Cumbria Cycleway   13

Essex Cycle Route   14

Icknield Way   15

Lancashire Cycleway   16

Leicestershire County Cycle Route   17

Oxfordshire Cycleway   18

Reivers Cycle Route   19

South Downs Way   20

Surrey Cycleway   21

Wiltshire Cycleway   22

Yorkshire Dales Cycleway   23

Sustrans Carlisle to Inverness

At 402 miles, this massive crossing of Scotland from south to north is the longest route featured in this book. The **Scottish National Cycle Route** is a section of the planned Inverness to Dover route, the backbone of the new UK National Cycle Network. It runs on traffic-free paths and traffic-calmed roads from the English border city of Carlisle through the western Lowlands and Galloway Forest Park to Ayr on the west coast before reaching Glasgow, Scotland's metropolis. The northern section of the way will take you down the north bank of the Clyde Estuary to Dumbarton and the southern shore of Loch Lomond before you strike out into the varied and truly breathtaking scenery of the Scottish Highlands, from Loch Venachar to Loch Tay and across the Drumochter Pass, continuing through Strathspey below the Cairngorms to Inverness on the Moray Firth. The route is signposted by blue direction signs with a cycle silhouette and the number 7 in a red rectangle.

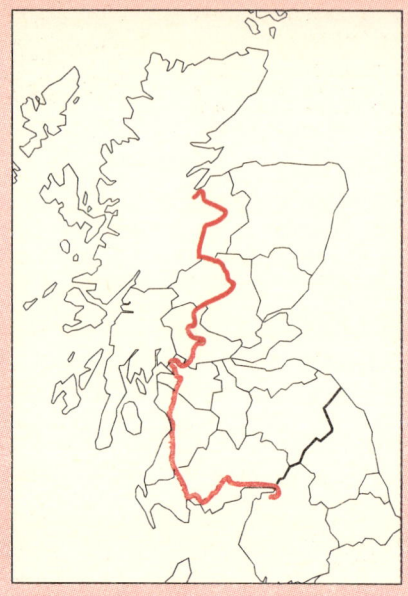

The indispensable **official route map and guide** for the Scottish National Cycle Route, which includes listings of cycle repair/hire shops along the route, comes in two parts, *Carlisle to Glasgow* and *Glasgow to Inverness*, and is available from Sustrans, 35 King Street, Bristol BS1 4DZ, tel 0117-926 8893, fax 0117-929 4173, @ £5.99 each (+ £1.50 p&p for both together or either one).

Maps: Ordnance Survey 1:50,000 Landranger series: 26, 27, 35, 36, 42, 43, 51, 52, 57, 63, 64, 70, 76, 77, 83, 84, 85

Transport: Carlisle, Glasgow and Inverness are all main termini on the Intercity network. There are connections to numerous other places on or near the route.

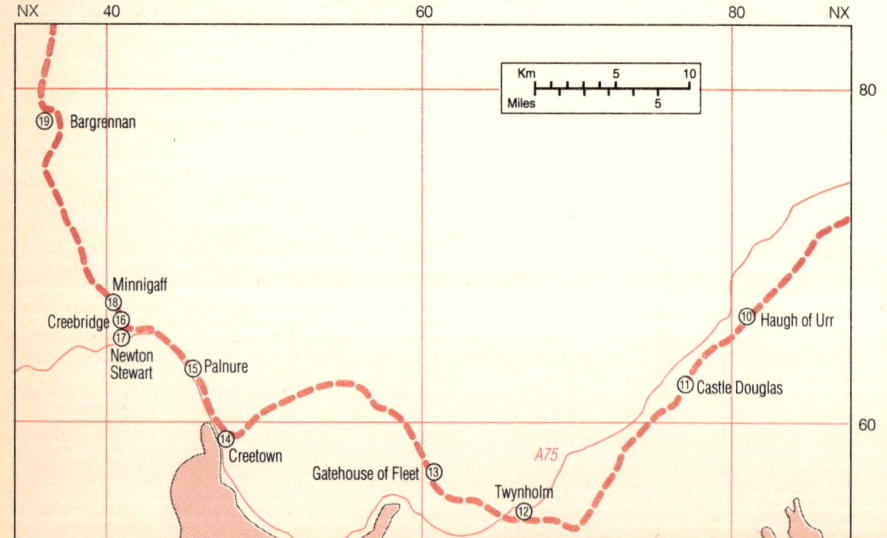

Carlisle 1

National Grid Ref: NY3955

🍴 🍺 Metal Bridge Inn, The Beehive, Mary's Pantry, Crown & Thistle, Coach & Horses, Golden Fleece, Black Lion

▲ *Carlisle Youth Hostel,*
University of Northumbria, The
Old Brewery Residences, Bridge
Lane, Caldegate, Carlisle,
Cumbria, CA2 5SR.
Actual grid ref: NY394560
Tel: 01228 597352. After 6pm:
01228 59486
Under 18: £12.00
Adults: £12.00
suitable for disabled people,
self-catering facilities, showers,
laundry facilities
Accommodation in an
award-winning conversion of the
former Theakston's brewery. Single
study bedrooms with shared
kitchen and bathroom in flats for
upto 7 people

Howard Lodge, 90 Warwick Road,
Carlisle, Cumbria, CA1 1JU.
Actual grid ref: NY407558
Grades: ETC 4 Diamond,
AA 3 Diamond
Tel: 01228 529842
Mr Hendrie.
D: £15.00-£25.00.
S: £20.00-£30.00.
Open: All Year
Beds: 2F 1D 2T 1S
Baths: 6 En 1 Sh
🛇 🅿 (6) 🖵 🏃 ✗ 🍽 💺 📺 🛡 ⚡ ♻
Friendly family-run guest house in
comfortable Victorian town house
in conservation area. Spacious
rooms all fully ensuite with
satellite TV, welcome tray,
hairdryer and clock radio. Large
breakfasts. 5 minutes' walk from
station and city centre. Evening
meals by prior arrangement.
Private car park

Craighead, 6 Hartington Place,
Carlisle, Cumbria, CA1 1HL.
Actual grid ref: NY405559
Grades: ETC 3 Diamond
Tel: 01228 596767 Mrs Smith.
D: £16.50 **S:** £16.50.
Open: All Year (not Xmas)
Beds: 1F 2D 1T 1S
Baths: 1 En 2 Sh
🛇 🖵 ✗ 💺 📺 🛡 ♻ 🚲
You will receive a warm welcome
at Craighead a grade II Listed
spacious Victorian town house with
comfortable rooms and original
features. CTV tea/coffee tray in all
rooms. Minutes' walk to city centre
bus and rail stations and all
amenities. Friendly personal
service

Angus Hotel & Almonds Bistro,
14 Scotland Road, Stanwix,
Carlisle, Cumbria, CA3 9DG.
Actual grid ref: NY400571
Grades: AA 4 Diamond
Tel: 01228 523546/0800 026 2046
Mr Webster. Fax no: 01228 531895
D: £20.00-£27.00 **S:** £26.00-£42.00.
Open: All Year
Beds: 4F 3D 4T 3S
Baths: 11 En 3 Sh
🛇 🅿 (6) 🖵 🏃 ✗ 💺 📺 🛡 🛡 ⚡ ♻
Victorian town house, foundations
on Hadrian's Wall. Excellent food,
Les Routiers Awards, local
cheeses, home baked bread.
Genuine warm welcome from
owners. Licensed, draught beer,
lounge, meeting room, internet
cafe, direct dial telephones, secure
garaging

All rates are subject to alteration at the owners' discretion.

Chatsworth Guest House,
22 Chatsworth Square, Carlisle,
Cumbria, CA1 1HF.
City centre Grade II Listed
building, close to shops, cathedral,
castle, all amenities
Grades: ETC 3 Diamond
Tel: 01228 524023 (also fax no)
Mrs Mackin.
D: £17.00-£22.00
S: £20.00-£26.00.
Open: All Year (not Xmas)
Beds: 1F 1D 3T 1S
Baths: 2 En 1 Sh
🛇 (2) ✗ 🖵 💺 📺 🛡

Avondale, 3 St Aidans Road,
Carlisle, Cumbria, CA1 1LT.
Attractive comfortable Edwardian
house. Quiet central position
convenient M6 J43
Grades: ETC 4 Diamond
RAC 4 Diamond
Tel: 01228 523012 (also fax no)
Mr & Mrs Hayes.
D: £20.00-£20.00 **S:** £20.00-£40.00.
Open: All Year (not Xmas)
Beds: 1D 2T
Baths: 1 En 1 Pr
🛇 🅿 (3) ✗ 🖵 ✗ 💺 📺 🛡 🛡 ⚡ ♻

Corner House Hotel & Bar,
4 Grey Street, Carlisle, CA1 2JP.
Grades: ETC 3 Diamond
Tel: 01228 533239
Mrs Anderson.
Fax no: 01228 546628
D: £17.50-£21.00 **S:** £25.00-£30.00.
Open: All Year
Beds: 3F 4D 4T 3S
Baths: 10 En
🛇 🖵 🏃 ✗ 💺 📺 ♿ 📺 🛡 🛡 ⚡ ♻
Small, friendly, licensed hotel. 10
mins to city centre attraction, bar,
large TV, lounge and games room.
Excellent base for golf, walking,
horse-riding, swimming, cycling or
touring by car, bus or train, the
lakes, Roman Wall or border
region

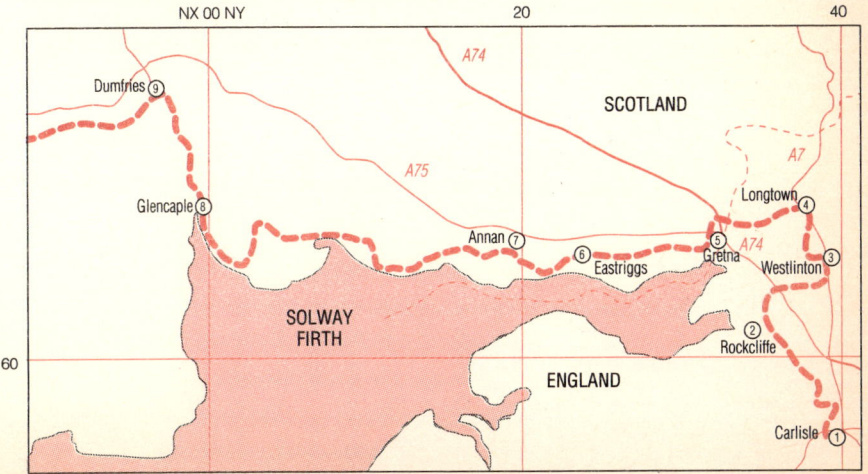

Courtfield Guest House,
*169 Warwick Road, Carlisle,
Cumbria, CA1 1LP.*
Short walk to historic city centre.
Close to M6, J43
Grades: ETC 4 Diamond
Tel: 01228 522767
Mrs Dawes.
D: £17.50-£20.00 **S:** £20.00.
Open: All Year (not Xmas)
Beds: 1F 2D 2T
Baths: 5 En
🛇 🅿 (4) ⅍ 🛏 🎂 🖳 Ⅳ ♿

East View Guest House,
*110 Warwick Road, Carlisle,
Cumbria, CA1 1JU.*
Actual grid ref: NY407560
10 minutes' walking distance from
city centre, railway station and
restaurants
Grades: ETC 2 Diamond
Tel: 01228 522112 (also fax no)
Mrs Glease.
D: £18.00-£20.00 **S:** £20.00-£25.00.
Open: All Year (not Xmas)
Beds: 3F 2D 1T 1S
Baths: 7 En
🛇 🅿 (4) ⅍ 🛏 🎂 🖳 Ⅳ ♿

Cherry Grove, *87 Petteril Street,
Carlisle, Cumbria, CA1 2AW.*
Lovely red brick building close to
golf club and town
Grades: AA 3 Diamond
Tel: 01228 541942
Mr & Mrs Houghton.
D: £17.50-£20.00 **S:** £20.00-£30.00.
Open: All Year
Beds: 3F 2D
Baths: 5 En
🛇 🅿 (3) ⅍ 🛏 🎂 🖳 Ⅳ 🛇 ♿

Cornerways Guest House,
*107 Warwick Road, Carlisle,
Cumbria, CA1 1EA.*
Large Victorian town house
Grades: ETC 4 Diamond
Tel: 01228 521733
Mrs Fisher.
D: £14.00-£18.00
S: £16.00-£18.00.
Open: All Year (not Xmas)
Beds: 2F 1D 4T 3S
Baths: 2 En 2 Sh
🛇 🅿 (4) 🞐 🛏 🎂 🖳 Ⅳ 🛇 ♿

Cambro House, *173 Warwick
Road, Carlisle, CA1 1LP.*
Grades: AA 3 Diamond
Tel: 01228 543094 (also fax no)
Mr & Mrs Mawson.
D: £17.00-£20.00
S: £20.00-£25.00.
Open: All Year
Beds: 2D 1T
Baths: 3 En
🅿 (2) 🞐 🛏 🖳 Ⅳ 🛇 ♿
Guests can expect warm hospitality
and friendly service at this
attractively decorated and
well-maintained guest house. Each
ensuite bedroom includes TV,
clock, radio, hairdryer and
welcome tray. Private off-road
parking available, non-smoking,
close to golf course

Kingstown Hotel, *246 Kingstown
Road, Carlisle, CA3 0DE.*
Grades: AA 3 Diamond
Tel: 01228 515292 (also fax no)
D: £18.50-£22.00. **S:** £29.00-£36.00.
Open: All Year (not Xmas)
Beds: 1F 5D 1T **Baths:** 7 En
🛇 🅿 (10) 🖵 🛏 🗙 🎂 🖳 ♿ Ⅳ ♿
Situated on the A7, only quarter
mile from M6 (J44), our small
family-run hotel offers weary
travellers comfortable
accommodation and a cosy lounge
bar in which to unwind. An ideal
base to explore historic Carlisle,
Hadrian's Wall and the Lake
District

Whitelea Guest House,
*191 Warwick Road, Carlisle,
CA1 1LP.*
Good base for lakes and Hadrian's
Wall. Friendly, family run
Tel: 01228 533139 Croskery.
D: £15.00-£18.00 **S:** £15.00-£18.00.
Open: All Year
Beds: 2F 1T 1S
🛇 🅿 🖵 🛏 🗙 🎂 🖳 Ⅳ ♿ 🛇

The Foxgloves, *73 Scotland Road,
Carlisle, Cumbria, CA3 9HL.*
Family-run elegant Victorian town
house, very suitable for Roman
Wall walkers
Tel: 01228 526365 Mrs Apcar.
D: £15.00 **S:** £15.00.
Open: All Year
Beds: 2T 1S
🛇 🖵 🛏 🎂 🖳 Ⅳ ♿

D = Price range per person
sharing in a double room

Pay B&Bs by
cash or cheque and
be prepared to
pay up front.

Howard House, *27 Howard Place,
Carlisle, Cumbria, CA1 1HR.*
Actual grid ref: NY407559
Elegant Victorian town house, 5
minutes' walk to city centre
Tel: 01228 529159
Mrs Fisher.
Fax no: 01228 512550
D: £16.00 **S:** £16.00.
Open: All Year
Beds: 2F 3D 3T
Baths: 2 Pr 2 Sh
🛇 🖵 🛏 🗙 🎂 🖳 Ⅳ 🛇 ♿

Rockcliffe 2

National Grid Ref: NY3561

🍴 🍺 Metal Bridge Inn

Metal Bridge House, *Metal
Bridge, Rockcliffe, Carlisle,
Cumbria, CA6 4HG.*
Actual grid ref: NY356649
In country, close to M6/A74,
quality accommodation, friendly
welcome
Grades: ETC 3 Diamond
Tel: 01228 674695 Mr Rae.
D: £16.00-£18.00 **S:** £20.00-£22.00.
Open: All Year (not Xmas)
Beds: 1D 2T
Baths: 1 Sh
🛇 🅿 (6) 🞐 🛏 🎂 🖳 Ⅳ ♿ 🛇

Carlisle to Dumfries

From the city centre of **Carlisle** (see the *Cumbria Cycleway*),
the route proceeds to Rockcliffe on the Eden Estuary and
Longtown on the Esk before crossing The Border to reach
Gretna Green, the renowned border village whose Old Smithy
was, during the eighteenth and nineteenth centuries, the site of
numerous clandestine marriages of English people, in whose
country marriage was the exclusive provenance of the Church.
Heading west along the Solway Firth you reach **Annan** and
then the village of Ruthwell, whose church houses a towering
magnificently carved seventh-century cross. A little way further,
Caerlaverock Castle is a beautiful thirteenth-century ruin built of
pink stone, with a twin-towered gatehouse and surrounded by a
moat. The nearby Wildfowl and Wetland Centre shelters bird
species including the barnacle goose. Cycling up the beautiful
Nith Estuary you reach the Queen of the South, **Dumfries**,
much of which is built in the local red sandstone. Here beneath
the neoclassical columns of his mausoleum in St Michael's
Churchyard lies Robert Burns, who lived in Dumfries for the last
five years of his life. The Burns House has a collection of his
paraphernalia and the Robert Burns Centre, located in a
converted water mill, is a themed museum, with a cafe.

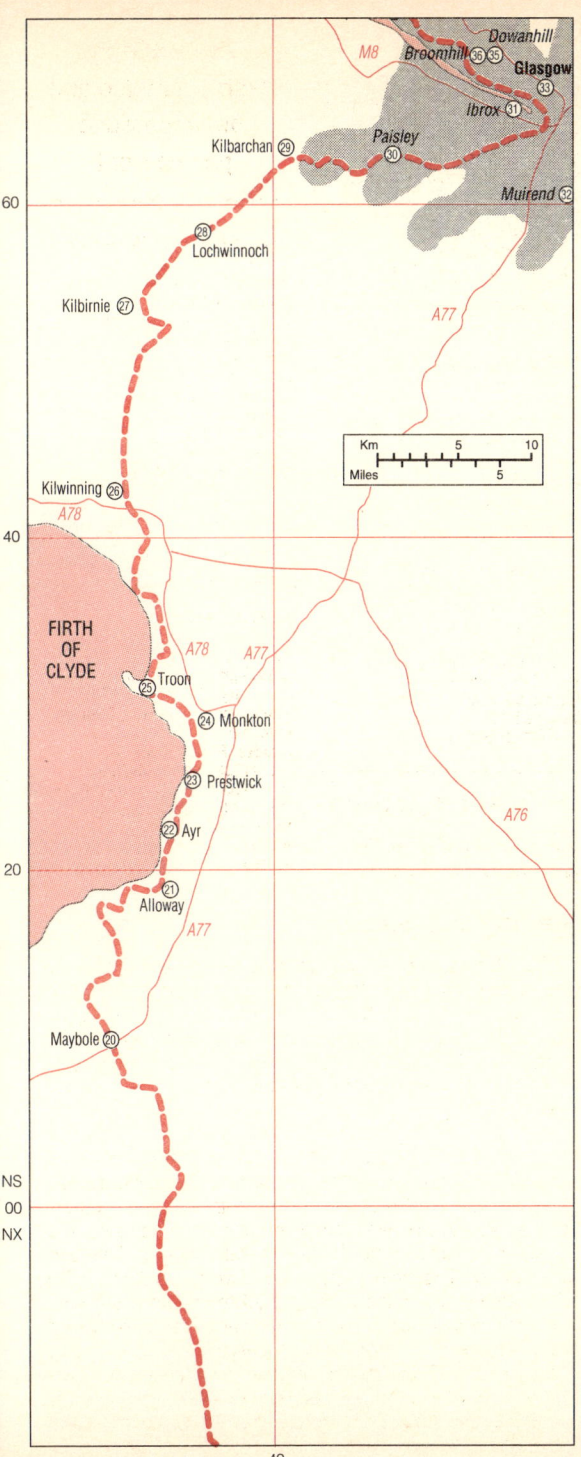

Westlinton 3

National Grid Ref: NY3964

Lynebank*, Westlinton, Carlisle, Cumbria, CA6 6AA.*
Family-run, excellent food, ideal stop for England/Scotland journey
Grades: ETC 4 Diamond
Tel: **01228 792820** (also fax no)
Mrs Butler.
D: £18.00-£22.00
S: £20.00-£24.00.
Open: All Year
Beds: 2F 3D 1T 3S
Baths: 9 En
🛇 🖻 (15) 🖵 ✕ 🎖 🎹 Ⅴ 🔒 ✦ 🚲

Longtown 4

National Grid Ref: NY3868

🍴 🍺 Crossways Inn, Graham Arms

Briar Lea House*, Brampton Road, Longtown, Carlisle, CA6 5TN.*
A substantial country house in 1.75 acres of attractive grounds
Grades: ETC 4 Diamond
Tel: **01228 791538** (also fax no)
Mr Gildert.
D: £19.50-£25.00
S: £25.00-£30.00.
Open: All Year (not Xmas)
Beds: 2D 1T
Baths: 3 En
🛇 🖻 (10) ✍ 🖵 🍴 ✕ 🎖 🎹 ♿ Ⅴ ✦ 🚲

Orchard House*, Blackbank, Longtown, Carlisle, Cumbria, CA6 5LQ.*
Spacious, tastefully furnished accommodation. Quiet wooded location near Gretna Green
Grades: ETC 4 Diamond
Tel: **01461 338596**
Mrs Payne.
D: £20.00-£22.50.
Open: All Year (not Xmas)
Beds: 1D 1T
Baths: 2 En
🛇 🖻 (4) ✍ 🖵 🎖 🎹 Ⅴ ✦ 🚲

Gretna 5

National Grid Ref: NY3167

🍴 🍺 Solway Lodge

The Braids*, Annan Road, Gretna, DG16 5DQ.*
Tel: **01461 337409** (also fax no)
Mrs Copeland.
D: £16.00-£18.00
S: £25.00-£25.00.
Open: All Year
Beds: 2T
Baths: 1 Sh
🛇 🖻 (2) 🖵 🎖 🎹 Ⅴ 🔒 ✦ 🚲
Small friendly family B&B in bungalow inside the entrance to our (BGHP VVVV) caravan park. Open all year. Gretna marriage centre, golf, Sunday market. Good area for bidwatching in winter months. Advice on fishing in the area

Hunters Lodge Hotel, *Annan Road, Gretna, Dumfriesshire, DG16 5DL.*
Closest hotel to the famous Registry Office and centre of Gretna, gateway to Scotland
Tel: 01461 338214
D: £25.00
S: £35.00.
Open: All Year
Beds: 2F 2T 5D 2S
Baths: 10 En 10 Pr 1 Sh
ﺡ ✑ (25) ☐ ✗ ▥ & ∮ ᨆ

Eastriggs 6

National Grid Ref: NY2466

Stanfield Farm, *Eastriggs, Annan, Dumfriesshire, DG12 6TF.*
Close to Gretna Green. Three golf courses and M74
Tel: 01461 40367
Mrs Mallinson.
D: £16.00 **S:** £16.00.
Open: Easter to Oct
Beds: 1F 2D
Baths: 1 Pr 1 Sh
ﺡ ✑ (3) ☐ ♄ ▤ ▥ Ⅵ ∮

Annan 7

National Grid Ref: NY1966

🐾 🍺 Queensbury Arms

The Old Rectory Guest House, *12 St Johns Road, Annan, Dumfriesshire, DG12 6AW.*
Tel: 01461 202029 (also fax no)
Buchanan & J Alexander.
D: £19.00-£22.00
S: £19.00-£22.00.
Open: All Year
Beds: 1F 3D 1T 3S
Baths: 1 En 2 Sh
ﺡ (4) ✑ (6) ✍ ☐ ♄ ✗ ▤ ▥ Ⅵ ♠ ∮ ᨆ
Charming C19th manse in the centre of Annan, gateway to south west Scotland, Rabbie Burns country. Be assured of a warm welcome, comfortable rooms, great Scottish breakfasts, home cooking, licensed. Main Euro & Irish routes. Walkers, cyclists welcome

Milnfield Farm, *Low Road, Annan, Dumfriesshire, DG12 5QP.*
Working farm, riverside walks, large garden; ideal for touring base
Grades: STB 2 Star
Tel: 01461 201811 Robinson.
D: £16.00-£18.00
S: £16.00-£18.00.
Open: All Year (not Xmas)
Beds: 1F 1D
ﺡ ✑ ✍ ☐ ♄ ▤ ▥ Ⅵ ∮ ᨆ

Pay B&Bs by cash or cheque and be prepared to pay up front.

The Craig, *18 St Johns Road, Annan, Dumfriesshire, DG12 6AW.*
Friendly Victorian house close to Motorways and station. Excellent breakfast
Tel: 01461 204665
Mrs Anderson.
D: £14.50 **S:** £14.50.
Open: All Year (not Xmas)
Beds: 1F 2T 1S
Baths: 1 Sh
ﺡ (1) ☐ ♄ ▤ ▥ Ⅵ ∮

Glencaple 8

National Grid Ref: NX9968

🐾 🍺 Nith Hotel

Riverside, *Shore Park, Glencaple, Dumfries, DG1 4RF.*
Detached house in small village, superb views over River Nith
Tel: 01387 770423
Mrs Anderson.
D: £17.50 **S:** £20.00.
Open: All Year (not Xmas)
Beds: 1F
Baths: 1 Pr
✑ (2) ✍ ☐ ▤ ▥ Ⅵ ♠ ∮ ᨆ

All cycleways are popular: you are well-advised to book ahead

All rates are subject to alteration at the owners' discretion.

Dumfries 9

National Grid Ref: NX9776

🐾 🍺 Hill Hotel, Auldgirth Inn, Station Hotel, The Courtyard

30 Hardthorn Avenue, *Dumfries, DG2 9JA.*
Grades: STB 2 Star B&B
Tel: 01387 253502 (also fax no)
Ms Sloan.
D: £16.00-£18.00 **S:** £23.00-£25.00
Open: All Year
Beds: 1D 1T **Baths:** 1 Sh
✑ (2) ✍ ☐ ▤ ▥ Ⅵ ∮
A warm Scottish welcome awaits you at no 30, a non-smoking private house with car parking in quiet residential area easy access from Dumfries bypass A75 and less than a mile from town centre ideal centre to explore SW Scotland

Fernwood, *4 Cassalands, Dumfries, DG2 7NS.*
Victorian sandstone villa, close to golf course and town centre
Grades: STB 3 Star
Tel: 01387 253701 (also fax no)
Mrs Vaughan.
D: £16.50-£17.50 **S:** £16.50-£17.50.
Open: All Year (not Xmas)
Beds: 1F 1D 2S **Baths:** 2 Sh
ﺡ ✑ (6) ✍ ☐ ▤ ▥ Ⅵ ∮ ᨆ

Dumfries to Maybole

From Dumfries you head southwest through Haugh of Urr to reach **Castle Douglas** and nearby Threave Garden (National Trust for Scotland), with the sumptuous colours of its flowers and woodland, where there is also a restaurant. On to Tongland on the Dee and Gatehouse of Fleet, a pretty town in the lovely Fleet Valley. Nearby fifteenth-century Cardoness Castle is a typical Scottish tower house. From Gatehouse you head on to Creetown, where the River Cree flows into Wigtown Bay, before reaching Palnure on the edge of **Galloway Forest Park**, a beautiful 300-square-mile area of peaks in surroundings of forested hills and moorland with numerous lochs and a network of rivers. The Park's Kirroughtree Visitor Centre is nearby. Newton Stewart is a centre for salmon and trout fishing in the Cree; from here you follow the river upstream before heading into Glen Trool. Continuing through the Forest Park, the route wends its way over fairly gentle hills before a steeper climb and descent over Nick of the Balloch to the River Stinchar, and another climb to the summit below White Scaurins. You now descend steadily to reach Crosshill and **Maybole**. The climb out of Maybole yields splendid views out to sea – your first sight of the Firth of Clyde.

Franklea Guest House, *Castle Douglas Road, Dumfries, DG2 8PP.*
Actual grid ref: NX955757
Grades: STB 3 Star
Tel: 01387 253004
Mrs Wild.
Fax no: 01387 259301
D: £18.00-£20.00 **S:** £20.00-£22.00.
Open: Easter to Nov
Beds: 1F 1D
Baths: 2 En
🛇 (5) 🅿 (5) 🗖 🖂 ✕ 🖴 🎹 ♿ 🖤 🖺 🖤 ⚡ ⚲
Bungalow 1 mile from Dumfries; ideal for golf next door, hill walking, Galloway park. Comfortable beds, log fire in winter, TV in all rooms. Will take full and partially disabled as we have only 2 steps in entrance hall. Lounge open all day

Fulwood Hotel, *Lovers Walk, Dumfries, DG1 1LX.*
Beautiful Victorian house opposite railway station in the heart of Burns country
Grades: STB 3 Star
Tel: 01387 252262 / 0411 260246
Fax no: 01387 252262
D: £17.00-£21.00 **S:** £20.00-£30.00.
Open: All Year (not Xmas)
Beds: 1F 2D 2T 1S
Baths: 3 En 1 Pr 1 Sh
⚲🗖🖴🎹🖤⚡⚲

Hazeldean Guest House, *4 Moffat Road, Dumfries, DG1 1NJ.*
Beautiful 4 star Victorian villa. Good area near station. Private parking
Grades: STB 4 Star
Tel: 01387 266178 (also fax no)
Mr Harper.
D: £19.00-£20.00
S: £25.00-£28.00.
Open: All Year (not Xmas)
Beds: 2F 2D 2T 1S
Baths: 6 En
🛇 🅿 (8) ⚲🗖✕🖴🎹♿🖺⚡⚲

Kirkton Villa, *8 Huntingdon Road, Dumfries, DG1 1NF.*
Attractive detached villa (some roughcast) with double glazing and CH
Tel: **01387 266859**
Mrs Hannah.
D: £17.50-£17.50 **S:** £20.00-£20.00.
Open: All Year
Beds: 1D 1T
Baths: 2 En
🛇 🅿 (3) 🗖 🖴 🎹 ♿ 🖤 ⚡ ⚲

All rooms full and
nowhere else to stay?
Ask the owner if
there's anywhere
nearby

Order your
packed lunches the
evening before you
need them.
Not at breakfast!

Mouswald Bank, *Carrutherstown Road, Dumfries, DG1 4JR.*
Superb views from bedrooms over Firth and Cumbrian coast
Grades: STB 2 Star B&B
Tel: 01387 830660
Mr & Mrs Wyllie.
D: £16.00-£18.00
S: £18.00-£20.00.
Open: Easter to Oct
Beds: 2F
Baths: 1 Sh
🛇 🅿 (3) ⚲🖴🎹🖤

Lochenlee, *32 Ardwall Road, Dumfries, DG1 3AQ.*
Quiet, warm, large Edwardian house in quiet residential street
Tel: **01387 265153**
Mrs Porteous.
D: £16.00
S: £14.00.
Open: All Year (not Xmas)
Beds: 2F 1S
Baths: 1 Sh
🛇⚲🗖🖴🎹🖤⚡

Haugh of Urr   10

National Grid Ref: NX8066

🍴🍺 The Grapes, Laurie Arms

Corbieton Cottage, *Haugh of Urr, Castle Douglas, Kirkcudbrightshire, DG7 3JJ.*
Actual grid ref: NX795695
Charming country cottage, lovely views, good food and a warm welcome
Grades: STB 4 Star
Tel: 01556 660413
Mr Jones.
D: £16.00-£18.00 **S:** £17.00-£18.00.
Open: Feb to Dec
Beds: 1D 1T
Baths: 1 Sh
🅿 (2) ⚲✕🖴🎹🖤

Old Hermitage, *Haugh of Urr, Castle Douglas, Kirkcudbrightshire, DG7 3LQ.*
Old Hermitage is a spacious country house with beautiful scenic views all around
Tel: **01556 660236**
Mrs Rennie.
D: £16.00 **S:** £20.00.
Open: Easter to Oct
Beds: 2D
Baths: 1 Pr
⚲🗖🖴🎹🖤⚲

Castle Douglas   11

National Grid Ref: NX7662

🍴🍺 Old Smugglers, Kings Arms Hotel, Laurie Arms, Douglas Arms, The Grapes

Craigadam, *Castle Douglas, Kirkcudbrightshire, DG7 3HV.*
Actual grid ref: NX801728
Grades: STB 3 Star
Tel: 01556 650233 (also fax no)
Mrs Pickup.
D: £23.00-£23.00 **S:** £28.00-£28.00.
Open: All Year (not Xmas)
Beds: 1F 2D 4T
Baths: 3 Pr
🛇 🅿 (10) 🗖 🖂 ✕ 🖴 🎹 🖤 ⚡ ⚲
Craigadam is an elegant country house within working farm. Antique furnishings, log fires and friendly atmosphere. All rooms ensuite - dine in our oak panelled dining room where we specialise in venison, pheasant, salmon, and other local produce. Sweets not for the calorie conscious

Imperial Hotel, *King Street, Castle Douglas, Kircudbrightshire, DG7 1AA.*
Grades: STB 3 Star, AA 2 Star
Tel: **01556 502086**
Fax no: 01556 503009
D: £27.00-£29.00 **S:** £35.00-£45.00.
Open: All Year (not Xmas)
Beds: 5D 5T 2S
Baths: 12 En
🛇 🅿 (20) 🗖 🖂 ✕ 🖴 🎹 🖤 🖺 ⚡ ⚲
Former coaching inn and Listed building. All rooms ensuite. Warm friendly welcome. Golf holiday specialists - itinerary organised for you. Central base for all leisure pursuits and for touring Galloway. Good Scottish fayre using local produce. Three bars, pool room, private car park

Dalcroy, *24 Abercromby Road, Castle Douglas, Kircudbrightshire, DG7 1BA.*
Tel: **01556 502674** Mrs Coates.
D: £16.50-£17.50 **S:** £13.00-£13.00.
Open: May to Oct
Beds: 1D 1T **Baths:** 1 Sh
🅿 (3) ⚲🗖🖴🎹🖤⚡⚲
A warm Scottish welcome assured in this long established spacious detached house, overlooking golf course, mins from attractive market town. Ideal base for Galloway Hills, lochs, forests, beaches, fishing, golf and birdwatching

---

Please don't camp
on *anyone's* land
without first obtaining
their permission.

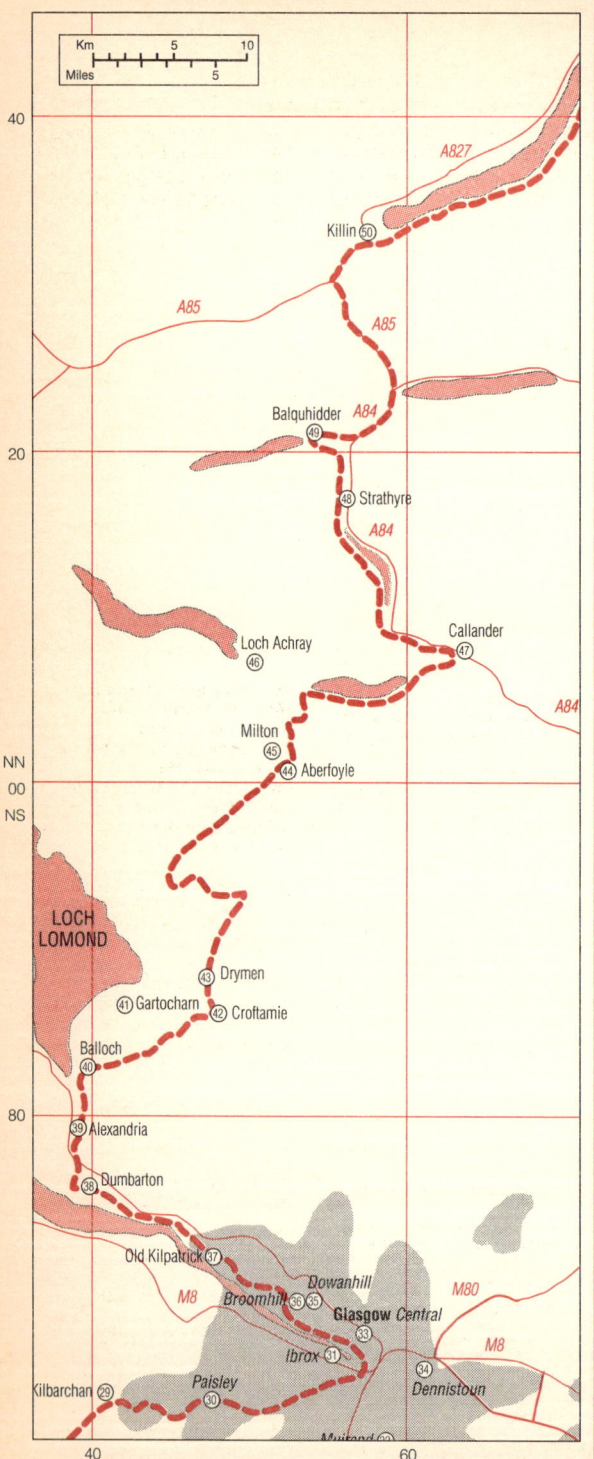

Milton Park Farm, *Castle Douglas, Kirkcudbrightshire,* *DG7 3JJ.*
Grades: STB 3 Star B&B
Tel: 01556 660212 Mrs Muir.
D: £18.00-£20.00 **S:** £18.00-£20.00.
Open: Easter to Oct
Beds: 2D 1T
Baths: 2 Sh
⛲ (9) ℗ (4) 🛏 👪 🎱 🖿 Ⓥ
A warm welcome and good food awaits you in this comfortable farmhouse. Superb outlook over large garden and down the Urr Valley. Centrally situated, ideal base for walking, golf, birdwatching and touring around Galloway. Free trout fishing on River Urr

Twynholm   12

National Grid Ref: NX6654

🍴 🍺 Murray Arms

Barbey Farm, *Twynholm, Kirkcudbright, Kirkcudbrightshire, DG6 4PN.*
Farmhouse accommodation with beautiful gardens in quiet rural area
Grades: STB 2 Star
Tel: 01557 860229 Miss Service.
D: £14.00-£14.00 **S:** £14.00-£14.00.
Open: Easter to Sep
Beds: 1F 1T
⛲ ℗ (2) 🛏 🎱 🖿 Ⓥ

Gatehouse of Fleet   13

National Grid Ref: NX6056

29 Fleet Street, *Gatehouse of Fleet, Castle Douglas, DG7 2BS.*
Friendly, comfortable Georgian House. Good walking, beaches, golf, birdwatching stb
Tel: 01557 814647
Mrs Carlisle.
D: £15.00-£17.50 **S:** £15.00-£20.00.
Open: All Year (not Xmas)
Beds: 1F 1D 1T 1S
Baths: 1 En 1 Sh
⛲ ℗ (1) ½ 🐾 🎱 🖿 Ⓥ ⚡ 🚲

Creetown   14

National Grid Ref: NX4758

Wal-d-mar, *Mill Street, Creetown, Newton Stewart, Wigtownshire, DG7 7JN.*
Tel: 01671 820369 Lockett.
Fax no: 01671 820266
D: £16.00-£16.00 **S:** £16.00-£16.00.
Open: All Year (not Xmas)
Beds: 1D 1S
Baths: 1 Sh
⛲ ℗ (3) 🛏 🐾 🎱 🖿 🛆 Ⓥ ⚡ 🚲
Modern bungalow in quiet village location, ideal base for touring, walking, golf, stb. Comfortable beds, good breakfasts, private off-road parking, warm Scottish welcome assured. Situated between Dumfries and Stranraer on the Cree estuary

Maybole to Glasgow

Descending to reach the coast at Doonfoot, you cycle along the seafront of its sandy beach into **Ayr**, birthplace of Robert Burns. The old town nestles around the fifteenth - century auld brig over the River Ayr, which features in Burns' poem 'Twa Brigs'. St John's Tower is the remnant of a church where Cromwell had an armoury. Scotland's most important racecourse is on the north bank of the river. The next stretch along the coast is peppered with golf courses – the game originated in Scotland. After Prestwick you reach Troon, one of the locations of the British Open golf championship. The Scottish Maritime Museum is at Irvine; from here you head inland to Kilwinning and up the Garnock Valley to Kilbirnie, before turning east through Lochwinnoch, Kilbarchan and Johnstone to **Paisley**. The interior of the town's abbey,

which was originally founded in the twelfth century but overhauled in the Victorian era, is richly decorated. The stained glass dates from various periods. The Museum and Art Gallery has a large exhibition of shawls documenting the history of the famous Paisley Pattern, which was developed from Indian designs. At the Sma' Shot Cottages, a large themed exhibition recreates different aspects of life in the eighteenth and nineteenth centuries. From Paisley you weave your way mostly through urban sprawl, but pass close to Pollok Country Park, where the fantastic Burrel Collection, which includes Chinese porcelain, Egyptian antiquities, medieval tapestries and furniture, stained glass and a large collection of paintings among much else, is flooded with sunlight in its superb purpose-built gallery. Proceeding to the south bank of the Clyde, cross Bell's Bridge to reach the centre of Scotland's powerhouse and largest city, Glasgow.

Palnure 15

National Grid Ref: NX4563

Crown Hotel, Bruce Hotel

The Stables Tearoom, *Palnure, Newton Stewart, Wigtownshire, DG8 6JB.*
Dinner, bed & breakfast. Country tearoom near Forest and walking paths
Grades: STB 2 Star B&B
Tel: 01671 404224 (also fax no)
Mrs Stables.
D: £18.00-£20.00
S: £18.00-£20.00.
Open: Easter to Nov
Beds: 1D 1T
Baths: 2 En

Creebridge 16

National Grid Ref: NX4165

Villa Cree, *Creebridge, Newton Stewart, Wigtownshire, DG8 6NR.*
Quiet riverside family house, excellent for walking, wildlife, touring or business
Grades: STB 3 Star
Tel: 01671 403914
Mr Rankin.
D: £18.00-£20.00 **S:** £18.00-£20.00.
Open: All Year (not Xmas)
Beds: 2D 1T 1S
Baths: 1 En 1 Pr

S = Price range for a single person in a room

Newton Stewart 17

National Grid Ref: NX4065

Kilwarlin, Corvisel Road, Newton Stewart, Wigtownshire, DG8 6LN.

Kilwarlin, *Corvisel Road, Newton Stewart, Wigtownshire, DG8 6LN.*
Actual grid ref: NX408650
Victorian house, beautiful garden, central location, home-baking, golf, fishing
Grades: STB 3 Star
Tel: 01671 403047 Mrs Dickson.
D: £16.50-£16.50 **S:** £16.50-£16.50.
Open: Easter to Oct
Beds: 1F 1D 1S **Baths:** 1 Sh

Eskdale, *Princess Avenue, Newton Stewart, DG8 6ES.*
Grades: STB 3 Star
Tel: 01671 404195 Mrs Smith.
D: £16.00-£18.00 **S:** £16.00-£20.00.
Open: All Year
Beds: 1D 1T 1S
Baths: 1 Pr 1 Sh
Eskdale is an attractive detached house in a very quiet residential area within five minutes' walk from the town centre, shops, supermarket and small cinema; golf course, sailing and access to Southern Upland Way all within easy reach

Rowallan House, *Corsbie Road, Newton Stewart, DG8 6JB.*
Visit our website - www.rowallan.co.uk - see what our guests say about Rowallan
Grades: STB 4 Star
Tel: 01671 402520 Mrs Henderson.
D: £27.00-£30.00 **S:** £27.00-£40.00.
Open: All Year
Beds: 2D 2T 1S
Baths: 5 En

Minnigaff 18

National Grid Ref: NX4166

Creebridge Hotel, Cree Inn

▲ **Minnigaff Youth Hostel**, *Minnigaff, Newton Stewart, Wigtownshire, DG8 6PL.*
Actual grid ref: NX411663
Tel: 01671 402211
Under 18: £4.95 **Adults:** £6.10
suitable for disabled people, self-catering facilities
Galloway Forest Park is nearby; fish in the River Cree; take a daytrip to the wild goat park and nature trails. The RSPB runs a reserve at Wood of Cree; scenic Glen Trool is nearby

Flowerbank Guest House, *Minnigaff, Newton Stewart, Wigtownshire, DG8 6PJ.*
A charming C18th house, private parking in extensive landscaped gardens
Tel: 01671 402629 Mrs Inker.
D: £18.50.
Open: All Year (not Xmas)
Beds: 1F 2D 2T
Baths: 4 En 1 Pr

Please respect a B&B's wishes regarding children, animals & smoking.

Bargrennan 19

National Grid Ref: NX3576

House O'Hill Hotel, Bargrennan,
Newton Stewart, Wigtownshire,
DG8 6RN.
Actual grid ref: NX351769
Small friendly family-run C19th
inn
Tel: **01671 840243** (also fax no)
Mrs Allwood.
D: £20.00-£25.00
S: £30.00-£40.00.
Open: All Year
Beds: 3F
Baths: 3 En
🛏 🅿 (50) 🛒 🏧 ✕ 🏃 📠 🕭 ⚡ 🚲

Maybole 20

National Grid Ref: NS2909

🍴🍺 Welltrees Inn

Homelea, 62 Culzean Road,
Maybole, Ayrshire, KA19 8AH.
Actual grid ref: NS295100
Grades: STB 3 Star
Tel: **01655 882736**
Mrs McKellar.
Fax no: 01655 883557
D: £17.50-£18.50
S: £20.00-£22.00.
Open: Easter to Oct
Beds: 1F 1T 1S
Baths: 2 Sh
🛏 🅿 (3) 💳 🏃 📠 🕭 📺 ⚡ 🚲
Homelea is a spacious red
sandstone Victorian family home,
retaining many original features.
Refreshment and home baking
welcome you on arrival. Ideal base
for touring Ayrshire - Culzean
Castle, Turnberry golf course,
Burns Heritage Park all within 6
mile radius

Nether Culzean Farm, Maybole,
KA19 7JQ.
Beautiful listed C18th farmhouse,
spacious and comfortable. Near
Culzean castle, beaches, golf
courses
Grades: STB 1 Star
Tel: **01655 882269** Mrs Blythe.
D: £15.00-£17.00 **S:** £15.00-£17.00.
Open: Easter to Oct
Beds: 2F
Baths: 1 Pr
🛏 🅿 (2) 💳 🏃 🐕 🏃 📠 🕭 📺 ⚡ 🚲

Alloway 21

National Grid Ref: NS3318

Garth Madryn, 71 Maybole Road,
Alloway, Ayr, KA7 4TB.
Alloway is a quiet residential area
of Ayr within easy reach of the
town
Grades: STB 2 Star
Tel: **01292 443346** Mrs MacKie.
D: £16.00-£17.00 **S:** £16.00-£17.00.
Open: All Year
Beds: 2T **Baths:** 2 En

Ayr 22

National Grid Ref: NS3422

🍴🍺 Tam O'Shanter, Kylestrome Hotel, Finlay's
Bar, Burrofield's Bar, Carrick Lodge, Durward
Hotel, Hollybush Inn, Balgarth, Littlejohns

🔺 *Ayr Youth Hostel, 5 Craigwell*
Road, Ayr, KA7 2XJ.
Actual grid ref: NS331211
Tel: **01292 262322**
Under 18: £6.50 **Adults:** £7.75
self-catering facilities, family bunk
rooms, shop, laundry facilities
An excellent family base, with a
barbecue, a 3-mile sandy beach
and plenty to see nearby, including
Burns Cottage, Culzean Castle and
a Gold Cup racecourse

Belmont Guest House, 15 Park
Circus, Ayr, KA7 2DJ.
Grades: STB 2 Star
Tel: **01292 265588**
Mr Hillhouse.
Fax no: 01292 290303
D: £18.50-£20.00
S: £22.00-£24.00.
Open: All Year (not Xmas)
Beds: 2F 2D 1T
Baths: 5 En
🛏 🅿 (5) 🛒 🏃 🏃 📠 🕭 📺 ⚡
Try a breath of fresh 'Ayr'. Warm,
comfortable hospitality assured in
this Victorian town house, situated
in a quiet residential area within
easy walking distance of the town
centre and beach. Ground floor
bedrooms available. Glasgow
(Preswick) Airport 6 miles. Green
Tourism Silver Award

Inverlea Guest House, 42 Carrick
Road, Ayr, KA7 2RB.
Tel: **01292 266756** (also fax no)
Mr & Mrs Bryson.
D: £15.00-£20.00
S: £18.00-£25.00.
Open: All Year
Beds: 3F 2D 2T 1S
Baths: 3 En 2 Pr 3 Sh
🛏 🅿 (5) 🛒 🏃 🏃 📠 🕭 📺 ⚡ 🚲
Family-run guest house which has
ensured personal attention for 14
years. Few minutes walk from
beach and town centre. Burns
Cottage and golf course nearby

Bringing children with
you? Always ask for
any special rates.

Glasgow

The great city of **Glasgow** has long been
Scotland's industrial hub, historically the centre
of the European tobacco trade until
shipbuilding and heavy industry took over. The
city's Victorian civic architecture was built on
wealth that flowed from industries whose
employees were crammed into its notorious
squalid and insanitary tenements. The grand
public architecture of the eighteenth and
nineteenth centuries includes the City
Chambers, elegantly colonnaded Stirling's
Library, Hutcheson's Hall with its white spire,
designed by David Hamilton (now National
Trust for Scotland) and Trades House,
Glasgow's only surviving Robert Adam
building, with a green dome and trade-inspired
internal decoration. The earlier history of the
city is reflected by Provand's Lordship, a
fifteenth-century house (now a museum) and

thirteenth-century **St Mungo's Cathedral**.
Close by, St Mungo's Museum of Religious Life
and Art is an excellent display of the art of the
world's religions. In addition to the Burrell
Collection, Glasgow's many superb museums
include the **Hunterian** (archaeology and
Scottish art), **Kelvingrove Art Gallery** and
Museum (Scottish and European art and
Scottish natural history), the **Museum of**
Transport (including bicycles, trains and
trams) and the **People's Palace** (the city's
social history). The considerable legacy of art
nouveau architect and designer Charles
Rennie Mackintosh includes the **Glasgow**
School of Art, which demonstrates inside and
out his concept of a building as total work of
art, Queen's Cross Church and Scotland Street
School. Mackintosh House, an impressive
recreation of the interior of his home, is at the
Hunterian.

Iona, *27 St Leonards Road, Ayr, KA7 2PS.*
Actual grid ref: NS341203
Welcome to Iona for comfortable rooms and full Scottish breakfast
Grades: STB 2 Star
Tel: 01292 269541 (also fax no)
Mr & Mrs Gibson.
D: £17.00-£20.00 **S:** £17.00-£20.00.
Open: Feb to Nov
Beds: 1D 1T 2S
Baths: 2 En 1 Sh

Monaco Guest House, *41 Seafield Drive, Ayr, KA7 4BJ.*
Grades: STB 3 Star B&B
Tel: 01292 264295 Lennon.
D: £19.00-£22.00 **S:** £20.00-£24.00.
Open: Easter to Oct
Beds: 1D 1T 1S
Baths: 1 En 1 Sh
Comfortable family-run B&B in quiet seafront location with superb panoramic views to Greenan Castle & the island of Arran. Central base for exploring Burns country, walking, golfing, 5 mins by car to town centre

Failte, *9 Prestwick Road, Ayr, KA8 8LD.*
Grades: STB 2 Star
Tel: 01292 265282 (also fax no)
Mrs Jennifer Thomson.
D: £19.00-£22.00
S: £19.00-£22.00.
Open: All Year (not Xmas)
Beds: 1D 1T
Baths: 1 En 1 Pr
This well-established B&B situated on the main road for Glasgow, 10 mins from Prestwick International Airport. (Drop off service). Ensuite room furnished to a high standard; twin room, furnished to a high standard, has its own luxury toilet & shower room

Deanbank, *44 Ashgrove Street, Ayr, KA7 3BG.*
Excellent highly commended 4 star B&B
Grades: STB 4 Star
Tel: 01292 263745
Ms Wilson.
D: £18.00-£20.00 **S:** £20.00-£25.00.
Open: All Year (not Xmas)
Beds: 1F 1T
Baths: 1 Sh

All rooms full and nowhere else to stay? Ask the owner if there's anywhere nearby

Tramore Guest House, *17 Eglinton Terrace, Ayr, KA7 1JJ.*
In C12th old fort area, 2 mins from town centre
Grades: STB 3 Star
Tel: 01292 266019 (also fax no)
D: £17.00-£17.00
S: £17.00-£19.00.
Open: All Year
Beds: 1D 2T
Baths: 2 Sh

The Dunn Thing Guest House, *13 Park Circus, Ayr, KA7 2DJ.*
Victorian House in quiet street near town centre
Tel: 01292 284531
Mrs Dunn.
D: £17.00-£20.00
S: £18.00-£22.00.
Open: All Year
Beds: 2D 1T
Baths: 3 En

Town Hotel, *9-11 Barns Street, Ayr, KA7 1XB.*
Family run hotel, close to town centre and 10 local golf courses
Tel: 01292 267595
D: £20.00-£25.00
S: £20.00-£25.00.
Beds: 3F 1D 14T
Baths: 18 En

Sunnyside, *26 Dunure Road, Doonfoot, Ayr, KA7 4HR.*
Actual grid ref: NS322185
Spacious rooms furnished to high standard, warm Scottish family welcome
Grades: STB 3 Star
Tel: 01292 441234 (also fax no)
Mrs Malcolm.
D: £20.00-£22.00
S: £26.00-£28.00.
Open: All Year (not Xmas)
Beds: 2F
Baths: 2 En

Kilkerran, *15 Prestwick Road, Ayr, KA8 8LD.*
Family-run guest house on main A74 Ayr - Prestwick
Tel: 01292 266477
Ms Ferguson.
D: £16.00
S: £16.00.
Open: All Year
Beds: 1F 1D 2T 1S
Baths: 2 Pr 1 Sh

9 Midton Road, *Ayr, KA7 2SE.*
In heart of Burns Country, beach and town centre nearby
Tel: 01292 288473
Mrs Horn.
D: £15.00 **S:** £15.00.
Open: All Year
Beds: 1F 1T 1S
Baths: 1 Sh

Lochinver , *32 Park Circus, Ayr, KA7 2DL.*
Long established family-run Victorian Guest House in quiet residential street in central Ayr
Tel: 01292 265086 (also fax no)
Mr Young.
D: £16.00 **S:** £18.00.
Open: All Year
Beds: 2F 2D 1T 1S
Baths: 3 En 1 Pr 1 Sh

Chalmers Bed & Breakfast, *34 Carrick Road, Ayr, KA7 2RB.*
Tasteful Victorian house. Ideally situated, beach, town, golf, Burns heritage
Tel: 01292 282841 (also fax no)
Mrs Macleay.
D: £16.00 **S:** £20.00.
Open: All Year (not Xmas)
Beds: 1F 1D 1T
Baths: 1 En 1 Sh

Prestwick 23
National Grid Ref: NS3425
North Beach Hotel, Golf Inn, Carlton Hotel

Knox Bed & Breakfast, *105 Ayr Road, Prestwick, Ayrshire, KA9 1TN.*
Superb accommodation, homely welcome, excellent value, close to all amenities, airport and Centrum Arena
Grades: STB 3 Star
Tel: 01292 478808
Mrs Wardrope.
D: £15.00-£18.00
S: £16.00-£20.00.
Open: All Year (not Xmas)
Beds: 1D 1T 1S
Baths: 1 Sh

Monkton 24
National Grid Ref: NS3627
The Wheatsheaf, North Beach Hotel

Crookside Farm, *Kerrix Road, Monkton, Prestwick, Ayrshire, KA9 2QU.*
Tel: 01563 830266
Mrs Gault.
D: £12.00 **S:** £12.00.
Open: All Year (not Xmas)
Beds: 1F 1D
Baths: 1 Sh
Comfortable farmhouse central heating throughout, ideal for golfing, close to airport

D = Price range per person sharing in a double room

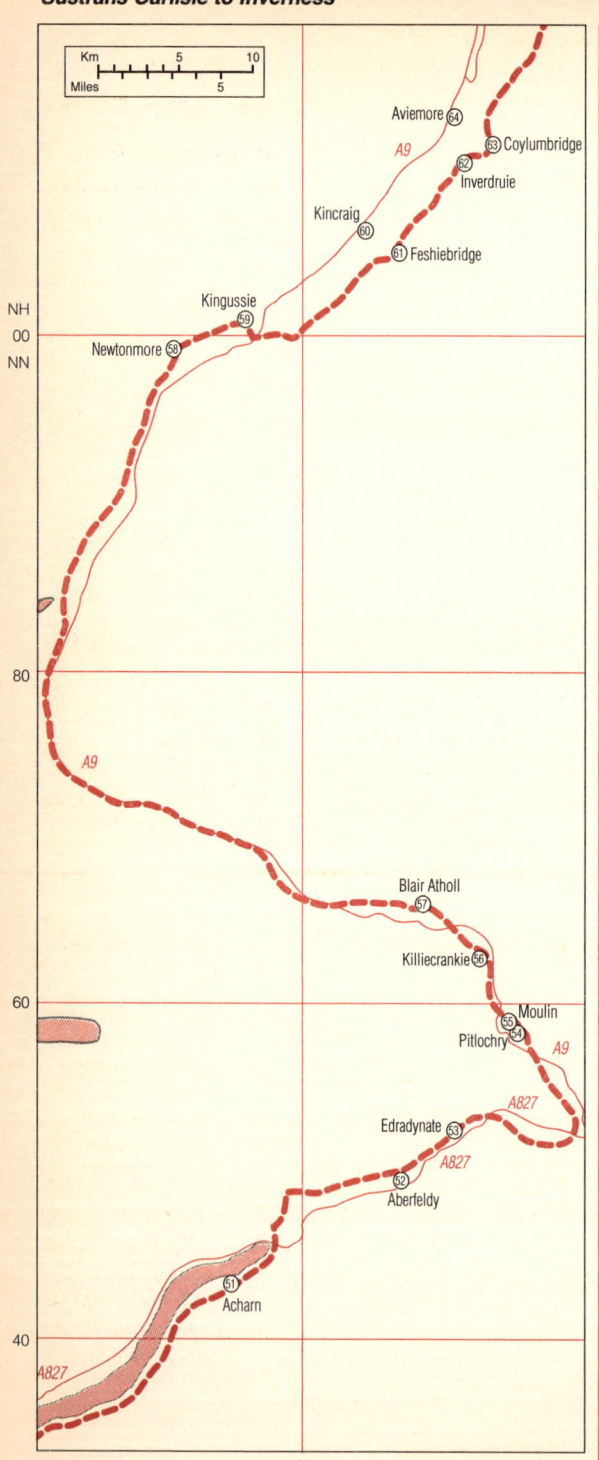

National Grid Ref: NS3230

🍴 🛏 Old Loans Inn, Lookout, Wheatsheaf, South Beach Hotel, The Anchorage

The Cherries, 50 Ottoline Drive, Troon, Ayrshire, KA10 7AW.
Beautiful quiet home on golf course near beaches and restaurants
Grades: STB 3 Star
Tel: **01292 313312** Mrs Tweedie.
Fax no: 01292 319007
D: £20.00-£23.00 **S:** £20.00-£25.00.
Open: All Year
Beds: 1F 1T 1S
Baths: 1 En 1 Pr 1 Sh
🛏 🅿 (5) ✠ ☐ 🐾 🛒 🎍 📖 Ⅴ ✦ 🚲

Bearsden House, 7 St Meddans Street, Troon, Ayrshire, KA10 6JU.
Sandstone Victorian house, close to sea, town; decorated in style
Tel: **01292 318804** Mrs Ely.
Fax no: 01292 318404
D: £24.00-£25.00 **S:** £24.00-£25.00.
Open: Mar to Nov
Beds: 1D 1T
Baths: 1 En 1 Pr
🛏 (12) 🅿 (3) ☐ 🐾 🎍 📖 Ⅴ 🚲

Mossgiel, 56 Bentinck Drive, Troon, KA10 6Y.
5 minutes from beach, 10 minutes' walk from golf courses
Grades: STB 2 Star
Tel: **01292 314937** (also fax no) Mrs Rankin.
D: £18.00-£22.00 **S:** £20.00-£24.00.
Beds: 1F 1D 1T
Baths: 1 En 1 Pr 1 Sh
🛏 🅿 (3) ☐ 🎍 📖 & Ⅴ 🔒 ✦ 🚲

The Beeches, 63 Ottoline Drive, Troon, KA10 7AN.
Bright spacious house, wooded gardens. Every amenity, beaches, golf, marina
Grades: STB 2 Star
Tel: **01292 314180**
D: £16.00-£18.00 **S:** £18.00-£20.00.
Open: All Year
Beds: 1D 1T 1S
Baths: 2 Pr
🛏 🅿 (4) ✠ ☐ 🎍 📖 Ⅴ 🚲

Rosedale, 9 Firth Road, Barassie, Troon, KA10 6TF.
Quiet seafront location - ideal for Sea Cat ferry to Ireland
Grades: STB 2 Star
Tel: **01292 314371** Mrs Risk.
D: £19.00-£21.00 **S:** £20.00-£20.00.
Open: All Year (not Xmas)
Beds: 1D 1T 1S
🛏 (5) ✠ ☐ 🎍 📖 Ⅴ ✦ 🚲

Bringing children with you? Always ask for any special rates.

All cycleways are popular: you are well-advised to book ahead

Kilwinning 26

National Grid Ref: NS3043

🏨 🍺 Blair Inn

Tarcoola, Montgreenan, Kilwinning, Ayrshire, KA13 7QZ.
Actual grid ref: NS344440
Attractive country setting convenient for Arran ferry and Ayrshire golf
Tel: **01294 850379**
Mrs Melville.
Fax no: 01294 850249
D: £16.00-£18.00 **S:** £16.00-£16.00.
Open: All Year
Beds: 1T
Baths: 1 Pr
🛏 (8) 🅿 (2) 🗶 ⌨ 🍽 🛉 🏛 �V ⚡ 🚲

Claremont Guest House,
27 Howgate, Kilwinning, Ayrshire, KA13 6EW.
Friendly family B&B close to town centre and public transport
Tel: **01294 553905** Mrs Filby.
D: £17.00-£20.00 **S:** £17.00-£20.00.
Open: All Year (not Xmas)
Beds: 1F 1S
Baths: 2 Sh
🛏 🅿 (10) 🗶 ⌨ 🍽 ⚡ 🚲

Kilbirnie 27

National Grid Ref: NS3154

🏨 🍺 Mossend Hotel, Dalby Inn, Haylie Hotel, Begattas

Alpenrose, 113 Herriot Avenue, Kilbirnie, Ayrshire, KA25 7JB.
Enjoy an 'Alpenrose' breakfast and you will be able to cope with anything
Tel: **01505 683122**
Mrs Cameron.
D: £11.00 **S:** £11.00.
Open: All Year
Beds: 1D 1T 1S
Baths: 1 Sh
🛏 🅿 (4) ⌨ 🗶 🛉 🏛 ⚡ 🛉 ⚡ V

Lochwinnoch 28

National Grid Ref: NS3559

Belltrees Guest House, Belltrees Farm, Lochwinnoch, Renfrewshire, PA12 4JN.
8 miles from Glasgow airport, wonderful views of the Loch
Tel: **01505 842376**
D: £17.00-£22.00 **S:** £20.00-£22.00.
Open: All Year
Beds: 1F 1D
Baths: 1 En
🛏 🅿 ⌨ 🛉 🛉 🏛 ⚡ V 🛉 ⚡ 🚲

Kilbarchan 29

National Grid Ref: NS4063

🏨 🍺 Trust Inn

Tower House, Milliken Park Road, Kilbarchan, Johnstone, Renfrewshire, PA10 2DB.
Historic home which Chopin visited. Excellent connections to motorway, railway airport
Tel: **01505 703299** (also fax no)
Mrs Van Breugel.
D: £25.00 **S:** £28.00.
Open: All Year (not Xmas)
Beds: 1F 1T 1S **Baths:** 3 En
🛏 (1) 🅿 (6) ⌨ 🍽 🛉 🏛 V ⚡ 🚲

Paisley 30

National Grid Ref: NS4863

🏨 🍺 Paraffin Lamp

Myfarrclan Guest House, 146 Corsebar Road, Paisley, Renfrewshire, PA2 9NA.
Grades: STB 4 Star B&B
Tel: **0141 884 8285**
Mr & Mrs Farr.
Fax no: 0141 581 1566
D: £32.50-£35.00 **S:** £40.00-£60.00.
Open: All Year
Beds: 2D 1T **Baths:** 2 En 1 Pr
🛏 🅿 (2) ⌨ 🗶 🛉 🏛 V
Nestling in leafy suburb of Paisley, lovingly restored bungalow offering many thoughtful extras

---

S = Price range for a single person in a room

Planning a longer stay? Always ask for any special rates.

Glasgow Ibrox 31

National Grid Ref: NS5564

Holly House, 54 Ibrox Terrace, Glasgow, G51 2TB.
Situated in an early Victorian tree-lined terrace in the city centre
Tel: **0141 427 5609**
Mr Divers.
Fax no: 0141 427 5608
D: £20.00 **S:** £25.00.
Open: All Year
Beds: 2F 2D 2T 2S
Baths: 5 En
🛏 (10) 🅿 (6) ⌨ 🗶 🛉 🏛 ⚡ V 🛉 ⚡

Glasgow Muirend 32

National Grid Ref: NS5760

16 Bogton Avenue, Glasgow, G44 3JJ.
Quiet red sandstone terraced private house adjacent station, 12 mins city centre
Grades: STB 2 Star
Tel: **0141 637 4402**
Mrs Paterson.
D: £20.00-£20.00 **S:** £22.00-£22.00.
Open: All Year (not Xmas)
Beds: 1D 2S
Baths: 2 Sh
🅿 (2) ⌨ 🗶 🛉 🏛 V

Glasgow to Loch Tay

Proceeding through the decaying shipyards of the north bank of the Clyde, you reach **Dumbarton** before heading north to Balloch Castle Country Park by Loch Lomond. Having left metropolitan Clydeside spectacularly behind, you continue to Drymen before cycling through Queen Elizabeth Forest Park, where be red deer, to reach Aberfoyle. Climbing northward you are in the heart of the Trossachs, a wild and wonderful region of craggy hills, forest and secluded waterfalls. Hugging the southern shore of Loch Venachar you arrive at **Callander**, a small town with excellent facilities, where the Rob Roy and Trossachs visitor centre introduces the region and offers an audiovisual presentation on its famous son, the most renowned of the MacGregors and hero of Sir Walter Scott's novel. From here you cycle along the west bank of Loch Lubnaig to reach Balquhidder at the eastern end of Loch Voil and Lochearnhead at the western end of Loch Earn. Climbing to the summit of Glen Ogle and descending to Lix Toll, you reach **Killin**, where the River Dochart cascades over the town's pretty waterfall into Loch Tay. The mountain **Ben Lawers** glowers across from the other side as you undertake the long ride down the southern shore of the loch.

Glasgow Central 33

National Grid Ref: NS5865

🏴🍴 Dorsey's, Park Bar, Mitchell's, Stravaigan's, Orchard Park, Bellahoustow Hotel, Garfield House, Highlanders Park, Snaffil Bit

▲ *Glasgow Youth Hostel,*
7/8 Park Terrace, Glasgow, G3 6BY.
Actual grid ref: NS575662
Tel: 0141 332 3004
Under 18: £9.95
Adults: £11.50
evening meals available, self-catering facilities, family bunk rooms, shop, laundry facilities *Glasgow's alive. There are the dear green places of the city parks, like Kelvingrove. There's great shopping, and things to see. A great base too for touring the Trossachs, the Clyde Coast and Loch Lomond*

Kirkland House, 42 St Vincent Crescent, Glasgow, G3 8NG.
Grades: STB 3 Star
Tel: 0141 248 3458
Mrs Divers.
Fax no: 0141 221 5174
D: £27.00-£30.00
S: £27.00-£30.00.
Open: All Year
Beds: 3D 2T 2S
Baths: 6 En 2 Sh
🛏🖰(1)✍🗖🛢🎨🖳Ⅴ
City centre guest house with excellent rooms on beautiful Victorian Crescent in Finnieston (Glasgow's 'little Chelsea'). Short walk to Scottish Exhibition Centre, Museum/Art Gallery, Kelvingrove Park and all West End facilities. Glasgow airport 10 minutes, member of the Harry James society

Kelvingrove Hotel,
944 Sauchiehall Street, Glasgow, G3 7TH.
Grades: STB 2 Star
Tel: 0141 339 5011
Mr Wills.
Fax no: 0141 339 6566
D: £24.00-£29.00
S: £33.00-£38.00.
Open: All Year (not Xmas)
Beds: 7F 13D 3T 2S
Baths: 23 En
🛏🖰🖰(20)✍🗖🖰🗙🛢🎨🖳Ⅴ🛢✦🚲
Centrally located family-run hotel, set in Glasgow's fashionable West End. Close to pubs, clubs, art galleries, museums, University, shops, rail and bus links - all within walking distance

Pay B&Bs by cash or cheque and be prepared to pay up front.

Please don't camp on *anyone's* land without first obtaining their permission.

Number Thirty Six, 36 St Vincent Crescent, Glasgow, G3 8NG.
Grades: STB 3 Star
Tel: 0141 248 2086
Mrs MacKay.
Fax no: 0141 221 1477
D: £25.00-£30.00
S: £30.00-£35.00.
Open: All Year (not Xmas)
Beds: 4D 2T
Baths: 4 En 2 Pr
✍🗖🛢🎨🖳Ⅴ
Situated in a Georgian terrace on the edge of Glasgow city centre, we are an ideal base for exploring Glasgow and the west of Scotland. Beside the Art Gallery, University and SECC. Individually designed rooms. Personal attention guaranteed

Glasgow Dennistoun 34

National Grid Ref: NS6065

Seton Guest House, 6 Seton Terrace, Glasgow, G31 2HU.
Warm and friendly welcome assured. Five minutes from city centre
Grades: STB 2 Star
Tel: 0141 556 7654
Fax no: 0141 402 3655
D: £15.00-£16.00 **S:** £17.00-£18.00.
Open: All Year (not Xmas)
Beds: 4F 2D 2T 1S
Baths: 3 Sh
🛏🗖🖰🛢🎨🖳Ⅴ🚲

Glasgow Dowanhill 35

National Grid Ref: NS5667

🏴🍴 Orchard Park Hotel, Bellahoustow Hotel

The Terrace House Hotel,
14 Belhaven Terrace, Glasgow, G12 0TG.
Grades: STB 2 Star
Tel: 0141 337 3377 (also fax no)
Ms Black.
D: £29.00-£39.00 **S:** £49.00-£65.00.
Open: All Year
Beds: 4F 3D 5T 1S
Baths: 12 En 1 Pr
🛏✍🗖🖰🗙🛢🎨🖳Ⅴ
Family run-licensed hotel situated in the green & leafy up market West End within 15 minutes of Glasgow's city centre. The fashionable Byres Road is 5 minutes' walk away, boasting some of the finest bars & restaurants

Glasgow Broomhill 36

National Grid Ref: NS5467

Lochgilvie House, 117 Randolph Road, Broomhill, Glasgow, G11 7DS.
Grades: STB 3 Star
Tel: 0141 357 1593
Mrs Ogilvie.
Fax no: 0141 334 5828
D: £25.00-£27.50
S: £25.00-£30.00.
Open: All Year
Beds: 1F 2D 3T
Baths: 4 En
🛏(10)🅿✍🗖🛢🎨🖳Ⅴ
Luxurious Victorian town house situated in Glasgow's prestigious West End, adjacent to rail station, convenient for art galleries, museums, International Airport, eight minutes by train to city centre

Old Kilpatrick 37

National Grid Ref: NS4672

🏴🍴 Old Kilpatrick Inn

Elmhurst, 2 Mount Pleasant Drive, Old Kilpatrick, Glasgow, G60 5HJ.
Victorian villa with exceptional views over the River Clyde
Tel: 01389 874341
Mr & Mrs Hunter.
D: £18.00 **S:** £16.00.
Open: All Year
Beds: 2T 1S
Baths: 1 En 2 Pr
🛏🗖🖰🛢🎨🖳Ⅴ🛢✦🚲

Dumbarton 38

National Grid Ref: NS4075

🏴🍴 Abbotsford Hotel

Kilmalid House, 17 Glen Path, Dumbarton, G82 2QL.
Large Victorian manse. Overlooking castle & River Clyde
Tel: 01389 732030
Mr & Mrs Muirhead.
D: £16.00 **S:** £16.00.
Open: All Year
Beds: 1F 2D 1S
Baths: 1 Sh
🛏🅿(12)🗖🖰🛢🎨🖳Ⅴ🛢✦

Alexandria 39

National Grid Ref: NS3979

Carnbo, Overton Road, Alexandria, Dunbartonshire, G83 0DN.
Modern, detached villa with warm friendly atmosphere situated near Balloch
Grades: STB 1 Star
Tel: 01389 754919
Mrs Ritchie.
D: £17.00-£19.00
S: £19.00-£21.00.
Open: Easter to Nov
🛏(1)🅿(3)✍🗖🗙🛢🎨🖳Ⅴ🚲

Balloch 40

National Grid Ref: NS3982

⚑ ⬅ Roundabout Inn, Balloch Hotel, Corries, The Stables

Glyndale, 6 McKenzie Drive,
Lomond Road Estate, Balloch,
Alexandria, Dunbartonshire,
G83 8HL.
Easy access to Loch Lomond,
Glasgow Airport, public transport
Grades: STB 3 Star B&B
Tel: **01389 758238**
Mrs Ross.
D: £16.00-£17.00
S: £19.00-£20.00.
Open: All Year (not Xmas)
Beds: 1D 1T
Baths: 1 Sh
🛏 🅿 (2) ⅒ ⬚ ★ ▥ Ⅵ ∦ ⚲

Anchorage Guest House, *Balloch*
Road, Balloch, Alexandria,
Dunbartonshire, G83 8SS.
Situated on the banks of Loch
Lomond. Ideal base for touring,
fishing, sailing & walking
Grades: STB 1 Star
Tel: **01389 753336**
Mr Bowman.
D: £18.00-£25.00.
Open: All Year
Beds: 1F 2D 4T
Baths: 5 En 2 Sh
🛏 (1) 🅿 (6) ⬚ ★ ✕ ★ ▥ ⅙ Ⅵ ∦ ⚲

Ballagan House, *Balloch,*
Alexandria, Dunbartonshire,
G83 8LY.
Modern building with Balloch
Country Park on our doorstep
Tel: **01389 759641** (also fax no)
D: £20.00-£28.00 **S:** £22.00-£25.00.
Beds: 2F 3D 1T 3S
Baths: 1 En 2 Sh
⅒ ⬚ ★ ▥ Ⅵ

7 Carrochan Crescent, *Balloch,*
Alexandria, Dunbartonshire,
G83 8PX.
A warm welcome awaits you;
ideally situated for touring stb
Grades: STB 3 Star
Tel: **01389 750078**
Mrs Campbell.
D: £16.00-£16.00 **S:** £18.00-£18.00.
Open: Easter to Oct
Beds: 2D
Baths: 1 Sh
🛏 🅿 (2) ⬚ ★ ▥ Ⅵ ∦ ⚲

24 Balloch Road, *Balloch,*
Alexandria, Dunbartonshire,
G83 8LE.
Superb hospitality offered in
luxurious accommodation central
to all amenities
Grades: STB 3 Star
Tel: **01389 752195**
Mrs Hamill.
D: £12.00-£25.00 **S:** £18.00-£25.00.
Open: All Year
Beds: 2F 2D
Baths: 4 En
🛏 🅿 (5) ⬚ ★ ★ ▥ ⅙ Ⅵ ∦ ⚲

Auchry, *24 Boturich Drive,*
Balloch, Alexandria,
Dunbartonshire, G83 8JP.
Actual grid ref: NS395822
Set in quiet cul de sac; walking
distance to loch Lomond
Grades: STB 3 Star
Tel: **01389 753208**
Mrs McIntosh.
D: £16.00-£18.00 **S:** £17.00-£19.00.
Open: Easter to Mar
Beds: 1D 1S
Baths: 1 Pr 1 Sh
🅿 (4) ⅒ ⬚ ★ ▥ Ⅵ ∦ ⚲

Westville, *Riverside Lane, Balloch,*
Alexandria, Dunbartonshire,
G83 8LF.
Bungalow overlooking River
Leven at southern end of Loch
Lomond
Tel: **01389 752307**
Mrs Oultram.
D: £18.50 **S:** £19.50.
Open: All Year (not Xmas)
Beds: 1F 1D
Baths: 1 Sh
🛏 (5) 🅿 (2) ⅒ ⬚ ★ ★ ▥ ⅙ Ⅵ ∦ ⚲

Dumbain Farm, *Balloch,*
Alexandria, Dunbartonshire,
G83 8DS.
Converted granary on dairy farm.
Great breakfasts, home-made
raspberry jam!
Tel: **01389 752263** Mrs Watson.
D: £17.00 **S:** £20.00.
Open: All Year
Beds: 1F 1T 1D
Baths: 3 En
🛏 (1) 🅿 (4) ⅒ ⬚ ★ ▥ Ⅵ ∦ ⚲

Oakvale, *Drymen Road, Balloch,*
Alexandria, Dunbartonshire,
G83 8JY.
Beautiful family home - pretty
rooms
Tel: **01389 751615**
Mrs Feltham.
D: £16.00 **S:** £20.00.
Open: All Year
Beds: 2D 1T
Baths: 3 En
🛏 🅿 (4) ⬚ ★ ▥ Ⅵ

Gartocharn 41

National Grid Ref: NS4286

⚑ ⬅ Hungry Monk, Clachan Inn

Mardella Farm, *Old School Road,*
Gartocharn, Loch Lomond,
Alexandria, Dunbartonshire,
G83 8SD.
Actual grid ref: NS438864
Friendly, welcoming, homely
atmosphere. Come and meet the
quackers (ducks)!
Grades: AA 4 Diamond
Tel: **01389 830428**
Mrs MacDonell.
D: £18.50-£22.00 **S:** £31.00-£37.00.
Open: All Year
Beds: 1F 1D 1T
Baths: 1 En 1 Sh
🛏 🅿 (4) ⅒ ⬚ ★ ★ ▥ Ⅵ ∦

Croftamie 42

National Grid Ref: NS4786

⚑ ⬅ Clachan Inn, Wayfarers

Croftburn, *Croftamie, Drymen,*
Glasgow, G63 0HA.
Actual grid ref: NS402860
Former gamekeeper's cottage in
one acre of beautiful gardens
overlooking Strathendrick Valley
& Campsie Fells
Grades: STB 3 Star,
AA 4 Diamond
Tel: **01360 660796** (also fax no)
Mrs Reid.
D: £18.00-£22.00 **S:** £20.00-£25.00.
Open: All Year
Beds: 2D 1T
Baths: 2 En 1 Pr
🛏 (12) 🅿 (20) ⅒ ⬚ ★ ✕ ★ ▥ Ⅵ ∦ ⚲

Drymen 43

National Grid Ref: NS4788

⚑ ⬅ Buchanan Arms, Clachan Inn, Wayfarers,
Winnock Hotel

Green Shadows, *Buchanan Castle*
Estate, Drymen, Glasgow, G63 0HX.
Tel: **01360 660289**
Mrs Goodwin.
D: £21.00-£21.00 **S:** £24.00-£24.00.
Open: All year (not Xmas)
Beds: 1F 1D 1S
Baths: 2 Sh
🛏 🅿 (8) ⅒ ⬚ ★ ▥ Ⅵ ∦ ⚲
Warm, friendly welcome in a
beautiful country house with
spectacular views over golf course
and the Lomond Hills. Buchanan
Castle to the rear. 1 mile from
Drymen Centre, 2 miles from Loch
Lomond. Glasgow Airport 40 mins
away

Easter Drumquhassle Farm,
Gartness Road, Drymen, Glasgow,
G63 0DN.
Actual grid ref: NS486872
Traditional farmhouse, beautiful
views, home cooking, excellent
base on the West Highland Way
Grades: STB 3 Star,
AA 3 Diamond
Tel: **01360 660893** Mrs Cross.
Fax no: 01360 660282
D: £18.00-£25.00 **S:** £25.00-£30.00.
Open: All Year
Beds: 1F 1D 1T
Baths: 3 En
🛏 🅿 (10) ⅒ ⬚ ★ ✕ ★ ▥ Ⅵ ∦ ⚲

17 Stirling Road, *Drymen,*
Glasgow, G63 0BW.
Actual grid ref: NS476883
Family home in village near West
Highland Way; lovely garden
Tel: **01360 660273** (also fax no)
Mrs Lander.
D: £15.00-£18.00 **S:** £18.00-£23.00.
Open: All Year
Beds: 1F 1T
Baths: 1 Sh
🛏 🅿 (1) ⬚ ★ ★ ▥ Ⅵ ∦ ⚲

Drymen House, 5/7 Stirling Road, Drymen, Glasgow, G63 0BW.
Friendly warm atmosphere - restaurant and bar facilities
Grades: STB 2 Star
Tel: 01360 660099
Fax no: 01360 661162
D: £20.00-£25.00 **S:** £20.00-£25.00.
Open: All Year
Beds: 5F 2D 2T 1S
🛏🅿🖵✕🏃⚕👪🖢Ⓥ🅰✦🚲

Glenava, Stirling Road, Drymen, Glasgow, G63 0AA.
Warm welcome, stunning scenery, comfortable rooms, lovely local Wales
Grades: STB 3 Star
Tel: 01360 660491 Ms Fraser.
D: £17.00-£18.00 **S:** £25.00-£25.00.
Open: Easter to Oct
Beds: 1D 1T
Baths: 1 Sh
🛏🅿(4)🍴🖵🏃⚕🖢Ⓥ🅰✦🚲

Aberfoyle 44

National Grid Ref: NN5200

🍽🍴 Black Bull, Old Coach House, Inverard Hotel, Forth Inn, The Byre

Oak Royal Guest House,
Aberfoyle, Stirling, FK8 3UX.
Beautiful Trossachs countryside. Ideal base for touring & outdoor enthusiasts
Grades: STB 3 Star B&B
Tel: 01877 382633 (also fax no)
D: £20.00-£22.50 **S:** £25.00-£30.00.
Open: All Year
Beds: 2D 1T
Baths: 2 En 1 Sh
🛏🅿(6)🍴🖵🏃⚕🖢Ⓥ🅰✦🚲

The Forth Inn, Main Street, Aberfoyle, Stirling, FK8 3UQ.
Family-run hotel set in the heart of The Trossachs
Tel: 01877 382372
Fax no: 01877 382488
D: £17.50 **S:** £20.00.
Open: All Year
Beds: 1F 2D 2T **Baths:** 6 En
🛏🅿(20)🖵🏃✕⚕👪🖢Ⓥ🅰✦🚲

Milton 45

National Grid Ref: NN5001

Creag Ard House B&B, Milton, Aberfoyle, Stirling, FK8 3TQ.
Actual grid ref: NN502015
Grades: STB 3 Star
Tel: 01877 382297 Mrs Wilson.
D: £25.00-£35.00 **S:** £25.00-£70.00.
Open: All Year
Beds: 4D 2T 1S
Baths: 4 En 1 Sh
🛏🅿(7)🍴🏃✕⚕🖢Ⓥ🅰✦🚲
A beautiful Victorian house with extensive and colourful gardens, set in some of the most magnificent scenery, overlooking Loch Ard and superb views of the mountains. Own trout fishing, boat hire, excellent home cooking, fine wines and the best Scotch whiskies

---

Planning a longer stay? Always ask for any special rates.

Loch Tay to the Pass of Drumochter

From Kenmore at the northeastern end of Loch Tay you follow the River Tay to the sixteenth-century fortified tower house Castle Menzies, historic seat of the Menzies clan, and Aberfeldy, where the restored water mill dates from the early nineteenth century. From here you continue to **Pitlochry**. Here the Edradour Distillery is Scotland's smallest whisky distillery and the Pitlochry Festival Theatre stages a different play every night from May to October. By the hydroelectric power station is a fish ladder, by which the salmon can bypass the dam on the Tummel to reach their breeding grounds. A short way through the Tummel Forest Park, the spectacular Pass of Killiecrankie was the setting in 1689 for the Battle of Killiecrankie, a great Jacobite victory in the period when such things happened. A little further on is Blair Atholl, where there is a working water mill, and nearby Blair Castle, seat of the Dukes of Atholl. Over the long period since its foundation in the thirteenth century, this striking white fortress has undergone much alteration. It is the scene every May for the parade of the Atholl Highlanders, Britain's only legal private army. The route through Glen Garry culminates in a steady ascent to the **Pass of Drumochter.** This will test your stamina. There is no alternative to the A9 and there is only one hotel listed in this book - at Dalwhinnie.

Loch Achray 46

National Grid Ref: NN5106

Glenbruach Country House, Loch Achray, Trossachs, Callander, Perthshire, FK17 8HX.
Tel: 01877 376216 (also fax no)
Mrs Lindsay.
D: £22.00-£25.00 **S:** £22.00-£25.00.
Open: All Year
Beds: 2D 1T **Baths:** 2 En 1 Pr
🛏(12)🅿(3)🍴🏃✕⚕🖢Ⓥ🅰✦🚲
Unique country mansion in the heart of Rob Roy country. All rooms with Loch views. Interesting interior design and collections in this Scots-owned home

Callander 47

National Grid Ref: NN6307

🍽🍴 Abbotsford Lodge Hotel, Myrtle Inn, Crags Hotel, Bracklin Fall, Bridge End

Riverview House, Leny Road, Callander, Perthshire, FK17 8AL.
Grades: STB 3 Star
Tel: 01877 330635 Mr Little.
D: £21.00-£22.00 **S:** £22.00-£24.00.
Open: All Year (not Xmas)
Beds: 3D 2T 1S **Baths:** 5 En
🅿(6)🍴🖵✕🏃⚕🖢Ⓥ🅰✦🚲
Attractive, stone-built villa in own grounds within easy walking of town centre and cycle/pathway. Good home cooking. We also offer self catering cottages in beautiful Trossachs area

Arden House , Bracklinn Road, Callander, Perthshire, FK17 8EQ.
Tel: 01877 330235 (also fax no)
Mr Mitchell & Mr W Jackson.
D: £25.00-£30.00 **S:** £27.50.
Open: Easter to Nov
Beds: 3D 2T 1S **Baths:** 6 En
🛏(14)🅿(6)🍴🖵🏃⚕🖢Ⓥ🅰
Peaceful Victorian country house in beautiful gardens with stunning views. Home of BBC TV's 'Dr Finlay's Casebook'. Comfortable ensuite rooms with TV. Tea/coffee and many thoughtful touches. Short walk to village centre. Generous breakfast

---

The Grid Reference beneath the location heading is for the village or town - *not* for individual houses, which are shown (where supplied) in each entry itself.

Glengarry Hotel, *Stirling Road, Callander, Perthshire, FK17 8DA.*
Tel: **01877 330216**
D: £22.00-£25.00.
Open: All Year
Beds: 2F 1D
Baths: 3 En
🛇 ᵽ (15) ⌿ ⌷ ⟲ ✕ ⚐ ▥ Ⅴ ▮ ⚡ ⟳
Family-run hotel in its own grounds in the picturesque town of Callander where the Lowlands meet the Highlands. Large comfortable bedrooms. A warm welcome, a hearty breakfast, traditional home-cooked evening meals. Easy access

Roslin Cottage, *Lagrannoch, Callander, Perthshire, FK17 8LE.*
Beautiful C18th stone cottage & garden on outskirts of town
Tel: **01877 330638**
Mrs Ferguson.
Fax no: 01877 331448
D: £15.50-£16.00
S: £18.50-£18.50.
Open: All Year
Beds: 1D 1T 2S
Baths: 1 Sh
🛇 ᵽ ᵽ ⌷ ⚐ ✕ ⚐ ▥ Ⅴ ⚡

East Mains House, *Bridgend, Callander, Perthshire, FK17 8AG.*
C18th mansion house, mature garden
Grades: STB 3 Star
Tel: **01877 330535** (also fax no)
Ms Alexander.
D: £22.00-£24.00
S: £29.00-£29.00.
Open: All Year
Beds: 2F 4D
Baths: 4 En
🛇 ᵽ (6) ⌿ ⌷ ⚐ ✕ ⚐ ▥ Ⅴ ⟳

Lamorna, *Ancaster Road, Callander, Perthshire, FK17 8JJ.*
Detached bungalow, panoramic views of Callander and surrounding countryside, quiet location, close all amenities
Grades: STB 3 Star B&B
Tel: **01877 330868**
D: £18.00-£20.00.
Open: Easter to Oct
Beds: 1D 1T
Baths: 1 Sh
ᵽ (2) ⌿ ⌷ ⚐ ▥ Ⅴ

Brook Linn Country House, *Callander, Perthshire, FK17 8AU.*
Lovely comfortable Victorian house with magnificent views and personal attention
Grades: STB 4 Star,
AA 4 Diamond
Tel: **01877 330103** (also fax no)
Mrs House.
D: £23.00-£27.00
S: £23.00-£27.00.
Open: Easter to Oct
Beds: 1F 2D 2T 2S
Baths: 6 En 1 Sh
🛇 ᵽ (8) ⌿ ⌷ ⚐ ⚐ ▥ Ⅴ ⚡ ⟳

White Cottage, *Bracklinn Road, Callander, FK17 8EQ.*
Situated in one acre garden. Magnificent views of Ben Ledi
Grades: STB 3 Star
Tel: **01877 330896**
Mrs Hughes.
Fax no: 01877 331866
D: £17.00-£20.00 **S:** £22.00-£25.00.
Open: Easter to Nov
Beds: 2D
Baths: 1 Sh
ᵽ (3) ⌿ ⌷ ⚐ ▥ Ⅴ ⟳

Auchinlea, *Ancaster Road, Callander, Perthshire, FK17 8EL.*
Quietly situated bungalow, few minutes walk from town & amenities
Tel: **01877 330769** Mrs McKenzie.
D: £16.00 **S:** £18.00.
Open: All Year
Beds: 1D 1T
Baths: 2 Sh
🛇 ᵽ (1) ⌿ ⌷ ⚐ ⚐ ▥ Ⅴ

Campfield Cottage, *138 Main Street, Callander, Perthshire, FK17 8BG.*
Modernised comfortable cottage. Breakfast served in conservatory overlooking patio & garden
Tel: **01877 330597** Mrs Harvey.
D: £15.00 **S:** £20.00.
Open: All Year
Beds: 2D 1T
Baths: 1 Sh
ᵽ ⌷ ⚐ ⚐ ▥ Ⅴ

The Lochans, *5 Lubnaig Drive, Callander, Perthshire, FK17 8JT.*
Outlook to hills, quiet, adjacent leisure centre and all amenities
Tel: **01877 330627** Mrs Lochans.
D: £19.50 **S:** £22.00.
Open: Easter to Oct
Beds: 1T 1D
Baths: 2 En
🛇 ᵽ (2) ⌷ ⚐ ✕ ⚐ ▥ Ⅴ ⚡ ⟳

Strathyre 48

National Grid Ref: NN5617

🍴 🍺 Strathyre Inn, Ben Shian Hotel

Rosebank House, *Strathyre, Callander, Perthshire, FK18 8NA.*
Actual grid ref: NN563174
Grades: STB 4 Star GH
Tel: **01877 384208**
Mr & Mrs Moor.
Fax no: 01877 384201
D: £18.00-£20.00
S: £18.00-£25.00.
Open: Mar to Dec
Beds: 1F 2D 1T 1S
Baths: 2 En 1 Pr
🛇 ᵽ (3) ⌿ ⌷ ⚐ ✕ ⚐ ▥ Ⅴ ▮ ⚡ ⟳
Rosebank house is a fine example of Victorian architecture. Jill and Pete Moor will welcome you to our comfortable home, where good food both evening and morning meals are a treat. Open fires. Cyclists and walkers are especially welcome

Dochfour, *Strathyre, Callander, FK18 8NA.*
Award-winning B&B in scenic glen, specialising in being the best!
Grades: STB 3 Star
Tel: **01877 384256** (also fax no)
Mr & Mrs Ffinch.
D: £17.00-£20.00 **S:** £23.00-£26.00.
Open: All Year
Beds: 2D 1T **Baths:** 2 En 1 Pr
🛇 ᵽ (6) ⌷ ✕ ⚐ ▥ Ⅴ ▮ ⚡ ⟳

The Inn At Strathyre, *Main Street, Strathyre, Callander, Perthshire, FK18 8NA.*
Lovely inn with recommended restaurant surrounded by beautiful scenery
Tel: **01877 384224** (also fax no)
Mr La Piazza.
D: £22.00 **S:** £25.00.
Open: All Year
Beds: 4D 3T **Baths:** 7 Pr
🛇 (5) ᵽ (15) ⌷ ✕ ⚐ ▥ Ⅴ ▮ ⚡

Coire Buidhe, *Strathyre, Callander, Perthshire, FK18 8NA.*
Former mill. Value for money. Repeat custom our recommendation. 1998 FHG Publications award winner
Tel: **01877 384288**
Mr & Mrs Reid.
D: £14.50 **S:** £15.00.
Open: All Year (not Xmas)
Beds: 2F 2D 2T 2S
Baths: 1 Pr 3 Sh
🛇 ᵽ (6) ⌷ ⚐ ▥ Ⅴ ▮ ⚡

Balquhidder 49

National Grid Ref: NN5320

Cragmhor, *Balquhidder, Lochearnhead, FK19 8PB.*
Surrounded by beautiful mountain scenery, close to loch and river
Grades: STB 3 Star
Tel: **01877 384204** Mrs Wagstaff.
Fax no: 01877 384374
D: £17.50-£20.00 **S:** £22.50-£25.00.
Open: All Year (not Xmas)
Beds: 1D 1T **Baths:** 2 En
🛇 ᵽ (8) ⌿ ⌷ ⚐ ⚐ ▥ Ⅴ ▮ ⟳

Killin 50

National Grid Ref: NN5732

🍴 🍺 Bridge of Lochay

▲ **Killin Youth Hostel,** *Killin, Perthshire, FK21 8TN.*
Actual grid ref: NN569338
Tel: **01567 820546**
Under 18: £4.85 **Adults:** £6.10
suitable for disabled people, self-catering facilities, shop
Picturesque Killin has the Falls of Dochart, beautiful in fine weather and impressive when in spate. There are standing stones from the Bronze Age, and the grave of Fingal, the Celtic hero. The area provides views of Ben Lawers and Loch Tay and a wide range of wildlife

Falls of Dochart Cottage, Killin, Perthshire, FK21 8SW.
Tel: **01567 820363**
Mr & Mrs Mudd.
D: £17.00–£17.00
S: £17.00.
Open: All Year (not Xmas)
Beds: 1D 1T 1S
Baths: 2 Sh
ॐ (1) 🅿 (4) ⅍ ☐ ⅄ ✕ 🎟 ♨
C17th cottage, overlooking the falls and river - home cooking - comfortable and friendly atmosphere. Open all year: central to magnificent mountain area - renowned for hill walking

Drumfinn House, Manse Road, Killin, Perthshire, FK21 8UY.
Grades: STB 2 Star
Tel: **01567 820900** (also fax no)
Mrs Semple.
D: £16.00–£20.00.
Open: All Year (not Xmas)
Beds: 1F 3D 2T
Baths: 3 En 1 Sh
ॐ (12) 🅿 (6) ⅍ ☐ ⅄ ♨ 🎟 ♥ ⅍ ♨
Warm, friendly country house in the centre of the highland village of Killin. Large airy rooms, some with open fires. Private off street parking with area for cyclists and motor cycles. Ideal touring centre with spectacular mountain and loch views

The Coach House Hotel, Lochay Road, Killin, Perthshire, FK21 8TN.
Tel: **01567 820349**
Fax no: 01567 820349 (ring first)
D: £20.00–£26.00 **S:** £20.00–£26.00.
Open: All Year
Beds: 1F 1D 2T **Baths:** 2 En 2 Sh
ॐ 🅿 (40) ⅍ ☐ ♨ ♨ 🎟 ♥ ⅍ ♨
Family run hotel surrounded by mountains overlooking the river extensive menu cooked by proprietor chef peter Shuttleworth fully licensed lounge bar also fully inclusive escorted holidays available min 2 max 6 persons Edinburgh Glasgow air/rail

Greenacre, Killin, Perthshire, FK21 8TY.
Peace and tranquillity in beautiful surroundings at the foot of Ben Lawers **Grades:** STB 3 Star
Tel: **01567 820466** (also fax no)
Dearie.
D: £20.00–£20.00.
Open: All Year (not Xmas)
Beds: 2D 1T **Baths:** 3 En
ॐ 🅿 (4) ☐ ♨ 🎟 ♿ 🎟 ⅍ ♨

D = Price range per person sharing in a double room

Breadalbane House, Main Street, Killin, Perthshire, FK21 8UT.
Large converted bank, home from home
Tel: **01567 820386** (also fax no)
Mrs Grant.
D: £18.00 **S:** £20.00.
Open: All Year (not Xmas)
Beds: 2F 2D 1T
Baths: 5 En
ॐ 🅿 (6) ⅍ ☐ ⅄ ✕ ♨ 🎟 ♿ 🎟 ⅍ ♨

Acharn 51

National Grid Ref: NN7543

🍴 🍺 Croft-na-caber Hotel

12 Ballinlaggan, Acharn, Aberfeldy, Perthshire, PH15 2HT.
Tel: **01887 830409** Mrs Spiers.
D: £16.00 **S:** £16.00–£16.00.
Open: All Year
Beds: 1T 1S
Baths: 1 Sh
ॐ 🅿 (2) ⅍ ☐ ✕ ♨ 🎟 🎟 ⅍ ♨
A warm welcome awaits you in the quiet lochside village of Acharn, surrounded by beautiful scenery. Local attractions abound, whether it be watersports, scuba diving, hill walking, golf, fishing, pony trekking, castles, cycle hire and much, much more

Old School House, Acharn, Aberfeldy, Perthshire, PH15 2HS.
Comfortable converted school-house near Loch Tay. Excellent touring/walking
Grades: STB 3 Star
Tel: **01887 830307** (also fax no)
Mrs Brodie.
D: £18.00–£20.00 **S:** £25.00–£25.00.
Open: Easter to Oct
Beds: 2D 1T
Baths: 2 En 1 Sh
ॐ 🅿 (10) ☐ ♨ 🎟 🎟 ⅍ ♨

Aberfeldy 52

National Grid Ref: NN8549

🍴 🍺 Black Watch, Aileen Chraggan Hotel, Coshieville Hotel

Carn Dris, Aberfeldy, Perthshire, PH15 2LB.
Large Edwardian private house, ex manse, overlooking Aberfeldy golf course
Tel: **01887 820250**
Mrs Bell Campbell.
D: £20.00–£25.00 **S:** £20.00–£25.00.
Open: Easter to Oct
Beds: 2D 1T **Baths:** 1 En 1 Sh
ॐ (10) 🅿 (4) ☐ ⅄ ♨ 🎟 ⅍ ♨

Bringing children with you? Always ask for any special rates.

The Pass of Drumochter to Inverness

The way through Glen Truim leads to **Newtonmore** and **Kingussie**, where Ruthven Barracks was built in the early eighteenth century by the ascendant royal family to suppress the Jacobites. From here you head on through Strathspey, haven of ospreys and salmon, past Loch Insh to **Inverdruie** near Aviemore, and on to **Boat of Garten**; before turning west and then north to Carrbridge, and on to Slochd Summit. After descending to Tomatin across the River Findhorn you proceed to **Culloden**. Here in 1746 the last battle fought anywhere in Britain finally crushed the Jacobite rebellion, leading to the flight of Prince Charles Edward Stuart and the mass murder and pillage of the Highland Clearances. Before you reach the town the Culloden Visitor Centre, at the site of the battle, offers an audiovisual presentation. It is but a short way to **Inverness**, capital of the Highlands, where the route ends on the west bank of the River Ness. In front of the Victorian castle, built on the site of the earlier edifice razed by the Jacobites, stands a statue of Flora MacDonald, the local heroine who helped 'Bonnie' Prince Charles Edward Stuart escape from Benbecula to Skye after Culloden. The Museum and Art Gallery has displays of local interest; and Balnain House, a museum of Highland music, is well worth a visit. To the south of town, the northern section of Thomas Telford's Caledonian Canal leads into Loch Ness. To the north, you can take a cruise around the Moray Firth to spot seals and perhaps dolphins traversing the bay.

Novar, *2 Home Street, Aberfeldy, Perthshire, PH15 2AJ.*
Novar is a comfortable stone house near golf course; good walks
Grades: STB 3 Star
Tel: 01887 820779
Mrs Malcolm.
D: £17.00-£19.00
S: £25.00-£25.00.
Open: All Year (not Xmas)
Beds: 1F 1D 1T
Baths: 2 En 5 Pr 1 Sh
♿ �ℙ (3) ⚡ ⌨ 🐾 🍴 🛗 ♿ 🛏 ⓥ ⓐ ✦ ♻

Tomvale, *Tom of Cluny Farm, Aberfeldy, Perthshire, PH15 2JT.*
Modern farmhouse with outstanding views of the Upper Tay Valley
Tel: 01887 820171 (also fax no)
Mrs Kennedy.
D: £17.00 **S:** £18.00.
Open: All Year (not Xmas)
Beds: 1F 1D
Baths: 1 Sh
♿ ℙ ⌨ 🐾 ✕ 🛗 ⓥ ⓐ ✦ ♻

Handa, *Taybridge Road, Aberfeldy, PH15 2BH.*
Quiet residential area. One minute river walks and golf courses
Tel: 01887 820334
Mrs Bassett-Smith.
D: £17.00-£18.50
S: £17.00-£17.00.
Open: All Year (not Xmas)
Beds: 1T 1D
♿ ℙ ⌨ ✕ 🛗 ⓥ ⓐ ♻

Balnearn House, *Aberfeldy, Perthshire, PH15 2BJ.*
Excellent Scottish breakfast. Aberfeldy outstanding centre for touring by car or walking
Tel: 01887 820431
Mr MacLaurin.
Fax no: 01887 829064
D: £18.50 **S:** £25.00.
Open: Easter to Nov
Beds: 1F 6D 2T
Baths: 8 En 1 Pr
♿ ℙ (20) ⌨ 🐾 🛗 ⓥ ⓐ ✦

2 Rannoch Road, *Aberfeldy, Perthshire, PH15 2BU.*
Large modern bungalow, comfortable and friendly. Quiet location near all amenities
Tel: 01887 820770 Mrs Ross.
D: £16.00 **S:** £16.00.
Open: Mar to Oct
Beds: 2D 1T
Baths: 1 En 1 Sh
ℙ (4) ⌨ 🐾 🛗 ⓥ

Caber Feidh Guest House, *56 Dunkeld Street, Aberfeldy, Perthshire, PH15 2AF.*
Friendly welcome, central Scotland. Ideal for touring, golf, fishing, walking
Tel: 01887 820342 (also fax no)
Mr Thain.
D: £18.50 **S:** £18.50.
Open: Mar to Jan
Beds: 1F 3D 1T 1S
Baths: 6 En
ℙ (5) ⌨ 🐾 🛗 ⓥ ⓐ

Edradynate 53
National Grid Ref: NN8852

Lurgan Farm, *Edradynate, Aberfeldy, Perthshire, PH15 2JX.*
Actual grid ref: NN880529
Traditional working farm, with stunning views over the Tay Valley
Grades: STB 2 Star B&B
Tel: 01887 840451 Mrs Kennedy.
D: £17.00-£22.00 **S:** £17.00-£22.00.
Open: All Year (not Xmas)
Beds: 1F
Baths: 1 En
♿ ℙ ⚡ ⌨ 🐾 🛗 ⓥ ♻

S = Price range for a single person in a room

Pitlochry 54
National Grid Ref: NN9458

� ⚑ Moulin Hotel, Westlands

▲ **Pitlochry Youth Hostel,**
Knockard Road, Pitlochry, PH16 5HJ.
Actual grid ref: NN943584
Tel: 01796 472308
Under 18: £6.50 **Adults:** £7.75
evening meals available, self-catering facilities, family bunk rooms, shop, laundry facilities
Pitlochry is a bustling small town at the very centre of Scotland. Scenic countryside ideal for climbing. The Festival Theatre is open May-October - outdoor shows all summer. The Highland Games are in September

Oakbank, *20 Lower Oakfield, Pitlochry, PH16 5DS.*
Tel: 01796 472080 Mr Hendry.
Fax no: 01796 473502
D: £18.00-£20.00 **S:** £20.00-£22.00.
Open: All Year (not Xmas)
Beds: 1F 1D 1T
Baths: 3 En
♿ ℙ (3) ⚡ ⌨ 🐾 🛗 ⓥ ⓐ ✦ ♻
Oakbank - well-appointed detached granite Victorian villa, overlooking beautiful Tummel Valley. Quality rooms, full Scottish breakfast. If you come by public transport ,we also provide car hire (discount to residents). We will meet you from Pitlochry train/bus stations

Balrobin Hotel, *Higher Oakfield, Pitlochry, Perthshire, PH16 5HT.*
Quality accommodation with panoramic views at affordable prices
Grades: STB 3 Star, RAC 2 Star
Tel: 01796 472901 Mr Hohman.
Fax no: 01796 474200
D: £25.00-£33.00 **S:** £25.00-£39.00.
Open: Apr to Oct
Beds: 1F 10D 3T 1S **Baths:** 15 En
♿ (5) ℙ (15) ⌨ 🐾 ✕ 🛗 ⓥ ⓐ ♻

Dundarave House, *Strathview Terrace, Pitlochry, PH16 5AT.*
Charm, character and serene atmosphere
Grades: STB 3 Star,
AA 4 Diamond
Tel: 01796 473109 (also fax no)
Mrs Waller.
D: £18.00-£26.00 **S:** £18.00-£26.00.
Open: All Year
Beds: 1F 2D 2T 2S
Baths: 5 En 2 Sh
🛇 (6) 🅿 (7) 🛏 ⌂ 🎱 📖 Ⅴ 🛡 ✗ 🚲

Dun-Donnachaidh, *9 Knockard Road, Pitlochry, Perthshire, PH16 5HJ.*
Victorian house of character, wonderful views, quiet, close to town centre
Grades: STB 4 Star B&B
Tel: 01796 474018 (also fax no)
Wallace.
D: £17.50-£25.00 **S:** £17.50-£38.00.
Open: Feb to Oct
Beds: 2D 1T
Baths: 3 En
🛇 (12) 🅿 (3) 🛏 ⌂ 🎱 📖 Ⅴ ✗ 🚲

Acair, *10 Craigower Crescent, Pitlochry, PH16 5HS.*
Modern house, 5 mins walk from town, offers Scottish hospitality
Grades: STB 3 Star
Tel: 01796 473898 Mrs Irvine.
D: £18.00-£20.00.
Open: May to Oct
Beds: 2D
Baths: 2 En
🅿 (3) 🛏 ⌂ 🎱 📖 Ⅴ 🚲

Poplars Hotel, *27 Lower Oakfield, Pitlochry, Perthshire, PH16 5DS.*
Impressive Victorian house set in a large garden, with spectacular views
Tel: 01796 472129 Ms Shepherd.
Fax no: 01796 472554
D: £18.00 **S:** £19.00.
Open: All Year
Beds: 3F 4D 4T
Baths: 11 En
🛇 🅿 (15) ⌂ 🛏 ✗ 🎱 📖 ♿ Ⅴ

Easter Dunfallandy Country House B&B, *Pitlochry, Perthshire, PH16 5NA.*
Quietly situated with wonderful views just 2 miles from Pitlochry in lovely highland Perthshire
Tel: 01796 474128 Mr Mathieson.
Fax no: 01796 473994
D: £26.00 **S:** £52.00.
Open: Mar to Nov
Beds: 1D 2T
Baths: 3 En
🅿 (6) 🛏 ⌂ 📖 ✗

Pay B&Bs by cash or cheque and be prepared to pay up front.

Grove Cottage, *10 Lower Oakfield, Pitlochry, Perthshire, PH16 5DS.*
Victorian house with lovely views, quiet road near town centre
Tel: 01796 472374 (also fax no)
Mrs Hawkes.
D: £14.50 **S:** £16.00.
Open: All Year
Beds: 1D 1T 2S
Baths: 2 Pr 1 Sh
🅿 (4) ⌂ 🛏 ✗ 🎱 📖 Ⅴ 🛡 ✗

Briar Cottage, *Wellbrae, Pitlochry, Perthshire, PH16 5HH.*
Bright modern house, suitable for disabled. Quiet location 5 minutes' walk from town centre
Tel: 01796 473678 Mrs Scott.
D: £14.50 **S:** £25.00.
Open: Easter to Oct
Beds: 1D 2T
Baths: 1 En 1 Sh
🛇 🅿 (3) ⌂ 🛏 🎱 📖 ♿ Ⅴ

Moulin 55

National Grid Ref: NN9459

🏨 🍺 Moulin Hotel

Baringa, *Craig Lunie Road, Moulin, Pitlochry, PH16 5QZ.*
Ideally situated, hospitable base for touring and outdoor pursuits
Grades: STB 2 Star
Tel: 01796 472868 Mrs Currie.
D: £16.00-£16.00 **S:** £16.00-£16.00.
Open: May to Oct
Beds: 1F 1D 2S
Baths: 2 Sh
🛇 🅿 (5) 🛏 ⌂ 🎱 📖 Ⅴ 🛡 ✗ 🚲

Lavalette, *Manse Road, Moulin, Pitlochry, Perthshire, PH16 5EP.*
Grades: STB 3 Star
Tel: 01796 472364 Mrs Robertson.
D: £16.00-£16.00 **S:** £15.00-£15.00.
Open: Mar to Oct
Beds: 1F 1D 1S
Baths: 2 En 1 Sh
🛇 🅿 (3) 🛏 ⌂ 🎱 📖 Ⅴ ✗
Modern bungalow in the quiet and historic village of Moulin where the scenery is superb. Ideal for theatre lovers, golfers, walkers and fishermen. Amongst many other interests, our full Scottish breakfast. Warm, friendly welcome guaranteed

Killiecrankie 56

National Grid Ref: NN9162

Tighdornie, *Killiecrankie, Pitlochry, Perthshire, PH16 5LR.*
Modern house in beautiful historic Killiecrankie. Famous Blair Castle nearby
Tel: 01796 473276 (also fax no)
Mrs Sanderson.
D: £21.00 **S:** £25.00.
Open: All Year
Beds: 1T 2D
Baths: 3 En
🛇 🅿 (5) 🛏 ⌂ 🎱 📖 Ⅴ ✗

Blair Atholl 57

National Grid Ref: NN8764

🏨 🍺 Tilt Hotel, The Roundhouse

Dalgreine, *off St Andrews Crescent, Blair Atholl, Pitlochry, PH16 5SX.*
Attractive comfortable guest house, set in beautiful surroundings near Blair Castle
Grades: STB 3 Star,
AA 4 Diamond
Tel: 01796 481276
Mr & Mrs Pywell & Mrs F Hardie.
D: £16.00-£20.00
S: £16.00-£20.00.
Open: All Year
Beds: 1F 2D 2T 1S
Baths: 2 En 1 Pr 1 Sh
🛇 🅿 (6) 🛏 ⌂ 🎱 📖 Ⅴ 🛡 ✗ 🚲

Lauchope House, *The Terrace, Bridge Of Tilt, Blair Atholl, Pitlochry, Perthshire, PH18 5SX.*
Situated in large garden. Superb views. Near Blair Castle and Pitlochry
Tel: 01796 481200
Mrs McFarlane.
D: £14.50 **S:** £14.50.
Open: Easter to Oct
Beds: 1F 1D
Baths: 1 Pr 1 Sh
🛇 🅿 (3) 🛏 ⌂ 🎱 📖 Ⅴ

Newtonmore 58

National Grid Ref: NN7199

🏨 🍺 Braeriach Hotel, Glen Hotel

▲ **Croft Holidays Hostel (Independent),** *Stone Road, Newtonmore, Inverness-shire, PH20 1BA.*
Actual grid ref: NH720001
Tel: 01540 673504 Adults: £9.00
self-catering facilities

▲ **Newtonmore Independent Hostel,** *Craigellachie House, Main Street, Newtonmore, Inverness-shire, PH20 1DA.*
Actual grid ref: NN713990
Tel: 01540 673360 Adults: £8.50
self-catering facilities, no smoking

The Pines, *Station Road, Newtonmore, Inverness-shire, PH20 1AR.*
Tel: 01540 673271
Mr Walker.
Fax no: 01540 673882
D: £22.50-£25.00 **S:** £22.50-£25.00.
Open: All Year
Beds: 2D 2T 1S
Baths: 5 En
🛇 (12) 🅿 (5) 🛏 ⌂ ✗ 🎱 Ⅴ 🛡 🚲
Situated in over one acre of mature pine gardens. Most rooms enjoying panoramic mountain views, ideal for touring, walking or cycling. RSPB reserves, Cairngorm mountains within easy driving distance. Discounts for three nights or longer

Tom An T'silidh, *Station Road, Newtonmore, Inverness-shire, PH20 1AR.*
Comfortable detached villa. Quiet location nearby River Spey and golf course
Grades: STB 2 Star
Tel: 01540 673554
Mrs Smith.
D: £19.00-£23.00
S: £20.00-£25.00.
Open: All Year (not Xmas)
Beds: 1F 1D 1T
Baths: 3 En
⑤ 🅿 (4) ⅍ 🗆 ⊼ ✕ 🚲 Ⅲ. Ⅵ 🛈 ≠ ⌖

Glenquoich House, *Glen Road, Newtonmore, Inverness-shire, PH20 1EB.*
Beautiful Victorian 150 metres from village centre. Mountain views
Tel: 01540 673461 (also fax no)
Watson.
D: £18.00 **S:** £18.00.
Open: All Year
Beds: 1F 2T 1D 1S
Baths: 1 En 2 Sh
⑤ (10) 🅿 (5) ⅍ 🗆 🚲 Ⅲ. Ⅵ 🛈 ≠ ⌖

Kingussie   59

National Grid Ref: NH7500

🏨 Scot House Hotel, Tipsy Laird, Osprey Hotel

▲ **Lairds Bothy Hostel
(Independent)**, *68 High Street, Kingussie, Inverness-shire, PH21 1HZ.*
Actual grid ref: NH758008
Tel: 01540 661334
Adults: £8.00
evening meals available, self-catering facilities, showers

The Osprey Hotel, *Kingussie, Inverness-shire, PH21 1EN.*
Grades: STB 3 Star Hotel, AA 2 Star
Tel: 01540 661510 (also fax no)
Mr Burrow.
D: £24.00-£30.00.
S: £24.00-£30.00.
Open: All Year
Beds: 3D 3T 2S
Baths: 8 En
⑤ 🅿 🗆 ⊼ ✕ 🚲 Ⅲ. & Ⅵ 🛈 ≠ ⌖
Small hotel in area of outstanding beauty, offering a warm welcome, ensuite accommodation and award-winning food. Aileen & Robert hold AA food rosettes and are members of the 'taste of Scotland'. Ideal base for touring, walking, golf, fishing, stb

Bringing children with
you? Always ask for
any special rates.

Homewood Lodge, *Kingussie, Inverness-shire, PH21 1HD.*
Grades: STB 4 Star GH
Tel: 01540 661507 Anderson.
D: £15.00 **S:** £15.00.
Open: All Year
Beds: 1F 1T 2D **Baths:** 4 En
🅿 (6) ⅍ 🗆 ✕ 🚲 Ⅲ. Ⅵ 🛈 ≠ ⌖
Homewood Lodge, a beautifully decorated Victorian house set in mature gardens. A tranquil base for touring in all directions. Splendid views of the Cairngorms from the dining room where only superb fresh food is served. Private off-street parking

Greystones, *Acres Road, Kingussie, Inverness-shire, PH21 1LA.*
Actual grid ref: NH758012
Victorian family home, pleasantly secluded, a five-minute walk from Kingussie
Grades: STB 3 Star
Tel: 01540 661052
Mr & Mrs Johnstone.
Fax no: 01540 662162
D: £18.50-£18.50 **S:** £18.50-£18.50.
Open: All Year (not Xmas)
Beds: 1F 1D 1T 1S
Baths: 1 Pr 2 Sh
⑤ 🅿 (6) ⅍ 🗆 ⊼ ✕ 🚲 Ⅲ. Ⅵ 🛈 ≠ ⌖

Arden House, *Newtonmore Road, Kingussie, Inverness-shire, PH21 1HE.*
Excellent food and accommodation, delightful centrally situated Victorian villa
Grades: STB 3 Star GH
Tel: 01540 661369 (also fax no)
Mrs Spry.
D: £19.00-£22.00 **S:** £19.00-£22.00.
Open: All Year
Beds: 2F 2D 1T 1S
Baths: 3 En 3 Sh
⑤ (1) 🅿 (7) ⅍ 🗆 ⊼ ✕ 🚲 Ⅲ. & Ⅵ 🛈 ≠ ⌖

Bhuna Monadh, *85 High Street, Kingussie, Inverness-shire, PH21 1HX.*
Listed building in scenic area with many outdoor activities
Tel: 01540 661186 Ms Gibson.
Fax no: 01540 661186
D: £15.00-£20.00 **S:** £20.00-£25.00.
Open: All Year
Beds: 1D 1T
Baths: 2 En
⑤ 🅿 (3) ⅍ 🗆 ⊼ 🚲 Ⅲ. Ⅵ 🛈 ≠ ⌖

The Hermitage, *Spey Street, Kingussie, Inverness-shire, PH21 1HN.*
Warm Highland welcome in heart of Badenoch & Strathspey. Log fires on cold evenings
Grades: STB 4 Star
Tel: 01540 662137 Mr Taylor.
Fax no: 01540 662177
D: £21.00-£23.00 **S:** £26.00-£28.00.
Open: All Year (not Xmas)
Beds: 1F 1T 3D
Baths: 5 En
⑤ 🅿 🗆 ⊼ ✕ 🚲 Ⅲ. Ⅵ 🛈 ≠ ⌖

Rowan House, *Homewood, Newtonmore Road, Kingussie, Inverness-shire, PH21 1HD.*
Quiet hillside position; outstanding views of Spey Valley and mountains
Grades: STB 4 Star
Tel: 01540 662153 Ms Smiter.
D: £17.00-£22.00 **S:** £17.00-£20.00.
Open: All Year (not Xmas)
Beds: 1D 2T
Baths: 1 En 2 Pr
⑤ (2) 🅿 (3) ⅍ 🗆 🚲 Ⅲ. Ⅵ ⌖

Glengarry, *East Terrace, Kingussie, Inverness-shire, PH21 1JS.*
Traditional stone villa, attractive gardens, in quiet residential location
Grades: STB 4 Star
Tel: 01540 661386 (also fax no)
Mr & Mrs Crawford.
D: £18.00-£21.00
S: £19.00-£19.00.
Open: All Year
Beds: 1D 1T 2S
Baths: 2 En 2 Sh
🅿 (4) ⅍ 🗆 ✕ 🚲 Ⅲ. Ⅵ

Dunmhor House, *67 High Street, Kingussie, Inverness-shire, PH21 1HX.*
Centrally situated for numerous attractions in beautiful scenic Highland village
Tel: 01540 661809 (also fax no)
D: £16.00-£18.00
S: £16.00-£20.00.
Open: All Year
Beds: 2F 2D 1S
Baths: 2 Sh
⑤ 🅿 (5) 🗆 ⊼ ✕ 🚲 Ⅲ. Ⅵ ⌖

Avondale Guest House, *Newtonmore Road, Kingussie, Inverness-shire, PH21 1HF.*
Splendid example of an Edwardian home now converted into a luxury family-run guest house
Tel: 01540 661731 (also fax no)
D: £18.00 **S:** £21.00.
Open: All Year
Beds: 1F 2T 2D 1S
Baths: 4 En 2 Sh
⑤ (10) 🅿 (6) ⅍ 🗆 ⊼ ✕ 🚲 Ⅲ. & Ⅵ 🛈 ⌖

The Grid Reference
beneath the location
heading is for the
village or town - *not*
for individual houses,
which are shown
(where supplied) in
each entry itself.

Kincraig 60

National Grid Ref: NH8305

Kith & Kin Inn, Ossian Hotel

▲ **Kirkbeag Hostel (Independent)**, *Kirkbeag, Kincraig, Kingussie, Inverness-shire, PH21 1ND.*
Actual grid ref: NH840068
Tel: **01540 651298**
Adults: £8.50
self-catering facilities

Kirkbeag, Milehead, Kincraig, Kingussie, Inverness-shire, PH21 1ND.
Freindly family B&B in converted C19th church. Quiet country location
Grades: STB 3 Star
Tel: **01540 651298** (also fax no)
Mrs Paisley.
D: £16.50-£17.50
S: £20.00-£23.00.
Open: All Year
Beds: 1D 1T
Baths: 2 Sh
ॐ 🅿 (6) ⌷ ✕ ஊ ▥ Ⅴ ⬥ ⚡

Ossian Hotel, Kincraig, Kingussie, Inverness-shire, PH21 1QD.
Warm welcome, good food, good whisky
Grades: STB 2 Star
Tel: **01540 651242**
Mrs Rainbow.
Fax no: 01540 651633
D: £20.00-£31.00
S: £20.00-£31.00.
Open: Feb to Dec
Beds: 2F 3D 2T 2S
Baths: 8 En 1 Pr
ॐ 🅿 (20) ⨶ ⌷ ★ ✕ ஊ ▥ Ⅴ ⬥ ⚡ ⮔

Braeriach Guest House, Kincraig, Kingussie, Inverness-shire, PH21 1QA.
Actual grid ref: NH824056
Beautiful riverside country house. Spacious comfortable rooms with incredible views
Grades: STB 3 Star
Tel: **01540 651369**
Mrs Johnson.
D: £20.00-£25.00
S: £20.00-£25.00.
Open: All Year
Beds: 2D 2T
Baths: 3 En 1 Pr
ॐ 🅿 (4) ⌷ ★ ✕ ஊ ▥ Ⅴ ⬥ ⚡ ⮔

Insh House, Kincraig, Kingussie, Inverness-shire, PH21 1NU.
Friendly family guest house in splendid rural location near loch & mountains
Grades: STB 3 Star GH
Tel: **01540 651377**
Mr & Mrs Thompson.
D: £17.00-£20.00
S: £17.00-£20.00.
Open: All Year (not Xmas)
Beds: 1F 1D 1T 2S
Baths: 2 En 1 Sh
ॐ 🅿 ⨶ ⌷ ★ ✕ ஊ ▥ Ⅴ ⬥ ⚡

Feshiebridge 61

National Grid Ref: NH8504

Balcraggan House, Feshiebridge, Kincraig, Kingussie, Inverness-shire, PH21 1NG.
Wonderful setting where wildlife, walks and cycle routes abound
Tel: **01540 651488**
Mrs Gillies.
D: £25.00-£25.00
S: £30.00-£30.00.
Open: All Year
Beds: 1D 1T
Baths: 2 En
ॐ (10) 🅿 ⨶ ⌷ ✕ ஊ ▥ Ⅴ ⬥

Inverdruie 62

National Grid Ref: NH9011

Old Bridge Inn

Avondruie Guest House, Inverdruie, Aviemore, Inverness-shire, PH22 1QH.
Modern house in riverside setting. Ideal for skiers and ramblers
Tel: **01479 810267**
Mr Black.
D: £17.50 **S:** £19.00.
Open: All Year
Beds: 2D 4T
Baths: 4 Pr 1 Sh
ॐ 🅿 (8) ⌷ ★ ஊ ⬥

Coylumbridge 63

National Grid Ref: NH9110

Bridge Inn, Cairgorm Hotel

Avalon, Coylumbridge, Aviemore, Inverness-shire, PH22 1RD.
Modern country setting, wonderful walks; near entrance to Larig Ghru
Grades: STB 2 Star
Tel: **01479 810158**
Mrs McCombie.
D: £18.00-£20.00 **S:** £18.00.
Open: All Year
Beds: 1D 1T
Baths: 2 En
ॐ (2) 🅿 (3) ⨶ ⌷ ★ ஊ ▥ Ⅴ ⬥

Aviemore 64

National Grid Ref: NH8912

Glenmore Lodge, Cairngorm Hotel, Old Bridge Inn, Mackenzie's

▲ **Aviemore Youth Hostel**, *25 Grampian Road, Aviemore, Inverness-shire, PH22 1PR.*
Actual grid ref: NH893119
Tel: **01479 810345**
Under 18: £7.10
Adults: £8.60
suitable for disabled people, self-catering facilities, family bunk rooms, shop, laundry facilities
Set in birch woodlands next to a nature reserve, an ideal base for you to explore the beauty of Strathspey

Ravenscraig Guest House, Aviemore, Inverness-shire, PH22 1RP.
Grades: STB 2 Star GH, AA 3 Diamond
Tel: **01479 810278**
Mr & Mrs Gatenby.
Fax no: 01479 812742
D: £18.00-£24.00 **S:** £18.00-£24.00.
Open: All Year
Beds: 2F 5D 4T 1S
Baths: 12 En
ॐ 🅿 (16) ⌷ ★ ✕ ஊ ▥ Ⅴ ⬥ ⚡ ⮔
Comfortable ensuite rooms and wonderful breakfasts make 'Ravenscraig' the place to stay in Strathspey. Our central location makes Aviemore a super location for touring the Highlands of Scotland. Available locally: golf, fishing, hill-walking, mountain biking, birdwatching

Ryvoan, Grampian Road, Aviemore, Inverness-shire, PH22 1RY.
Beautiful modern bungalow with patio overlooking the Cairngorms situated at north end of village
Tel: **01479 810805** Mrs Cristall.
D: £16.00-£16.00 **S:** £18.00-£18.00.
Open: Dec to Oct
Beds: 1T 1D
Baths: 2 En
🅿 (3) ⌷ ★ ஊ ▥ Ⅴ ⬥ ⚡ ⮔

Eriskay, Craig-na-gower, Aviemore, Inverness-shire, PH22 1RW.
Quietly situated warm and comfortable house good base for touring
Grades: STB 4 Star
Tel: **01479 810717**
Fax no: 01479 812312
D: £16.00-£20.00 **S:** £22.00-£26.00.
Open: All Year
Beds: 2D 1T
Baths: 3 En
🅿 (4) ⌷ ஊ ▥ Ⅴ ⬥ ⚡ ⮔

Kinapol Guest House, Dalfaber Road, Aviemore, Inverness-shire, PH22 1PY.
Friendly, modern, quiet, central, mountain views, riverside walks, bike hire
Tel: **01479 810513** (also fax no)
Mr & Mrs Hall.
D: £15.00 **S:** £16.00.
Open: All Year
Beds: 2F 3D
Baths: 2 Sh
ॐ 🅿 (5) ⌷ ஊ ▥ Ⅴ ⬥ ⚡

All rooms full and
nowhere else to stay?
Ask the owner if
there's anywhere
nearby

Boat of Garten 65

National Grid Ref: NH9418

🍴🍺 Boat Hotel, Craigard Hotel, The Heatherbank

Heathbank - The Victorian House,
Drumuillie Road, Boat of Garten,
Inverness-shire, PH24 3BD.
Grades: STB 4 Star
Tel: **01479 831234**
Mr Burge.
D: £25.00-£35.00 **S:** £30.00-£50.00.
Open: All Year
Beds: 5D 2T
Baths: 7 En
🛇 (8) 🅿 (8) ⅍□✕⚑🎖🕮Ⅴ🛈⌁⚷♿
Beautiful of character, house full of
curiosities; each bedroom is
different in style and atmosphere -
the romantic Victorian room, the
Oriental room stb.; some four
posters, even a sunken bathroom.
Magnificent breakfasts and dinners
(Taste of Scotland); calorie-laden
puddings a speciality

The Old Ferrymans House, *Boat*
of Garten, Inverness-shire, PH24 3BY.
Tel: **01479 831370** (also fax no)
Ms Matthews.
D: £19.00 **S:** £19.00.
Open: All Year
Beds: 1T 1D 2S
Baths: 2 Sh
🛇 🅿 (4) ⅍🕿🎖🕮Ⅴ🛈⌁
Which? recommended former
ferryman's house, just across River
Spey from village, welcoming,
homely, comfortable. Sitting room
with wood stove, many books, no
TV. No set breakfast times,
home-cooked meals with Highland
specialities. Numerous walks,
beautiful Strathspey countryside
and Cairngorm mountains, castles,
distilleries

Avingormack Guest House, *Boat*
of Garten, Inverness-shire, PH24 3BT.
Breathtaking views of the moun-
tains, award winning food - just
perfect
Grades: STB 3 Star
Tel: **01479 831614**
Mrs Ferguson.
D: £19.00-£22.00 **S:** £19.50.
Open: All Year
Beds: 1F 2D 1T
Baths: 2 En 1 Sh
🛇 🅿 (6) ⅍□✕🎖🕮Ⅴ🛈⌁⚷♿

Glen Sanda, *Street Of Kincardine,*
Boat of Garten, Inverness-shire,
PH24 3BY.
Modern bungalow, rural setting,
near RSPB and all sporting
amenities
Grades: STB 4 Star
Tel: **01479 831494**
Mrs Lyons.
D: £20.00-£22.00 **S:** £20.00-£24.00.
Open: All Year
Beds: 2D 1T
Baths: 3 En
🅿 (3) ⅍□🎖🕮Ⅴ⚷♿

Mullingarroch Croft, *Boat of*
Garten, Inverness-shire, PH24 3BY.
Actual grid ref: NH947182
Excellent area for fishing, walking,
golf and bird watching
Tel: **01479 831645** Mrs Grant.
D: £15.50 **S:** £15.50.
Open: Apr to Oct
Beds: 2D 1S **Baths:** 1 Sh
🛇 🅿 (3) ⅍□🎖🕮Ⅴ

Carrbridge 66

National Grid Ref: NH9022

🍴🍺 The Cairn Hotel, The Rowanlea, Struan Hotel

Cairn Hotel, *Main Road,*
Carrbridge, Inverness-shire,
PH23 3AS.
Actual grid ref: NH907228
Grades: STB 3 Star
Tel: **01479 841212** Mr Kirk.
Fax no: 01479 841362
D: £19.00-£22.00 **S:** £19.00-£26.00.
Open: All Year (not Xmas)
Beds: 2F 2D 1T 2S
Baths: 4 En 1 Sh
🛇 🅿 (15) □🎖Ⅴ🛈⌁⚷♿
Enjoy the country pub atmosphere;
log fire, malt whiskies, real ales and
affordable food in this
family-owned village centre hotel
close to the historic bridge. A
perfect base for touring
Cairngorms, Loch Ness, Whisky
Trail and beyond

Carrmoor Guest House, *Carr*
Road, Carrbridge, Inverness-shire,
PH23 3AD.
Actual grid ref: NH908227
Licensed, family-run, warm
welcome. Popular restaurant, chef
proprietor
Grades: STB 3 Star
Tel: **01479 841244** (also fax no)
Mrs Stitt.
D: £19.50-£21.50 **S:** £22.00.
Open: All Year
Beds: 1F 3D 2T **Baths:** 6 En
🛇 🅿 (6) □🕿✕🎖🕮Ⅴ🛈⌁⚷♿

Craigellachie House, *Main Street,*
Carrbridge, Inverness-shire,
PH23 3AS.
Traditional house in centre of small
Highland village on main tourist
routes
Grades: STB 3 Star GH
Tel: **01479 841641** Mrs Pedersen.
D: £16.00-£19.00 **S:** £16.00-£25.00.
Open: All Year
Beds: 2F 2D 2T 1S
Baths: 3 En 2 Sh
🛇 🅿 (8) ⅍□✕🎖🕮Ⅴ🛈⌁⚷♿

Pine Ridge, *Carrbridge, Inverness-*
shire, PH23 3AA.
Pine Ridge, formerly The Manse,
nestles amongst the pine trees
Grades: STB 3 Star
Tel: **01479 841646** Mrs Weston.
D: £16.00-£20.00 **S:** £20.00-£25.00.
Open: All Year
Beds: 1F 1D 1T **Baths:** 1 En 1 Sh
🛇 🅿 (6) ⅍□🕿🎖🕮Ⅴ🛈⌁⚷♿

Fairwinds Hotel, *Carrbridge,*
Inverness-shire, PH23 3AA.
Former Victorian manse mod-
ernised to highest standards. Quiet
location surrounded by woods
Tel: **01479 841240** (also fax no)
D: £24.00 **S:** £25.00.
Open: Dec to Oct
Beds: 2T 2D 1S
Baths: 5 En
🛇 (12) 🅿 (8) □✕🎖🕮Ⅴ🛈⌁⚷♿

Tomatin 67

National Grid Ref: NH8029

🍴🍺 Tomatin Inn

Millcroft, *Old Mill Road, Tomatin,*
Inverness, IV13 7YN.
1850 modernised crofthouse in
quiet village. Ideal base for touring
Grades: STB 3 Star,
AA 4 Diamond
Tel: **01808 511405** Mrs Leitch.
D: £18.00-£18.00 **S:** £18.00-£18.00.
Open: All Year
Beds: 1D 1T
Baths: 1 En 1 Pr
🛇 🅿 (3) □🎖🕮🛈⌁⚷♿

Daviot 68

National Grid Ref: NH7239

🍴🍺 Deerstalker, Tomatin Inn

Torguish House, *Daviot,*
Inverness, IV2 5XQ.
Tel: **01463 772208**
Mr & Mrs Allan.
Fax no: 01463 772308
D: £16.00-£22.00 **S:** £20.00-£25.00.
Open: All Year
Beds: 3F 3D 1T
Baths: 5 En 2 Pr
🛇 🅿 (20) □🕿🎖🕮Ⅴ
Torguish: Former manse set in
quiet rural area once the childhood
home of late author Alistair
McLean, who wrote novels such as
'Guns of Navarone', stb

Crofthill, *Daviot, Inverness, IV1 2XQ.*
Actual grid ref: NH723395
Rural modern family home. Garden
and parking, good Highland base
Grades: STB 4 Star
Tel: **01463 772230**
Mrs Lees.
D: £20.00-£24.00 **S:** £20.00.
Open: Easter to Oct
Beds: 1D 1T
Baths: 2 En
🛇 🅿 (2) ⅍□🕿🎖🕮♿Ⅴ⚷

Always telephone
to get directions to
the B&B - you will
save time!

Culloden Moor 69

National Grid Ref: NH7345

🍴 🍺 Cawdor Tavern

Westhill House, *Westhill, Inverness, IV1 5BP.*
Spacious, comfortable family home amidst trees, wildlife and with glorious views. One mile Culloden Battlefield, three miles Inverness. Perfect centre for touring Highlands
Grades: STB 2 Star
Tel: 01463 793225 Mrs Honnor.
Fax no: 01463 792225
D: £18.00-£20.00 **S:** £16.00-£18.00.
Open: Easter to Oct
Beds: 1F 1T 1S
Baths: 2 En 1 Sh
🛏 🅿 (4) ✚ ☐ 🐾 ♿ 📺 🔽 ⚡ 🚲

King of Clubs, *Tigh-Na-Ceard, Culloden Moor, Inverness, IV1 2EE.*
Grades: STB 3 Star
Tel: 01463 790476 (also fax no) Fraser.
D: £17.00-£19.00
S: £17.00-£19.00.
Open: All Year
Beds: 1F 1D 1T 1S
Baths: 2 En 1 Sh
🛏 🅿 (6) ☐ 🐾 ♿ 📺 🔽 ⚡ 🚲
A warm, friendly welcome awaits you at King of Clubs. Central to all amenities but out in the countryside for a quiet and peaceful stay. From the dining room window there is some of the beautiful scenery you expect to find in Scotland

Smithton 70

National Grid Ref: NH7145

3a Resaurie, *Smithton, Inverness, IV2 7NH.*
Actual grid ref: NH718452
Grades: STB 2 Star
Tel: 01463 791714 Mrs Mansfield.
D: £17.00-£21.00 **S:** £17.00-£21.00.
Open: All Year
Beds: 2D 1T
Baths: 1 En 1 Sh
🛏 🅿 (3) ✚ ☐ 🐾 ✗ ♿ 📺 🔽 📖 ⚡ 🚲
Quiet residential area 3 miles east of Inverness. Public transport nearby. GB National Cycle Route 7 passes door. Adjacent to Farmland. Views to Moray Firth, Ben Wyvis and Rossshire Hills. Home baking, high tea, Evening meals. A CHRISTIAN HOME

Please respect
a B&B's wishes
regarding children,
animals & smoking.

High season,
bank holidays and
special events mean
low availability
everywhere.

Inverness 71

National Grid Ref: NH6645

🍴 🍺 Finlay's, The Waterfront, The Harlequin, Kilcoy Arms, The Redcliffe, Heathmount Hotel, Johnny Foxs', Loch Ness House Hotel, Craigmonie Hotel, Mairten Lodge, Cawdor Tavern, Girvans

🔺 **Inverness Milburn Youth Hostel**, *Victoria Drive, Inverness, IV2 3BQ.*
Actual grid ref: NH667449
Tel: 01463 231771
Under 18: £9.95
Adults: £11.50
suitable for disabled people, evening meals available, self-catering facilities, family bunk rooms, laundry facilities
New modern hostel situated close to the town centre and all its amenities, the shops, cafes and the lively Eden Court Theatre. The gateway to the Highlands

Torridon Guest House, *59 Kenneth Street, Inverness, IV3 5PZ.*
Grades: STB 2 Star B&B
Tel: 01463 236449 (also fax no) Mrs Stenhouse.
D: £17.00.
Open: All Year
Beds: 3F
Baths: 2 En 1 Pr
🛏 (5) 🅿 (4) ☐ 📖 📺 🔽 ♿
Comfortable, family-run house, 5 minutes from town centre, good food, good beds, and a warm welcome assured

Pitfaranne, *57 Crown Street, Inverness, IV2 3AY.*
Grades: STB 2 Star
Tel: 01463 239338
Mr & Mrs Morrison.
D: £16.00-£20.00
S: £18.00-£26.00.
Open: All Year
Beds: 1F 2D 4T
Baths: 1 En 1 Pr 2 Sh
🛏 🅿 (5) ☐ ♿ 📖 📺 🔽 ⚡ 🚲
5 minutes from town centre/rail/bus stations. Find true Highland hospitality in friendly relaxed atmosphere of 100-year-old town house in quiet location. Private showers in all cosy guest rooms. Daily room service. Extensive varied menu. Full Scottish breakfast our speciality

---

Edenview, *26 Ness Bank, Inverness, IV2 4SF.*
Grades: STB 3 Star
Tel: 01463 234397 Mrs Fraser.
Fax no: 01463 222742
D: £18.00-£24.00 **S:** £22.00-£28.00.
Open: Mar to Oct
Beds: 1F 1D 1T
Baths: 2 En 1 Pr
🛏 🅿 (4) ☐ 🐾 ♿ 📺 🔽
Comfortable friendly Victorian home on River Ness within 5 minutes town, 7 miles airport; excellent touring centre for viewing the beautiful Scottish Highlands (including Glen Affric, Loch Ness and the Black Isle), castles, exhibitions, shopping, golf, dolphin watching, monster hunting

Strathmhor Guest House, *99 Kenneth Street, Inverness, IV3 5QQ.*
Grades: STB 2 Star
Tel: 01463 235397
Mr & Mrs Reid.
D: £20.00-£25.00 **S:** £18.00-£25.00.
Open: All Year
Beds: 2D 2T 1S
Baths: 2 En 1 Pr 1 Sh
🛏 🅿 (5) ☐ 🐾 ♿ 📺 🔽 🚲
Warm welcome awaits at refurbished Victorian home. Comfortable bedrooms and good food. 10 minutes walk into town centre, theatres, restaurants, leisure centre; golf course and fishing nearby

Tanera, *8 Fairfield Road, Inverness, IV3 5QA.*
Warm, comfortable house, close to River Ness, theatre and all amenities
Tel: 01463 230037 (also fax no) Mrs Geddes.
D: £18.00-£25.00 **S:** £20.00-£30.00.
Open: All Year
Beds: 2D 1T
Baths: 2 En 1 Pr 1 Sh
🛏 (10) 🅿 (3) ✚ ☐ 🐾 ♿ 📺 🔽 ⚡ 🚲

Charden Villa, *11 Fairfield Road, Inverness, IV3 5QA.*
Tel: 01463 222403 Mrs Munro.
D: £18.00-£20.00 **S:** £22.00-£25.00.
Open: All Year
Beds: 4F, 3T or 1D
Baths: 2 En, 1 Sh
🛏 ☐ ♿ 📺 📖 ♿ 🔽 📖 ⚡
Charden Villa is a warm and comfortable family-run house situated 10 minutes walk from Town Centre. Places of interest such as Culloden Battlefield, Loch Ness, The Isle of Skye is about a 2 hour drive through some beautiful scenery

---

D = Price range per person
sharing in a double room

Clach Mhuilinn, *7 Harris Road, Inverness, IV2 3LS.*
Grades: STB 4 Star
Tel: **01463 237059** Mrs Elmslie.
Fax no: 01463 242092
D: £24.00-£27.50 **S:** £35.00-£40.00.
Open: Easter to Oct
Beds: 1D 1T
Baths: 2 En
⌖ (10) **P** (3) ⌿ ⌷ ⌑ ▥ Ⓥ
Comfortable no smoking B&B with luxury, charming ensuite bedrooms. 1 double and 1 twin suite with sitting room including TV hairdryer, tea and coffee facilities, electric blankets, flowers stb. Delicious breakfasts served overlooking the beautiful garden. Excellent Highland touring base

St Anns House, *37 Harowden Road, Inverness, IV3 5QN.*
Actual grid ref: NH658453
Friendly, small, clean, family-run hotel, 10 minutes' walk from town centre, bus & rail stations
Grades: STB 3 Star, AA 3 Diamond, RAC 3 Diamond
Tel: **01463 236157** (also fax no)
D: £22.00-£24.00 **S:** £20.00-£30.00.
Open: Mar to Oct
Beds: 1F 2D 2T 1S
Baths: 5 En 1 Pr
⌖ **P** (4) ⌿ ⌷ ⌑ ▥ Ⓥ ∎ ⚡ ⊶

Hawthorn Lodge House, *15 Fairfield Road, Inverness, IV3 5QA.*
Tel: **01463 715516** Mrs Davidson.
Fax no: 01463 221578
D: £20.00-£26.00 **S:** £20.00-£26.00.
Open: All Year
Beds: 2F 1D 1T
Baths: 3 En 1 Sh
⌖ **P** (6) ⌿ ⌷ ⌑ ▥ Ⓥ ∎ ⊶
The real taste of Scotland at Hawthorn Lodge

Taigh Na Teile, *6 Island Bank Road, Inverness, IV2 4SY.*
Grades: STB 4 Star
Tel: **01463 222842**
Mr & Mrs Menzies.
Fax no: 01463 226844
D: £20.00-£20.00 **S:** £25.00-£30.00.
Open: All Year (not Xmas)
Beds: 1D 2T
Baths: 2 En 1 Pr
P (4) ⌿ ⌷ ⌑ ▥ Ⓥ ∎ ⊶
Overlooking the river Ness, this beautifully appointed Victorian-style house is situated just ten minutes' walk from the town centre. Variety of restaurants all within easy walking distance, as is Eden Court Theatre, aquadome & sports centre, and floral hall

---

All cycleways are popular: you are well-advised to book ahead

---

S = Price range for a single person in a room

Kinkell House, *11 Old Edinburgh Road, Inverness, IV2 3HF.*
Grades: STB 3 Star
Tel: **01463 235243**
Fax no: 01463 225255
D: £18.00-£46.00 **S:** £20.00-£24.00.
Open: All Year
Beds: 4F 1D 1S
Baths: 3 En 2 Sh
P (8) ⌷ ⌖ ⌑ ▥ Ⓥ ∎ ⚡
Traditional Georgian family home full of charm and character. Spacious rooms which are tastefully decorated and comfortably furnished. 5 mins' walk from town centre and all amenities an ideal touring base. Garden for guests' use. A warm welcome guaranteed

East Dene, *6 Ballifeary Road, Inverness, IV3 5PJ.*
Near Eden Court Theatre
Grades: STB 3 Star,
AA 3 Diamond
Tel: **01463 232976** (also fax no)
Mrs Greig.
D: £22.00-£27.00 **S:** £29.00-£35.00.
Open: All Year
Beds: 3D 1T **Baths:** 3 En
P (4) ⌷ ⌖ ✗ ⌑ ▥ Ⓥ

The Tilt, *26 Old Perth Road, Inverness, IV2 3UT.*
Family home convenient for A9. Ideal touring base
Grades: STB 3 Star B&B
Tel: **01463 225352** (also fax no)
Mrs Fiddes.
D: £14.00 **S:** £16.00.
Open: All Year (not Xmas)
Beds: 1F 1D 1T 1S **Baths:** 1 Sh
⌖ **P** (4) ⌿ ⌷ ▥.

Crown Hotel, *19 Ardconnel Street, Inverness, IV2 3EU.*
Clean, warm, friendly. Excellent breakfast, four minutes from the station
Grades: STB 2 Star
Tel: **01463 231135** (also fax no)
D: £17.00-£20.00 **S:** £17.00-£25.00.
Open: All Year (not Xmas)
Beds: 2F 2D 1T 2S
Baths: 3 En 2 Sh
⌖ ⌷ ⌑ ▥ Ⓥ ⊶

Ivanhoe Guest House, *68 Lochalsh Road, Inverness, IV3 6HW.*
Family-run, 10 mins' walk town centre. 'Highland Hospitality'
Tel: **01463 223020** (also fax no)
Crerer.
D: £16.00-£18.00 **S:** £16.00-£18.00.
Open: All Year (not Xmas)
Beds: 2F 1T 2S
Baths: 2 En 3 Sh
⌖ (5) ⌿ ⌷ ⌑ ▥ Ⓥ

Kendon, *9 Old Mill Lane, Inverness, IV2 3XP.*
Grades: STB 3 Star
Tel: **01463 238215** Mrs Kennedy.
D: £21.00-£25.00.
Open: Apr to Oct
Beds: 2D 1T
Baths: 3 En
P (4) ⌿ ⌷ ⌑ ▥ Ⓥ ∎
Family bungalow in peaceful location with large garden and private parking. All rooms ensuite with TV and tea/coffee facilities. Totally non-smoking. Excellent restaurants nearby

Eskdale Guest House, *41 Greig Street, Inverness, IV3 5PX.*
Grades: STB 3 Star
Tel: **01463 240933** (also fax no)
Mrs Mazurek.
D: £16.00-£25.00 **S:** £22.00-£25.00.
Open: All Year (not Xmas)
Beds: 2F 2D 1T 1S
Baths: 3 En 1 Sh
⌖ **P** (5) ⌿ ⌷ ⌑ ▥ Ⓥ
Situated in the heart of Inverness only 5 minutes from bus/rail stations, this impeccably run guest house offers all the comforts of home and a warm Highland welcome. Private parking, discounts for stays over 3 days. Please phone Vera & Alex

Kerrisdale, *4 Muirfield Road, Inverness, IV2 4AJ.*
Spacious, comfortable Victorian house
Grades: STB 4 Star
Tel: **01463 235489** (also fax no)
Mrs Donald.
D: £20.00-£22.00.
Open: All Year (not Xmas)
Beds: 1F 1D 1T **Baths:** 2 En 1 Pr
⌖ **P** (3) ⌿ ⌷ ⌑ ▥ Ⓥ

Roseneath Guest House, *39 Greig Street, Inverness, IV3 5PX.*
Grades: STB 3 Star
Tel: **01463 220201**
Fax no: 01463 712555
D: £15.00-£25.00.
Open: All Year
Beds: 3F 1T 2D
Baths: 5 En 1 Pr
⌖ (7) **P** (3) ⌷ ⌑ ▥ Ⓥ ∎ ⊶
Over 100 year old building in centre location 200 yards from River Ness and Greig Street Bridge. Only 5 minutes to town centre and all tourist excursions. Recently refurbished to very high standards

Carbisdale, *43 Charles Street, Inverness, IV2 3AH.*
Victorian family home, central location, ideal base for touring highlands
Grades: STB 4 Star B&B
Tel: **01463 225689** (also fax no)
Mrs Chisholm.
D: £16.00-£18.00 **S:** £20.00-£25.00.
Open: All Year
Beds: 2D 1T **Baths:** 2 Sh
⌷ ⌑ ▥ Ⓥ

Abbotsford, 7 *Fairfield Road,*
Inverness, IV3 5QA.
Comfortable friendly home, cen-
trally situated, 2 mins town centre
Tel: **01463 715377** Mr Griffin.
D: £16.00-£20.00 **S:** £18.00-£25.00.
Open: All Year (not Xmas)
Beds: 1F 1D
Baths: 2 En
ॐ (12) 🅿 (1) 🖵 🎍 🎟 🖳

Winmar House Hotel, *Kenneth*
Street, Inverness, IV3 5QG.
Full Scottish breakfast and friendly
welcome. Ample parking
Tel: **01463 239328** (also fax no)
Mrs Maclellan.
D: £16.00-£22.00 **S:** £16.00-£22.00.
Open: All Year (not Xmas)
Beds: 1D 6T 3S
Baths: 1 En 4 Pr 2 Sh
ॐ 🅿 (10) ✝🖵🗙🎍🎟 🖳 ఠ్

Hebrides, *120a Glenurquhart*
Road, Inverness, IV3 5TD.
Quality graded B&B offering high
standards, no smoking, private
parking
Grades: STB 4 Star
Tel: **01463 220062**
Mrs MacDonald.
D: £18.00-£25.00.
Open: All Year
Beds: 2D 1T
Baths: 2 En
🅿 (3) ✝🖵🎍🖳 ✦

Abb Cottage, *11 Douglas Row,*
Inverness, IV1 1RE.
Central, quiet, riverside listed ter-
raced cottage. Easy access public
transport
Tel: **01463 233486**
Miss Storrar.
D: £16.00-£18.00
S: £18.00-£25.00.
Open: Feb to Dec
Beds: 3T
Baths: 1 Sh
ॐ (12) 🅿 (2) ✝🖵🗙🎍🎟 ఠ 🖳

MacGregor's, *36 Ardconnel Street,*
Inverness, IV2 3EX.
We are situated minutes from River
Ness, shops and castle
Tel: **01463 238357**
Mrs MacGregor.
D: £14.00-£18.00
S: £15.00-£20.00.
Open: All Year (not Xmas)
Beds: 1F 3D 1T 3S
Baths: 2 En 3 Sh
🖵🎍🎍🎟 🖳

Cambeth Lodge, *49 Fairfield*
Road, Inverness, IV3 5QP.
Comfortable detached Victorian
house. Warm Scottish welcome
assured
Grades: STB 3 Star
Tel: **01463 231764**
Mrs Carson-Duff.
D: £17.00-£20.00.
Open: All Year (not Xmas)
Beds: 2D 1T
Baths: 1 En 1 Pr 1 Sh
ॐ 🅿 (5) ✝🖵🎍🎟 ✦ ఠ్

Hazeldean House, *125 Lochalsh*
Road, Inverness, IV3 5QS.
Friendly highland welcome. Only
10 mins' walk to town centre
Grades: STB 3 Star
Tel: **01463 241338** (also fax no)
Mr Stuart.
D: £14.00-£20.00 **S:** £16.00-£22.00.
Open: All Year
Beds: 2F 4D 3T 2S
Baths: 3 En 2 Sh
ॐ 🅿 (6) ✝🖵🗙🎍🎟 🖳 ఠ్

6 Broadstone Park, *Inverness,*
IV2 3LA.
Family-run B&B. Victorian house
10 mins town centre, bus and
railway station
Grades: STB 2 Star
Tel: **01463 221506**
Mrs Mackinnon.
D: £20.00-£25.00 **S:** £21.00-£25.00.
Open: All Year (not Xmas)
Beds: 1F 1D 1T 1S
Baths: 2 En 1 Pr
ॐ (5) 🅿 (3) ✝🖵🎍🎟 ✦ ఠ్

Marry Ann Villa, *Ardross Place,*
Inverness, IV3 5BZ.
Victoria house situated in quiet
private court in town centre
Grades: STB 2 Star B&B
Tel: **01463 230187**
Mr & Mrs Findlay.
Fax no: 01463 714224
D: £15.00-£17.00 **S:** £17.00-£20.00.
Open: All Year (not Xmas)
Beds: 1F 1T 1S **Baths:** 2 Sh
ॐ (2) 🖵🎍🎟 🖳 ఠ్

Lyndon, *50 Telford Street,*
Inverness, IV3 5LE.
A warm and friendly welcome
awaits you at the Lyndon
Grades: STB 3 Star
Tel: **01463 232551** Smith.
D: £15.00-£22.00 **S:** £30.00-£40.00.
Open: All Year (not Xmas)
Beds: 4F 1D 1T
Baths: 5 En 1 Pr
ॐ 🅿 (6) 🖵🎍🎍🎟 ✦ ఠ్

Strathisla, *42 Charles Street,*
Inverness, IV2 3AH.
2 minutes' walk to high street. 5
mins to rail and bus stations
Grades: STB 2 Star
Tel: **01463 235657** (also fax no)
Mr & Mrs Lewthwaite.
D: £15.00-£18.00 **S:** £16.00-£20.00.
Open: All Year (not Xmas)
Beds: 1D 1T 2S
Baths: 1 Sh
ॐ (8) 🅿 (2) ✝🖵🗙🎍🎟 🖳 ఠ్

101 Kenneth Street, *Inverness,*
IV3 5QQ.
Warm friendly, within easy reach
to town centre
Grades: STB 2 Star
Tel: **01463 237224** Mrs Reid.
Fax no: 01463 712249
D: £16.00-£25.00 **S:** £20.00-£25.00.
Open: All Year
Beds: 2F 2D 1T 1S
Baths: 1 En 1 Pr 2 Sh
ॐ 🅿 (6.) ✝🖵🎍🎟 ఠ 🖳

Corrbheinn, *Viewmount Brae,*
Culloden Road, Inverness, IV1 2BP.
Quiet, comfortable family home.
Good breakfasts, excellent centre
for touring
Tel: **01463 791356**
Mr & Mrs Mcmaster.
D: £18.00-£20.00 **S:** £20.00-£25.00.
Open: Easter to Oct
Beds: 2D 1T
Baths: 3 En
🅿 (6) ✝🖵🎍🎟 🖳 ✦ ఠ్

An Airidh, *65 Fairfield Road,*
Inverness, IV3 5LH.
In a quiet but central part of town.
Close to all amenities
Tel: **01463 240673** (also fax no)
Mrs MacDonald.
D: £12.00 **S:** £13.00.
Open: Nov to Sep
Beds: 1F 1D 1T 1S
Baths: 1 En 1 Sh
ॐ (12) 🅿 (1) ✝🖵🎍🎟 ఠ 🖳 ఠ్

3 Cawdor Road, *Inverness, IV2 3NR.*
Victorian detached house within 6
min walk to town centre & trains
Tel: **01463 220049** Mr McKay.
Fax no: 01463 233454
D: £18.00 **S:** £18.00.
Open: All Year
Beds: 1F 1T 1D 1S
Baths: 3 En
ॐ 🅿 (2) ✝🖵🎍🎟 🖳 ఠ్

The Borve, *9 Old Edinburgh Road,*
Inverness, IV2 3HF.
Quiet residential area and only 2
minutes from the castle and River
Ness
Tel: **01463 234728** Mrs White.
Fax no: 01463 711017
D: £22.00 **S:** £25.00.
Open: All Year (not Xmas)
Beds: 1F 2T 2D
Baths: 2 En 2 Sh
ॐ 🅿 (4) ✝🖵🎍🎍🎟 🖳 ✦

16 Fairfield Road, *Inverness,*
IV3 5QA.
Town centre location - 1 mile from
sportscentre, ice rink, boating pond
Tel: **01463 240309** (also fax no)
Ms Phyfer.
D: £16.00 **S:** £16.00.
Open: All Year
Beds: 1F 1D1T 1S
Baths: 4 En
ॐ 🅿 (5) ✝🖵🎍🗙🎍🎟 🖳 ఠ

Always telephone

to get directions to

the B&B - you will

save time!

STILWELL'S BRITAIN BED & BREAKFAST 2000

The Bed & Breakfast is one of the great British institutions. Like warm beer and the changing of the guard at Buckingham Palace, it's known by people around the world. Of course, you don't have to be a tourist to enjoy this traditional accommodation. Whether you're travelling, on holiday, away on business or just escaping from it all, the B&B is a great value alternative to expensive hotels and a world away from camping and caravanning. And there's no better way of choosing a convenient and desirable B&B than by consulting **Stilwell's Britain: Bed & Breakfast 2000.**

Stilwell's Britain: Bed & Breakfast 2000, the most comprehensive guide of its kind, contains over 7,750 entries - private houses, country halls, farms, cottages, inns, small hotels and guest houses - listed by county and location, in England, Scotland and Wales. Each entry includes room rates, facilities, tourist grades and a brief description of the B&B and its location and surroundings. The average charge per person per night is £18. The listings also provide the names of local pubs and restaurants which serve food in the evening. As with all Stilwell publications, the book has local maps and listings of tourist information offices.

The indispensable guide to great value accommodation: **Stilwell's Britain: Bed and Breakfast 2000**

£9.95 from all good bookstores (ISBN 1-900861-14-3) or £11.95 (inc p&p) from Stilwell Publishing Ltd, 59 Charlotte Road, London EC2A 3QW (020 7739 7179)

Sustrans Clyde to Forth

The **Clyde to Forth Cycle Route** is a new section of the developing National Cycle Network, running for 90 miles on traffic-free paths and traffic-calmed roads through Scotland's central belt, linking the west and east coasts and the country's two most major cities, Glasgow, the metropolis, and Edinburgh, the capital. The route intersects with the Scottish National Cycle Route (Carlisle to Inverness) in Glasgow and Paisley. It is clearly signposted by blue direction signs with a cycle silhouette and the number 75 in a red rectangle.

Having started at the port of **Gourock**, with excellent views across the Firth of Clyde both north and west to the highlands of Argyll, the route from **Greenock** follows an almost entirely traffic-free railway path through Port Glasgow, Kilmalcolm and Bridge of Weir as far as **Paisley;** then alternates between shorter traffic-free paths and minor roads through **Glasgow**'s South Side to reach the Clyde at Bell's Bridge,which you cross to reach the city centre. The route now meanders with the river eastwards out of town through Rutherglen to reach Uddingston, from where you head north through Coatbridge to Airdrie. The central link in the route is the **Airdrie to Bathgate Railway Path**, a superb traffic-free path built out of the industrial decay of the former Junction Railway. Interspersed with the disused mines and quarries there is now a sculpture trail, featuring works which aim to use use their industrial and natural setting to aesthetic advantage. The path takes you to Caldercruix and around the Hillend Reservoir across the country's central plateau via Blackridge and Armadale. After Bathgate the route crosses **Livingston** on landscaped paths

into Almondell and Calderwood Country Park, with its attractive wooded valleys. From East Calder there is a section on roads via Kirknewton to Currie, where you join the Water of Leith Walkway which you follow into outer **Edinburgh**. The Union Canal towpath takes you to the city centre, from where it's a short ride to the end of the route at **Leith**.

The indispensable **official route map and guide** for the route is available from Sustrans, 35 King Street, Bristol BS1 4DZ, tel 0117-926 8893, fax 0117-929 4173, @ £5.99 (+ £2.00 p&p).

Maps: Ordnance Survey 1:50,000 Landranger series: 63, 64, 65, 66

Trains: Glasgow and Edinburgh are both major termini on the Intercity network. Numerous other places on or near to the route are served by trains, including Gourock, from where there are also frequent ferry departures to Dunoon in Argyll.

All rooms full and nowhere else to stay? Ask the owner if there's anywhere nearby

Greenock   1

National Grid Ref: NS2777

Lindores Manor Guest House, 61 Newark Street, Greenock, PA16 7TE.
Beautiful Victorian manor house. Private parking, large garden, quality accommodation. Licensed
Tel: **01475 783075** Mrs Nellis.
D: £22.00 **S:** £25.00.
Open: All Year
Beds: 2F 4T 5D **Baths:** 11 En
♿ **P** (11) □ **✔ ✖** 🍵 **📽 ⛿ V**

Please don't camp on *anyone's* land without first obtaining their permission.

Greenock has a couple of interesting museums – the Custom House Museum, on the history of Customs and Excise, and the Mclean Museum of shipping and steam power, commemorating James Watt, the local boy who revolutionised the technology by inventing the first steam engine with separate condenser in 1765.

For information on **Paisley** and **Glasgow** see under *Sustrans Carlisle to Inverness.*

Kilmacolm 2

National Grid Ref: NS3669

🍴🍺 The Pullman

Margaret's Mill Farm, High Greenock Road, Kilmacolm, Renfrewshire, PA13 4TG.
Tel: **01505 873716** Mrs Henderson.
D: £15.00-£18.00 **S:** £15.00-£18.00.
Open: All Year
Beds: 1F 1D 1T
🛏 🅿 (8) ⳨ 🗖 🎂 🎇 ♦ ⚲
200-year-old farmhouse set in beautiful valley. Comfortable spacious bedrooms with colour TV. Private off-road parking, golf, fishing, clay-pigeon shooting and horse-riding nearby. Convenient for Burns country and Argyll ferries.

Kilbarchan 3

National Grid Ref: NS4063

🍴🍺 Trust Inn

Tower House, Milliken Park Road, Kilbarchan, Johnstone, Renfrewshire, PA10 2DB.
Historic home which Chopin visited. Excellent connections to motorway, railway airport
Tel: **01505 703299** (also fax no)
Mrs Van Breugel.
D: £25.00 **S:** £28.00.
Open: All Year (not Xmas)
Beds: 1F 1T 1S
Baths: 3 En
🛏 (1) 🅿 (6) ⳨ 🗖 🎂 🎇 ♦ ⚲

Paisley 4

National Grid Ref: NS4863

🍴🍺 Paraffin Lamp

Myfarrclan Guest House, 146 Corsebar Road, Paisley, Renfrewshire, PA2 9NA.
Grades: STB 4 Star B&B
Tel: **0141 884 8285** Mr & Mrs Farr.
Fax no: 0141 581 1566
D: £32.50-£35.00 **S:** £40.00-£60.00.
Open: All Year
Beds: 2D 1T
Baths: 2 En 1 Pr
🛏 🅿 (2) ⳨ 🗖 ✗ 🎂 🎇 🎇
Nestling in leafy suburb of Paisley, lovingly restored bungalow offering many thoughtful extras

---

D = Price range per person sharing in a double room

All cycleways are popular: you are well-advised to book ahead

---

Glasgow Ibrox 5

National Grid Ref: NS5564

Holly House, 54 Ibrox Terrace, Glasgow, G51 2TB.
Situated in an early Victorian tree-lined terrace in the city centre
Tel: **0141 427 5609**
Mr Divers.
Fax no: 0141 427 5608
D: £20.00
S: £25.00.
Open: All Year
Beds: 2F 2D 2T 2S
Baths: 5 En
🛏 (10) 🅿 (6) ⳨ 🗖 ✗ 🎂 🎇 👶 🎇 🔒 ♦

Glasgow Muirend 6

National Grid Ref: NS5760

16 Bogton Avenue, Glasgow, G44 3JJ.
Quiet red sandstone terraced private house adjacent station, 12 mins city centre
Grades: STB 2 Star
Tel: **0141 637 4402**
Mrs Paterson.
D: £20.00-£20.00
S: £22.00-£22.00.
Open: All Year (not Xmas)
Beds: 1D 2S
Baths: 2 Sh
🅿 (2) ⳨ 🗖 ✗ 🎂 🎇 🎇

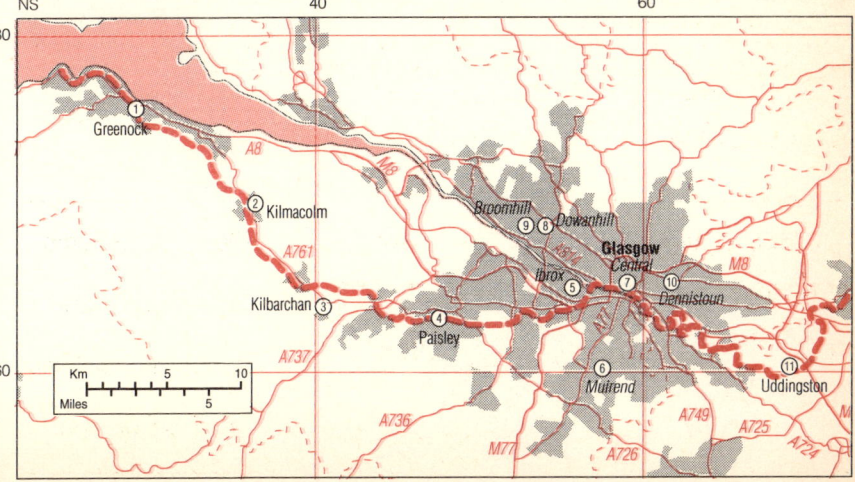

Glasgow Central   7

National Grid Ref: NS5865

🍴🍺 Dorsey's, Park Bar, Mitchell's, Stravaigan's, Orchard Park, Bellahouston Hotel, Garfield House, Highlanders Park, Snaffil Bit

🔺 **Glasgow Youth Hostel,**
7/8 Park Terrace, Glasgow, G3 6BY.
Actual grid ref: NS575662
Tel: **0141 332 3004**
Under 18: £9.95 **Adults:** £11.50
evening meals available, self-catering facilities, family bunk rooms, shop, laundry facilities
Glasgow's alive. There are the dear green places of the city parks, like Kelvingrove. There's great shopping, and things to see. A great base too for touring the Trossachs, the Clyde Coast and Loch Lomond

Kirkland House, *42 St Vincent Crescent, Glasgow, G3 8NG.*
Grades: STB 3 Star
Tel: **0141 248 3458**
Mrs Divers.
Fax no: 0141 221 5174
D: £27.00-£30.00 **S:** £27.00-£30.00.
Open: All Year
Beds: 3D 2T 2S
Baths: 6 En 2 Sh
🛇 (1) 🕭⊁⬚🏠🖳🛍️💷 Ⅴ
City centre guest house with excellent rooms on beautiful Victorian Crescent in Finnieston (Glasgow's 'little Chelsea'). Short walk to Scottish Exhibition Centre, Museum/Art Gallery, Kelvingrove Park and all West End facilities. Glasgow airport 10 minutes, member of the Harry James society

Kelvingrove Hotel,
944 Sauchiehall Street, Glasgow, G3 7TH.
Grades: STB 2 Star
Tel: **0141 339 5011** Mr Wills.
Fax no: 0141 339 6566
D: £24.00-£29.00
S: £33.00-£38.00.
Open: All Year (not Xmas)
Beds: 7F 13D 3T 2S
Baths: 23 En
🛇 🅿 (20) ⊁🐾🍽️🛍️💷Ⅴ⚡🚲
Centrally located family-run hotel, set in Glasgow's fashionable West End. Close to pubs, clubs, art galleries, museums, University, shops, rail and bus links - all within walking distance

---

All rooms full and nowhere else to stay? Ask the owner if there's anywhere nearby

---

S = Price range for a single person in a room

Number Thirty Six, *36 St Vincent Crescent, Glasgow, G3 8NG.*
Grades: STB 3 Star
Tel: **0141 248 2086** Mrs MacKay.
Fax no: 0141 221 1477
D: £25.00-£30.00
S: £30.00-£35.00.
Open: All Year (not Xmas)
Beds: 4D 2T
Baths: 4 En 2 Pr
⊁🕭🏠🖳💷Ⅴ
Situated in a Georgian terrace on the edge of Glasgow city centre, we are an ideal base for exploring Glasgow and the west of Scotland. Beside the Art Gallery, University and SECC. Individually designed rooms. Personal attention guaranteed

Glasgow Dowanhill   8

National Grid Ref: NS5667

🍴🍺 Orchard Park Hotel, Bellahoustan Hotel

The Terrace House Hotel,
14 Belhaven Terrace, Glasgow, G12 0TG.
Grades: STB 2 Star
Tel: **0141 337 3377** (also fax no)
Ms Black.
D: £29.00-£39.00
S: £49.00-£65.00.
Open: All Year
Beds: 4F 3D 5T 1S
Baths: 12 En 1 Pr
🛇⊁🕭🏠🍽️🛍️💷Ⅴ
Family run-licensed hotel situated in the green & leafy up market West End within 15 minutes of Glasgow's city centre. The fashionable Byres Road is 5 minutes' walk away, boasting some of the finest bars & restaurants

Glasgow Broomhill   9

National Grid Ref: NS5467

Lochgilvie House, *117 Randolph Road, Broomhill, Glasgow, G11 7DS.*
Grades: STB 3 Star
Tel: **0141 357 1593**
Mrs Ogilvie.
Fax no: 0141 334 5828
D: £25.00-£27.50
S: £25.00-£30.00.
Open: All Year
Beds: 1F 2D 3T
Baths: 4 En
🛇 (10) 🅿⊁🏠🛍️💷Ⅴ
Luxurious Victorian town house situated in Glasgow's prestigious West End, adjacent to rail station, convenient for art galleries, museums, International Airport, eight minutes by train to city centre

Glasgow Dennistoun   10

National Grid Ref: NS6065

Seton Guest House, *6 Seton Terrace, Glasgow, G31 2HU.*
Warm and friendly welcome assured. Five minutes from city centre
Grades: STB 2 Star
Tel: **0141 556 7654**
Fax no: 0141 402 3655
D: £15.00-£16.00
S: £17.00-£18.00.
Open: All Year (not Xmas)
Beds: 4F 2D 2T 1S
Baths: 3 Sh
🛇🕭🐾🛍️💷Ⅴ🚲

Uddingston   11

National Grid Ref: NS6960

🍴🍺 The Windmill

Northcote Guest House,
2 Holmbrae Avenue, Uddingston, Glasgow, G71 6AL.
Large Victorian private house, quiet locality. Easily accessible
Tel: **01698 813319** (also fax no)
Mrs Meggs.
D: £15.00-£16.00
S: £15.00-£16.00.
Open: All Year (not Xmas)
Beds: 1F 1D 1S
Baths: 1 Sh
🛇 🅿 (3) 🕭🖳

Airdrie   12

National Grid Ref: NS7665

Rosslee Guest House, *107 Forrest Street, Airdrie, Lanarkshire, ML6 7AR.*
Former church manse
Grades: STB 3 Star
Tel: **01236 765865**
Mr McFadzean.
Fax no: 01236 748535
D: £20.00-£25.00
S: £18.00-£25.00.
Open: All Year
Beds: 1F 3T 2S
Baths: 4 En 2 Pr
🛇 (2) 🅿 (8) 🕭🐾🛍️💷🗡️⚡🚲

Armadale   13

National Grid Ref: NS9368

Tarrareoch Farm, *Armadale, Bathgate, W Lothian, EH48 3BJ.*
C17th farmhouse all on one level. Midway Edinburgh/Glasgow. Beautiful countryside
Grades: STB 3 Star
Tel: **01501 730404**
Mrs Gibb.
D: £16.00-£20.00
S: £20.00-£26.00.
Open: All Year
Beds: 1F 2T
Baths: 1 En 1 Sh
🛇 🅿 (10) 🕭🐾🛍️💷Ⅴ⚡🚲

Bathgate 14

National Grid Ref: NS9769

�__🍴 Kaim Park

Hillview, 35 The Green, Bathgate, W Lothian, EH48 4DA.
Quality and friendly accommodation with spectacular views of West Lothian
Grades: STB 2 Star
Tel: 01506 654830 (also fax no)
Mrs Connell.
D: £15.00-£16.00 **S:** £20.00-£22.00.
Open: All Year (not Xmas)
Beds: 1F 1T
Baths: 1 Sh
🛇🍴🗁🛏🔥💻▥⌂🚲

Blackburn 15

National Grid Ref: NS9865

Cruachan Guest House, 78 East Main Street, Blackburn, Bathgate, West Lothian, EH47 7QS.
Relaxed, friendly, high-quality. Airport nearby, rail service to Edinburgh
Grades: STB 3 Star
Tel: 01506 655221
Mr Harkins.
Fax no: 01506 652395
D: £20.00-£23.00 **S:** £25.00-£30.00.
Open: All Year (not Xmas)
Beds: 1F 3D
Baths: 3 En 1 Pr
🛇🅿(5)🍴🗁🔥💻▥⌂🚲

Balerno 16

National Grid Ref: NT1666

�__🍴 Tanners, Kestrel

Newmills Cottage, 472 Lanark Road West, Balerno, EH14 5AE.
Grades: STB 4 Star B&B
Tel: 0131 449 4300 (also fax no)
Mrs Linn.
D: £20.00-£27.50 **S:** £25.00-£35.00.
Open: All Year
Beds: 2T
Baths: 1 En 1 Pr
🅿🍴🗁🔥💻▥⌂🚲
Delightful house set in own grounds with ample, private off road parking & lovely garden. The traditional style cottage was built in 1992 & offers very spacious comfortable rooms with excellent facilities. A very warm welcome & a delicious breakfast

---

**All details shown
are as supplied
by B&B owners in
Autumn 1999.**

Edinburgh Morningside 17

National Grid Ref: NT2471

�__🍴 Montpeliers

Dunedin, 21-23 Colinton Road, Edinburgh, EH10 5DR.
Victorian terraced villa, furnished in period-style. Princess street, 15 mins
Grades: STB 2 Star
Tel: 0131 447 0679 Mr Fortune.
Fax no: 0131 446 9358
D: £20.00-£30.00 **S:** £20.00-£30.00.
Open: All Year (not Xmas)
Beds: 4F 2D 1T 2S
Baths: 6 En 1 Pr 2 Sh
🛇🍴🗁🔥💻▥&⌂🚲

Sandeman House, 33 Colinton Road, Edinburgh, EH10 5DR.
Non-smoking Victorian family home, conveniently situated, unrestricted street parking
Grades: STB 4 Star
Tel: 0131 447 8080 (also fax no)
Ms Sandeman.
D: £28.00-£36.00 **S:** £25.00-£45.00.
Open: All Year (not Xmas)
Beds: 1D 1T 1S
Baths: 3 Pr
🛇🅿🍴🗁🔥💻▥⌂

Edinburgh Corstorphine 18

National Grid Ref: NT1972

Zetland Guest House, 186 St Johns Road, Edinburgh, EH12 8SG.
A splendid Victorian house situated on the west side of Edinburgh
Grades: STB 2 Star GH, AA 4 Diamond
Tel: 0131 334 3898 Mr Stein.
Fax no: 0131 538 0162
D: £20.00-£27.50 **S:** £20.00-£50.00.
Open: All Year
Beds: 1F 2D 4T 1S
Baths: 4 En 2 Sh
🛇🅿(7)🗁🔥💻▥

Finlaystone, 19 Meadowplace Road, Edinburgh, EH12 7UJ.
Detached bungalow, midway between city/airport. Excellent bus services to city
Tel: 0131 334 8483 (also fax no)
Mrs Mitchell.
D: £15.00 **S:** £20.00.
Open: All Year (not Xmas)
Beds: 1F 2T
🛇🅿(3)🗁🛏💻

Glenturret, 18 Downie Terrace, Edinburgh, EH12 7AU.
Traditional Stone-built Victorian terraced villa. A panoramic view of Pentland Hills to rear
Tel: 0131 334 5434 Mrs Hall.
Fax no: 0131 334 3690
D: £23.00 **S:** £24.00.
Open: All Year (not Xmas)
Beds: 1F 2T 1D
Baths: 2 En 1 Sh
🛇🅿(3)🗁🔥💻▥

On the way in **Livingston**, the Almond Valley Heritage Centre at Mill Farm has reconstructions tracing different aspects of past life in the West Lothian region, including an exhibition on the shale oil industry, a working water mill and a narrow-gauge railway. This one is particularly suitable for young children, with farm animals in child-friendly closures.

Just before **Currie**, Malleny Garden contains Scotland's national collection of bonsai trees, a large array of roses and four 400-year-old yew trees.

Edinburgh Slateford 19

National Grid Ref: NT2271

�__🍴 Tickled Trout

13 Moat Street, Edinburgh, EH14 1PE.
Comfortable accommodation, colour TV, each room.
Grades: STB 2 Star
Tel: 0131 443 8266 Mrs Hume.
D: £15.00-£20.00 **S:** £18.00-£20.00.
Open: Easter to Mar
Beds: 1D 1T
🛇🅿🗁🔥💻▥

Edinburgh Gorgie 20

National Grid Ref: NT2272

Orwell Lodge Hotel, 29 Polwarth Terrace, Edinburgh, EH11 1NH.
Elegant Victorian mansion. Quiet location close to city centre. Bar, restaurant
Tel: 0131 229 1044 Mr Thommen.
Fax no: 0131 228 9492
D: £35.00 **S:** £45.00.
Open: All Year
Beds: 3T 3D 4S
Baths: 10 En
🛇🅿(35)🍴🗁✕🔥💻▥🔒

**Please respect
a B&B's wishes
regarding children,
animals & smoking.**

Edinburgh Merchiston 21

National Grid Ref: NT2472

▲ **Edinburgh Bruntsfield Youth
Hostel,** *7 Bruntsfield Crescent,
Edinburgh, EH10 4EZ.*
Actual grid ref: NT249720
Tel: **0131 447 2994**
Under 18: £7.10 **Adults:** £8.60
self-catering facilities, laundry
facilities

Nova Hotel, *5 Bruntsfield
Crescent, Edinburgh, EH10 4EZ.*
Tel: **0131 447 6437** Mr McBride.
Fax no: 0131 452 8126 (preferred
for bookings)
D: £25.00-£55.00 **S:** £45.00-£70.00.
Open: All Year
Beds: 6F 2D 2T 2S **Baths:** 12 En
🛇 🄿 🗶 🗖 🟊 🗶 🚼 📷 🕭 Ⓥ 🔆 ↻
Victorian, city centre, quiet area,
free parking, fully licensed, all
rooms ensuite bath & shower
upgraded 1998. Close to all tourist
attractions, conference centres,
theatres. Train station 1 mile,
airport 5 miles. Perfect for business
and tourists. Lovely views

Villa Nina Guest House,
*39 Leamington Terrace,
Edinburgh, EH10 4JS.*
Grades: STB 1 Star
Tel: **0131 229 2644** (also fax no)
Mr Cecco.
D: £17.00-£24.00.
Open: All Year (not Xmas/
New Year)
Beds: 1F 2D 2T **Baths:** 2 Sh
🄿 🗖 🚼 📷 Ⓥ
Very comfortable Victorian terrace
house situated in quiet residential
part of city yet 15 minutes' walk
Princes Street, Castle, theatres. TV
in all rooms. Private showers. Full
cooked breakfast. Rates from
£16.50

Finlay Guest House, *4 Hartington
Place, Edinburgh, EH10 4LE.*
Elegant four-poster room. Central,
friendly, comfortable. Excellent
breakfast. Great value
Tel: **0131 229 1620** (also fax no)
Mrs Hazzard.
D: £18.00 **S:** £23.00.
Open: All Year
Beds: 1F 1T 2D 2S
Baths: 2 Sh
🛇 🗖 🚼 📷 Ⓥ

Gillsland Hotel, *Gillsland Road,
Edinburgh, EH10 5BW.*
Victorian mansion family-run with
lots of atmosphere. Spacious
ensuite rooms
Tel: **0131 337 1058** Mrs Ranaldi.
Fax no: 0131 337 5735
D: £20.00 **S:** £35.00.
Open: All Year
Beds: 3F 3D 4T **Baths:** 8 En 2 Sh

Edinburgh Murrayfield 22

National Grid Ref: NT2273

14 Lennel Avenue, *Murrayfield,
Edinburgh, EH12 6DW.*
Beautiful home quietly situated
near city centre and bus routes
Tel: **0131 337 1979** Mrs Smith.
D: £20.00 **S:** £25.00.
Open: Easter to Nov
Beds: 2T 1D **Baths:** 2 Pr
🛇 (14) 🄿 (3) 🔆 🗖 📷 🔆 ↻

Craigelachie Hotel,
*21 Murrayfield Avenue, Edinburgh,
EH12 6AU.*
Elegant Victorian town house hotel
Tel: **0131 337 4076** Mr Oag.
Fax no: 0131 313 3305
D: £27.50 **S:** £27.00.
Open: All Year
Beds: 3F 1D 2T 2S
Baths: 3 En 2 Sh
🛇 (1) 🄿 🔆 🗖 🚼 📷 Ⓥ

Edinburgh Newington 23

National Grid Ref: NT2671

Rowan Guest House,
*13 Glenorchy Terrace, Edinburgh,
EH9 2DQ.*
Grades: STB 3 Star,
AA 3 Diamond
Tel: **0131 667 2463** (also fax no)
Mr & Mrs Vidler.
D: £23.00-£32.00.
S: £24.00-£29.00.
Open: All Year (not Xmas)
Beds: 1F 3D 2T 3S
Baths: 3 En 3 Sh
🛇 (2) 🄿 (2) 🗖 🚼 📷 Ⓥ
Comfortable Victorian home in
quiet, leafy, conservation area, a
mile and a half from city centre,
castle and Royal Mile. Delicious
breakfast, including porridge and
freshly baked scones. A warm
welcome and personal service
from Alan and Angela. Free
parking

Gifford House, *103 Dalkeith Road,
Edinburgh, EH16 5AJ.*
Grades: STB 3 Star
Tel: **0131 667 4688** (also fax no)
Mrs Dow.
D: £20.00-£38.00.
S: £23.00-£50.00.
Open: All Year
Beds: 2F 2D 2T 1S
Baths: 7 En
🛇 🔆 🗖 🟊 🚼 📷 Ⓥ 🕭 🔆 ↻
David and Margaret assure you of
good Scottish hospitality. Warm
welcome, comfortable
surroundings, centrally located for
all Edinburgh's attractions.
Edinburgh conference centre
within easy access, extensive
breakfast menu

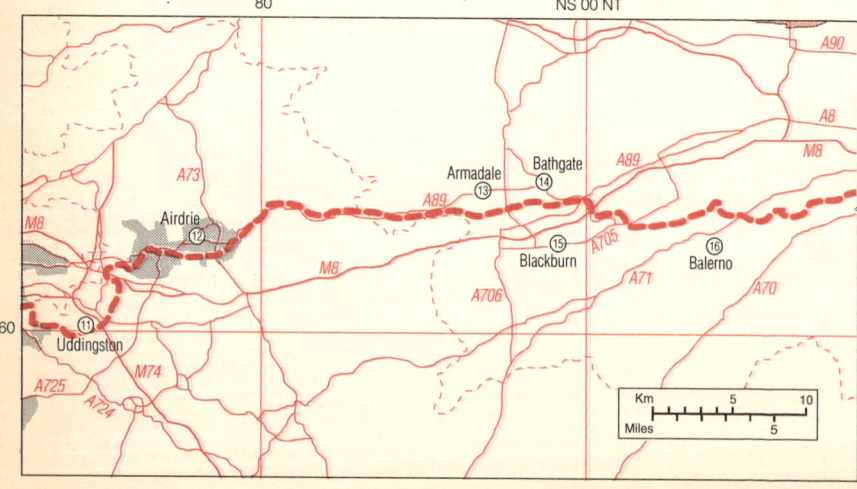

Edinburgh, for unbroken centuries the centre of Scotland's judicial system and church, has just been restored to pre-eminence in the country's administration and legislature. The new Scottish Parliament will eventually sit in a brand new building, currently under construction, designed by the Catalan architects Enric Miralles Benedetta Tagliabue. It will stand close by the Palace of Holyroodhouse, at the eastern end of the Old Town's historic main thoroughfare, the Royal Mile, and will be an open, fragmented arrangement which is designed to complement both the Palace itself, and Salisbury Crags to the south. Holyrood Palace itself, official residence of the monarch in Scotland, is a mainly sixteenth- and seventeenth-century building with a turreted façade and Palladian courtyard. Access is restricted to guided tours, which include the rooms once inhabited by Mary, Queen of Scots. In the grounds stand the ruins of Holyrood Abbey, which arose in the twelfth century from origins shrouded in mystery. Of the earliest, Norman part of the building there survives one doorway. The Royal Mile leads westwards up to the rock, with sheer drops on three sides and yielding the best views over the city, on which stands Edinburgh Castle. It was here that the city began, and for centuries the castle had enoromus strategic importance; its military significance remains, as the headquarters of the Scottish Division. The castle's oldest building is St Margaret's Chapel, an atmospheric small Norman church.

There is much to explore long the Royal Mile itself, including the churches of St Giles, a hotch-potch of styles thanks to multiple restorations, and Canongate, built in the seventeenth century to an anachronistic Renaissance design, which has a number of notables buried in its graveyard, including Adam Smith. Elsewhere in the Old Town, Greyfriars Kirkyard is one of the most atmospheric graveyards you're likely to find, and is famous for Greyfriars Bobby, the archetypal loyal dog who refused to leave his master's grave. The Old Town's museums include the wide-ranging Royal Museum of Scotland, the Museum of Childhood and the Scotch Whisky Heritage Centre – yes, they have got a shop. Stretching north from Princes Street, in Edinburgh's smart Georgian New Town you can find the excellent National Gallery of Scotland and the Scottish National Portrait Gallery and Museum of Antiquities. Further afield, the Scottish National Gallery of Modern Art was the first purely twentieth-century galley in Britain when it opened forty years ago.

Edinburgh's port of **Leith** has a high concentration of pubs and eateries on or near the waterfront, and is, as such, the ideal journey's end.

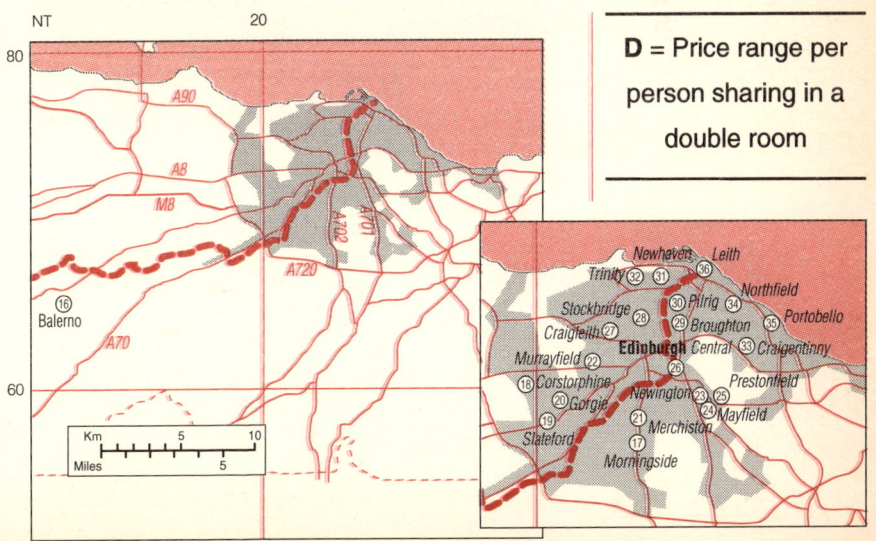

D = Price range per person sharing in a double room

Brothaigh House, *18 Craigmillar Park, Edinburgh, EH16 5PS.*
Victorian house of character.
Warm and elegant. Situated on
A701
Grades: STB 3 Star,
AA 3 Diamond
Tel: 0131 667 2202 (also fax no)
Mr & Mrs Brodie.
D: £22.00-£35.00 **S:** £25.00-£45.00.
Open: All Year (not Xmas)
Beds: 1F 4D 1T
Baths: 4 En 1 Pr 1 Sh
🛇 🅿 (6) ⊁ 🗆 🌡 🎟 🖻

7 Crawfurd Road, Newington,
Edinburgh, EH16 5PQ.
Beautiful centrally located house.
Guest rooms overlook well-main-
tained gardens
Grades: STB 2 Star
Tel: 0131 667 2283 Mrs McLean.
D: £19.00-£25.00 **S:** £22.00-£25.00.
Open: Easter to Oct
Beds: 1F 1T 1S **Baths:** 1 Sh
⊁ 🗆 🎟

17 Crawfurd Road, Edinburgh,
EH16 5PQ.
Victorian family home, friendly
welcome - easy access to city
centre
Grades: STB 2 Star
Tel: 0131 667 1191 Ms Simpson.
D: £17.50-£25.00 **S:** £17.50-£25.00.
Open: May to Sep
Beds: 1D 1T 1S
Baths: 2 Sh
🛇 🅿 (1) ⊁ 🗆 🌡 🎟 🖻

Edinburgh Mayfield 24

National Grid Ref: NT2672

Ⓜ ◁ Leasley

Ben Doran Guest House,
*11 Mayfield Gardens, Edinburgh,
EH9 2AX.*
Grades: STB 4 Star, AA 4
Diamond, RAC 4 Diamond
Tel: 0131 667 8488 Dr Labaki.
Fax no: 0131 667 0076
D: £25.00-£60.00 **S:** £25.00-£60.00.
Open: All Year
Beds: 4F 3D 2T 1S
Baths: 6 En 3 Sh
🛇 🅿 (6) ⊁ 🗆 🗙 🌡 🎟 🖻 🔒
Beautiful refurbished Listed
Georgian building for visitors who
want more than a place to sleep.
Charming, elegant, cosy and
comfortable, family-run, excellent
service. Centrally located and on
bus routes. Sumptuous Scottish
breakfast and lovely architectural
and hillside views await!

Planning a longer
stay? Always ask for
any special rates.

Hopetoun Guest House, *15
Mayfield Road, Edinburgh, EH9 2NG.*
Actual grid ref: NT265717
Grades: STB 3 Star
Tel: 0131 667 7691 Mrs Mitchell.
Fax no: 0131 466 1691
D: £20.00-£27.00 **S:** £25.00-£40.00.
Open: All Year (not Xmas)
Beds: 1F 1D 1T
Baths: 1 En 1 Pr 1 Sh
🛇 (6) 🅿 (2) ⊁ 🗆 🌡 🎟 🖻
Completely non-smoking. Small,
friendly, family-run guest house,
close to Edinburgh University.
Excellent bus service. Royal
Mile/Castle 25 mins, on foot.
Personal attention in a relaxed,
informal atmosphere. Good choice
of breakfast. Owner a fund of local
information! Which? Books B&B
Guide

Kingsway Guest House, *5 East
Mayfield, Edinburgh, EH9 1SD.*
Grades: STB 2 Star
Tel: 0131 667 5029 (also fax no)
D: £18.00-£35.00 **S:** £25.00-£35.00.
Open: All Year
Beds: 2F 2D 2T 1S
Baths: 1 En 1 Pr 1 Sh
🗆 🗙 🌡 🎟 🖻 ⚡ 🚲
Warm, friendly terraced Victorian
villa quietly situated 1.5m from
Princes Street, close to all major
attractions and walking distance to
Commonwealth Pool, Holyrood
Park, Parliament buildings and
Edinburgh's latest attraction the
Dynamic Earth. Quality shops and
restaurants nearby

Glenalmond Guest House,
*25 Mayfield Gardens, Edinburgh,
EH9 2BX.*
Grades: STB 4 Star
Tel: 0131 668 2392 (also fax no)
Mr & Mrs Fraser.
D: £20.00-£35.00 **S:** £25.00-£40.00.
Open: All Year (not Xmas)
Beds: 3F 4D 2T 1S **Baths:** 10 En
🛇 (5) 🗆 🌡 🎟 & 🖻 🚲
Deb & Dave warmly welcome you
to their superb accomodations.
Ground, four poster, en-suite rooms
available. Close to Waverley
Station. Varied breakfast served
daily with home-made scones

Lauderville Guest House, *52
Mayfield Road, Edinburgh, EH9 2NH.*
Grades: STB 4 Star
Tel: 0131 667 7788 Mrs Marriott.
Fax no: 0131 667 2636
D: £25.00-£40.00 **S:** £28.00-£48.00.
Open: All Year
Beds: 2F 5D 2T 1S
Baths: 10 En
🛇 🅿 (6) ⊁ 🗆 🗙 🌡 🎟 🖻 🚲
Brian and Yvonne welcome visi-
tors to Edinburgh to stay in taste-
fully restored (Listed) Victorian
house. Enjoy Scottish or vegetarian
breakfast in our traditional dining
room and relax in our guest lounge
with access to secluded garden.
Centrally located for attractions

Lorne Villa Guest House, *9 East
Mayfield, Edinburgh, EH9 1SD.*
Grades: STB 3 Star
Tel: 0131 667 7159 (also fax no)
Mr McCulloch.
D: £18.00-£32.00 **S:** £18.00-£32.00.
Open: All Year
Beds: 1F 2D 3T 1S
Baths: 3 En 1 Pr 3 Sh
🛇 🅿 (6) 🗆 🗙 🌡 🎟 🖻 🖻
Festival city residence, serving fine
Scottish cuisine with Scottish
hospitality. 1 mile to city centre.
Quiet location off main route to
city and close to main bus service.
Many well-known attractions, close
by universities, concert halls,
swimming pools

Classic Guest House, *50 Mayfield
Road, Edinburgh, EH9 2NH.*
Grades: STB 3 Star
Tel: 0131 667 5847 Mrs Mail.
Fax no: 0131 662 1016
D: £20.00-£30.00 **S:** £20.00-£40.00.
Open: All Year
Beds: 7F 1D 1T 3S
Baths: 7 En
🛇 (3) 🅿 ⊁ 🗆 🌡 🎟 & 🖻 🚲
Friendly, family-run Victorian
house, totally non-smoking.
Personal service, Scottish hospitali-
ty. On main bus routes. Perfect for
exploring the capital. Warm wel-
come awaits, excellent value

Abcorn Guest House, *4 Mayfield
Gardens, Edinburgh, EH9 2BU.*
Detached Victorian villa, one mile
from Edinburgh city centre
Grades: STB 3 Star
Tel: 0131 667 6548
D: £25.00-£35.00 **S:** £25.00-£35.00.
Open: All Year
Beds: 2F 2D 2T 1S **Baths:** 7 En
🛇 🅿 (6) 🗆 🌡 🎟 🖻

Ivy Guest House, *7 Mayfield
Gardens, Edinburgh, EH9 2AX.*
Grades: STB 3 Star, AA 3
Diamond, RAC 4 Diamond
Tel: 0131 667 3411 Mr Green.
Fax no: 0131 620 1422
D: £17.00-£35.00 **S:** £17.00-£65.00.
Open: All Year
Beds: 2F 3D 2T 1S
Baths: 6 En 2 Pr
🛇 🅿 (7) 🗆 🗙 🌡 🎟 🖻
Quiet, family-run Victorian villa
guest house, many local
restaurants, close to all Edinburgh's
major cultural attractions, golf
courses, Commonwealth
swimming pool and university. A
hearty Scottish breakfast and a
warm welcome is assured

Bringing children with
you? Always ask for
any special rates.

The International, *37 Mayfield Gardens, Edinburgh, EH9 2BX.*
Grades: STB 4 Star, AA 4 Diamond
Tel: 0131 667 2511 Mrs Niven.
Fax no: 0131 667 1112
D: £20.00-£40.00 **S:** £25.00-£45.00.
Open: All Year
Beds: 2F 2D 2T 3S
Baths: 9 Pr
🛇 🄿 🖵 🛏 🏔 ᴴ ⅋ ♨
Stone-built Victorian house, 1.5 miles south of Princes Street on main A701. Private parking, ensuite facilities, TV and coffee makers. International is a haven of luxury

St Conan's Guest House, *30 Minto Street, Edinburgh, EH9 1SB.*
Grades: STB 2 Star GH
Tel: 0131 667 8393 (also fax no)
Mr Bryce.
D: £20.00-£27.00 **S:** £20.00-£30.00.
Open: All Year
Beds: 3F 1D 3T
Baths: 1 En 4 Pr 1 Sh
🛇 🄿 (7) 🖵 🛏 🏔 ᴴ ⅋ ♨
A handsome, stone-built, Listed, end-terrace Georgian town house on three floors, lying approx 1 mile south from Princes Street and the main rail and bus stations. An ideal location for exploring Edinburgh's Old and New Towns

Parklands Guest House, *20 Mayfield Gardens, Edinburgh, EH9 2BZ.*
Comfortable well maintained Victorian guest house near city centre
Grades: STB 3 Star, AA 3 Star
Tel: 0131 667 7184
Mr Drummond.
Fax no: 0131 667 2011
D: £22.00-£30.00 **S:** £30.00-£40.00.
Open: All Year
Beds: 1F 3D 2T
Baths: 5 En 1 Pr
🛇 🄿 (1) 🖵 🏔 🏔 ᴴ ⅋

Tania Guest House, *19 Minto Street, Edinburgh, EH9 1RQ.*
Comfortable Georgian guest house, very good bus route, Italian spoken
Grades: STB 1 Star
Tel: 0131 667 4144
Mrs Roscilli.
D: £18.00-£25.00 **S:** £20.00-£27.50.
Open: All Year (not Xmas)
Beds: 3F 1D 1T 1S
Baths: 2 En
🛇 🄿 🖵 🏔 🏔 ᴴ ⅋

Avondale Guest House, *10 South Gray Street, Edinburgh, EH9 1TE.*
Quiet location on good bus route to centre (1.25 miles)
Grades: STB 2 Star
Tel: 0131 667 6779 (also fax no)
Mrs Fraser.
D: £20.00-£30.00.
Open: All Year
Beds: 2F 2D 1T
Baths: 2 En 2 Sh
🛇 🄿 (3) ⅋ 🖵 🛏 🏔 🏔 ᴴ ⅋ ♨

Sonas, *3 East Mayfield, Edinburgh, EH9 1SD.*
Comfortable Victorian terraced villa built in 1876, retains many original features
Tel: 0131 667 2781 Mrs Robins.
Fax no: 0131 667 0454
D: £19.00 **S:** £22.00.
Open: All Year
Beds: 1F 3D 3T **Baths:** 7 En
🛇 🄿 🖵 🏔 🏔 ᴴ ⅋

Barony House, *4 Queens Crescent, Edinburgh, EH9 2AZ.*
Lovely Victorian house near city centre. Very quiet. Excellent hospitality
Tel: Freephone 0800 980 4806
Mrs Berkengoff.
Fax no: 0131 667 6833
D: £18.00 **S:** £18.00.
Open: All Year (not Xmas)
Beds: 3F 1D 2T 2S
Baths: 3 Pr 2 Sh
🛇 🄿 (6) ⅋ 🖵 🛏 🏔 🏔 ᴴ ⅋

Aros House, *1 Salisbury Place, Edinburgh, EH9 1SL.*
15 mins' walk to historic city centre. Rooms have hairdryers, ironing facilities & fridges
Tel: 0131 667 1585 Mrs Jameson.
D: £19.00 **S:** £25.00.
Open: Mar to Oct
Beds: 1D 2T **Baths:** 2 En 1 Pr
🖵 🏔 🏔 ᴴ

Edinburgh Prestonfield 25

National Grid Ref: NT2771

🍴 Physilian & Firkin

Santa Lucia Guest House, *14 Kilmaurs Terrace, Edinburgh, EH16 5DR.*
Value for those who don't want hotels or expensive accommodation
Grades: STB 1 Star
Tel: 0131 667 8694
D: £14.00-£22.00 **S:** £17.00-£23.00.
Open: All Year
Beds: 1D 4T 1S **Baths:** 2 Sh
⅋ 🖵 🏔 🏔 ᴴ

The Rosehall Hotel, *101 Dalkeith Road, Edinburgh, EH16 5AJ.*
Close to city centre. Family run. Warm welcome assured
Tel: 0131 667 9372 Mr Gallagher.
D: £25.00 **S:** £25.00.
Open: All Year
Beds: 4F 1D 3T 2S
Baths: 1 Pr 3 Sh
🛇 🖵 🛏 🗡 🏔 🏔 ᴴ 🎒 ⅋

Highland Park Guest House, *16 Kilmaurs Terrace, Edinburgh, EH16 5DR.*
Quiet residential area off Dalkeith Road (A7/A68) convenient for city centre
Tel: 0131 667 9204 (also fax no)
Mr & Mrs Love.
D: £17.00 **S:** £18.00.
Open: All Year (not Xmas)
Beds: 2F 2T 2S **Baths:** 1 En 2 Sh
🛇 ⅋ 🖵 🏔 🏔 ᴴ

Edinburgh Central 26

National Grid Ref: NT2573

🍴 Golf Tavern, Bennets Bar, Minto Hotel, Navaar Hotel, Allison Hotel, Seahaven Hotel

▲ **Edinburgh Eglinton Youth Hostel,** *18 Eglinton Crescent, Edinburgh, EH12 5DD.*
Actual grid ref: NT238735
Tel: 0131 337 1120
Under 18: £9.95 **Adults:** £11.50
evening meals available, self-catering facilities, shop, laundry facilities

▲ **Edinburgh Central Youth Hostel,** *Robertson Close/College Wynd, Cowgate, Edinburgh, EH1 1LY.*
Tel: 0131 337 1120
Under 18: £9.95 **Adults:** £11.50
self-catering facilities, family bunk rooms, laundry facilities

▲ **Edinburgh Pleasance Youth Hostel,** *New Arthur Place, Edinburgh, EH8 9TH.*
Tel: 0131 337 1120
Under 18: £9.95 **Adults:** £11.50
self-catering facilities, family bunk rooms, laundry facilities

Rothesay Hotel, *8 Rothesay Place, Edinburgh, EH3 7SL.*
Grades: STB 2 Star, AA 3 Diamond
Tel: 0131 225 4125 Mr Borland.
D: £25.00-£45.00 **S:** £38.00-£65.00.
Open: All Year
Beds: 2F 4D 18T 12S
Baths: 36 Pr
🛇 🖵 🛏 🗡 🏔 ᴴ
Set in the heart of Edinburgh's Georgian new town in the city centre, the hotel is just a short walk from Princes Street, Edinburgh's shopping and commercial centre, and from museums galleries theatres and concert halls

Averon Guest House, *44 Gilmore Place, Edinburgh, EH3 9NQ.*
Grades: STB 1 Star, AA 2 Diamond, RAC 3 Diamond
Tel: 0131 229 9932 Mr Cran.
D: £18.00-£38.00 **S:** £25.00-£38.00.
Open: All Year
Beds: 3F 2D 3T 1S
Baths: 6 Pr
🛇 🄿 (10) 🖵 🛏 🏔 🏔 ᴴ ⅋ ♨
Fully restored Georgian town house, built in 1770. Central Edinburgh with car park. Standard and ensuite rooms available. STB, AA, RAC, Les Routiers recommended. 10 minute walk to Castle and Princes Street

S = Price range for a single person in a room

Aries Guest House, 5 Upper Gilmore Place, Edinburgh, EH3 9NW.
Small central friendly, all attractions walkable. TV, tea in rooms
Grades: STB 1 Star
Tel: **0131 229 4669**
Mrs Robertson.
D: £17.00-£28.00 **S:** £25.00-£35.00.
Open: All Year (not Xmas)
Beds: 1F 2D 2T **Baths:** 2 Sh
🛇🏠🍴🔥🛁📖🕭🐾📺

17 Hope Park Terrace, Edinburgh, EH8 9LZ.
Fifteen minutes' walk city centre.
H&c in bedrooms
Tel: **0131 667 7963**
Mrs Frackelton.
D: £25.00-£25.00
S: £25.00-£25.00.
Open: All Year
Beds: 2D **Baths:** 1 Sh
🛇 (10) 🕭📖📺🕯

Amaryllis Guest House, 21 Upper Gilmore Place, Edinburgh, EH3 9NL.
Warm, comfortable, friendly, central all attractions. Walkable but quietly situated
Grades: STB 2 Star
Tel: **0131 229 3293** (also fax no)
Melrose.
D: £25.00-£50.00
S: £40.00-£100.00.
Open: All Year (not Xmas)
Beds: 4F 1D **Baths:** 4 En 1 Pr
🛇 (10) 🅿 (2) 🏠🛁📖📺

Kingsview Guest House, 28 Gilmore Place, Edinburgh, EH3 9NQ.
Grades: STB 2 Star
Tel: **0131 229 8004** (also fax no)
D: £18.00-£30.00 **S:** £18.00-£30.00.
Open: All Year
Beds: 4F 2D 2T 1S
Baths: 2 En 1 Pr 1 Sh
🛇🛏🏠🔥✗🛁📖📺🚴
Our family-run guest house is located in the heart of our historic capital's city centre, close to all major attractions. Our famous Kingsview grill breakfast is not for the faint-hearted. Small groups welcome. A warm Scottish welcome awaits

6 Dean Park Crescent, Edinburgh, EH4 1PN.
Warm friendly home. Large rooms. 10 mins walk to centre
Grades: STB 3 Star B&B
Tel: **0131 332 5017**
Mrs Kirkland.
D: £22.00-£29.00 **S:** £40.00-£55.00.
Open: Easter to Oct
Beds: 1F 1D 1T
Baths: 1 En 1 Pr 1 Sh
🛇🕯🏠🛁📖🕭📺

D = Price range per person sharing in a double room

Pay B&Bs by cash or cheque and be prepared to pay up front.

Castle Park Guest House, 75 Gilmore Place, Edinburgh, EH3 9NU.
Family run, close to city centre, conference centre. A warm welcome awaits you
Tel: **0131 229 1215**
Fax no: 0131 229 1223
D: £17.50-£25.00 **S:** £17.50-£22.50.
Open: All Year
Beds: 1F 4D 1T 2S
Baths: 4 En 2 Sh
🛇🅿 (4) 🏠🔥🛁📖📺

Ailsa Craig Hotel, 24 Royal Terrace, Edinburgh, EH7 5AH.
Elegant city centre Georgian town house hotel. Walking distance major attractions
Grades: STB 3 Star
Tel: **0131 556 1022**
Fax no: 0131 556 6055
D: £25.00-£45.00 **S:** £25.00-£60.00.
Open: All Year
Beds: 5F 5D 3T 4S
Baths: 14 En 1 Pr 2 Sh
🛇🏠✗🛁📖📺🕭

Greenside Hotel, 9 Royal Terrace, Edinburgh, EH7 5AB.
City centre Georgian town house hotel within walking distance of Prince Street and the castle
Grades: STB 3 Star,
AA 4 Diamond
Tel: **0131 557 0022** (also fax no)
D: £22.50-£45.00 **S:** £25.00-£55.00.
Open: All Year
Beds: 8F 4D 2T 2S
Baths: 16 En
🛇🏠✗🛁📖📺🕭

37 Howe Street, Edinburgh, EH3 6TF.
Quiet Georgian garden flat few mins' walk to Princes Street
Grades: RAC 2 Star
Tel: **0131 557 3487** (also fax no)
Mrs Collie.
D: £20.00-£20.00.
Open: Easter to Oct
Beds: 1D
Baths: 1 Sh
🏠🛁📖🕭📺

Ellesmere House, 11 Glengyle Terrace, Edinburgh, EH3 9LN.
Central Edinburgh, enviable location overlooking golf links within walking distance to all major attractions
Tel: **0131 229 4823** Mrs Leishman.
Fax no: 0131 229 5285
D: £25.00 **S:** £25.00.
Open: All Year
Beds: 1F 2D 2T 1S
Baths: 6 En
🛇 (10) 🅿🏠🛁📖📺

Lyncliff Hotel, 4 Windsor Street, Edinburgh, EH7 5JR.
Family-run hotel, excellent location. Playfair Building, overlooking Calton Hill
Tel: **0131 556 6972**
Mr & Mrs Fernandez.
Fax no: 0131 478 7059
D: £25.00 **S:** £27.50.
Open: All Year
Beds: 4D 3T 2S
Baths: 3 Sh
🛇🅿🏠🛁📺🕯

Edinburgh Craigleith 27

National Grid Ref: NT2374

St Bernards Guest House, 22 St Bernards Crescent, Edinburgh, EH4 1NS.
Victorian town house. 15 minute walk from city centre. Quiet location
Grades: STB 2 Star
Tel: **0131 332 2339**
Mr & Mrs Alsop.
D: £22.50-£30.00 **S:** £25.00-£30.00.
Open: All Year
Beds: 3D 4T 1S
Baths: 4 En 2 Sh
🕯🏠🛁📖📺🕭🐾

Edinburgh Stockbridge 28

National Grid Ref: NT2474

Dene Guest House, 7 Eyre Place, Edinburgh, EH3 5ES.
Enjoy a comfortable stay and a hearty breakfast in a relaxed and informal atmosphere
Tel: **0131 556 2700**
McDougall.
Fax no: 0131 557 9876
D: £19.50 **S:** £19.50.
Open: All Year
Beds: 2F 2D 3T 3S
Baths: 4 Pr 2 Sh
🛇🏠🔥🛁📖📺

Edinburgh Broughton 29

National Grid Ref: NT2575

Brodies Guest House, 22 East Claremont Street, Edinburgh, EH7 4JP.
Grades: STB 2 Star, AA 3 Diamond
Tel: **0131 556 4032**
Mrs Olbert.
Fax no: 0131 556 9739
D: £22.00-£35.00 **S:** £22.00-£30.00.
Open: All Year (not Xmas)
Beds: 1F 1D 1T 1S
Baths: 2 Pr 1 Sh
🛇🏠🛁📖📺
A warm Scottish welcome awaits you at our Victorian town house. Only 10 minutes' walk to city centre, bus & rail stations. Full choice breakfasts (including vegetarian). Fresh Scottish produce. Unrestricted street parking

Edinburgh Pilrig 30

National Grid Ref: NT2675

Balmoral Guest House, 32 Pilrig Street, Edinburgh, EH6 5AL.
Excellent location for city centre, Leith Port and Royal Yacht 'Britannia'
Grades: STB 2 Star
Tel: 0131 554 1857
Fax no: 0131 553 5712
D: £17.00-£30.00
S: £25.00-£25.00.
Open: All Year (not Xmas)
Beds: 1F 2D 2T
Baths: 1 En 2 Sh
🛇 🅿 ⊬ ☐ 🏃 🎜 🎹 Ⓥ ⚡ ⚲

Sunnyside Guest House, 13 Pilrig Street, Edinburgh, EH6 5AN.
Beautiful Georgian family-run guest house. An easy atmosphere and ample breakfast
Grades: STB 2 Star
Tel: 0131 553 2084
Mr Wheelaghan.
D: £17.00-£27.00 **S:** £17.00-£27.00.
Open: All Year (not Xmas)
Beds: 2F 4D 2T 1S
Baths: 4 En 1 Pr 1 Sh
🛇 🅿 ⊬ ☐ 🎜 🎹 Ⓥ ⚲

Claymore Guest House, 68 Pilrig Street, Edinburgh, EH6 5AS.
Warm, welcoming, personally run, centrally situated, close to all attractions
Grades: STB 2 Star GH
Tel: 0131 554 2500 (also fax no)
Mrs Dorrian.
D: £18.00-£30.00 **S:** £22.00.
Open: All Year (not Xmas)
Beds: 2F 2D 2T
Baths: 3 En 1 Pr 2 Sh
🛇 ⊬ ☐ 🎜 🎹 Ⓥ

Glenburn Guest House, 22 Pilrig Street, Edinburgh, EH6 5AJ.
Clean, welcoming, budget accommodation. 15 minutes city centre
Tel: 0131 554 9818 (also fax no)
Mrs McVeigh.
D: £19.00-£26.00
S: £20.00-£36.00.
Open: All Year (not Xmas)
Beds: 3F 3D 4T 3S
Baths: 1 En 6 Sh
☐ 🎜 🎹 Ⓥ

Edinburgh Newhaven 31

National Grid Ref: NT2576

The Muffin Guest House, 164 Ferry Road, Edinburgh, EH6 4NS.
Stone-built family house 1.5 miles city centre, good bus routes
Tel: 0131 554 4162
Miss Pryde.
D: £16.00 **S:** £18.00.
Open: All Year (not Xmas)
Beds: 1F 3D 1T 2S
Baths: 2 Pr 2 Sh
🛇 🅿 (4) ☐ ✗ 🎜 🎹 Ⓥ ♿ Ⓥ

Edinburgh Trinity 32

National Grid Ref: NT2476

🚾 🚲 Old Chain Pier

Dunedin, 109 Trinity Road, Edinburgh, EH5 3JY.
Friendly welcome in elegant Victorian house in quiet residential area
Tel: 0131 552 3752 Mrs Marshall.
Fax no: 0131 551 4653
D: £22.00-£27.00 **S:** £25.00-£27.00.
Open: All Year (not Xmas)
Beds: 1T 1D
Baths: 2 Pr
🅿 (1) ⊬ ☐ 🎜 🎹 Ⓥ ⚡ ⚲

Ardleigh Guest House, 260 Ferry Road, Edinburgh, EH5 3AN.
Family-run guest house with panoramic view of city skyline
Tel: 0131 552 1833 (also fax no)
D: £20.00 **S:** £25.00.
Open: All Year (not Xmas)
Beds: 2F 3T 2D
Baths: 5 En 2 Pr
🛇 (5) ☐ 🎜 🎹 Ⓥ

Edinburgh Craigentinny 33

National Grid Ref: NT2974

Glenfarrer House, 36 Farrer Terrace, Edinburgh, EH7 6SG.
Grades: STB 2 Star
Tel: 0131 669 1265 Mrs Smith.
D: £21.00 **S:** £17.00.
Open: Easter to Oct
Beds: 1D 1T 2S
Baths: 2 En 1 Sh
🅿 (2) ⊬ ☐ 🎜 🎹 Ⓥ ⚡
Chalet bungalow close to excellent bus services. City centre 2 miles. End of city by-pass 3 minutes. Join Bet & Bill for our unique Ceilidh breakfast. Good home cooking. A warm welcome awaits you. Singles welcome

Edinburgh Northfield 34

National Grid Ref: NT2973

Failte Guest House, 117 Willowbrae Road, Edinburgh, EH8 7HN.
Small friendly guest-house. 10 mins by bus to city centre
Tel: 0131 661 3629 Chiekrie.
Fax no: 0131 620 1102
D: £18.00 **S:** £22.00.
Open: All Year (not Xmas)
Beds: 2F 2D 2T 1S
Baths: 2 En 2 Sh
🛇 🅿 ☐ 🚹 🎜 🎹 ♿ Ⓥ

All rates are subject to alteration at the owners' discretion.

D = Price range per person sharing in a double room

Edinburgh Portobello 35

National Grid Ref: NT3074

🚾 🚲 Peacock Inn

Hopebank, 33 Hope Lane North, Portobello, Edinburgh, EH15 2PZ.
Tel: 0131 657 1149
Ms Williamson.
D: £20.00 **S:** £20.00.
Open: Easter to Oct
Beds: 2D 1T
Baths: 3 Pr 1 Sh
🛇 🅿 ⊬ ☐ 🎜 🎹 Ⓥ ⚡
Edinburgh is an excellent centre for touring from, with many golf courses, indoor bowls fitness, clubs, art galleries, museums and other sports activities

Cruachan, 6 Pittville Street, Edinburgh, EH15 2BY.
Elegant Georgian villa adjacent to beach, promenade, city centre 2.5 miles. Good parking
Grades: STB 2 Star B&B
Tel: 0131 669 2195
Mrs Thom.
D: £20.00-£22.00
S: £19.00-£21.00.
Open: Easter to Oct
Beds: 2D 1T 1S
Baths: 2 Sh
🛇 (12) 🅿 (3) ⊬ ☐ 🚹 🎜 Ⓥ

Edinburgh Leith 35

National Grid Ref: NT2776

🚾 🚲 Persevere

Sandaig Guest House, 5 East Hermitage Place, Edinburgh, EH6 8AA.
Overlooks Leith Links. Full Scottish breakfast included in price
Grades: STB 3 Star, AA 3 Diamond
Tel: 0131 554 7357
D: £18.00-£35.00
S: £20.00-£40.00.
Open: All Year
Beds: 3F 3D 2T 2S
Baths: 4 En 1 Pr 3 Sh
🛇 ☐ 🚹 🎜 🎹 Ⓥ

Crioch Guest House, 23 East Hermitage Place, Edinburgh, EH6 8AD.
Leith's restored waterfront offers excellent bars and restaurants nearby
Tel: 0131 554 5494
Mrs Marshall.
D: £16.50 **S:** £18.00.
Open: All Year
Beds: 1F 2T 2D 1S
Baths: 2 Sh
🛇 ⊬ ☐ 🎜 🎹 Ⓥ

Sustrans Devon Coast to Coast

The new **Devon Coast to Coast Cycle Route** is a recently opened section of the developing National Cycle Network, running on traffic-free paths and traffic-calmed roads for 90 miles from Ilfracombe on Devon's rugged north coast to the historic city and port of Plymouth, in the south western corner of the county. The southern part of the route skirts the west side of Dartmoor National Park. A high proportion is on railway paths, exemplary of the work Sustrans has been engaged in over recent years in creating safe, enjoyable routes for cyclists. The route coincides with the West Country Way from Barnstaple through Bideford and up the Torridge Valley as far as Sheepwash. It is clearly signposted by blue direction signs with a cycle silhouette, numbered 31 from Ilfracombe to Barnstaple, 3 for the length of the intersection with the West Country Way and 27 from Sheepwash to Plymouth. There is a fair amount of up-and-down involved throughout.

The route starts with a climb inland before descending back to the coast to reach the attractive stone-built village of **Mortehoe** and then **Woolacombe**, from where you cycle beside the beach as far as Putsborough before the reide to **Braunton**,which involves a few climbs and descents. From Braunton the route shares a traffic-free path with the Tarka Trail walk into **Barnstaple**. This continues west along the coast through Instow and up the Torridge Estuary to the eastern part of **Bideford**, East-the-Water, where the Tarka Trail Centre is located; and on a railway path up the Torridge Valley to East Yarde and as far as Moormill, close by **Petrockstowe**, from where you follow roads to Sheepwash and Hatherleigh. On to Jacobstowe in the Okement Valley and through Abbeyford Woods to **Okehampton**, on the northern edge of **Dartmoor**. A bridleway leads to the Meldon Viaduct, which you cross to reach **Bridestowe**. From here you head on to **Lydford**, and pass above the gorge to reach **North Brentor**, where the route divides to give two alternatives through the south western edge of Dartmoor. The western route takes you below the bleak outcrop of Brent Tor, crowned by St Michael's church, and is reasonably straightforward as far as **Tavistock** but gets tougher and rather muddy between there and Yelverton. The eastern route, through Mary Tavy,

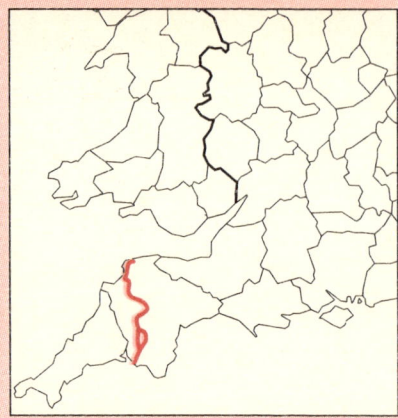

Peter Tavy, Walkhampton, Dousland and Meavy, is a little way up onto the moor so a bit more up-and-down throughout. The routes meet at Clearbrook, from where most of the rest of the way runs on another traffic-free railway path, the Plym Valley Path, as far as the mouth of the Plym. Cross the bridge into **Plymouth** and ride along the seafront to the Hoe and on to the end of the route at Millbay Docks.

The indispensable **official route map and guide** for the route is available from Sustrans, 35 King Street, Bristol BS1 4DZ, tel 0117-926 8893, fax 0117-929 4173, @ £5.99 (+ £2.00 p&p).

Maps: Ordnance Survey 1:50,000 Landranger series: 180, 181, 190, 191, 192, 201, 202

Transport: Plymouth is a main line rail terminus; Okehampton and Barnstaple are also served by trains. The **Devon Bike Bus** scheme, operated by Devon County Council between Barnstaple and Okehampton, and connecting from Okehampton to Exeter, runs throughout the months of June, July, August and September. This innovative new scheme makes use of specially converted buses to carry cyclists with their bicycles. Contact Devon County Council on 01392 383223 for details. Unfortunately the stretch from Ilfracombe to Barnstaple is not served, and drivers on regular bus services will not accept bicycles. Cycling the whole route from the designated start may therefore prove impractical.

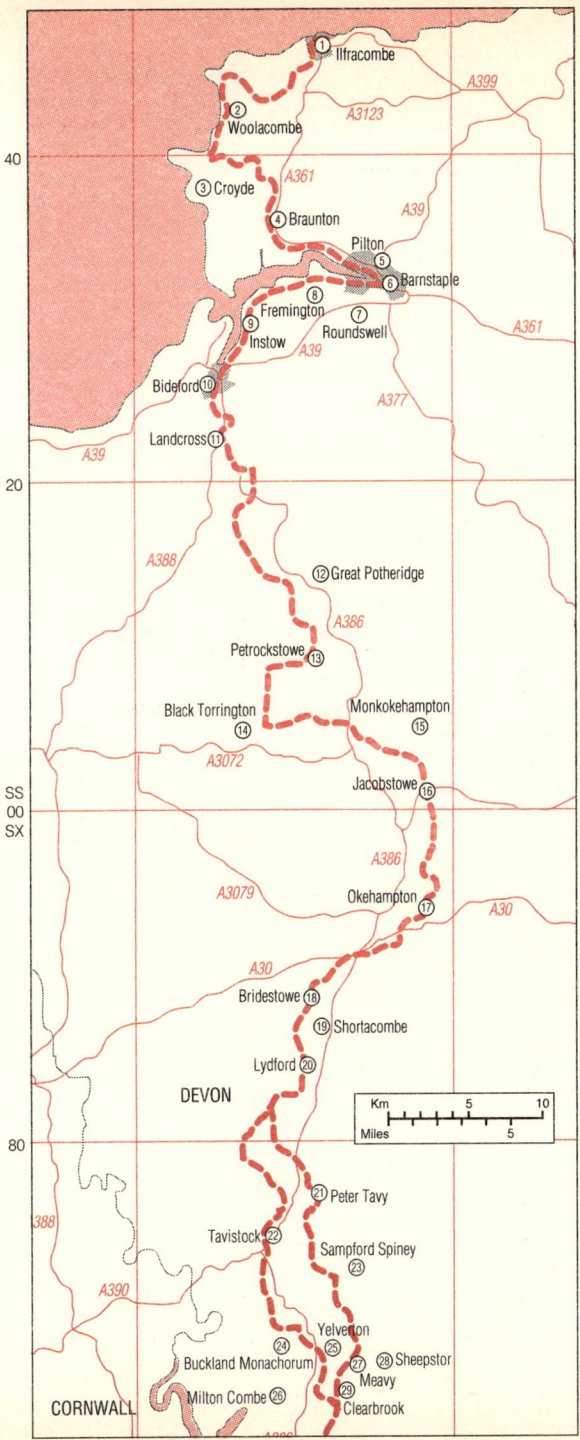

Ilfracombe 1

National Grid Ref: SS5147

🍴 Williams Arms, Agricultural Inn, Cider Apple, The Crown, Sherbourne Lodge

🔺 *Ilfracombe Youth Hostel, Ashmour House, 1 Hillsborough Terrace, Ilfracombe, Devon, EX34 9NR.*
Actual grid ref: SS524476
Tel: **01271 865337**
Under 18: £6.20
Adults: £9.15
evening meal at 7.00pm, family bunk rooms, television, games room, showers, central heating, shop
End house on a fine Georgian terrace, overlooking the picturesque harbour and the Bristol Channel

Lyncott Guest House, 56 St Brannock's Road, Ilfracombe, Devon, EX34 8EQ.
Actual grid ref: SS517463
Tel: **01271 862425** (also fax no)
Mr & Mrs Holdsworth.
D: £17.00-£20.00 **S:** £17.00-£20.00.
Open: All Year
Beds: 2F 3D 1S
Baths: 6 En
🛏 🅿 (5) ⊬ ⊡ ✕ 🛓 Ⓥ ∮ ♂
Join David and Marianna in their charming, lovingly refurbished Victorian house pleasantly situated near lovely Bicclescombe Park. Relax in elegant, smoke-free surroundings. Enjoy delightful, spacious, individually designed ensuite bedrooms and sample their scrumptious home-made fare

Ilfracombe is a relatively unspoilt Victorian and Edwardian holiday resort with the usual seaside attractions. The harbour offers pleasure trips, and day trips to Lundy Island. There is also a museum and a theatre, the Landmark.

Woolacombe is good for cafés and shops, and the beach of Morte Bay has been named as one of the world's top ten beaches.

Just off the route, **Croyde** is a thatched village with numerous tea rooms and attractive old pubs. At **Georgeham** you can visit the house of Henry Williamson, author of *Tarka the Otter* (see under Bideford).

Westwell Hall, *Torrs Park,*
Ilfracombe, Devon, EX34 8AZ.
Elegant Victorian gentleman's
residence in own grounds - superb
views
Grades: ETC 1 Star, AA 1 Star,
RAC 1 Star
Tel: **01271 862792** (also fax no)
Mr & Mrs Lomas.
D: £22.00-£24.00 **S:** £22.00-£24.00.
Open: All Year
Beds: 7D 2T 1S
Baths: 10 En
ॐ📞🅿🖵🛋✕🏃🕯📺Ⓥ

Combe Lodge Hotel,
Chambercombe Park, Ilfracombe,
Devon, EX34 9QW.
Actual grid ref: SS530473
Quiet position, overlooking
harbour, ideal for walking, cycling,
golf holidays
Tel: **01271 864518**
Mr & Mrs Wileman.
D: £16.50-£18.50 **S:** £20.50-£22.50.
Open: All Year (not Xmas)
Beds: 2F 4D 2S
Baths: 4 En 1 Pr 1 Sh
ॐ(1)🅿(8)⅄🖵🏃✕🏃🕯📺Ⓥ🛡⚡

Sherborne Lodge Hotel, *Torrs*
Park, Ilfracombe, Devon, EX34 8AY.
Grades: ETC 1 Star
Tel: **01271 862297**
Mr & Mrs Millington.
Fax no: 01271 865520
D: £15.50-£21.50
S: £15.50-£21.50.
Open: All Year
Beds: 1F 8D 2T 1S
ॐ🅿(10)🖵🏃🕯📺Ⓥ🛡⚡♿
Friendly, fully-licensed family
hotel providing good food, wine,
comfortable accommodation and
excellent service. Located yards
from the coastal path and close to
the tunnels, beaches, theatre, town
and harbour. We guarantee you a
relaxing stay

Varley House, *Chambercombe*
Park, Ilfracombe, Devon, EX34 9QW.
Period house with attractive ensuite
accommodation, close to coastal
walks
Tel: **01271 863927**
Mrs S O'Sullivan & Mr D Small.
Fax no: 01271 879299
D: £24.00-£25.00
S: £23.00-£24.00.
Open: Easter to Oct
Beds: 2F 4D 1T 2S
Baths: 7 En 1 Pr
ॐ(5)🅿(7)🖵🏃✕🏃🕯📺Ⓥ

Harcourt Hotel, *Fore Street,*
Ilfracombe, Devon, EX34 9DS.
Friendly licensed hotel ensuite
rooms TV tea coffee, sea views
Tel: **01271 862931**
Mr Doorbar.
D: £17.00-£24.00 **S:** £17.00-£24.00.
Open: All Year
Beds: 3F 4D 1T 2S
Baths: 8 En 2 Sh
ॐ🅿(4)🖵🏃✕🏃🕯📺🛡⚡♿

Cairn House Hotel,
43 St Brannocks Road, Ilfracombe,
Devon, EX34 8EH.
Beautiful Victorian hotel, delight-
fully situated in its own grounds
Tel: **01271 863911** Mrs Tupper.
D: £18.00 **S:** £20.00.
Open: All Year (not Xmas)
Beds: 3F 6D 1S
Baths: 10 En
ॐ(2)🅿🖵🏃✕🏃🕯📺Ⓥ🛡

Slipway Cottage, *2 Hierns Lane,*
The Harbour, Ilfracombe, Devon,
EX34 9EH.
Situated in excellent level position
overlooking lovely harbour
Tel: **01271 863035**
Mr & Mrs Furber.
D: £17.00 **S:** £17.00.
Open: All Year
Beds: 1T 3D
Baths: 2 En 1 Sh
🖵✕🏃🕯📺Ⓥ🛡⚡

Woolacombe — 2

National Grid Ref: SS4543

🍴🍺 Jubilee Inn, Chichester Arms, Red Barn,
Stables, Golden Hind, The Mill

Barton Lea, *Beach Road,*
Woolacombe, Devon, EX34 7BT.
Warm welcome, sea views, big
breakfast menu, close to Coastal
Foot Path
Tel: **01271 870928** Mrs Vickery.
D: £15.50-£18.00 **S:** £20.00-£25.00.
Open: Easter to Oct
Beds: 1F 1D 1T
Baths: 3 En
ॐ🅿(7)⅄🖵🏃🕯📺Ⓥ🛡⚡♿

Sunny Nook, *Beach Road,*
Woolacombe, Devon, EX34 7AA.
Actual grid ref: SS466438
Delightful home in lovely situation,
wonderful views and excellent
breakfasts. No smoking
throughout.
Tel: **01271 870964** Mr Fenn.
D: £17.50-£22.00 **S:** £22.50-£30.00.
Open: All Year (not Xmas)
Beds: 1F 1D 1T
Baths: 2 En 1 Pr
ॐ(8)🅿(5)⅄🖵✕🏃🕯📺Ⓥ🛡⚡

Clyst House, *Rockfield Road,*
Woolacombe, Devon, EX34 7DH.
Friendly, comfortable guest house
close excellent beach. Delicious
English breakfast. Beautiful walks
& surfing
Tel: **01271 870220** Mrs Braund.
D: £18.00-£20.00 **S:** £18.00-£20.00.
Open: Mar to Nov
Beds: 1F 1D 1T
Baths: 1 Sh
ॐ(7)🅿⅄🖵✕🏃🕯📺Ⓥ⚡

D = Price range per person
sharing in a double room

Camberley, *Beach Road,*
Woolacombe, Devon, EX34 7AA.
Actual grid ref: SS465437
Large Victorian house with views
to sea and NT land
Grades: ETC 3 Diamond
Tel: **01271 870231**
Mr & Mrs Riley.
D: £19.00-£24.00 **S:** £19.00-£24.00.
Open: All Year (not Xmas)
Beds: 3F 3D 1T **Baths:** 6 En 1 Pr
ॐ🅿(6)🖵🕯📺Ⓥ🛡♿

Caertref, *Beach Road,*
Woolacombe, Devon, EX34 7BT.
Family run 3 mins from sandy
beach. Relaxed friendly
atmosphere
Tel: **01271 870361** Mr & Mrs Bret.
D: £19.00 **S:** £21.00.
Open: Easter to Oct
Beds: 3F 2T 6D **Baths:** 11 En
ॐ🅿(11)🖵✕🏃🕯📺Ⓥ♿

Sands Hotel, *Bay View Road,*
Woolacombe, Devon, EX36 7DQ.
Beautiful sea views overlooking
Woolacombe, beach fifty yards.
Family run
Tel: **01271 870550** (also fax no)
D: £25.00 **S:** £22.00.
Open: All Year (not Xmas)
Beds: 2F 4T 11D 4S
Baths: 8 En 5 Sh
ॐ🖵🏃🕯📺Ⓥ♿

Ivycott Mews, *Woolacombe,*
Devon, EX34 7HL.
Actual grid ref: SS429476
Comfortable converted Victorian
barn. Relaxed homely atmosphere.
Beaches 2 miles
Tel: **01271 871048** Mrs Collis.
D: £15.00 **S:** £16.00.
Open: Easter to Oct
Beds: 1F 1T **Baths:** 1 Sh
ॐ🅿(3)⅄🖵🏃🕯📺Ⓥ⚡

Fircroft, *Station Road,*
Woolacombe, Devon, EX34 7AW.
A warm welcome awaits you at our
family-run guest house, offering
excellent accommodation
Tel: **01271 870542** (also fax no)
Mrs Keiff.
D: £17.00 **S:** £22.00.
Open: All Year
Beds: 1F 1T 3D
Baths: 3 En 2 Sh
ॐ🅿(6)⅄🖵✕🏃🕯📺Ⓥ🛡⚡♿

Croyde — 3

National Grid Ref: SS4439

🍴🍺 The Thatch

Chapel Farm, *Hobbs Hill, Croyde,*
Braunton, Devon, EX33 1NE.
Actual grid ref: SS444390
C16th thatched farmhouse, 10 min-
utes to beach
Tel: **01271 890429** Mrs Windsor.
D: £18.00-£26.00 **S:** £18.00-£30.00.
Open: Easter to Nov
Beds: 1F 2D **Baths:** 3 En
🅿(6)⅄🖵🏃🕯📺Ⓥ🛡⚡♿

Braunton 4

National Grid Ref: SS4936

🍴🍺 The Argicultural Inn, Mariners Arms

Pixie Dell, *1 Willand Rd,*
Braunton, N. Devon, EX33 1AX.
Large chalet bungalow and garden.
Warm welcome assured
Tel: **01271 812233**
Mrs Dale.
D: £18.00-£18.00 **S:** £18.00-£20.00.
Open: All Year (not Xmas)
Beds: 1D 2T 1S
Baths: 2 Sh
🏃🅿(4)✒🛏🗢🕯🖾♿🛒♿🎱⚡

Rozel, *43 Saunton Road, Braunton,*
Devon, EX33 1HD.
1930s dormer bungalow with
award-winning hidden garden
Tel: **01271 812679**
Mr & Mrs Hopkins.
D: £17.50.
Open: All Year (not Xmas)
Beds: 1F 1D
Baths: 2 En
🏃(10)🅿(3)✒🛏🕯🖾♿🎱

Stockwell Lodge, *66 South Street,*
Braunton, Devon, EX33 2AS.
Charming family home with leaded
lights and balcony. Beautiful walks
Tel: **01271 814338**
Mrs Saunders.
D: £16.00 **S:** £16.00.
Open: All Year
Beds: 2F 1T 2D 1S
Baths: 2 En 1 Sh
🏃🅿(10)🛏🛋🕯🖾♿🛒♿🎱

North Cottage, *14 North Street,*
Braunton, Devon, EX33 1AJ.
Actual grid ref: SS486367
Old picturesque cottage near
village
Tel: **01271 812703**
Mrs Watkins.
D: £14.00 **S:** £14.00.
Open: All Year
Beds: 1F 2D 1S
Baths: 1 En 1 Sh
🏃🅿(3)✒🛏🕯🖾♿🛒♿

Pilton 5

National Grid Ref: SS5534

🍴🍺 Windsor Arms, Williams Arms

Bradiford Cottage, *Halls Mill*
Lane, Pilton, Barnstaple, Devon,
EX31 4DP.
Actual grid ref: SS551345
C17th cottage set in the peaceful
countryside just one mile from
Barnstaple
Tel: **01271 345039** (also fax no)
Mrs Hare.
D: £15.00 **S:** £15.00.
Open: All Year (not Xmas/
New Year)
Beds: 2D 1T 1S
Baths: 1 Sh
🏃(8)🅿(4)✒🛏🕯🖾♿

Barnstaple 6

National Grid Ref: SS5633

🍴🍺 Windsor Arms, Williams Arms, Rolle Quay
Inn, North Country Inn, Pyne Arms,
Ring o' Bells, Chichester Arms

Mount Sandford, *Mount Sandford*
Road, Barnstaple, Devon, EX32 0HL.
Tel: **01271 342354** Mrs White.
D: £18.00-£22.00 **S:** £20.00.
Open: All Year (not Xmas)
Beds: 1F 1D 1T
Baths: 3 En
🏃(3)🅿(3)✒🛏🕯🖾♿⚡🎱
Georgian house in 1.5 acres
gardens. 2 double, 1 twin, all
ensuite, TV, tea-making, central
heated. Winner of Barnstaple in
Bloom Garden 1998. Easily reach
of all North Devon Coast. 500
yards from 18-hole Golf Park. £18
B&B

Crossways, *Braunton Road,*
Barnstaple, Devon, EX31 1JY.
Actual grid ref: SS555333
Detached house - town & Tarka
Trail 150 yards, bicycle hire
Tel: **01271 379120**
Mr & Mrs Tysn.
D: £15.00 **S:** £17.00.
Open: All Year
Beds: 1F 1D 1T
Baths: 2 Pr 1 Sh
🏃🅿(6)✒🛏✗🕯🖾♿⚡

Kingston House, *Rumsam Road,*
Rumsam, Barnstaple, Devon,
EX32 9EW.
Victorian house, peaceful location,
Tarka trail nearby, good food,
cleanliness assured
Tel: **01271 373957** Mrs Miller.
D: £18.00-£20.00.
Open: All Year (not Xmas)
Beds: 1F 1D
Baths: 2 En
🏃(10)✒🛏🕯🖾♿🎱

West View, *Pilton Causeway,*
Barnstaple, Devon, EX32 7AA.
Modernised Victorian property
overlooking park
Tel: **01271 342079** (also fax no)
Mrs Rostock.
D: £17.00 **S:** £17.00.
Open: All Year
Beds: 3F 3D 10T 7S
Baths: 5 En 7 Sh
🏃🅿(12)🛏🛏✗🕯🖾♿⚡🎱

Nelson House, *99 Newport Road,*
Rock Park, Barnstaple, Devon,
EX32 9BA.
Spacious Georgian house, close to
town centre, Rock Park, leisure
centre, River Taw
Tel: **01271 345929**
D: £16.00 **S:** £18.00.
Open: All Year
Beds: 1F 1T 1D
Baths: 1 En 1 Pr
🏃✒🛏🕯🖾♿🎱

Roundswell 7

National Grid Ref: SS5431

🍴🍺 Hunters Inn, New Inn

The Red House, *Roundswell,*
Barnstaple, Devon, EX31 3NP.
A period country house situated in
an elevated position with
panoramic views
Tel: **01271 345966** Mrs Cox.
D: £17.00 **S:** £20.00.
Open: Feb to Nov
Beds: 1T 1D
Baths: 1 Sh
🏃(12)🅿(5)✒🛏🕯🖾♿⚡🎱

S = Price range for a single
person in a room

The pretty old market town of **Barnstaple** has some interesting buildings, such as the medieval timber-framed Pannier Market, where the market is still held, the eighteenth-century colonnades of Queen Anne's Walk and fourteenth-century St Anne's Chapel, a school where John Gay, who wrote *The Beggar's Opera*, was once a pupil – it now houses a museum of education. The town also hosts the Museum of North Devon, and the Queen's Theatre.

At **Bideford**, on the Torridge Estuary, you will find a fourteenth-century bridge and a statue commemorating Charles Kingsley, who wrote the historical romance *Westward Ho!*, set in the town (the eponymous nearby coastal resort was named after the book). The Tarka Trail Centre in East-the-Water provides information on the popular walk which shares this part of the cycle route: named after Henry Williamson's classic 1927 novel, *Tarka the Otter* (which has been a bestseller ever since), it explores the varied North Devon countryside through which Tarka was pursued.

Fremington   8

National Grid Ref: SS5132

🍴 🍺 Cedars Inn, New Inn

Muddlebridge House, *Fremington, Barnstaple, Devon, EX31 2NQ.*
Actual grid ref: SS522326
Large Regency house
Tel: **01271 376073** (also fax no)
Mr & Mrs Macdonald.
D: £23.00 **S:** £27.00.
Open: Easter to Nov
Beds: 1F 1D 1T
Baths: 3 En 1 Sh
🛇 (3) 🅿 (4) ⅍ 🗆 📺 🛏 📖 🔽 🛒 ⚡ 🚲

Instow   9

National Grid Ref: SS4730

🍴 🍺 Quay Inn, Boathouse, Wayfarer Inn

🔺 **Instow Youth Hostel,**
Worlington House, New Road, Instow, Bideford, Devon, EX39 4LW.
Actual grid ref: SS482303
Tel: **01271 860394**
Under 18: £6.20 **Adults:** £9.15
evening meal at 7.00pm, family
bunk rooms, television, showers,
shop
Large Victorian country house with fine views across the Torridge Estuary

Pilton Cottage, *Victoria Terrace, Marine Parade, Instow, Bideford, Devon, EX39 4JW.*
Victorian house, beautiful estuary
view, yards from sandy beach
Tel: **01271 860202**
Mr & Mrs Gardner.
D: £17.50 **S:** £18.50.
Open: Easter to Oct
Beds: 1F 2D 1T 1S
Baths: 1 Pr 1 Sh
🅿 (3) ⅍ 🗆 🛏 📖 🔽 ⚡

Bideford   10

National Grid Ref: SS4526

🍴 🍺 Tanton's Hotel, Farmers Arms, Crab & Ale,
Royal Hotel, Swan Inn, Joiners' Arms, Hunters'
Inn, Sunset Hotel

The Mount Hotel, *Northdown Road, Bideford, Devon, EX39 3LP.*
Actual grid ref: SS449269
Grades: AA 4 Diamond
Tel: **01237 473748**
Mr & Mrs Laugharne.
D: £22.00-£24.00
S: £25.00-£33.00.
Open: Jan to Dec
Beds: 1F 3D 1T 2S
Baths: 7 En
🛇 🅿 ⅍ 🗆 🛏 📖 🔽 🔽 🛒 ⚡ 🚲
Charming Georgian licensed guest
house only 5 minutes' walk to town
centre, private lounge for guests'
use, all rooms ensuite, attractive
garden, car parking for guests.
Convenient for touring N Devon
coastline, Clovelly, Lundy, Exmoor
and Dartmoor. No smoking

Corner House, *14 The Strand, Bideford, Devon, EX39 2ND.*
Actual grid ref: SS4426
Family-run guest house. Clean,
comfortable accommodation. Town
centre location
Tel: **01237 473722**
Stone.
D: £16.00 **S:** £17.50.
Open: All Year
Beds: 1F 2D 1T 1S
Baths: 1 Sh
🛇 ⅍ 🗆 🗙 🛏 📖 🔽 🛒 ⚡

Landcross   11

National Grid Ref: SS4623

Sunset Hotel, *Landcross, Bideford, Devon, EX39 5JA.*
Actual grid ref: SS461239
Grades: ETC 3 Diamond,
AA 3 Diamond
Tel: **01237 472962**
Mrs Lamb.
D: £26.00-£30.00
S: £25.00-£30.00.
Open: Easter to Nov
Beds: 2F 2D 2T
Baths: 4 En
🅿 (8) ⅍ 🗆 🗙 🛏 📖 🔽 🛒 🚲
Somewhere special: small country
hotel, quiet peaceful location,
overlooking spectacular scenery

Great Potheridge   12

National Grid Ref: SS5114

🔺 **Great Potheridge YHA
Camping Barn**, *Great Potheridge, Merton, Okehampton, Devon.*
Actual grid ref: SS513146
Adults: £3.35+
evening meals available, camping
available
*Located at an outdoor Education
Centre, this barn provides excellent
bunk-house accommodation with
outdoor activities available.*
*ADVANCE BOOKING
ESSENTIAL*

Petrockstowe   13

National Grid Ref: SS5109

🍴 🍺 The Laurels

Aish Villa, *Petrockstowe, Okehampton, Devon, EX20 3HL.*
Actual grid ref: SS514089
Peaceful location, superb views,
ideal for visiting Dartmoor,
Exmoor, coast
Tel: **01837 810581**
Ms Gordon.
D: £15.00-£15.00
S: £15.00-£15.00
Open: All Year
Beds: 1F 1T
Baths: 1 Sh
🛇 🅿 (4) ⅍ 🗆 🛏 📖 ♿ 🔽 ⚡ 🚲

Black Torrington   14

National Grid Ref: SS4605

🍴 🍺 Golden Inn Half Moon

Coham Manor, *Black Torrington, Beaworthy, Devon, EX21 5HT.*
Actual grid ref: SS456058
Beautiful old manor house in own
farmland and woods beside River
Torridge
Tel: **01409 231514** (also fax no)
Mr Coham-Maclaren.
D: £25.00-£25.00
S: £27.50-£27.50.
Open: All Year (not Xmas)
Beds: 2T
Baths: 1 En 1 Pr
🛇 🅿 (10) ⅍ 🗆 🛏 📖 🔽 ⚡ 🚲

All rooms full and
nowhere else to stay?
Ask the owner if
there's anywhere
nearby

Just off the route (there is a link route) at **Great
Torrington**, *Torrington 1646* reconstructs the battle, in which
Cromwell's New Model Army was instrumental, which saw
this Royalist stronghold fall finally to the forces of Parliament.
You can also visit the Dartington Crystal factory (tours are
available) and shop.

At **Hatherleigh** there is a gallery of local arts and crafts,
and a pottery.

Okehampton has a ruined castle with a Norman keep,
and the Museum of Dartmoor Life, with interactive exhibits.

Lydford Gorge, owned by the National Trust, boasts
some impressive natural features, from the raging Devil's
Cauldron whirlpool to the White Lady, a slender water drop
of 90 feet. The gorge shelters a wealth of wildlife, including
woodpeckers, herons and butterflies galore.

Monkokehampton 15

National Grid Ref: SS5805

🏠 Duke of York

Seldon Farm, *Monkokehampton, Winkleigh, Devon, EX19 8RY.*
Grades: ETC 2 Diamond
Tel: 01837 810312
Mrs Case.
D: £16.00-£17.00
S: £16.00-£17.00.
Open: Easter to Oct
Beds: 1F 2D
Baths: 1 Sh
🛌🅿️🖳🔭🛏📺♿📺👜⚡🚲
Charming C17th farmhouse in beautiful, tranquil, rural setting within 3 miles from the market town of Hatherleigh. Follow the Tarka trail or visit Rosemoor Gardens, Dartington Glass, Lydford Gorge or Castle Drogo. Central for touring Dartmoor or Exmoor

Jacobstowe 16

National Grid Ref: SS5801

🔺 **Higher Cadham YHA Camping Barn**, *Cadham, Jacobstowe, Okehampton, Devon.*
Actual grid ref: SS585025
Adults: £3.35+
evening meals available, shop
Converted barn in peaceful farmyard setting.
ADVANCE
BOOKING ESSENTIAL

Higher Cadham Farm,
Jacobstowe, Okehampton, Devon, EX20 3RB.
Superb farmhouse accommodation with country walks. Hearty farmhouse food
Grades: ETC 4 Diamond,
AA 4 Diamond
Tel: **01837 851647** Mrs King.
Fax no: 01837 851410
D: £18.50-£25.00 **S:** £18.50-£25.00.
Open: All Year (not Xmas)
Beds: 3F 2D 3T 1S
Baths: 5 En 1 Sh
🛌🅿️(10)🖳🛏✗🔭📺♿📺👜⚡🚲

Okehampton 17

National Grid Ref: SX5895

🏠 Oxenham Arms, River Inn, Tors Hotel, New Inn

🔺 **Okehampton Youth Hostel,**
The Goods Yard, Okehampton Station, Okehampton, Devon, EX20 1EJ.
Actual grid ref: SX591942
Tel: **01837 53916**
Under 18: £6.85 **Adults:** £10.15
evening meal at 7.00pm, self-catering facilities, family bunk rooms, showers, laundry facilities
Converted Victorian railway goods shed on northern edge of Dartmoor National Park

---

S = Price range for a single person in a room

North Lake, *Exeter Road, Okehampton, Devon, EX20 1QH.*
Grades: ETC 3 Diamond
Tel: **01837 53100**
Mrs Jones.
D: £20.00-£20.00 **S:** £20.00-£20.00.
Open: All Year (not Xmas)
Beds: 2D 1T
Baths: 2 En 1 Pr
🛌(6)🅿️(10)🖳🛏🔭📺♿📺👜⚡🚲
Set in large grounds with panoramic views across Dartmoor. Tastefully furnished, good food, with a personal friendly touch; come and go as you please. Superb walking and riding base, stunning scenery and cascading rivers

Heathfield House, *Okehampton, Devon, EX20 1EW.*
Grades: AA 4 Diamond
Tel: **01837 54211** (also fax no)
Mrs Seigal.
D: £35.00-£35.00 **S:** £35.00-£40.00.
Open: All Year (not Xmas)
Beds: 1F 1D 2T 4S
Baths: 20 Sh
🛌🅿️(8)🖳🛏✗🔭📺♿📺👜⚡🚲
Situated high on north face of Dartmoor, tucked away & private although only 10 mins from market town of Okehampton. Chef owner, direct access Dartmoor, spectacular views right across to Exmoor. Famous for food

Bourna Farmhouse, *Okehampton, Devon, EX20 3EJ.*
Traditional newly thatched Devon longhouse, many original features, very comfortable
Tel: **01805 804584**
Mrs Andrews.
D: £13.50-£17.00
S: £13.50-£17.00.
Open: All Year
Beds: 1F 1D 1T 1S
Baths: 1 En 1 Pr 1 Sh
🛌🅿️(10)🖳🛏✗🔭📺📺

Arnley House, *7 Oaklands Park, Okehampton, Devon, EX20 1LN.*
Modern luxury house, warm welcome, discount for 3 days plus
Tel: **01837 53311**
D: £22.00-£22.00
S: £23.50-£23.50.
Open: Jan to Nov
Beds: 1D
Baths: 1 En
🅿️(1)🖳🛏📺📺👜⚡🚲

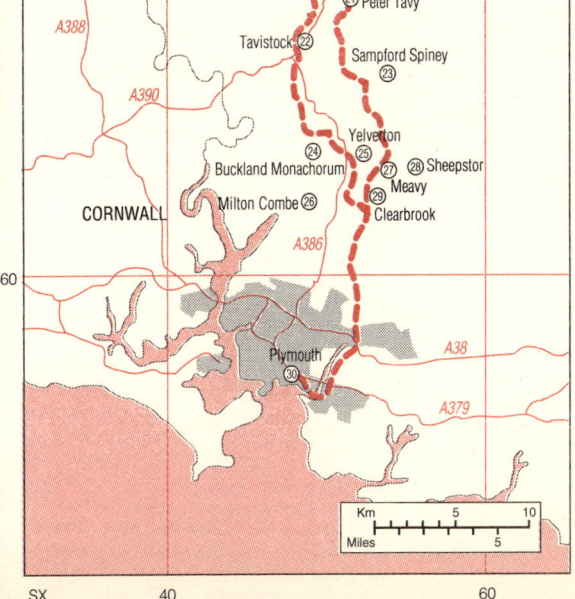

Order your packed lunches the *evening before* you need them. Not at breakfast!

Bridestowe 18

National Grid Ref: SX5189

🍺 🍴 White Hart

Week Farm, *Bridestowe, Okehampton, Devon, EX20 4HZ.*
Actual grid ref: SX519913
Grades: AA 4 Diamond
Tel: **01837 861221**
Ms Hockridge.
D: £23.00-£24.00 **S:** £23.00-£24.00.
Open: All Year (not Xmas)
Beds: 2F 3D
Baths: 5 En
🛏 🅿 ⏰ 🛏 🐾 ✕ 👤 🏠 ⚿ 🛗 👤 ∅ ⚲
C17th farmhouse home-from-home, guests returning annually for our delicious home cooking and glorious surrounding countryside. Ideal touring centre for Dartmoor and coasts (walking, cycling, horse, riding, fishing) outdoor heated swimmimg pool. Come and spoil yourselves

The White Hart Inn, *Fore Street, Bridestowe, Okehampton, Devon, EX20 4EL.*
Actual grid ref: 5X513893
C17th country inn, close to Dartmoor. Same owners for 37 years
Grades: ETC 3 Diamond
Tel: **01837 861318** (also fax no)
Mr Owen.
D: £23.00-£23.00 **S:** £29.00-£29.00.
Open: All Year
Beds: 2D
Baths: 2 En
🅿 (20) ⏰ ✕ 👤 👤 ∅ ⚲

Way Barton Barn, *Bridestowe, Okehampton, Devon, EX20 4QH.*
200-year-old converted barn in peaceful location with extensive views
Tel: **01837 861513**
Mrs Kemp.
D: £15.00 **S:** £15.00.
Open: Jan to Nov
Beds: 1F 1D 1T
Baths: 1 Sh
🛏 🅿 ⏰ ✕ 👤 🛗 👤 ∅ ⚲

Shortacombe 19

National Grid Ref: SX5286

▲ **Fox & Hounds YHA Camping Barn**, *Shortacombe, Okehampton, Devon.*
Actual grid ref: SX525866
Adults: £3.35+
showers, camping available
Ideally situated on the western edge of Dartmoor.
ADVANCE BOOKING ESSENTIAL

Pay B&Bs by

cash or cheque and

be prepared to

pay up front.

Lydford 20

National Grid Ref: SX5184

🍺 🍴 Dartmoor Inn

Moor View House, *Vale Down, Lydford, Okehampton, Devon, EX20 4AU.*
Licensed country house; reputation for good food, ideal touring centre
Grades: AA 5 Diamond,
RAC 5 Diamond
Tel: **01822 820220** (also fax no)
Mr Sharples.
D: £25.00-£36.00
S: £30.00-£45.00.
Open: All Year
Beds: 3D 1T **Baths:** 4 Pr
🛏 (12) 🅿 ⚿ ⏰ 🐾 ✕ 👤 🛗 👤 ∅ ⚲

The Springs, *Lydford, Okehampton, Devon, EX20 4BA.*
Warm and welcoming accommodation. Direct access onto Dartmoor, great breakfasts
Tel: **01822 820297**
Mrs Wray.
D: £20.00-£22.00 **S:** £20.00-£22.00.
Open: All Year (not Xmas)
Beds: 1D 1T 1S
Baths: 2 En 1 Pr 1 Sh
🅿 (8) ⚿ ⏰ 🐾 ✕ 👤 🛗 ⚿ 👤 ∅ ⚲

Peter Tavy 21

National Grid Ref: SX5177

🍺 🍴 Peter Tavy Inn

Churchtown, *Peter Tavy, Tavistock, Devon, PL19 9NP.*
Detached Victorian house standing in own large quiet garden
Tel: **01822 810477**
Mrs Lane.
D: £17.00-£18.00 **S:** £17.00-£18.00.
Open: All Year (not Xmas)
Beds: 2D 1S
Baths: 1 En 1 Sh
🛏 (10) 🅿 (6) ⏰ 🐾 🛗 👤 ∅ ⚲

Tavistock 22

National Grid Ref: SX4874

🍺 🍴 Blacksmiths' Arms, Cornish Arms, Peter Tavy Inn, Montery Jacks, Chip Shop Inn

Hele Farm, *Tavistock, Devon, PL19 8PA.*
Comfortable accommodation at fully organic dairy farm dated 1780
Grades: ETC 3 Diamond
Tel: **01822 833084**
Mrs Steer.
D: £18.00-£20.00 **S:** £20.00-£25.00.
Open: Apr to Oct
Beds: 1D 1T
Baths: 2 Pr
🛏 🅿 (3) ⚿ ⏰ 🐾 🛗 👤 ∅ ⚲

At **Tavistock**, visit the church of St Eustace, where, close by the remains of eleventh-century Tavistock Abbey, the fifteenth-century church building is adorned by a William Morris window.

A couple of miles off the route, **Buckland Abbey**, a former Cistercian abbey, was converted to become the home of Francis Drake. There is an array of Drake memorabilia on show in the house, which stands amid beautiful grounds.

Between **Plympton** and Plymouth, Saltram House, the largest country house in Devon, features Robert Adam architecture, Chippendale furniture and portraits by Joshua Reynolds.

Plymouth is one of Britain's most important maritime cities. Plymouth Hoe, the historic promenade from which the city spreads out, gives magnificent views across Plymouth Sound, also at times catching strong winds. Here in 1588, having caught wind of the approaching Spanish Armada whilst in the middle of a game of bowls, Sir Francis Drake declared, "There is plenty of time to win this game and to thrash the Spaniards too". Allegedly. Close by are the Barbican, whose Tudor and Jacobean buildings form the heart of old Plymouth, with the Mayflower Steps from which the Pilgrim Fathers set sail; and the Royal Citadel, a fortification built during the Restoration to keep this Parliamentarian town in check.

D = Price range per person
sharing in a double room

Acorn Cottage, Tavistock, Devon,
PL19 0LQ.
Actual grid ref: SX463787
Grades: ETC 4 Diamond
Tel: **01822 810038 / 07899 954400**
D: £15.00-£18.00 **S:** £20.00-£30.00.
Open: All Year
Beds: 1D 2T
Baths: 3 En 1 Pr
🏃 (3) 🅿 (20) ⛄🛏🏠🔥📷📺🍴💷🚲
C17th Grade II Listed, many
original features retained. Peaceful,
rural location, beautiful views, just
3 miles from Tavistock on the
Chillaton road. Quality
accommodation near Lydford
Gorge and Brentor medieval
church. Central to beaches, golf
courses, theme parks, Dartmoor,
walking, riding, gliding and
fishing

Kingfisher Cottage, Mount Tavy
Road, Vigo Bridge, Tavistock,
Devon, PL19 9JB.
Riverside accommodation in
characterful cottage near town and
beautiful Dartmoor
Tel: **01822 613801** Mrs Toland.
D: £16.00-£21.00 **S:** £16.00-£35.00.
Open: All Year
Beds: 2D 1T
Baths: 1 En
🏃 🅿 (5) ⛄🛏🏠🔥📺💷🚲

Mount Tavy Cottage, Tavistock,
Devon, PL19 9JL.
Stone cottage in ten acres, own
walled garden, close to Dartmoor
Tel: **01822 614253** Mr Moule.
D: £20.00-£22.50 **S:** £18.00-£22.50.
Open: All Year
Beds: 2D 1S **Baths:** 2 Pr
🏃 🅿 (6) ⛄🛏🏠✗🔥📺💷💷🚲

Sampford Spiney   23

National Grid Ref: SX5372

🍴🍺 London Inn, Horrabridge

Withill Farm, Sampford Spiney,
Yelverton, Devon, PL20 6LN.
Actual grid ref: SX548727
Tel: **01822 853992** (also fax no)
D: £17.00-£20.00 **S:** £18.00-£22.00.
Open: All Year
Beds: 1D 2T
Baths: 1 En 1 Sh
🏃 🅿 (6) 🏠🔥✗🔥📺💷💷🚲
West Dartmoor. Relax at our
friendly, small working farm in an
secluded setting, surrounded by
woods, a tumbling brook, moorland
and granite tors. Ideal for walking,
riding, cycling, central for visiting
Devon & Cornwall.

All rates are subject
to alteration at the
owners' discretion.

Bringing children with
you? Always ask for
any special rates.

Buckland Monachorum 24

National Grid Ref: SX4968

Uppaton Country Guest House,
Coppicetown Road, Buckland
Monachorum, Yelverton, Devon,
PL20 7LL.
Grades: ETC 4 Diamond,
AA 4 Diamond
Tel: **01822 855511**
Mr & Dr McQueen.
D: £20.00-£25.00 **S:** £20.00-£25.00.
Open: All Year
Beds: 1F 2D 2T 1S
Baths: 3 En 2 Sh
🏃 🅿 ⛄🛏🏠✗🔥📺💷🚲
Beautiful Victorian mansion
between Tavistock & Plymouth on
the edge of Dartmoor National
Park. Uppaton House occupies a
delightful position on the moor.
Elegantly appointed bedrooms,
most with panoramic views, period
furnishings throughout; tranquillity
with style and excellent cuisine. We
look forward to welcoming you
to Uppaton House

Yelverton   25

National Grid Ref: SX5267

🍴🍺 Rock Inn

The Rosemont Guest House,
Greenbank Terrace, Yelverton,
Devon, PL20 6DR.
Grades: ETC 3 Diamond
Tel: **01822 852175**
Fax no: 01822 855214
D: £20.00-£22.00 **S:** £20.00-£32.00.
Open: All Year (not Xmas)
Beds: 2F 2D 2T 1S **Baths:** 7 En
🏃 🅿 (5) ⛄🛏🔥🔥📺💷🚲
Overlooking moorland village
green within the glorious Dartmoor
National Park. Historic Plymouth,
Tavistock, Buckland Abbey,
Garden House and Lydford Gorge
all nearby. Excellent free range
breakfast using local produce. Pubs,
restaurants and other
amenities within village

Knightstone Tea Rooms,
Crapstone Road, Yelverton, Devon,
PL20 6BT.
Quiet, secluded, of historic interest,
overlooking moors. Ideal for
sightseeing
Grades: ETC 2 Diamond
Tel: **01822 853679**
D: £17.50-£17.50 **S:** £17.50-£17.50.
Open: All Year
Beds: 1F 1T 1S **Baths:** 1 Sh
🏃 🅿 (20) ⛄🛏✗🔥📺💷💷🚲

Rettery Bank, Harrowbeer Lane,
Yelverton, PL20 6EA.
Actual grid ref: SX519684
Quiet house with wonderful views,
comfortable beds, jacuzzi, English
breakfast
Tel: **01822 855088** (also fax no)
Leavey.
D: £20.00-£25.00 **S:** £16.00-£20.00.
Open: All Year (not Xmas)
Beds: 1D 1T **Baths:** 1 En 1 Sh
🏃 (5) 🅿 (2) 🏠✗🔥📺💷🚲

Milton Combe   26

National Grid Ref: SX4865

🍴🍺 Who'd Have Thought It

▲ *Lopwell YHA Camping Barn,*
Lopwell, Milton Combe, Yelverton,
Devon, PL6 7BZ.
Actual grid ref: SX475650
Tel: **01752 696408 Adults:** £3.35+
self-catering facilities, showers
Converted barn on the banks of the
River Tamar on the edge of
Dartmoor. ADVANCE BOOKING
ESSENTIAL

Blowiscombe Barton, Milton
Combe, Yelverton, Devon, PL20 6HR.
Farmhouse, rolling countryside.
Beautiful garden & swimming
pool. Close Plymouth, Dartmoor
Tel: **01822 854853** (also fax no)
Mrs Fisk.
D: £18.00 **S:** £24.00.
Open: All Year (not Xmas)
Beds: 2D 1T **Baths:** 3 Pr
🏃 🅿 (6) 🏠✗🔥📺💷

Meavy   27

National Grid Ref: SX5467

🍴🍺 Royal Oak

Greenwell Farm, Meavy,
Yelverton, Devon, PL20 6PY.
Actual grid ref: SX534659
Offering fresh country air
breathtaking views & scrumptious
farmhouse cuisine
Tel: **01822 853563** (also fax no)
Mrs Cole.
D: £21.00 **S:** £25.00.
Open: All Year (not Xmas)
Beds: 2D 1T **Baths:** 2 En 1 Pr
🏃 🅿 (8) 🏠✗🔥📺💷💷

The Grid Reference
beneath the location
heading is for the
village or town - *not*
for individual houses,
which are shown
(where supplied) in
each entry itself.

Sheepstor 28

National Grid Ref: SX5567

|⊖| ⊖ The Royal Oak

Burrator House, *Sheepstor, Yelverton, PL20 2PD.*
Secluded historic country house. Guest rooms overlook lake and gardens. Dartmoor Tourist Association Member
Tel: **01822 855669** (also fax no)
Mr Flint.
D: £25.00-£27.50 **S:** £35.00-£37.50.
Open: All Year (not Xmas)
Beds: 3D 1T 1S **Baths:** 3 En 1 Pr
ち (8) 目 (12) 乡 ロ ★ × ± ▥ Ⅵ ▮ ⊁ ⊙

Clearbrook 29

National Grid Ref: SX5265

|⊖| ⊖ Skylark Inn

Sunbeam House, *Clearbrook, Yelverton, Devon, PL20 6JD.*
Actual grid ref: SX521656
Tel: **01822 853871** Ms Newberry.
Fax no: 01822 855672
D: £17.50-£17.50 **S:** £20.00-£20.00.
Open: All Year (not Xmas)
Beds: 1D 1T **Baths:** 2 Sh
ち 目 (6) 乡 ロ ± ▥ Ⅵ ⊁ ⊙
Direct access to Dartmoor. Large double fronted family house offering peace and tranquillity. Good-sized bay-windowed double bedrooms overlooking Dartmoor. Friendly welcome, hearty country breakfast. Close to local pub for evening meals. Ideal for walking, cycling, fishing, golf

Plymouth 30

National Grid Ref: SX4756

|⊖| ⊖ West Hoe, Brown Bear, Odd Wheel, Eddystone Inn, The Walrus, Sippers, The Yardarm

▲ **Plymouth Youth Hostel,** *Belmont House, Devonport Road, Stoke, Plymouth, Devon, PL3 4DW.*
Actual grid ref: SX461555
Tel: **01752 562189**
Under 18: £6.85 **Adults:** £10.15
evening meal at 7.00pm, family bunk rooms, television, games room, showers, shop
Classical Grecian-style house built in 1820 for a wealthy banker, set in own grounds, within easy walking distance of the city centre

---

All rooms full and nowhere else to stay? Ask the owner if there's anywhere nearby

---

▲ ▲ **Plymouth Backpackers' Hostel (Independent),** *172 Citadel Road, The Hoe, Plymouth, Devon, PL1 3DB.*
Actual grid ref: SX483537
Tel: **01752 225158 Adults:** £7.50
self-catering facilities

Sea Breezes, *28 Grand Parade, West Hoe, Plymouth, Devon, PL1 3DJ.*
Actual grid ref: SX483538
Tel: **01752 667205** (also fax no)
Mr & Mrs Tregidgo.
D: £15.00-£15.00 **S:** £15.00-£15.00.
Open: All Year
Beds: 3F 2D 2T 1S
Baths: 2 En 2 Pr 2 Sh
ち 目 (1) ロ ★ × ± ▥ Ⅵ ▮ ⊙
A warm welcome assured in our elegant Victorian town-house on sea front. Theatres, shopping centre, historic Hoe and Barbican close by. Ideal touring centre for South-West Peninsula

Mountbatten Hotel, *52 Exmouth Road, Stoke, Plymouth, Devon, PL1 4QH.*
Grades: ETC 3 Diamond
Tel: **01752 563843** Mr Hendy.
Fax no: 01752 606014
D: £23.00-£23.00 **S:** £19.00-£25.00.
Open: All Year
Beds: 3F 6D 2T 4S
Baths: 7 En 2 Sh
ち 目 (4) ロ ★ × ± ▥ Ⅵ ▮ ⊙
Small licensed Victorian hotel overlooking parkland with river views. Quiet cul de sac. Close city centre/ferryport. Good access Cornwall. Walking distance Naval base, Royal Fleet Club, FE College. Secure parking. Well appointed rooms. Tea/coffee, CTVs, telephones. Credit cards accepted

Rusty Anchor, *30 Grand Parade, West Hoe, Plymouth, Devon, PL1 3DJ.*
Tel: **01752 663924** (also fax no)
Ms Turner.
D: £15.00-£25.00 **S:** £15.00-£30.00.
Open: All Year (not Xmas)
Beds: 4F 1D 2T 2S
Baths: 3 En 3 Pr 2 Sh
ち ロ ★ × ± ▥ Ⅵ ⊁ ⊙
Situated on the sea front, walking distance city centre, Hoe. Excellent reputation for cleanliness, friendly atmosphere and good food. Holiday or business, all are welcome in our family-run establishment

Cassandra Guest House, *13 Crescent Avenue, The Hoe, Plymouth, Devon, PL1 3AN.*
Ideally situated for city centre, seafront, Barbican, Ferry, port, theatres, stations
Tel: **01752 220715** (also fax no)
D: £17.00-£20.00 **S:** £17.00-£26.00.
Open: All Year
Beds: 3F 1D 1T 1S
Baths: 2 En 1 Pr 1 Sh
ち 乡 ロ ★ ± ▥ Ⅵ ⊁ ⊙

Hotspur Guest House, *108 North Road East, Plymouth, Devon, PL4 6AW.*
Grades: ETC 2 Diamond
Tel: **01752 663928** Taylor.
Fax no: 01752 261493
D: £16.00-£17.00 **S:** £16.50-£17.50.
Open: All Year (not Xmas)
Beds: 2F 1D 2T 3S
ち ロ ★ × ± ▥ Ⅵ ▮
Victorian property, adjacent city centre; bus/rail stations, historic Barbican, Hoe, seafronts, 10 mins walk. Ideal touring centre for Dartmoor and the Southwest. Tastefully decorated inside and out. Family run. Try us for your home-from-home holiday or business stay

Osmond Guest House, *42 Pier Street, West Hoe, Plymouth, Devon, PL1 3BT.*
Grades: ETC 4 Diamond
Tel: **01752 229705** Mrs Richards.
Fax no: 01752 269655
D: £16.00-£20.00 **S:** £17.00-£25.00.
Open: All Year
Beds: 3D 2T 1S
Baths: 4 En
目 (2) 乡 ロ ± ▥ & Ⅵ ▮ ⊙
Seafront Edwardian house. Walking distance to all attractions. Courtesy pick-up from stations

Sydney Guest House, *181 North Road West, Plymouth, Devon, PL1 5DE.*
Situated in the heart of the city near the railway, ferry, port, university
Tel: **01752 266541**
Mrs Puckey.
Fax no: 01333 310573
D: £25.00-£45.00
S: £14.00-£25.00.
Open: All Year
Beds: 1F 2D 2T 3S
Baths: 3 En
ち ロ × ▥

Athenaeum Lodge, *4 Athenaeum St, The Hoe, Plymouth, PL1 2RQ.*
A welcoming highly commended guest house by resident owners
Grades: ETC 4 Diamond
Tel: **01752 665005** (also fax no)
Rowe.
D: £18.00-£21.00
S: £25.00-£34.00.
Open: All Year (not Xmas)
Beds: 4D 5T
Baths: 7 En 2 Sh
ち (5) 目 (5) 乡 ロ ± ▥ Ⅵ

Georgian House Hotel, *51 Citadel Road, The Hoe, Plymouth, PL1 3AU.*
Family-run hotel in central location near all Plymouth's amenities
Grades: AA 3 Diamond
Tel: **01752 663237**
D: £19.00-£22.00
S: £22.00-£29.00.
Open: Feb to Dec
Beds: 6D 2T 2S
Baths: 10 En
ち 乡 ロ ± ▥ Ⅵ ▮

The Dudley, 42 Sutherland Road, Mutley, Plymouth, Devon, *PL4 6BN*.
Actual grid ref: SX484555
Charming Victorian town house. Good breakfasts and comfortable, homely accommodation
Tel: **01752 668322**
Mr Punter & Miss A Hayes.
Fax no: 01752 673763
D: £17.00 **S:** £18.00.
Open: All Year
Beds: 2F 2T 1D 2S
Baths: 6 En 1 Sh
🛏 🅿 (3) 🖵 🛏 ✕ ♨ 🕮 Ⓥ 🛆 ⚡

Pay B&Bs by cash or cheque and be prepared to pay up front.

Allington House, 6 St James Place East, The Hoe, Plymouth, Devon, *PL1 3AS*.
Quiet, small but central. Recommended, comfortable plus excellent breakfast
Tel: **01752 221435**
Mrs Budziak.
D: £16.00 **S:** £20.00.
Open: All Year
Beds: 4D 1T 1S
Baths: 3 En 1 Sh
🅿 (2) 🖵 ♨ 🕮 Ⓥ

Rainbow Lodge, 29 Athenaeum Street, The Hoe, Plymouth, Devon, *PL1 2RQ*.
You won't be disappointed. Give us a try. NOW
Tel: **01752 229699** Mrs Graham.
Fax no: 01752 229357
D: £13.00 **S:** £15.00.
Open: All Year (not Xmas)
Beds: 2F 2D 5T 1S
Baths: 7 Pr 🛏 (3) 🅿 (6) 🖵 🛏 ♨ 🕮 Ⓥ

West Hoe Guest House, 26 Pier Street, West Hoe, Plymouth, Devon, *PL1 3BT*.
Comfortable family-run guest house on Plymouth's famous hoe and seafront
Tel: **01752 252006**
D: £13.00 **S:** £15.00.
Open: Easter to Oct
Beds: 2F 3T
Baths: 1 Sh
🛏 🖵 🛏 ✕ ♨ 🕮 Ⓥ 🛆 ⚡ 🚲

All cycleways are popular: you are well-advised to book ahead

---

Sustrans Hull to Harwich

The **Hull to Harwich Cycle Route** is a section of the new National Cycle Network, running on traffic-free paths and traffic-calmed roads between the Continental ferry ports of Hull in the East Riding of Yorkshire and Harwich in the northeastern corner of Essex. 370 miles long, it links the towns of Lincoln and Boston in Lincolnshire, Wisbech in Cambridgeshire and King's Lynn, Fakenham and Norwich in Norfolk with Beccles, Woodbridge and Ipswich in Suffolk and Colchester in Essex. The flat landscape of the Eastern counties yields long views and makes excellent cycling country: the only up-and-down of any degree (and this undemanding) comes in the route through the northern reaches of the Lincolnshire Wolds. The route is clearly signposted by blue direction signs with a cycle silhouette and the number 1 in a red rectangle.

The indispensable **official route map and guide** for the route comes in two parts, *Hull to Fakenham* and *Fakenham to Harwich*, and is available from Sustrans, 35 King Street, Bristol BS1 4DZ, tel 0117-926 8893, fax 0117-929 4173, @ £5.99 each (+ £1.50 p&p for both together or either one).

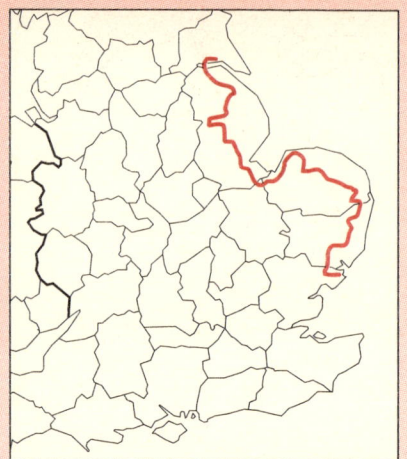

Maps: Ordnance Survey 1:50,000 Landranger series: 107, 112, 113, 121, 122, 131, 132, 133, 134, 155, 156, 168, 169

Trains: Hull, King's Lynn, Norwich, Ipswich, Colchester and Harwich are all main line termini; there are connecting services to many other places on or near the route.

Hull to Market Rasen

Kingston-upon-Hull is the major port of the Humber, the great deepwater estuary of England's East Coast. The poet Philip Larkin said the only good thing about the place is that it is 'very nice and flat for cycling'. For your purposes, that's a recommendation. The Streetlife Transport Museum may be of interest, as it has a recreation of a bicycle repair workshop from the early days of the beautiful machine. Of more general interest are the Town Docks Museum, the Ferens Art Gallery and the birthplace of William

Wilberforce, who achieved the abolition of slavery in Britain. From the docks you head west, staying close to the river, to Hessle, where you join the Humber Bridge cyclepath to cross the resplendent Humber Bridge. The longest suspension bridge in the world, it was completed in 1981. The best view of the bridge is from the waterside at Barton-upon-Humber, on the other side. From Barton you head south, and into the Lincolnshire Wolds. From here it's a brief climb and then descent to Walesby, before you head down to the small market town of **Market Rasen**.

Hull   1

National Grid Ref: TA0929

🍴 🍺 Hanorth Arms, The Zoological

Marlborough Hotel, 232 Spring Bank, Hull, HU3 1LU.
Family run, near city centre
Tel: **01482 224479** (also fax no)
Mr Norman.
D: £17.00 **S:** £17.00.
Open: All Year
Beds: 2 F 2D 7T 5S
Baths: 3 Sh
🛇 🅿 (10) 🔌 🐾 ✗ 🛏

Beck House , 628 Beverley High Road, Hull, HU6 7LL.
Traditional town house, B&B, fine accommodation, close to university etc
Tel: **01482 445468** Mrs Aylwin.
D: £19.00-£22.00 **S:** £19.00-£22.00.
Open: All Year
Beds: 3S **Baths:** 2 En 5 Pr
🛇 🅿 (4) 🔌 🛏 🛀 🛏 Ⓥ 🖧

D = Price range per person
sharing in a double room

S = Price range for a single
person in a room

The Tree Guest House, 132 Sunny Bank, Spring Bank West, Hull, HU3 1LE.
Close to the city centre and universities
Tel: **01482 448822** (also fax no)
D: £15.00-£18.00 **S:** £16.00-£24.00.
Open: All Year
Beds: 1F 3D 3S **Baths:** 2 En 2 Sh
🛇 🅿 🔌 🐾 🛀 🛏 ♿ Ⓥ

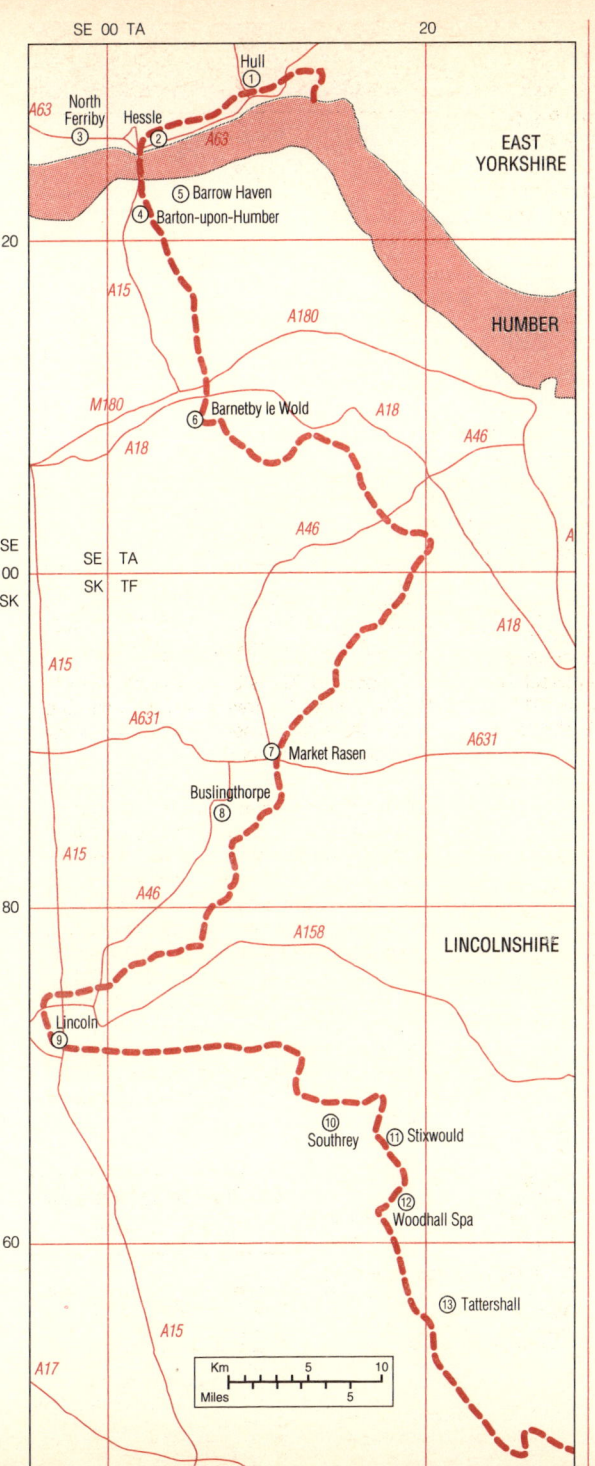

80 Riversdale Road, Beverley High Road, Hull, North Humberside, HU6 7HB.
Attractive house built 1932, back lawn facing playing fields; luxury accommodation
Tel: **01482 859750** Mrs Drake.
D: £15.00-£16.00 **S:** £16.00-£17.00.
Open: All Year (not Xmas)
Beds: 1D 1S
Baths: 1 En

Town House, 102 Sunny Bank, Spring Bank West, Hull, HU3 1LF.
Guest house, quiet location
Tel: **01482 446177** Mr Hogg.
D: £15.00 **S:** £16.00.
Open: All Year
Beds: 1D 2T 4S
Baths: 1 Sh

Admiral Wyndham, 52-54 Sunny Bank, Spring Bank West, Hull, HU3 1LQ.
A Victorian town house in a tranquil tree-lined avenue. A warm welcome is assured
Tel: **01482 443168**
Fax no: 01482 341889
D: £16.00 **S:** £18.00.
Open: All Year
Beds: 2F 3T 3D 7S
Baths: 2 En 2 Sh

Hessle   2

National Grid Ref: TA0326

Country Park Inn

Sandford, 79 Ferriby Road, Hessle, E Yorks, HU13 0HU.
Friendly luxurious Edwardian home quiet location yet close to amenities
Tel: **01482 648655**
D: £19.00-£20.00 **S:** £26.00-£30.00.
Open: All Year (not Xmas)
Beds: 2F 1T
Baths: 1 En 1 Sh

The Grid Reference beneath the location heading is for the village or town - *not* for individual houses, which are shown (where supplied) in each entry itself.

North Ferriby 3

National Grid Ref: SE9826

B&B at 103, *103 Ferriby High Road, North Ferriby, East Yorks, HU14 3LA.*
Comfortable house, large garden, overlooking river near Humber Bridge and Hull
Grades: ETC 3 Diamond
Tel: **01482 633637** Mrs Simpson.
D: £15.00-£15.00 **S:** £15.00-£15.00.
Open: All Year
Beds: 1D 1T 1S
Baths: 1 Sh
ⓣ (7) 𝕇 (2) ⊬▢🛌🛏🌠▥Ⓥ🛆🚲

Barton-upon-Humber 4

National Grid Ref: TA0321

🍴🍺 White Swan

White Swan Hotel, *Fleetgate, Barton-upon-Humber, Lincs, DN18 5.*
Local friendly pub, pool, darts, doms etc
Tel: **01652 632459**
D: £23.50-£23.50
S: £30.00-£30.00.
Open: All Year (not Xmas)
Beds: 1D 3T
Baths: 2 En 1 Sh
𝕇 (10) ▢✗🛌🌠▥Ⓥ🚲

All rooms full and nowhere else to stay? Ask the owner if there's anywhere nearby

Barrow Haven 5

National Grid Ref: TA0622

Haven Inn, *Ferry Road, Barrow Haven, Barton-upon-Humber, Lincs, DN19 7EX.*
Welcoming olde worlde inn, set in rural hamlet. Good views
Tel: **01469 530247**
Fax no: 01469 530625
D: £24.80 **S:** £39.50.
Open: All Year
Beds: 1F 3D 5T **Baths:** 9 En
ⓣ𝕇▢🛌✗🌠🛌▥Ⓥ🛆⊬🚲

Barnetby le Wold 6

National Grid Ref: TA0509

🍴🍺 Station Hotel

Reginald House, *27 Queen Road, Barnetby le Wold, DN38 6JH.*
Grades: ETC 4 Diamond
Tel: **01652 688566**
Fax no: 01652 688510
D: £17.50-£20.00 **S:** £22.50-£25.00.
Open: All Year
Beds: 1D 1T **Baths:** 2 En
𝕇 (4) ⊬▢✗🌠▥Ⓥ🛆⊬🚲
Beautiful modern bungalow with newly-built first floor ensuite guest accommodation. Good home cooking, private garden. Quiet location in the village of Barnetby le Wold

Holcombe Guest House, *34 Victoria Road, Barnetby le Wold, Lincs, DN38 6JR.*
Actual grid ref: TA059097
Homely accommodation near Lincoln, Scunthorpe, Hull, Grimsby and Humberside Airport
Tel: **0850 764002 (M)** Mrs Vora.
Fax no: 01652 680841
D: £16.30 **S:** £17.50.
Open: All Year
Beds: 2F 1T 5S **Baths:** 4 Pr 2 Sh
ⓣ𝕇 (7) ▢🛌✗🌠▥🛆Ⓥ🛆⊬

Market Rasen 7

National Grid Ref: TF1089

🍴🍺 The Chase, Gordon Arms

Waveney Cottage Guest House, *Willingham Road, Market Rasen, Lincs, LN8 3DN.*
Small Tudor-style cottage close to National Hunt racecourse
Grades: ETC 3 Diamond
Tel: **01673 843236**
Mrs Dawson-Margrave.
D: £16.00 **S:** £18.00.
Open: All Year
Beds: 1D 2T
Baths: 3 Pr
ⓣ𝕇 (6) ⊬▢🌠🛌▥Ⓥ🛆⊬

Buslingthorpe 8

National Grid Ref: TF0885

🍴🍺 White Hart

East Farm House, *Middle Rasen Road, Buslingthorpe, Market Rasen, Lincs, LN3 5AQ.*
Spacious C18th farmhouse overlooking farmland, quiet location, near Market Rasen
Grades: ETC 4 Diamond
Tel: **01673 842283** Mrs Grant.
D: £20.00-£23.00 **S:** £25.00-£27.00.
Open: All Year
Beds: 1D 1T
Baths: 2 Pr
ⓣ (5) 𝕇 (5) ⊬▢🛌✗🌠🛌▥Ⓥ🛆⊬

Please don't camp on *anyone's* land without first obtaining their permission.

Market Rasen to Boston

From Market Rasen it's a leisurely jaunt through a series of Lincolnshire villages to **Lincoln**. Here you can find the largest collection of bicycles in Britain at the National Cycle Museum. The massive cathedral, whose three towers dominate the flat landscape for miles around, originated in the Norman period, but was ruined by an earthquake in the twelfth century. The reconstruction dates from the Early English period of the Gothic age. Most noteworthy is the intricate narrative carving of the frieze on the west front. Lincoln Castle also dates from the Norman period, and houses one of only four existing original copies of the Magna Carta; but from 1787 until 1878 it was used as the city jail.

The pews in the prison chapel resemble coffins – a reminder of the era's not-so-progressive attitudes towards criminal justice. The route through southern Lincolnshire brings you to Tattershall Bridge, close to Tattershall Castle, an early brick building put up in the fifteenth century, with late Gothic fireplaces and tapestries. With the Boston Stump, the 288-foot tower of the church of St Botolph (nicknamed from its lack of a spire), rising ahead, you cycle on to *St Botolph's Town*. **Boston**, standing close to where the Witham flows into The Wash, was the starting point for the first abortive voyage of the Pilgrim Fathers, who were imprisoned in the Guildhall, now a museum. The link remains strong with the town's greater namesake in Massachussetts.

Lincoln 9

National Grid Ref: SK9771

🏠 🍺 Lord Tennyson, Sun Inn, The Barge, Royal William

🔺 *Lincoln Youth Hostel,*
77 South Park, Lincoln, LN5 8ES.
Actual grid ref: SK980700
Tel: **01522 522076**
Under 18: £6.20 **Adults:** £9.15
evening meal at 7.00pm, family bunk rooms, television, showers, shop
Victorian villa in a quiet road opposite South Common open parkland

Admiral Guest House, 16 Nelson Street, Lincoln, LN1 1PJ.
Actual grid ref: SK968715
Grades: RAC 3 Diamond
Tel: **01522 544467** (also fax no)
Mr Robertson.
D: £16.00-£20.00
S: £16.00-£20.00.
Open: All Year (not Xmas)
Beds: 1F 3D 2T 3S
Baths: 7 En 2 Pr
🛇 🅿 (12) 🗆 🛏 ✕ 🎄 ▥ & Ⅴ 🛆 ✦ 🚲
Admiral Guest House, also known as Nelsons Cottages, situated just off main A57 close to city centre and Lincoln University, offering large floodlit car park, also close to Brayford pool, cathedral and castle and all amenities. All rooms ensuite and private bath

Newport Guest House, 26-28 Newport, Lincoln, LN1 3DF.
Tel: **01522 528590** Mr Clarke.
Fax no: 01522 544502
D: £16.00-£20.00 **S:** £16.00-£28.00.
Open: All Year (not Xmas)
Beds: 2D 5T 1S
Baths: 3 En 2 Sh
🛇 (6) 🅿 (5) 🗠 🗆 🛏 🎄 ▥ & Ⅴ ✦ 🚲
A double-fronted Victorian house recently renovated to an excellent stadard. Easy to find. Parking available and just minutes away from Lincoln's historic centre. Enjoy our superb Lincolnshire breakfasts and stroll around the medieval buildings and streets nearby

Ridgeways Guest House,
243 Burton Road, Lincoln, LN1 3UB.
Actual grid ref: SK972727
Tel: **01522 546878** (also fax no)
Mr Barnes.
D: £17.50-£25.00 **S:** £20.00-£25.00.
Open: All Year
Beds: 2F 1D 1T
Baths: 3 En 1 Pr
🅿 (6) 🗠 🗆 🛏 🎄 & Ⅴ 🚲
Situated uphill within easy walking distance to the historic heart of Lincoln's cathedral, castle, Lawn Conference Centre. Also uphill Lincoln's shops, pubs and restaurants. Private car park and garden for guests' use. Credit cards accepted

Edward King House, The Old Palace, Minster Yard, Lincoln, LN2 1PU.
Actual grid ref: SK978718
Tel: **01522 528778**
Rev Adkins.
Fax no: 01522 527308
D: £18.50-£20.50
S: £19.00-£21.00.
Open: All Year (not Xmas)
Beds: 1F 11T 5S
Baths: 8 Sh
🛇 🅿 (12) 🗠 🗆 🛏 🎄 ▥ Ⅴ 🚲
A former residence of the Bishops of Lincoln at the historic heart of the city and next to the cathedral and medieval old palace. We offer a peaceful haven with a secluded garden and superb views

The Old Rectory, 19 Newport, Lincoln, LN1 3DQ.
Large Edwardian home near cathedral, castle, pubs and restaurants
Tel: **01522 514774**
Mr Downes.
D: £20.00-£20.00
S: £20.00-£25.00.
Open: All Year (not Xmas)
Beds: 2F 4D 1T 1S
Baths: 5 En 1 Sh
🛇 🅿 (8) 🗠 🗆 🎄 ▥ Ⅴ 🚲

Eardleys Hotel, 21 Cross O'Cliff Hill, Lincoln, LN5 8PN.
Homely hotel, overlooking parkland & golf course. Guest bar & parking
Tel: **01522 523050** (also fax no)
Mr Hill.
D: £17.50-£20.00.
S: £20.00-£25.00.
Open: All Year
Beds: 2F 2D 1T 1S
Baths: 2 En 2 Sh
🛇 🅿 (10) 🗆 🛏 ✕ 🎄 ▥ Ⅴ 🛆 ✦ 🚲

31 Newland Street West, Lincoln, LN1 1QQ.
Tel: **01522 532934**
Mrs Ward.
D: £15.00-£15.00
S: £15.00-£15.00.
Open: All Year (not Xmas)
Beds: 1D 1S
Baths: 1 Sh
🛇 🗠 🗆 🛏 🎄 ▥ Ⅴ 🚲
Easy reach from Newark showground and Swinderby. A46, A57. In close proximity to all city attractions, pleasant walk along Roman canal, local pubs for evening meal. Single room adapts to twin/double, takes child's bed. Cot, highchair, child minding available

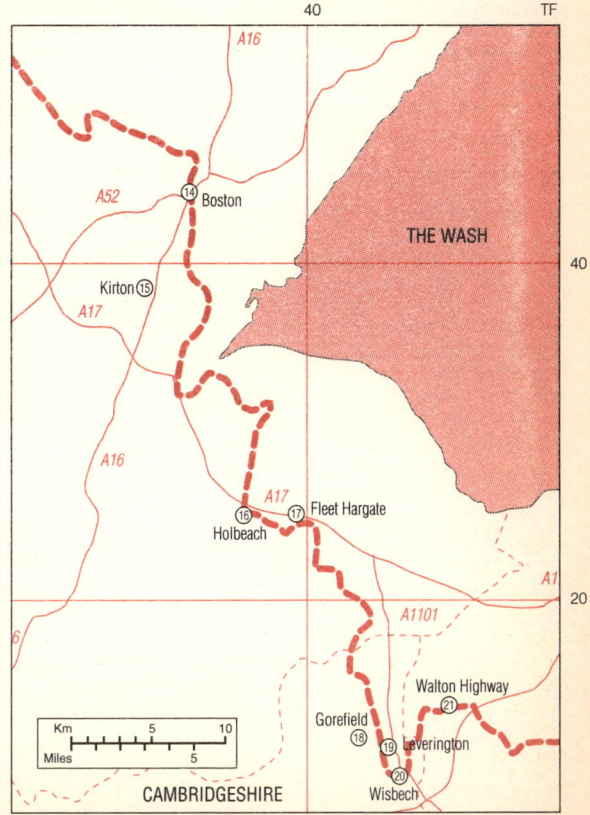

The Barbican Hotel, *11 St Marys Street, Lincoln, LN5 7EQ.*
Victorian Hotel. Refurbished. Opposite railway station. An ideal central location
Tel: **01522 543811**
D: £26.00
S: £39.00-£39.00.
Open: All Year (not Xmas)
Beds: 5D 2T 5S
Baths: 12 En
🛏 🖵 🛠 🍴 👤 📷 Ⅲ Ⅴ 👶 ᧰

Elma Guest House, *14 Albion Crescent, off Long Leys Road, Lincoln, LN1 1HS.*
Quiet location, friendly family home with garden pond and willow tree
Tel: **01522 529792** (also fax no)
Mrs Guymer.
D: £17.00-£20.00.
S: £17.00-£20.00.
Open: All Year
Beds: 1D 1T 1S
Baths: 2 Sh
🛏 🅿 (5) 🖵 🛠 👤 📷 Ⅲ Ⅴ 🎒 ᧰

The Bakery Guest House,
26-28 Burton Road, Lincoln, LN1 3LB.
Converted bakery only two minutes from Lincoln castle and cathedral
Tel: **01522 576057** (also fax no)
D: £25.00-£30.00
S: £35.00-£40.00.
Open: All Year
Beds: 1F 2D 1T
Baths: 3 En 1 Pr
🛏 🖵 🛠 👤 📷 Ⅲ Ⅴ ᧰

Mayfield Guest House, *213 Yarborough Road, Lincoln, LN1 3NQ.*
Comfortable Victorian House close to castle, cathedral and Old City
Tel: **01522 533732** (also fax no)
Mr Benson.
D: £18.50 **S:** £19.00.
Open: All Year (not Xmas)
Beds: 2F 1D 1T 1S
Baths: 4 En 1 Pr
🛏 (5) 🅿 (5) 🖵 🛠 👤 📷 Ⅲ Ⅴ 🎒 👶

Linholme Guest House, *116 West Parade, Lincoln, LN1 1LA.*
Beautiful Victorian home. Enjoy a delicious traditional or vegetarian breakfast
Tel: **01522 522930** Mrs Holme.
D: £18.00 **S:** £20.00.
Open: All Year (not Xmas)
Beds: 1D 2T
Baths: 2 En 1 Sh
🛏 🅿 (3) 🛠 👤 📷 Ⅲ Ⅴ ᧰

Southrey 10

National Grid Ref: TF1366

🍴 🍺 Riverside Inn

Riverside Inn, *Ferry Road, Southrey, Lincoln, LN3 5TA.*
Small, peaceful, country inn by river. Log fires, beer garden
Tel: **01526 398374** Mrs Walley.
D: £18.00-£18.00 **S:** £18.00-£18.00.
Open: All Year
Beds: 1D 1T
Baths: 1 Sh
🛏 🅿 (10) 🖵 🛠 🍴 👤 📷 Ⅲ Ⅴ 🎒 🎒 ᧰

Stixwould 11

National Grid Ref: TF1766

🍴 🍺 Abbey Lodge

Orchard House, *Station Road, Stixwould, Lincoln, LN3.*
Actual grid ref: TF164651
Family farmhouse, peaceful countryside location, near delightful attractions of Woodhall Spa
Tel: **01526 353596**
D: £19.00 **S:** £19.00.
Open: All Year (not Xmas)
Beds: 1F **Baths:** 1 En
🛏 🅿 (2) 🛠 👤 📷 Ⅲ Ⅴ 🎒 ᧰

Woodhall Spa 12

National Grid Ref: TF1963

🍴 🍺 The Mall, Abbey Lodge Inn

Claremont Guest House,
9-11 Witham Road, Woodhall Spa, Lincs, LN10 6RW.
Friendly personal service in a traditional unspoilt Victorian guest house
Grades: ETC 2 Diamond
Tel: **01526 352000**
Mrs Brennan.
D: £15.00-£20.00.
S: £13.50-£20.00.
Open: All Year
Beds: 4F 2D 1T 3S
Baths: 3 En 2 Sh
🛏 🅿 (4) 🖵 🛠 👤 📷 Ⅴ 🎒 ᧰

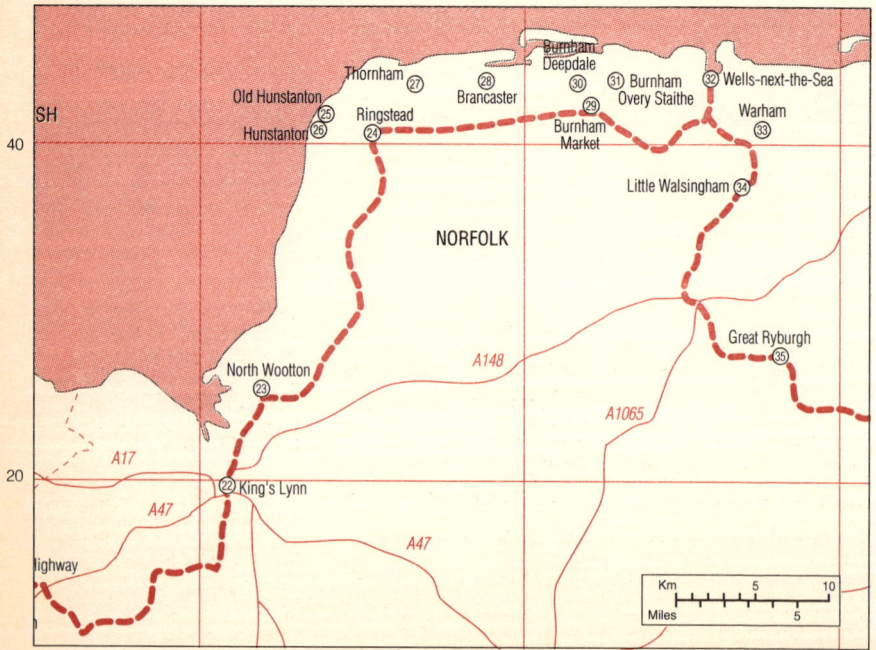

Boston to Beccles

Now you strike out southwards across the Fens, the low-lying country of southern Lincolnshire and northern Cambridgeshire which, before it was drained in the seventeenth century by Dutchmen, was inhospitable marshland. After crossing the River Welland at Fosdyke Bridge, it's over three marshes to Holbeach, before crossing into Cambridgeshire at Tydd St Giles and proceeding to **Wisbech** on the River Nene, the 'capital of the fens'. Here the Fenland Museum sports, among other things, a reconstructed Victorian post office. Leaving Wisbech to the north you come into Norfolk and head eastwards. After crossing the River Great Ouse at Wiggenhall St Germans, you cycle into **King's Lynn**, which lies a short way upstream from where the Ouse flows into the Wash. There is much to see here: St George's Guildhall, one of England's largest, dates from the fifteenth century and now houses an arts centre and a restaurant, the Customs House at Purfleet Quay is a small seventeenth-century Palladian building, and St Margaret's church boasts two impressive Flemish brasses. The Old Gaol House holds a display of treasures from the town's past; the True's Yard museum offers a glimpse of life in the old fishing community through two tiny preserved cottages. Attractions on the route northeast out of King's Lynn include **Castle Rising**, where the impressively well-preserved twelfth-century keep is surrounded by a large earthwork, and the village has a group of seventeenth-century almshouses. A little way further on stands **Sandringham House**, a private country retreat of the Royal family (but open to the public) built in the late nineteenth century in the neo-Jacobean style, set in sixty acres of pretty grounds. From here it's on to Ringstead, not far from the spectacular cliffs of Hunstanton, then Burnham Market, birthplace of Admiral Nelson (with three pubs carrying his worthy name), before you reach the market town of **Fakenham**. The route now takes you along the line of the River Wensum to the attractive village of Reepham, with its Georgian and half-timbered houses and the redbrick Old Brewery House, and on to **Norwich**. The capital of East Anglia was economically important for centuries before the Industrial Revolution; the city bears traces of every period of English history. Tombland is the old Saxon market place, close to the picturesque half-timbered houses of Elm Hill. The Norman keep of Norwich Castle, dating from the twelfth century, ranks with the Tower of London as England's best surviving Norman fortification. The city's cathedral is also a Norman foundation, with later additions - the vaulted roof, with illustratively carved bosses, and the spire (the tallest in England after Salisbury) date from the fifteenth century. The most important modern building is the Sainsbury Centre for the Visual Arts, designed in the 1970s by Norman Foster, which houses a brilliant display in which central figures of western modern art (Picasso, Modigliani, Giacometti) share space with African, Pacific and Native American exhibits. Having cycled through the city centre, you cross the River Yare and skirt the Norfolk Broads as far as Loddon, before heading south to the banks of the Waveney, which you follow downstream until the route enters Suffolk at **Beccles**.

Newlands, *56 Woodland Drive, Woodhall Spa, Lincs, LN10 6YG.*
Grades: ETC 4 Diamond
Tel: 01526 352881
D: £18.00-£20.00
S: £20.00-£20.00.
Open: All Year (not Xmas)
Beds: 1D 2T **Baths:** 2 En 1 Pr
🛏 🅿 (8) ⅍ 🖵 🔌 🎞 Ⓥ ⚲
Luxury accommodation in quiet tree-lined lane. Very convenient for village and international golf courses. Special aviation room and guest lounge. Very attractive gardens, excellent centre for visiting Lincolnshire

Tattershall 13

National Grid Ref: TF2158

🍴🍺 Prattington Arms

Lodge House, *Market Place, Tattershall, Lincoln, Lincs, LN4 4LQ.*
Clean comfortable accommodation. Close RAF Coningsby. Walking, Cycling, Angling, Golf
Tel: 01526 342575 (also fax no)
Mr Palethorpe.
D: £14.00-£15.00 **S:** £13.00-£16.00.
Open: All Year
Beds: 1D 1T 2S **Baths:** 2 En 1 Sh
🛏 (1) 🅿 (3) ⅍ 🖵 🔌 🎞 Ⓥ ⚲

Boston 14

National Grid Ref: TF3344

🍴🍺 The Mill, White Hart, Four Crossroads, Red Cow

Lochiel Guest House, *69 Horncastle Road, Boston, Lincs, PE21 9HY.*
Comfortable, friendly, picturesque waterside setting. Large garden
Tel: 01205 363628
Mr & Mrs Lynch.
D: £16.00-£18.00 **S:** £18.00-£20.00.
Open: All Year
Beds: 1D 1T 1S **Baths:** 1 Sh
🛏 🅿 (3) ⅍ 🖵 🔌 🎞 Ⓥ 🛈 ⚲

Bramley House, *267 Sleaford Road, Boston, Lincs, PE21 7PQ.*
Excellent former farmhouse; large garden and car park. Good value
Tel: 01205 354538 (also fax no)
Mrs Tilke.
D: £17.50 **S:** £20.00.
Open: All Year (not Xmas)
Beds: 3D 2T 4S **Baths:** 4 En 2 Sh
🅿 (15) ⅍ 🖵 ✕ 🔌 🎞 🅖 Ⓥ

S = Price range for a single person in a room

Bringing children with you? Always ask for any special rates.

Kirton 15

National Grid Ref: TF3038

🍴🍺 Merry Monk

Westfield House, *31 Willington Rd, Kirton, Boston, Lincs, PE20 1EP.*
Victorian house in large village, 4 miles from historic Boston
Tel: 01205 722221 Mrs Duff.
D: £15.00-£15.00 **S:** £15.00-£15.00.
Open: All Year
Beds: 1F 1D 1S **Baths:** 1 Sh
🛏 🅿 (5) 🖵 🐾 🔌 🎞 Ⓥ

The Nook, *45 Boston Road, Kirton, Boston, Lincolnshire, PE20 1ES.*
Farm cottage C1900, village location, 3 miles from historic Boston
Tel: 01205 723419
D: £16.00-£16.00 **S:** £16.00-£16.00.
Open: All Year (not Xmas)
Beds: 1F 1S **Baths:** 1 Sh
⅍ 🖵 ✕ 🔌 🎞 Ⓥ 🛈

Holbeach 16

National Grid Ref: TF3625

⚫ Chequers Hotel

Barrington House, *Barrington Gate, Holbeach, Spalding, Lincs, PE12 7LB.*
Spacious Georgian house 3 minutes walk from pubs and restaurants
Grades: ETC 4 Diamond
Tel: **01406 425178** (also fax no)
Mrs Symonds.
D: £25.00-£22.50 **S:** £23.00-£25.00.
Open: All Year
Beds: 2D 1T 1S **Baths:** 3 En 2 Pr
⏚ 🅿 (4) 🗗 🛏 ✕ 🗚 🎬 Ⅵ ⅋ ⟷

Elloe Lodge, *37 Barrington Gate, Holbeach, Spalding, Lincs, PE12 7LB.*
Spacious house, old market town, close pubs & restaurants. Snooker room, drawing room, delightful gardens
Tel: **01406 423207** (also fax no)
Mrs Vasey.
D: £19.00-£19.00 **S:** £25.00-£25.00.
Open: All Year (not Xmas)
Beds: 3D **Baths:** 2 Pr
⏚ 🅿 (10) ⅋ 🗗 ✕ 🗚 🎬 Ⅵ ⅋ ⟷

Cackle Hill House, *Cackle Hill Lane, Holbeach, Spalding, Lincs, PE12 8BS.*
Actual grid ref: TF352262
Spacious, comfortable, tastefully-furnished farmhouse set in a rural position. **Grades:** ETC 4 Diamond
Tel: **01406 426721** Mrs Biggadike.
Fax no: 01406 424659
D: £20.00-£22.00 **S:** £22.00-£24.00.
Open: All Year (not Xmas)
Beds: 1D 2T **Baths:** 2 En 1 Pr
⏚ (10) 🅿 (5) ⅋ 🗗 🛏 🗚 🎬 Ⅵ ⅋

Fleet Hargate 17

National Grid Ref: TF3925

⚫ The Bull, Rose & Crown

Willow Tea Rooms And B&b, *Old Main Road, Fleet Hargate, Spalding, Lincs, PE12 8LL.*
Pretty English tea rooms renowned for good food. Comfortable accommodation. Tel: **01406 423112**
D: £16.00-£18.00 **S:** £20.00-£22.00.
Open: All Year
Beds: 2F 3D 1T **Baths:** 5 En 1 Pr
⏚ 🅿 (6) 🗗 🛏 ✕ 🗚 🎬 Ⅵ ⟷

Gorefield 18

National Grid Ref: TF4211

Maison De La Chien, *35 Churchill Road, Gorefield, Wisbech, Cambs, PE13 4NA.*
Actual grid ref: TF422122
Quiet village location overlooking farmland on the beautiful Cambridgeshire fens
Tel: **01945 870789** Mrs Barnard.
D: £15.00-£15.00 **S:** £15.00-£15.00.
Open: All Year
Beds: 1D 1T **Baths:** 1 Sh
🅿 (2) ⅋ 🗗 🛏 ✕ 🗚 🎬 Ⅵ 🛆 ⅋ ⟷

Leverington 19

National Grid Ref: TF4411

⚫ Rising Star

Wheatmalt Farm House, *Gadds Lane, Leverington Common, Leverington, Wisbech, Cambs, PE13 5BL.*
Ex-farmhouse in quiet lane
Tel: **01945 584856**
Mr & Mrs Samuel.
D: £16.00-£16.00 **S:** £20.00-£20.00.
Open: All Year (not Xmas)
Beds: 1D
Baths: 1 Pr
🅿 (5) 🗗 🛏 🗚 🎬 Ⅵ ⟷

Wisbech 20

National Grid Ref: TF4609

⚫ Blackfriars, Red Lion

Algethi Guest House, *136 Lynn Road, Wisbech, Cambs, PE13 3DP.*
Friendly family-run guest house near town centre and river
Tel: **01945 582278** Mrs McManus.
Fax no: 01945 466456
D: £15.00-£17.50 **S:** £15.00-£17.50.
Open: All Year
Beds: 2F 1D 2S
Baths: 2 Pr
⏚ 🅿 (3) 🗗 🛏 ✕ 🗚 🎬 Ⅵ ⅋ ⟷

Marmion House Hotel, *11 Lynn Road, Wisbech, Cambs, PE13 3DD.*
Georgian town house hotel located in the capital of the Fens
Grades: ETC 3 Diamond
Tel: **01945 582822**
Mrs Lilley.
Fax no: 01945 475889
D: £18.00-£22.00 **S:** £20.00-£26.00.
Open: All Year (not Xmas)
Beds: 20F 10D 2T 6S
Baths: 18 En 1 Pr 2 Sh
⏚ 🅿 🗗 🗚 🎬 Ⅵ ⟷

Deben Guest House, *146 Lynn Road, Wisbech, Cambs, PE13 3DP.*
Edwardian house, five minutes from town centre. Double glazed, friendly atmosphere
Tel: **01945 583121**
Mr Potter.
D: £16.00-£16.00 **S:** £16.00-£16.00.
Open: All Year
Beds: 1D 1T 1S
Baths: 1 Sh
⏚ 🅿 (6) 🗗 ✕ 🗚 🎬 Ⅵ

Ravenscourt, *138 Lynn Road, Wisbech, Cambs, PE13 3DP.*
Actual grid ref: TF466102
Edwardian house, original features located walking distance from town centre
Tel: **01945 585052** (also fax no)
Mr Parish.
D: £15.00 **S:** £17.50.
Open: All Year
Beds: 2F 1D 1T
Baths: 4 Pr
⏚ 🅿 ⅋ 🗗 🗚 🎬 Ⅵ 🛆 ⅋

Walton Highway 21

National Grid Ref: TF4912

⚫ King of Hearts

Maple Lodge, *Lynn Road, Walton Highway, Wisbech, Cambs, PE14 7QE.*
Modern family home on outskirts of village, overlooking open fields
Tel: **01945 461430**
D: £17.00-£20.00 **S:** £17.00-£20.00.
Open: All Year
Beds: 2D 1T 1S
Baths: 1 En 1 Sh
⏚ 🅿 (5) ⅋ 🗗 ✕ 🗚 🎬 Ⅵ ⟷

Homeleigh Guest House, *Lynn Road, Walton Highway, Wisbech, Cambs, PE14 7DE.*
Homeleigh Guest House built 1880s. All rooms ensuite
Tel: **01945 582356** Mrs Wiseman.
Fax no: 01945 587006
D: £20.00 **S:** £20.00.
Open: All Year
Beds: 2D 2T 2S
Baths: 6 En
⏚ 🅿 (6) 🗗 🛏 ✕ 🗚 🎬 🛆 Ⅵ 🛆 ⅋

King's Lynn 22

National Grid Ref: TF6120

⚫ The Wildfowler

▲ **King's Lynn Youth Hostel,** *Thoresby College, College Lane, King's Lynn, Norfolk, PE30 1JB.*
Actual grid ref: TF616199
Tel: **01553 772461**
Under 18: £5.65 **Adults:** £8.35
self-catering facilities, showers, no smoking
Traditional hostel in a wing of the 500-year-old Chantry college building in the historic part of King's Lynn. Discover heritage buildings and museums and other attractions in the varied West Norfolk countryside

Guanock Hotel, *Southgates, London Road, King's Lynn, Norfolk, PE30 5JG.*
Grades: ETC 2 Diamond
RAC 2 Diamond
Tel: **01553 772959** (also fax no) Mr Parchment.
D: £18.00-£19.00 **S:** £21.00-£24.00.
Open: All Year
Beds: 5F 4D 3T 5S
Baths: 5 Sh
⏚ 🅿 (8) 🗗 ✕ 🗚 🎬 Ⅵ 🛆
Warm friendly hotel noted for cleanliness and good food. Close to town centre and all industrial estates, adjacent to historic Southgates, near Sandringham House

D = Price range per person sharing in a double room

Maranatha Guest House,
115 Gaywood Road, King's Lynn,
Norfolk, PE30 2PU.
Friendly family run. Special rates
for children, groups catered for
Grades: ETC 2 Diamond
Tel: 01553 774596 Mr Bastone.
D: £15.00-£20.00 **S:** £20.00.
Open: All Year
Beds: 2F 2D 3T 2S
Baths: 3 En 2 Sh
🛏 🅿 (9) 🗋 ⊁ ✕ 🎨 🔲 ♿ 🎥 🛡 ⚡ 🚲

The Old Rectory, *33 Goodwins*
Road, King's Lynn, Norfolk,
PE30 5QX.
Grades: ETC 3 Diamond
Tel: 01485 768544
D: £21.00-£21.00 **S:** £32.00-£32.00.
Open: All Year
Beds: 2F 2T
Baths: 4 En
🛏 🅿 (5) ⊁ 🗋 🎨 🔲 🎥 🚲
Elegant former rectory. Well-
appointed, high quality ensuite
accommodation. Guests have free-
dom of access at all times. Off
street parking, storage for cycles,
non-smoking, quietly situated,
close to centre of historic attractive
market town. Well-behaved pets
welcome

Havana Guest House, *117*
Gaywood Road, King's Lynn,
Norfolk, PE30 2PU.
Actual grid ref: TF627204
Large Victorian house, comfort-
able, well-appointed bedrooms,
ample parking
Tel: 01553 772331
Mr & Mrs Breed.
D: £16.00 **S:** £18.00.
Open: All Year (not Xmas)
Beds: 1F 2D 3T 1S
Baths: 4 Pr 1 Sh
🛏 (2) 🅿 (8) ⊁ 🗋 🎨 🔲 🎥 🛡

North Wootton 23

National Grid Ref: TF6424

Red Cat Hotel, *Station Road,*
North Wootton, Kings Lynn,
Norfolk, PE30 3QH.
Country hotel renowned for its
hospitality and atmosphere. Dogs
welcome
Grades: ETC 3 Diamond
Tel: 01553 631244 Mr Irwin.
Fax no: 01553 631574
D: £22.50-£22.50 **S:** £25.00.
Open: All Year (not Xmas)
Beds: 1F 3D 1T 3S
Baths: 8 En 4 Pr 1 Sh
🛏 🅿 (50) 🗋 🦅 ✕ 🎨 🔲 🎥 🛡 ⚡ 🚲

Pay B&Bs by cash or
cheque and be prepared
to pay up front.

Ringstead 24

National Grid Ref: TF7040

▲ **Courtyard Farm Bunkhouse**
Barn (Independent), *Ringstead,*
Hunstanton, Norfolk, PE36 5LQ.
Actual grid ref: TF729400
Tel: 01485 525369 Adults: £4.00
self-catering facilities

Old Hunstanton 25

National Grid Ref: TF6842

🍴 🍺 Mariners Inn

Cobbler's Cottage, *3 Wodehouse*
Road, Old Hunstanton,
Hunstanton, Norfolk, PE36 6JD.
Tel: 01485 534036 Ms Poore.
D: £20.00-£27.00 **S:** £27.00-£32.00.
Open: Feb to Nov
Beds: 1D 2T
Baths: 3 En
🅿 (8) 🗋 🦅 🎨 🔲 🎥 ⚡
Quietly situated 500 yards from
sandy natural beach. Birdwatching
at Titchwell, Snettisham Holme. 3
pubs, restaurants in village. Royal
Sandringham, Norfolk lavender 15
mins drive. Quality
accommodation, highly
recommended by returning valued
guests. Rooms booked in advance;
sorry, no spontaneous callers

Hunstanton 26

National Grid Ref: TF6740

🍴 🍺 Golden Lion, Marine Bar, Le Strange Arms,
Ancient Mariner

▲ **Hunstanton Youth Hostel,**
15 Avenue Road, Hunstanton,
Norfolk, PE36 5BW.
Actual grid ref: TF674406
Tel: 01485 532061
Under 18: £6.20
Adults: £9.15
evening meal at 7.00pm, family
bunk rooms, television, showers,
shop
Victorian carrstone house in
seaside resort with Blue Flag
beach, famous for birdwatching
and ecology studies

Kiama Cottage, *23 Austin Street,*
Hunstanton, Norfolk, PE36 6AN.
Grades: ETC 3 Diamond
Tel: 01485 533615
Mr & Mrs Gardiner.
D: £18.00-£25.00
S: £20.00-£25.00.
Open: All year (not Xmas)
Beds: 2F 2D
Baths: 3 En 1 Pr
🛏 ⊁ 🗋 🎨 🔲 🎥 🛡 ⚡ 🚲
A warm welcome awaits you at our
Victorian-style cottage located in a
quiet residential area and ideally
situated for visiting Hunstanton
attractions and West Norfolk
generally

Sutton House Hotel, *24 Northgate,*
Hunstanton, Norfolk, PE36 6AP.
Edwardian house near town/sea
Tel: 01485 532552 (also fax no)
Mr Emsden.
D: £20.00-£27.00
S: £25.00-£25.00.
Open: All Year
Beds: 2F 2D 3T 1S
Baths: 8 En
🛏 (1) 🅿 (5) 🗋 🦅 ✕ 🎨 🔲 🎥 🛡 ⚡ 🚲

Rosamaly Guest House, *14 Glebe*
Avenue, Hunstanton, Norfolk,
PE36 6BS.
Warm, friendly atmosphere. Hearty
breakfasts, tasty evening meals.
Comfy ensuite bedrooms, quiet,
convenient location
Grades: ETC 3 Diamond
Tel: 01485 534187
Mrs Duff Dick.
D: £18.00-£23.00
S: £20.00-£25.00.
Open: All Year (not Xmas)
Beds: 1F 2D 1T 1S
Baths: 4 En
🛏 🗋 🦅 ✕ 🎨 🔲 🎥 🛡 🚲

The Gables, *28 Austin Street,*
Hunstanton, PE36 6AW.
Tel: 01485 532514
Mrs Bamfield.
D: £17.00-£23.00.
Open: All Year
Beds: 5F 1D 1T
Baths: 5 En
🛏 ⊁ 🎨 ✕ 🎨 🔲 🎥 🛡 ⚡ 🚲
Recently refurbished attractive
Edwardian home retaining many
original features combined with
comfortable modern facilities
within easy reach of local
amenities and seafront, overlooking
new Boston sensory park and the
sea, nominated ETB best B&B

Ellinbrook Guest House,
37 Avenue Road, Hunstanton,
Norfolk, PE36 5HW.
Friendly family establishment
situated 5 minutes from seafront
and shops
Tel: 01485 532022
Mr & Mrs Vass.
D: £15.00-£21.00
S: £15.00-£21.00.
Open: All Year (not Xmas)
Beds: 2F 2D 1T 1S
Baths: 1 Sh
🛏 🅿 (5) ⊁ 🗋 ✕ 🎨 🔲 🎥 🛡 🚲

Avocet House, *44 Greevegate,*
Hunstanton, Norfolk, PE36 6AG.
Family run B&B near RSPB
reserves, cycleway, beautiful sandy
beaches
Grades: ETC 3 Diamond
Tel: 01485 533118
Mr & Mrs Sykes.
D: £15.00-£22.50.
Open: All Year (not Xmas)
Beds: 3D
Baths: 2 En
⊁ 🗋 🎨 🔲 🎥 🛡 🚲

Caltofts, *15 Austin Street, Hunstanton, Norfolk, PE36 6AJ.*
Guest house situated in quiet road, 2 mins sea and shops
Tel: **01485 533759**
Mr & Mrs Vass.
D: £18.00 **S:** £18.00.
Open: All Year
Beds: 2F 2D 1T 1S
Baths: 2 Pr 1 Sh
🛏 🅿 (3) ⅍ 🗆 ✕ 👤 ▥ Ⓥ

Gemini Lodge Guest House,
5 Alexandra Road, Hunstanton, Norfolk, PE36 5BT.
Attractive family-run guest house with good food and accommodation
Tel: **01485 533902** (also fax no)
Mr & Mrs Harrison.
D: £18.50.
Open: All Year (not Xmas)
Beds: 1F 1D 1T
Baths: 3 En
🛏 (3) 🗆 ▥ ⅍ 🚲

Thornham   27

National Grid Ref: TF7343

🍴 ◁ King's Head, The Lifeboat, Titchwell Manor

Kings Head Hotel, *High Street, Thornham, Hunstanton, Norfolk, PE36 6LY.*
C16th inn, open log fires
Tel: **01485 512213** Mrs John.
D: £18.00 **S:** £18.00.
Open: All Year (not Xmas)
Beds: 2D 1T
Baths: 1 Sh
🛏 🅿 ⅍ 🗆 ✕ 👤 Ⓥ ⅍

Greenwoods, *High Street, Thornham, Hunstanton, Norfolk, PE36 6QY.*
Actual grid ref: TF737434
Attractive modern property with pretty secluded garden
Tel: **01485 512310** (also fax no)
Miss Leary.
D: £20.00 **S:** £20.00.
Open: All Year
Beds: 2D 1T
Baths: 2 Pr 1 Sh
🛏 (8) 🅿 (5) ⅍ 🗆 ⌐↑ ✕ 👤 ▥ Ⓥ 🔒 ⅍

Brancaster   28

National Grid Ref: TF7743

🍴 ◁ Jolly Sailors

The Old Bakery, *Main Road, Brancaster, Kings Lynn, Norfolk, PE31 8AA.*
Delightful converted old bakery and cottage set in grounds of one acre
Tel: **01485 210501**
Mrs Townshend.
D: £18.00 **S:** £22.50.
Open: All Year (not Xmas)
Beds: 1F 2D 1S
Baths: 2 En 2 Sh
🛏 🅿 (3) 🗆 ⌐ 👤 ▥ Ⓥ 🔒 ⅍

Burnham Market   29

National Grid Ref: TF8342

🍴 ◁ Host Arms

Millwood, *Herrings Lane, Burnham Market, King's Lynn, Norfolk, PE31 8DP.*
Peaceful, luxurious coastal lodge
Tel: **01328 730152** Mrs Leftley.
Fax no: 01328 730158
D: £27.50-£30.00 **S:** £35.00-£45.00.
Open: All Year (not Xmas)
Beds: 1D 1T
🛏 (8) 🅿 ⅍ 🗆 ⌐↑ 👤 ▥ Ⓥ 🚲

Burnham Deepdale   30

National Grid Ref: TF8044

▲ **Deepdale Granary Bunkhouse (Independent),** *Deepdale Farm, Burnham Deepdale, Norfolk, PE31 8DD.*
Actual grid ref: TF803443
Tel: **01485 210256 Adults:** £7.50
self-catering facilities, showers

Burnham Overy Staithe   31

National Grid Ref: TF8444

🍴 ◁ The Hero

Domville Guest House, *Glebe Lane, Burnham Overy Staithe, Kings Lynn, Norfolk, PE31 8JQ.*
Quietly situated family-run guest house
Grades: ETC 3 Diamond
Tel: **01328 738298** (also fax no)
Mrs Smith.
D: £18.00-£23.00 **S:** £18.00-£23.00.
Open: All Year (not Xmas)
Beds: 2T 3S
Baths: 4 En
🛏 (6) 🅿 (10) ⅍ 🗆 ✕ 👤 Ⓥ 🔒 ⅍ 🚲

Wells-next-the-Sea   32

National Grid Ref: TF9143

🍴 ◁ Crown Hotel, The Edinburgh, Ark Royal, Lifeboat Inn, Three Horseshoes

Mill House, *Northfield Lane, Wells-next-the-Sea, Norfolk, NR23 1JZ.*
Mill House: a former mill-owner's house in secluded gardens
Tel: **01328 710739** Mr Downey.
D: £17.00 **S:** £17.50.
Open: All Year
Beds: 1F 3D 3T 2S
Baths: 7 En 2 Pr
🛏 (8) 🅿 (10) 🗆 ⌐↑ 👤 ▥ ♿ Ⓥ ⅍

Pay B&Bs by cash or cheque and be prepared to pay up front.

Please respect a B&B's wishes regarding children, animals & smoking.

St Heliers Guest House, *Station Road, Wells-next-the-Sea, Norfolk, NR23 1EA.*
Actual grid ref: TF917436
Central Georgian family house in secluded gardens with excellent breakfasts
Tel: **01328 710361** (also fax no)
Mrs Kerr.
D: £16.00-£22.00 **S:** £18.00-£30.00.
Open: All Year (not Xmas)
Beds: 3F 1D 1T 1S
Baths: 2 Sh
🅿 (4) ⅍ 🗆 👤 ▥ Ⓥ 🔒 ⅍ 🚲

East House, *East Quay, Wells-next-the-Sea, Norfolk, NR23 1LE.*
Actual grid ref: TF921437
Old house overlooking marsh, creeks and boats to distant sea
Tel: **01328 710408**
Mrs Scott.
D: £22.50-£22.50 **S:** £26.00-£26.00.
Open: All Year (not Xmas)
Beds: 2T
Baths: 2 En
🛏 (7) 🅿 (2) 🗆 👤 ▥ Ⓥ ⅍ 🚲

The Warren, *Warham Road, Wells-next-the-Sea, Norfolk, NR23 1NE.*
Actual grid ref: TF922430
Ideally situated for ornithologists, walkers, cyclists, beach lovers and historians
Tel: **01328 710273** Mrs Wickens.
D: £20.00-£20.00 **S:** £22.00-£25.00.
Open: All Year (not Xmas)
Beds: 1D 1T
Baths: 1 En 1 Pr
🅿 (2) ⅍ 🗆 👤 ▥ Ⓥ

Brooklands, *31 Burnt Street, Wells-next-the-Sea, Norfolk, NR23 1HP.*
Charming beamed 250-year-old house. Delightful cottage garden
Tel: **01328 710768** Mrs Wykes.
D: £16.00-£16.00 **S:** £20.00.
Open: Apr to Oct
Beds: 1F 1D **Baths:** 1 Sh
🛏 (7) 🅿 (2) ⅍ 🗆 ⌐↑ 👤 ▥ Ⓥ

Greengates, *Stiffkey Road, Wells-next-the-Sea, Norfolk, NR23 1QB.*
Actual grid ref: TF9243
C18th cottage of character with views over salt marshes
Tel: **01328 711040** Mrs Jarvis.
D: £17.00-£22.00 **S:** £20.00-£25.00.
Open: All Year (not Xmas)
Beds: 1D 1T
Baths: 1 En 1 Pr 1 Sh
🅿 (2) ⅍ 🗆 👤 ▥ Ⓥ 🚲

Brambledene, Warham Road, Wells-next-the-Sea, Norfolk, NR23 1NE.
Nicely decorated bedrooms. Comfortable beds. 1929 bungalow. Wonderful breakfasts
Tel: **01328 711143**
Mr & Mrs Bramley.
D: £13.00-£15.00 **S:** £14.00.
Open: All Year (not Xmas)
Beds: 1F 1D
Baths: 1 Sh
🛏 🅿 (4) ⤺ 🗆 🛌 🖥 & 🔟 🛡 ⚡ 🚲

Eastdene Guest House, Northfield Lane, Wells-next-the-Sea, Norfolk, NR23 1LH.
Close to coastal path. Good birdwatching area
Tel: **01328 710381** Mrs Court.
D: £18.00 **S:** £20.00.
Open: All Year
Beds: 1D 2T 1S
Baths: 3 Pr 1 Sh
🛏 (9) 🅿 (5) ⤺ 🗆 🛌 🖥 🔟 🛡 ⚡

Warham 33
National Grid Ref: TF9441
🍴 🍺 Three Horseshoes

The Three Horseshoes / The Old Post Office, 69 Bridge Street, Warham, Wells-next-the-Sea, Norfolk, NR23 1NL.
Dream country cottage adjoining award-winning village pub
Tel: **01328 710547** Mr Salmon.
D: £24.00-£26.00 **S:** £24.00-£24.00.
Open: All Year (not Xmas)
Beds: 3D 1S
Baths: 1 En 1 Sh
🛏 (14) 🅿 (10) ⤺ 🗆 🛌 ✕ 🖥 🔟 🚲

S = Price range for a single person in a room

D = Price range per person sharing in a double room

Little Walsingham 34
National Grid Ref: TF9337
🍴 🍺 White Horse

St Davids House, Friday Market, Little Walsingham, Walsingham, Norfolk, NR22 6BY.
Actual grid ref: TF9437
Tudor house in medieval village; five miles from coast
Grades: ETC 2 Diamond
Tel: **01328 820633** Mrs Renshaw.
D: £20.00-£22.00 **S:** £20.00-£20.00.
Open: All Year
Beds: 3F 1D 1T
Baths: 1 En 2 Sh
🛏 🅿 🗆 🛌 ✕ 🖥 🔟 🛡 ⚡ 🚲

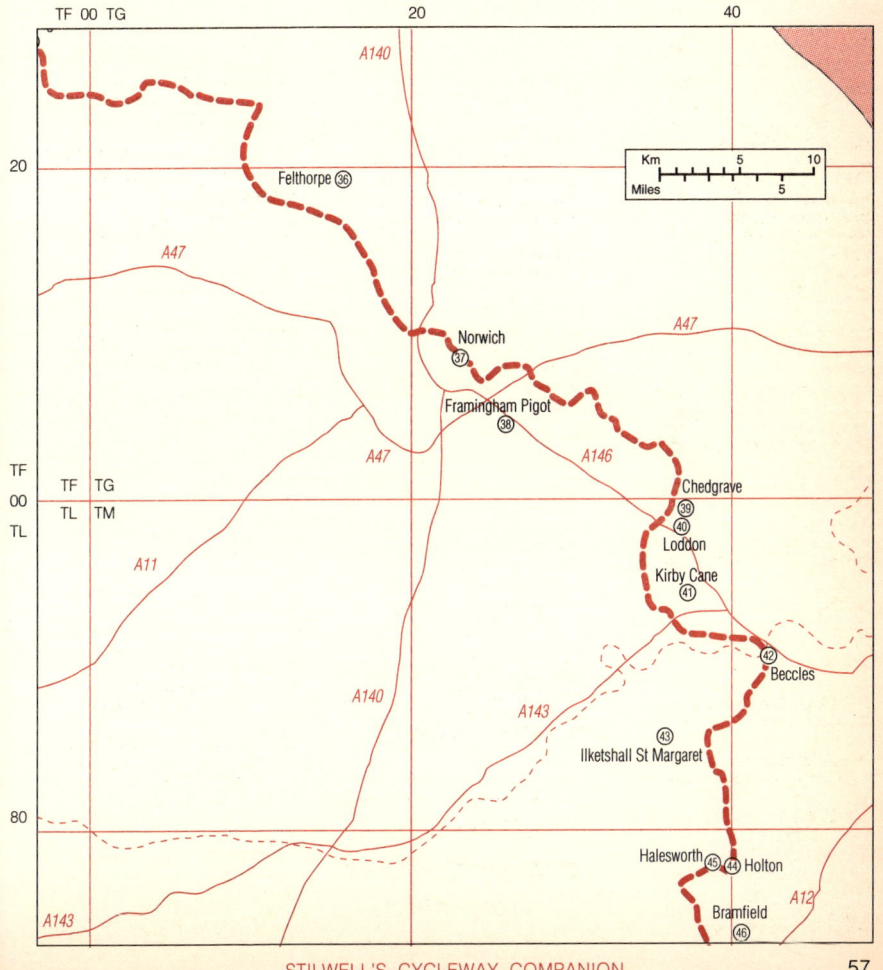

The Old Bakehouse, *33 High Street, Little Walsingham, Norfolk, NR22 6BZ.*
Restaurant with good food and attractive rooms in historic village
Tel: **01328 820454** Mrs Padley.
D: £22.50-£22.50 **S:** £27.50-£27.50.
Open: All Year (not Xmas)
Beds: 2D 1T **Baths:** 3 En
⛺ 🏠 🛏 ✕ ⚒ ⛛ Ⓥ

Great Ryburgh 35

National Grid Ref: TF9527

Highfield Farm, *Great Ryburgh, Fakenham, Norfolk, NR21 7AL.*
Actual grid ref: TF947279
Beautiful large farmhouse, peaceful location, welcoming hosts
Grades: ETC 4 Diamond
Tel: **01328 829249** Mrs Savory.
Fax no: 01328 829422
D: £20.00 **S:** £25.00.
Open: All Year (not Xmas)
Beds: 1D 2T
Baths: 1 En 1 Sh
⛺ (12) 🅿 (8) ⚒ 🏠 ✕ ⚒ ⛛ Ⓥ

The Boar Inn, *Great Ryburgh, Fakenham, Norfolk, NR21 0DX.*
300-year-old village inn, within easy reach of coast, Broads and Norwich
Tel: **01328 829212**
D: £24.50 **S:** £25.00.
Open: All Year (not Xmas)
Beds: 1F 2T 1D 1S
Baths: 5 En
⛺ 🅿 (25) 🏠 ✕ ✕ ⚒ ⛛ Ⓥ

Felthorpe 36

National Grid Ref: TG1618

🍺 🍴 Red Lion, Parson Woodforde, The Blacksmiths, Yeast & Feast, The Ratcatchers, Marsham Arms, The Dog

Spinney Ridge, *Hall Lane, Felthorpe, Norwich, NR10 4BX.*
Actual grid ref: TG168183
Tel: **01603 754833**
Mr & Mrs Thompson.
D: £18.00-£20.00 **S:** £18.00-£20.00.
Open: All Year (not Xmas)
Beds: 2D 2T 1S
Baths: 2 En 1 Sh
⛺ (1) 🅿 (6) ⚒ 🏠 ⚒ ⛛ Ⓥ ♣
Charactered quiet house in a wooded rural setting with a warm and friendly welcome and service 6 miles North of Norwich off the A1149. Centre for North Norfolk and the Broads convenient to recommended restaurants. No smoking, no dogs

---

Bringing children with you? Always ask for any special rates.

Lodge Farmhouse, *The Street, Felthorpe, Norwich, NR10 4BY.*
Actual grid ref: TG170182
Comfortable friendly family house, edge of village location, good breakfast
Tel: **01603 754896** Mrs Howe.
D: £15.00-£15.00 **S:** £15.00-£15.00.
Open: All Year (not Xmas)
Beds: 1D 1T **Baths:** 1 Sh
⛺ 🅿 (4) ⚒ 🏠 ⚒ ⛛ Ⓥ ♣ ⚲

Flitcham Cottage, *Fir Covert Road, Felthorpe, Norwich, NR10 4DT.*
Cottage style accommodation in beautiful open farmland. Warm welcome
Tel: **01603 867493** Mr Smith.
D: £15.50 **S:** £15.50.
Open: All Year (not Xmas)
Beds: 2D 1T **Baths:** 1 Sh
⛺ 🅿 (9) ⚒ 🏠 ⚒ ⛛ Ⓥ ♣ ⚲

Norwich 37

National Grid Ref: TG2308

🍺 🍴 The Pickwick, Black Horse, The Tuns, The Falcon, Town House

🔺 **Norwich Youth Hostel,** *112 Turner Road, Norwich, Norfolk, NR2 4HB.*
Actual grid ref: TG213095
Tel: **01603 627647**
Under 18: £6.20 **Adults:** £9.15
evening meal at 6.30-7.15pm, self-catering facilities, television, showers
In quiet suburban street outside the city centre, a good place for exploring Norwich. Within easy reach of East Anglian countryside, from seaside to the Broads

Earlham Guest House, *147 Earlham Road, Norwich, NR2 3RG.*
Grades: ETC 3 Diamond, AA 3 Diamond
Tel: **01603 454169** (also fax no)
Mr & Mrs Wright.
D: £20.00-£23.00 **S:** £22.00-£25.00.
Open: All Year (not Xmas)
Beds: 1F 3D 1T 3S
Baths: 2 En 2 Sh
⛺ (10) ⚒ 🏠 ⚒ ⛛ Ⓥ ♣ ⚲
Susan & Derek Wright offer welcoming and friendly hospitality with comfortable modern facilities, close historic Norwich and University. Vegetarian choices, personal keys. Short break rates available 1 Oct - 31 Mar. No smoking throughout. Amex, MasterCard and Visa welcome

Rosedale, *145 Earlham Road, Norwich, NR2 3RG.*
Comfortable, family-run guest house. Easy access to city, coast & university
Tel: **01603 453743** Mrs Curtis.
Fax no: 01603 408473
D: £17.00 **S:** £16.00.
Open: All Year (not Xmas)
Beds: 1F 1D 3T 3S **Baths:** 2 Sh
⛺ (4) 🏠 ⚒ ⛛ Ⓥ

Trebeigh House, *16 Brabazon Road, Hellesdon, Norwich, NR6 6SY.*
Warm welcome to quiet friendly house convenient city country airport
Tel: **01603 429056** Mrs Jope.
Fax no: 01603 414247
D: £17.00-£18.00 **S:** £17.00-£19.00.
Open: All Year (not Xmas)
Beds: 1D 1T
Baths: 1 Sh
⛺ 🅿 (3) ⚒ 🏠 ⚒ ⛛ Ⓥ ⛾

Harvey House Guest House, *50 Harvey Lane, Norwich, NR7 0AQ.*
Comfy, no smoking with easy access to city and Broads
Grades: ETC 3 Diamond, AA 3 Diamond
Tel: **01603 436575** (also fax no)
D: £20.00-£21.50 **S:** £18.50-£25.00.
Open: All Year
Beds: 1F 1D 2T 1S
Baths: 3 En 1 Pr 1 Sh
⛺ (3) 🅿 (6) ⚒ 🏠 ⚒ ⛛ Ⓥ

EdMar Lodge, *64 Earlham Road, Norwich, NR2 3DF.*
Only 10 mins' walk from city centre. 2 car parks bordering neat garden
Tel: **01603 615599** Mrs Lovatt.
Fax no: 01603 495599
D: £17.00 **S:** £25.00.
Open: All Year
Beds: 2F 1D 1T 1S
Baths: 3 Pr 2 Sh
⛺ 🅿 (6) 🏠 ⚒ ⛛ Ⓥ

Aylwyne House, *59 Aylsham Road, Norwich, NR3 2HF.*
Comfortable, modern, private house, walking distance city, cathedral, parks outlook
Tel: **01603 665798** Mrs Adams.
D: £18.00 **S:** £20.00.
Open: All Year
Beds: 1F 1D 1S **Baths:** 2 En 1 Pr
⛺ (3) 🅿 (3) ⚒ 🏠 ⚒ ⛛ Ⓥ

Framingham Pigot 38

National Grid Ref: TG2703

🍺 🍴 The Gull

The Old Rectory, *Rectory Lane, Framingham Pigot, Norwich, NR14 7QQ.*
Friendly comfortable Victorian Rectory. Large garden. 10 mins Norwich centre
Tel: **01508 493082** Mrs Thurman.
D: £21.00-£21.00 **S:** £21.00-£21.00.
Open: All Year (not Xmas)
Beds: 1F 1D 1T **Baths:** 2 En 1 Sh
⛺ 🅿 (6) ⚒ 🏠 ⚒ ⛛ Ⓥ ♣ ⚲

Planning a longer stay? Always ask for any special rates.

Chedgrave 39

National Grid Ref: TM3599

🍴 🍺 Kingshead the Swan

Chedgrave House, 2 Norwich Road, Chedgrave, Norwich, NR14 6HB.
Traditionally furnished Victorian town house with Aga breakfasts. Riverside walks nearby
Tel: **01508 520320**
Fax no: 01508 521095
D: £20.00-£25.00 **S:** £25.00-£27.50.
Open: All Year
Beds: 1F 1D 1T
Baths: 2 En 1 Sh
🛏 🅿 (4) 🍴 🗖 🛉 🐾 🎿 🏛 🖾 🚲

Loddon 40

National Grid Ref: TM3698

🍴 🍺 Kings Head

Poplar Farm, Sisland, Loddon, Norwich, NR14 6EF.
Working farm pigs, cows. Quiet, rural setting near broads
Tel: **01508 520706** Mrs Hemmant.
D: £17.00-£25.00 **S:** £18.00-£25.00.
Open: All Year (not Xmas)
Beds: 1F 1D 1T
Baths: 1 En 1 Pr
🛏 🅿 (4) 🍴 🗖 🗙 🛉 🏛 🖾

Kirby Cane 41

National Grid Ref: TM3794

Butterley House, Leet Hill Farm, Yarmouth Road, Kirby Cane, Bungay, Suffolk, NR35 2HJ.
Dairy farm situated in the Waveney Valley - quiet location
Tel: **01508 518301** Mrs Cook.
D: £16.50 **S:** £18.00.
Open: All Year
Beds: 1F 1T 1D
Baths: 1 En 1 Sh
🛏 🅿 🍴 🗖 🗙 🛉 🏛 🖾 🛉 🖾 🎿 🚲

Beccles 42

National Grid Ref: TM4289

🍴 🍺 Bear & Bells

Catherine House, 2 Ringsfield Road, Beccles, Suffolk, NR34 9PQ.
Well furnished family home, excellent facilities, view over Waveney Valley
Tel: **01502 716428** Mrs Renilson.
D: £18.00-£20.00
S: £18.00-£20.00.
Open: All Year
Beds: 1F 1D 1S
Baths: 1 En 1 Sh
🛏 🅿 (4) 🗖 🛉 🏛 🖾 🎿 🚲

D = Price range per person sharing in a double room

Ilketshall St Margaret 43

National Grid Ref: TM3585

🍴 🍺 Rumburgh Buck

Shoo-Devil Farmhouse, Ilketshall St Margaret, Bungay, Suffolk, NR35 1QU.
Actual grid ref: TM351858
Enchanting thatched C16th farm house in secluded garden near St. Peters Brewery
Tel: **01986 781303** (also fax no)
Mrs Lewis.
D: £18.50-£20.00 **S:** £20.00-£25.00.
Open: All Year (not Xmas)
Beds: 1D 1T **Baths:** 2 En
🅿 (4) 🍴 🗖 🗙 🛉 🏛 🖾 🚲

Holton 44

National Grid Ref: TM4077

🍴 🍺 Queens Head

Gavelcroft, Holton, Halesworth, Suffolk, IP19 8LY.
Actual grid ref: TM3978
Grade II Listed C16th farmhouse set in own extensive grounds of garden & apple orchard
Tel: **01986 873117** Mrs Hart.
Fax no: 01986 784643
D: £20.00-£25.00 **S:** £25.00-£30.00.
Open: All Year (not Xmas)
Beds: 1F 1T
Baths: 2 En
🛏 🅿 (6) 🍴 🗖 🛉 🐾 🏛 🖾 🛉 🖾 🚲

All rates are subject to alteration at the owners' discretion.

Halesworth 45

National Grid Ref: TM3877

🍴 🍺 Rumburgh Buck, Huntsman & Hound

Rumburgh Farm, Halesworth, Suffolk, IP19 0RU.
Grades: ETC 3 Diamond
Tel: **01986 781351** (also fax no)
D: £16.50-£19.00.
S: £21.00-£25.00.
Open: All Year (not Xmas)
Beds: 1F 1D
Baths: 2 En
🛏 🅿 (3) 🍴 🗖 🛉 🏛 🖾 🎿 🚲
Attractive C17th timber framed farmhouse on a mixed enterprise farm, peaceful location, surrounded by countryside. Comfortable accommodation and hearty breakfasts, easy reach - Southwold RSPB, Minsmere and Heritage coast. We look forward to welcoming you

Bramfield 46

National Grid Ref: TM4073

🍴 🍺 Queens Head Bramfield

Broad Oak Farm, Bramfield, Halesworth, Suffolk, IP19 9AB.
Comfortable farmhouse surrounded by meadow land and extensive gardens, peaceful setting
Grades: ETC 4 Diamond
Tel: **01986 784232**
Mrs Kemsley.
D: £18.00-£22.00
S: £20.00-£24.00.
Open: All Year
Beds: 2T
Baths: 2 En 1 Pr 3 Sh
🛏 🅿 (4) 🗖 🛉 🗙 🏛 🖾 🛉 🖾 🎿 🚲

Halesworth to Dedham Vale

The way through the gently sloping rich farmland of Suffolk brings you to the market town of **Halesworth** and then the village of Peasenhall before you reach **Framlingham,** whose twelfth-century castle has a continuous curtain wall, from which there are fine views of the small town. From here it's on to the attractive town of **Woodbridge**, before you pass through the northwestern outskirts of **Ipswich**, Suffolk's county town. Ipswich Museum contains replicas of the Roman Mildenhall Treasure and the Sutton Hoo ship burial, both important local archaeological finds (the originals are in the British Museum in London), local studies exhibitions and anthropological galleries on Africa, Asia and the Americas. Christchurch Mansion is a Tudor house with substantial collections of Gainsborough and Constable, both local painters. The town's other celebrated Tudor building is the 'ancient house', faced with an outstanding seventeenth-century example of pargeting (sculpted plasterwork). Leaving town to the west, you go on to Whatfield and turn south through **Hadleigh**, before reaching **Stratford St Mary** in Constable's **Dedham Vale.**

Darsham 47

National Grid Ref: TM4169

Priory Farm, *Priory Lane, Darsham, Saxmundham, Suffolk, IP17 3QD.*
Comfortable C17th farmhouse ideal for exploring Suffolk. Cycle hire available
Grades: ETC 3 Diamond
Tel: **01728 668459** (also fax no)
Mrs Bloomfield.
D: £20.00-£25.00
S: £25.00-£30.00.
Open: Easter to Oct
Beds: 1D 1T **Baths:** 2 Pr
🛏 (12) 🅿 (2) ⌿☐ 🍴 ▥ Ⓥ

Pay B&Bs by cash or cheque and be prepared to pay up front.

Sibton 48

National Grid Ref: TM3669

Sibton White Horse, *Halesworth Road, Sibton, Saxmundham, Suffolk, IP17 2JJ.*
Grades: ETC 2 Diamond
Tel: **01728 660337** Mr Dyke.
D: £22.50-£22.50 **S:** £27.00-£27.00.
Open: All Year
Beds: 3D 2T 3S **Baths:** 7 En 1 Sh
🛏 🅿 🍴 ✕ ▥ ⅏ Ⓥ
C16th inn. 3 acres secluded grounds. 8 rooms with private facilities. Full of character. Separate modern accommodation. Close Minsmer, Southwold. Log fire. Customers' comments: 'fantastic' 'lovely pub', 'good food, good company', 'super time in great company'. Restaurant , bar menu

Park Farm, *Sibton, Saxmundham, Suffolk, IP17 2LZ.*
Enjoy a friendly farmhouse welcome with your every comfort assured
Tel: **01728 668324** Gray.
Fax no: 01728 668564
D: £19.00-£21.00
S: £19.00-£21.00.
Open: All Year (not Xmas)
Beds: 1D 2T
Baths: 2 En 1 Pr
🅿 (6) ⌿☐ ✕ 🍴 ▥ Ⓥ 🚲

All cycleways are popular: you are well-advised to book ahead

---

Order your packed lunches the *evening before* you need them.
Not at breakfast!

Cransford 49

National Grid Ref: TM3164

🍴 🍺 White Horse, The Crown

High House Farm, *Cransford, Woodbridge, Suffolk, IP13 9PD.*
Tel: **01728 663461**
Mrs Kindred.
Fax no: 01728 663409
D: £18.00 S: £18.00.
Open: All Year
Beds: 1F 1D
Baths: 1 En 1 Pr
🛇 🅿 (4) 🖵 🛏 🏃 🎫 🛒 Ⅴ 🖤 ♦ ⌀
Beautiful oak-beamed C15th farmhouse on family farm. Very large family room, children welcome. You can expect comfortable beds and hearty breakfasts using local & homemade produce. Inglenook fireplaces with logfires in winter. Cosy guest lounge with colour TV, central heating. Attractive gardens, farm/woodland walks

Framlingham 50

National Grid Ref: TM2863

🍴 🍺 The Crown, Queen's Head

Shimmens Pightle, *Dennington Road, Framlingham, Woodbridge, Suffolk, IP13 9JT.*
Grades: ETC 3 Diamond
Tel: **01728 724036** Mrs Collett.
D: £20.00-£22.00 S: £23.00-£25.00.
Open: Easter to Nov
Beds: 1F 1D 1T
Baths: 1 Sh
🛇 (8) 🅿 (5) ⅙ 🖵 🏃 🎫 🛒 Ⅴ
Comfortable family home set in an acre of landscaped garden, overlooking fields. Within a mile of the historic castle town of Framlingham with its famous castle and church. Ground floor rooms with wash basins. Local cured bacon & home preserves. Guests lounge with TV

Boundary Farm, *off Saxmundham Road, Framlingham, Woodbridge, Suffolk, IP13 9NU.*
C17th farmhouse, open countryside, ideal touring base. Brochure on request
Tel: **01728 723401** Mrs Cook.
Fax no: 01728 723877
D: £18.00-£25.00 S: £20.00-£25.00.
Open: All Year (not Xmas)
Beds: 2D 1T
Baths: 1 En 1 Sh
🛇 🅿 (4) 🖵 ✕ 🏃 🎫 🛒 Ⅴ 🖤 ♦ ⌀

Always telephone to get directions to the B&B - you will save time!

Dallinghoo 51

National Grid Ref: TM2655

🍴 🍺 The Castle

Old Rectory, *Dallinghoo, Woodbridge, Suffolk, IP13 0LA.*
Actual grid ref: TM263551
Rare, restful, rural retreat, relaxing, remedial, regularly revisited. Room service
Grades: ETC 3 Diamond
Tel: **01473 737700**
Mrs Quinlan.
D: £16.00-£18.00.
Open: All Year (not Xmas)
Beds: 1D 1T
Baths: 1 Pr 1 Sh
🛇 🅿 (6) ⅙ 🎫 ♦ ⌀

Woodbridge 52

National Grid Ref: TM2649

Grove House Hotel, *39 Grove Road, Woodbridge, Suffolk, IP12 4LG.*
Grades: ETC 3 Diamond
Tel: **01394 382202**
D: £25.00-£27.50 S: £25.00-£37.50.
Open: All Year
Beds: 1F 5D 3T 3S
Baths: 11 En 1 Sh
🛇 🅿 (15) 🖵 🛏 ✕ 🏃 🎫 🛒 Ⅴ 🖤 ♦ ⌀
A warm welcome awaits everyone at our newly extended and renovated hotel, 10 minutes walk from the market square. All bedrooms comfortable, individually decorated and well-appointed. Great breakfast menu. Superb area for walking, birdwatching, golf, fishing and painting

Playford 53

National Grid Ref: TM2147

🍴 🍺 Admirals Head

Glenham, *Hill Farm Road, Playford, Ipswich, Suffolk, IP6 9DU.*
Actual grid ref: TM215478
Situated in the Fynn valley. Warm welcome extended to all
Grades: ETC 3 Diamond
Tel: **01473 624939**
Mr & Mrs Booker.
D: £16.00-£25.00 S: £16.00-£20.00.
Open: All Year (not Xmas)
Beds: 1F 1T 1S
Baths: 1 Pr 1 Sh
🛇 🅿 (3) ⅙ 🖵 🛏 🎫 ♦ ⌀

All rates are subject to alteration at the owners' discretion.

Ipswich 54

National Grid Ref: TM1644

🍴 🍺 Royal George, The Westerfield, The Swan, The Greyhound, The Ram, The Railway, Beagle Inn

Sidegate Guest House, *121 Sidegate Lane, Ipswich, IP4 4JB.*
Grades: ETC 4 Diamond, Silver
Tel: **01473 728714**
Mr & Mrs Marriott.
Fax no: 01473 728714 (phone first)
D: £20.00-£25.00
S: £27.00-£30.00.
Open: All Year
Beds: 1F 2D 1T
Baths: 4 En
🛇 🅿 (5) ⅙ 🖵 🛏 🏃 🎫 🛒 Ⅴ 🖤 ♦ 🚲 ⌀
High quality ensuite rooms in beautiful house and gardens, family run. Extensive breakfast menu, close to town centre, hospital, Suffolk college and showground. On route 66 rail station to Martlesham. Ideal location for touring Suffolk's heritage coast and Constable country

Colchester to Harwich

Crossing the River Stour into Essex, continue into **Colchester**, the oldest town in Britain. *Camulodunum* was the first capital of Roman Britain, and there are remains of the Roman walls. The town was sacked by Queen Boudicca ('Boadicea') of the Iceni tribe after the Romans killed her husband and raped her daughters. The honey-coloured Norman castle keep, the biggest in Europe, was built on the foundations of a Roman temple, and now houses a museum with Roman mosaics and statues. There is a museum of social history in the Saxon Holy Trinity Church. Also worth visiting is the Dutch Quarter, established by Flemish refugee weavers in the sixteenth century, which has tall Dutch-style houses. The route out of town goes to Wivenhoe, from where the final stretch leads to **Harwich**. The Harwich Redoubt, a circular fort currently undergoing restoration, was built against a feared invasion by Napoleon.

Stelvio Guest House, Crane Hill, London Road, Ipswich, Suffolk, IP2 0SS.
Red brick Edwardian house close to A12, A14 junction
Tel: **01473 602982**
Mr & Mrs Patrick.
D: £20.00-£25.00 **S:** £21.00-£25.00.
Open: All Year
Beds: 1F 1T 1S
Baths: 2 En 1 Pr
🛇 🅿 (10) ⅒ 🗆 🏯 📖 Ⓥ ⬛

Maple House, 114 Westerfield Road, Ipswich, Suffolk, IP4 2XW.
Attractive house one mile to town centre; close to park
Tel: **01473 253797** Mrs Seal.
D: £14.00-£28.00 **S:** £15.00-£15.00.
Open: All Year (not Xmas)
Beds: 2D 2S
Baths: 2 En 1 Sh
🛇 🅿 (3) ⅒ 🗆 🏯 🛋 📖 ⬛ Ⓥ ⊕

Redholme, 52 Ivry Street, Ipswich, IP1 3QP.
Grades: ETC 4 Diamond
Tel: **01473 250018** (also fax no)
Mr & Mrs McNeil.
D: £20.25-£24.00 **S:** £24.30-£27.50.
Open: All Year
Beds: 1F 2D 2T 1S
Baths: 5 En 1 Pr
🛇 🅿 (5) ⅒ 🗆 ✕ 🛋 📖 ⬛ ⬛ Ⓥ ⬛ ⊕ ⊕
Elegant Victorian house in large well maintained garden in quiet conservation area. 10 minutes' walk from town centre near Christchurch Park. Spacious bedrooms with complete bathrooms, we offer comfort in a friendly and helpful atmosphere. Good centre for visiting Suffolk

107 Hatfield Road, Ipswich, Suffolk, IP3 9AG.
Large Victorian guest house, modern facilities
Tel: **01473 723172**
Mrs Debenham.
Fax no: 01473 270876
D: £17.00 **S:** £17.00.
Open: All Year
Beds: 1D 2T
Baths: 1 Pr 2 Sh
🛇 🅿 🅿 🏯 ✕ 🛋 📖 ⬛ Ⓥ

Craigerne, Cauldwell Avenue, Ipswich, Suffolk, IP4 4DZ.
Tastefully restored large Victorian house, secluded grounds, parking
Tel: **01473 714061**
Mrs Krotunas.
D: £16.00 **S:** £18.00.
Open: All Year (not Xmas)
Beds: 1D 1T 3S
Baths: 3 En 2 Sh
🅿 (6) 🗆 🛋 📖 Ⓥ

Kersey 55

National Grid Ref: TM0044

🍴 🍺 The Bell

Red House Farm, Kersey, Ipswich, Suffolk, IP7 6EY.
Comfortable farmhouse (c.1840)
Tel: **01787 210245**
Mrs Alleston.
D: £18.00 **S:** £20.00.
Open: All Year
Beds: 1D 1T
Baths: 1 Pr 1 Sh
🅿 (4) 🗆 🏯 ✕ 🛋 📖 Ⓥ

Fairview, Priory Hill, Kersey, Ipswich, Suffolk, IP7 6DU.
Converted C17th cottages. Stunning views of countryside, church and village
Tel: **01473 828606** Mrs Worsley.
Fax no: 01473 828602
D: £19.00 **S:** £20.00.
Open: All Year
Beds: 2D
Baths: 1 En 1 Sh
🅿 (2) ⅒ 🗆 🛋 📖 Ⓥ ⬛ ⊕ ⊕

Holton St Mary 56

National Grid Ref: TM0636

🍴 🍺 Kings Head

Stratford House, Holton St Mary, Colchester, Essex, CO7 6NT.
A welcoming home with luxury accommodation in Constable country
Grades: ETC 4 Diamond
Tel: **01206 298246** (also fax no)
Mrs Selleck.
D: £20.00-£20.00
S: £20.00-£20.00.
Open: All Year (not Xmas)
Beds: 1D 1T 1S
Baths: 1 Sh
🛇 (10) 🅿 (10) ⅒ 🗆 🛋 📖 Ⓥ ⊕ ⊕

Dedham 57

National Grid Ref: TM0533

🍴 🍺 Marlborough Head

Mays Barn Farm, Mays Lane, Dedham, Colchester, Essex, CO7 6EW.
Actual grid ref: TM0531
Grades: ETC 4 Diamond
Tel: **01206 323191**
Mrs Freeman.
D: £20.00-£22.00
S: £25.00-£30.00.
Open: All Year (not Xmas)
Beds: 1D 1T
Baths: 1 En 1 Pr
🛇 (12) 🅿 (3) ⅒ 🗆 🛋 📖 Ⓥ ⊕
Do you want peace and quiet away from all traffic? Wonderful views of Dedham Vale? A comfortable well-furnished old house and friendly hospitality? Then stay at Mays Barn Farm - ideal for exploring the unspoilt Essex and Suffolk border lands

---

Langham 58

National Grid Ref: TM0233

🍴 🍺 Shepherd & Dog

Oak Apple Farm, Greyhound Hill, Langham, Colchester, Essex, CO4 5QF.
Actual grid ref: TM023320
Comfortable farmhouse tastefully decorated with large attractive garden
Grades: ETC 4 Diamond
Tel: **01206 272234** Mrs Helliwell.
D: £20.00 **S:** £20.00.
Open: All Year (not Xmas)
Beds: 2T 1S
Baths: 1 Sh
🛇 🅿 (6) 🗆 🛋 📖 Ⓥ ⬛ ⊕ ⊕

Colchester 59

National Grid Ref: TL9925

🍴 🍺 Forresters, George, Siege House, Red Lion, Roverstye, Peveril Hotel

8 Broadmead Road, Parsons Heath, Colchester, Essex, CO4 3HB.
Grades: ETC 3 Diamond
Tel: **01206 861818** (also fax no)
Mr & Mrs Smith.
D: £18.50-£18.50 **S:** £25.00-£25.00.
Open: All Year
Beds: 1D
Baths: 1 Sh
🅿 ⅒ 🗆 ✕ 🛋 📖 Ⓥ
Friendly family home, quiet residential area. 10 min by bus or car from town centre, bus station, castle, leisure complex, or university. Very convenient for touring Constable country, only 20 min from the sea or zoo

St John's Guest House, 330 Ipswich Road, Colchester, Essex, CO4 4ET.
Well situated close to town, convenient for A12 and A120 Harwich
Tel: **01206 852288** Mrs Knight.
D: £20.00-£25.00 **S:** £26.00-£45.00.
Open: All Year
Beds: 2F 2D 2T 2S
Baths: 5 En 3 Sh
🛇 🅿 (10) ⅒ 🗆 🏯 🛋 📖 Ⓥ ⊕

Peveril Hotel, 51 North Hill, Colchester, Essex, CO1 1PY.
Grades: AA 1 Star
Tel: **01206 574001** (also fax no)
D: £27.00-£45.00 **S:** £27.00-£45.00.
Open: All Year (not Xmas)
Beds: 4F 6D 2T 5S
Baths: 6 En 4 Sh
🛇 🅿 (10) 🗆 🏯 🛋 📖 Ⓥ ⬛ ⊕
Town centre holiday accommodation. Superb food, near castle

D = Price range per person sharing in a double room

S = Price range for a single person in a room

11a Lincoln Way, *Colchester, Essex, CO1 2RL.*
Grades: ETC 3 Diamond
Tel: **01206 867192**
Mr & Mrs Edwards.
Fax no: 01206 799993
D: £18.00-£20.00
S: £18.00-£22.00.
Open: All Year
Beds: 1T 1S
Baths: 1 Sh
⏳ (4) 🅿 (1) ⊬ 🗗 🛏 ✗ 🛒 🔳 Ⓥ 🔒 🚲
Friendly, comfortable modern house in quiet residential area, five minutes walk from town centre, bus station, castle and leisure complex. Close to university and railway station. Convenient for Harwich port and touring Constable country. Colour TVs, washbasins, tea/coffee in bedrooms

Hampton House, *224 Maldon Road, Colchester, Essex, CO3 3BD.*
Friendly family home, tastefully furnished - books - games - on bus route
Tel: **01206 579291** Ms Morgan.
D: £17.00 **S:** £18.00.
Open: All Year
Beds: 1T 2S
Baths: 1 Sh
🗗 🛒 🔳 Ⓥ 🗲

D = Price range per person
sharing in a double room

The Old Manse, *15 Roman Road, Colchester, Essex, CO1 1UR.*
Quiet town centre location beside Castle Park. 3 minutes' walk bus station, town, castle
Tel: **01206 545154** Mrs Anderson.
D: £18.00 **S:** £25.00.
Open: All Year (not Xmas)
Beds: 1D 2T **Baths:** 1 Pr 2 Sh
⏳ (3) 🅿 (1) ⊬ 🗗 🛒 🔳 Ⓥ

The Red House, *29 Wimpole Road, Colchester, Essex, CO1 2DL.*
Elegant, comfortable Victorian house. Short walk to town centre and stations
Tel: **01206 509005**
Mrs Harrington.
Fax no: 01206 795077
D: £18.00 **S:** £20.00.
Open: All Year
Beds: 1T 2D **Baths:** 3 En
⏳ ⊬ 🗗 ✗ 🛒 🔳 Ⓥ 🔒

Wix   60

National Grid Ref: TM1628

🍴 🍺 Village Maid

Dairy House Farm, *Bradfield Road, Wix, Manningtree, Essex, CO11 2SR.*
Spacious quality, rural accommodation. A really relaxing place to stay
Grades: ETC 4 Diamond, Gold, AA 4 Diamond
Tel: **01255 870322** Mrs Whitworth.
Fax no: 01255 870186
D: £18.50-£20.00 **S:** £26.00-£26.00.
Open: All Year (not Xmas)
Beds: 1D 2T **Baths:** 2 En 1 Pr
⏳ (12) 🅿 (4) 🗗 🛒 🔳 Ⓥ 🔒 🗲 🚲

New Farm House, *Spinnells Lane, Wix, Manningtree, Essex, CO11 2UJ.*
Actual grid ref: TM165289
Country guest house in 4 acres of grounds. Residents' license
Tel: **01255 870365** Mrs Mitchell.
Fax no: 01255 870837
D: £21.00 **S:** £22.00.
Open: All Year
Beds: 5F 1D 3T 2S
Baths: 9 Pr 1 Sh
⏳ 🅿 (20) 🗗 🛏 ✗ 🛒 🔳 ♿ Ⓥ 🔒 🗲

Harwich   61

National Grid Ref: TM2431

🍴 🍺 The Royal Oak

Tudor Rose, *124 Fronks Road, Dovercourt, Harwich, CO12 4EQ.*
Harwich international port. Seafront, Railway 5 minutes. London 1 hour
Tel: **01255 552398**
D: £17.50-£17.50 **S:** £20.00-£30.00.
Open: May to Aug
⏳ 🅿 (2) ⊬ 🗗 🛒 🔳 Ⓥ 🗲 🚲

High season,
bank holidays and
special events mean
low availability
everywhere.

Kingfisher Cycle Trail

The **Kingfisher Cycle Trail** is a new long-distance cycleway through Ireland's beautiful border lakelands, where the kingfisher is king. It straddles the Irish Border, running mainly through Fermanagh and Leitrim but with briefer forays into Cavan, Monaghan, Donegal and Tyrone. It has been developed primarily by Leitrim County Council in the Republic of Ireland and Fermanagh District Council in Northern Ireland, with assistance from Sustrans in Britain. The northern section forms part of the UK's National Cycle Network; the route as a whole is the first long distance cyleway in Ireland and the first link in a proposed All Ireland Cycle Network. The total length is 280 miles, and the route is signposted by a brown direction sign bearing a cycle silhouette and the image of a kingfisher, fish in bill.

The route is set out in a figure of eight. The northern circle takes you from **Enniskillen** through Fermanagh's south western corner to the shores of **Loch Melvin**, then north to **Belleek** and around the north bank of **Lower Lough Erne** through **Pettigo**, **Kesh** and the **Castle Archdale Forest** to **Irvinestown** and back to Enniskillen. The southern circle starts in **Carrick-on-Shannon** and takes you through Leitrim village and **Drumshanbo** past the shores of **Loch Allen**, and below the Cuilcagh Mountains to Derrylin before crossing **Upper Lough Erne** by ferry and continuing through Newtownbutler to **Clones**, County Monaghan, at the eastern extremity of the route. From here you head west through Cavan to **Belturbet** and **Ballyconnel** before you reach **Ballinamore** in County Leitrim and return to Carrick-on-Shannon. The two circles overlap in the Fermanagh countryside, through Florencecourt Forest and Marlbank National Nature Reserve.

The indispensable **official route map and guide** for the route is available from Sustrans, 35 King Street, Bristol BS1 4DZ, tel 0117-926 8893, fax 0117-929 4173, @ £5.99 (+ £2.00 p&p). The Kingfisher Cycle Trial Holiday Guide, with information on organised cycle tours of varying lengths around the trail, is available free of charge from the Kingfisher Cycle Trail Office, Tourist Information Centre, Wellington Road, Enniskillen, Co Fermanagh BT74 7EF, tel 028 6632 0121, fax 028 6632 5511, email pat@cycleireland.com or visit them on the internet at www.cycleireland.com

Maps: 1:50,000 Irish OS Discovery/OSNI Discoverer series: 12, 17, 26, 27, 33 (both ranges use the same system of serial numbers – some border country maps are available in both)

Transport links: Carrick-on-Shannon can be reached by rail form Dublin. Enniskillen can be reached by bus from Belfast (Ulsterbus) or from Dublin (Bus Eireann), both of which can carry bicycles in the luggage boot.

Enniskillen   1

National Grid Ref: H2344

⚑ The Horseshoe, Manor House, The Inishclare, Mulligan's

Mountview Guest House,
61 Irvinestown Road, Enniskillen, Co Fermanagh, BT74 6DN.
Victorian house, large ensuite. Half mile to town. Sky TV, snooker room
Grades: NITB 2 Star
Tel: 028 6632 3147
Fax no: 028 6632 9611
D: £20.00-£21.00 **S:** £25.00-£30.00.
Open: All Year (not Xmas)
Beds: 3T **Baths:** 3 En
🛇 🅿 (6) ❐ ✕ 🛏 🛋 📺

Drumcoo House, 32 Cherryville, Cornagrade Road, Enniskillen, Co Fermanagh, BT74 4FY.
Actual grid ref: H237458
Family-run B&B in Enniskillen, central to beautiful Lakeland county. **Grades:** NITB Grade B
Tel: **028 6632 6672** Mrs Farrell.
D: £17.00-£19.00 **S:** £19.00-£24.00.
Open: All Year (not Xmas)
Beds: 1F 1D 1T 1S
Baths: 3 En 1 Sh
🛇 🅿 (10) ❐ 🛏 🛋 📺 🔒 ⚲ 🚲

D = Price range per person sharing in a double room

S = Price range for a single person in a room

Abbeyville, 1 Willoughby Court, Portora, Enniskillen, Co Fermanagh, BT74 7EX.
Modern B&B, convenient to National Trust properties, leisure facilities and Marble Arch Caves
Grades: NITB Approv
Tel: **028 6632 7033**
Mrs McMahon.
D: £17.00-£20.00.
Open: All Year (not Xmas)
Beds: 2T 1D **Baths:** 3 En
🛇 🅿 (6) ⚲ ❐ 🛏 🛋 📺 🔒

Tamlaght 2

National Grid Ref: H2741

🍴🍺 Mulligan's

*Dromard House, Tamlaght,
Enniskillen, Co Fermanagh,*
BT74 4HR.
Award-winning B&B beautifully
situated with woodland walk to
lake shore
Grades: NITB Approv,
AA 4 Diamond
Tel: 028 6638 7250
Mrs Weir.
D: £17.50-£17.50
S: £20.00-£20.00.
Open: All Year (not Xmas)
Beds: 1F 2D 1T
Baths: 4 En
🛏 (8) 🅿 (4) ⌿🖵🏠🕯🖵📺♿

Letterbreen 3

National Grid Ref: H1840

Abocurragh Farmhouse,
*Abocurragh, Letterbreen,
Enniskillen, Co Fermanagh,*
BT94 9AG.
Farm guest house in picturesque
setting
Grades: NITB Approv
Tel: 028 6634 8484
Mrs Mullally.
D: £18.00 **S:** £18.00.
Open: All Year
Beds: 2F 1D
Baths: 4 En
🛏🅿⌿🖵✗🕯🖵📺🛢⚡

Enniskillen, *Inis Ceithleann*, means 'the island of
Kathleen', the wife of Balor, the Celtic king who once took
refuge from his enemies on the island upon which stands
the town. Here you can find the Watergate, a
seventeenth-century construction with Scottish
characteristics, built by William Cole on the site of the old
Maguire Castle. The building hosts a Heritage Centre,
which contains exhibitions on the history and natural
history of the area; and for military enthusiasts, the
Regimental Museum of the Royal Inniskilling Fusilliers,
boasting a wealth of paraphernalia including the bugle
that sounded the charge at the Somme in 1916. Castle
Coole is a late eighteenth-century Palladian house built in
Portland stone by James Wyatt, with original plasterwork
decoration intact; set in landscaped parkland with oak
trees. The town's old buttermarket has been renovated to
house a craft centre, where you can see craftspeople at
work on vases, ceramics and Celtic jewellery, which are
on sale in the shop.

Kiltyclogher 4

National Grid Ref: G9744

⛺ *Leitrim Lakes Hostel
(Independent), Kiltyclogher, Sligo.*
Tel: **072 54044 Adults:** £7.00
self-catering facilities, family bunk
rooms, showers, camping available

**All rates are subject to alteration
at the owners' discretion.**

Pettigoe 5

National Grid Ref: H1066

Hill Top View, Pettigoe, Donegal.
Spectacular view of Lough Erne.
Anglers', walkers' paradise. Lough
Derg pilgrimage
Grades: BF Approv
Tel: **072 61535** Mrs O'Shea.
D: £16.00 **S:** £19.00.
Open: All Year (not Xmas)
Beds: 1F 1T
Baths: 4 En
🛏 (1) 🅿 (6) ⌿🖵🏠✗🖵🛢⚡

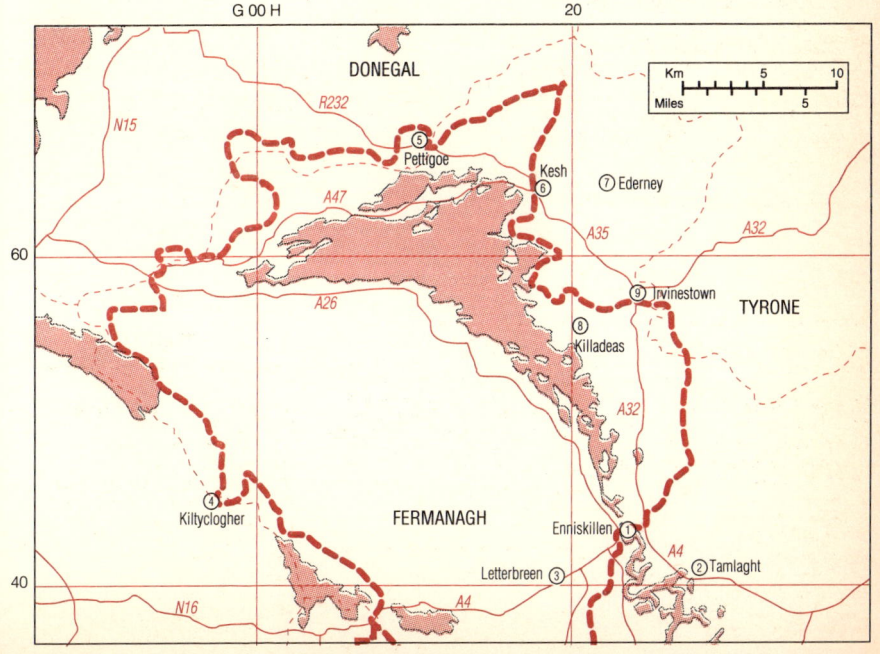

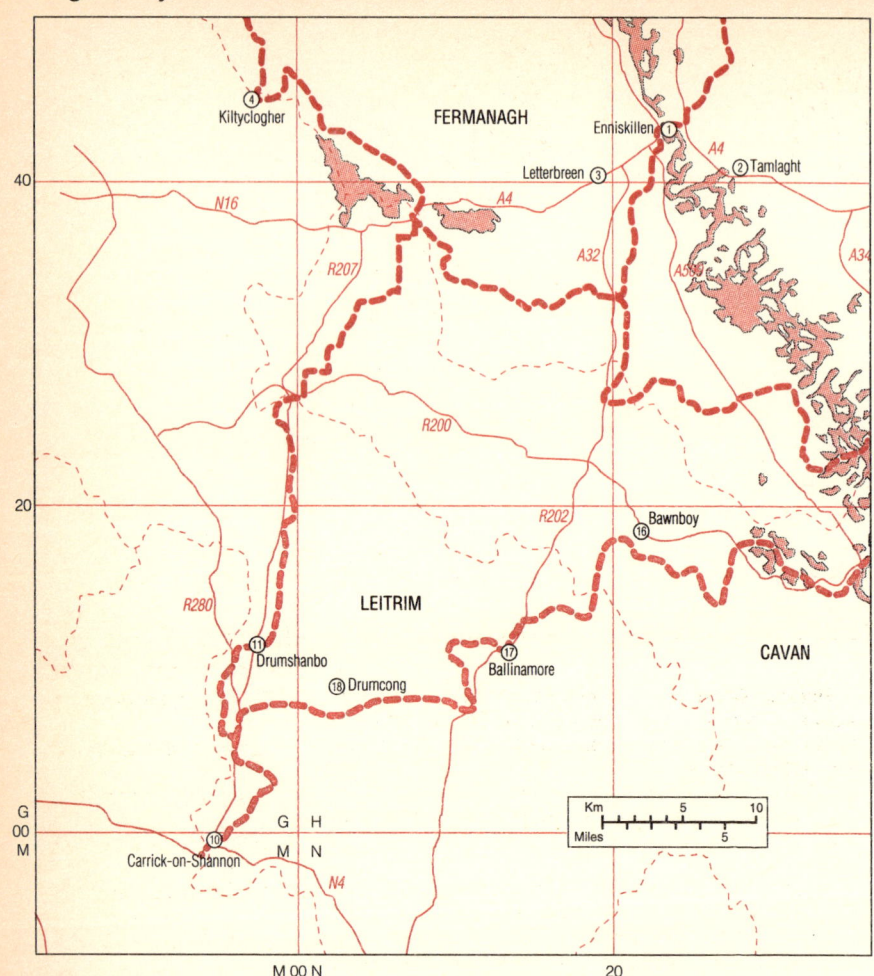

Kesh 6

National Grid Ref: H1863

Lough Erne Hotel

Roscolban House, *Enniskillen Road, Kesh, Enniskillen, Co Fermanagh, BT93 1TF.*
Modern comfortable guest house. Quiet and conveniently situated for touring with a friendly welcome
Tel: **028 6863 1096** Mrs Stronge.
D: £16.00 **S:** £18.50.
Open: All Year (not Xmas)
Beds: 2F 1T **Baths:** 2 En 1 Sh

S = Price range for a single
person in a room

D = Price range per person sharing in a double room

Ederney 7

National Grid Ref: H2264

Greenwood Lodge, *Erne Drive, Ederney, Kesh, Enniskillen, Co Fermanagh, BT93 0EF.*
Well-appointed guest house, good food, personal service. Ideal for touring
Grades: NITB Approv
Tel: **028 6863 1366** (also fax no)
Mrs McCord.
D: £16.00-£18.00 **S:** £18.00-£20.00.
Open: All Year (not Xmas)
Beds: 3D 2T 1S
Baths: 5 En 1 Sh

Killadeas 8

National Grid Ref: H2054

Manor House, The Inishclare

Rossfad House, *Killadeas, Enniskillen, Co Fermanagh, BT94 2LS.*
A Georgian country house on Lower Lough Erne. Lake views
Grades: NITB Approv
Tel: **028 6638 8505** Mrs Williams.
D: £17.50-£20.00 **S:** £20.00-£25.00.
Open: Mar to Nov
Beds: 1F 1D **Baths:** 1 En 1 Pr

Planning a longer
stay? Always ask for
any special rates.

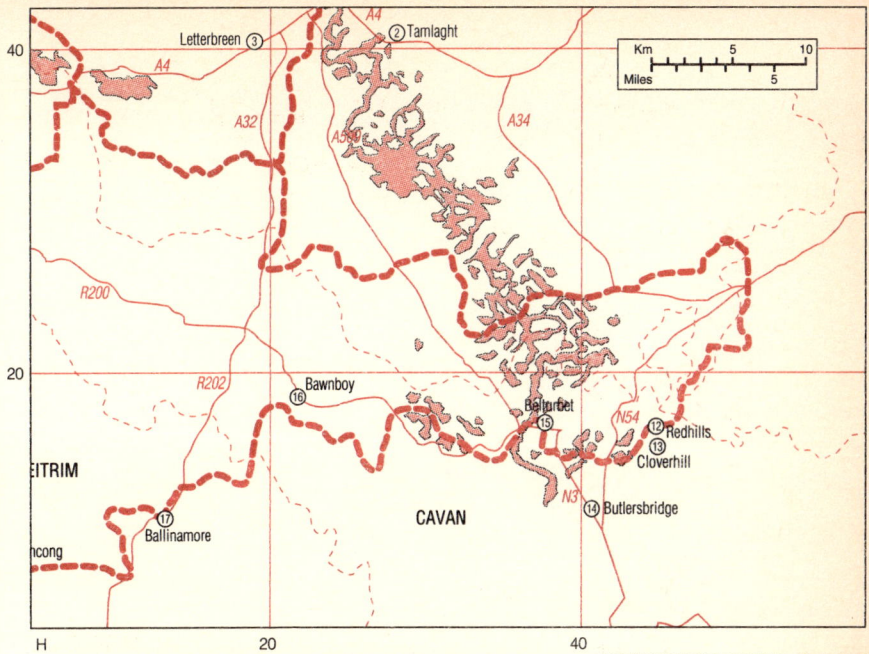

Florence Court, on the route south from Enniskillen, is an eighteenth-century mansion built by John Cole, noted for its lavish rococo plasterwork, and the grounds including a water-powered sawmill.

A little further on, in the Marlbank National Nature Reserve, tours are available through the stalactite-clad **Marble Arch Caves**, the most impressive of the many famous caves of County Fermanagh.

At **Garrison**, on the shores of Loch Melvin, the Loch Melvin Activity Centre offers a range of outdoor pursuits including caving and watersports.

A little way off the route beyond **Belleek** (take care on the busy road if you make this detour), the nature reserve at Castle Caldwell is the breeding ground of a number of rare birds, including the common scoter and the peregrine falcon.

From Castle Archdale Forest you can take a ferry to **White Island**, renowned for its ruined twelfth-century abbey with an eery collection of early Christian sculptures, believed to be caryatids (carved columns) from an earlier church on the site.

The Grid Reference beneath the location heading is for the village or town - *not* for individual houses, which are shown (where supplied) in each entry itself.

The Olde Schoolhouse, Tully Road, Killadeas, Enniskillen, Co Fermanagh, BT94 1RE.
Central for touring Fermanagh, Tyrone and Donegal. Good food, homely atmosphere
Grades: NITB Approv
Tel: **028 6862 1688** (also fax no)
Mrs Moore.
D: £19.00-£21.00 **S:** £20.00-£29.00.
Open: All Year
Beds: 2F 3D 1T **Baths:** 6 En
♿ 🅿 (10) 🖵 ✕ 🛏 🛒 & Ⅴ 🛎 ✓

All details shown are as supplied by B&B owners in Autumn 1999.

Irvinestown 9

National Grid Ref: H2358

▲ *Irvinestown Youth Hostel, Castle Archdale, Irvinestown, Enniskillen, County Fermanagh,* BT94 1PP.
Tel: **028 6862 8118**
Under 18: £7.50
Adults: £8.50
evening meals available, self-catering facilities, television, central heating, shop, laundry facilities
Centre of Castlelodge Country Park, situated in cobbled courtyard. 2 minutes' walk to shore

Carrick-on-Shannon, County Letrim's main town, sits picturesquely on both sides of a wide stretch of the Shannon, and is a good location for watersports enthusiasts. Worth seeing here: the Costello Mortuary Chapel is the smallest chapel in Ireland and the second smallest in the world. Built in 1879 by a local businessman to commemorate his wife, the interior is beautifully tiled with Bath stone, with the couple's coffins on either side of the miniature aisle. The Irish Potato Famine is commemorated by a memorial garden behind the old St Patrick's Workhouse (now a hospital), whose inmates suffered particularly badly.

At **Drumshanbo**, on the south of Loch Allen, the Sliabh an Iarann Visitor Centre includes exhibits on the area's mining history.

On the site of the sixth-century monastery founded by St Tiernach at **Clones**, the vestiges of the twelfth-century Augustinian abbey can be found in Abbey Street. The town's religious heritage is further reflected in the richly carved (although weathered by age) High Cross, at 'the Diamond' in the centre of town, depicting biblical scenes.

Fenagh has a ruined monastery and two seventh-century churches founded by St Caillain.

Close to **Keshcarrigan**, where the route passes Loch Scur, the cairn and stone circle at Sheebeg is believed by some to be the grave of the Irish hero Finn MacCool.

Carrick-on-Shannon   10

National Grid Ref: M9499

🍴 🚲 Riverside Bar, Cryan's, Tig Brid

▲ *Town Clock Hostel (Independent)*, *Town Centre, Carrick-on-Shannon, County Leitrim.*
Tel: **078 20068 Adults:** £6.00
self-catering facilities, showers

Gortmor House, Lismakeegan, Carrick-on-Shannon, Co Leitrim.
Excellent home cooking, good wines, quiet scenic location, laundry facilities on request
Grades: BF Approv
Tel: **078 20489**
Mrs McMahon.
Fax no: 078 21439
D: £18.50-£18.50
S: £25.00-£25.00.
Open: Jan to Nov
Beds: 2F 1D 1T
Baths: 1 En 3 Pr
🛇 🅿 (8) 🗲 🖵 🗶 🎟 🛢 ⚡ 🚴

Always telephone

to get directions to

the B&B - you will

save time!

D = Price range per person
sharing in a double room

Corbally Lodge, Dublin Road N4, Carrick-on-Shannon, Co Leitrim.
Country peacefulness, antique furnishings, laundry, breakfast service. Fishing and walking
Grades: BF Approv
Tel: **078 20228** (also fax no)
Mr & Mrs Rowley.
D: £16.00-£18.00
S: £20.00-£23.00.
Open: All Year (not Xmas)
Beds: 1D 3T
Baths: 3 En
🛇 🅿 🖵 🗢 🗶 🎟 🛢 ⚡

Drumshanbo   11

National Grid Ref: G9710

🍴 🚲 Sorohan's

Mooney's B&B, 2 Carick Road, Drumshanbo, Carrick-on-Shannon, Co Leitrim.
Stone two-storey house, home from home, scenic area in lovely Leitrim
Grades: BF Approv
Tel: **078 41013**
Mrs Mooney.
Fax no: 078 41237
D: £12.00 **S:** £12.00.
Open: All Year (not Xmas)
Beds: 2D 1T 1S **Baths:** 1 Sh
🛇 (12) 🗲 🖵 🎟 🚴

Redhills   12

National Grid Ref: H4416

🍴 🚲 Old Post Inn

Hillside, Shannon Wood, Redhills, Cavan.
Beautiful modern home half mile Redhills village, 2 music pubs, horseriding, golf, fishing locally
Grades: BF Approv
Tel: **047 55125**
Mrs Smith.
D: £17.00-£17.00 **S:** £20.00-£20.00.
Open: Apr to Oct
Beds: 2F 1T
Baths: 3 En 3 Pr 1 Sh
🛇 🅿 🖵 🗶 🎟 🛢 ⚡

Cloverhill   13

National Grid Ref: H4114

🍴 🚲 Derragarra Inn

Fortview House, Drumbran, Cloverhill, Belturbet, Co Cavan.
Beautiful country house. Excellent home cooking. Farm walks. First class fishing
Tel: **049 4338185**
Mrs Smith.
Fax no: 049 4338834
D: £16.00-£16.00
S: £18.00-£18.00.
Open: Easter to Oct
Beds: 3F 1D 2T
Baths: 1 Pr 2 Sh
🛇 🅿 🗲 🖵 🗶 🛢 🎟 Ⓥ

Butlersbridge   14

National Grid Ref: H4110

🍴 🚲 Dennagaria Inn

Ford House, Deredis, Butlersbridge, Cavan.
Grades: BF Approv
Tel: **049 4331427** Mrs Mundy.
D: £15.00-£18.00.
Open: All Year
Beds: 6F
Baths: 3 En 1 Pr 1 Sh
🛇 🅿 🖵 🗢 🗶 🛢 🎟 Ⓥ
Modern farm guest house, overlooking rivers and lakes in what is truly scenic countryside, Quiet walks, country lanes, forests and woods. Or take a trip downstream in one of our boats. Perfect for anglers - Butlersbridge is surrrounded by water - so is the house.

High season,

bank holidays and

special events mean

low availability

everywhere.

Belturbet 15

National Grid Ref: H3617

Erne View House, 9 Bridge Street, Belturbet, Co Cavan.
Town house by River Erne convenient to pubs, shops and bistros
Grades: BF Approv
Tel: **049 9522289**
Mrs McGreevey.
D: £15.00 **S:** £18.00.
Open: All Year (not Xmas)
Beds: 4 F
Baths: 2 En 2 Sh
🛏 🅿 (5) 🗙 ✗ 🎴 🛏 Ⓥ

Bawnboy 16

National Grid Ref: H2119

The Keepers' Arms, Bawnboy, Ballyconnell, Belturbet, Co Cavan.
The charm of a restored coaching house, situated in scenic, tranquil surroundings
Tel: **049 9523318** Mrs McKiernan.
D: £16.00 **S:** £22.00.
Open: All Year
Beds: 3D 1T **Baths:** 2 En 2 Sh
🛏 🅿 (15) 🍴 ✗ 🎴 🛏 Ⓥ 🗝 ⚡

Ballinamore 17

National Grid Ref: H1211
🍴 🍷 Smyth's

▲ *Ballinamore Holiday Hostel (Independent), Main Street, Ballinamore, County Leitrim.*
Tel: **078 44955 Adults:** £7.50
evening meals available, self-catering facilities, showers

Riversdale, Ballinamore, Co Leitrim.
Grades: BF 3 Star, RAC 3 Diamond
Tel: **078 44122** Ms Thomas.
Fax no: 078 44813
D: £26.00-£26.00 **S:** £31.00-£31.00.
Open: All Year (not Xmas)
Beds: 4F 3D 2T 1S **Baths:** 10 En
🛏 (5) 🅿 (12) 🗙 🍴 ✗ 🎴 🛏 🗝 ⚡ 🐎
Comfortable spacious residence in parkland setting alongside Shannon-Erne Waterway. Indoor heated swimming pool, squash, sauna, games room on premises. Local golf, horse-riding, dude ranch, canoeing, boat trips. Good touring centre. Brochure available. Weekly terms. Canal barge holidays

Please respect
a B&B's wishes
regarding children,
animals & smoking.

Drumcong 18

National Grid Ref: H0209

Lakeview, Drumcong, Carrick-on-Shannon, Co Leitrim.
Relaxing, comfortable Georgian home, overlooking two lakes
Tel: **078 42034** Mrs McKeown.
D: £17.50 **S:** £20.00.
Open: All Year
Beds: 2F 1T **Baths:** 3 En
🛏 🅿 (6) 🗙 ✗ 🎴 🛏 Ⓥ ⚡

S = Price range for a single
person in a room

Sustrans Lon Las Cymru

The **Welsh National Cycle Route** is a section of the new UK National Cycle Network, running on traffic-free paths and traffic-calmed roads across the full length of Wales from the southeastern coast to the ferry port of Holyhead at the northwest of the Isle of Anglesey. It will take you through the full range of the Principality's breathtaking landscape, including two National Parks, the Brecon Beacons in the south and Snowdonia in the north. Much of the route is through sparsely populated regions. You should be prepared for a fair amount of climbing, particularly in the northern reaches, but don't let this put you off – Sustrans have designed the route with novice cyclists in mind. You can start at Cardiff, or at Chepstow on the English border; there are western and eastern alternative routes for most of the way, meeting and parting twice before meeting again for the final stretch from Porthmadog to Holyhead. The maximum distance is 288 miles; most of the route is signposted by blue direction signs with a cycle silhouette and the number 8 in a red rectangle.

The indispensable **official route map and guide** in English and Welsh for the Welsh National Cycle Route, which includes listings of cycle repair/hire shops along the route, comes in two parts, *Lon Las Cymru: Chepstow & Cardiff to Builth Wells* and *Lon Las Cymru: Builth Wells to Holyhead*, and is available from

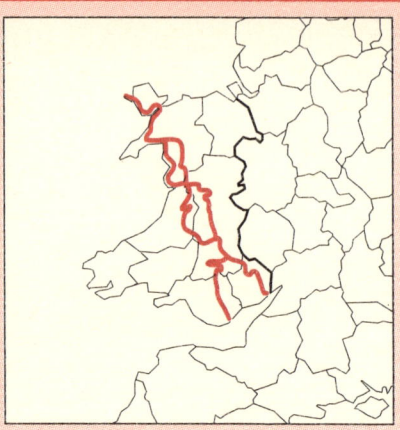

Sustrans, 35 King Street, Bristol BS1 4DZ, tel 0117-926 8893, fax 0117-929 4173, @ £5.99 each (+ £1.50 p&p for both together or either one).

Maps: Ordnance Survey 1:50,000 Landranger series: 114, 123, 124, 135, 136, 147, 160, 161, 171, 172

Transport: Cardiff, Bangor and Holyhead are all main line rail termini; Chepstow is a stop on the line between Cardiff and Gloucester; there are connections to many other places on or near the route. Holyhead is a major ferry port to Ireland, serving Dublin and Dun Laoghaire.

Cardiff   1

National Grid Ref: ST1677

🏨 🍴 Robin Hood, Halfway Hotel, The Beverley, Allensbank

▲ *Cardiff Youth Hostel, 2 Wedal Road, Roath Park, Cardiff, CF2 5PG.*
Actual grid ref: ST185788
Tel: **029 2046 2303**
Under 18: £6.85 **Adults:** £10.15
suitable for disabled people, evening meal at 7.00pm, family bunk rooms, shop, security lockers, parking, laundry facilities
Conveniently located hostel near the city centre and Roath Park lake, with cycling & sailing facilities

---

D = Price range per person sharing in a double room

Bringing children with you? Always ask for any special rates.

Rambler Court Hotel,
188 Cathedral Road, Pontcanna, Cardiff, S Glam, CF1 9JE.
Grades: WTB 2 Star
Tel: **029 2022 1187** (also fax no)
Ms Oxley & L Cronin.
D: £17.00-£20.00 **S:** £17.00-£25.00.
Open: All Year
Beds: 3F 3D 1T 3S
Baths: 4 En 5 Sh
🛇 🅿 (4) 🖵 🛋 📶 🎽 🖤 ✦ ♒
Friendly family-run hotel, ideally situated in a tree-lined conservation area, close to all of the city's main attractions, 10 minutes' walk to the city centre and Millennium Stadium. Good local restaurants & pubs

---

Preste Gaarden Hotel,
181 Cathedral Road, Pontcanna, Cardiff, S Glam, CF11 9PN.
Highly recommended, modernised ex-Norwegian consulate offering olde-worlde charm
Grades: WTB 2 Star Hotel
Tel: **029 2022 8607** Mr Nicholls.
Fax no: 029 2037 4805
D: £18.00-£22.00 **S:** £22.00-£27.00.
Open: All Year (not Xmas)
Beds: 1F 2D 3T 4S
Baths: 7 En 3 Pr
🛇 🅿 (3) 🖵 🛋 📶 🖤

Austins, 11 Coldstream Terrace, Cardiff, S Glam, CF11 6LJ.
In the centre of the city 300 yards from Cardiff Castle
Grades: WTB 2 Star
Tel: **029 2037 7148**
Mr Hopkins.
Fax no: 029 2037 7158
D: £17.50-£19.50 **S:** £20.00-£27.50.
Open: All Year
Beds: 1F 5T 5S
Baths: 4 En 2 Sh
🛇 🖵 🛏 🛋 📶 🖤 ♒

The Beeches Hotel, 73 Ninian Road, Roath Park, Cardiff, CF2 5EN. Family-run establishment overlooking Roath Park. Warm welcome. Lock-up car park
Grades: WTB 1 Star
Tel: **029 2049 1803** Mr Sainsbury.
Fax no: 029 2049 5968
D: £17.50-£24.00 **S:** £19.00-£26.00.
Open: All Year
Beds: 2F 3D 5S **Baths:** 2 En 2 Sh
♿ P □ ✕ 🏃 ▥ Ⓥ ⏟ ⚡ ♿

Clayton Hotel, 65 Stacey Road, Roath, Cardiff, S Glam, CF2 1DS. Excellent family-run comfortable, homely hotel
Tel: **029 2049 2345**
Mr Milliner.
D: £14.00 **S:** £14.00.
Open: All Year (not Xmas)
Beds: 1F 2D 3T 4S
Baths: 4 Pr 1 Sh
♿ (3) P (6) ✂ □ ✕ 🏃 ▥ Ⓥ

All rooms full and nowhere else to stay? Ask the owner if there's anywhere nearby

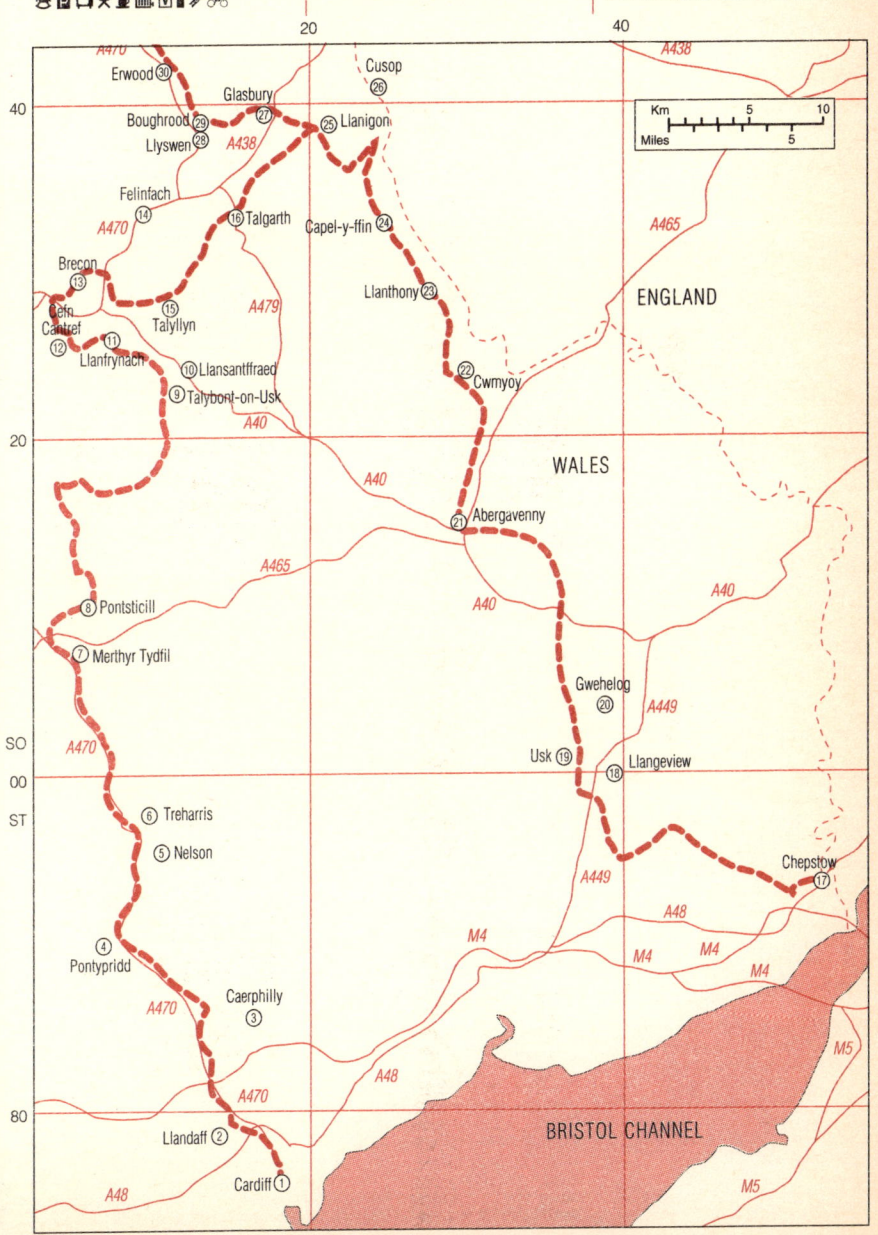

The Routes

The **western route** runs from **Cardiff** up the River Taff through the industrial heartland of South Wales to Pontypridd, Abercynon and Merthyr Tydfil, before wending through the beautiful wooded valleys below the Brecon Beacons range itself, within the **Brecon Beacons National Park**, to Brecon, where it turns east to join the other route close to the River Wye. From **Chepstow**, at the mouth of the Wye, the **eastern route** turns west to the River Usk, which it follows upstream to Usk before heading on to **Abergavenny**, where it enters the Brecon Beacons National Park to follow the River Honddu up the idyllic Vale of Ewyas to its source in the Black Mountains range, passing below Offa's Dyke and the border for much of the way until the two routes converge. After the stretch through the beautiful Wye Valley as far as **Builth Wells**, the route parts again as it heads into Mid Wales: the eastern way pursues the Wye Valley to Newbridge-on-Wye, Rhayader and Llangurig before turning eastwards to Llanidloes. The western section of this part of the route is unsignposted and tough going – only for experienced cyclists, preferably on a mountain bike: after **Llanwrtyd Wells** you take the Abergwysyn Pass up the 'Devil's Staircase' through dense forest, to reach the valley of the Towi with its breathtaking scenery. After following the Towi to its source you proceed to Devil's Bridge.

The two routes pass either side of the peak of **Plynlimon Fawr** in the Cambrian Mountains before they converge again at **Machynlleth**, where you cross the River Dovey into **Snowonia National Park**. The western alternative turns west to Tywyn on the coast before heading north and crossing the Barmouth viaduct bridge into **Barmouth**. From here you continue to Dyffryn Ardudwy and Llanbedr, and proceed to the toll bridge over the River Dwyryd into Penrhyndeudraeth, and on to Garreg, where the routes finally join. The eastern route from Machynlleth goes to Corris, and continues, with the majestic mass of Cader Idris towering away to the left, to **Dolgellau**. From here you cycle through the lovely Coed-y-Brenin Forest Park, in the heart of southern Snowdonia, and on to Trawsfynydd, Gellilydan and Maentwrog on the Dwyryd before reaching Garreg. The final stretch of the way proceeds through **Porthmadog** and around the western side of the Snowdon massif to Caernarfon and Bangor; having crossed the great Menai Suspension Bridge, you traverse the southern side of Anglesey, an island scattered with the remains of ancient Celtic settlements, to reach **Holyhead**.

Georgian Hotel, 179 Cathedral Road, Pontcanna, Cardiff, S Glam, CF1 9PL.
Grades: WTB 2 Star
Tel: **029 2023 2594** Mr Menin.
D: £20.00-£27.50 **S:** £27.50-£35.00.
Open: All Year (not Xmas)
Beds: 1F 2D 3T 2S
Baths: 8 En
All the rooms have been tastefully restored to today's standards, each having a colour television, ensuite bathroom and hospitality tray. The Georgian Hotel is c nveniently close to all the major place of interest in Cardiff

---

Llandaff 2

National Grid Ref: ST1577

Plymouth Arms, St Fagan's

Plas-Y-Bryn, 93 Fairwater Road, Llandaff, Cardiff, S Glam, CF5 2LG.
Comfortable Edwardian semi-detached - quiet bedrooms, TV, tea/coffee fac. Landaff Cathedral & public transport near
Tel: **029 2056 1717** Mrs Lougher.
D: £17.00 **S:** £17.50.
Open: All Year
Beds: 2T 1S **Baths:** 1 Sh

Caerphilly 3

National Grid Ref: ST1586

Traveller's Rest, The Moat, Black Cock

Lugano, Hillside Mountain Road, Caerphilly, Mid Glamorgan, CF83 1HN.
Grades: WTB 3 Star
Tel: **029 2085 2672**
D: £16.50-£17.50 **S:** £22.50-£25.00.
Open: All Year (not Xmas)
Beds: 1D 2T **Baths:** 3 En
Charming character house, residents' own private garden and entrance; upstairs bedrooms overlooking Caerphilly Castle, all rooms ensuite. Minutes' walk to town centre, castle, train and bus stations for regular services to the capital, Cardiff. Warm friendly welcome assured. No smoking

Dugann, Springfield Bungalow, Rudry Road, Caerphilly, Mid Glam, CF83 3DW.
Quiet lounge, bathroom, good breakfast, garden, pub nearby, Caerphilly Castle 5 mins
Tel: **029 2086 6607** Mrs Powell.
D: £18.00 **S:** £25.00.
Open: All Year
Beds: 1F 2D 2S **Baths:** 1 Pr

Y-Fron Guest House, Pwllypant, Caerphilly, Mid Glam, CF83 3HW.
Family-run guest house with panoramic views of Welsh countryside
Tel: **029 2088 2896** Mrs Walton.
D: £13.50 **S:** £16.00.
Open: All Year
Beds: 4F 3T 1S **Baths:** 2 Sh 2 Pr

Denehurst, 16 St Martins Road, Caerphilly, Mid Glam, CF83 1ED.
Tastefully decorated family run guest house. 5 mins from town centre
Tel: **029 2088 3724**
D: £16.00 **S:** £17.50.
Open: All Year (not Xmas)
Beds: 1T 1D 1S **Baths:** 1 En 2 Sh

Watford Fach Farm Guesthouse, Watford Road, Caerphilly, Mid Glam, CF83 1NE.
300-year-old farmhouse. Amenities - railway station, bus station. Close to Caerphilly Castle
Tel: **029 2085 1500**
Mr & Mrs Fahey.
Fax no: 029 2086 5021
D: £18.00 **S:** £16.00.
Open: All Year (not Xmas)
Beds: 3F 2D 1T 2S
Baths: 5 En 3 Sh

Pontypridd 4

National Grid Ref: ST0789

⊮ ◀ Market Tavern

Market Tavern Hotel, Market Street, Pontypridd, Mid Glam, CF37 2ST.
Tel: **01443 485331**
Mr John.
Fax no: 01443 402806
D: £19.00-£20.00 **S:** £30.00-£30.00.
Open: All Year (not Xmas)
Beds: 4D 3T 4S **Baths:** 11 En
🛏 🖵 🗙 🏃 ▥ 🕭 Ⅴ
All bedrooms ensuite and delightfully furnished. Traditional bar offers wide selection of food, ales and wines. The Chilli Pepper cocktail bar offers Mexican food and live entertainment. Disabled facilities offered, centrally located, 20 minutes from Cardiff

All details shown
are as supplied
by B&B owners in
Autumn 1999.

Nelson 5

National Grid Ref: ST1195

⊮ ◀ Rowan Tree

Wern Ganol Farm, Nelson, Treharris, Mid Glam, CF46 6PS.
Working farm with pleasant views
Grades: WTB 2 Star
Tel: **01443 450413**
Mrs Portlock.
D: £19.00-£19.00 **S:** £20.00-£25.00.
Open: All Year
Beds: 2F 2D 2T
Baths: 6 En 2 Pr
🛏 🅿 (7) 🖵 🏃 🏃 ▥ Ⅴ 🚲

Treharris 6

National Grid Ref: ST0997

⊮ ◀ Railway Inn, Cross Inn

Fairmead, 24 Gelligaer Road, Treharris, Nelson, Mid Glam, CF46 6DN.
A small family run quiet haven, offering a warm welcome
Grades: WTB 4 Star
Tel: **01443 411174**
Mrs Kedward.
Fax no: 01443 411430
D: £21.50-£35.00 **S:** £27.50-£35.00.
Open: All Year
Beds: 2D 1T **Baths:** 2 En 1 Pr
🛏 🅿 (5) ⚡ 🖵 🏃 🗙 🏃 ▥ Ⅴ 🛈 ⚡ 🚲

Merthyr Tydfil 7

National Grid Ref: SO0506

⊮ ◀ Mountain Ash Inn, The Brunswick, White Horse Inn

Brynawel Guest House, Queens Road, Merthyr Tydfil, Mid Glam, CF47 0HD.
Actual grid ref: SO053065
Grades: WTB 3 Star
Tel: **01685 722573** Mrs Johnson.
D: £20.00-£20.00 **S:** £25.00-£25.00.
Open: All Year
Beds: 1D 2T **Baths:** 3 En
🛏 🅿 (5) ⚡ 🖵 🏃 ▥ Ⅴ 🛈 ⚡ 🚲
Large Victorian house, tastefully furnished, adjoining parks, family home, friendly atmosphere. Ensuite rooms, TV tea/coffee. Non-smoking, 10 mins Brecon Beacons National Park. Excellent Welsh breakfast. Ideal location for walkers, cyclists, business or quiet break

Planning a longer
stay? Always ask for
any special rates.

Cardiff to Brecon

Cardiff, the national capital, was in the past important for its docks, which shipped out coal from the South Wales mines. With the decline of the docks, Cardiff Bay is now undergoing extensive redevelopment, including the construction of a barrage to create a giant freshwater marina. There is a visitors' centre, built into a hollow tube that overlooks the bay, which has displays on the various projects underway. Also at Cardiff Bay is the Welsh Industrial and Maritime Museum, with prominence given to mining and to the railways. Other museums in and around Cardiff are the National Museum of Wales, including the natural history of Wales and a sizeable art collection, which includes Italian and Flemish Renaissance paintings, Impressionism, and sculpture; and the fantastic Welsh Folk Museum at St Fagan's, just west of town. This is a large site with reconstructed buildings, of all sorts and various periods, from all over the country. Other attractions are Cardiff Castle, an amalgam of Norman motte and bailey with an extensive Victorian

Neo-Gothic fantasy by William Burges; and Llandaff Cathedral, originally twelfth century but with substantial nineteenth-century restoration, including work by prominent Pre-Raphaelites.

On the route just north of Cardiff, **Castell Coch** is a Victorian medieval fantasy also by William Burges, constructed out of a thirteenth-century ruined fortress.

At **Pontypridd** you can find the Pontypridd Historical and Cultural Centre, dedicated to life in the Valleys.

Merthyr Tydfil has another Neo-Gothic castle, Cyfartha, a gallery of Welsh modern art and a museum which records the harsh conditions of nineteenth-century industrial life, the Ynysfach Engine House.

Every self-respecting Celtic nation produces whisky. If you've only heard of the Scotch and Irish varieties, you will be surprised to find the Welsh Whisky Visitor Centre at **Brecon**. The town also offers the Brecknock Museum, a document of past life in the region, and an intriguing cathedral, originally Norman but restored in the Victorian era.

Maes Y Coed, *Park Terrace, Pontmorlais West, Merthyr Tydfil, Mid Glam,* CF47 8UT.
Tel: **01685 722246** (also fax no)
D: £16.00-£18.00 **S:** £18.00-£22.00.
Open: All Year
Beds: 4F 5T 1S
Baths: 4 En
Large comfortable house on edge of Brecon Beacons in 0.25 acre of gardens. Edging the Taff Trail. Friendly welcome, good home cooked breakfast, evening meals. Ideal for golfing, fishing, walking and all outdoors pursuits.

Pontsticill   8
National Grid Ref: SO0511
Butcher's Arms

Butchers Arms, *Pontsticill, Merthyr Tydfil,* CF48 2UE.
Actual grid ref: SO056113
Grades: WTB 3 Star
Tel: **01685 723544**
Fax no: 01685 388820
D: £18.50-£22.50.
Open: All Year
Beds: 2D 1T
Baths: 3 En
Set in the beautiful surroundings of the Brecon Beacons National Park. Ideal for walking, cycling, fishing and relaxing - situated opposite side of the valley to the Brecon Mountain Railway. Good food served 7 days and 7 nights a week. Real ales

Talybont-on-Usk   9
National Grid Ref: SO1122

Llanddety Hall Farm, *Talybont-on-Usk, Brecon, Powys,* LD3 7YR.
C17th Listed farmhouse in Brecon Beacons National Park, beautiful views
Grades: WTB 3 Star Farm, AA 4 Diamond
Tel: **01874 676415** Mrs Atkins.
D: £20.00-£24.00 **S:** £24.00-£25.00.
Open: All Year (not Xmas)
Beds: 2D 1T **Baths:** 2 En 1 Pr

Llansantffraed   10
National Grid Ref: SO1223
Traveller's Rest

The Allt, *Llansantffraed, Talybont-on-Usk, Brecon, Powys,* LD3 7YF.
Actual grid ref: SO123234
C18th farmhouse overlooking River Usk with magnificent mountain views
Tel: **01874 676310**
Mrs Hamill-Keays.
D: £15.00-£16.50 **S:** £12.00-£15.00.
Open: All Year (not Xmas)
Beds: 1F 1D 1S **Baths:** 1 Sh

Llanfrynach   11
National Grid Ref: SO0725
White Swan

Llanbrynean Farm, *Llanfrynach, Brecon, Powys,* LD3 7BQ.
Actual grid ref: SO076254
Beautiful countryside, traditional family farmhouse, ideal location for Brecon Beacons
Grades: WTB 2 Star
Tel: **01874 665222** Mrs Harpur.
D: £19.00-£21.00 **S:** £20.00-£25.00.
Open: Easter to Nov
Beds: 1F 1D 1T
Baths: 2 En 1 Pr

Cefn Cantref   12
National Grid Ref: SO0426

Held Bunkhouse Barn (Independent), *Cefn Cantref, Brecon, Powys,* LD3 8LT.
Actual grid ref: SO036266
Tel: **01874 624646 Adults:** £7.50
self-catering facilities

Upper Cantref Farm Bunkhouse (Independent), *Cefn Cantref, Brecon, Powys,* LD3 8LR.
Actual grid ref: SO057258
Tel: **01874 665223 Adults:** £9.00
suitable for disabled people, self-catering facilities, showers

Brecon   13
National Grid Ref: SO0428
Three Horseshoes Inn, The Clarence, George Hotel, Red Lion, Camden Arms, Castle Inn, Lion Inn, Bentley's, Traveller's Rest, Tai 'R' Bull

Lansdowne Hotel, *39 The Watton, Brecon, Powys,* LD3 7EG.
Grades: WTB 2 Star, AA 2 Star
Tel: **01874 623321** Mrs Mulley.
Fax no: 01874 610438
D: £23.50-£25.00 **S:** £27.50-£30.00.
Open: All Year
Beds: 2F 5D 2T
Baths: 9 Pr
Our warm and friendly family-run hotel and restaurant is located in the centre of Brecon. You can enjoy comfortable accommodation and delicious freshly prepared food in our fully licensed restaurant. The perfect location for touring the beautiful National Park

Pay B&Bs by cash or cheque and be prepared to pay up front.

S = Price range for a single person in a room

Beacons Guest House, *16 Bridge Street, Brecon, Powys,* LD3 8AH.
Actual grid ref: SO142285
Grades: WTB 3 Star GH, AA 3 Diamond, RAC 3 Diamond
Tel: **01874 623339** (also fax no)
Mr & Mrs Jackson.
D: £18.00-£29.50 **S:** £20.00.
Open: All Year (not Xmas)
Beds: 6F 4D 3T 1S
Baths: 11 En 1 Sh
Georgian guest house of great character with excellent restaurant. Delightful, well-equipped bedrooms, cosy cellar bar, car park and lock-up. Centrally located for National Park

Glanyrafon, *1 The Promenade, Kensington, Brecon, Powys,* LD3 9AY.
Riverside Edwardian house, view of Beacons, near town centre
Grades: WTB 3 Star
Tel: **01874 623302** (also fax no)
Mrs Roberts.
D: £17.50-£19.00 **S:** £20.00-£22.00.
Open: Easter to Oct
Beds: 2D 1T **Baths:** 2 Sh

Pen-y-Bryn House, *Llangorse, Brecon,* LD3 7UG.
Actual grid ref: SO137275
Grades: WTB 4 Star
Tel: **01874 658606** Mrs Thomas.
Fax no: 01874 658215
D: £20.00-£20.00 **S:** £25.00-£25.00.
Open: All Year (not Xmas)
Beds: 1F 1T 1D **Baths:** 2 En 1 Pr
Situated in the Brecon Beacons National Park, overlooking Llangorse Lake, with large gardens and mountains beyond. Also, we have nearby our own acitvity centre which offers riding, climbing indoor and out (best indoor climbing in Britain) and so much more

Brecon Canal Guest House, *Canal Bank, The Watton, Brecon, Powys,* LD3 7HG.
Grades: WTB 2 Star
Tel: **01874 623464**
Fax no: 01874 610930
D: £17.00-£20.00 **S:** £17.00-£17.00.
Open: Easter to Oct
Beds: 1D 2T 1S **Baths:** 2 En
Small, friendly, cottage-style guest house, situated adjacent to the Brecon canal close to new theatre. Quiet, semi-rural position, yet only 5 minutes walk from town centre. All rooms have TV, tea/coffee, some ensuite. Private parking

*County House, 100 The Struet,
Brecon, LD3 7LS.*
Grades: WTB 4 Star
Tel: 01874 625844 (also fax no)
D: £27.50-£27.50 **S:** £35.00.
Open: All Year
Beds: 2D 1T **Baths:** 3 En
⛺ ♿ (6) ⌨ ♞ ✗ 🍴 Ⅲ. Ⅴ ✦ ♿ ♽
C18th Georgian Grade II Listed
town house - served as the judge's
lodgings for 150 years, completely
restored to a high standard. Situated
between cathedral and castle with
easy access to surrounding National
Park. Walled garden to river.
Private car park. Licensed

*Tir Bach Guest House,
13 Alexandra Road, Brecon,
Powys, LD3 7PD.*
Panoramic view of Brecon
Beacons. Quiet road near town
centre
Grades: WTB 2 Star
Tel: 01874 624551
D: £14.00-£17.00 **S:** £18.00-£22.00.
Open: All Year (not Xmas)
Beds: 1F 1D 1T **Baths:** 1 Sh
⛺ ⌨ ♞ 🍴 Ⅲ. Ⅴ ♽

*Canal Bridge B&B, 1 Gasworks
Lane, Brecon, LD3 7HA.*
Actual grid ref: S0048282
Grades: WTB 3 Star B&B
Tel: 01874 611088
D: £17.00-£20.00 **S:** £20.00-£25.00.
Open: Mar to Nov
Beds: 1F 3D 1T 1S
Baths: 4 En 2 Pr
⛺ (5) ♿ (6) ⌨ ♞ 🍴 Ⅲ. Ⅴ ✦ ♽
Whether walking, cycling or simply
relaxing, enjoy a stay at our spa-
cious and comfortable B&B close
to historic town centre,
museums, theatre and River Usk, a
stone's throw from scenic Brecon
canal. Discover the Brecon
Beacons! A warm welcome awaits

Blaencar Farm, Brecon, LD3 8HA.
Actual grid ref: SN933287
Grades: WTB 5 Star Farm
Tel: 01874 636610
D: £20.00-£22.00 **S:** £24.00-£24.00.
Open: Easter to Nov
Beds: 2D 1T **Baths:** 3 En
♿ ♿ ⌨ ♞ 🍴 Ⅲ. Ⅴ ♽
Tastefully restored farmhouse on
working family farm. Quality
ensuite accommodation in
peaceful, accessible location in the
Heart of the Brecon Beacons
National Park. Birds and wildlife in
abundance including Red Kite.
Private fishing on River Usk

*Brynawel Guest House, 13 Cradoc
Road, Brecon, LD3 9LH.*
Impressive Victorian residence.
Beautiful views, ensuites, TVs,
tea/coffee facilities
Grades: WTB 3 Star
Tel: 01874 624363 (also fax no)
D: £20.00-£25.00 **S:** £20.00-£25.00.
Open: All Year (not Xmas)
Beds: 2D 1T **Baths:** 3 En
⛺ (6) ♿ (5) ⌨ ✗ Ⅲ. Ⅴ ♽

Tir Bach, Brecon, LD3 8NE.
Beautiful C17th Welsh Longhouse
in Brecon Beacons National Park
Grades: WTB 3 Star
Tel: 01874 625675 Mrs Norris.
Fax no: 01874 611198
D: £20.00-£20.00 **S:** £23.00-£25.00.
Open: All Year (not Xmas)
Beds: 1T 2D
Baths: 2 En 2 Pr
⛺ (12) ♿ (6) ⌨ ♞ Ⅲ. Ⅴ ♽

Highgrove Farm, Brecon, LD3 7SU.
Actual grid ref: SO097279
Superb position overlooking
Brecon. Comfortable, restored
C16th farmhouse
Grades: WTB 4 Star
Tel: 01874 655489
D: £20.00-£25.00 **S:** £25.00-£40.00.
Open: All Year
Beds: 2D 1T
Baths: 1 En 1 Sh
⛺ ♿ (3) ⌨ 🍴 Ⅲ. Ⅴ ♽

*Flag & Castle Guest House,
11 Orchard Street, Llanfaes,
Brecon, Powys, LD3 8AN.*
Convenient town/National Park
amenities, near Taff Trail. Parking
Tel: 01874 625860 Mrs Jones.
D: £16.00 **S:** £17.50.
Open: All Year
Beds: 1F 2D 1T 2S
Baths: 1 Pr 2 Sh
⛺ ♿ ⌨ ♞ 🍴 Ⅲ. Ⅴ

*Cambridge House, St David Street,
Llanfaes, Brecon, Powys, LD3 8BB.*
Family-run. Off main road. Superb
breakfasts. Evening meals. Friendly
Tel: 01874 624699 (also fax no)
Mr Lomas.
D: £15.00 **S:** £16.00.
Open: All Year
Beds: 2D 1T 1S **Baths:** 1 Pr 1 Sh
⛺ ♿ (4) ⌨ ♞ ✗ 🍴 Ⅲ. Ⅴ

Felinfach 14

National Grid Ref: SO0933

🍴 Griffin Inn, Old Ford Inn, Plough & Harrow

*Plough & Harrow Inn, Felinfach,
Brecon, LD3 0UB.*
Grades: WTB 3 Star Inn
Tel: 01874 622709
D: £18.00-£20.00 **S:** £25.00-£25.00.
Open: All Year
Beds: 1F 1D 1T
Baths: 2 En 1 Pr
⛺ ♿ (20) ⌨ ♞ ✗ 🍴 Ⅲ. ♿ Ⅴ ♿ ✦ ♽
Village inn offering comfortable
ensuite accommodation, located 4
miles north of Brecon off the A470.
Within easy reach of the Black
Mountains and the Beacons. A
variety of energetic or sedate
activities are on offer - golf,
fishing, cycling, gliding, trekking,
birdwatching

*The Old Mill, Felinfach, Brecon,
Powys, LD3 0UB.*
C16th converted corn mill, within
easy reach of Brecon Beacons
Tel: 01874 625385 Mrs Boxhall.
D: £16.00 **S:** £18.00.
Open: Feb to Nov
Beds: 1D 2T
Baths: 2 En 1 Pr
⛺ ♿ ⌨ ♞ Ⅲ. Ⅴ ♿ ✦

*Llwyncynog Farm, Felinfach,
Brecon, Powys, LD3 0UG.*
Llwyncynog Farm, ideally situated,
nestling between Brecon Beacons
and Black Mountains
Tel: 01874 623475 Mrs Phillips.
D: £18.00 **S:** £20.00.
Open: Easter to Oct
Beds: 1F 1D 1T
Baths: 3 Pr
⛺ ♿ (4) ⌨ ♞

Chepstow to Llanidloes

Chepstow Castle, built in the twelfth century, was the first
stone castle in Britain. Its strategic location on a cliff
overlooking the Wye, with a panorama of the area around the
border, lends it considerable drama.

After flying to Scotland in 1941, Rudolf Hess was imprisoned
in **Abergavenny** – Spandau was definitely a considerable
comedown. The main attraction today is the Museum of
Childhood and the Home, which has a haunted doll's house.
The restored eleventh-century castle keep hosts a museum of
local history.

Llanthony Priory in the Vale of Ewyas is a romantic ruin in an
unworldly setting. An Augustine foundation dating from the
twelfth century, the ruined arches frame the mountains to
create a picture of tranquillity.

Rhayader is an attractive town with eighteenth-century
coaching inns.

At picturesque **Llanidloes** there is a rare free-standing
Tudor market hall and an interesting museum, as well as a
church with a hammerbeam roof dating from the fifteenth
century.

Talyllyn 15

National Grid Ref: SO1027

🍴 🍺 Red Lion, White Swan, The Castle

Glascwm, Talyllyn, Brecon, *LD3 7SY.*
Tranquil rural setting, close to the
Brecon Beacons and Llangorse
Lane **Grades:** WTB 3 Star
Tel: **01874 658659**
D: £20.00-£20.00.
Open: All Year (not Xmas)
Beds: 1F 1D 1T **Baths:** 3 En
🛏 🅿 (4) ✂ 🖵 🎴 ⬇ 🎞 Ⓥ 🛢

Glynderi, Talyllyn, Brecon, Powys,
LD3 7SY.
Actual grid ref: SO107273
Regency house set in 4 acres of
mature gardens
Tel: **01874 658263**
Fax no: 01874 658363
D: £20.00 **S:** £25.00.
Open: All Year (not Xmas)
Beds: 2D 1T
Baths: 3 En
🛏 🅿 (4) 🖵 🎴 ✕ ⬇ 🎞 Ⓥ 🛢 ⚡

Order your
packed lunches the
evening before you
need them.
Not at breakfast!

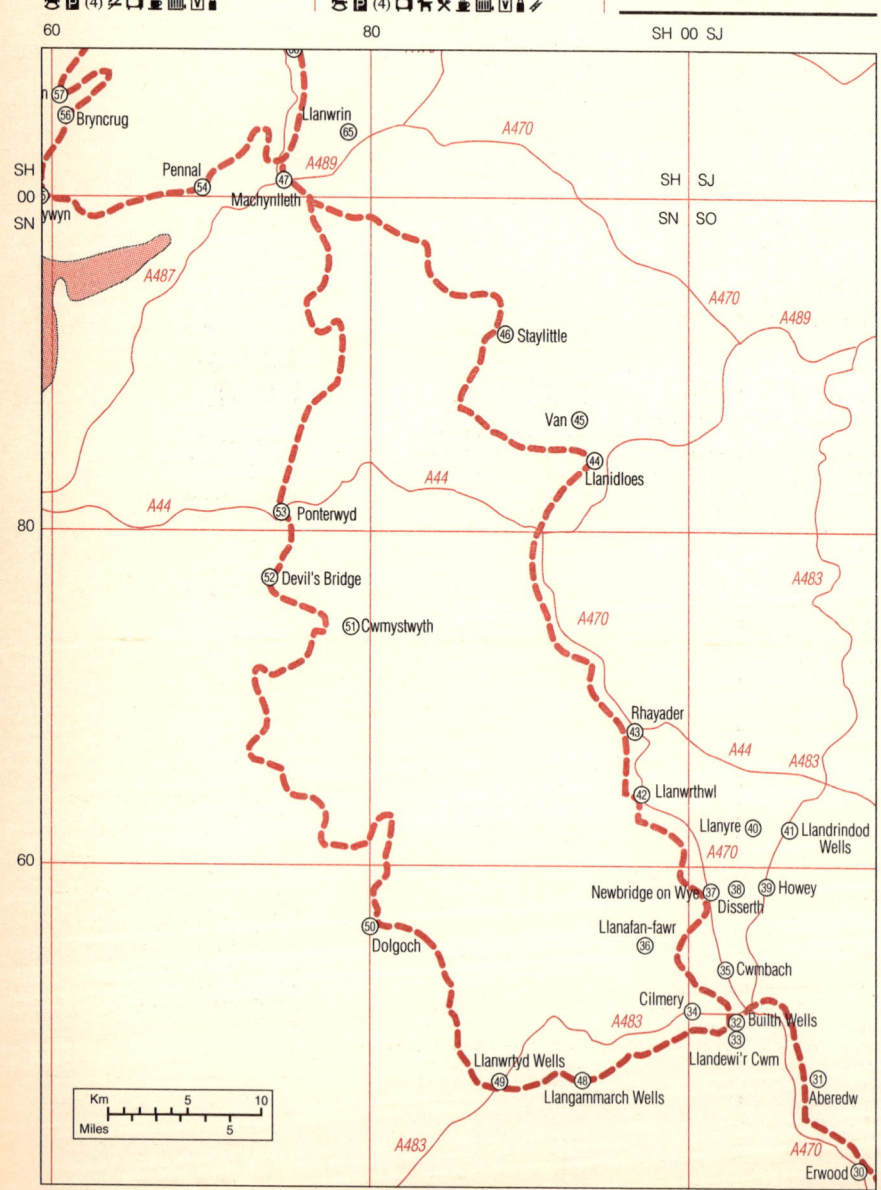

Talgarth 16

National Grid Ref: SO1533

🍴 🍺 Mason's Arms, Castle Inn

Castle Inn, *Pengenffordd, Talgarth, Brecon, Powys, LD3 0EP.*
Actual grid ref: SO174296
Traditional country inn with the Brecon Beacons national park
Grades: WTB 2 Star Inn, AA 3 Diamond
Tel: **01874 711353** Mr Mountjoy.
D: £20.00-£23.00 **S:** £20.00-£31.00.
Open: All Year (not Xmas)
Beds: 1F 2D 1T 1S
Baths: 2 En 1 Sh
🛏 🅿 (50) 🛏 ✕ 🌰 🍴 📺 🔒 ⚡ 🚲

The Old Masons Arms, *Hay Road, Talgarth, Brecon, Powys, LD3 0AL.*
C16th hotel with country cottage ambience. Ideal for walking amidst Black Mountains & Brecon Beacons
Grades: WTB 3 Star
Tel: **01874 711688**
D: £26.50-£29.50 **S:** £29.50-£32.50.
Open: All Year
Beds: 2F 2D 1T 2S **Baths:** 7 En
🛏 🅿 (10) 🛏 🛏 ✕ 🌰 🍴 📺 ⚡

Chepstow 17

National Grid Ref: ST5393

🍴 🍺 White Lion, Coach & Horses, Cross Keys

Langcroft, *71 St Kingsmark Avenue, Chepstow, Monmouthshire, NP6 5LY.*
Actual grid ref: ST529938
Grades: WTB 1 Star
Tel: **01291 625569** (also fax no)
Mrs Langdale.
D: £18.00-£20.00 **S:** £20.00-£20.00.
Open: All Year
Beds: 1D 1T 1S **Baths:** 1 Sh
🛏 🅿 (2) 🛏 🛏 🌰 🍴 📺 ⚡ 🚲
Modern family friendly home.
Town centre, four minutes' walk

Pendine Guest House, *6 Bridge Street, Chepstow, Monmouthshire, NP16 5EY.*
Actual grid ref: ST535941
Beside historic castle in town centre, picturesque walks close by
Grades: WTB 2 Star
Tel: **01291 623308** Mrs Jones.
D: £18.00-£19.50 **S:** £25.00-£28.00.
Open: All Year
Beds: 2F 3D 2T 3S
Baths: 1 En 1 Pr 1 Sh
🛏 🅿 (3) ⚡ 🛏 🌰 🍴 📺 ⚡ 🚲

The First Hurdle, *9-10 Upper Church St, Chepstow, Gwent, NP16 5EX.*
Enjoy comfortable,ensuite accommodation. Centrally situated, family owned B&B
Tel: **01291 622189** Mrs Westwood.
Fax no: 01291 628421
D: £23.00-£25.00 **S:** £25.00-£27.50.
Open: Easter to Nov
Beds: 2D 1T 1S **Baths:** 5 En
⚡ 🛏 🌰 🍴 📺 ⚡ 🚲

The Old Course Hotel, *Newport Road, Chepstow, Gwent, NP16 5PR.*
Modern hotel, convenient for the Wye Valley, Chepstow races and more. **Grades:** AA 3 Star
Tel: **01291 626261**
Fax no: 01291 626263
D: £28.75-£30.25 **S:** £47.00-£52.50.
Open: All Year
Beds: 4F 10D 7T 10S
Baths: 31 En
🛏 🅿 (18) 🛏 🛏 ✕ 🌰 🍴 📺 🔒 ⚡

Lower Hardwick House, *Mount Pleasant, Chepstow, Monmouthshire, NP6 5PT.*
Actual grid ref: ST531935
Beautiful Georgian house, walled garden. Free car parking for duration walk
Tel: **01291 622162** Mrs Grassby.
D: £15.00 **S:** £18.00.
Open: All Year
Beds: 2F 1D 1T 1S
Baths: 2 Pr 2 Sh
🛏 🅿 (12) 🛏 🛏 🌰 🍴 📺 ⚡

Llangeview 18

National Grid Ref: SO3900

The Rat Trap, *Chepstow Road, Llangeview, Usk, Monmouthshire, NP5 1EY.*
Grades: WTB 2 Star
Tel: **01291 673288**
Mr & Mrs Rabaiotti.
Fax no: 01291 673305
D: £29.50-£34.50 **S:** £20.00-£24.00.
Open: All Year
Beds: 1F 5D 5T 1S
Baths: 12 En
🛏 (2) 🅿 (50) 🛏 🛏 🌰 🍴 ♿ 📺 🚲
In the beautiful setting of the Vale of Usk (adjacent to the Wye Valley)

Usk 19

National Grid Ref: SO3700

New Court Hotel, *62 Maryport Street, Usk, Monmouthshire, NP5 1AD.*
Small village pub/hotel. Play area, garden, restaurant, lounge & bar
Tel: **01291 673364** Hunt.
D: £20.00 **S:** £20.00.
Open: All Year
Beds: 1F 3D 2T 1S
🛏 🛏 ✕ 🌰 🍴 📺 🔒 ⚡ 🚲

Gwehelog 20

National Grid Ref: SO3804

🍴 🍺 The Hall

Oak Farm, *Gwehelog, Usk, Monmouthshire, NP5 1RB.*
Pretty, self-contained cottage in beautiful country. Usk, 2 miles
Tel: **01291 672830** Mrs Dean.
Fax no: 01291 673569
D: £18.00-£18.00 **S:** £25.00-£25.00.
Open: All Year
Beds: 1F **Baths:** 1 En
🛏 🅿 📺 🛏 🛏 ✕ 🌰 🍴 📺 🔒 ⚡ 🚲

Ty-Gwyn Farm, *Gwehelog, Usk, Monmouthshire, NP5 1RG.*
Quiet countryside location with magnificent views, surrounded by secluded lawns
Tel: **01291 672878** (also fax no)
Mr & Mrs Arnett.
D: £19.00-£20.00 **S:** £25.00-£30.00.
Open: All Year (not Xmas)
Beds: 2D 1T
Baths: 2 En 1 Pr
🛏 (5) 🅿 ⚡ 🛏 🌰 🍴 📺 🔒 ⚡ 🚲

Abergavenny 21

National Grid Ref: SO2914

🍴 🍺 King's Arms, Crown Inn, Old Mitre, Lamb & Flag, Walnut Treem, Bear Hotel, Nant -y-fyn, Red Hart

Pentre House, *Brecon Road, Abergavenny, Monmouthshire, NP7 7EW.*
Actual grid ref: SO283151
Charming small Georgian award-winning country house in wonderful gardens
Grades: WTB 3 Star
Tel: **01873 853435**
Mrs Reardon-Smith.
Fax no: 01873 852321
D: £17.00-£18.00 **S:** £20.00-£25.00.
Open: All Year (not Xmas)
Beds: 1F 1D 1T
Baths: 2 Sh
🛏 🅿 (6) 🛏 🛏 ✕ 🌰 🍴 📺 🔒 ⚡

Tyn-y-bryn, *Deriside, Abergavenny, Monmouthshire, NP7 7HT.*
Actual grid ref: SO301165
Magnificent views, a homely atmosphere. Comfortable accommodation & warm welcome
Grades: WTB 2 Star Farm
Tel: **01873 856682** (also fax no)
Ms Belcham.
D: £20.00 **S:** £25.00.
Open: Easter to Nov
Beds: 1F 1T 1D
Baths: 2 En
🅿 (6) 🛏 🛏 ✕ 🌰 🍴 📺 🔒 ⚡

Maes Glas, *Monmouth Road, Abergavenny, NP7 9SP.*
Grades: WTB 3 Star
Tel: **01873 854494** (also fax no)
Mrs Haynes.
D: £17.50-£20.00 **S:** £17.50-£20.00.
Open: All Year
Beds: 1F 1D
Maes Glas is a detached bungalow, within easy walking distance of town centre, railway and bus stations. It has a 3 star rating with the Welsh Tourist Board. Your host, Mrs Kathy Haynes, will provide you with a very warm welcome

---

D = Price range per person sharing in a double room

The Guest House & Mansel Restaurant, 2 Oxford Street, Abergavenny, Monmouthshire, NP7 5RP.
Actual grid ref: SO303147
Near bus, railway station, town; excellent accommodation, choice of breakfast
Grades: WTB 2 Star
Tel: **01873 854823**
Mrs Cook.
D: £16.00-£19.00 **S:** £19.50-£27.00.
Open: Mar to Dec
Beds: 3F 6D 6T 2S
Baths: 3 Sh
🛇 (6) 🅿 (10) 🗗 🕸 🎄 🖿 🎟 🛡 ✦ 🐾

Kings Head Hotel, Cross Street, Abergavenny, NP7 5EW.
C16th coaching inn in centre of picturesque market town
Grades: WTB 2 Star
Tel: **01873 853575**
D: £22.50-£25.00 **S:** £25.00-£25.00.
Open: All Year
Beds: 2D 2T 1S
Baths: 4 En 1 Sh
🗗 🗙 🎄 🖿 🎟

Milfield, Old Monmouth Road, Abergavenny, NP7 8BU.
Newly built house. Fantastic views of town and surrounding mountains
Grades: WTB 3 Star
Tel: **01873 858095**
Mr & Mrs Trinder.
D: £20.00-£20.00.
Open: All Year (not Xmas)
Beds: 1F 1D 1T
🛇 🅿 (5) ⚡ 🎄 🖿 🎟 ✦ 🐾

Cwmyoy 22

National Grid Ref: SO2923

Gaer Farm, Cwmyoy, Abergavenny, Monmouthshire, NP7 7NE.
Actual grid ref: SO298219
Special views and breakfasts. Remote hilltop farm. Llanthony Valley
Tel: **01873 890345** Mrs Judd.
D: £20.00 **S:** £24.00.
Open: All Year (not Xmas)
Beds: 3D
Baths: 3 En
🛇 (10) 🅿 (4) ⚡ 🗗 🕸 🎄 🖿 🎟 🛡 ✦

Llanthony 23

National Grid Ref: SO2827

The Half Moon, Llanthony, Abergavenny, Monmouthshire, NP7 7NN.
Actual grid ref: SO286278
C17th, beautiful countryside. Serves good food and real ales
Tel: **01873 890611**
Mrs Smith.
D: £17.50 **S:** £20.00.
Open: All Year (not Xmas)
Beds: 1F 4D 2T
Baths: 2 Sh
🛇 🅿 (5) 🗗 🕸 🗙 🎄 🖿 🎟 🛡 ✦

Capel-y-ffin 24

National Grid Ref: SO2531

▲ **Capel-y-Ffin Youth Hostel**, Capel-y-Ffin, Abergavenny, Monmouthshire, NP7 7NP.
Actual grid ref: SO250328
Tel: **01873 890650**
Under 18: £4.65 **Adults:** £6.80
evening meal at 7.30pm, showers, central heating, shop, no smoking
Old hill farm set in 40-acre grounds on mountainside in Brecon Beacons National Park

The Grange, Capel-y-Ffin, Abergavenny, NP7 7NP.
Actual grid ref: SO251315
Small Victorian guest house situated in the beautiful Black Mountains
Grades: WTB 1 Star
Tel: **01873 890215**
Mrs Griffiths. Fax no: 01873 890157
D: £22.50-£23.00 **S:** £22.50-£23.00.
Open: Easter to Nov
Beds: 1F 1D 1T 1S
Baths: 3 En
🛇 (6) 🅿 (10) 🗗 🕸 🗙 🎄 🖿 🛡 🎟 🛡 ✦ 🐾

Llanigon 25

National Grid Ref: SO2139

🏮 🍴 Black Lion

The Old Post Office, Llanigon, Hay-on-Wye, Hereford, HR3 5QA.
A very special find in Black Mountains, superb vegetarian breakfast
Grades: WTB 3 Star GH
Tel: **01497 820008** Mrs Webb.
D: £17.00-£25.00 **S:** £20.00-£45.00.
Open: All Year
Beds: 1F 1D 1T
Baths: 2 En 1 Sh
🛇 🅿 (3) ⚡ 🗗 🕸 🎄 🖿 🎟 ✦ 🐾

Llwynbrain, Llanigon, Hay-on-Wye, Hereford, HR3 5QF.
Warm, friendly family farmhouse with views of Black Mountains
Tel: **01497 847266**
D: £18.00-£25.00 **S:** £18.00-£25.00.
Open: All Year (not Xmas)
Beds: 2F 1S **Baths:** 1 Sh
🛇 🅿 (6) 🗗 🕸 🖿 🎟 🛡 ✦ 🐾

Cusop 26

National Grid Ref: SO2341

Fernleigh, Hardwick Road, Cusop, Hay-on-Wye, Hereford, HR3 5QX.
Quiet location walking distance of the famous book town of Hay-on-Wye
Tel: **01497 820459**
Mr Hughes.
D: £15.00-£19.00 **S:** £19.00-£19.00.
Open: Easter to Oct
Beds: 2D 1S **Baths:** 1 En 1 Sh
🛇 🅿 (4) ⚡ 🗗 🗙 🎄 🖿 🎟 🛡 ✦ 🐾

Glasbury 27

National Grid Ref: SO1739

Maes-Mawr, Glasbury, Hereford, HR3 5ND.
Tel: **01497 847308**
D: £15.00-£17.00
S: £16.00-£18.00.
Open: Easter to Nov
Beds: 1F 2D 1T
Baths: 1 Sh
🛇 🅿 (5) 🗗 🕸 🎄 🖿 🎟 🛡 ✦ 🐾
10 mins' off A438 road on a farm in the countryside. Panoramic views of Black Mountains. Within easy reach of walking, canoeing, pony trekking, golf. 7 miles from Hay on Wye, well noted for book shops. 15 Brecon, 28 Hereford, 13 Builth Wells

Llyswen 28

National Grid Ref: SO1337

🏮 🍴 Griffin Inn

Lower Rhydness Bungalow, Llyswen, Brecon, Powys, LD3 0AZ.
Very comfortable centrally-heated bungalow, working farm, views into valley
Tel: **01874 754264**
Mrs Williams.
D: £16.00 **S:** £16.00.
Open: Easter to Dec
Beds: 1D 1T 1S
Baths: 1 Sh
🛇 🅿 (3) 🗗 🕸 🗙 🎄 🖿 🛡 🎟 🛡 ✦

Boughrood 29

National Grid Ref: SO1339

🏮 🍴 Bridgend Inn, Griffin Inn

Upper Middle Road, Boughrood, Brecon, Powys, LD3 0BX.
Actual grid ref: SO140392
Quietly situated, 180-year-old cottage, mountains, panorama, homely atmosphere
Grades: WTB 3 Star Farm
Tel: **01874 754407**
Mrs Kelleher.
D: £17.00-£17.00
S: £17.00-£25.00.
Open: All Year (not Xmas)
Beds: 1D 1T
Baths: 1 En 1 Pr
🛇 🅿 (3) ⚡ 🗗 🗙 🎄 🖿 🎟 🛡 ✦ 🐾

Erwood 30

National Grid Ref: SO0942

🏮 🍴 Erwood Inn, Wheelwrights' Arms

▲ **Trericket Mill Bunkhouse (Independent)**, Erwood, Builth Wells, Powys, LD2 3TQ.
Actual grid ref: SO112415
Tel: **01982 560312**
Adults: £8.00
evening meals available, self-catering facilities, showers, camping available

Trericket Mill Vegetarian Guesthouse, *Erwood, Builth Wells, Powys, LD2 3TQ.*
Actual grid ref: SO112414
Listed C19th watermill in Wye Valley, friendly and informal
Grades: WTB 2 Star GH
Tel: **01982 560312** Mr Legge.
Fax no: 01982 560768
D: £14.00-£20.00 **S:** £16.00.
Open: All Year (not Xmas)
Beds: 2F 2D 2T
Baths: 4 En 2 Sh
⛺ 🅿 (8) 🛏 ✕ 🎖 ⅲ Ⓥ 🖴 ∦ ♿

Orchard Cottage, *Erwood, Builth Wells, Powys, LD2 3EZ.*
Actual grid ref: SO096431
C18th tastefully modernised Welsh stone cottage. Gardens overlooking river
Grades: WTB 4 Star B&B,
AA 4 Diamond
Tel: **01982 560600**
Mr & Mrs Prior.
D: £17.00-£19.50 **S:** £20.00-£20.00.
Open: All Year (not Xmas)
Beds: 1F 1D 1T
Baths: 1 En 1 Sh
⛺ 🅿 (6) 🛏 🎖 ⅲ Ⓥ ∦ ♿

Hafod-y-Gareg, *Erwood, Builth Wells, Powys, LD2 3TQ.*
Actual grid ref: SO107415
Secluded medieval farmhouse in idyllic Welsh hillside locality. Tranquillity personified
Tel: **01982 560400**
D: £13.50-£17.50 **S:** £13.50-£17.50.
Open: All Year (not Xmas)
Beds: 1F 2D 1T **Baths:** 3 En
⛺ 🅿 (6) 🛏 🐾 ✕ 🎖 ⅲ Ⓥ 🖴 ∦ ♿

Aberedw 31

National Grid Ref: SO0847

🍽 🍺 Seven Stars

Court Farm, *Aberedw, Builth Wells, Powys, LD2 3UP.*
Actual grid ref: SO091479
Strictly non-smoking, peaceful, picturesque. Hill-walking, birds and wildlife in abundance
Tel: **01982 560277** Mr Davies.
D: £17.00-£19.00 **S:** £18.00-£20.00.
Open: Easter to Nov
Beds: 2D 1S **Baths:** 1 En 1 Pr 1 Sh
⤢ 🛏 🎖 ⅲ Ⓥ ♿

Builth Wells 32

National Grid Ref: SO0350

🍽 🍺 Prince Llewelyn Inn, Llanclwedd Arms, Greyhound Hotel

Bron Wye, *Church Street, Builth Wells, Powys, LD2 3BS.*
Actual grid ref: SO039512
Christian family-run guest house. Overlooking River Wye
Grades: WTB 2 Star
Tel: **01982 553587** Mrs Wiltshire.
D: £17.00-£17.00 **S:** £17.00-£17.00.
Open: All Year
Beds: 1F 2D 1T 2S **Baths:** 6 En
⛺ 🅿 (7) ⤢ 🛏 🐾 🎖 ⅲ Ⓥ 🖴 ∦ ♿

Dollynwydd Farm, *Builth Wells, Powys, LD2 3RZ.*
Grades: WTB 2 Star
Tel: **01982 553660** Mrs Williams.
D: £18.00-£20.00 **S:** £18.00-£20.00.
Open: All Year (not Xmas)
Beds: 1D 2T 2S **Baths:** 1 En 2 Sh
⛺ (14) 🅿 (6) ⤢ 🛏 ✕ ⅲ 🖴 ∦ ♿
C17th farmhouse lying beneath Eppyut hills. Superb area for walking, bird-watching within easy distance, Breacon Beacons, Elan Valley, Hay-on-Wye, bookshops, very comfortable in quiet area, ample parking, lockup garage for bikes. 1 mile Butler Wells, B4520 just left on our farm lane

Pencerring Gardens Hotel, *Llandrindod Road, Builth Wells, Powys, LD2 3TF.*
Country house retaining many unusual features in its own grounds
Grades: WTB 2 Star, AA 2 Star
Tel: **01982 553226**
Fax no: 01982 552347
D: £25.00-£40.00 **S:** £35.00-£75.00.
Open: All Year
Beds: 4F 7T 5D 4S **Baths:** 20 En
⛺ 🅿 ⤢ 🛏 🐾 🎖 ⅲ Ⓥ 🖴

The Cedar Guest House, *Hay Road, Builth Wells, Powys, LD2 3AR.*
On A470 outside market town of Builth Wells in the heart of Wales
Tel: **01982 553356** Mr Morris.
D: £20.00 **S:** £22.50.
Open: All Year
Beds: 1F 1D 3T 2S
Baths: 5 En 1 Sh
⛺ 🅿 (10) ⤢ 🛏 🐾 ✕ 🎖 ⅲ Ⓥ 🖴 ∦ ♿

Llanddewi'r Cwm 33

National Grid Ref: SO0348

🍽 🍺 Griffin Inn

Newhall, *Llanddewi'r Cwm, Builth Wells, Powys, LD2 3RX.*
Actual grid ref: SO034487
Farmhouse overlooking Wye Valley, comfortable accommodation, ensuite rooms
Tel: **01982 552483** Mrs James.
D: £18.00 **S:** £18.00.
Open: All Year (not Xmas)
Beds: 1F 3D 1T **Baths:** 3 Pr 2 Sh
⛺ 🅿 (6) 🛏 ✕ 🎖 ⅲ Ⓥ

Cilmery 34

National Grid Ref: SO0051

🍽 🍺 Prince Llewelyn Inn

Halcyon House, *Cilmery, Builth Wells, Powys, LD2 3NU.*
Actual grid ref: SO003514
Jacuzzi, snooker, views, hospitality, inn; cows, sheep; self-catering, camping
Tel: **01982 552838** Mr Johnson.
Fax no: 01982 551090
D: £16.00-£20.00 **S:** £18.00-£22.00.
Open: All Year
Beds: 2F 1S **Baths:** 2 Sh
⛺ 🅿 (7) 🛏 🐾 ✕ 🎖 ⅲ ♿ Ⓥ 🖴 ∦ ♿

Cwmbach 35

National Grid Ref: SO0254

Rhydfelin, *Cwmbach, Builth Wells, Powys, LD2 3RT.*
1725 cosy stone guest house, restaurant and bar
Grades: WTB 3 Star
Tel: **01982 552493**
Moyes.
Fax no: 01982 55382
D: £18.00-£22.00
S: £26.00-£44.00.
Open: All Year (not Xmas)
Beds: 1F 2D 1T
Baths: 1 En 1 Sh
⛺ 🅿 (12) ⤢ 🛏 🐾 ✕ 🎖 ⅲ Ⓥ 🖴 ♿

Western Route to Machynlleth

Llanwrtyd Wells is a pretty spa town, developed in the eighteenth century around the sulphur spring named Ffynon Droellwyd. Mr Green at The Neuadd Arms is the organiser of the world famous 'Man v. Horse' race.

Strata Florida Abbey is the very impressive ruin of a twelfth-century Cistercian foundation. Although a victim of the Dissolution, there is a fair amount to see, including a great Norman arch at the western end.

At **Devil's Bridge** three stone bridges, the earliest reputedly built by the Knights Templars, are set against the stunning backdrop of the Mynach Falls.

It was at **Machynlleth** in 1404 that Owain Glyndwr, leader of the resistance to English rule, summoned a parliament and proclaimed himself Prince of Wales. The Parliament House contains themed displays. The town also hosts the Celtica exhibition, with a reconstructioin Celtic settlement and audio-visual displays. The Y Tabernacl building houses a cultural centre which includes the Wales Museum of Modern Art.

Llanafan-fawr   36

National Grid Ref: SN9655

🍴🍺 Red Lion

*Gwern-Y-Mynach, Llanafan-fawr,
Builth Wells, Powys, LD2 3PN.*
Lovely walks from farm near Red
Lion Inn. Working sheep farm
Tel: **01597 860256** Mrs Davies.
D: £12.00 **S:** £12.00.
Open: All Year
Beds: 1F 1S **Baths:** 1 Pr 1 Sh
🛇🅿️🗪🏧🍴✕🍷🎞️Ⅴ🛈

Newbridge on Wye   37

National Grid Ref: SO0158

*Lluest Newydd, Llysdinam,
Newbridge on Wye, Llandrindod
Wells, Powys, LD1 6ND.*
Luxury remote farmhouse. Ideal
for walking and birdwatching. Elan
Valley close by
Grades: WTB 4 Star
Tel: **01597 860435**
D: £18.00-£22.00 **S:** £22.00-£26.00.
Open: All Year
Beds: 1F 1T 2D **Baths:** 2 En 1 Pr
🛇🅿️(6)🖚🗪✕🍷🎞️Ⅴ🛈🚲

Disserth   38

National Grid Ref: SO0358

🍴🍺 Drover's Arms

*Disserth Mill, Disserth, Builth
Wells, Powys, LD2 3TN.*
Actual grid ref: SO040551
A sun trap by a stream
Grades: WTB 2 Star
Tel: **01982 553217**
Mrs Worts.
D: £17.00-£20.00
S: £18.00-£20.00.
Open: Easter to Oct
Beds: 1T 1S
Baths: 1 En
🛇🅿️(4)🐕🏧🎞️Ⅴ🛈🚲

Pay B&Bs by
cash or cheque and
be prepared to
pay up front.

Howey   39

National Grid Ref: SO0558

🍴🍺 Three Wells, Drover's Arms

*Holly Farm, Howey, Llandrindod
Wells, Powys, LD1 5PP.*
Actual grid ref: SO050589
Comfortable old farmhouse, dates
back to Tudor times, bedrooms
have lovely views of countryside
Grades: WTB 3 Star Farm,
AA 4 Diamond
Tel: **01597 822402**
Mrs Jones.
D: £18.00-£22.00
S: £22.00-£24.00.
Open: All Year (not Xmas)
Beds: 1F 2D 2T
Baths: 3 En 2 Sh
🛇🅿️(6)🗪✕🏧🎞️Ⅴ🛈🚲

*Brynhir Farm, Chapel Road,
Howey, Llandrindod Wells, Powys,
LD1 5PB.*
Actual grid ref: SO067586
Remote farm, 1 mile off A483 - 4
star accommodation, good walks
Grades: WTB 4 Star,
AA 4 Diamond
Tel: **01597 822425** (also fax no)
Mrs Nixon.
D: £22.00-£25.00.
S: £23.00-£26.00.
Open: All Year
Beds: 3F 1D 1T 1S
Baths: 4 En 1 Pr 1 Sh
🛇🅿️(10)🖚🗪🏧✕🍷🎞️♿Ⅴ🛈🚲

*Acorn Court, Chapel Road,
Howey, Llandrindod Wells, Powys,
LD1 5PB.*
A beautiful country house in
peaceful unspoilt countryside. An
ideal setting for a romantic break
Tel: **01597 823543** (also fax no)
Mr & Mrs Bufton.
D: £22.00
S: £25.00.
Open: All Year (not Xmas)
Beds: 2T 1D
Baths: 3 En
🛇(10)🅿️(10)🖚🗪✕🏧🎞️Ⅴ🛈

Llanyre   40

National Grid Ref: SO0462

🍴🍺 Bell Inn

*Highbury Farm, Llanyre,
Llandrindod Wells, Powys, LD1 6EA.*
Actual grid ref: SO044628
Peaceful spacious Victorian
farmhouse with short farm trail
excellent food
Grades: WTB 3 Star
Tel: **01597 822716** (also fax no)
Mrs Evans.
D: £18.00-£21.00
S: £21.00-£24.00.
Open: Mar to Nov
Beds: 1F 2D
Baths: 2 En 1 Pr
🛇(1)🅿️(3)🖚🗪✕🏧🎞️Ⅴ🛈🚲

60

Ffestiniog 71

A487   Maentwrog 72   70

74 Criccieth   73   Gellilydan
Porthmadog

Trawsfynydd 69

Harlech
64

Llandanwg
63

A470

Dyffryn Ardudwy
62

Llanaber
61   Brithdir 67
Barmouth   Dolgellau 68
60

59   Islaw'r Dref
58

Km   5   10
Miles   5

Arthog   A487

Corris
66

Llanegryn 57
58 Bryncrug   Llanwrin
65

CARDIGAN BAY

Pennal   47   A489
54
55   Machynlleth
Tywyn

40

20

SH
00
SN

Greenglades, *Llanyre, Llandrindod Wells, Powys, LD1 6EA.*
Beautiful country house in tranquil setting near village inn
Grades: WTB 4 Star
Tel: 01597 822950
D: £18.00-£22.00 **S:** £20.00-£24.00.
Open: All Year (not Xmas)
Beds: 1F 1D 1T **Baths:** 2 En
🛇 🛏 (3) ⏚🖵🏠�🕹 🎹 Ⓥ ✦ 🚲

Llandrindod Wells   41

National Grid Ref: SO0561

🍴🍺 Builder's Arms, Llanerch Inn, Three Wells, Drover's Arms

Builders Arms, *Crossgates, Llandrindod Wells, Powys, LD1 6RB.*
Family run village inn. Garden, patio, large car park
Grades: WTB 2 Star
Tel: 01597 851235
D: £17.50-£17.50 **S:** £19.50-£19.50.
Open: All Year
Beds: 1D 1T **Baths:** 1 En
🛇 🅿 🏠🌙🕹 🎹 Ⓥ 🚲

Llanerch Inn, *Llanerch Lane, Llandrindod Wells, Powys, LD1 6BG.*
C16th inn with relaxed atmosphere
Tel: 01597 822086 Mr Leach.
Fax no: 01597 824618
D: £25.00 **S:** £27.50.
Open: All Year
Beds: 2F 5D 3T 2S
Baths: 11 En 1 Pr
🛇 🅿 🏠🌙🕹 🎹 Ⓥ 🛊✦

The Cottage, *Spa Road, Llandrindod Wells, Powys, LD1 5EY.*
Most unusual Edwardian Arts & Crafts house with welcoming friendly atmosphere
Tel: 01597 825435 (also fax no)
Mr Taylor.
D: £17.00 **S:** £18.00.
Open: All Year (not Xmas)
Beds: 1F 2D 4T **Baths:** 4 En 1 Sh
🛇 🖵🕹 🎹 Ⓥ

Llanwrthwl   42

National Grid Ref: SN9763

🍴🍺 Vulcan Arms

Dyffryn Farm, *Llanwrthwl, Llandrindod Wells, Powys, LD1 6NU.*
Actual grid ref: SN972645
Grades: WTB 2 Star Farm
Tel: 01597 811017 Mrs Tyler.
Fax no: 01597 810609
D: £20.00-£22.00 **S:** £20.00-£22.00.
Open: Mar to Oct
Beds: 1D 1T 1S
Baths: 1 En 1 Pr 1 Sh
🛇 (5) 🅿 (6) ⏚🖵🏠🌙🕹 🛊✦ 🚲
Idyllically situated above the Upper Wye valley, near the Elan Lakes. Wonderful hillwalking, cycling, birdwatching. Ideal touring centre. Enjoy our warm hospitality and wholesome country cooking. Relax in the delightful Hayloft lounge - unwind in this lovely old C17th farmhouse

Rhayader   43

National Grid Ref: SN9768

🍴🍺 Bear's Head, Crown Inn, Triangle Inn

Bryncoed, *Dark Lane, Rhayader, Powys, LD6 5DA.*
Tel: 01597 811082
D: £14.50-£20.00 **S:** £15.00-£21.00.
Open: All Year
Beds: 3F 2D 2T
Baths: 1 En 2 Pr 1 Sh
🛇 🅿 (4) ⏚🖵🏠🌙🍴🕹 🎹 Ⓥ 🛊✦ 🚲
Victorian house set in 0.33 acre, originally built for local doctor. Panoramic hill views, close to leisure centre, large swimming pool, fitness facilities. 40 mins to coast. Stair chair for less able. Off-road parking. Special deal senior cits & families

Gigrin Farm, *Rhayader, Powys, LD6 5BL.*
Actual grid ref: SN980677
Superb views; working farm, nature trail, feeding red kites every day
Grades: WTB 2 Star
Tel: 01597 810243 Mrs Powell.
Fax no: 01597 810357
D: £16.00-£17.50 **S:** £17.50-£20.00.
Open: All Year
Beds: 2D
Baths: 1 Sh
🛇 (5) 🅿 (3) ⏚🖵🕹 🎹 Ⓥ

Brynteg, *East Street, Rhayader, Powys, LD6 5EA.*
Comfortable Edwardian guest house, overlooking hills and gardens
Grades: WTB 2 Star
Tel: 01597 810052 Mrs Lawrence.
D: £16.00-£16.00 **S:** £16.00-£16.00.
Open: All Year (not Xmas)
Beds: 2D 1T 1S
Baths: 3 En 1 Pr
🛇 🅿 (4) 🖵🕹 🎹 🛊 🚲

Brynafon Country House Hotel, *South Street, Rhayader, Powys, LD6 5BL.*
Grades: WTB 2 Star
Tel: 01597 810735 Mrs Collins.
Fax no: 01597 810111
D: £18.00-£30.00 **S:** £30.00.
Open: All Year
Beds: 2F 11D 9T
Baths: 14 En 8 Sh
🛇 🅿 ⏚🖵🏠🌙🍴🕹 🎹 ⓖ Ⓥ 🛊✦ 🚲
A former Victorian workhouse built in 1876, this impressive building is now a comfortable, relaxed, family-run Hotel. Set amid glorious hills and mountains near Rhayader and the beauiful Elan Valley with a rare red kite feeding centre next door

---

S = Price range for a single person in a room

Beili Neuadd, *Rhayader, Powys, LD5 5NS.*
Actual grid ref: SN994698
Award-winning accommodation in farmhouse - secluded position with stunning views
Grades: WTB 3 Star
Tel: 01597 810211 (also fax no)
Mrs Edwards.
D: £19.50-£21.00 **S:** £19.50.
Open: All Year (not Xmas)
Beds: 2D 1T 1S
Baths: 2 En 2 Pr
🛇 (8) 🅿 🏠🌙🍴🕹 🎹 ⓖ Ⓥ 🛊✦ 🚲

The Horseshoe Guest House, *Church Street, Rhayader, Powys, LD6 5AT.*
Actual grid ref: SN969680
Spacious Welsh stone house. Beams, log fire. Member of 'Taste of Wales'
Grades: WTB 3 Star GH
Tel: 01597 810982 (also fax no)
Mrs Stubbs.
D: £18.00-£19.00 **S:** £18.00-£18.00.
Open: All Year (not Xmas)
Beds: 2D 1T 1S
Baths: 2 En 1 Sh
🛇 🅿 (6) 🏠🌙🍴🕹 🎹 Ⓥ 🛊✦ 🚲

Liverpool House, *East House, Rhayader, Powys, LD6 5EA.*
Large pleasant double-fronted guest house. Private, secure car park on premises
Tel: 01597 810706
Mrs Griffiths.
Fax no: 01597 810964
D: £14.50 **S:** £16.50.
Open: All Year (not Xmas)
Beds: 2F 5D 1S
Baths: 7 En 1 Sh
🛇 🅿 (6) 🏠🌠🕹 🎹 Ⓥ

Llanidloes   44

National Grid Ref: SN9584

🍴🍺 The Unicorn

Lloyds, *Cambrian Place, Llanidloes, Powys, SY18 6BX.*
Actual grid ref: SN955844
Long-established Victorian hotel in centre of attractive market town
Grades: WTB 2 Star
Tel: 01686 412284
Mr Lines.
Fax no: 01686 412666
D: £22.00-£22.00
S: £17.50-£29.50.
Open: Mar to Jan
Beds: 3D 2T 4S **Baths:** 6 En 1 Sh
🛇 🖵🍴🕹 🎹 Ⓥ ✦ 🚲

Gorphwysfa Guest House, *Westgate Street, Llanidloes, Powys, SY18 6HL.*
Actual grid ref: SN954845
Large Victorian house & garden
Tel: 01686 413356
Mrs Lines.
D: £14.00 **S:** £14.00.
Open: All Year
Beds: 1F 1D 1T 1S **Baths:** 2 Sh
🛇 (1) 🅿 (5) ⏚🏠🍴🕹 🎹 🛊

Dyffryn Glyn, Llanidloes, Powys,
SY18 6NE.
Actual grid ref: SN930865
Homely atmosphere. Beautiful
scenery. Excellent food. Ideal
touring and walking
Tel: **01686 412129** Mrs Evans.
D: £16.00 **S:** £18.00.
Open: Easter to Dec
Beds: 1T 2D **Baths:** 1 En 1 Sh
⏲ ᴘ (4) ⌷ ✕ ♨ ▥ Ⅴ 🛇 ∅ ⌁

Van 45

National Grid Ref: SN9587

⋈ ◫ Star Inn, Red Lion

Esgairmaen, Van, Llanidloes,
Powys, SY18 6NT.
Actual grid ref: SN925904
Modern comfortable farmhouse
Tel: **01686 430272**
D: £17.00-£19.00 **S:** £17.00-£19.00.
Open: Easter to Oct
Beds: 1F 1D **Baths:** 2 En
⏲ (1) ᴘ (4) ⌁ ⌷ 🛏 ✕ ♨ ▥ Ⅴ 🛇 ∅ ⌁

Staylittle 46

National Grid Ref: SN8892

⋈ ◫ Star Inn

Maesmedrisiol Farm, Staylittle,
Llanbrynmair, Powys, SY19 7BN.
Actual grid ref: SN8894
Friendly, comfortable, stone-built
farmhouse
Tel: **01650 521494** Mrs Anwyl.
D: £15.00-£16.00 **S:** £15.00-£16.00.
Open: Easter to Nov
Beds: 1F 1D 1T **Baths:** 2 Pr
⏲ (1) ᴘ (20) ⌁ ⌷ ✕ ♨ ▥ Ⅴ 🛇 ∅ ⌁

Western Route through Snowdonia

From **Tywyn** you can take
a steam train on the Talyllyn
Railway to Abergynolwyn.

Barmouth is a pleasant
seaside resort where you can
find the Ty Gwyn Museum, a
museum on the Tudors.

Harlech Castle is a World
Heritage Site with a
spectacular clifftop location
overlooking the sea. Built by
Edward I at the time of the
conquest of Wales in the late
thirteenth century, it was taken
by Owain Glyndwr in 1404.
The future Henry VII was
besieged here for seven years
during the Wars of the Roses.
The most impressive feature is
the gatehouse, with its two
huge half-round towers.

Machynlleth 47

National Grid Ref: SH7400

⋈ ◫ White Lion, Black Lion, Glyndwyr Hotel,
White Horse, The Wynnastay, Skinner's Arms

Maenllwyd, Newtown Road,
Machynlleth, Powys, SY20 8EY.
Actual grid ref: SH752009
Home from home, within walking
distance all amenities, safe parking
Grades: WTB 3 Star GH,
AA 3 Diamond
Tel: **01654 702928** (also fax no)
Mr Vince.
D: £19.00-£22.00
S: £25.00-£25.00.
Open: All Year (not Xmas)
Beds: 1F 4D 3T
Baths: 8 En
⏲ ᴘ (10) ⌁ ⌷ 🛏 ♨ ▥ Ⅴ 🛇 ∅ ⌁

Awelon, Heol Powys, Machynlleth,
Powys, SY20 8AY.
Centrally situated, small, comfort-
able private house. Warm welcome
Grades: WTB 2 Star
Tel: **01654 702047**
Ms Williams.
D: £16.00-£17.00 **S:** £16.00-£17.50.
Open: All Year (not Xmas)
Beds: 1T 1S
Baths: 1 Sh
⏲ (2) ⌁ 🛏 ▥ 🛇 ∅

Gwelfryn, 6 Green Fields,
Machynlleth, Powys, SY20 8DR.
Quiet but central near alternative
energy centre, Celtica and RSPB
Grades: WTB 2 Star
Tel: **01654 702532**
D: £17.00-£19.50 **S:** £17.00.
Open: Easter to Oct
Beds: 1D 1T 1S
Baths: 1 En 1 Pr
⏲ ⌁ ⌷ 🛏 ♨ ▥ Ⅴ 🛇 ∅ ⌁

Cwmdylluan Forge, Machynlleth,
Powys, SY20 8RZ.
Actual grid ref: SH764000
Modern riverside bungalow, rooms
overlook lovely garden and river
Grades: WTB 3 Star
Tel: **01654 702684** Hughes.
Fax no: 01654 700133
D: £15.50-£17.50
S: £16.50-£18.00.
Open: All Year
Beds: 1D 1T 1S
Baths: 2 Pr 2 Sh
⏲ (5) ᴘ (5) ⌷ 🛏 ✕ ♨ ▥ & Ⅴ 🛇 ∅ ⌁

Pendre Guest House, Maengwym
Street, Machynlleth, Powys,
SY20 8EF.
Actual grid ref: SH748007
Georgian house, in historic market,
Machynlleth, warm friendly atmos-
phere
Tel: **01654 702088**
Ms Petrie.
D: £17.00 **S:** £24.00.
Open: All Year (not Xmas)
Beds: 2F 1D 1T
Baths: 2 Pr 2 Sh
⏲ ᴘ (3) ⌷ 🛏 ♨ ▥ Ⅴ 🛇 ∅

Llangammarch Wells 48

National Grid Ref: SN9347

Irfon View, Llangammarch Wells,
Powys, LD4 4BT.
Clean comfortable accommodation
with homely atmosphere
Grades: WTB 2 Star
Tel: **01591 620554** (also fax no)
Mrs Jones.
D: £15.50-£15.50.
Open: All Year
Beds: 2D 1T
Baths: 1 Sh
⏲ ᴘ (2) ⌁ ⌷ 🛏 ♨ ▥ Ⅴ 🛇 ∅ ⌁

Llanwrtyd Wells 49

National Grid Ref: SN8746

⋈ ◫ Stonecroft Inn, New Inn

▲ *Stonecroft Hostel*
(Independent), Dolecoed Road,
Llanwrtyd Wells, Powys.
Actual grid ref: SN878467
Tel: **01591 610332 Adults:** £8.00
self-catering facilities, central
heating

Carlton House Hotel, Dolycoed
Road, Llanwrtyd Wells, Powys,
LD5 4SN.
Edwardian restaurant with rooms.
Excellent dining, comfortable
rooms, warm welcome
Grades: AA 2 Star
Tel: **01591 610248** Dr Gilchrist.
Fax no: 01591 610242
D: £30.00-£35.00 **S:** £30.00-£40.00.
Open: All Year (not Xmas)
Beds: 1F 4D 1T 1S
Baths: 5 En 2 Pr
⏲ ⌷ 🛏 ✕ ♨ ▥ Ⅴ 🛇

Haulwen, Beulah Road, Llanwrtyd
Wells, Powys, LD5 4RF.
Actual grid ref: SN881468
Grades: WTB 2 Star
Tel: **01591 610449** (also fax no)
D: £15.00-£20.00 **S:** £15.00-£20.00.
Open: All Year
Beds: 1D 1S
Baths: 1 Sh
⌁ 🛏 ♨ ▥ & Ⅴ 🛇 ∅ ⌁
Small & friendly, comfortable
rooms, hairdryers, toiletries, robes,
electric radio alarms wtb in rooms.
Choice for breakfast. Red kite
country, excellent area for cycling,
walking, pony trekking, birds &
nature. Smallest town in Britain,
home of unusual events

Oakfield House, Dol-y-coed Road,
Llanwrtyd Wells, Powys, LD5 4RA.
Comfortable Edwardian house in
Britain's smallest town. Red kite
country
Grades: WTB 3 Star
Tel: **01591 610605**
D: £17.00-£17.00 **S:** £17.00-£20.00.
Open: Easter to Oct
Beds: 1D 1T 1S
Baths: 2 Sh
⏲ (5) ᴘ (1) ⌁ ⌷ 🛏 ♨ ▥ Ⅴ 🛇 ∅ ⌁

Dolgoch   50

National Grid Ref: SN8056

▲ *Dolgoch Youth Hostel,*
Dolgoch, Tregaron, Cardiganshire,
SY25 6NR.
Actual grid ref: SH806561
Tel: 01974 298680
Under 18: £4.65
Adults: £6.80
self-catering facilities, showers,
shop, no smoking
Remote farmhouse in the wild and
lonely Tywi Valley providing
simple yet spacious mountain hut
type accommodation. No electrici-
ty. Open fire, gas lighting. Twm
Shon Cattis Cave and Llyn Brianne
Reservoir nearby

Cwmystwyth   51

National Grid Ref: SN7874

🍴🍺 Miners' Arms

Hafod Lodge, Cwmystwyth,
Aberystwyth, Ceredigion, SY23 4AD.
Actual grid ref: SN784742
Grades: WTB 3 Star B&B
Tel: 01974 282247
Mr & Mrs Davis.
D: £18.50-£24.00
S: £18.50-£24.00.
Open: All Year
Beds: 1D 1T
Baths: 1 En 1 Pr
🅿 (6) ⚲🗇🛏🌰🕎🎨Ⅴ🗸✦🚲
Picturesque, peaceful location,
ideal for touring river valleys,
lakes, mountains and coast. Kite
Country. Walkers and birdwatchers
paradise. Welcoming, comfortable
and very well-appointed. Guest
lounge with open-fire. Traditional
or vegetarian breakfasts. Transport
to excellent evening meal

Devil's Bridge   52

National Grid Ref: SN7376

🍴🍺 Hafway Inn

Mount Pleasant, Devil's Bridge,
Aberystwyth, Ceredigion, SY23 4QY.
Actual grid ref: SN736769
Grades: WTB 3 Star GH
Tel: 01970 890219
Mr & Mrs Connell.
Fax no: 01970 890239
D: £21.00-£23.00
S: £21.00-£29.00.
Open: All Year (not Xmas)
Beds: 2D 2T
Baths: 3 En 1 Pr
🛏 (12) 🅿 (4) ⚲🗇🗙🌰🕎🎨Ⅴ🗸✦🚲
Lose the crowds amidst stunning
scenery where red kites soar. Relax
in our comfortable lounge, then
wine and dine by candlelight.
Guests write 'wonderful hospitality,
excellent food' and keep returning.
Ideal location for birdwatching,
walking or visiting many
surrounding attractions

Ponterwyd   53

National Grid Ref: SN7480

The George Borrow Hotel,
Ponterwyd, Aberystwyth,
Ceredigion, SY23 3AD.
Grades: WTB 2 Star Hotel,
AA 2 Star
Tel: 01970 890230
Fax no: 01970 890587
D: £23.00-£25.00
S: £23.00-£25.00.
Open: All Year (not Xmas)
Beds: 2F 3D 2T 2S
Baths: 9 En
🛏 🅿 (40) 🗇🛏🗙🌰🕎🎨Ⅴ🗸✦🚲
Famous old hotel set in beautiful
countryside, overlooking Eagle
Falls and the Rheidol Gorge. 3
miles Devils Bridge, 12 miles
Aberystwyth. An ideal centre to
explore mid-Wales. Good fishing,
birdwatching and walking. Home
made food and fine beer, log fires
and a friendly welcome

Pennal   54

National Grid Ref: SH6900

Marchlyn, Aberdovey Road,
Pennal, Machynlleth, SY20 9YS.
Quiet location near Aberdovey on a
Welsh-speaking working farm
Tel: 01654 702018
D: £17.00-£20.00 **S:** £17.00-£20.00.
Open: All Year
Beds: 1F 4D 1T 1S
Baths: 2 En 1 Pr

Tywyn   55

National Grid Ref: SH5800

🍴🍺 Peniarth Arms, Tredegar Arms

Greenfield Hotel & Restaurant,
High Street, Tywyn, LL36 9AD.
Small friendly licensed hotel. Close
Talyllyn Steam and Main Railway
Grades: AA 1 Star, RAC 1 Star
Tel: 01654 710354 (also fax no)
Mrs Jenkins.
D: £16.00-£18.50
S: £17.00-£19.50.
Open: Feb to Dec
Beds: 2F 3D 3T
Baths: 6 Pr 1 Sh
🛏🗇🗙🌰🕎Ⅴ🗸

Hendy Farm, Tywyn, LL36 9RU.
Actual grid ref: SH597015
Comfortable farmhouse near farm
and beach. Own halt on Talyllyn
railway
Grades: WTB 3 Star Farm
Tel: 01654 710457 (also fax no)
Mrs Lloyd-Jones.
D: £18.00-£24.00
S: £22.00-£27.00.
Open: Easter to Oct
Beds: 2D 1T
Baths: 2 En 1 Pr
🛏🅿⚲🗇🛏🌰🕎Ⅴ✦🚲

Eastern Route through Snowdonia

On the eastern route out of
Machynlleth, the **Centre for
Alternative Technology** is a
self-sufficient community
started in the 1970s on the
site of a disused slate quarry,
where you can see renew-
able energy generation
(wind, water and solar power)
in action, as well as organic
gardens and numerous other
attractions.

Dolgellau was the site of a
Quaker community; entry to
the Quaker Heritage Centre is
free. To the north of town, the
Gwynfynydd Gold Centre and
Mine is the only working gold
mine open to the public.

Bryncrug   56

National Grid Ref: SH6003

Dolgoch Falls Hotel, Dolgoch,
Bryncrug, Tywyn, Gwynedd,
LL36 9UW.
Actual grid ref: SH650046
Grades: WTB 2 Star
Tel: 01654 782258 Mr Lycett.
Fax no: 01654 782209
D: £25.00-£30.00 **S:** £25.00.
Open: Mar to Dec
Beds: 3D 2T 1S **Baths:** 4 En 1 Sh
🛏 (12) 🅿 (50) 🗇🛏🗙🌰🕎🎨Ⅴ🗸✦🚲
One of Wales' most comfortable
family-run hotels, set at the foot of
magnificent waterfalls and ravine.
Excellent home cooking is served
in the 600-year-old restaurant.
Whether exploring or just relaxing,
this peaceful little haven awaits
your pleasure

Llanegryn   57

National Grid Ref: SH6005

Cefn Coch Guest House,
Llanegryn, Tywyn, LL36 9SD.
Actual grid ref: SH592050
Grades: WTB 3 Star
Tel: 01654 712193 (also fax no)
Mrs Sylvester.
D: £20.00-£23.00 **S:** £20.00-£28.00.
Open: Mar to Oct
Beds: 2D 3T **Baths:** 3 En 2 Sh
🛏 (10) 🅿 (11) ⚲🗇🛏🌰🕎🎨Ⅴ🗸✦🚲
Cefn Coch is a traditional Welsh
coaching inn, carefully restored to
modern comfortable standards;
enjoy the garden and the spectac-
ular views over the Dysynni Valley;
after discovering the many local
attractions, relax and unwind with
real home cooked food

Islaw'r Dref 58

National Grid Ref: SH6815

▲ *Kings (Dolgellau) Youth Hostel*, Islaw'r Dref, Penmaenpool, Dolgellau, Gwynedd, *LL40 1TB*.
Actual grid ref: SH683161
Tel: **01341 422392**
Under 18: £5.65 **Adults:** £8.35
evening meal at 7.00pm,
self-catering facilities, grounds
available for games, shop, parking,
camping available, no smoking
*Traditional hostel set in idyllic
wooded valley, with magnificent
views up to Cader Idris and Rhinog
mountain ranges*

▲ *Caban Cader Idris
(Independent Hostel)*, Islaw'r
Dref, Dolgellau, *LL40 1TS*.
Actual grid ref: SH682169
Tel: **01248 600478 / 01766 762588**
Adults: £4.00
self-catering facilities, showers

Pay B&Bs by cash or
cheque and be prepared
to pay up front.

All cycleways are
popular: you are
well-advised to
book ahead

Arthog 59

National Grid Ref: SH6414

🍴🛏 Fairbourne Hotel

Graig Wen Guest House, Arthog, *LL39 1BQ*.
Grades: WTB 2 Star
Tel: **01341 250900** Mrs Ameson.
Fax no: 01341 250482
D: £17.00-£19.00 **S:** £18.00-£20.00.
Open: All Year
Beds: 1F 4D 1T 1S
Baths: 3 En 2 Sh
🛇 (4) ℙ (20) ⅍⌖⍾✕🍽🛆🍴🚲
In 42 acres of woodland leading to
Mawddach Estuary. Spectacular
view of mountains, estuary, sea
from house. Ideal for ramblers,
cyclists, climbers, bird watchers.
Cader Mountain, lakes, beaches,
pony trekking, golf course, fishing,
stream trains nearby. Disabled
welcome

Barmouth 60

National Grid Ref: SH6115

🍴🛏 The Last

The Gables, Fford Mynach,
Barmouth, Gwynedd, *LL42 1RL*.
Actual grid ref: SH609166
Victorian house of character lovely
position near mountains - warm
welcome
Grades: WTB 2 Star
Tel: **01341 280553**
Mr & Mrs Lewis.
D: £18.00-£20.00. **S:** £18.00-£20.00.
Open: Easter to Nov
Beds: 1F 2D 1S
Baths: 2 En 1 Sh
🛇 ℙ (4) ⅍⌖⍾✕🍽🛆🍴🖭🗔🚲✦

Wavecrest Hotel, 8 Marine
Parade, Barmouth, *LL42 1NA*.
Actual grid ref: SH609160
Welcoming and relaxing *Which?*
B&B. Excellent food, wine and
whiskey
Grades: WTB 3 Star, AA 2 Star
Tel: **01341 280330** (also fax no)
Mr & Mrs Jarman.
D: £18.00-£27.00 **S:** £22.00-£37.00.
Open: Easter to Oct
Beds: 2F 3D 2T 2S
Baths: 8 En 1 Pr
🛇 ℙ (2) ⅍⌖⍾✕🍽🛆🍴🖭🗔✦

Tal-Y-Don Hotel, High Street,
Barmouth, *LL42 1DL*.
Families welcome. Home cooking,
bar meals and good beer
Tel: **01341 280508**
Mrs Davies.
D: £17.00-£20.00
S: £20.00-£25.00.
Open: All Year (not Xmas)
Beds: 2F 4D 2T
Baths: 4 En 2 Sh
🛇 ℙ⅍⌖✕🛆🍴🖭🗔🛈🚲

Endeavour Guest House, Marine
Parade, Barmouth, *LL42 1NA*.
Actual grid ref: SH611159
Sea front location, beach 75 yards,
railway station 150 yards
Tel: **01341 280271**
Mr & Mrs Every.
D: £16.00-£20.00
S: £16.00-£16.00.
Open: All Year (not Xmas)
Beds: 7F 1S
Baths: 4 En 1 Sh
🛇 (3) ℙ (3) ⌖🛆🍴🖭🗔✦🚲

Bryn Melyn Hotel, Panorama
Road, Barmouth, *LL42 1DQ*.
Actual grid ref: SH620158
A warm welcome, relaxed
atmosphere and stunningly
magnificent views of the
Mawddach Estuary
Tel: **01341 280556**
Mr Jukes MBII.
Fax no: 01341 280342
D: £29.00 **S:** £36.00.
Open: Jan to Dec
Beds: 2F 4D 3T
Baths: 9 En
🛇 (5) ℙ (9) ⌖🍴✕🛆🍴🖭🗔✦✦

Porthmadog to Holyhead

From **Porthmadog** you can take the spectacular norrow-gauge Ffestiniog Railway to Blaenau Ffestiniog, up the route between the old slate mines and the coast. A detour to the southeast of town will bring you to the famous Italianate fantasy village of **Portmeirion**, assembled in the 1920s by Sir Clough Williams-Ellis out of buildings in a myriad styles brought here from different parts of Britain, and elsewhere.

Thirteenth-century **Criccieth** Castle was ruined by Owain Glyndwr in 1404. The ruins yield views across Cardigan Bay to Harlech.

The superlatively well-preserved **Caernarfon** Castle, with its polygonal towers, was built to be the royal seat in conquered Wales by Edward I. It was the scene in 1969 for a made-to-order, pseudo-medieval ceremony marking Prince Charles' investiture as Prince of Wales.

At **Bangor**, the cathedral contains the famous sixteenth-century wooden carving, the Mostyn Christ. The main building of the university mirrors the design of the cathedral; the museum and art gallery has a Welsh national flavour; and the renovated Victorian pier gives excellent views of the Menai Suspension Bridge, built by Thomas Telford in 1826.

The reason for the fame of **Llanfairpwllgwyngyllgogerychwyrndrobwll-llantisiliogogogoch** should be self-evident even if this is the first you've ever heard of the place.

Plas Newydd, just beyond Llanfairetc, is an eighteenth-century house in the Gothic style – a rare thing. Designed by James Wyatt, the interior is eclectic; and there is a huge mural by Whistler. The grounds, which include a fine spring garden, yield splendid views to Snowdonia.

If the cycle route has failed to expend all your energy reserves, you can climb the 700-foot Holyhead mountain above **Holyhead**; at the top you will find a large Iron Age hill fort, Caer y Tawr. Below the mountain at South Stack, the Ellin's Tower Seabird Centre offers observation of the abundant bird life on the cliffs.

Llanaber 61

National Grid Ref: SH6017

Llwyndu Farmhouse, Llanaber, Barmouth, Gwynedd, LL42 1RR.
Actual grid ref: SH600185
Grades: WTB 3 Star,
AA 4 Diamond
Tel: 01341 280144 Mrs Thompson.
D: £27.50-£32.00 **S:** £27.50-£32.00.
Open: All Year (not Xmas)
Beds: 2F 4D 1T
Baths: 7 En
🛇 🅿 (10) ⌿ 🖵 ♛ ✕ 🔥 📖 🖤 🛡 ⚡
C16th Llwyndu nestles in a spectacular location with panoramic views over Cardigan Bay in front & Rhinogs Mountains behind. The cooking is imaginative, with a good wine list, Llwyndu has a relaxing & restful atmosphere - great after a good walk

Dyffryn Ardudwy 62

National Grid Ref: SH5822

🍴 🍺 Hel Y Bryn

Parc yr Onnen, Dyffryn Ardudwy, Gwynedd, LL44 2DU.
Actual grid ref: SH592242
Rural setting; superb sea and mountain views by peaceful lane
Grades: WTB 3 Star
Tel: 01341 247033
Mr & Mrs Bethell.
D: £18.00-£20.00 **S:** £20.00-£20.00.
Open: All Year
Beds: 1D 1T **Baths:** 2 En
🛇 🅿 (3) ⌿ 🖵 ♛ ✕ 🔥 📖 🖤 🛡 ⚡ 🚲

The Old Farmhouse, Tyddyn Du, Dyffryn Ardudwy, Gwynedd, LL44 2DW.
Secluded luxury farmhouse; heated pool and hot spa; informal, friendly atmosphere. **Grades:** WTB 3 Star
Tel: 01341 242711
Fax no: 01341 247881
D: £16.66-£25.00 **S:** £16.66-£25.00.
Open: All Year
Beds: 1F 2D 2T **Baths:** 5 En
🛇 (5) 🅿 (10) ⌿ 🖵 ♛ ✕ 🔥 📖 🖤 🛡 ⚡ 🚲

Byrdir, Dyffryn Ardudwy, LL44 2EA.
Actual grid ref: SH597243
Peaceful farmhouse, pretty converted barns, superb views, warm welcome/croeso cynnes
Tel: 01341 247200 Mrs Jones.
Fax no: 01341 247889
D: £19.00 **S:** £19.00.
Open: Easter to Sep
Beds: 3F 3D 2T 2S
Baths: 9 En 1 Pr
🛇 🅿 (14) ⌿ 🖵 ✕ 🔥 📖 🖤

Llandanwg 63

National Grid Ref: SH5628

🍴 🍺 The Victoria

Glan-Y-Gors, Llandanwg, Harlech, LL46 2SD.
3 star guest house near beach, with panoramic views
Grades: WTB 3 Star
Tel: 01341 241410 Mrs Evans.
D: £16.00-£17.00 **S:** £16.00-£17.00.
Open: All Year
Beds: 1F 1D 1T **Baths:** 1 En 1 Sh
🛇 (1) 🅿 (6) 🖵 ♛ 🔥 📖 🖤 🛡 ⚡ 🚲

Harlech 64

National Grid Ref: SH5831

🍴 🍺 The Lion

Tyddyn Y Gwynt, Harlech, LL46 2TH.
Actual grid ref: SH593298
Perfect setting for peaceful holidays; warm welcome, tourist attractions, mountain scenery, beaches. Car essential
Grades: WTB 2 Star
Tel: 01766 780298
Mrs Jones.
D: £16.00-£16.00
S: £16.00-£18.00.
Open: All Year
Beds: 1F 1D 1T 1S
Baths: 1 Sh
🛇 🅿 (8) 🖵 ♛ 🔥 📖 🖤 🛡 ⚡ 🚲

Godre'R Graig, Fford Newydd, Harlech, Gwynedd, LL46 2UD.
Grades: WTB 3 Star
Tel: 01766 780905 (also fax no)
Mr Lynch.
D: £16.00-£18.00
S: £16.00-£25.00.
Open: All Year (not Xmas)
Beds: 2F 4D 2T 1S
Baths: 4 Sh
🛇 🅿 (8) 🖵 ♛ ✕ 🔥 📖 🕭 🖤 🛡 ⚡ 🚲
A gracious Edwardian house nestling at the foot of Harlech Castle. Close to Royal St Davids Golf Club. A superb base for walking, fishing (sea/freshwater), pony trekking, rock climbing, golf & eating. The most relaxing place in the world (probably)

Lion Hotel, *Harlech, LL46 2SG.*
2 bars & restaurant. Double rooms
ensuite
Tel: **01766 780731** Mr Morris.
D: £18.00 **S:** £20.00.
Open: All Year
Beds: 4D 1T 1S
Baths: 5 Pr
🅿 (3) ⌨ 🖤 ✕ ♨ 🏠, 🆅

Maes yr Hebog, *Heol y Bryn,
Harlech, Gwynedd, LL46 2TU.*
Quality bungalow accommodation,
great food, spectacular views,
mountains and coast
Tel: **01776 780885**
Mr & Mrs Clark.
D: £20.00-£24.00 **S:** £32.00-£42.00.
Open: Easter to Oct
Beds: 2D **Baths:** 2 En
🅿 (2) ⌁ ⌨ ✕ ♨ 🏠, 🆅 ⨝

Llanwrin 65

National Grid Ref: SH7803

🍴 🍺 Penrho's Arms

Mathafarn, *Llanwrin,
Machynlleth, Powys, SY20 8QJ.*
Elegant country house, part of a
working farm
Grades: WTB 4 Star Farm
Tel: **01650 511226** Mrs Hughes.
D: £19.00-£20.00 **S:** £25.00-£25.00.
Open: All Year
Beds: 1D 1T 1S
Baths: 1 En 1 Pr 1 Sh
⛷ 🅿 ⌁ ⌨ ♨ 🏠, 🆅

Corris 66

National Grid Ref: SH7507

▲ **Corris Youth Hostel,** *Old
School, Old Road, Corris,
Machynlleth, Powys, SY20 9QT.*
Actual grid ref: SH753080
Tel: **01654 761686**
Under 18: £5.65 **Adults:** £8.35
evening meal at 7.00pm, self-catering facilities, family bunk rooms,
central heating, security lockers,
parking, laundry facilities, no
smoking
*Picturesque former village school,
recently renovated, with panoramic
views of Corris*

Brithdir 67

National Grid Ref: SH7618

🍴 🍺 Cross Foxes

Llwyn Talcen, *Brithdir, Dolgellau,
LL40 2RY.*
Country house in rhododendron
gardens, mountains on doorstep,
home cooking
Grades: WTB 1 Star
Tel: **01341 450276**
Mrs Griffiths.
D: £18.00-£20.00 **S:** £18.00-£20.00.
Open: Easter to Oct
Beds: 1D 1S
Baths: 1 En 1 Sh
⛷ (3) 🅿 (3) ⌨ 🖤 ✕ ♨ 🏠, 🆅 🛡 ⨝ ⨝

Y Goedlan, *Brithdir, Dolgellau,
LL40 2RN.*
Victorian vicarage in peaceful
countryside. Spacious bedrooms.
Hearty breakfast
Tel: **01341 423131** (also fax no)
Mrs Evans.
D: £16.00 **S:** £18.00.
Open: Feb to Nov
Beds: 1F 1D 1T
Baths: 1 Sh
⛷ (4) 🅿 (3) ⌨ ♨ 🏠, 🆅

Dolgellau 68

National Grid Ref: SH7217

🍴 🍺 Cross Foxes, Dylanwad Da, The George,
Royal Ship, Ivy House, The Unicorn

Glyn Farm House, *Dolgellau,
LL40 1YA.*
Actual grid ref: SH704178
Bedrooms with views, riverside
path to Dogellau, near organised
bicycle track
Grades: WTB 1 Star
Tel: **01341 422286** (also fax no)
Mrs Price.
D: £16.00-£20.00 **S:** £14.00-£20.00.
Open: Mar to Nov
Beds: 1D 1T
Baths: 1 En 1 Sh
⛷ 🅿 (6) ⌨ 🖤 ♨ 🏠, 🆅 ⨝ ⨝

Tanyfron, *Arran Road, Dolgellau,
LL40 2AA.*
Modernised, former stone farm-
house, beautiful views. Wales in
Bloom Winners 1999
Grades: WTB 3 Star
Tel: **01341 422638** Mrs Rowlands.
Fax no: 01341 421251
D: £20.00-£20.00 **S:** £25.00-£40.00.
Open: Feb to Nov
Beds: 1D 2T
Baths: 3 En
⛷ (5) 🅿 (6) ⌁ ⌨ ♨ 🏠, 🆅 ⨝ ⨝

Ivy House, *Finsbury Square,
Dolgellau, LL40 1RF.*
Actual grid ref: SH728177
Attractive country town guest
house, licensed restaurant, good
home-made food
Grades: WTB 2 Star GH
Tel: **01341 422535** Mrs Bamford.
Fax no: 01341 422689
D: £18.50-£24.50 **S:** £21.00-£28.00.
Open: All Year
Beds: 1F 3D 2T
Baths: 3 En 2 Sh
⛷ ⌨ 🖤 ✕ ♨ 🏠, 🆅 🛡 ⨝ ⨝

Arosfyr Farm, *Penycefn Road,
Dolgellau, LL40 2YP.*
Homely friendly, farmhouse,
flower, gardens, mountainous,
views, self-catering available
Grades: WTB 1 Star
Tel: **01341 422355** Mr Skeel Jones.
D: £15.00-£16.50 **S:** £18.00-£20.00.
Open: All Year
Beds: 1F 1D 1T
Baths: 2
⛷ 🅿 (4) ⌨ 🖤 ♨ 🏠, 🆅 🛡 ⨝ ⨝

Esgair Wen Newydd, *Garreg
Feurig, Llanfachreth Road,
Dolgellau, LL40 2YA.*
Actual grid ref: SH736185
Bungalow, mountain views, very
quiet. Friendly relaxed atmosphere.
High standards
Grades: WTB 3 Star
Tel: **01341 423952** Mrs Westwood.
D: £17.50-£17.50 **S:** £19.50-£19.50.
Open: Feb to Nov
Beds: 2D 1T
Baths: 1 Sh
⛷ (3) 🅿 (3) ⌨ ✕ ♨ 🏠, 🆅 🛡 ⨝ ⨝

Bryn Yr Odyn Guest House,
Maescaled, Dolgellau, LL40 1UG.
Secluded C17th longhouse, 0.5
mile town centre, tour/walking
guidance
Grades: WTB 2 Star
Tel: **01341 423470** Mr Jones.
D: £17.00 **S:** £20.00.
Open: All Year
Beds: 1D 2T
Baths: 2 Sh
⛷ 🅿 (3) ⌁ ⌨ 🖤 ♨ 🏠, 🆅 🛡 ⨝ ⨝

Aber Cafe, *Smithfield Street,
Dolgellau, Gwynedd, LL40 1DE.*
Town centre situation, many walks
in area, also Cader Idris
Tel: **01341 422460**
D: £16.00-£16.00 **S:** £16.00-£16.00.
Open: All Year (not Xmas)
Beds: 1F 1D 1T 2S
Baths: 2 En 1 Pr 2 Sh
⛷ (5) 🅿 (6) ⌨ 🖤 ♨ 🏠, 🆅 🛡 ⨝ ⨝

Gwelafon, *Caedeintur, Dolgellau,
LL40 2YS.*
Beautiful, high-standard, spacious
house. Panoramic views of town
and mountains
Grades: WTB 3 Star
Tel: **01341 422634**
D: £20.00-£25.00 **S:** £17.00-£20.00.
Open: Easter to Oct
Beds: 1D 2S
Baths: 1 En 1 Sh
⛷ (7) 🅿 (3) ⌁ ⌨ ♨ 🏠, 🆅 🛡 ⨝ ⨝

Dwy Olwyn, *Coed Y Fronallt,
Dolgellau, LL40 2YG.*
Actual grid ref: SH734183
Situated on an acre of landscaped
gardens, boasting magnificent
views
Tel: **01341 422822** Mrs Jones.
D: £15.00 **S:** £20.00.
Open: Feb to Dec
Beds: 1F 1D 1T **Baths:** 1 Pr 1 Sh
⛷ 🅿 ⌁ ⌨ ✕ ♨ 🏠, 🆅 🛡 ⨝

Gwernan Lake Hotel, *Islaw'r Dref,
Dolgellau, LL40 1TL.*
Actual grid ref: SH704159
Situated between the slopes of
Cader Idris and own 12-acre trout
fishing lake
Tel: **01341 422488** Ms Lathaen.
D: £22.50 **S:** £22.50.
Open: All Year
Beds: 3D 2T 2S
Baths: 1 En 2 Sh
🅿 (20) ⌨ 🖤 ✕ ♨ 🏠, 🆅 🛡 ⨝ ⨝

Trawsfynydd 69

National Grid Ref: SH7035

Old Mill Farm, Fron Oleu, Trawsfynydd, Blaenau Ffestiniog, LL41 4UN.
Actual grid ref: SH7135
Olde Worlde charm, wonderful scenery, friendly animals, large good breakfasts
Grades: WTB 2 Star Farm
Tel: 01766 540397 (also fax no)
Miss Roberts & Mrs P Osborne.
D: £20.00-£25.00 **S:** £20.00-£25.00.
Open: All Year
Beds: 2F 3D 2T **Baths:** 7 En
🛏 🅿 (10) 🖉 🔲 🏠 ✕ 🖳 🛖 👶 ♿ 🔣 ⚡ ♿

Gellilydan 70

National Grid Ref: SH6839

🍴 🍺 Bryn Arms

Tyddyn Du Farm, Gellilydan, Blaenau Ffestiniog, Gwynedd, LL41 4RB.
Actual grid ref: SH691398
Enchanting C17th farmhouse; deluxe barn suites with jacuzzi, patio window, gardens wtb
Grades: WTB 4 Star,
AA 4 Diamond
Tel: 01766 590281 Mrs Williams.
D: £20.00-£28.00.
Open: All Year (not Xmas)
Beds: 3F 1D **Baths:** 3 Pr 2 Sh
🛏 🅿 (8) 🖉 🔲 🏠 ✕ 🖳 🛖 👶 🔣 ⚡ ♿

Gwynfryn, Gellilydan, Blaenau Ffestiniog, LL41 4EA.
Actual grid ref: SH685398
Detached, comfortable, clean, quiet period house
Tel: 01766 590225
Mrs Jones.
D: £15.00 **S:** £15.00.
Open: All Year (not Xmas)
Beds: 1F 1D 1S **Baths:** 1 Sh
🛏 🅿 🖉 🔲 ✕ 🖳 🛖 🔣 ⚡

Ffestiniog 71

National Grid Ref: SH7041

🍴 🍺 The Grapes

🔺 *Abbey Arms Hostel (Independent), Ffestiniog, Blaenau Ffestiniog, LL41 4LS.*
Actual grid ref: SH700419
Tel: 01766 762444 Adults: £12.50
evening meals available

Tyddyn Pant Glas, Ffestiniog, Blaenau Ffestiniog, LL41 4PU.
Actual grid ref: SH709413
Self-contained annexe - superb views: excellent centre for all attractions
Tel: 01766 762442
Mrs Langdale-Pope.
D: £17.50-£17.50 **S:** £17.50-£20.00.
Open: All Year (not Xmas)
Beds: 1D **Baths:** 1 En
🅿 (1) 🖉 🔲 🖳 🛖 🔣 ⚡

Maentwrog 72

National Grid Ref: SH6640

The Old Rectory Hotel, Maentwrog, Blaenau Ffestiniog, LL41 4HN.
Actual grid ref: SH665407
Main house/budget annexe, 3 acre garden. Informal, peaceful
Tel: 01766 590305 (also fax no)
Ms Herbert.
D: £22.50-£32.50
S: £30.00-£45.00.
Open: All Year (not Xmas)
Beds: 2F 6D 2T
Baths: 10 En
🛏 🅿 🔲 🏠 ✕ 🖳 🛖 🔣 ⚡

Porthmadog 73

National Grid Ref: SH5638

🍴 🍺 The Ship

35 Madog Street, Porthmadog, LL49 9BU.
Modern terraced house
Tel: 01766 512843
Mrs Skellern.
D: £14.00-£15.00
S: £14.00-£15.00.
Open: All Year (not Xmas)
Beds: 1F 1D 1T 1S
Baths: 1 En 2 Sh
🛏 (3) 🔲 🏠 🖳 🛖 🔣

Llwyn Derw, Morfa Bychan Road, Porthmadog, LL49 9UR.
Period house, own grounds, town centre 1 km, beach 2 km
Grades: WTB 2 Star B&B
Tel: 01766 513869
D: £18.00-£23.00 **S:** £21.00-£26.00.
Open: Easter to Oct
Beds: 1F 1D
Baths: 1 En
🛏 (3) 🅿 (3) 🖉 🔲 🖳 🛖 🔣 ⚡ ♿

Criccieth 74

National Grid Ref: SH4938

🍴 🍺 The Poachers, Prince of Wales, The Moelwyn

🔺 *Stone Barn Bunkhouse Barn (Independent), Tyddyn Morthwyl, Criccieth, LL52 0NF.*
Actual grid ref: SH495402
Tel: 01766 522115 Adults: £5.00
self-catering facilities

Mor Heli Guest House, Min Y Mor, Criccieth, LL52 0EF.
Tel: 01766 522802
Fax no: 01766 522878
D: £18.00 **S:** £18.00.
Open: All Year (not Xmas)
Beds: 2F 2D 1T
Baths: 5 Pr
🛏 🅿 🔲 🏠 ✕ 🖳 🔣 ⚡
Situated on sea front overlooking 100 miles of coastline. All bedrooms sea views, full ensuite facilities, colour TV and hospitality trays. Recommended by guests since 1972

Min Y Gaer Hotel, Porthmadog Road, Criccieth, LL52 0HP.
Actual grid ref: SH502382
Pleasant hotel with delightful coastal views ideal for touring Snowdonia
Grades: WTB 2 Star Hotel,
AA 4 Diamond, RAC 4 Diamond
Tel: 01766 522151
Fax no: 01766 523540
D: £21.50-£24.50.
S: £21.50-£24.50.
Open: Easter to Oct
Beds: 3F 4D 2T 1S
Baths: 10 En
🛏 🅿 (12) 🖉 🔲 🏠 🖳 🛖 🔣 ⚡ ♿

Y Rhoslyn, 8 Marine Terrace, Criccieth, LL52 0EF.
Comfortable seafront guest house in unspoilt seaside town, close to beach, castle
Grades: WTB 2 Star GH
Tel: 01766 522685
D: £13.50-£18.00
S: £16.00-£25.00.
Open: Feb to Nov
Beds: 2F 2D 1T 1S
Baths: 2 En 1 Sh
🛏 🖉 🔲 🏠 ✕ 🖳 🛖 🔣

Bron Rhiw Hotel, Caernarfon Road, Criccieth, LL52 0AP.
Cosy, comfortable non-smoking hotel; a truly warm welcome awaits you
Grades: WTB 2 Star Hotel
Tel: 01766 522257
Ms Woodhouse &
Ms Williams.
D: £20.00-£22.50 **S:** £20.00-£22.50.
Open: Mar to Nov
Beds: 5F 2D 2T 0S
Baths: 7 En 2 Pr
🛏 🅿 (4) 🖉 🔲 🏠 ✕ 🖳 🛖 🔣 ⚡ ♿

Craig Y Mor Guest House, West Parade, Criccieth, LL52 0EN.
Tastefully upgraded Victorian house overlooking sea into Tremadoc Bay
Grades: WTB 3 Star GH
Tel: 01766 522830 Mr Williamson.
D: £20.00-£21.00 **S:** £20.00.
Open: Mar to Oct
Beds: 4F 2D
Baths: 6 En
🛏 🅿 (6) 🔲 🏠 🖳 🛖 🔣 ⚡

Muriau, Criccieth, LL52 0RS.
C17th gentleman's residence, secluded garden
Grades: WTB 3 Star
Tel: 01766 522337 Mrs Neville.
D: £16.50-£21.00 **S:** £16.50-£21.00.
Open: Mar to Oct
Beds: 3D 2T
Baths: 3 En 1 Sh
🛏 (12) 🅿 (6) 🖉 🔲 ✕ 🖳 🛖 🔣 ⚡ ♿

D = Price range per person sharing in a double room

Cardigan Hotel, 29 Marine Terrace, Criccieth, *LL52 0EL*.
Welcome to our friendly seafacing hotel ideal for touring Snowdonia, Llyn Peninsula
Tel: **01766 522086**
Mr & Mrs Woodger.
D: £16.00 **S:** £16.00.
Open: All Year
Beds: 3F 2D 2T 2S
Baths: 5 En 2 Pr 1 Sh
🖵 ⼻ ✕ ♨ ⛿ Ⅶ ⚡ ⟲

Pant-glas   75

National Grid Ref: SH4747

▲ *Old School Bunkhouse (Independent),* Hen Ysgol, Pant-glas, *LL51 9EQ*.
Actual grid ref: SH456474
Tel: **01286 660701 Adults:** £4.50
self-catering facilities, showers

Bwlch Derwin   76

National Grid Ref: SH4547

Hen Ysgol/Old School, Bwlch Derwin, Garndolbenmaen, *LL51 9EQ*.
Actual grid ref: SH456474
Grades: WTB 2 Star
Tel: **01286 660701** Gibbins.
D: £17.00-£20.00 **S:** £20.00-£25.00.
Open: All year
Beds: 2F 1D 1T
Baths: 1 En 1 Sh
🖰 ⛿ (6) ⼻ 🖵 ⼻ ✕ ♨ ⛿ & Ⅶ ⚡ ⟲
Beautiful mid C19th Welsh country school. Perfectly situated for the attractions of Snowdonia and Lleyn Peninsula. Set in a peaceful location, off the A487, between Caernarfon and Porthmadog. Sue and Terry offer a warm welcome.

Penygroes   77

National Grid Ref: SH4753

🍴 🍺 Bryneisteddfod Clynnog

Lleuar Fawr, Penygroes, Caernarfon, Gwynedd, *LL54 6PB*.
Actual grid ref: SH455520
Peaceful location, substantial farmhouse breakfast, comfortable bedrooms. Warm Welsh welcome
Grades: WTB 3 Star
Tel: **01286 660268** (also fax no)
Mrs Lloyd Jones.
D: £18.00-£20.00 **S:** £25.00-£25.00.
Open: All Year (not Xmas)
Beds: 1D 1T **Baths:** 2 En
🖰 ⛿ ⼻ 🖵 ⼻ ♨ Ⅶ ⚡ ⟲

D = Price range per person sharing in a double room

Rhostryfan   78

National Grid Ref: SH4957

🍴 🍺 Newborough Arms

Hafoty, Rhostryfan, Caernarfon, *LL54 7PH*.
Converted farmhouse on the edge of Snowdonia overlooking Caernarfon castle
Grades: WTB 4 Star Farm, AA 4 Diamond
Tel: **01286 830144** (also fax no)
Mrs Davies.
D: £24.00-£26.00 **S:** £28.00-£28.00.
Open: Feb to Nov
Beds: 1F 2D 1S
Baths: 4 En
🖰 ⛿ (20) 🖵 ♨ Ⅶ ⚡ ⟲

Saron   79

National Grid Ref: SH4658

Pengwern Farm, Saron, Llanwnda, Caernarfon, *LL54 5UH*.
Charming spacious farmhouse of character
Grades: WTB 4 Star, AA 4 Diamond
Tel: **01286 831500** (also fax no)
Mr & Mrs Rowlands.
D: £20.00-£25.00 **S:** £30.00-£35.00.
Open: Easter to Feb
Beds: 2D 1T
Baths: 3 En
🖰 ⛿ (3) ⼻ 🖵 ✕ ♨ Ⅶ ⚡ ⟲

Llanfaglan   80

National Grid Ref: SH4760

🍴 🍺 The Harp

The White House, Llanfaglan, Caernarfon, *LL54 5RA*.
Quiet, isolated country house. Magnificent views to mountains and sea
Grades: WTB 3 Star
Tel: **01286 673003**
Mr Bayles.
D: £19.00-£21.00 **S:** £23.00-£25.00.
Open: Mar to Nov
Beds: 2D 2T
Baths: 3 En 1 Pr
🖰 ⛿ (8) 🖵 ⼻ ♨ Ⅶ ⚡ ⟲

Caernarfon   81

National Grid Ref: SH4862

🍴 🍺 Black Boy, Harp Inn, Newborough Arms

Princes Of Wales Hotel, Bangor Street, Caernarfon, *LL55 1AR*.
Centrally located, perfect stopover en-route for Ireland's ferries or exploring Snowdonia
Grades: WTB 1 Star Hotel
Tel: **01286 673367** Ms Parry.
Fax no: 01286 676610
D: £19.00-£26.00 **S:** £19.00-£26.00.
Open: All Year (not Xmas)
Beds: 2F 8D 7T 4S
Baths: 19 En 2 Sh
🖰 ⛿ (6) 🖵 ⼻ ✕ ♨ Ⅶ ⚡ ⟲

Cadnant Valley Caravan Park, Llanberis Road, Caernarfon, *LL55 2DF*.
Clean comfortable and friendly house 0.25 mile Caernarfon town
Tel: **01286 673196** Mrs Noon.
D: £15.00-£15.00 **S:** £15.00-£15.00.
Open: Easter to Sep
Beds: 1D 1T
Baths: 1 Sh
⛿ (4) 🖵 ♨ Ⅶ

Swn-Y-Fenai, 8 Church Street, Caernarfon, *LL55 1SW*.
Conveniently situated 100 metres from the famous Caernarfon Castle
Tel: **01286 671677** Mr Newell.
Fax no: 01745 334513
D: £12.00-£20.00 **S:** £12.00-£20.00.
Open: All Year
Beds: 1F 2D 5T 1S
Baths: 2 Sh
🖰 ⼻ ✕ ♨ Ⅶ ⟲

Marianfa, St David's Road, Caernarfon, Gwynedd, *LL55 1EL*.
Ideal base touring Snowdonia, Llyn Peninsula, Anglesey, Llandudno, Conwy valley
Grades: WTB 3 Star
Tel: **01286 675589**
D: £16.00-£22.00 **S:** £17.00-£25.00.
Open: All Year
Beds: 2F 1D 1T 1S
Baths: 4 En 1 Pr
🖰 (10) ⛿ (5) ⼻ 🖵 ♨ Ⅶ ⟲

Marteg, High Street, Caernarfon, Gwynedd, *LL55 4HA*.
Within walking distance of Snowdon mountain railway and all amenities
Grades: WTB 3 Star B&B
Tel: **01286 870207**
Mr & Mrs Torr.
D: £20.00-£22.00
S: £20.00-£22.00.
Open: Easter to Dec
Beds: 2D 1T 1S
Baths: 3 En 1 Pr
⛿ (4) ⼻ 🖵 ♨ Ⅶ ⚡ ⟲

Menai Bank Hotel, North Road, Caernarfon, *LL55 1BD*.
Elegant town house overlooking Menai Straits. Close Snowdonia and Anglesey
Tel: **01286 673297** (also fax no)
D: £17.00 **S:** £20.00.
Open: All Year
Beds: 4F 3T 7D 3S
Baths: 11 En 2 Sh
🖰 ⛿ (10) 🖵 ⼻ ✕ ♨ Ⅶ ⟲

High season, bank holidays and special events mean low availability *everywhere.*

Pentir   82

National Grid Ref: SH5667

⊯ ⊲ Yaynol Arms

Rainbow Court Guest House,
Village Square, Pentir, Bangor,
LL57 4UY.
Actual grid ref: SH574670
1999 award-winning guest
house/restaurant. Mountains,
attractions, peace, friendly
Grades: WTB 3 Star
Tel: **01248 353099** (also fax no)
Mrs Lorrimer Riley.
D: £16.00-£20.00 **S:** £16.00-£27.00.
Open: All Year (not Xmas)
Beds: 1F 1D 1T 1S
Baths: 1 En 1 Pr 1 Sh
⼘ ⃣P (3) ⼧ ⃞ ✗ ⃧ ⃤ Ⅴ ⃞

Menai Bridge   83

National Grid Ref: SH5572

⊯ ⊲ Penrhos Arms

Wern Farm Guest House,
Pentraeth Road, Menai Bridge,
Anglesey, LL59 5RR.
Grades: WTB 4 Star Farm
Tel: **01248 712421** (also fax no)
Mr & Mrs Brayshaw.
D: £21.00-£27.00 **S:** £25.00-£50.00.
Open: Feb to Nov
Beds: 2F 1T
Baths: 1 En 1 Sh
⼘ ⃣P ⼧ ⃞ ⃧ ⃤ Ⅴ ⃞ ⼁ ⼢
Great hospitality. Hearty breakfasts
and everything you could possibly
need for a relaxing holiday in a
lovely C18th farmhouse.
Comfortable surroundings,
wonderful views. Traditional
games, antique three-quarter
snooker table, tennis court and
beautiful landscaped gardens make
this a perfect venue

Gaerwen   84

National Grid Ref: SH4771

⊯ ⊲ Penrhos Arms Sailors Return

Benlas, *Llandaniel, Gaerwen,*
Anglesey, LL65 6HB.
Actual grid ref: SH499710
Pretty cottage, quiet country road,
superb views to Snowdonia
Tel: **01248 421543** Mrs Taylor.
D: £18.00-£20.00 **S:** £20.00-£20.00.
Open: Easter to Oct
Beds: 2D
Baths: 1 Sh
⼘ ⃣P (3) ⼧ ⼁ ⃧ ⃤ Ⅴ ⼁ ⼢

Llangaffo   85

National Grid Ref: SH4468

Plas Llangaffo, *Llangaffo,*
Gaerwen, Anglesey, LL60 6LR.
Set in a peaceful location
Grades: WTB 1 Star Farm
Tel: **01248 440452** Mrs Lamb.
D: £16.00-£20.00 **S:** £16.00-£20.00.
Open: All Year
Beds: 1F 2D 2T
Baths: 1 En 1 Sh
⼘ ⃣P (8) ⃞ ⼧ ✗ ⃧ ⃤ ⃞ ⃤ Ⅴ

Llanfair-yn-Neubwll   86

National Grid Ref: SH3076

⊯ ⊲ Valley Hotel

Ty Gwrthyn, *Llanfair-yn-Neubwll,*
Holyhead, Anglesey, LL65 3LD.
Country guest house by the sea.
Near Irish ferries. Relaxing!
Tel: **01407 741025**
Mrs Montgomery Croft.
D: £20.00 **S:** £23.00.
Open: All Year
Beds: 1F 1D 2T
Baths: 3 En
⃣P (8) ⃞ ⼧ ⃧ ⃤ ⃞ ⃤ Ⅴ

Holyhead   87

National Grid Ref: SH2482

⊯ ⊲ Valley Hotel, Boat House, Kings Arms

Roselea, *26 Holborn Road,*
Holyhead, Anglesey, LL65 2AT.
Homely family-run B&B - warm
welcome guaranteed to our visitors.
2 mins from ferries
Grades: WTB 2 Star
Tel: **01407 764391** (also fax no)
Mrs Foxley.
D: £16.00-£20.00 **S:** £20.00.
Open: All Year (not Xmas)
Beds: 1D 1T
Baths: 1 Sh
⼘ ⼧ ⃞ ⃧ ⃤ Ⅴ ⼁ ⼢

Order your
packed lunches the
evening before you
need them.
Not at breakfast!

Monravon Guest House, *Port-y-*
felin Road, Holyhead, LL65 1PL.
Grades: WTB 3 Star GH
Tel: **01407 762944** (also fax no)
D: £15.00-£18.50.
Open: All Year (not Xmas)
Beds: 3F 3D 3T
Baths: 9 En
⼘ ⼧ ⃞ ⃧ ⃤ ⃞ ⃤ Ⅴ ⼢
A family-run business offering bed
& breakfast in this 9 bedroom all
ensuite guest house. 3 minutes to
ferry & train terminals. 3 ground
floor bedrooms, car parking just off
the main street. adjacent to town
park & beach. We cater 97% for
ferry passengers

Hendre, *Porth y Felin Road,*
Holyhead, Anglesey, LL65 1AH.
Grades: WTB 4 Star,
AA 4 Diamond
Tel: **01407 762929** (also fax no)
D: £20.00-£22.50 **S:** £25.00-£30.00.
Open: All Year
Beds: 2D 1T
Baths: 3 En
⼘ ⃣P (6) ⼧ ⃞ ⼧ ✗ ⃧ ⃤ ⃞ ⃤ Ⅴ ⼁ ⼁ ⼢
Large detached house in its own
grounds facing park. All rooms
individually designed with views of
Holyhead Mountain and the sea.
Country walks in all directions. 3
mins from ferry terminal, 2 mins
walk from promenade. Parking in
grounds

Wavecrest, *93 Newry Road,*
Holyhead, Anglesey, LL65 1HU.
Actual grid ref: SH248828
Ideal ferry stopover for Ireland;
close to the South Stack
Grades: WTB 3 Star
Tel: **01407 763637** (also fax no)
Mr Hiltunen.
D: £16.00-£20.00
S: £18.00-£20.00.
Open: All Year (not Xmas)
Beds: 3F 1D 1S
Baths: 2 En 1 Pr 1 Sh
⼘ ⃣P (4) ⼧ ⃞ ⼧ ✗ ⃧ ⃤ ⃞ ⃤ Ⅴ ⼁ ⼢

Tasma, *31 Walthew Avenue,*
Holyhead, Anglesey, LL65 1AG.
Comfortable accommodation.
Conveniently situated for ferries,
railway, beaches and shops
Tel: **01407 762291** Mrs Jones.
D: £17.00-£17.00
S: £20.00-£17.00.
Open: All Year (not Xmas)
Beds: 2F
Baths: 2 Sh
⼘ ⃣P (1) ⼧ ⃞ ✗ ⃧ ⃤ ⃞ ⃤ Ⅴ ⼁ ⼁ ⼢

Sustrans Sea to Sea (C2C)

The **Sea to Sea** cycle route is both a section of the new National Cycle Network and an award-winning leisure route. 140 miles long, it starts on the Cumbrian west coast at Workington or Whitehaven, proceeds through the northern Lake District via Keswick to Penrith, and continues through eastern Cumbria to Allenheads in Northumberland; and then through the north of County Durham to Consett, from where it heads either to Newcastle and Tynemouth or to Sunderland. The route is clearly signposted by blue direction signs bearing a cycle silhouette and the legend 'C2C'.

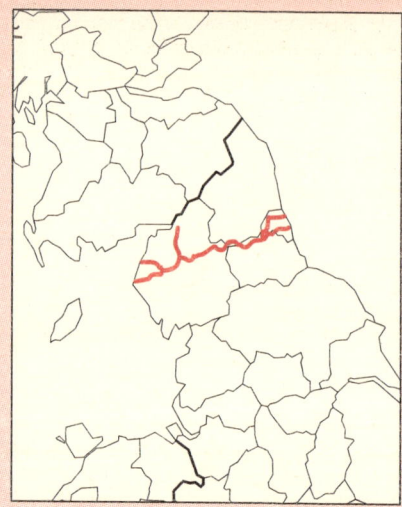

The indispensable **official route map and guide** for the Sea to Sea cycle route is available from Sustrans, 35 King Street, Bristol BS1 4DZ, tel 0117-926 8893, fax 0117-929 4173, @ £5.99 (+ £1.50 p&p).

Maps: Ordnance Survey 1:50,000 Landranger series: 86, 87, 88, 89, 90, 91; and for the Penrith-Carlisle link, 85

Trains: The Intercity west coast main line goes to Carlisle, from where you can connect to Workington, Whitehaven or Penrith; or to Langwathby via the famous scenic Leeds-Settle-Carlisle Railway. The Intercity east coast main line goes to Newcastle, from where you can connect to Tynemouth or Sunderland.

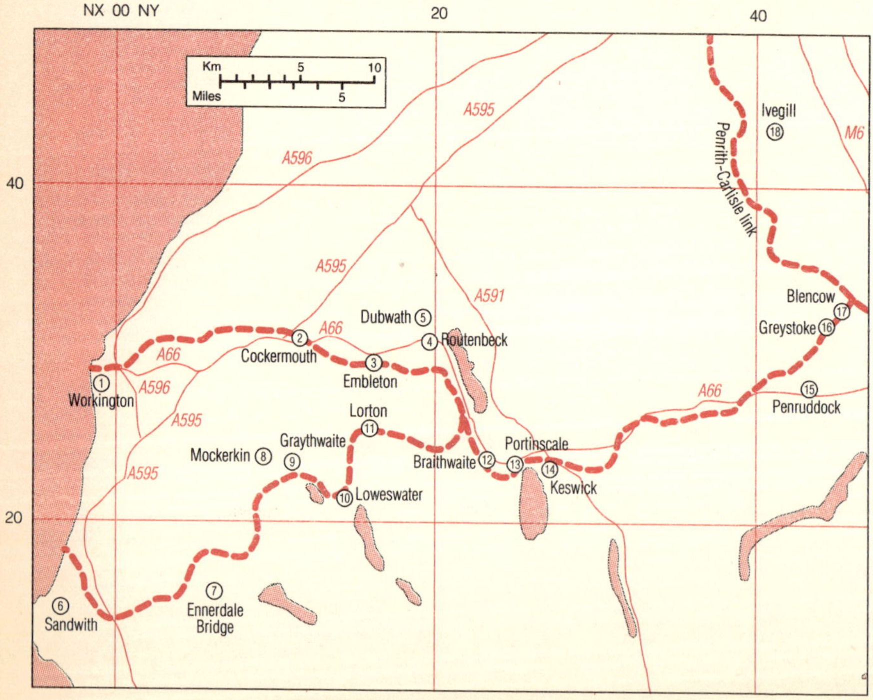

Workington or Whitehaven to Braithwaite

From the mid-nineteenth to mid-twentieth century, **Workington** was a major centre of the iron and steel industry, its particular success due to the fact that Henry Bessemer's steelmaking process depended on a supply of phosphorous free ores, in which this area is rich. The Helena Thompson Museum houses a display of costumes and embroidery. The first stretch of the way takes you up the Derwent Valley to Cockermouth, where the Wordsworth House is the birthplace of the region's most famous son. Elsewhere, the Printing House offers a myriad different types of printing press, and you can tour Jenning's Brewery on the banks of the Cocker. From here you head into the **Lake District National Park**, and on to Wythorp Woods, where you cycle down the west bank of **Bassenthwaite Lake**, with the imposing mass of **Skiddaw** towering above the opposite side, and on to Braithwaite. **Whitehaven** lies to the north of St Bees Head, a Heritage Coast with sandstone cliffs and nature reserves for the important bird life it supports. The town has been through a number of incarnations - harbour for St Bees Priory, major tobacco port, during which time the many Georgian buildings went up, and then coal and shipbuilding centre. The initial stage of the southern route takes you east by way of Cleator Moor to Kirkland, from where you ascend to the edge of the National Park. Here you ride northwards to the northwestern end of **Loweswater**, where you cycle down the northeast bank and then downstream alongside the River Cocker to Low Lorton, from where you ascend into Whinlatter Forest and then descend (steeply) to Thornthwaite, where you turn south to **Braithwaite**.

Workington   1

National Grid Ref: NX9927

🍴 🍺 Ye Old Sportsman, Traveller's Rest, Miners' Arms

Silverdale, 17 Banklands, Workington, Cumbria, CA14 3EL.
Large Victorian private house. Near start C2C cycleway and lakes
Tel: **01900 61887** Mrs Hardy.
D: £11.00-£13.50 **S:** £12.50-£15.00.
Open: All Year (not Xmas)
Beds: 2T 2S
Baths: 2 Sh
🛇 🖰 🎗 🏊 ▥ Ⓥ

The Green Dragon Hotel, Portland Square, Workington, Cumbria, CA14 4BJ.
Delightful 1728 coaching house overlooking a Georgian courtyard
Tel: **01900 603803** Mrs Roberts.
Fax no: 01900 872659
D: £20.00-£25.00 **S:** £25.00-£40.00.
Open: All Year
Beds: 3D 3T 4S
Baths: 8 En 2 Pr
🛇 ⅄ 🖰 🎗 ✗ 🏊 ▥ Ⓥ 🛈 🚲 ♿

D = Price range per person sharing in a double room

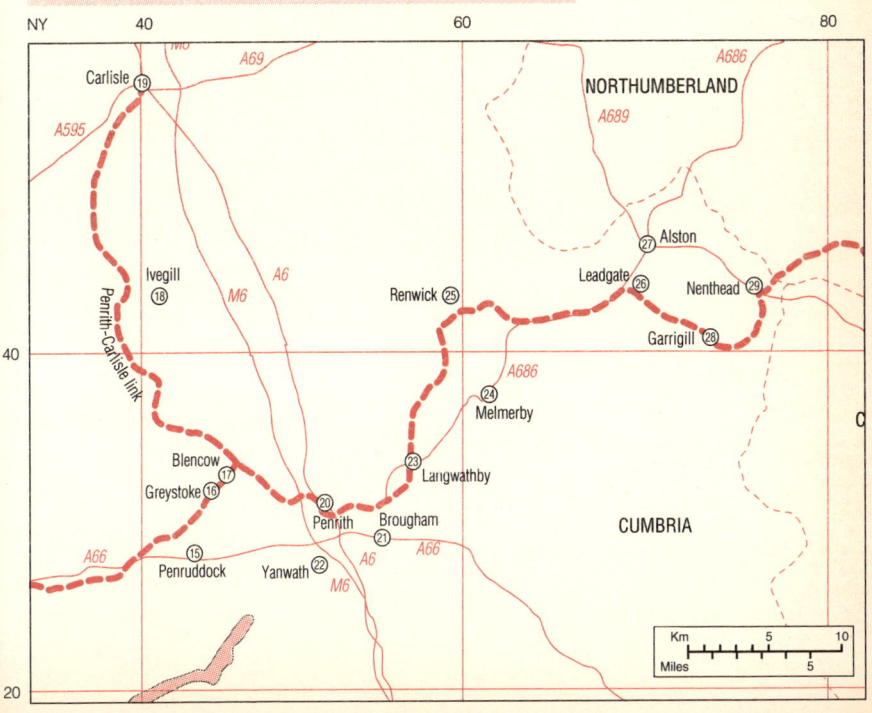

NY   40   60   80

Cockermouth 2

National Grid Ref: NY1230

🍴 🍺 The Bitter End, Shepherds Hotel

▲ **Cockermouth Youth Hostel,**
*Double Mills, Cockermouth,
Cumbria, CA13 0DS.*
Actual grid ref: NY118298
Tel: **01900 822561**
Under 18: £5.65 **Adults:** £8.35
evening meal at 7.00pm, self-cater-
ing facilities, showers, no smoking
*Simple accommodation in restored
C17th watermill, convenient for
northern and western fells and
Cumbrian coastline*

Shepherds Hotel, *Egremont Road,
Cockermouth, Cumbria, CA13 0QX.*
Tel: **01900 822673** (also fax no)
D: £18.75-£20.00 **S:** £37.50-£40.00.
Open: All Year (not Xmas)
Beds: 4D 9T
Baths: 13 En
🛏 🅿 (99) 🍴 🗀 ✕ 🛢 🎞 🕭 ♥ 🛢 ♦ 🚲
Modern hotel with views towards
Lake District, close to gem town of
Cockermouth and bustling
Keswick. Excellent hot and cold
food available all day. Attached to
visitors centre and large gift shop.
Ideal for touring on business or
pleasure

Benson Court Cottage, *10 St
Helen's Street, Cockermouth,
Cumbria, CA13 9HX.*
Tel: **01900 822303** Mrs Townley.
D: £15.00-£18.00 **S:** £15.00-£19.00.
Open: All Year
Beds: 1F 1S
🛏 (6) 🍴 🗀 🛢 🎞 🕭 ♥ ♦ 🚲
Homely 1727 cottage in town
centre conservation area, log fires.
Welcome Host Resident owner.
Over 25 eating places within a 5
minute stroll. Tourists and
commercial guests equally wel-
come. Own key. Healthy & hearty
breakfasts from 0700 hrs. Room
only from £10.

The Rook Guest House,
*9 Castlegate, Cockermouth,
Cumbria, CA13 9EU.*
Actual grid ref: NY122307
Cosy C17th town house. Spiral
staircase. Convenient for all
amenities
Tel: **01900 828496** Mrs Waters.
D: £15.00-£17.50 **S:** £20.00-£20.00.
Open: All Year (not Xmas)
Beds: 2D 1T
Baths: 1 En 1 Pr 1 Sh
🛏 (5) 🍴 🗀 🛢 🎞 🕭 ♥ ♦ 🚲

**Pay B&Bs by cash or
cheque and be prepared
to pay up front.**

Holme Lea, *17 Skiddaw View,
Cockermouth, Cumbria, CA13 0DQ.*
Friendly acommodation near all
amenities on fringe of Northern
Lakes
Tel: **01900 828039**
Hewitson.
D: £16.00-£18.00.
Open: All Year (not Xmas)
Beds: 1T 2D
Baths: 2 En 1 Pr
🛏 🅿 (3) 🍴 🗀 🛢 🎞 🕭 ♥ ♦ 🚲

Embleton 3

National Grid Ref: NY1630

🍴 🍺 Wheatsheaf Inn

Lambfoot House, *Embleton,
Cockermouth, Cumbria, CA13 9XL.*
Actual grid ref: NY164303
Grades: AA 4 Diamond
Tel: **017687 76424**
Mr & Mrs Holden.
Fax no: 017687 76721
D: £22.00-£23.00
S: £22.00-£23.00.
Open: All Year
Beds: 1D 1T 1S
Baths: 3 En
🅿 (5) 🍴 🗀 🛢 🎞 🕭 ♥ 🚲
Relax in elegant and spacious
ensuite rooms, lounge or
conservatory, all with fell views.
The emphasis here is on quality and
personal attention. Well located
between Keswick and
Cockermouth for discovering the
lakes and fells of the English Lake
District

Routenbeck 4

National Grid Ref: NY1930

Riggs Cotage, *Routenbeck,
Cockermouth, Cumbria, CA13 9YN.*
Very quiet C16th Lakeland cottage,
off the beaten track, garden,
orchard, naturalised pond & stream
Tel: **017687 76580** (also fax no)
Mrs Wilkinson.
D: £20.00 **S:** £25.00.
Open: All Year
Beds: 1F 1D 1T
Baths: 1 En 1 Pr 1 Sh
🛏 (5) 🅿 (3) 🍴 🗀 ✕ 🛢 🎞 🅥

Dubwath 5

National Grid Ref: NY1931

Ouse Bridge Hotel, *Dubwath,
Cockermouth, CA13 9YD.*
Ouse Bridge looks across
Bassenthwaite Lake toward
Skiddaw
Tel: **017687 76322** (also fax no)
Mr & Mrs Patrick.
D: £19.00 **S:** £19.00.
Open: Feb to Dec
Beds: 2F 1T 5D 2S
Baths: 8 En 2 Sh
🛏 (5) 🅿 (20) 🗀 ✕ 🛢 🅥 🛢

Sandwith 6

National Grid Ref: NX9614

🍴 🍺 Lowther Arms

▲ **Tarn Flatt YHA Camping
Barn,** *Tarnflat Hall, Sandwith,
Whitehaven, Cumbria.*
Actual grid ref: NX947146
Tel: **Adults:** £3.35+
*Situated on St Bees Head overlook-
ing Scottish coastline and the Isle
of Man. RSPB seabird reserve and
lighthouse nearby. ADVANCE
BOOKING ESSENTIAL*

The Old Granary, *Spout Howse,
Sandwith, Whitehaven, Cumbria,
CA28 9UG.*
Actual grid ref: NX964147
Tastefully converted barn on C2C
route and Coast to Coast path
Tel: **01946 692097** Mrs Buchanan.
D: £17.00 **S:** £16.00.
Open: All Year
Beds: 1F 1D 1T **Baths:** 2 En
🛏 🅿 (2) 🗀 🛢 🎞 🅥 ♦ 🚲

Ennerdale Bridge 7

National Grid Ref: NY0715

🍴 🍺 Shepherds Arms

The Shepherds Arms Hotel,
*Ennerdale Bridge, Cleator,
Cumbria, CA23 3AR.*
Grades: ETC 2 Star
Tel: **01946 861249** (also fax no)
Mr Stanfield.
D: £26.50-£27.50 **S:** £28.00-£32.00.
Open: All Year
Beds: 1F 3D 3T 1S
Baths: 6 En 2 Pr
🛏 🅿 (6) 🗀 🍴 🛢 🎞 🅥 🛢 ♦ 🚲
A small friendly hotel in the Lake
District National Park which has
been completely refurbished. Real
ale, real fires, home cooking, bar
meals, restaurant, extensive
vegetarian menu, lounge. On
Wainwright's coast to coast
footpath

Mockerkin 8

National Grid Ref: NY0923

▲ **Swallow YHA Camping Barn,**
*Waterend, Mockerkin,
Cockermouth, Cumbria.*
Actual grid ref: NY116226
Adults: £3.35+
showers
*In picturesque valley of
Loweswater, on a 200-acre work-
ing farm. Permits for fishing and
boat hire on Loweswater available.
ADVANCE BOOKING ESSENTIAL*

S = Price range for a single
person in a room

D = Price range per person sharing in a double room

Graythwaite 9

National Grid Ref: NY1123

Silverholme, Graythwaite, Ulverston, Cumbria, LA12 8AZ.
Small Georgian mansion set against wooded backdrop with panoramic views of Lake Windermere
Tel: **015395 31332** (also fax no) Walker.
D: £23.00 **S:** £33.00.
Open: All Year
Beds: 2F 1D **Baths:** 2 En 1 Pr
🛏 🅿 (6) ⊬ 🗖 🏠 ✕ 🎄 🛋 Ⅶ 🗲 🚲

Loweswater 10

National Grid Ref: NY1420

🍴 🍺 Kirkstyle Inn

Graythwaite, Loweswater, Cockermouth, Cumbria, CA13 0SU.
Actual grid ref: NY115232
Tel: **01946 861555** Mrs Beebe.
Fax no: 01946 862300
D: £17.00-£18.00 **S:** £17.00-£20.00.
Open: All Year (not Xmas)
Beds: 1D 1T 1S
Baths: 1 Sh
🛏 🅿 (4) ⊬ 🗖 ✕ 🎄 🛋 Ⅶ 🗲 🚲
Lovely home half mile off road in elevated position at northern end of Loweswater. Ideal walking/ touring area for northern lakes, Solway coast, borders. Large garden, fishing, horse riding, tennis within five miles. Nearest pub 2 miles dbl has wash basin and shower; twin wash basin

Askhill Farm, Loweswater, Cockermouth, Cumbria, CA13 0SU.
Beef and sheep rearing farm, quiet valley, Loweswater. Ideal country walking area
Tel: **01946 861640** Mrs Vickers.
D: £17.00-£19.00
S: £18.00-£20.00.
Open: Easter to Oct
Beds: 1F 1D
Baths: 1 Sh
🛏 🅿 (3) ⊬ 🗖 🏠 🎄 🛋 Ⅶ 🗲 🚲

Order your packed lunches the *evening before* you need them. Not at breakfast!

Lorton 11

National Grid Ref: NY1525

🍴 🍺 The Wheatsheaf

The Old Vicarage, Church Lane, Lorton, Cockermouth, Cumbria, CA13 9UN.
Grades: AA 4 Diamond
Tel: **01900 85656** (also fax no) Mr Humphreys.
D: £22.00-£30.00 **S:** £22.00-£30.00.
Open: All Year (not Xmas)
Beds: 5D 3T
Baths: 7 En 1 Pr
🛏 🅿 (10) ⊬ 🗖 ✕ 🎄 🛋 Ⅶ 🗲 🚲 ♿
Elegant Victorian country house with stunning views, wooded grounds, log fires and historic charm; lovely rooms including four poster, ground floor and family suite, excellent four course dinners and wine list, local pub 5 minutes' walk

Cragg End Farm, Rogerscale, Lorton Vale, Cockermouth, Cumbria, CA13 0RG.
Tel: **01900 85658** Mrs Steel.
D: £18.00-£18.00 **S:** £18.00.
Open: All Year
Beds: 1F 1D 2T **Baths:** 3 Sh
🛏 🅿 ⊬ 🗖 🏠 ✕ 🗲 🚲
Beautiful views, ideal situation for walking. Quiet, working, family farm.

Braithwaite 12

National Grid Ref: NY2323

🍴 🍺 Royal Oak, Middle Ruddings Hotel, Coledale Inn

Cottage In The Wood Hotel, Whinlatter Pass, Braithwaite, Keswick, Cumbria, CA12 5TW.
Actual grid ref: NY213245
Grades: ETC 4 Diamond
Tel: **01768 78409** Mrs Littlefair.
Fax no: 017687 78064
D: £25.00-£33.00 **S:** £25.00-£47.00.
Open: Mar to Nov
Beds: 3F 3D 1T
Baths: 7 En
🛏 🅿 (15) ⊬ 🗖 🏠 ✕ 🎄 🛋 & Ⅶ 🗲 ♿
Superb location in the Whinlatter Forest Park. Wonderful views, excellent home cooking in idyllic surroundings. Log fires, very well appointed bedrooms, cottage-style decor with many added facilities. Tennis, golf, bowls can be arranged locally. A walkers' paradise

Coledale Inn, Braithwaite, Keswick, Cumbria, CA12 5TN.
Large Georgian/Victorian family inn. Superb mountain views. Real ales
Tel: **017687 78272** Mr Mawdsley.
D: £26.00 **S:** £20.00.
Open: All Year
Beds: 4F 6D 1T 1S
Baths: 12 Pr
🛏 🅿 (15) 🗖 🏠 ✕ 🎄 🛋 & Ⅶ 🗲

Thelmlea Country Guest House, Braithwaite, Keswick, Cumbria, CA12 5TD.
Friendly relaxed atmosphere. Superb views, large garden. Ideal base touring / walking
Tel: **017687 78305** Mrs Robinson.
D: £16.50 **S:** £20.00.
Open: All Year
Beds: 1F 1D
Baths: 2 En
🛏 (3) 🅿 (6) 🗖 🏠 🎄 🛋 & Ⅶ 🗲

Portinscale 13

National Grid Ref: NY2523

🍴 🍺 Farmers Arms

Rickerby Grange, Portinscale, Keswick, Cumbria, CA12 5RH.
Grades: ETC 4 Diamond
RAC 4 Diamond, Sparkling
Tel: **017687 72344**
Mrs Bradley.
D: £28.00-£30.00 **S:** £28.00-£30.00.
Open: All Year
Beds: 3F 9D 2S
Baths: 14 En
🛏 (5) 🅿 (14) 🗖 🏠 ✕ 🎄 🛋 Ⅶ 🗲 🚲
Set within own garden, private parking. In the pretty village of Portinscale near the shores of Lake Derwentwater, within walking distance of Keswick. Offering comfort, good service, a well-stocked bar, comfortable lounge, restaurant where a five-course dinner can be enjoyed

Thirnbeck Guest House, Portinscale, Keswick, Cumbria, CA12 5RD.
Comfortable Georgian guest house with fine views over Derwentwater
Tel: **017687 72869**
Savage.
D: £22.00-£22.00 **S:** £22.00-£22.00.
Open: All Year (not Xmas)
Beds: 4D 1T 1S
Baths: 5 En 1 Pr
🛏 (3) 🅿 (4) ⊬ 🗖 🏠 🎄 🛋 Ⅶ 🗲 🚲

Keswick 14

National Grid Ref: NY2623

🍴 🍺 The Packhorse, Sun Inn, Four in Hand, Twa Dogs, Chaucer House, George Hotel, Kitchin's Cellar Bar, Skiddaw Hotel, Dog & Gun, Golden Lion, Farmers Arms

▲ *Keswick Youth Hostel, Station Road, Keswick, Cumbria, CA12 5LH.*
Actual grid ref: NY267235
Tel: **017687 72484**
Under 18: £6.85
Adults: £10.15
evening meal at 7.00pm, family bunk rooms, games room, grounds available for games, showers, central heating, parking, laundry facilities
Standing above the River Greta, this hostel is ideally placed in Keswick - the northern hub of the Lake District - for superb views across the park to Skiddaw

Braithwaite to Penrith

Two miles beyond **Braithwaite** you come to Portinscale, a village fringed by woodland on the banks of **Derwent Water**. From Nichol End, just off your road into the village, there is a boat service on this attractive lake. From Portinscale the route takes you into **Keswick**, the principal (and very popular) town of the northern Lake District. The town has been a major tourist centre since Victorian times, and its buildings date mostly from this period. Attractions include the Cumberland Pencil Museum, harking back to the days when Borrowdale graphite was the draughtsman's favourite substance; the *Beatrix Potter's Lake District* multimedia experience; and the Museum and Art Gallery, most notable for its manuscript collection featuring Wordsworth, Southey et al. Your road east from Keswick takes you (steeply) past Castlerigg Stone Circle, a neolithic site whose fantastic location sets it apart from those in Wiltshire. From here it's on to Threlkeld, below **Blencathra**, and then Troutbeck, before leaving the National Park and heading on to Greystoke and Little Blencow. From here you can make a detour to Hutton-in-the-Forest, a magnificent house built around a thirteenth-century tower, with an attractive eighteenth-century walled garden. From Little Blencow you come to **Penrith**, an attractive old town built of red sandstone, as is its ruined fourteenth-century castle. From Penrith there is a link route via Skelton, Stockdalewath on the Roe Beck and Dalston in the Caldew Valley to **Carlisle**, where you can join the *Sustrans Carlisle-Inverness* route.

Chaucer House Hotel, Ambleside Road, Keswick, Cumbria, CA12 4DR.
Grades: RAC 2 Star
Tel: 017687 72318
Mr Pechartscheck.
Fax no: 017687 75551
D: £30.00-£40.00 **S:** £30.00-£40.00.
Open: Feb to Dec
Beds: 4F 9D 12T 8S
Baths: 2En 4 Pr
Enjoy the informal tranquillity of this Victorian house hotel. Close to town and lake. Overlooked by Skiddow, Blencathra and Cat Bells. Superb food in PLENTY, all freshly prepard daily. Also self-catering available

Hall Garth, 37 Blencathra Street, Keswick, Cumbria, CA12 4HX.
Tel: 017687 72627 Mr Flint.
D: £18.00-£22.00. **S:** £17.00.
Open: All Year
Beds: 1F 3D 1T
Baths: 2 En 1 Pr 2 Sh
Select family-run and non-smoking guest house in quiet, yet convenient location, quality spacious pine bedrooms, all with fell views. Delicious full English breakfast in a relaxed friendly atmosphere

D = Price range per person sharing in a double room

Foye House, 23 Eskin Street, Keswick, Cumbria, CA12 4DQ.
Grades: ETC 3 Diamond
Tel: 017687 73288
Mr & Mrs Sharpe.
D: £19.00-£21.00 **S:** £16.00-£17.00.
Open: All Year
Beds: 1F 2D 1T 2S
Baths: 4 Pr 2 Sh
Foye house is a well-appointed, small, friendly Victorian guest house quietly located 5 minutes' walk from the town centre and 10 minutes from the Lake. We are ideally situated for walking, cycling and motoring holidays. Hearty traditional breakfast served

Cumbria House, 1 Derwentwater Place Ambleside Road, Keswick, Cumbria, CA12 4DR.
Grades: ETC 3 Diamond
Tel: 017687 73171 (also fax no)
Mr Colam.
D: £18.00-£23.50 **S:** £18.00-£23.50.
Open: Feb to Nov
Beds: 1F 3D 2T 3S
Baths: 4 En 2 Sh
Ideal base for a Lakeland holiday - quiet, 3 minutes from centre of Keswick. Our library of walking/climbing books and advice on suitable routes ensures our popularity with walkers and cyclists. Individually cooked breakfast includes home-made rolls. Drying room, residents license

Brookfield, Penrith Road, Keswick, Cumbria, CA12 4LJ.
Tel: 017687 72867 (also fax no)
Mr Gregory.
D: £16.00-£20.00. **S:** £16.00-£20.00.
Open: All Year
Beds: 2F 2D
Baths: 2 En 1 Sh
A warm welcome awaits you at this family run Victorian guest house. Walking distance to the historic stone circle. Ample street parking. Some rooms with a view of Latrigg. Local information books and videos. Walking boots welcome. Family discounts

Beckside, 5 Wordsworth Street, Keswick, Cumbria, CA12 4HU.
Quality ensuite accommodation. Hearty breakfasts. Close to all amenities
Grades: ETC 4 Diamond
Tel: 017687 73093
Mr & Mrs Helling.
D: £15.00-£19.50 **S:** £22.00.
Open: All Year (not Xmas)
Beds: 1F 2D 1T
Baths: 4 En

Hunters Way, 4 Eskin Street, Keswick, Cumbria, CA12 4DH.
Spacious comfortable ensuite rooms, close to Keswick Centre and countryside
Grades: ETC 4 Diamond
Tel: 017687 72324
D: £20.00-£23.00 **S:** £17.00-£20.00.
Open: All Year (not Xmas)
Beds: 3D 1T 2S
Baths: 4 En 1 Sh

Claremont House, Chestnut Hill, Keswick, Cumbria, CA12 4LT.
Grades: AA 3 Diamond
Tel: 017687 72089 Werfel.
D: £21.00-£25.00.
Open: Easter to Nov
Beds: 3D 1T
Baths: 4 En
Claremont House, built about 150 years ago as a lodge house to the Fieldside estate, stands elevated about one mile from Keswick centre. Fine accommodation in pleasant surroundings, all tastes catered for with our substantial breakfasts

High season, bank holidays and special events mean low availability *everywhere*.

Greystoke House, *9 Leonard Street, Keswick, Cumbria,* CA12 4EL.
Tel: **017687 72603** Mrs Harbage.
D: £19.00-£20.00 **S:** £16.00-£17.00.
Open: All Year
Beds: 4D 2S
Baths: 4 En 2 Sh
🛇 ⅄ ▢ 🐾 🛉 Ⅲ. Ⓥ 🛆 ⚡ ⚲
Traditional Lakeland town house. Two minutes walk from the heart of the town and doorstep to your Lakeland holiday. Ideal base for walking, cycling and touring. Friendly relaxed atmosphere providing a good hearty English breakfast

Clarence House, *14 Eskin Street, Keswick, Cumbria,* CA12 4DQ.
Lovely detached Victorian house, excellent ensuite accommodation. Cleanliness guaranteed. No smoking
Tel: **017687 73186**
Mr & Mrs Robertson.
Fax no: 017687 72317
D: £20.00-£28.00 **S:** £20.00-£28.00.
Open: All Year (not Xmas)
Beds: 1F 4D 3T 1S
Baths: 8 Pr
🛇 (5) ⅄ ▢ 🛉 Ⅲ. Ⓥ

Avondale, *20 Southey Street, Keswick, Cumbria,* CA12 4EF.
Actual grid ref: NY268233
Quality accommodation; great breakfasts & close to all amenities
Grades: ETC 4 Diamond,
AA 4 Diamond
Tel: **Freephone 0800 0286831**
Mr Williams.
Fax no: 017687 75431
D: £19.75-£21.50
S: £19.75-£21.50.
Open: All Year (not Xmas)
Beds: 4D 1T 1S
Baths: 6 En
🛇 (12) ⅄ ▢ 🛉 Ⅲ. Ⓥ 🛆

Glaramara Guest House, *9 Acorn Street, Keswick, Cumbria,* CA12 4EA.
Actual grid ref: NY269232
Cosy family B&B. Good food, central, bike hire, C2C storage/ holiday stabling
Tel: **017687 73216** (also fax no)
Mrs Harbage (BHSII).
D: £17.00-£22.00
S: £17.00-£25.00.
Open: All Year
Beds: 1F 1D 1T 1S
Baths: 2 Pr 2 Sh
🛇 🄿 (3) ⅄ ▢ 🐾 🛉 Ⅲ. Ⓥ 🛆

Please respect
a B&B's wishes
regarding children,
animals & smoking.

Daresfield, *Chestnut Hill, Keswick, Cumbria,* CA12 4LS.
Actual grid ref: NY279236
Homely accommodation - good views
Tel: **017687 72531** Mrs Spencer.
D: £16.00-£18.00 **S:** £16.00-£18.00.
Open: All Year (not Xmas)
Beds: 1F 1D 1S
Baths: 1 Sh
🛇 🄿 (3) ⅄ ▢ 🛉 Ⅲ. Ⓥ ⚡ ⚲

Watendlath, *15 Acorn Street, Keswick, Cumbria,* CA12 4EA.
Grades: ETC 3 Diamond
Tel: **017687 74165**
D: £16.00-£19.00.
Open:
Beds: 1F 3D 1T
Baths: 2 En 1 Sh
🛇 ▢ 🛉 Ⅲ. ⚡ ⚲
Just a few mins from Keswick town centre, Watendlath is a quiet and relaxed retreat, small, tasteful and renowned for its superb traditional English breakfasts. The attractive rooms have everything to make your holiday a home-from-home experience

Sunnyside Guest House,
25 Southey Street, Keswick, Cumbria, CA12 4EF.
Grades: ETC 4 Diamond,
AA 4 Diamond, RAC 4 Diamond
Tel: **017687 72446**
Mr & Mrs Newton.
Fax no: 017687 74447
D: £18.00-£24.00 **S:** £24.00-£24.00.
Open: All Year (not Xmas)
Beds: 1F 4D 1T 1S
Baths: 5 En 2 Sh
🛇 🄿 (7) ⅄ ▢ 🐾 🛉 Ⅲ. Ⓥ 🛆 ⚡
This recently refurbished Victorian building is situated just five minutes walk from the town centre and ten minutes walk from the lake, yet provides quiet and comfortable accommodation throughout

Melbreak House, *29 Church Strett, Keswick, Cumbria,* CA12 4DX.
Close to town centre. Arrive a guest - leave as a friend
Tel: **017687 73398**
Mr & Mrs Hardman.
D: £17.00 **S:** £17.00.
Open: All Year
Beds: 3F 6D 1T 1S
Baths: 10 En
🛇 ⅄ ▢ 🐾 ✕ 🛉 Ⅲ. Ⓥ ⚡

Badgers Wood Guest House,
30 Stanger Street, Keswick, Cumbria, CA12 5JU.
Warm, friendly Victorian house. Close to town, bus station, restaurants, pubs
Grades: ETC 4 Diamond
Tel: **017687 72621**
D: £17.50-£22.00 **S:** £17.50.
Open: All Year (not Xmas)
Beds: 4D 1T 1S
Baths: 3 En 1 Sh
⅄ ▢ 🛉 Ⅲ. Ⓥ ⚡ ⚲

Portland House, *19 Leonard Street, Keswick, Cumbria,* CA12 4EL.
Comfortable and quiet Edwardian house, short walk from town centre
Grades: ETC 3 Diamond
Tel: **017687 74230**
D: £20.00-£20.00 **S:** £20.00-£20.00.
Open: All Year (not Xmas)
Beds: 1F 2D 1T 1S
Baths: 5 En
🛇 (3) 🄿 (3) ⅄ ▢ 🐾 🛉 Ⅲ. 🛆 Ⓥ 🛆 ⚲

Lynwood House, *35 Helvellyn Street, Keswick, Cumbria,* CA12 4EP.
Victorian-style with modern comforts. Traditional or home-made organic breakfasts
Grades: ETC 4 Diamond, Silver
Tel: **017687 72398** Mr Picken.
D: £16.50-£20.00 **S:** £22.50-£17.50.
Open: All Year
Beds: 1F 2D 1S
Baths: 1 En
🛇 (3) ⅄ ▢ 🛉 Ⅲ. Ⓥ 🛆 ⚡ ⚲

Lairbeck Hotel, *Vicarage Hill, Keswick, Cumbria,* CA12 5QB.
Secluded setting, attractive mountain views
Grades: ETC 2 Diamond,
AA 2 Star, RAC 2 Star
Tel: **017687 73373**
Fax no: 017687 73144
D: £29.00-£37.00 **S:** £29.00-£37.00.
Open: Mar to Jan
Beds: 1F 8D 1T 4S
Baths: 14 En
🛇 (6) 🄿 (16) ⅄ ▢ ✕ 🛉 Ⅲ. Ⓥ 🛆 ⚡

High Hill Farm, *High Hill, Keswick, Cumbria,* CA12 5NY.
Modernised former farmhouse, special breaks, available all year, lovely views
Tel: **017687 74793**
Ms Davies.
D: £18.00-£19.00.
Open: All Year
Beds: 2D 1T
Baths: 3 En
🄿 (3) ⅄ ▢ 🛉 Ⅲ. Ⓥ ⚡ ⚲

Dolly Waggon Guest House,
17 Helvellyn Street, Keswick, Cumbria, CA12 4EN.
Actual grid ref: NY269233
Friendly 'home from home' guest house. Walkers welcome. Own keys
Tel: **017687 73593** (also fax no)
Mrs Osborn.
D: £19.50 **S:** £19.50.
Open: Feb to Nov
Beds: 1F 4D 1T **Baths:** 6 Pr
🛇 (7) ⅄ ▢ 🛉 Ⅲ. Ⓥ 🛆 ⚡

Always telephone
to get directions to
the B&B - you will
save time!

Penrith to Consett

The route out of **Penrith** heads northeastwards to **Langwathby** in the Eden Valley, and on to **Little Salkeld**. Close to here stand Long Meg and Her Daughters, a late neolithic stone circle - Long Meg herself stands 18 feet high and is named from her eerily humanoid profile. From here you head onto Viol Moor, from where you make the climb to **Hartside**, where there is a cafe during the summer months with a spectacular panorama. There is a great deal of up-and-down in the route through the Pennines, which takes you to **Garrigill** on the River South Tyne, on to **Nenthead** and up to Black Hill on the county boundary, the highest point on the route. From here you descend through Northumberland over Coalcleugh Moor and Allendale Common to **Allenheads**. Now you enter County Durham and follow the Rookhope Burn stream down to **Rookhope**, from where there is a brief steep climb to the start of the Waskerley Way, a reclaimed railway path, which you follow down to **Consett**.

Latrigg House, *St Herbert Street, Keswick, Cumbria, CA12 4DF.*
Actual grid ref: NY270233
Quiet, convenient, friendly Victorian house. Excellent home cooking
Tel: **017687 73068**
Mr & Mrs Townsend.
Fax no: 017687 72801
D: £18.00 **S:** £18.00.
Open: All Year
Beds: 3D 1T 2S **Baths:** 6 En
🛇 🅿 (1) ⅙ ⬚ ✗ ⬚ 🎟 Ⅴ 🛈 ⚡

The Cartwheel, *5 Blencathra Street, Keswick, Cumbria, CA12 4HW.*
Actual grid ref: NY268234
Family-run guest house ideally situated for northern Lakes
Tel: **017687 73182** Mr Gladas.
D: £16.00 **S:** £16.00.
Open: All Year
Beds: 4D 1T 1S
Baths: 3 En 1 Sh
🛇 ⅙ ⬚ ✗ ⬚ 🎟 Ⅴ 🛈 ⚡

Easedale Hotel, *Southey Street, Keswick, Cumbria, CA12 4EG.*
An owner-managed hotel, with emphasis on comfort & cleanliness
Tel: **017687 72710**
Mr Barraclough.
Fax no: 017687 71127
D: £18.00 **S:** £18.00.
Open: All Year
Beds: 3F 4D 2T 1S
Baths: 3 Pr 2 Sh
🛇 ⬚ ✗ ⬚ 🎟 Ⅴ 🛈 ⚡

Littlefield, *32 Eskin Street, Keswick, Cumbria, CA12 4DG.*
Convenient for walks, lake and shops. Early breakfast if required
Tel: **017687 72949**
D: £16.00 **S:** £16.00.
Open: All Year
Beds: 2D 1T 2S
Baths: 1 Pr 1 Sh

Bringing children with

you? Always ask for

any special rates.

The Paddock Guest House, *Wordsworth Street, Keswick, Cumbria, CA12 4HU.*
Personally run, our charming and friendly guest house dates from mid C19th
Tel: **017687 72510**
D: £16.00 **S:** £27.00.
Open: All Year (not Xmas)
Beds: 1F 1T 3D
Baths: 4 En 1 Pr
🛇 🅿 (5) ⅙ ⬚ 🎟 ⬚ 🎟 Ⅴ 🛈 ⚡

Braemar, *21 Eskin Street, Keswick, Cumbria, CA12 4DQ.*
Guest house for non-smokers. Conveniently situated for exploring area
Tel: **017687 73743** Welch.
D: £20.00 **S:** £16.00.
Open: All Year (not Xmas)
Beds: 3D 1T 2S
Baths: 3 En 1 Sh
⅙ ⬚ ⬚ 🎟 Ⅴ 🛈 ⚡ 🚲

Cranford House, *18 Eskin Street, Keswick, Cumbria, CA12 4DG.*
Friendly B&B aimed at walkers and cyclists; lounge with open fire
Tel: **017687 71017**
Fax no: 017687 72335
D: £16.00 **S:** £16.00.
Open: All Year
Beds: 1T 1D 2S
⅙ ⬚ ⬚ 🎟 Ⅴ 🛈 🚲

Erinville, *57 Eskin Street, Keswick, Cumbria, CA12 4DG.*
Small and friendly, cosy rooms. Comfy beds, great breakfasts, central
Tel: **017687 71365**
D: £17.00 **S:** £17.00.
Open: All Year
Beds: 1T 2D 1S
Baths: 2 En 1 Sh
⅙ ⬚ 🎟 ⬚ 🎟 Ⅴ 🚲

Langdale, *14 Leonard Street, Keswick, Cumbria, CA12 4EL.*
Quality accommodation, all rooms ensuite with good food and cleanliness in comfortable surroundings
Tel: **017687 73977** Mrs Vickers.
D: £19.00 **S:** £19.00.
Open: All Year (not Xmas)
Beds: 3D
Baths: 3 En
⅙ ⬚ ⬚ 🎟 Ⅴ 🛈 ⚡

Penruddock   15

National Grid Ref: NY4227

🍴 🍺 **Herdwick Inn**

Low Garth, *Penruddock, Penrith, Cumbria, CA11 0QU.*
Actual grid ref: NY425284
Converted C18th barn offering a warm welcome in peaceful surroundings
Tel: **017684 83492**
Mrs Barritt.
D: £17.00-£20.00 **S:** £17.00-£20.00.
Open: All Year
Beds: 1F 1T
Baths: 2 En
🛇 🅿 ⅙ ⬚ 🎟 ✗ ⬚ 🎟 Ⅴ 🛈 ⚡ 🚲

Greystoke   16

National Grid Ref: NY4430

🍴 🍺 **Clickham Inn**

Lattendales Farm, *Greystoke, Penrith, Cumbria, CA11 0UE.*
Actual grid ref: NY436307
Comfortable farmhouse in pleasant quiet village
Tel: **017684 83474**
Mrs Ashburner.
D: £16.00-£17.00 **S:** £17.00-£18.00.
Open: Mar to Oct
Beds: 2D 1T
Baths: 1 Sh
🛇 (1) 🅿 (5) ⅙ ⬚ 🎟 ⬚ 🎟 ⚡ 🚲

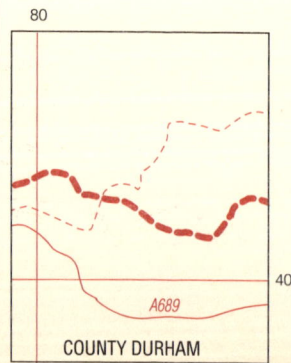

80

40

A689

COUNTY DURHAM

Blencow 17

National Grid Ref: NY4532

|¶| ◀| Crown Inn

Little Blencow Farm, *Blencow, Penrith, Cumbria, CA11 0DG.*
Working farm in small village. Comfortable home with friendly welcome
Tel: **017684 83338** Mrs Fawcett.
Fax no: 017684 83054
D: £16.00-£18.00 **S:** £16.00-£18.00.
Open: All Year (not Xmas)
Beds: 1F 1D 1T
Baths: 1 Pr 1 Sh
👁 🅿 (4) ⊬⌷🕯️🏃🛏 🎟 📷 ⚡ ♻ 👟

Ivegill 18

National Grid Ref: NY4143

|¶| ◀| The Bluebell, Crown Inn

Streethead Farm, *Ivegill, Carlisle, Cumbria, CA4 0NG.*
Tel: **016974 73327** (also fax no)
Mrs Wilson.
D: £20.00-£22.00 **S:** £22.00-£25.00.
Open: All Year (not Xmas)
Beds: 2D **Baths:** 2 En
👁 🅿 (7) 🅿 (2) ⌷🕯️🛏 🎟 📷 ⚡ ♻ 👟
Farm house midway between Penrith and Carlisle, M6 (J41/42) 10 minutes' drive, ideal for break en route to Scotland. Ensuite bedrooms with bed canopies and window seats to admire our marvellous views, real fires, home baking, choice of breakfasts, brochure

Croft End Hurst, *Ivegill, Carlisle, CA4 0NL.*
Rural bungalow situated midway between J41/42 of M6
Grades: ETC 3 Diamond
Tel: **017684 84362**
D: £17.00-£19.00
S: £17.00.
Open: All Year
Beds: 1D 1T
Baths: 1 Sh
👁 (1) 🅿 (4) ⊬⌷🕯️🏃🛏 ♿ 🎟 ♻ 👟

Carlisle 19

National Grid Ref: NY3955

|¶| ◀| Metal Bridge Inn, The Beehive, Mary's Pantry, Crown & Thistle, Coach & Horses, Golden Fleece, Black Lion

🔺 **Carlisle Youth Hostel,**
University of Northumbria, The Old Brewery Residences, Bridge Lane, Caldewgate, Carlisle, Cumbria, CA2 5SR.
Actual grid ref: NY394560
Tel: **01228 597352.**
After 6pm: 01228 59486
Under 18: £12.00
Adults: £12.00
suitable for disabled people, self-catering facilities, showers, laundry facilities
Accommodation in an award-winning conversion of the former Theakston's brewery. Single study bedrooms with shared kitchen and bathroom in flats for upto 7 people

Howard Lodge, *90 Warwick Road, Carlisle, Cumbria, CA1 1JU.*
Actual grid ref: NY407558
Grades: ETC 4 Diamond,
AA 3 Diamond
Tel: **01228 529842**
Mr Hendrie.
D: £15.00-£25.00
S: £20.00-£30.00.
Open: All Year
Beds: 2F 1D 2T 1S
Baths: 6 En 1 Sh
👁 🅿 (6) ⌷🕯️🏃🛏 🎟 📷 📷 ⚡ 👟
Friendly family-run guest house in comfortable Victorian town house in conservation area. Spacious rooms all fully ensuite with satellite TV, welcome tray, hairdryer and clock radio. Large breakfasts. 5 minutes' walk from station and city centre. Evening meals by prior arrangement. Private car park

---

Order your
packed lunches the
evening before you
need them.
Not at breakfast!

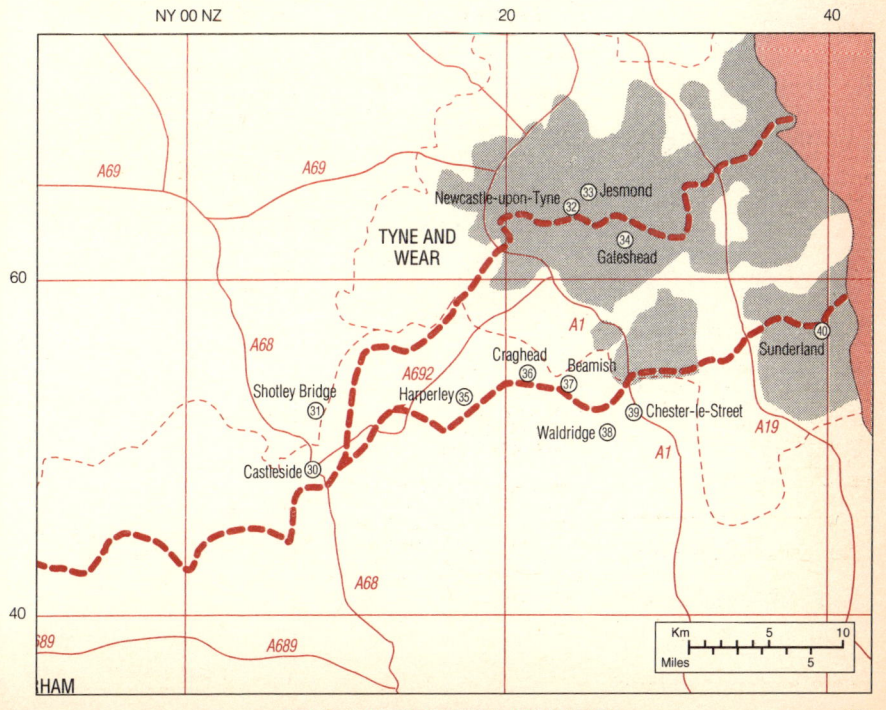

NY 00 NZ   20   40

A69 · A69 · TYNE AND WEAR · Newcastle-upon-Tyne ㉜ · ㉝ Jesmond · Gateshead ㉞
60
A68 · A1 · Sunderland ㊵
Craghead ㊱ · Beamish · A19
Shotley Bridge ㉛ · A692 · Harperley ㉟ · ㊲ · Chester-le-Street ㊳
Castleside ㉚ · Waldridge ㊳ · A1
A68
40
A689 · A689
HAM

Km 0 5 10
Miles 0 5

Craighead, *6 Hartington Place,
Carlisle, Cumbria, CA1 1HL.*
Actual grid ref: NY405559
Grades: ETC 3 Diamond
Tel: 01228 596767
Mrs Smith.
D: £16.50 **S:** £16.50.
Open: All Year (not Xmas)
Beds: 1F 2D 1T 1S
Baths: 1 En 2 Sh
♿☐🛏🚉🖫Ⅴ✦🚲
You will receive a warm welcome
at Craighead a grade II Listed
spacious Victorian town house with
comfortable rooms and original
features. CTV tea/coffee tray in all
rooms. Minutes' walk to city centre
bus and rail stations and all
amenities. Friendly personal
service

Angus Hotel & Almonds Bistro,
*14 Scotland Road, Stanwix,
Carlisle, Cumbria, CA3 9DG.*
Actual grid ref: NY400571
Grades: AA 4 Diamond
**Tel: 01228 523546 /
0800 026 2046** Mr Webster.
Fax no: 01228 531895
D: £20.00-£27.00
S: £26.00-£42.00.
Open: All Year
Beds: 4F 3D 4T 3S
Baths: 11 En 3 Sh
♿☐🛏🗙🚉🖫Ⅴ🗐✦🚲
Victorian town house, foundations
on Hadrian's Wall. Excellent food,
Les Routiers Awards, local
cheeses, home baked bread.
Genuine warm welcome from
owners. Licensed, draught beer,
lounge, meeting room, internet
cafe, direct dial telephones, secure
garaging

Chatsworth Guest House,
*22 Chatsworth Square, Carlisle,
Cumbria, CA1 1HF.*
City centre Grade II Listed
building, close to shops, cathedral,
castle, all amenities
Grades: ETC 3 Diamond
Tel: 01228 524023 (also fax no)
Mrs Mackin.
D: £17.00-£22.00
S: £20.00-£26.00.
Open: All Year (not Xmas)
Beds: 1F 1D 3T 1S
Baths: 2 En 1 Sh
♿ (2)✁☐🚉🖫Ⅴ

Avondale, *3 St Aidans Road,
Carlisle, Cumbria, CA1 1LT.*
Attractive comfortable Edwardian
house. Quiet central position
convenient M6 J43
Grades: ETC 4 Diamond
RAC 4 Diamond
Tel: 01228 523012 (also fax no)
Mr & Mrs Hayes.
D: £20.00-£20.00
S: £20.00-£40.00.
Open: All Year (not Xmas)
Beds: 1D 2T
Baths: 1 En 1 Pr
♿🅿 (3)✁☐🗙🚉🖫Ⅴ🗐✦🚲

Please respect
a B&B's wishes
regarding children,
animals & smoking.

All rooms full and
nowhere else to stay?
Ask the owner if
there's anywhere
nearby

Corner House Hotel & Bar,
4 Grey Street, Carlisle, CA1 2JP.
Grades: ETC 3 Diamond
Tel: 01228 533239 Mrs Anderson.
Fax no: 01228 546628
D: £17.50-£21.00 **S:** £25.00-£30.00.
Open: All Year
Beds: 3F 4D 4T 3S
Baths: 10 En
♿☐🛏🗙🚉🖫&Ⅴ🗐♦🚲
Small, friendly, licensed hotel. 10
mins to city centre attraction, bar,
large TV, lounge and games room.
Excellent base for golf, walking,
horse-riding, swimming, cycling or
touring by car, bus or train, the
lakes, Roman Wall or border
region

Courtfield Guest House,
*169 Warwick Road, Carlisle,
Cumbria, CA1 1LP.*
Short walk to historic city centre.
Close to M6, J43
Grades: ETC 4 Diamond
Tel: 01228 522767 Mrs Dawes.
D: £17.50-£20.00 **S:** £20.00.
Open: All Year (not Xmas)
Beds: 1F 2D 2T
Baths: 5 En
♿🅿 (4)✁☐🚉🖫Ⅴ🚲

Consett to Tynemouth or Sunderland

From Consett the northern route passes close to the impressively complete Derwentcote Steel Furnace (just beyond **Hamsterley**), a remnant of the Industrial Revolution; and follows the Derwent to the Tyne, which it crosses into **Newcastle**. The capital of the Northeast was built on coal and shipbuilding, rising to a position of importance in the nineteenth century. Sights from the earlier centuries of the city's history include the twelfth-century castle from which it gets its name, and the cathedral, notable for its fifteenth-century lantern tower. The Laing Gallery is the region's foremost art gallery, including a major display of British art. Newcastle's material icon is the Tyne Bridge, the great steel arch whose famous daughter spans Sydney Harbour. You get a view of the bridge to your left as the cycle route crosses the Tyne into Gateshead over the Swing Bridge. From here you head east to **Jarrow**, famed for the 1936 hunger march, where you cross the Tyne again through the pedestrian tunnel, and reach the North Sea at **Tynemouth**

The southern route out of Consett takes you to **Stanley**, and the Beamish Museum beyond. This is a large open-air re-creation of early twentieth-century life in the region, including tours of a reopened drift mine, a period High Street, a train station and a farmyard with rare old breeds of cattle and sheep. The Consett and Sunderland Railway Path takes you to **Chester-le-Street** and **Washington**, where the Old Hall was the ancestral home of the family of the eponymous founder of a certain country. There is also an Arts Centre; and the Washington Wildfowl and Wetlands Centre is east of town. The cycle route east crosses the River Wear over a footbridge to the village of Cox Green and leads into **Sunderland**, another old shipbuilding town. Here you cross back over the Wear into Monkwearmouth, and reach the North Sea by Roker Pier.

East View Guest House,
110 Warwick Road, Carlisle,
Cumbria, CA1 1JU.
Actual grid ref: NY407560
10 minutes' walking distance from
city centre, railway station and
restaurants
Grades: ETC 2 Diamond
Tel: 01228 522112 (also fax no)
Mrs Glease.
D: £18.00-£20.00 **S:** £20.00-£25.00.
Open: All Year (not Xmas)
Beds: 3F 2D 1T 1S
Baths: 7 En
🛇 🅿 (4) ⅏ 🗆 🌲 🖤 🎟 Ⓥ ⸕ ♻

Cherry Grove, 87 Petteril Street,
Carlisle, Cumbria, CA1 2AW.
Lovely red brick building close to
golf club and town
Grades: AA 3 Diamond
Tel: 01228 541942
Mr & Mrs Houghton.
D: £17.50-£20.00 **S:** £20.00-£30.00.
Open: All Year
Beds: 3F 2D
Baths: 5 En
🛇 🅿 (3) ⅏ 🗆 🌲 🖤 🎟 Ⓥ 🖿 ⸕ ♻

Cornerways Guest House,
107 Warwick Road, Carlisle,
Cumbria, CA1 1EA.
Large Victorian town house
Grades: ETC 4 Diamond
Tel: 01228 521733 Mrs Fisher.
D: £14.00-£18.00 **S:** £16.00-£18.00.
Open: All Year (not Xmas)
Beds: 2F 1D 4T 3S
Baths: 2 En 2 Sh
🛇 🅿 (4) 🗆 🌲 🗙 🎟 Ⓥ 🖿 ♻

Cambro House, 173 Warwick
Road, Carlisle, CA1 1LP.
Grades: AA 3 Diamond
Tel: 01228 543094 (also fax no)
Mr & Mrs Mawson.
D: £17.00-£20.00 **S:** £20.00-£25.00.
Open: All Year
Beds: 2D 1T
Baths: 3 En
🅿 (2) ⅏ 🗆 🌲 🎟 Ⓥ 🖿 ⸕ ♻
Guests can expect warm hospitality
and friendly service at this attrac-
tively decorated and well-main-
tained guest house. Each ensuite
bedroom includes TV, clock, radio,
hairdryer and welcome tray.
Private off-road parking available,
non-smoking, close to golf course

Kingstown Hotel, 246 Kingstown
Road, Carlisle, CA3 0DE.
Grades: AA 3 Diamond
Tel: 01228 515292 (also fax no)
D: £18.50-£22.00. **S:** £29.00-£36.00.
Open: All Year (not Xmas)
Beds: 1F 5D 1T
Baths: 7 En
🛇 🅿 (10) 🗆 🌲 🗙 🎟 Ⓥ & ⸕ ♻
Situated on the A7, only quarter
mile from M6 (J44), our small family-run hotel offers weary travellers
comfortable accommodation and a
cosy lounge bar in which to
unwind. An ideal base to explore
historic Carlisle, Hadrian's Wall
and the Lake District

Whitelea Guest House,
191 Warwick Road, Carlisle,
CA1 1LP.
Good base for lakes and Hadrian's
Wall. Friendly, family run
Tel: 01228 533139 Croskery.
D: £15.00-£18.00 **S:** £15.00-£18.00.
Open: All Year
Beds: 2F 1T 1S
🛇 🅿 🗆 🌲 🗙 🎟 Ⓥ ⸕ ♻

The Foxgloves, 73 Scotland Road,
Carlisle, Cumbria, CA3 9HL.
Family-run elegant Victorian town
house, very suitable for Roman
Wall walkers
Tel: 01228 526365 Mrs Apcar.
D: £15.00 **S:** £15.00.
Open: All Year **Beds:** 2T 1S
🛇 🗆 🌲 🎟 Ⓥ ⸕

Howard House, 27 Howard Place,
Carlisle, Cumbria, CA1 1HR.
Actual grid ref: NY407559
Elegant Victorian town house, 5
minutes' walk to city centre
Tel: 01228 529159 Mrs Fisher.
Fax no: 01228 512550
D: £16.00 **S:** £16.00.
Open: All Year
Beds: 2F 3D 3T **Baths:** 2 Pr 2 Sh
🛇 🗆 🌲 🗙 🎟 Ⓥ 🖿 ⸕

Penrith 20

National Grid Ref: NY5130

🐾 🍴 Royal Hotel, Lowther Arms, Glen Cottage,
Dog & Duck, Gloucester Arms, Cross Keys,
Agricultural Hotel, Beacon Bank, Herdwick Inn

Norcroft Guest House, Graham
Street, Penrith, Cumbria, CA11 9LQ.
Grades: ETC 3 Diamond
Tel: 01768 862365 (also fax no)
Mrs Jackson.
D: £16.00-£21.50 **S:** £16.00.
Open: All Year
Beds: 2F 2D 4T 1S
Baths: 7 En 2 Sh
🛇 🅿 (9) ⅏ 🗆 🌲 🗙 🎟 & Ⓥ 🖿 ⸕ ♻
Charming Victorian house with
relaxed friendly atmosphere ideal
centre or stop over (M6 junction 40
just 10 mins away) for English
lakes or Scottish borders. Enjoy our
hearty Cumbria food or 5 mins'
walk to town centre for
alternatives. Ample private parking

Blue Swallow, 11 Victoria Road,
Penrith, Cumbria, CA11 8HR.
Grades: ETC 3 Diamond
Tel: 01768 866335 Mrs Hughes.
D: £17.00-£20.00 **S:** £22.00-£27.00.
Open: All Year (not Xmas)
Beds: 1F 2D 2T
Baths: 3 En 1 Sh
🛇 🅿 (5) 🗆 🌲 🎟 Ⓥ 🖿 ⸕ ♻
Victorian town house situated in
lovely market town of Penrith;
ideal location for beautiful Eden
Valley and Lakeland. Close to
Carlisle to Settle Steam Railway.
Barbara and David look forward to
meeting you whether on business
or touring the area

Beacon Bank Hotel, Beacon Edge,
Penrith, Cumbria, CA11 7BD.
Grades: ETC 4 Diamond
Tel: 01768 862633
Mrs Black.
D: £25.00-£30.00 **S:** £35.00-£35.00.
Open: All Year
Beds: 2F 4D 2T
Baths: 8 En
🛇 🅿 (10) ⅏ 🗆 🌲 🎟 Ⓥ 🖿 ♻
Beacon Bank is a beautiful
Victorian house in an acre of
landscaped gardens. Ideally
situated (5 mins M6) for touring
Lake District, Southern Scotland
and Pennines. Relax and enjoy
comfortable, spacious
accommodation in a non-smoking
enviroment

The Friarage, Friargate, Penrith,
Cumbria, CA11 7XR.
Clean, comfortable historical
house, town centre. Ideal
North/South, East/West travellers
Grades: ETC 4 Diamond
Tel: 01768 863635 (also fax no)
Mrs Clark.
D: £15.00-£20.00 **S:** £17.00-£18.00.
Open: Mar to Oct
Beds: 1F 1D 1T 1S
Baths: 1 En 2 Sh
🛇 🅿 (3) 🗆 🌲 🎟 Ⓥ 🖿 ⸕ ♻

Grosvenor House, 3 Lonsdale
Terrace, Meeting House Lane,
Penrith, Cumbria, CA11 7TS.
Large comfortable town house
convenient for lakes and fells
Tel: 01768 863813
Mrs Fitzpatrick.
D: £14.00-£18.00
S: £20.00-£20.00.
Open: Easter to Nov
Beds: 1D 2T
Baths: 1 Sh
🛇 ⅏ 🗆 🌲 🖿 ♻

Albany House, 5 Portland Place,
Penrith, Cumbria, CA11 7QN.
Friendly, comfortable Victorian
house, good breakfast, town centre
m6 5 minutes
Grades: ETC 3 Diamond,
AA 3 Diamond
Tel: 01768 863072 (also fax no)
Mrs Blundell.
D: £17.50-£25.00
S: £20.00-£27.50.
Open: All Year
Beds: 4F 1D
Baths: 2 En 2 Sh
🛇 🅿 (1) 🗆 🌲 🎟 Ⓥ 🖿 ⸕ ♻

Cumrew, Graham Street, Penrith,
Cumbria, CA11 9LG.
Grades: ETC 4 Diamond
Tel: 01768 867923 (also fax no)
Mrs Ablewhite.
D: £15.00-£16.00
S: £15.00-£16.00.
Open: Mar to Oct
Beds: 1D 1S
Baths: 1 Sh
🛇 (5) 🅿 (1) ⅏ 🗆 🌲 🎟 Ⓥ ⸕ ♻
Home from home B&B 5 minutes'
walk from town centre

The White House, *94 Lowther Street, Penrith, Cumbria,* CA11 7UW.
Tel: **01768 892106**
D: £19.00-£24.00 **S:** £25.00-£30.00.
Open: All Year
Beds: 1F 1D
Baths: 2 En
🛇 ⊬ 🖵 🖿 🎟 🗓 ✿ ♦ 🚲
Two very comfortable and spacious rooms in lovely Victorian home, crisp cotton sheets, ensuite facilities with shower and bath, splendid cooked breakfast with quality local produce, a cafetiere of fresh coffee, or quality tea, relaxed and friendly atmosphere

7 Alexandra Road, *Penrith, Cumbria,* CA11 9AL.
Attractive sandstone house in residential area, near town and railway
Tel: **01768 863950** Allison.
D: £14.00-£14.00 **S:** £14.00-£14.00.
Open: Easter to Oct
Beds: 2D 1S **Baths:** 1 Sh
🖿 ✿ ♦ 🚲

Voreda View, *2 Portland Place, Penrith, Cumbria,* CA11 7QN.
Provides comfortable stay, good food, spacious accommodation and Sky Sports
Tel: **01768 863395** (also fax no)
D: £15.00-£18.00 **S:** £15.00-£19.50.
Open: All Year
Beds: 4F 2S
Baths: 2 Sh
🛇 🅿 (1) 🖵 ♛ 🏧 🖿 🎟 ♦ 🚲

Roundthorn Country House, *Beacon Edge, Penrith, Cumbria,* CA11 8SJ.
Beautiful Georgian mansion with spectacular views of the surrounding area
Grades: ETC 3 Diamond
Tel: **01768 863952** Carruthers.
Fax no: 01768 864100
D: £25.00-£30.00 **S:** £37.50-£45.00.
Open: All Year
Beds: 2F 6D
Baths: 8 En
🛇 🅿 ⊬ 🖵 ♛ ✕ 🏧 🖿 🎟 ✿ ♦ 🚲

Caledonia Guest House, *8 Victoria Road, Penrith, Cumbria,* CA11 8HR.
Comfortable family-run Victorian house close to all amenities
Tel: **01768 864482**
D: £18.00-£20.00 **S:** £25.00-£30.00.
Open: All Year
Beds: 1F 2D 2T 1S
Baths: 4 En 2 Pr
🛇 🅿 (5) ⊬ 🖵 🏧 🖿 🎟 ✿ ♦ 🚲

Barco House, *Carleton Road, Penrith, Cumbria,* CA11 8LR.
Actual grid ref: NY523298
Victorian house in own grounds with off street parking
Tel: **01768 863176** Mrs Stockdale.
D: £17.00 **S:** £19.00.
Open: All Year
Beds: 2F 1T
Baths: 2 En
🛇 🅿 (8) 🖵 ♛ ✕ 🏧 🖿 🎟

Brougham 21

National Grid Ref: NY5328

🍴 🍺 Beehive Inn

Keepers Cottage, *Brougham, Penrith, Cumbria,* CA10 2DE.
Beamed period cottage in rural setting. Heated indoor swimming pool
Grades: ETC 3 Diamond
Tel: **01768 865280** (also fax no)
D: £20.00-£24.50 **S:** £24.50-£30.00.
Open: All Year
Beds: 1F 1T 1D
Baths: 3 En
🅿 (4) ⊬ 🖵 ♛ 🏧 🖿 🎟 ✿ ♦ 🚲

Yanwath 22

National Grid Ref: NY5128

🍴 🍺 Yanwath Gate Inn

Yanwath Gate Farm, *Yanwath, Penrith, Cumbria,* CA10 2LF.
Comfortable C17th farmhouse, good food, near a pub
Tel: **01768 864459**
Mr & Mrs Donnelly.
D: £17.00-£20.00 **S:** £17.00-£20.00.
Open: All Year
Beds: 1F 1D
Baths: 2 En
🛇 🅿 (9) ⊬ 🖵 🖿 🎟 ✿ ♦

Langwathby 23

National Grid Ref: NY5733

▲ **Hay Loft B&B Bunkhouse (Independent),** *Langwathby Hall, Langwathby, Penrith, Cumbria,* CA10 1PD.
Actual grid ref: NY568338
Tel: **01768 881771 Adults:** £11.50
evening meals available, showers

Melmerby 24

National Grid Ref: NY6137

🍴 🍺 Shepherds Inn

Gale Hall Farm, *Melmerby, Penrith, Cumbria,* CA10 1HN.
Actual grid ref: NY6236
Large comfortable farmhouse near Pennines and Lake District
Tel: **01768 881254**
Mrs Toppin.
D: £15.00-£15.00 **S:** £15.00-£15.00.
Open: JUN to Nov
Beds: 1F 1T 1S
Baths: 1 Sh
🛇 🅿 (3) 🖵 ♛ 🏧 🚲

All cycleways are popular: you are well-advised to book ahead

---

Renwick 25

National Grid Ref: NY5943

Scalehouse Farm, *Scalehouses, Renwick, Penrith, Cumbria,* CA10 1JY.
Actual grid ref: NY588451
Tel: **01768 896493** (also fax no)
D: £14.00-£18.00 **S:** £16.00-£20.00.
Open: All Year (not Xmas)
Beds: 2D 1T 1Pr 1 Sh
🛇 🅿 (6) ⊬ 🖵 ✕ 🏧 🖿 🎟 ✿ ♦ 🚲
Old farmhouse with period features, open fires and beams, tastefully renovated, cosy rooms and period furniture, peaceful setting with wonderful views of the Pennines and Lake District fells, wholesome cooking with produce from our garden in season and home-made bread

Leadgate 26

National Grid Ref: NY7043

🍴 🍺 Angel Inn

Brownside House, *Leadgate, Alston, Cumbria,* CA9 3EL.
Warm welcome at this peaceful country house outside Alston, North Pennines
Grades: ETC 3 Diamond
Tel: **01434 382169** (also fax no)
Mrs Le Marie.
D: £18.00-£18.00 **S:** £18.00-£18.00.
Open: All Year
Beds: 1D 2T 1S **Baths:** 1 Sh
🛇 🅿 (4) ⊬ 🖵 ♛ ✕ 🏧 🖿 🎟 ✿ ♦ 🚲

Alston 27

National Grid Ref: NY7146

🍴 🍺 Blue Bell Inn, Angel Inn, Turks Head

▲ **Alston Youth Hostel,** *The Firs, Alston, Cumbria,* CA9 3RW.
Actual grid ref: NY717461
Tel: **01434 381509**
Under 18: £5.65 **Adults:** £8.35
evening meal at 7.00pm, family bunk rooms, showers, shop, no smoking
Purpose-built hostel overlooking River South Tyne, on outskirts of Alston, the highest market town in England

Greycroft, *Middle Park, The Raise, Alston, Cumbria,* CA9 3AR.
Actual grid ref: NY747408
Grades: ETC 4 Diamond
Tel: **01434 381383** (also fax no)
Mrs Dent.
D: £18.00-£22.00 **S:** £20.00-£24.00.
Open: All Year (not Xmas)
Beds: 1D 1T **Baths:** 2 En
🛇 🅿 (2) ⊬ 🖵 ✕ 🏧 🖿 ♿ 🎟 ✿ ♦ 🚲
In North Pennines with open views south to Crossfell. 1 mile from historic town of Alston. Ideal area for walking or touring, Pennine Way and Alternative Coast to Coast walks. All home cooking, furnished to high standard

High Field, *Brunteley Meadows, Alston, Cumbria, CA9 3UX.*
Beautiful Pennine views. Remedial massage available. German and French spoken
Tel: **01434 382182** Mrs Pattison.
D: £14.50 **S:** £14.50.
Open: All Year (not Xmas)
Beds: 1T 1D 1S
Baths: 1 En 1 Sh
🛇 🅿 (2) 🔌 ❑ ✗ ♨ Ⅲ. Ⅴ 🛈 ✦ ♻

Garrigill 28

National Grid Ref: NY7441

🍴 🍺 George & Dragon

▲ **Ivy Farmhouse Bunkhouse Barn (Independent),** *Garrigill, Alston, Cumbria, CA9 3DU.*
Actual grid ref: NY744414
Tel: **01434 382501 Adults:** £5.00 evening meals available, self-catering facilities

Ivy House, *Garrigill, Alston, Cumbria, CA9 3DU.*
C17th converted farmhouse. Comfortable, friendly atmosphere. Picturesque North Pennines village
Grades: AA 4 Diamond
Tel: **01434 382501** Mrs Humble.
Fax no: 01434 382660
D: £17.00-£19.50 **S:** £26.00-£29.00.
Open: All Year
Beds: 2F 1T
Baths: 3 En
🛇 🅿 (10) 🔌 ❑ ♉ ✗ ♨ Ⅲ. Ⅴ 🛈 ✦ ♻

High Windy Hall Hotel, *Middleton In Teesdale Road, Garrigill, Alston, Cumbria, CA9 3EZ.*
Peaceful, panoramic views. Good fresh food. Family run, licensed
Tel: **01434 381547** Mrs Platts.
Fax no: 01434 382477
D: £26.00 **S:** £34.00.
Open: Mar to Nov
Beds: 1F 2D 1T
Baths: 4 Pr
🛇 (1) 🅿 (5) ❑ ✗ ♨ Ⅲ. Ⅴ 🛈 ✦

Nenthead 29

National Grid Ref: NY7843

Mill Cottage Bunkhouse, *Nenthead, Alston, Cumbria, CA9 3PD.*
Bunkhouse in spectacular landscape, part of Nenthead Mines heritage site
Tel: **01434 382037**
D: £12.00-£12.00 **S:** £12.00-£12.00.
Open: All Year (not Xmas)
Beds: 2F
🛇 🅿 (4) 🔌 ✗ ♨ Ⅲ. Ⅴ 🛈 ✦ ♻

Pay B&Bs by cash or cheque and be prepared to pay up front.

Castleside 30

National Grid Ref: NZ0849

Bee Cottage Farm, *Castleside, Consett, Co Durham, DH8 9HW.*
Actual grid ref: NZ068453
Ideally situated for Beanish Museum, Durham Cathedral, C2C cycle track and Metro Centre
Grades: ETC 3 Diamond
Tel: **01207 508224**
Mrs Lawson.
D: £22.00-£70.00.
S: £28.00-£35.00.
Open: All Year
Beds: 4F 3D 2T 1S
Baths: 5 En 2 Sh
🛇 🅿 (20) 🔌 ❑ ♉ ✗ ♨ Ⅲ. Ⅴ 🛈

Castleneuk Guest House, *18 Front Street, Castleside, Consett, Co Durham, DH8 9AR.*
Rural village: Beamish Museum, Metro Centre, Hadrian's Wall, Durham 20 mins
Tel: **01207 506634**
McGuigan.
D: £20.00 **S:** £20.00.
Open: All Year (not Xmas)
Beds: 4D 2T 1S
Baths: 4 Pr
🛇 (4) 🅿 (5) ❑ ♉ ✗ ♨ Ⅲ. Ⅴ 🛈 ✦

Shotley Bridge 31

National Grid Ref: NZ0852

🍴 🍺 Punchbowl & Manor House

Redwell Hall Farm, *Shotley Bridge, Consett, Co Durham, DH8 9TS.*
Tel: **01207 255216** Mrs Ward.
D: £19.50 **S:** £21.00.
Open: All Year
Beds: 1F 1D 1T 1S
Baths: 1 Sh
🛇 🅿 (10) 🔌 ❑ ♉ ✗ ♨ Ⅲ. Ⅴ 🛈 ✦ ♻
Redwell Hall Farm is situated 1 mile west of the A68 in the beautiful Derwent Valley near Derwent reservoir. Fishing & sailing, panoramic views & lovely quiet countryside accommodation ensure a relaxing holiday in an Area of Outstanding Beauty

Newcastle-upon-Tyne 32

National Grid Ref: NZ2564

🍴 🍺 Prince of Wales

▲ **Newcastle-upon-Tyne Youth Hostel,** *107 Jesmond Road, Newcastle-upon-Tyne, NE2 1NJ.*
Actual grid ref: NZ257656
Tel: **0191 281 2570**
Under 18: £6.20
Adults: £9.15
evening meal at 7.00pm, self-catering facilities, family bunk rooms, games room, shop, parking
A large town house conveniently located for the centre of this vibrant city, the regional capital of the North East

---

Chirton House Hotel, *46 Clifton Road, Newcastle-upon-Tyne, NE4 6SH.*
Victorian-style house, conveniently situated for city, airport, Northumberland and Durham
Grades: ETC 3 Diamond
Tel: **0191 273 0407** (also fax no)
Mrs Turnbull.
D: £18.00-£23.00 **S:** £26.00-£36.00.
Open: All Year
Beds: 3F 2D 3T 3S
Baths: 6 En 5 Sh
🛇 🅿 ❑ ♉ ♨ Ⅲ. Ⅴ ✦

Jesmond 33

National Grid Ref: NZ2566

Jesmond Park Hotel, *74-76 Queens Road, Jesmond, Newcastle-upon-Tyne, NE2 2PR.*
Very clean, quiet, comfortable hotel offering good full English breakfast
Tel: **0191 281 2821**
Fax no: 0191 281 0515
D: £20.00 **S:** £24.00.
Open: All Year
Beds: 3F 4D 3T 5S
Baths: 9 En 3 Sh
🛇 ❑ ♉ ♨ Ⅲ. Ⅴ 🛈 ✦ ♻

Gateshead 34

National Grid Ref: NZ2561

🍴 🍺 Nine Pins, The Victoria

Bellevue Guest House, *31-33 Belle Vue Bank, Low Fell, Gateshead, Tyne & Wear, NE9 6BQ.*
Victorian terrace, centrally located for Metro Centre, Newcastle stadium, Beamish Museum
Tel: **0191 487 8805**
Mr Wallace.
D: £18.00-£20.00 **S:** £18.00-£28.00.
Open: All Year
Beds: 1F 1D 2T 2S
Baths: 2 En 1 Sh
🛇 🅿 ❑ ✗ ♨ Ⅲ. ♿ Ⅴ ✦ ♻

Cox Close House, *Ravensworth, Gateshead, NE11 0HQ.*
Actual grid ref: NZ228600
Unique C16th. Secluded yet near city and tourist attractions
Tel: **0191 488 7827**
D: £18.00-£22.00 **S:** £18.00-£22.00.
Open: All Year
Beds: 1F 1D 1T
Baths: 1 En 1 Sh
🛇 🅿 🔌 ❑ ♉ ✗ ♨ Ⅲ. Ⅴ 🛈 ✦ ♻

All rooms full and nowhere else to stay? Ask the owner if there's anywhere nearby

---

Harperley 35

National Grid Ref: NZ1753

⚑ Harperley Hotel

Bushblades Farm, *Harperley, Stanley, Co Durham, DH9 9UA.*
Actual grid ref: NZ1653
Georgian farmhouse, rural setting, close Beamish Museum and Durham City
Grades: ETC 3 Diamond
Tel: **01207 232722** Mrs Gibson.
D: £17.00-£19.50 **S:** £20.00-£25.00.
Open: All Year (not Xmas)
Beds: 2D 1T **Baths:** 1 En 2 Sh
🐾 (12) ☑ (4) ⌨ 🎍 ⅲ ⅋ Ⅴ ⚡ ⚲

Craghead 36

National Grid Ref: NZ2151

⚑ Punch Bowl

The Punch Bowl, *Craghead, Stanley, DH9 6EF.*
Village public house providing a good hearty breakfast and friendly welcome
Grades: ETC 2 Diamond
Tel: **01207 232917**
D: £15.00-£20.00 **S:** £15.00-£20.00.
Open: All Year (not Xmas)
Beds: 1F 1T 2S
Baths: 1 Sh
🐾 ☑ (20) ⌨ ✕ 🎍 ⅲ Ⅴ ⚲

Pay B&Bs by cash or cheque and be prepared to pay up front.

All rates are subject to alteration at the owners' discretion.

Beamish 37

National Grid Ref: NZ2253

⚑ Beamish Mary Inn

No Place House, *Beamish, Stanley, Co Durham, DH9 0QH.*
Converted co-operative store, close to Beamish Museum. Friendly warm welcome
Grades: ETC 2 Diamond
Tel: **0191 370 0891**
Mr & Mrs Wood.
D: £18.00-£19.50 **S:** £20.00-£23.00.
Open: All Year
Beds: 2D 1T
Baths: 2 En 1 Sh
🐾 (3) ☑ (5) ⌨ 🍴 🎍 ⅲ Ⅴ ⚡

Waldridge 38

National Grid Ref: NZ2550

Waldridge Fell House, *Waldridge Lane, Waldridge, Chester-le-Street, Co Durham, DH2 3RY.*
Converted village chapel with panoramic views and country walks. Private parking
Tel: **0191 389 1908**
Mrs Sharratt.
D: £20.00 **S:** £24.00.
Open: All Year (not Xmas)
Beds: 5F
Baths: 1 Pr 1 Sh
🐾 ☑ (8) ⌨ 🍴 🎍 ⅲ ⅰ Ⅴ

Chester-le-Street 39

National Grid Ref: NZ2751

⚑ Waldridge Tavern

16 St Cuthberts Avenue, Holmlands Park, *Chester-le-Street, Co Durham, DH3 3PS.*
Semi-detached house, drive for 2 cars. Extremely central to main High Street
Tel: **0191 387 3071** (also fax no)
Mrs McCann.
D: £25.00 **S:** £25.00.
Open: All Year (not Xmas)
Beds: 2F 1D 1S **Baths:** 4 En
🐾 (10) ⌨ ✕ 🎍 ⅲ Ⅴ ⅰ ⚲

Sunderland 40

National Grid Ref: NZ3957

The Chaise, *Sea Front, 5 Roker Terrace, Roker, Sunderland, Tyne & Wear, SR6 9NB.*
Large Victorian guest house, spectacular sea views, excellent breakfast, car parking
Tel: **0191 565 9218** (also fax no)
Mrs Corbyn.
D: £14.00 **S:** £16.00.
Open: All Year
Beds: 7F 2D 2T 1S **Baths:** 4 Pr 2 Sh
🐾 ☑ (12) ⌨ ✕ 🎍 ⅲ Ⅴ ⅰ ⚡

Felicitations Guest House & Art Studio, *94 Ewesley Road, High Barnes, Sunderland, Tyne & Wear, SR4 7RJ.*
Lovely atmosphere. Aromatic treats. An oasis for the body and mind
Tel: **0191 522 0960** Mrs Lindsay.
Fax no: 0191 551 8915
D: £25.00 **S:** £20.00.
Open: All Year
Beds: 1F 1D 1S **Baths:** 1 Pr
🐾 (5) ☑ (1) ⌨ ✕ 🎍 ⅲ Ⅴ ⅰ

ROUTES FOR PEOPLE

Sustrans - it stands for sustainable transport - is a charity working on practical projects to encourage people to walk and cycle more, so as to reduce motor traffic and its adverse effects.

National Cycle Network

Sustrans' flagship project will open in June 2000 with 5000 miles of continuous traffic-free routes and traffic-calmed and minor roads, running right through urban centres and reaching all parts of the UK. The National Cycle Network is a Millennium Commission project and will open with a nationwide celebration called Ride The Net during Midsummer week in June.

Safe Routes to Schools

Safe Routes to Schools is a project to enable and encourage children to cycle and walk to school by improving street design, calming traffic, creating traffic-free spaces and linking with the National Cycle Network.

Sustrans Information Service

Sustrans publish and stock a range of maps, leaflets, information sheets and technical publications. For a free catalogue with further information about Sustrans and the National Cycle Network, and details on how to become a supporter, please contact the Sustrans Information Service, PO Box 21, Bristol BS99 2HA, tel 0117-929 0888, or surf the Web and visit us at **www.sustrans.org.uk**.

Sustrans Severn & Thames

The **Severn & Thames Cycle Route** is a new section of the developing National Cycle Network, running on traffic-free paths and traffic-calmed roads through 140 miles of the South of England, following the Severn from the ancient city of Gloucester before turning inland at Bristol, visiting beautiful Bath and traversing northern Wiltshire with its prehistoric sites to finish at Newbury in Berkshire. An extension of the route from Newbury to Reading is currently at the planning stage. The route connects to the **West Country Way** in Bristol and Bath and the **Welsh National Cycle Route** via the Severn Bridge; it also intersects with the **Wiltshire Cycleway** and the **Round Berkshire Cycle Route**. It is clearly signposted by blue direction signs with a cycle silhouette, numbered 41 from Gloucester to the Severn Bridge and 4 from the Severn Bridge to Newbury.

The route south from **Gloucester** strikes out across the Severn flood plain before running for a short distance along the Gloucester and Sharpness Canal towpath after Frampton on Severn. After **Slimbridge**, **Berkeley** and Oldbury-on-Severn, the junction to the Severn Bridge is at Elberton, before you cycle on, with views of the two Severn Bridges to your right, towards **Avonmouth**, Bristol's port. Here you cross the Avon on a cyclepath alongside the M5 to reach Pill, and head along the traffic-free path up the Avon Gorge. This takes you through the Avon Gorge Nature Reserve and under Brunel's Clifton Suspension Bridge before you reach **Bristol** city centre. From here you follow the traffic-free Bristol and Bath Railway Path, the first Sustrans project (shared with the West Country Way), to historic **Bath**, and the Kennet and Avon Canal towpath to lovely **Bradford-on-Avon**. Here the route through Wiltshire divides into two: the northern route through **Corsham**, **Chippenham** and **Calne** heads up into the Marlborough Downs and close by the neolithic

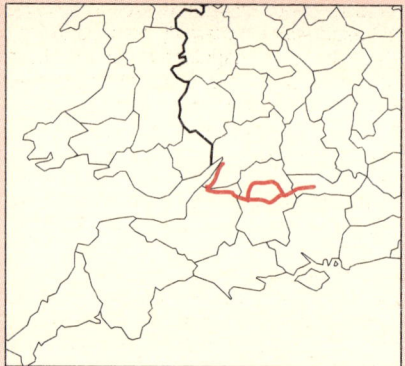

sites of Avebury before reaching Marlborough and taking the Grand Avenue through ancient Savernake Forest to join up with the southern branch. The southern route continues along the Kennet and Avon Canal towpath past the edge of **Trowbridge**, and descends alongside the 'staircase' of 29 locks at Caen Hill to **Devizes** before heading through the Vale of Pewsey to Wootton Rivers and joining up with the northern branch before **Great Bedwyn**. The final stretch of the way follows the Kennet and Avon Canal through the sleepy Berkshire villages of **Hungerford** and **Kintbury** into the Thames Valley to reach **Newbury**.

The indispensable **official route map and guide** for the route is available from Sustrans, 35 King Street, Bristol BS1 4DZ, tel 0117-926 8893, fax 0117-929 4173, @ £5.99 (+ £2.00 p&p).
Maps: Ordnance Survey 1:50,000 Landranger series: 162, 172, 173, 174
Trains: Bristol, Bath, Gloucester, Chippenham and Newbury are served by main line train services; there are connections to several other places on or near to the route.

Gloucester   1

National Grid Ref: SO8318

🍴 🍺 Linden Tree

Rotherfield House Hotel, *5 Horton Road, Gloucester, GL1 3PX.*
Immaculate, extended detached Victorian property. Friendly atmosphere, excellent choice food
Grades: AA 1 Star
Tel: **01452 410500** Mr Eacott.
D: £22.00-£25.00 **S:** £24.00-£36.00.
Open: All Year
Beds: 2F 3D 1T 7S
Baths: 4 En 2 Pr
🛇 🅿 (9) 🛏 🍽 ✕ 🎦 🕯 🛢 ⚡ 🔗

Georgian Guest House, *85 Bristol Road, Gloucester, GL1 5SN.*
Part-Georgian terraced house, 15 minutes walk city centre
Tel: **01452 413286** (also fax no) Nash.
D: £14.50-£15.50 **S:** £14.50-£15.50.
Open: All Year
Beds: 4F 3T 2S
Baths: 2 En 1 Sh
🛇 🅿 (3) 🛏 🛏 🕯 🎦 Ⓥ 🔗

D = Price range per person sharing in a double room

Slimbridge   2

National Grid Ref: SO7303

▲ ***Slimbridge Youth Hostel,***
Shepherd's Patch, Slimbridge, Gloucester, GL2 7BP.
Actual grid ref: ST730043
Tel: **01453 890275**
Under 18: £6.85 **Adults:** £10.15
evening meal at 7.00pm, family bunk rooms, games room, showers, shop, parking
Purpose-built youth hostel, with its own pond & wildfowl collection, next to the Sharpness Canal and Sir Peter Scott's famous wildfowl reserve

Gloucester, important since Roman times, is most notable for its fantastically preserved cathedral, among England's best examples of the Perpendicular style. The tomb of King Edward II (see under Berkeley), with alabaster statue, is largely responsible for the wealth on which the most magnificent parts of the cathedral were built, as it became a place of pilgrimage. The city also has a wealth of specialist museums, many of them converted warehouses in the redundant docks. The most notable are the National Waterways Museum, recording the heyday of the country's canal network, and the Regiments of Gloucestershire Museum, much more interesting than it sounds thanks to its empathetic approach.

At **Slimbridge**, the Wildfowl and Wetlands Trust offers access to a large variety of birdlife all year round, as in winter migratory Arctic birds arrive. The centre is particularly notable for its large numbers of flamingos.

Bristol 5

National Grid Ref: ST6075

|●| ◀ Port of Call

▲ *Bristol International Youth Hostel, Hayman House, 14 Narrow Quay, Bristol, BS1 4QA.*
Actual grid ref: ST586725
Tel: **0117 922 1659**
Under 18: £8.00 **Adults:** £11.65
evening meal at 6.00-7.30pm, self-catering facilities, television, games room, showers, shop, laundry facilities
With views over the waterways, this hostel has been sympathetically and imaginatively restored to create a relaxing yet cosmopolitan atmosphere

Arches Hotel, 132 Cotham Brow, Bristol, BS6 6AE.
Actual grid ref: ST588745
Friendly, non-smoking city centre hotel, close to shops and restaurants
Grades: ETC 3 Diamond
Tel: **0117 924 7398** (also fax no)
Mr Lambert.
D: £20.50-£25.00 **S:** £23.50-£37.00.
Open: All Year (not Xmas)
Beds: 3F 2D 1T 3S
Baths: 4 En 2 Sh
☎ (6) ⊁ ☐ ★ ♨ Ⅲ ☑ ✦

Planning a longer stay? Always ask for any special rates.

Berkeley 3

National Grid Ref: ST6899

|●| ◀ Black Horse North Nibley

Pickwick Farm, Berkeley, Glos, GL13 9EU.
C18th inn now comfortable farm house warm welcome close castle wildfowl trust
Grades: ETC 3 Diamond
Tel: **01453 810241** Mrs Jordan.
D: £18.00-£19.00 **S:** £18.00-£19.00.
Open: All Year (not Xmas)
Beds: 1F 1D 1T **Baths:** 1 En 1 Sh
☎ (2) ℗ (4) ⊁ ☐ ♨ Ⅲ ☑ ✦ ♻

Easter Compton 4

National Grid Ref: ST5782

|●| ◀ The Fox, The Plough

Firwood House, Main Road, Easter Compton, Bristol, BS35 5RA.
Small village 5 mins M5, 5 mins Severn Bridge, only 15 mins central Bristol
Tel: **01454 633394** Mrs Griffiths.
Fax no: 01454 633323
D: £20.00 **S:** £22.50.
Open: All Year
Beds: 1F 2T 1D 1S **Baths:** 3 Sh
☎ ℗ (5) ⊁ ☐ ★ ♨ Ⅲ ☑ ⓘ ✦

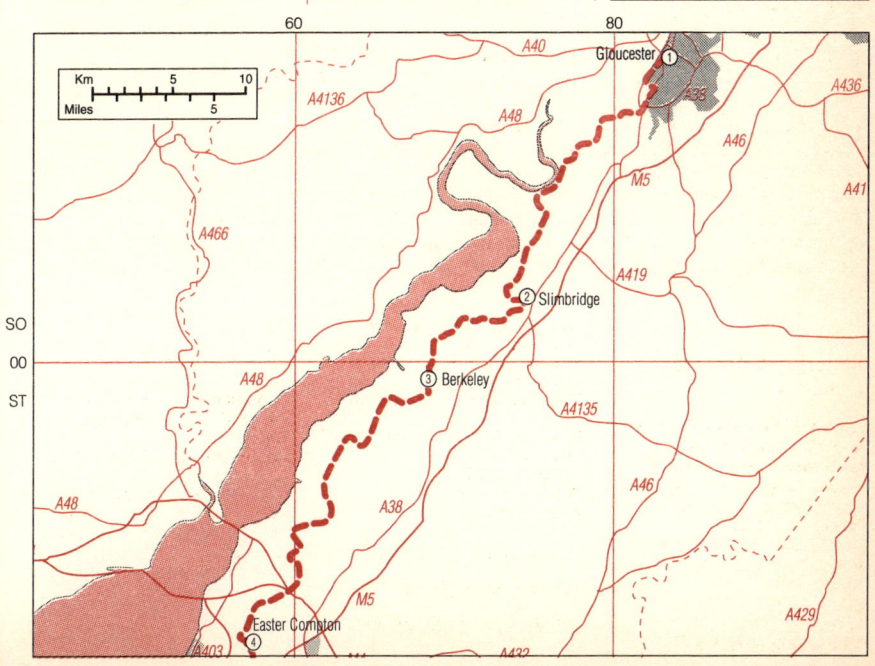

Downs View Guest House,
*38 Upper Belgrave Road, Clifton,
Bristol, BS8 2XN.*
Centrally situated. Overlooking
Durdham Down. Near Zoo and
Clifton Suspension Bridge
Tel: **0117 973 7046** Ms Cox.
Fax no: 0117 9738169
D: £20.00-£22.50 **S:** £25.00-£27.50.
Open: All Year (not Xmas)
Beds: 2F 4D 3T 6S
Baths: 7 En 2 Sh
🛏 (2) ♿ 🛐 🕏 ⬛ ▥

Maison George, *10 Greville Road,
Southville, Bristol, BS3 1LL.*
Large Victorian town-house within
walking distance of city centre
Tel: **0117 963 9416** (also fax no)
Mr Evans.
D: £20.00-£30.00 **S:** £20.00-£30.00.
Open: All Year
Beds: 1F 1D 2T 1S **Baths:** 2 Sh
🛏 🖂 🛐 🕏 ⬛ ▥

Basca House, *19 Broadway Road,
Bishopston, Bristol, BS7 8ES.*
Lovely Victorian home in quiet
residential area. 1 mile city centre
Tel: **0117 942 2182**
Mrs Chawdhary.
D: £19.50 **S:** £20.00.
Open: All Year (not Xmas)
Beds: 2T 2S **Baths:** 2 Sh
🛏 🖂 🛐 🕏 ⬛ ▥

S = Price range for a single

person in a room

All cycleways are popular: you are well-advised to book ahead

---

Norfolk House, *577 Gloucester
Road, Horfield, Bristol, BS7 0BW.*
Actual grid ref: ST596774
Pleasant Victorian house over-
looking park
Tel: **0117 951 3191** (also fax no)
Mr Thomas.
D: £18.00 **S:** £20.00.
Open: All Year (not Xmas)
Beds: 2D 1T
Baths: 1 En 2 Sh
🛏 🖂 🛐 ✕ ⬛ ▥ 🔒

Keynsham 6

National Grid Ref: ST6568

🍴 🍺 The Talbot

Fiorita, *91 Bath Road, Keynsham,
Bristol, BS31 1SR.*
Warm welcome, comfortable
family home midway between
Bristol and Bath
Tel: **0117 986 3738** (also fax no)
Mrs Poulter.
D: £14.50-£16.00 **S:** £16.00-£18.00.
Open: Jan to Dec
Beds: 1D 1T **Baths:** 1 En 1 Sh
🛏 🅿 (4) 🖂 🛐 ⬛ ▥ 🔒 ⚡ 🚲

Bath 7

National Grid Ref: ST7464

🍴 🍺 Royal Oak, The Dolphin, Wheelwrights
Arms, Old Crown, The Huntsman, The George,
Devonshire Arms, The Sportsman, Waldergrave
Arms, The Bear, Park Tavern, Rose & Crown,
Weston Walk, The Boathouse

▲ **Bath Youth Hostel,** *Bathwick
Hill, Bath, North East Somerset,
BA2 6JZ.*
Actual grid ref: ST766644
Tel: **01225 465674**
Under 18: £6.85 **Adults:** £10.15
evening meal at 5.30-7.30pm,
family bunk rooms, television,
games room, showers, shop,
security lockers
*Handsome Italianate mansion, set
in beautiful, secluded gardens, with
views of historic city and
surrounding hills*

Bailbrook Lodge, *35-37 London
Road West, Bath, BA1 7HZ.*
Grades: ETC 3 Diamond,
AA 3 Diamond
Tel: **01225 859090** (also fax no)
Mrs Sexton.
D: £29.00-£40.00 **S:** £39.00-£50.00.
Open: All Year
Beds: 4F 4D 4T **Baths:** 12 En
🛏 🅿 (14) 🖂 ✕ 🛐 ⬛ ▥ ⚡ 🚵
A warm welcome is assured at
Bailbrooke Lodge, an imposing
Georgian House set it its own
gardens. The elegant period
bedroms (some four posters) offer
ensuite facilities, TV and hospit-
ality trays. Situated 1.5 miles from
Bath centre. Close to M4.

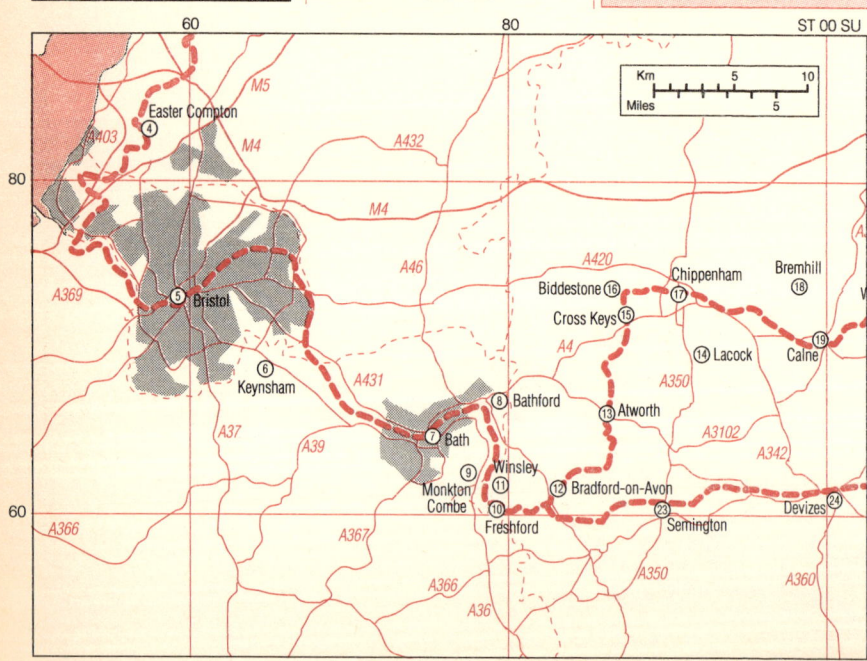

Koryu B&B, *7 Pulteney Gardens, Bath, BA2 4HG.*
Tel: **01225 337642** (also fax no)
Mrs Shimizu.
D: £22.00-£25.00 **S:** £22.00-£25.00.
Open: All Year
Beds: 1F 2D 2T 2S
Baths: 5 En 2 Sh
♿ 🅿 (2) ⊬ 🗔 ✕ 🎐 🏛 Ⓥ ⚲
Completely renovated Victorian home run by a young Japanese lady, extremely clean, delicious breakfasts with wide menu, beautiful linens; a bright, cheerful and welcoming house. Abbey and Roman baths 5 mins, gorgeous Kennet and Avon canal 2 mins

Sarnia, *19 Combe Park, Weston, Bath, BA1 3NR.*
Actual grid ref: ST730656
Grades: AA 4 Diamond
Tel: **01225 424159**
Mr & Mrs Fradley.
Fax no: 01225 337689
D: £22.50-£30.00 **S:** £25.00-£40.00.
Open: All Year (not Xmas/New Year)
Beds: 1F 1D 1T
Baths: 2 En 1 Pr
♿ 🅿 (3) ⊬ 🗔 🎐 🏛 Ⓥ 🛆 ⚲
Superb bed & breakfast in large Victorian home, easy reach of town centre. Spacious bedrooms, private facilities, newly decorated, attractively furnished. Breakfast in sunny dining room, English, Continental and vegetarian menus, home made jams, marmalades, comfortable lounge, secluded garden, private parking & children welcome

Berkeley Castle is a medieval castle set in Elizabethan gardens. It is most famous as the scene of the murder in 1327 of Edward II, who, unpopular with the barons on account of his homosexuality and the advancement he granted first to Piers Gaveston and then to Hugh le Despenser, was deposed by his wife Queen Isabel with Roger de Mortimer. Read about it in Christopher Marlowe's play. You can visit the room where the deed was done (it involved a red-hot poker). Thereafter, his body was denied burial in both Bristol and Malmesbury, and Gloucester reaped the rewards in later years.

For **Bristol** and **Bath** see under the *Sustrans West Country Way.*

The Old Red House, *37 Newbridge Road, Bath, BA1 3HE.*
Grades: AA 3 Diamond
Tel: **01225 330464**
Fax no: 01225 331661
D: £22.00-£33.00 **S:** £30.00-£45.00.
Open: Mar to Dec
Beds: 1F 4D 1T 1S
Baths: 3 En 1 Pr 1 Sh
♿ 🅿 (4) ⊬ 🗔 🍴 🎐 🏛 Ⓥ ⚲
A romantic Victorian gingerbread house with stained glass windows, comfortable bedrooms with canopied or king size beds, superbly cooked breakfasts around large family dining table. Sunny conservatory. Special rates for 3 or more nights - well-lit car park. No smoking

14 Raby Place, *Bathwick Hill, Bath, BA2 4EH.*
Grades: ETC 3 Diamond
Tel: **01225 465120**
Mrs Guy.
Fax no: 01225 465283
D: £22.50-£25.00
S: £25.00-£25.00.
Open: All Year
Beds: 1F 2D 1T 1S
Baths: 3 En 2 Pr
♿ ⊬ 🗔 🎐 🏛 Ⓥ 🛆 ⚲
Charming Georgian terraced house with beautiful interior rooms. Healthy breakfasts, fresh fruit salads, yoghurts, organic eggs, granary bread and a selection of home made jams. We are a no smoking house

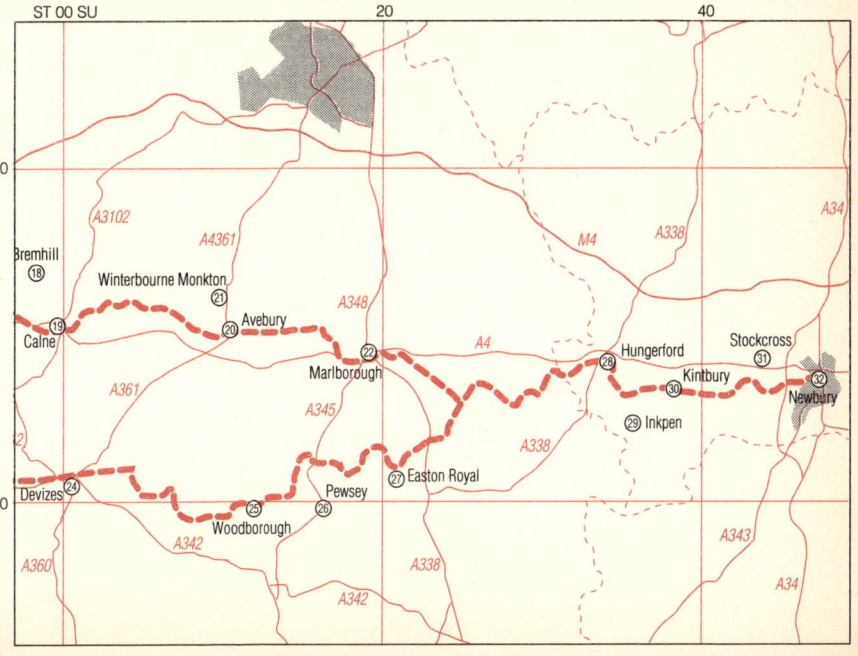

Kinlet Guest House, *99 Wellsway, Bath, BA2 4RA.*
Actual grid ref: ST745636
Home from home. Friendly, comfortable, easy walk into the city
Tel: **01225 420268** (also fax no)
Mrs Bennett.
D: £19.00-£20.00 **S:** £22.00-£27.00.
Open: All Year
Beds: 1F 1D 1S
Baths: 1 Sh
🛇 ⅏ ☐ 🖳 Ⅷ Ⅴ ⅋ ⚲

Cedar Lodge, *13 Lambridge London Road, Bath, BA1 6BJ.*
Come, stay, enjoy. Welcoming, comfortable lovely, well-placed period house
Tel: **01225 423468**
Mr & Mrs Beckett.
D: £25.00 **S:** £30.00.
Open: All Year
Beds: 1T 2D
Baths: 2 En 1 Pr
🛇 (10) 🅿 (6) ⅏ ☐ 🖳 Ⅷ Ⅴ ⅋ ⚲

Glan y Dwr, *14 Newbridge Hill, Bath, BA1 3PU.*
Grades: ETC 3 Diamond
Tel: **01225 317521**
D: £16.00-£24.00 **S:** £18.00-£35.00.
Open: All Year
Beds: 2D 1T 3S
Baths: 1 En 1 Pr 1 Sh
🛇 (11) 🅿 (3) ⅏ ☐ 🖳 Ⅷ Ⅴ ⅋ ⚲
We pride ourselves on personal attention to ensure you have a comfortable stay in Bath. Comfortable rooms with a good selection of breakfasts

Georgian Guest House,
34 Henrietta Street, Bath, BA2 6LR.
Grades: ETC 3 Diamond
Tel: **01225 424103**
Fax no: 01225 425279
D: £28.00-£35.00 **S:** £28.00-£50.00.
Open: All Year (not Xmas)
Beds: 7D 2T 2S
Baths: 7 En 1 Sh
🛇 ⅏ ☐ 🖳 Ⅷ Ⅴ ⚲
Grade I Listed town house, situated just 2 mins walk to city centre in a peaceful location. Enjoy your English/continental breakfast in our sunny dining room overlooking the garden. Winter breaks available

Wellsway Guest House,
51 Wellsway, Bath, BA2 4RS.
Walking distance to city. Clean, comfortable
Tel: **01225 423434** Mrs Strong.
D: £20.00-£20.00 **S:** £20.00-£20.00.
Open: All Year
Beds: 1F 1D 1T 1S
Baths: 4 Sh
🛇 🅿 (4) ☐ 🖳 ⅋ ⚲

D = Price range per person sharing in a double room

S = Price range for a single person in a room

Dene Villa, *5 Newbridge Hill, Bath, BA1 3PW.*
Victorian family-run guest house, a warm welcome is assured
Tel: **01225 427676** Mrs Surry.
Fax no: 01225 482684
D: £20.00-£22.50 **S:** £19.00-£22.00.
Open: All Year
Beds: 1F 1D 1T 1S
Baths: 3 En
🛇 (3) 🅿 (4) ☐ 🖳 Ⅷ Ⅴ ⚲

Joanna House, *5 Pulteney Avenue, Bath, BA2 4HH.*
City centre Victorian house near railway, Kennet and Avon canal
Tel: **01225 335246** Mr House.
D: £16.00-£19.00 **S:** £15.00-£18.00.
Open: All Year
Beds: 1F 1D 1T 1S
🛇 ⅏ ☐ 🖳 Ⅷ Ⅴ

The Terrace Guest House,
3 Pulteney Terrace, Bath, BA2 4HJ.
Mid-terrace house, 7 minutes from city centre and railway station
Tel: **01225 316578** Mrs Gould.
D: £16.00-£17.50 **S:** £18.00-£20.00.
Open: All Year (not Xmas)
Beds: 1D 1T **Baths:** 1 Sh
🛇 (6) ☐ 🖳 Ⅷ Ⅴ ⅋ ⚲

Brinsley Sheridan Guest House,
95 Wellsway, Bearflat, Bath, BA2 4RU.
Lovely friendly guest house only short walk from city centre
Grades: ETC 4 Diamond
Tel: **01225 429562**
Fax no: 01225 429616
D: £17.50-£25.00 **S:** £17.50-£30.00.
Open: All Year
Beds: 1F 2D 1T
Baths: 1 En 1 Pr 2 Sh
🛇 ⅏ ☐ 🖳 Ⅷ Ⅴ ⚲

Flaxley Villa, *9 Newbridge Hill, Bath, BA1 3PW.*
Victorian house on west side of Bath in residential area
Tel: **01225 313237** Mrs Cooper.
D: £20.00-£25.00 **S:** £18.00-£36.00.
Open: All Year
Beds: 3D 1T 1S
Baths: 3 En
🛇 🅿 (5) ☐ 🖳 Ⅷ Ⅴ ⚲

Cairngorm, *3 Gloucester Road, Lower Swainswick, Bath, BA1 7BH.*
Charming detached home with beautiful views over city and countryside
Grades: AA 2 Diamond
Tel: **01225 429004** Mrs Biggs.
D: £16.50-£20.00 **S:** £18.00.
Open: All Year (not Xmas)
Beds: 2D 1T
Baths: 3 En
🛇 (2) 🅿 (3) ⅏ ☐ 🖳 & Ⅷ Ⅴ ⅋ ⚲

Westerlea, *87 Greenway Lane, Bath, BA2 4LN.*
Georgian style house, large gardens, friendly, ensuite accommodation, cars garaged
Grades: ETC 4 Diamond
Tel: **01225 311543** (also fax no)
D: £22.50-£30.00 **S:** £35.00-£50.00.
Open: All Year (not Xmas)
Beds: 2D
Baths: 2 En
🛇 (12) 🅿 (2) ⅏ ☐ 🖳 Ⅷ Ⅴ ⅋ ⚲

Cheery Tree Villa, *7 Newbridge Hill, Bath, BA1 3PW.*
Small, friendly Victorian home. 1 mile from Bath city centre
Grades: ETC 3 Diamond
Tel: **01225 331617**
D: £16.00-£48.00 **S:** £18.00-£25.00.
Open: All Year (not Xmas)
Beds: 1D 1T 1S
Baths: 1 Sh
🛇 (4) 🅿 (4) ☐ 🖳 Ⅷ Ⅴ ⚲

The White Guest House,
23 Pulteney Gardens, Bath, BA2 4HG.
Ideally situated for all of Bath's famous attractions (great breakfast)
Grades: AA 3 Diamond
Tel: **01225 426075** (also fax no)
Wynne.
D: £22.50-£22.50 **S:** £25.00.
Open: All Year
Beds: 2D 1T
Baths: 3 En
🛇 (3) ⅏ ☐ 🖳 Ⅷ Ⅴ ▮

Fyfield, *Ralph Allen Drive, Combe Down, Bath, BA2 5AE.*
Attractive comfortable 1950s house, large garden, 1.5 miles from city centre
Tel: **01225 833561** Mrs Waterman.
D: £18.00 **S:** £18.00.
Open: All Year (not Xmas)
Beds: 1D 1T 1S
Baths: 1 Sh
🛇 🅿 (4) ☐ 🖳 Ⅷ Ⅴ

Marisha's Guest House,
68 Newbridge Hill, Bath, BA1 3QA.
Offering a warm welcome in the relaxed atmosphere of this beautifully restored Victorian house
Tel: **01225 446881** (also fax no)
Mrs Webb.
D: £17.00 **S:** £17.00.
Open: All Year (not Xmas)
Beds: 2F 2T 2D 1S
Baths: 4 En 3 Pr
🛇 (5) 🅿 (3) ⅏ ☐ 🖳 & Ⅷ Ⅴ ▮ ⅋ ⚲

Wentworth House Hotel,
106 Bloomfield Road, Bath, BA2 2AP.
Imposing Victorian Bath stone mansion (1887) in secluded grounds with stunning views from rear
Tel: **01225 339193** Mrs Kitching.
Fax no: 01225 310460
D: £30.00 **S:** £45.00.
Open: All Year (not Xmas)
Beds: 2F 8 D 5T
Baths: 13 En 2 Pr
🛇 (5) 🅿 (20) ☐ 🖳 Ⅷ ▮ 🖳 Ⅷ Ⅴ ▮

Bradford on Avon centres on an arched stone bridge over the Avon, and also features a tithe barn and the ancient Saxon Church of St Laurence.

Corsham Court is a sixteenth-century house, purchased in the late eighteenth century by Paul Methuen, and extensively developed over the following decades by Nash and Bellamy. It now houses an extensive art collection including Michelangelo, Caravaggio, Rubens and Reynolds. There is also a landscaped garden by Brown and Repton. The village itself has weavers' cottages and a Brunel railway tunnel.

Just before **Calne**, Bowood House is a Georgian mansion partly designed by Robert Adam. It was here that Joseph Priestly discovered oxygen in 1774. The house is set in a magnificent landscaped garden designed by 'Capability' Brown, notable for its Rhododendron gardens.

Bathford 8

National Grid Ref: ST7966

🍴 🍺 The Crown

Bridge Cottage, Northfield End, Ashley Road, Bathford, Bath, BA1 7TT.
Pretty cottage with lovely gardens. Village location near Bath city
Tel: **01225 852399**
Mrs Bright.
D: £20.00-£27.50 **S:** £25.00-£40.00.
Open: All Year (not Xmas)
Beds: 2D 1T
Baths: 2 Pr
🛇 🅿 🗲 ☐ 🏠 🖢 📖 🗹

Garston Cottage, Ashley Road, Bathford, Bath, N E Somerset, BA1 7TT.
Country cottage, 2 miles from Bath, courtyard garden with jacuzzi
Grades: ETC 3 Diamond
Tel: **01225 852510**
Ms Smart.
Fax no: 01225 852793
D: £20.00-£25.00 **S:** £25.00-£30.00.
Open: All Year
Beds: 1F 1D 1T
Baths: 3 En
🛇 🅿 (2) 🗲 ☐ 🏠 🖢 📖 🗹 🚲

Monkton Combe 9

National Grid Ref: ST7762

🍴 🍺 Wheelwrights Arms

The Manor House, Monkton Combe, Bath, BA2 7HD.
Grades: ETC 3 Diamond
Tel: **01225 723128** Mrs Hartley.
Fax no: 01225 722972
D: £22.50-£35.00 **S:** £30.00-£35.00.
Open: All Year
Beds: 2F 5D 1T
Baths: 8 En
🛇 🅿 (12) ☐ 🏠 ✕ 🖢 📖 🗹 🕭 🚲 🐎
Restful rambling medieval manor by millstream in rural Area of Outstanding Natural Beauty

Freshford 10

National Grid Ref: ST7860

🍴 🍺 The Inn, Old Coaching Inn

Tyning House, Freshford, Bath, BA3 6DR.
Great hospitality in beautiful surroundings!
Tel: **01225 723288** (also fax no)
Mrs Harward.
D: £16.00 **S:** £21.00.
Open: All Year
Beds: 2D
Baths: 1 Sh
🛇 🅿 (6) ☐ 🖢 📖 🗹

Winsley 11

National Grid Ref: ST7961

🍴 🍺 Seven Stars

3 Corners, Cottles Lane, Winsley, Bradford-on-Avon, Wilts, BA15 2HJ.
House in quiet village edge location, attractive rooms and gardens
Tel: **01225 865380** Mrs Cole.
D: £22.50-£25.00 **S:** £26.00-£30.00.
Open: All Year (not Xmas)
Beds: 1F 1D
Baths: 1 En 1 Pr
🛇 🅿 (4) 🗲 ☐ ✕ 🖢 📖 🗹 🕭 🚲 🐎

Bradford-on-Avon 12

National Grid Ref: ST8261

🍴 🍺 Seven Stars, Barge Inn, Cross Guns, King's Arms, Bear Inn, The Beehive, The Plough, Hop Pole, Three Horse Shoes

Great Ashley House, Ashley Lane, Bradford-on-Avon, Wilts, BA15 2PP.
A warm welcome to our 200-year-old former family farmhouse
Tel: **01225 863381** (also fax no)
Mrs Rawlings.
D: £17.50-£20.00 **S:** £25.00-£30.00.
Open: All Year (not Xmas)
Beds: 1F 2D
Baths: 1 En 1 Sh
🛇 🅿 (3) 🗲 ☐ 🖢 📖 🗹 🚲 🐎

Great Ashley Farm, Ashley Lane, Bradford-on-Avon, Wilts, BA15 2PP.
Actual grid ref: ST813619
Grades: ETC 4 Diamond
Tel: **01225 864563** (also fax no)
Mrs Rawlings.
D: £20.00-£24.00
S: £25.00-£45.00.
Open: All Year (not Xmas)
Beds: 1F 2D
Baths: 3 En
🛇 🅿 🗲 ☐ 🏠 🖢 📖 🗹 🕭 🚲 🐎
Come and enjoy our lovely secluded farmhouse set between Bath and Bradford on Avon, offering delightful ensuite rooms, great hospitality and a delicious breakfast. Golf, cycle-hire, Kennet and Avon Canal close by. Convenient for M4, Glastonbury Wells, Stonehenge, Lacock, Castle Combe, making this the ideal touring base. Children welcome, working farm

Chard's Barn, Leigh Grove, Bradford-on-Avon, Wilts, BA15 2RF.
Tel: **01225 863461**
Mr & Mrs Stickney.
D: £20.00-£23.00
S: £20.00-£20.00.
Open: All Year (not Xmas)
Beds: 1D 1T 1S
Baths: 2 En 1 Pr
🛇 🅿 (4) 🗲 ☐ 🏠 🖢 📖 🕭 🗹 🐎
Quiet C17th barn in unspoilt countryside with lovely gardens, view and walks. All ground floor, individually styled bedrooms, choice of breakfasts. Historic town and golf course, one mile. Close - Bath, Castle Combe, Longleat. Easy for Salisbury Plain and Stonehenge

The Locks, 265 Trowbridge Road, Bradford-on-Avon, Wilts, BA15 1UA.
Private house alongside restored canal
Tel: **01225 863358**
Mrs Benjamin.
D: £16.00-£19.00 **S:** £20.00-£30.00.
Open: All Year
Beds: 1F 2T
Baths: 1 En 1 Pr 1 Sh
🛇 (3) 🅿 (6) 🗲 ☐ 🖢 📖 🗹 🕭 🚲 🐎

Atworth 13

National Grid Ref: ST8665

🍴 🍺 The Golden Fleece

Church Farm, Atworth, Melksham, Wilts, SN12 8JA.
Working dairy farm, large garden. Easy access Bath, Lacock, Bradford-on-Avon
Tel: **01225 702215**
Mrs Hole.
D: £17.50-£20.00
S: £20.00-£25.00.
Open: Easter to Oct
Beds: 1F 1D
Baths: 1 Sh
🛇 🅿 (4) ☐ 🏠 🖢 🗹

Lacock 14

National Grid Ref: ST9168

🍴 🍺 The George, Red Lion, Carpenters' Arms, The Angel

The Old Rectory, *Lacock, Chippenham, Wilts, SN15 2JZ.*
Grades: ETC 4 Diamond
Tel: **01249 730335** Mrs Sexton.
Fax no: 01249 730166
D: £22.50-£25.00 **S:** £25.00-£27.50.
Open: All Year
Beds: 1F 1D 1T
Baths: 3 En
🛇 🄿 (6) 🕭 ⌨ ⌂ 🕭 👤 🖤 🛋 🖤 ⚡ ♿
Superb Gothic Victorian
architecture, set in 8 acres of
grounds and gardens, many original
features and 4 poster beds.
Excellent pubs a stroll away in
famous Lacock location for tourists
and businessmen, M4 (J17), close
by. Bath 12 miles, London 2 hours.
Recomm in 'Off the Beaten Track'

Videl, *6A Bewley Lane, Lacock, Chippenham, Wiltshire, SN15 2PG.*
Detached bungalow with annexe.
Quiet position, rural location
Grades: ETC 3 Diamond
Tel: **01249 730279** Mrs Joad.
D: £20.00-£22.50 **S:** £25.00-£25.00.
Open: All Year
Beds: 1F 1T
Baths: 1 En 1 Pr
🛇 🄿 (2) 🕭 ⌨ 🕭 👤 🖤 🖤 ♿

Cross Keys 15

National Grid Ref: ST8671

🍴 🍺 White Horse

Spiders Barn, *Cross Keys, Corsham, Wiltshire, SN13 0DT.*
Extremely well-appointed house.
Large comfortable rooms
overlooking lovely garden
Tel: **01249 712012**
Ms Thornton-Norris.
D: £20.00-£20.00 **S:** £25.00-£30.00.
Open: All Year (not Xmas)
Beds: 1D 1T
Baths: 2 En
🄿 (6) 🕭 ⌨ 🕭 🖤 🖤 ⚡

Biddestone 16

National Grid Ref: ST8673

Home Farm, *Biddestone, Chippenham, Wilts, SN14 7DQ.*
Listed C17th farmhouse working
farm, picturesque village. Stroll to
pubs
Grades: ETC 4 Diamond,
AA 4 Diamond
Tel: **01249 714475**
Mr & Mrs Smith.
Fax no: 01249 701488
D: £20.00-£22.50 **S:** £25.00-£30.00.
Open: All Year (not Xmas)
Beds: 2F 1D
Baths: 2 En 1 Pr
🛇 🄿 (4) 🕭 ⌨ 🕭 🖤 👤 🖤 ⚡ ♿

At **Avebury** stands a large neolithic stone circle;
nearby are Silbury Hill, Europe's largest man-made
prehistoric mound, and West Kennet Long Barrow, a
burial complex dating from the fourth millennium BC.

Marlborough has the widest high street in England,
with a fine display of Georgian buildings and half-
timbered cottages.

Devizes has a number of pretty old coaching inns,
Elizabethan houses and an originally Norman church.
The town's superb museum specialises in prehistoric
finds, including from Avebury and Stonehenge.

Newbury was the site of two battles of the Civil War,
one of which (1643) is commemorated by the Falkland
Memorial.

Chippenham 17

National Grid Ref: ST9173

🍴 🍺 Rowden Arms, Biddestone Arms, White Horse, Three Crowns,

Bramleys, *73 Marshfield Road, Chippenham, Wilts, SN15 1JR.*
Large Victorian house, Grade II
Listed
Grades: ETC 1 Diamond
Tel: **01249 653770** Mrs Swatton.
D: £16.00-£18.00 **S:** £17.00-£19.00.
Open: All Year
Beds: 1F 3T 1S **Baths:** 1 Pr 1 Sh
🛇 🄿 (4) 🕭 ⌨ 🕭 🖤 🖤 👤 ⚡ ♿

Frogwell House, *132 Hungerdown Lane, Chippenham, Wilts, SN14 0BD.*
Family-run C19th stone-built house
providing comfortable
accommodation
Grades: ETC 4 Diamond
Tel: **01249 650328** (also fax no)
Mrs Burgess.
D: £17.50-£19.00 **S:** £25.00-£25.00.
Open: All Year
Beds: 1F 1D 2T 1S
Baths: 2 En 1 Sh
🛇 🄿 (6) 🕭 ⌨ 🕭 ✕ 🕭 🖤 🖤 ⚡ 🚲

Bremhill 18

National Grid Ref: ST9773

🍴 🍺 The George

Lowbridge Farm, *Bremhill, Calne, Wilts, SN11 9HE.*
Old thatched farmhouse. Varied
stock. Scenic views. Places to visit
Tel: **01249 815889** Miss Sinden.
D: £18.00-£18.50 **S:** £18.00-£18.50.
Open: All Year
Beds: 1F 1D **Baths:** 1 Sh
🛇 🄿 (8) 🕭 ⌨ 🕭 ✕ 🕭 🖤 🖤 ⚡ ♿

Planning a longer
stay? Always ask for
any special rates.

Bringing children with
you? Always ask for
any special rates.

Calne 19

National Grid Ref: ST9971

🍴 🍺 Black Horse

Lower Sands Farm, *Low Lane, Calne, Wilts, SN11 8TR.*
Old farmhouse, v. quiet homely and
friendly. Good breakfast, large gar-
den
Grades: ETC 1 Diamond
Tel: **01249 812402** Mrs Henly.
D: £16.00-£16.00 **S:** £16.00-£16.00.
Open: All Year (not Xmas)
Beds: 1D 1T 1S **Baths:** 1 Sh
🄿 (10) ⌨ 🕭 🖤 🖤 ♿

White Hart Hotel, *2 London Road, Calne, Wiltshire, SN11 0AB.*
Old coaching inn dating back to
1575
Grades: ETC 1 Diamond
Tel: **01249 812413** Miss Orlandi.
Fax no: 01249 812467
D: £18.00-£20.00 **S:** £18.00-£23.00.
Open: All Year
Beds: 3F 5D 4T 2S
Baths: 14 En
🄿 (10) ⌨ ✕ 🕭 🖤 🖤 👤 ⚡ ♿

Avebury 20

National Grid Ref: SU1069

🍴 🍺 Waggon & Horses, Red Lion

6 Beckhampton Road, *Avebury, Marlborough, Wilts, SN8 1QT.*
Close to Ridgeway Walk and bus
route
Tel: **01672 539588** Mrs Dixon.
D: £16.00-£20.00 **S:** £25.00-£30.00.
Open: All Year (not Xmas)
Beds: 1D 1T
Baths: 1 Sh
🛇 🄿 (6) ⌨ 🕭 🖤 🖤 👤 ⚡

Winterbourne Monkton 21

National Grid Ref: SU1072

The New Inn, Winterbourne Monkton, Swindon, Wilts, SN4 9NW.
Traditional country inn
Tel: **01672 539240**
D: £22.50 **S:** £28.00.
Open: All Year
Beds: 2D 3T **Baths:** 5 Pr
🛇 🅿 (25) ✕ 🏊 🛏 Ⅴ 🎴 ✦

Marlborough 22

National Grid Ref: SU1869

📶 ◀ The Bear, The Roebuck

Cartref, 63 George Lane, Marlborough, Wilts, SN8 4BY.
Family home near town centre.
Ideal for Avebury, Savernake,
Wiltshire Downs
Grades: ETC 3 Diamond
Tel: **01672 512771** Mrs Harrison.
D: £18.00-£18.00 **S:** £20.00-£20.00.
Open: All Year (not Xmas)
Beds: 1F 1D 1T
Baths: 1 Sh
🛇 (6) 🅿 (2) 🏇 🛏 🎴 ✦ ♂

Beam End, 67 George Lane, Marlborough, Wilts, SN8 4BY.
Comfortable detached house within easy walking distance of historic town
Tel: **01672 515048** (also fax no)
Mrs Drew.
D: £20.00-£27.50 **S:** £20.00-£20.00.
Open: All Year (not Xmas)
Beds: 1T 2S
Baths: 1 En 1 Sh
🅿 (3) ✔ 🗆 🏊 🛏 Ⅴ 🎴 ♂

Redlands, Elcot Lane, Marlborough, Wilts, SN8 2BA.
Warm welcome, rural views, excellent food
Tel: **01672 515477** Mrs Camm.
Fax no: 01672 516523
D: £17.50 **S:** £25.00.
Open: Easter to Nov
Beds: 2D 1T
Baths: 1 En 1 Sh
🛇 🅿 (4) ✔ 🗆 🏊 🛏 Ⅴ 🎴

Semington 23

National Grid Ref: ST8960

📶 ◀ The Linnet

New House Farm, Littleton, Semington, Trowbridge, Wilts, BA14 6LF.
Actual grid ref: ST910600
Victorian former farmhouse, open countryside, lovely gardens, good touring centre
Grades: ETC 3 Diamond
Tel: **01380 870349** Mrs Ball.
D: £20.00-£20.00 **S:** £25.00-£25.00.
Open: All Year
Beds: 2D 1T
Baths: 3 En
🛇 🅿 (10) ✔ 🗆 ✕ 🏊 🛏 & Ⅴ

Devizes 24

National Grid Ref: SU0061

📶 ◀ The Churchill, The Bridge, Royal Oak, The Bear, Black Swan, Stage Post, The Moonrakers, Elm Tree, Four Seasons

The Chestnuts, Potterne Road, Devizes, Wiltshire, SN10 5DD.
Actual grid ref: SU006608
Good base for Bath, Salisbury, Stonehenge, Avebury and Kennet & Avon Canal
Grades: ETC 4 Diamond
Tel: **01380 724532**
Mrs Mortimer.
D: £20.00-£25.00
S: £25.00-£25.00.
Open: All Year (not Xmas)
Beds: 1F 1T
Baths: 2 En
🛇 🅿 (2) ✔ 🗆 🏊 🛏 Ⅴ 🎴 ✦ ♂

Glenholme Guest House, 77 Nursteed Road, Devizes, Wilts, SN10 3AJ.
Friendly, comfortable house. Warm welcome. Lovely historic town
Grades: ETC 2 Diamond
Tel: **01380 723187**
Mrs Bishop.
D: £18.00-£18.00 **S:** £20.00-£20.00.
Open: All Year
Beds: 1F 1T
Baths: 1 Sh
🛇 🅿 🗆 ✔ ✕ 🏊 🛏 Ⅴ 🎴

Craven House, Station Road, Devizes, Wilts, SN10 1BZ.
Victorian house 50 yards from centre for restaurants and pubs
Tel: **01380 723514** Mrs Shaw.
D: £20.00 **S:** £20.00.
Open: All Year
Beds: 1F 1D 2T
Baths: 2 En 1 Pr 1 Sh
🛇 🗆 ✕ 🏊 🛏 Ⅴ 🎴 ✦ ♂

Gate House, Wick Lane, Devizes, Wilts, SN10 5DW.
Large house and garden, not on main road. Bath/Salisbury 25 miles
Grades: ETC 3 Diamond
Tel: **01380 725283**
Mrs Stratton.
Fax no: 01380 722382
D: £20.00-£20.00
S: £22.50-£22.50.
Open: All Year (not Xmas)
Beds: 1D 1T 1S
Baths: 1 En 1 Sh
🅿 (6) ✔ 🗆 🏊 🛏 Ⅴ ✦ ♂

Asta, 66 Downlands Road, Devizes, Wilts, SN10 5EF.
Comfortable, modern house in quiet road, 15 minutes from town centre
Grades: ETC 2 Diamond
Tel: **01380 722546**
Mrs Milne-Day.
D: £16.00 **S:** £16.00.
Open: All Year
Beds: 1D 2S
Baths: 1 Sh
🛇 🅿 (2) 🏇 ✕ 🏊 🛏

Woodborough 25

National Grid Ref: SU1159

📶 ◀ Seven Stars

St Cross, Woodborough, Pewsey, Wilts, SN9 5PL.
Pewsey Vale - heart of crop circles, beautiful countryside, Kennet & Avon Canal 8 mins' walk
Tel: **01672 851346** (also fax no)
Mrs Gore.
D: £25.00-£35.00.
Open: All Year
Beds: 1D 1T
Baths: 1 Sh
🛇 (6) 🅿 (1) ✔ 🗆 🏇 🎴 ✦ ♂

Pewsey 26

National Grid Ref: SU1660

📶 ◀ French Horn

Old Dairy House, Sharcott, Pewsey, Wilts, SN9 5PA.
Thatched dairy house with river lake wood in four acres
Tel: **01672 562287**
Mr & Mrs Barker.
D: £25.00-£25.00 **S:** £30.00-£30.00.
Open: All Year
Beds: 2T
Baths: 2 En

Easton Royal 27

National Grid Ref: SU2060

📶 ◀ Royal Oak, Three Horseshoes

Hook Cottage, Easton Royal, Pewsey, Wilts, SN9 5LY.
Actual grid ref: SU207608
Comfortable chalet bungalow in large garden with views to Downs
Tel: **01672 810275** (also fax no)
Mrs McNaught.
D: £17.50 **S:** £20.00.
Open: All Year
Beds: 1F 1T 1S **Baths:** 1 En 1 Pr
🛇 🅿 (5) ✔ 🗆 🏇 ✕ 🏊 🛏 & Ⅴ 🎴 ✦

Hungerford 28

National Grid Ref: SU3368

📶 ◀ Just Williams, John O'Gaunt

The Honeybones, 33 Bourne Vale, Hungerford, Berkshire, RG17 0LL.
Actual grid ref: SU333682
Tel: **01488 683228**
Mr & Mrs Honeybone.
D: £16.00-£17.50 **S:** £17.50-£22.50.
Open: All Year
Beds: 2T 1S
Baths: 1 Pr 1 Sh
🛇 (5) 🅿 (3) ✔ 🗆 🏊 🛏 Ⅴ ✦ ♂
Modern detached family house, southern edge of town, within walking distance town centre, railway and canal. Conservatory breakfast room with panoramic views of local countryside, ideal touring and walking base, 3 miles M4 (J14), guided walks by prior arrangement

Wilton House, *33 High Street, Hungerford, Berks, RG17 0NF.*
Elegant C15th town house in popular antiques centre
Grades: ETC 4 Diamond
Tel: **01488 684228** Mrs Welfare.
Fax no: 01488 685037
D: £25.00-£27.50 **S:** £35.00-£38.00.
Open: All Year (not Xmas)
Beds: 2F 1D 1T
Baths: 2 En
🛏 (8) 🅿 (3) ⅋ 🛏 🔥 🏛 🖳 🖳 ⅋

15 Sanden Close, *Hungerford, Berks, RG17 0LA.*
Semi-detached bungalow in quiet close. Short walk to shops and station
Tel: **01488 682583** Mrs Hook.
D: £15.00-£16.00 **S:** £17.00-£18.00.
Open: All Year (not Xmas)
Beds: 1D 1S
Baths: 1 Sh
🛏 (5) 🅿 (3) ⅋ 🛏 🏛

Brae House, *Salisbury Road, Hungerford, RG17 0LH.*
We warmly welcome you to our family home
Tel: **01488 682747** Mrs Rock.
D: £20.00-£20.00 **S:** £25.00-£35.00.
Open: All Year (not Xmas)
Beds: 1F
Baths: 1 En
🛏 🅿 (2) ⅋ 🛏 🔥 🏛 🖳 ⅋ 🚲

Wasing, *35 Sanden Close, Hungerford, Berkshire, RG17 0LA.*
Warm welcome to the home of ex farmers. 3 miles M4
Tel: **01488 684127** Mrs Smalley.
D: £15.50-£16.00 **S:** £17.00-£18.00.
Open: All Year (not Xmas)
Beds: 1D 1T 1S
Baths: 1 En 1 Sh
🛏 🅿 🛏 🔥 🏛 🖳 ⅋ 🚲

D = Price range per person sharing in a double room

Wynbush, *135 Priory Road, Hungerford, Berks, RG17 0AP.*
Detached house, large garden, quiet. 3 miles M4
Tel: **01488 682045** Mrs Simmonds.
D: £15.00 **S:** £17.00.
Open: All Year
Beds: 1D 1S
Baths: 1 Sh
🛏 🅿 (3) ⅋ 🛏 🔥 🏛 🖳

Inkpen   29

National Grid Ref: SU3764

Beacon House, *Bell Lane, Upper Green, Inkpen, Hungerford, Berks, RG17 9QJ.*
Actual grid ref: SU368634
Grades: AA 3 Diamond
Tel: **01488 668640**
Mr & Mrs Cave.
D: £20.00-£20.00 **S:** £20.00-£20.00.
Open: All Year
Beds: 1T 2S
Baths: 2 Sh
🛏 (7) 🅿 (6) 🛏 🔥 ✕ 🔥 🏛 🖳 🖳 ⅋ 🚲
Visit our 1930's country home on Berks/Wilts/Hants border. Maximum four guests ensures our personal attention. Lovely countryside for walking, garden for relaxing, studio for art work. Oxford, Windsor, Winchester, Salisbury one hour by car

---

Kintbury   30

National Grid Ref: SU3866

🍴 🍺 Crown & Garter

The Forbury, *Crossways, Kintbury, Hungerford, Berks, RG17 9SU.*
Extended C17th cottage. Lovely position facing south, overlooking own woodlands
Tel: **01488 658377** Mr Cubitt.
D: £20.00-£25.00 **S:** £20.00-£25.00.
Open: All Year (not Xmas)
Beds: 1F **Baths:** 1 Pr 1 Sh
🛏 🅿 (10) 🛏 🔥 ✕ 🔥 🏛 🖳 🖳 ⅋ 🚲

Stockcross   31

National Grid Ref: SU4368

🍴 🍺 Lord Lyon

79 Glebe Lane, *Stockcross, Newbury, Berks, RG19 8AD.*
Spacious detached Edwardian house. Easy reach of Chievely Interchange/Newbury
Tel: **01488 608561**
Mr & Mrs Tipple.
D: £25.00-£25.00 **S:** £25.00-£25.00.
Open: All Year
Beds: 1F 1T
Baths: 1 Sh
🛏 🅿 (5) ⅋ 🛏 🔥 🔥 🏛 🖳 ⅋

Newbury   32

National Grid Ref: SU4767

🍴 🍺 Lord Lyon, Red Lion, Gun Inn

15 Shaw Road, *Newbury, Berks, RG14 1HG.*
Late Georgian terraced house near town centre, rail and canal
Tel: **01635 44962** Mrs Curtis.
D: £17.00-£18.00 **S:** £17.00-£18.00.
Open: All Year
Beds: 1D, 1T
Baths: 1 Sh
🛏 🅿 ⅋ 🛏 🔥 🏛 🖳 ⅋ 🚲

Laurel House, *157 Andover Road, Newbury, RG14 6NB.*
A warm welcome awaits you in our delightful Georgian house
Tel: **01635 35931**
Mr & Mrs Dixon.
D: £18.00-£18.00.
Open: All Year (not Xmas)
Beds: 1D 1T
Baths: 1 Sh
🅿 (2) ⅋ 🛏 🔥 🏛 🖳 🚲

S = Price range for a single person in a room

STILWELL'S IRELAND BED & BREAKFAST

Think of Ireland and you think of that world famous Irish hospitality. The warmth of the welcome is as much a part of this great island as are the wild and beautiful landscapes, the traditional folk music, the Guinness and the architecture and lifestyle of Dublin and Belfast. Everywhere you go, North or South, you can't escape it. There are few better ways of experiencing this renowned hospitality, when travelling through Ireland, than by staying at one of the country's many Bed and Breakfasts. And there's no better way of choosing a convenient and desirable B&B than by consulting **Stilwell's Ireland: Bed and Breakfast 2000**.

Stilwell's Ireland: Bed and Breakfast 2000 contains over 1,400 entries - private houses, country halls, farms, cottages, inns, small hotels and guest houses - listed by county, in both Northern Ireland and the Republic of Ireland. Each entry includes room rates, facilities, tourist board grades or notices of approval and a brief description of the B&B, its location and surroundings. The average charge per person per night is £17.50. The listings also provide the names of local pubs and restaurants which serve food in the evening. As with all Stilwell B&B guides, **Stilwell's Ireland** has maps, listings of tourist information offices and rail, bus, air and ferry information.

Treat yourself to some Irish hospitality with **Stilwell's Ireland: Bed and Breakfast 2000**.

£6.95 from all good bookstores (ISBN 1-900861-16-X) or
£7.95 (inc p&p) from Stilwell Publishing Ltd,
59 Charlotte Road, London EC2A 3QW (020 7739 7179)

Sustrans West Country Way

The **West Country Way** is a recently-opened section of the new National Cycle Network, running on traffic-free paths and traffic-calmed roads from Padstow in Cornwall to Bristol, linking many historic towns in Devon and Somerset and passing through a great deal of this beautiful region's varied countryside, from the open heather-clad elevations of Bodmin Moor and Exmoor to the lowland of the Somerset Levels with its network of canals, which abruptly gives rise to the Mendip Hills. The route is clearly signposted by blue direction signs with a cycle silhouette and the number 3 in a red rectangle. The total distance is 230 miles.

The indispensable **official route map and guide** for the West Country Way is available from Sustrans, 35 King Street, Bristol BS1 4DZ, tel 0117-926 8893, fax 0117-929 4173, @ £5.99 (+ £1.50 p&p).

Maps: Ordnance Survey 1:50,000 Landranger series: 172, 180, 181, 182, 190, 193, 200, 201

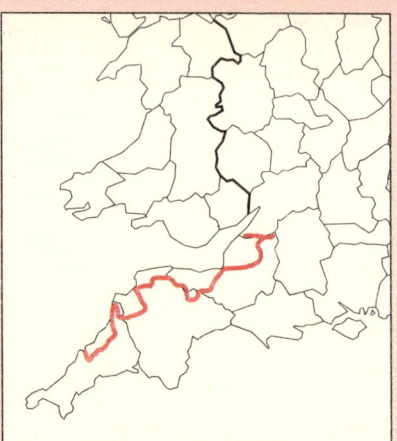

Trains: Bristol and Bath are main termini on the Intercity network; Bodmin, Tiverton, Taunton and Bridgwater are main line stations, as is Exeter, from where you can connect to Barnstaple.

Padstow to Camelford

The typical pretty Cornish fishing port of **Padstow** sits enclosed from the Atlantic Ocean by the Camel Estuary. Here you will find the fifteenth-century Church of St Petroc, the Celtic monk who founded the town in the sixth century. The route takes you up the estuary to Wadebridge and then follows the river upstream. From the village of **Dunmere** you can make a detour into Bodmin, the historic county town. Here you will find *another* Church of St Petroc, with an elaborate twelfth-century carved font, and Bodmin Jail, a notorious nineteenth-century death row. Bodmin Town Museum covers archaeology of the town as well as Bodmin Moor. From Dunmere the route follows the Camel Trail through Dunmere Wood before turning off to **Blisland**. Here you head north along quiet roads through the western reaches of **Bodmin Moor**, passing close to remains of some of the Bronze Age settlements which are scattered over the moor. As you near the Camelford turning, you can see rising away to your right Rough Tor, the moor's second highest peak, one of the eroded granite outcrops which make the landscape of Bodmin Moor and Dartmoor so dramatic. There is a designated detour to Camelford, one of the many sole authentic locations of King Arthur's court of Camelot.

Padstow   1

National Grid Ref: SW9175

🏴 🍺 Old Customs House, London Inn, Ring of Bells

Rosehill, High Street, Padstow, Cornwall, *PL28 8BB*.
Elevated, peaceful, old town location. Adjacent deerpark; five minutes harbour
Tel: **01841 532761** Mrs Meyer.
Fax no: 001603 7197744
D: £17.00-£20.00 **S:** £17.00-£20.00.
Open: All Year (not Xmas)
Beds: 1T 1D **Baths:** 1 Sh
🛏 🅿 (1) 🖤🗠🏇🛁🛗🎰 Ⅴ 🖍 ♿

Mother Ivey Cottage, *Trevose Head, Padstow, Cornwall, PL28 8SL.*
Actual grid ref: SW859763
Tel: **01841 520329** (also fax no)
Mrs Woosnam Mills.
D: £20.00-£22.50 **S:** £30.00-£35.00.
Open: Easter to Oct
Beds: 2T **Baths:** 2 En
🛏 (6) 🅿 (6) 🖤🗠🏇🗙🛁 Ⅴ 🖍 ♿
Traditionally-built Cornish clifftop house with stunning sea views, overlooking Trevose Head with a beach below. The area is renowned for swimming, fishing, surfing and walking. A championship golf course - Trevose - is nearby. The Cornwall Coastal Path is adjacent

20 Grenville Road, *Padstow, Cornwall, PL28 8EX.*
All full ensuite, on-site parking, 10 mins from harbour
Grades: AA 3 Diamond
Tel: **01841 532756** (also fax no)
Green.
D: £20.00-£25.00 **S:** £25.00.
Open: Easter to Oct
Beds: 1D 1T 1S **Baths:** 2 Pr
🛏 🅿 (5) 🖍🗠🛁🛗🎰 Ⅴ 🖍 ♿

S = Price range for a single person in a room

Treann House, *24 Dennis Road, Padstow, Cornwall, PL28 8DE.*
Elegant Edwardian house. Stunning estuary views, few mins to harbour
Grades: ETC 4 Diamond
Tel: **01841 532714**
Mrs Mitchell.
D: £22.50-£30.00
S: £22.50-£30.00.
Open: All Year
Beds: 2D 1T
Baths: 2 En 1 Pr
🛇 🖤☐🛉🎹.Ⓥ🛡⚡ 🚲

Althea Library B&B, *27 High Street, Padstow, Cornwall, PL28 8BB.*
Unique accommodation, short walk from harbour, quiet part of town
Tel: **01841 532717**
D: £26.00-£28.00
S: £26.00-£56.00.
Open: All Year (not Xmas)
Beds: 2D 1T
Baths: 3 En
🅿(3) 🖤☐🛉🎹.Ⓥ 🕭

Cross House Hotel, *Church Street, Padstow, Cornwall, PL28 8BG.*
Charming Georgian house, beautifully furnished to a high standard offering every comfort
Tel: **01841 532391**
Miss Gidlow.
D: £20.00 **S:** £50.00.
Open: All Year
Beds: 2F 7D
Baths: 9 En
🛇 (5) 🅿 (4) ☐🛉🎹.Ⓥ🛡⚡

St Issey 2

National Grid Ref: SW9271

🍴🍺 Ring of Bells

Trevorrick Farm, *St Issey, Wadebridge, Cornwall, PL27 7QH.*
Near camel trail and Padstow, centrally situated in North Cornwall for touring
Grades: ETC 3 Diamond
Tel: **01841 540574** Mr Mealing.
Fax no: 01841 540834
D: £18.00-£25.00 **S:** £27.00-£36.00.
Open: All Year (not Xmas)
Beds: 1F 1D 1T **Baths:** 3 En
🛇🅿(6)🖤☐🍴🎹.Ⓥ

Menhinick House, *St Issey, Wadebridge, Cornwall, PL27 7QA.*
Crawling distance from pub, good food, comfortable beds, warm welcome
Tel: **01841 541210** Mrs Sander.
D: £15.00-£18.00 **S:** £18.00-£20.00.
Open: Apr to Nov
Beds: 3T **Baths:** 2 Sh
🅿☐🛉🎹.Ⓥ

Pay B&Bs by cash or cheque and be prepared to pay up front.

Wadebridge 3

National Grid Ref: SW9872

🍴🍺 Earl of St Vincent, The Ship

West Park House, *106 Egloshale Road, Wadebridge, Cornwall, PL27 7AG.*
Tel: **01208 813279**
Mrs Bishop.
D: £22.50-£28.50
S: £18.00-£28.00.
Open: Mar to Dec
Beds: 1D 2T 1S
Baths: 2 En 1 Pr 1 Sh
🛇 (14) 🅿 (4) 🖤☐🍴🛉🎹.Ⓥ🛡⚡ 🚲
Welcome to West Park House, ideally placed to visit and explore Cornwall. The Camel Trail for cycling or walking to and from Bodmin and Padstow. Wadebridge offers good amenities. 3 Day breaks and small receptions offered upon request

Little Pound, *Bodieve, Wadebridge, Cornwall, PL27 6EG.*
Quiet hamlet, terraced gardens to stream, close to Camel Trail
Tel: **01208 814449**
Mrs Crook.
D: £16.00-£20.00
S: £16.00-£22.00.
Open: All Year (not Xmas)
Beds: 1D 1T 1S
Baths: 1 En 1 Sh
🛇 (3) 🅿 (4) 🖤☐🛉🎹.Ⓥ🚲

Camelford to Exmoor

The route now leads to the coast at Millook, where there is some steep up-and-down cycling over the clifftops before the descent to Widemouth Bay with its wonderful sandy beach, and the ride into **Bude**, a noted surfing centre. From here you strike out eastwards through Marhamchurch and come into Devon, arriving at the village of Bridgerule on the Tamar. Then it's on to Sheepwash in the Torridge Valley, where you turn north. The way now runs along a former railway line - this stretch is shared with the Tarka Trail, named after Henry Williamson's classic 1927 novel, *Tarka the Otter* - to **Bideford**, on the Torridge Estuary. Here you will find a fourteenth-century bridge and a statue commemorating Charles Kingsley, who wrote the historical romance *Westward Ho!*, set in the town (the eponymous nearby coastal resort was named after the book). Now it's down the Torridge Estuary and up the Taw Estuary to Barnstaple, where John Gay, who wrote *The Beggar's Opera*, went to school at St Anne's Chapel, which can be visited. Then you head inland and on to Bratton Fleming, from where it's a climb into **Exmoor National Park.** The route ascends swiftly to Mole's Chamber, atop the lonely high grass and heather plateau, before turning southeastwards along a particularly stupendous section of road which runs along the Devon-Somerset border. You would be very lucky to see some of Exmoor's indigenous red deer, the largest wild animal native to England; the magnificent views, however, are guaranteed.

Trevanion House, Trevanion Road, Wadebridge, Cornwall,
PL27 7JY.
C18th house, casual bookings welcome, specialist holidays for adults with learning disability
Tel: **01208 814903** Mrs Todd.
Fax no: 01208 816268
D: £19.00-£21.00 **S:** £20.00-£22.00.
Open: All Year
Beds: 10T 5S
Baths: 13 Pr 2 Sh
🛇 (5) 🅿 (8) ⊁⌷✗🔟♨🖳🖵&Ⅴ🌢⚲

Bodmin   4

National Grid Ref: SX0667

🍴 🍺 Borough Arms, Halfway House, St Benet's Abbey, Crown Inn, Lanivet Arms, Hole in the Wall, The Weavers

Wilbury Guest House, Fletchers Bridge, Bodmin, Cornwall, PL30 4AN.
Wilbury - beautiful spacious house situated 1 mile from Bodmin. Dogs welcome
Tel: **01208 74001** Mrs Harrison.
D: £15.00-£15.00 **S:** £15.00.
Open: All Year
Beds: 1F 2T 1S
Baths: 1 Sh
🛇 🅿 (6) ⊁⌷🛏✗🖳🖵🌢⚲

D = Price range per person
sharing in a double room

Order your packed lunches the *evening before* you need them. Not at breakfast!

Cromarty, 11 Priory Rd, Bodmin, Cornwall, PL31 2AF.
Home from home centrally located for visiting Cornwall's many treasures
Tel: **01208 74691**
Mrs Noyce.
D: £15.00-£16.00
S: £15.00-£16.00.
Open: All Year
Beds: 1D 1T 1S
Baths: 1 Sh
🛇 (5) 🅿 (4) ⊁⌷🖳🖵Ⅴ🌢⚲

Agan Chy, 68 Castle Street, Bodmin, Cornwall, PL31 2DY.
Quiet location. Easy access to coasts, moors and Camel Trail
Tel: **01208 75339**
D: £15.00 **S:** £17.00.
Open: All Year (not Xmas)
Beds: 3D
Baths: 1 Sh
🅿 (3) ⊁⌷♨🖳Ⅴ

Row   5

National Grid Ref: SX0976

Tarny Guest House, Row, St Breward, Bodmin, Cornwall, PL30 4LW.
Grades: ETC 4 Diamond
Tel: **01208 850583**
Mrs Turner.
D: £17.00-£22.00
S: £18.00-£25.00.
Open: All Year (not Xmas)
Beds: 2F 1D 1T
Baths: 2 En 1 Sh
🛇 🅿 (8) ⊁⌷♨🖳🖳Ⅴ🌢⚲
Warm welcome, large luxury rooms, magnificent views, acres of private gardens with wood side waterfalls. Area of outstanding beauty, wonderful walks, traffic-free cycling, the spectacular Cornish coast 6 miles, the moor with ancient standing stones. Ideal for visiting all of Cornwall

St Breward   6

National Grid Ref: SX0977

🍴 The Old Inn

Treswallock Farm, St Breward, Bodmin, Cornwall, PL30 4PL.
Beef and sheep farm on peaceful location of Bodmin Moor
Grades: ETC 3 Diamond
Tel: **01208 850255** (also fax no)
D: £17.50-£17.50 **S:** £18.00-£18.00.
Open: May to Oct
Beds: 1D 1S
Baths: 1 Sh
🛇 🅿 ⊁⌷🛏♨🖳Ⅴ🌢⚲

Camelford   7

National Grid Ref: SX1083

🍴 Masons' Arms, Darlington Inn, The Bridge, Osiers

Trenarth, Victoria Road, Camelford, Cornwall, PL32.
Actual grid ref: SX1184
Friendly comfortable country home, open views
Tel: **01840 213295**
Mrs Hopkins.
D: £15.00-£17.00 **S:** £15.00-£17.00.
Open: All Year
Beds: 1F 1D 1S
Baths: 1 En 1 Sh
🛇 (2) 🅿 (4) ⊁⌷🛏♨🖳&Ⅴ🌢⚲

Penlea House, Station Road, Camelford, Cornwall, PL32 9UR.
Actual grid ref: SX101837
Beautiful Edwardian house set in pretty gardens with panoramic views
Tel: **01840 212194** (also fax no)
Mrs Andrews.
D: £13.50 **S:** £15.00.
Open: All Year (not Xmas)
Beds: 1F 1D 1T
Baths: 2 En 2 Sh
🛇 🅿 (4) ⌷🛏♨🖳Ⅴ

Bude 8

National Grid Ref: SS2106

🍴 🍺 The Crooklets, The Sportsman, Preston Gate, Bencoolen Inn, Inn on the Green, Falcon Inn, Kings Arms

St Merryn, *Coastview, Bude, Cornwall, EX23 8AG.*
Tel: **01288 352058** Miss Abbot.
Fax no: 01288 359050
D: £14.00-£16.00 **S:** £20.00-£25.00.
Open: All Year
Beds: 1F 1D 1T 1S
Baths: 2 Sh
🛏 🅿 (4) ⅏ ❑ 🏠 🛏 🕮 ♿ 🆅 ⚡ ♻
A large dormer bungalow with good sized ground floor bedrooms each having vanity unit with hot/cold water, colour TV with remote and tea/coffee making facilities situated on A3072 approximately 500 yards from A39 Atlantic highway, off-road parking

Kisauni, *4 Downs View, Bude, Cornwall, EX23 8RF.*
Bright, airy Victorian house. 2 minutes beach. Romantic four poster bed. Home cooking
Tel: **01288 352653**
Mrs Kimpton.
D: £14.00-£16.00 **S:** £14.00-£16.00.
Open: All Year (not Xmas)
Beds: 2F 1D 1T 1S
Baths: 3 En 3 Sh
🛏 🅿 (5) ❑ 🏠 ✗ 🛏 ♿ 🆅 ⚡

Laundry Cottage, *Higher Wharf, Bude, Cornwall, EX23 8LW.*
Tel: **01288 353560**
Mrs Noakes.
D: £16.00-£17.00
S: £16.00-£20.00.
Open: All Year (not Xmas)
Beds: 1D 1T
Baths: 1 Sh
🛏 (10) 🅿 (2) ❑ 🏠 🛏 🕮 🆅 ⚡ ♻
Grade II Listed cottage in two acres of garden on historic Bude canal. Secluded yet only a few minutes' walk from town centre, restaurant, coastal path, beach, cycle routes etc. Rooms overlook garden and canal. Quiet, many extras, private parking

---

The Grid Reference beneath the location heading is for the village or town - *not* for individual houses, which are shown (where supplied) in each entry itself.

Pencarrol Guest House, *21 Downs View, Bude, Cornwall, EX23 8RF.*
Grades: AA 3 Diamond
Tel: **01288 352478**
Mr & Mrs Payne.
D: £17.00-£19.00
S: £15.00-£22.00.
Open: All Year (not Xmas)
Beds: 1F 3D 1T 2S
Baths: 3 En 1 Pr 3 Sh
⅏ ❑ 🛏 🕮 🆅 ⚡ ♻
Pencarrol overlooks Bude's 18-hole golf course and offers comfortable B&B accommodation; most rooms ensuite all rooms with TV tea/coffee facilities and central heating. Ground floor rooms available. Pencarrol is a non-smoking establishment

Sunrise Guest House, *6 Burn View, Bude, Cornwall, EX23 8BY.*
Grades: ETC 3 Diamond
Tel: **01288 353214** Mr Masters.
D: £17.00-£22.00 **S:** £17.00-£25.00.
Open: Feb to Nov
Beds: 1F 3D 1T 1S
Baths: 6 En
🛏 (3) 🅿 (2) ⅏ ❑ 🛏 🕮 ♿ 🆅 ⚡ ♻
The general standards are high and many of the features are delightful. The hospitality of the owners and the cleanliness experienced count for a lot. English Tourist Board Assessment 1999. Come see for yourselves! Centrally located. All rooms ensuite

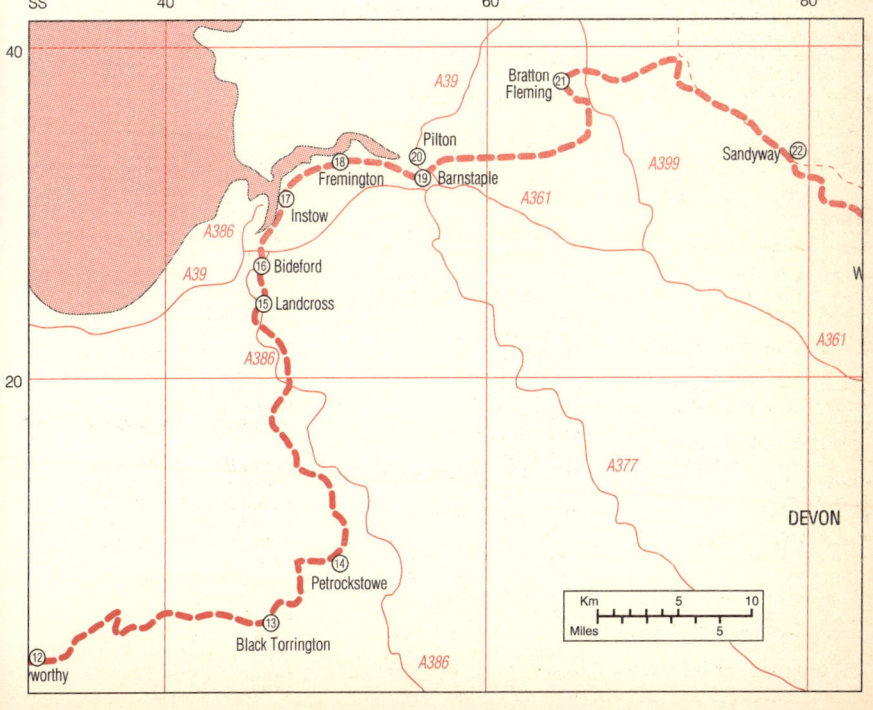

Saint Margarets, Killerton Road, Bude, Cornwall, EX23 8EN.
Victorian family-run hotel close to facilities yet in quiet area
Tel: **01288 352252**
Mr & Mrs Holmes.
Fax no: 01288 353122
D: £20.00-£35.00 **S:** £20.00-£35.00.
Open: All Year
Beds: 2F 4D 2T 2S
Baths: 9 En 1 Pr
🛏 🅿 (5) 🖵 🗶 🎍 📖 🔥 Ⅴ ♦ 🚲

Link's Side Guest House, Burn View, Bude, Cornwall, EX23 8BY.
Victoria house town centre, beaches, path, overlooking golf course
Grades: ETC 3 Diamond
Tel: **01288 352410**
Mr & Mrs Dockrill.
D: £16.00-£20.00 **S:** £16.00-£20.00.
Open: All Year
Beds: 1F 4D 1T 1S
Baths: 4 En 1 Sh
🛏 ⅍ 🖵 🏶 🎍 📖 ♿ Ⅴ 🗝 ♦ 🚲

Raetor, Stratton Road, Bude, Cornwall, EX23 8AQ.
Modern detached house situated on the main road. Bude one mile
Tel: **01288 354128** Barnard.
D: £14.00-£14.00 **S:** £14.00-£14.00.
Open: All Year
Beds: 1D 1T
Baths: 1 Sh
🅿 (2) 🖵 🎍 📖 Ⅴ 🚲

Meadow View, Kings Hill Close, Bude, Cornwall, EX23 8RR.
A large house 400 yds from canal.
Room overlooks garden and fields
Tel: **01288 355095**
Shepherd.
D: £15.00-£16.00 **S:** £15.00-£16.00.
Open: All Year
Beds: 1D
Baths: 1 Pr
⅍ 🖵 🎍 📖 Ⅴ ♦ 🚲

Serendipity, Burn View, Bude, Cornwall, EX23 8BY.
Comfortable accommodation and friendly. Fast becoming famous for our breakfasts
Tel: **01288 355797**
Mr & Mrs Wood.
D: £14.00-£15.00
S: £15.00-£17.00.
Open: All Year (not Xmas)
Beds: 1F 1D 1T
Baths: 2 Sh
🛏 🅿 (2) 🖵 🏶 🎍 📖 🗝 🚲

All rooms full and nowhere else to stay? Ask the owner if there's anywhere nearby

---

Order your packed lunches the *evening before* you need them. Not at breakfast!

Trenance, Crackington Haven, Bude, Cornwall, EX23 0JQ.
Close to coast path and beaches.
Quiet location, ideal for walking, touring
Tel: **01840 230273** (also fax no)
Mr & Mrs Beldman.
D: £18.00-£25.00
S: £19.00-£19.00.
Open: All Year
Beds: 3D 1T 1S
Baths: 2 En 1 Pr 1 Sh
🅿 (10) ⅍ 🖵 🗶 🎍 📖 Ⅴ 🗝 ♦ 🚲

Crooklets 9

National Grid Ref: SS2006

🍴 🍺 Inn on the Green

Inn on the Green, Crooklets Beach, Crooklets, Bude, Cornwall, EX23 8NF.
Actual grid ref: SS210617
Comfortable family hotel, good food
Grades: ETC 2 Diamond
Tel: **01288 356013**
Mr & Mrs Bellward.
Fax no: 01288 356244
D: £17.50-£45.00
S: £20.00-£48.00.
Open: All Year (not Xmas)
Beds: 2F 6D 9T 3S
Baths: 16 En 3 Sh
🛏 🅿 (6) 🖵 🏶 🗶 🎍 📖 Ⅴ 🗝 ♦

Marhamchurch 10

National Grid Ref: SS2203

🍴 🍺 Bullers Arms

Floraldene, Marhamchurch, Bude, Cornwall, EX23 0HE.
Actual grid ref: SS225036
Tel: **01288 361118**
Mrs Sibley.
D: £12.00-£16.00 **S:** £16.00-£18.00.
Open: All Year (not Xmas)
Beds: 2D 1T
Baths: 1 En
🛏 🅿 (2) 🖵 🎍 📖 Ⅴ 🗝 ♦ 🚲
Lovely and peaceful character cottage in picturesque village of Marhamchurch. 2 miles Bude/beaches, nearby popular country pub/restaurant, local shop/farm produce. Antiques abound in our tastefully furnished lounge, TV, videos, large rooms, own driveway, gardens hearty breakfast served

---

Clawton 11

National Grid Ref: SX3599

Churchtown House, Clawton, Holsworthy, Devon, EX22 6PS.
Actual grid ref: SX347993
Tel: **01409 271467** Mrs Farrow.
D: £16.00-£18.00 **S:** £16.00.
Open: All Year
Beds: 1F 1D 1T
Baths: 1 En 1 Sh
🛏 🅿 (6) 🗶 🎍 📖 Ⅴ 🗝 🚲
An elegant part-Georgian C17th farmhouse with a friendly atmosphere. Large South-facing rooms and far reaching views overlooking private garden and paddocks.
Perfect location for North Devon coast, Bodmin Moor and Dartmoor.
Good cycling, walking, in both Devon and Cornwall

Pyworthy 12

National Grid Ref: SS3103

🍴 🍺 Molesworth Arms

Little Knowle Farm, Pyworthy, Holsworthy, Devon, EX22 6JY.
Actual grid ref: SX323028
Friendly relaxed farmhouse, home cooking, children welcome
Tel: **01409 254642** Mrs Aston.
D: £16.00-£17.50 **S:** £16.00-£17.50.
Open: Easter to Oct
Beds: 1D 1T
Baths: 1 Sh
🛏 🅿 (3) 🖵 🗶 🎍 Ⅴ 🗝 ♦ 🚲

Black Torrington 13

National Grid Ref: SS4605

🍴 🍺 Golden Inn Half Moon

Coham Manor, Black Torrington, Beaworthy, Devon, EX21 5HT.
Actual grid ref: SS456058
Beautiful old manor house in own farmland and woods beside River Torridge
Tel: **01409 231514** (also fax no)
Mr Coham-Maclaren.
D: £25.00-£25.00 **S:** £27.50-£27.50.
Open: All Year (not Xmas)
Beds: 2T
Baths: 1 En 1 Pr
🛏 🅿 (10) ⅍ 🖵 🎍 📖 Ⅴ ♦ 🚲

Petrockstowe 14

National Grid Ref: SS5109

🍴 🍺 The Laurels

Aish Villa, Petrockstowe, Okehampton, Devon, EX20 3HL.
Actual grid ref: SS514089
Peaceful location, superb views, ideal for visiting Dartmoor, Exmoor, coast
Tel: **01837 810581** Ms Gordon.
D: £15.00-£15.00 **S:** £15.00-£15.00.
Open: All Year
Beds: 1F 1T **Baths:** 1 Sh
🛏 🅿 (4) ⅍ 🖵 🎍 📖 ♿ Ⅴ ♦ 🚲

Landcross 15

National Grid Ref: SS4623

Sunset Hotel, Landcross, Bideford, Devon, EX39 5JA.
Actual grid ref: SS461239
Grades: ETC 3 Diamond,
AA 3 Diamond
Tel: **01237 472962**
Mrs Lamb.
D: £26.00-£30.00
S: £25.00-£30.00.
Open: Easter to Nov
Beds: 2F 2D 2T
Baths: 4 En
🅿 (8) ⊬ 🗆 ✕ ♨ 📖 ▥ 🛊 🖈 ♿
Somewhere special: small country
hotel, quiet peaceful location,
overlooking spectacular scenery

Bideford 16

National Grid Ref: SS4526

🍴 ◀ Tanton's Hotel, Farmers Arms, Crab & Ale,
Royal Hotel, Swan Inn, Joiners' Arms, Hunters'
Inn, Sunset Hotel

*The Mount Hotel, Northdown
Road, Bideford, Devon, EX39 3LP.*
Actual grid ref: SS449269
Grades: AA 4 Diamond
Tel: **01237 473748**
Mr & Mrs Laugharne.
D: £22.00-£24.00
S: £25.00-£33.00.
Open: Jan to Dec
Beds: 1F 3D 1T 2S
Baths: 7 En
🛏 🅿 (4) ⊬ 🗆 ♨ 📖 ♿ 🛊 🖈 ♿
Charming Georgian licensed
guest house only 5 minutes' walk to
town centre, private lounge for
guests' use, all rooms ensuite,
attractive garden, car parking for
guests. Convenient for touring N
Devon coastline, Clovelly, Lundy,
Exmoor and Dartmoor. No
smoking

*Corner House, 14 The Strand,
Bideford, Devon, EX39 2ND.*
Actual grid ref: SS4426
Family-run guest house. Clean,
comfortable accommodation. Town
centre location
Tel: **01237 473722** Stone.
D: £16.00 **S:** £17.50.
Open: All Year
Beds: 1F 2D 1T 1S
Baths: 1 Sh
🛏 ⊬ 🗆 ✕ ♨ 📖 ▥ 🛊 🖈

Instow 17

National Grid Ref: SS4730

🍴 ◀ Quay Inn, Boathouse, Wayfarer Inn

▲ *Instow Youth Hostel,*
Worlington House, New Road,
Instow, Bideford, Devon, EX39 4LW.
Actual grid ref: SS482303
Tel: **01271 860394**
Under 18: £6.20 **Adults:** £9.15
evening meal at 7.00pm, family
bunk rooms, television, showers,
shop
*Large Victorian country house with
fine views across the Torridge
Estuary*

*Pilton Cottage, Victoria Terrace,
Marine Parade, Instow, Bideford,
Devon, EX39 4JW.*
Victorian house, beautiful estuary
view, yards from sandy beach
Tel: **01271 860202**
Mr & Mrs Gardner.
D: £17.50 **S:** £18.50.
Open: Easter to Oct
Beds: 1F 2D 1T 1S
Baths: 1 Pr 1 Sh
🅿 (3) ⊬ 🗆 ♨ 📖 ▥ 🛊 🖈

D = Price range per person
sharing in a double room

Planning a longer
stay? Always ask for
any special rates.

Fremington 18

National Grid Ref: SS5132

🍴 ◀ Cedars Inn, New Inn

*Muddlebridge House, Fremington,
Barnstaple, Devon, EX31 2NQ.*
Actual grid ref: SS522326
Large Regency house
Tel: **01271 376073** (also fax no)
Mr & Mrs Macdonald.
D: £23.00 **S:** £27.00.
Open: Easter to Nov
Beds: 1F 1D 1T
Baths: 3 En 1 Sh
🛏 (3) 🅿 (4) ⊬ 🗆 ♨ 📖 ▥ 🛊 🖈 ♿

Barnstaple 19

National Grid Ref: SS5633

🍴 ◀ Windsor Arms, Williams Arms, Rolle Quay
Inn, North Country Inn, Pyne Arms, Ring
O'Bells, Chichester Arms

*Mount Sandford, Mount Sandford
Road, Barnstaple, Devon, EX32 0HL.*
Tel: **01271 342354**
Mrs White.
D: £18.00-£22.00 **S:** £20.00.
Open: All Year (not Xmas)
Beds: 1F 1D 1T
Baths: 3 En
🛏 (3) 🅿 (3) ⊬ 🗆 ♨ 📖 ▥ 🛊 🖈 ♿
Georgian house in 1.5 acres gar-
dens. 2 double, 1 twin, all ensuite,
TV, tea-making, central heated.
Winner of Barnstaple in Bloom
Garden 1998. Easily reach of all
North Devon Coast. 500 yards
from 18-hole Golf Park. £18 B&B

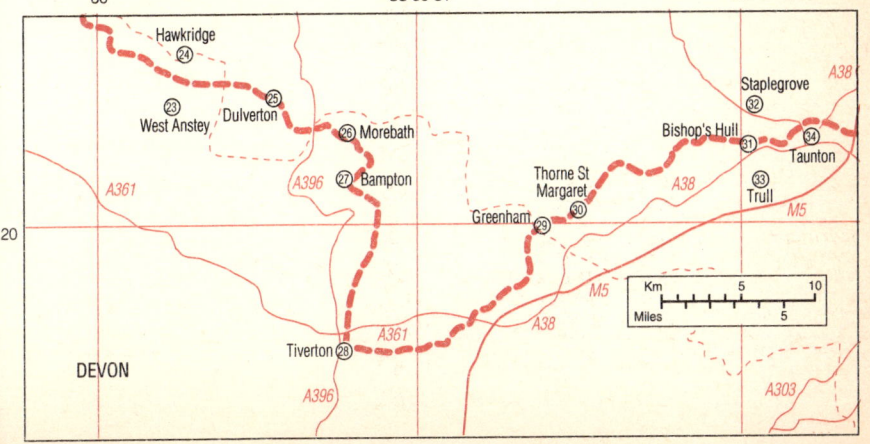

*Crossways, Braunton Road,
Barnstaple, Devon, EX31 1JY.*
Actual grid ref: SS555333
Detached house - town & Tarka
Trail 150 yards, bicycle hire
Tel: **01271 379120**
Mr & Mrs Tysn.
D: £15.00 **S:** £17.00.
Open: All Year
Beds: 1F 1D 1T
Baths: 2 Pr 1 Sh
🛇 ₽ (6) ⅏ ☐ ✗ 🛏 Ⅲ. Ⅴ ♦ ⚡

*Kingston House, Rumsam Road,
Rumsam, Barnstaple, Devon,
EX32 9EW.*
Victorian house, peaceful location,
Tarka trail nearby, good food,
cleanliness assured
Tel: **01271 373957**
Mrs Miller.
D: £18.00-£20.00.
Open: All Year (not Xmas)
Beds: 1F 1D
Baths: 2 En
🛇 (10) ⅏ ☐ 🛏 Ⅲ. Ⅴ ♦ ⚡ 🚲

*West View, Pilton Causeway,
Barnstaple, Devon, EX32 7AA.*
Modernised Victorian property
overlooking park
Tel: **01271 342079** (also fax no)
Mrs Rostock.
D: £17.00 **S:** £17.00.
Open: All Year
Beds: 3F 3D 10T 7S
Baths: 5 En 7 Sh
🛇 ₽ (12) ☐ 🛏 ✗ 🛏 Ⅲ. Ⅴ ⚋ ⚡

Bringing children with
you? Always ask for
any special rates.

High season,
bank holidays and
special events mean
low availability
everywhere.

*Nelson House, 99 Newport Road,
Rock Park, Barnstaple, Devon,
EX32 9BA.*
Spacious Georgian house, close to
town centre, Rock Park, leisure
centre, River Taw
Tel: **01271 345929**
D: £16.00 **S:** £18.00.
Open: All Year
Beds: 1F 1T 1D
Baths: 1 En 1 Pr
🛇 ⅏ ☐ 🛏 Ⅲ. Ⅴ ♦ 🚲

Pilton 20

National Grid Ref: SS5534

🍴 🍺 Windsor Arms, Williams Arms

*Bradiford Cottage, Halls Mill
Lane, Pilton, Barnstaple, Devon,
EX31 4DP.*
Actual grid ref: SS551345
C17th cottage set in the peaceful
countryside just one mile from
Barnstaple
Tel: **01271 345039** (also fax no)
Mrs Hare.
D: £15.00 **S:** £15.00.
Open: All Year (not Xmas/
New Year)
Beds: 2D 1T 1S
Baths: 1 Sh
🛇 (8) ₽ (4) ⅏ ☐ 🛏 Ⅲ. Ⅴ ⚡

Exmoor to Bridgwater

You eventually descend (steeply) to **Dulverton**, a pretty village where the National Park Visitors' Centre is located. From here you head down the Barle Valley to Brushford, where you leave Exmoor and head on to Morebath and Bampton. Cycling south from here you pass near to Knightshayes Court, a Victorian Gothic house with gardens divided into formal sections themed by scent or colour, before reaching **Tiverton**. The route now strikes out east along the Grand Western Canal, through Halberton and Sampford Peverell, crossing into Somerset and heading on to the county town, **Taunton**, in the heart of cider country. Taunton Castle was the scene of two fatal trials, that of the royal pretender Perkin Warbeck at the end of the fifteenth century; and the 'bloody assizes' of 1685, where the infamous Judge Jeffries ordered the executions of the Duke of Monmouth and his followers, who had attempted to seize the throne of England from James II. From Taunton you head northwards to **Bridgwater**, close to where the battle of Sedgemoor, fought in 1685, brought the Monmouth Rebellion to an end.

Bratton Fleming 21

National Grid Ref: SS6437

🍴 🍺 Black Venus

*Haxton Down Farm, Bratton
Fleming, Barnstaple, Devon,
EX32 7JL.*
Peaceful working farm in central
position. Warm welcome, good
food
Tel: **01598 710275** Mrs Burge.
D: £17.00-£20.00 **S:** £18.00-£20.00.
Open: Easter to Nov
Beds: 1F 1D
Baths: 2 En
🛇 ₽ (3) ⅏ 🛏 ✗ 🛏 Ⅲ. Ⅴ ⚡ 🚲

Sandyway 22

National Grid Ref: SS7933

*Barkham, Sandyway, South
Molton, Devon, EX36 3LU.*
Actual grid ref: SS787337
Grades: ETC 4 Diamond,
AA 4 Diamond
Tel: **01643 831370** (also fax no)
Mr Adie.
D: £23.00-£28.00.
Open: All Year (not Xmas)
Beds: 2D 1T
Baths: 1 En 1 Sh
🛇 ₽ (6) ⅏ ☐ ✗ Ⅲ. 🔔 ⚡
Tucked away in a hidden valley in the heart of Exmoor, you can relax and enjoy the tranquillity of our Georgian farmhouse. Panelled dining room, patio overlooking croquet lawn, log fires in the drawing room, excellent dinners. Licensed

West Anstey 23

National Grid Ref: SS8527

*Jubilee House, Highaton Farm,
West Anstey, South Molton, Devon,
EX36 3PJ.*
Actual grid ref: SS844254
Grades: ETC 4 Diamond
Tel: **01398 341312**
Fax no: 01398 341323
D: £18.00-£21.00 **S:** £18.00-£21.00.
Open: All Year
Beds: 2D 3S
Baths: 2 Sh
🛇 ₽ (4) ⅏ ☐ 🛏 ✗ 🛏 Ⅲ. Ⅴ 🔔 ⚡ 🚲
Elegant modern farmhouse, close edge Exmoor National Park, situated on Two Moors Way. Peaceful surroundings, easily accessible, has a great atmosphere. Large lounge (with log fire), dining room available for guests, local produce/home preserves. Bill is an international chef. Facilities to bring your horse on holiday

---

S = Price range for a single
person in a room

Hawkridge 24

National Grid Ref: SS8530

East Hollowcombe Farm,
Hawkridge, Dulverton, Somerset,
TA22 9QL.
Working farm, beautiful scenery,
ideal stopover for Two Moors Way
Tel: **01398 341622** Floyd.
D: £17.00-£18.00 **S:** £17.00-£18.00.
Open: Easter to Oct
Beds: 1F 1D 1S
Baths: 1 Sh
♿ 🅿 (8) 🛏 🍽 🏃 ▥ ▨ ⌨ ✦ 🚲

Dulverton 25

National Grid Ref: SS9128

🍴 🍺 Tarr Farm Inn, The Bridge, Lion Hotel,
White Horse

▲ ***Northcombe YHA Camping***
Barn, *Northcombe, Dulverton,*
Somerset.
Actual grid ref: SS916292
Adults: £3.35+
self-catering facilities, showers,
camping available
Beautifully converted windmill.
ADVANCE BOOKING ESSENTIAL

Highercombe Farm, *Dulverton,*
Somerset, TA22 9PT.
Tel: **01398 323616** (also fax no)
Mrs Humphrey.
D: £19.00 **S:** £28.00.
Open: Mar to Nov
Beds: 2D 1T **Baths:** 3 En
♿ (6) 🅿 🛏 🍽 🏃 ▥ ▨ ⌨ ✦
On the very edge of expansive
moorland, you will find our wel-
coming farmhouse home. All
ensuite rooms beautifully co-ordi-
nated overlooking our 450 acres of
working farm. Wonderful farmer's
breakfasts, optional evening meals.
A quiet and relaxing place to stay

Town Mills, *Dulverton, Somerset,*
TA22 9HB.
Mill house. Full breakfast served in
bedroom, some with log fires
Grades: ETC 4 Diamond,
AA 4 Diamond
Tel: **01398 323124**
Mrs Buckingham.
D: £18.50-£25.00
S: £22.00-£38.00.
Open: All Year
Beds: 4D 1T
Baths: 3 Pr 2 Sh
♿ 🅿 (5) 🛏 ▥ ▨ ⌨ ▨

Springfield Farm, *Ashwick Lane,*
Dulverton, Somerset, TA22 9QD.
Actual grid ref: SS878308
Peaceful farmhouse, magnificent
moorland/woodland views. 1.5 mile
walk to Tarr Steps
Tel: **01398 323722**
Mrs Vellacott.
D: £19.00 **S:** £25.00.
Open: Easter to Nov
Beds: 2D 1T
Baths: 2 En 1 Pr
♿ 🅿 ✂ 🛏 🍽 🏃 ▥ ▨ ⌨ ▨ ✦

Morebath 26

National Grid Ref: SS9524

🍴 🍺 Exeter Inn

Lodfin Farm, *Morebath, Tiverton,*
Devon, EX16 9BD.
Actual grid ref: SS955237
Peaceful, welcoming farmhouse.
Large gardens, hearty breakfast,
ideal location for Exmoor
Tel: **01398 331400** (also fax no)
Mrs Goodwin.
D: £20.00-£23.00
S: £20.00-£23.00.
Open: All Year (not Xmas)
Beds: 1F 1D 1S
Baths: 1 En 1 Sh
♿ (9) 🅿 (4) ✂ 🛏 🏃 ▥ ▨ ⌨ ✦ 🚲

Bampton 27

National Grid Ref: SS9522

🍴 🍺 Seahorse

Manor Mill House, *Bampton,*
Devon, EX16 9LP.
Welcoming C17th home in historic
Bampton, winner of Britain in
Bloom awards
Grades: ETC 4 Diamond
Tel: **01398 332211** Ayres.
D: £22.50-£25.00.
Open: All Year
Beds: 2D 1T
Baths: 3 En
🅿 (20) ✂ 🛏 ▥ ▨ ⌨ ✦ 🚲

Tiverton 28

National Grid Ref: SS9512

🍴 🍺 Twyford Inn, Trout Inn, The Seahorse, The
Anchor, White Ball

Lodgehill Farm Hotel, *Tiverton,*
Devon, EX16 5PA.
Actual grid ref: SS946111
Good parking, tranquil setting on
A396, 1 mile south of Tiverton,
with Dartmoor, Exmoor
Grades: ETC 3 Diamond
Tel: **01884 251200**
Mr & Mrs Reader.
Fax no: 01884 242090
D: £23.50-£27.50 **S:** £25.00-£29.50.
Open: All Year
Beds: 2F 2D 2T 3S
Baths: 9 En
♿ 🅿 (12) 🛏 🍽 🏃 ▥ ▨ ⌨ ✦ 🚲

Angel Guest House, *13 St Peter*
Street, Tiverton, Devon, EX16 6NU.
Town centre: Georgian house, large
cycle shed, ideal touring centre
Tel: **01884 253392**
Mr & Mrs Evans.
Fax no: 01884 251154
D: £16.00-£18.00 **S:** £16.00-£18.00.
Open: All Year
Beds: 2F 3D 1T 1S
Baths: 3 Pr 2 Sh
♿ 🅿 (4) 🛏 ▥ ▨ ⌨ 🚲

Greenham 29

National Grid Ref: ST0720

🍴 🍺 Globe Inn

Greenham Hall, *Greenham,*
Wellington, Somerset, TA21 0JJ.
Actual grid ref: ST076202
Impressive Victorian turreted house
with informal friendly atmosphere.
Central location in beautiful
countryside
Grades: ETC 2 Diamond
Tel: **01823 672603**
Mrs Ayre.
Fax no: 01823 672307
D: £21.00-£28.00.
S: £27.00-£30.00.
Open: All Year
Beds: 1F 3D 2T 1S
Baths: 4 En 1 Pr 2 Sh
♿ (all) 🅿 (10) 🛏 🏃 ▥ ▨ ⌨ ▨ ✦

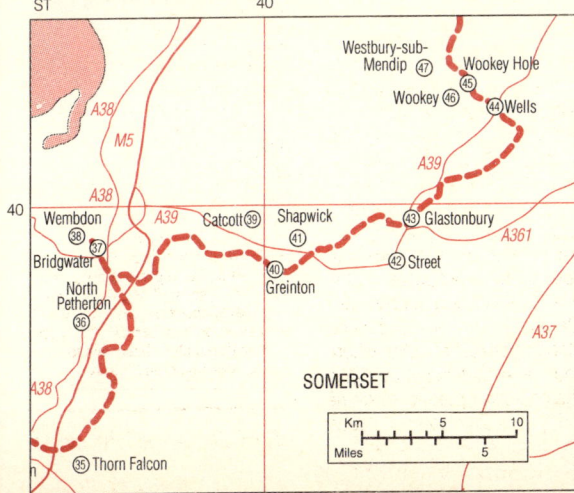

Bridgwater to the Mendips

From here it's east to **Glastonbury**, a small town more redolent with mythology of various kinds than anywhere in England. The towering ruins of the Benedictine abbey are all that remains of one of Britain's earliest Christian foundations. According to legend it was founded by Christ himself, brought here as a child by Joseph of Arimathea, who later returned with the Holy Grail and stuck his staff into the ground, which sprouted spontaneously into a thorn tree. The Glastonbury Thorn, in the abbey grounds, is descended from that original. Nearby Glastonbury Tor is said to be the Isle of Avalon, where King Arthur was brought after being mortally wounded in battle - the tomb of Arthur and Guinevere lies in the abbey grounds. Allegedly. From Glastonbury the route passes through the pancake-flat Somerset Levels to **Wells**, where stands one of England's most magnificent cathedrals, renowned for its ornately carved west front. Northwest of Wells you come to **Wookey Hole**, a striking group of caves, before ascending onto the limestone ridge of the Mendip Hills; after cycling along the ridge as far as **Charterhouse** you turn east to **East Harptree** and **Hinton Blewett**.

Thorne St Margaret   30

National Grid Ref: ST0921

🍴 🍺 Holywell Inn

Thorne Manor, *Thorne St Margaret, Wellington, Somerset, TA21 0EQ.*
Jacobean manor house, working farm 175 acres, peaceful countryside
Tel: **01823 672954** Mrs Hasell.
D: £20.00-£25.00
S: £22.00-£22.00.
Open: Easter to Oct
Beds: 1F
Baths: 1 En
🛇 🅿 (1) ⌿ 🖵 🌡 Ⅵ ⚲ ♿

Bishop's Hull   31

National Grid Ref: ST2024

🍴 🍺 Old Inn, The Cavalier

Hillview Guest House, *Bishop's Hull, Taunton, Somerset, TA1 5EG.*
Spacious accommodation, warm and friendly atmosphere in attractive village near Taunton
Grades: ETC 3 Diamond
Tel: **01823 275510** (also fax no)
Mr Morgan.
D: £17.50-£22.50
S: £17.50-£25.00.
Open: All Year
Beds: 2F 1D 1T 1S
Baths: 2 En 1 Pr 1 Sh
🛇 🅿 (6) ⌿ 🖵 🍴 🌡 🕮 ♿ Ⅵ ⚲ ♿

Staplegrove   32

National Grid Ref: ST2126

🍴 🍺 Cross Keys

Yallands Farmhouse, *Staplegrove, Taunton, Somerset, TA2 6PZ.*
Actual grid ref: ST209259
Grades: ETC 4 Diamond
Tel: **01823 278979** Mr & Mrs Kirk.
Fax no: 01823 278983
D: £26.00-£27.00 **S:** £28.00-£30.00.
Open: All Year
Beds: 1F 2D 1T 2S
Baths: 6 En
🛇 🅿 (6) 🖵 🌡 🕮 Ⅵ ⚲
Warm welcome assured at our delightful C16th house. An oasis of 'Old England'

Trull   33

National Grid Ref: ST2122

Winchester Arms, *Church Road, Trull, Taunton, Somerset, TA3 7LG.*
Traditional old world inn, full of character & charm - rural
Tel: **01823 284723**
D: £18.00 **S:** £18.00.
Open: All Year (not Xmas)
Beds: 3T **Baths:** 1 Sh

Taunton   34

National Grid Ref: ST2324

🍴 🍺 Square & Compass, Greyhound Inn, Cross Keys, Pen & Quill, King's Arms, Old Inn

The Old Mill, *Bishops Hull, Taunton, Somerset, TA1 5AB.*
Tel: **01823 289732** (also fax no)
Mr & Mrs Slipper.
D: £22.00-£24.00 **S:** £30.00-£35.00.
Open: All Year (not Xmas)
Beds: 2D **Baths:** 1 En 1 Pr
🅿 ⌿ 🖵 🌡 🕮 Ⅵ 🛈
A former corn mill retaining many original workings and features, riverside setting and large garden. A warm welcome awaits all our guests, extensive breakfast menu and good pubs nearby, brochure available

---

Blorenge Guest House,
57 Staplegrove Road, Taunton, Somerset, TA1 1DL.
We are situated within 10 mins of all Taunton's amenities
Tel: **01823 283005** Mr Painter.
D: £20.00-£35.00 **S:** £26.00-£40.00.
Open: All Year
Beds: 3F 9D 5T 7S
Baths: 17 En 2 Sh
🛇 🅿 (18) 🖵 🐾 🍴 ✕ 🌡 🕮 Ⅵ ⚲

Bryngwyn, *15 Wellington Road, Taunton, Somerset, TA1 5AN.*
Family-run. Excellent value. No smoking. Close to town centre
Tel: **01823 254953** Mrs Evans.
D: £15.00 **S:** £15.50.
Open: All Year (not Xmas)
Beds: 1T 1D 1S
Baths: 1 Sh
🛇 (12) 🅿 (5) ⌿ 🖵 🌡 🕮 Ⅵ ⚲

Thorn Falcon   35

National Grid Ref: ST2723

Lower Farm, *Thorn Falcon, Taunton, Somerset, TA3 5NR.*
Grades: AA 4 Diamond
Tel: **01823 443549** (also fax no)
Mrs Titman.
D: £22.00-£25.00 **S:** £24.00-£28.00.
Open: All Year (not Xmas)
Beds: 1F 1D 1T
Baths: 1 En 1 Pr
🛇 🅿 (10) ⌿ 🖵 ✕ 🕮 🛈 ⚲ ♿
Only 5 mins M5 (J25), yet in a peaceful location - a late C15th Somerset long house, with a wealth of antiquity throughout, standing in attractive gardens. Cattle and poultry in paddocks. Adjoining kitchen garden supplies our fresh vegetables

---

Please don't camp

on *anyone's* land

without first obtaining

their permission.

Pay B&Bs by cash or

cheque and be prepared

to pay up front.

North Petherton 36

National Grid Ref: ST2832

🍴🍺 Maypole Inn

Lower Clavelshay Farm, North Petherton, Bridgwater, Somerset, TA6 6PJ.
Actual grid ref: ST255310
Grades: AA 3 Diamond
Tel: **01278 662347** (also fax no)
Mrs Milverton.
D: £20.00-£23.00 **S:** £23.00-£26.00.
Open: March-Nov
Beds: 1F 2D
Baths: 2 En 1 Pr
🐾 🅿 (4) ⅏ 🗙 🛏 🗙 🛏 🎖 🎹 🔟 ⚡ ♿
Buzzards, badgers and beautiful countryside surround our C17th farmhouse hidden in its own peaceful valley in the Quantock Hills. Beautiful views, peace and tranquillity. Relaxed family atmosphere. Ideal for walking, riding or exploring the area. Close Hestercombe Gardens. Stabling available

Quantock View House, Bridgwater Road, North Petherton, Bridgwater, Somerset, TA6 6PR.
Actual grid ref: ST301342
Central for Cheddar, Wells, Glastonbury, the Quantocks and the sea
Grades: ETC 3 Diamond,
AA 3 Diamond
Tel: **01278 663309**
Mr & Mrs George.
D: £16.00-£18.00 **S:** £18.00-£22.00.
Open: All Year
Beds: 2F 1D 1T **Baths:** 3 En 1 Pr
🐾 🅿 (8) ⅏ 🗙 🛏 🗙 🛏 🎹 🔟 ⚡ ♿

The Walnut Tree Hotel, North Petherton, Bridgwater, TA6 6QA.
Set in heart of Somerset; fully modernised coaching inn, 2 restaurants; ideal touring location
Grades: AA 3 Star, RAC 3 Star
Tel: **01278 662255** Mr Goulden.
Fax no: 01278 663946
D: £28.00-£95.00 **S:** £30.00.
Open: All Year (not Xmas)
Beds: 5F 21D 5T 1S
Baths: 32 En
🐾 🅿 (72) ⅏ 🗙 🛏 🎖 🎹 ⚡ ♿

Bridgwater 37

National Grid Ref: ST3037

🍴🍺 Hope Inn, Tudor Hotel, Quantock Gateway, Malt Shovel Inn, Kings Head

The Acorns, 61 Taunton Road, Bridgwater, Somerset, TA6 3LP.
Large Victorian house overlooking Bridgwater & Taunton Canal, views to Quantock Hills, 1.5 miles M5
Tel: **01278 445577**
D: £15.00-£17.50 **S:** £15.00-£25.00.
Open: All Year (not Xmas)
Beds: 3F 2D 5T 3S
Baths: 5 En 3 Sh
🐾 🅿 (15) 🗙 🐾 🛏 🎹 🔟 ⚡

Cokerhurst Farm, 87 Wembdon Hill, Bridgwater, Somerset, TA6 7QA.
Three pretty, ensuite bedrooms. Friendly, peaceful, comfortable, with pleasant outlook
Tel: **01278 422330**
Mr & Mrs Chappell.
D: £21.00 **S:** £21.00.
Open: All Year (not Xmas)
Beds: 1F 1D 1T
Baths: 3 En
🐾 🅿 (3) ⅏ 🗙 🛏 🎖 🎹 🔟 ⚡ ♿

Wembdon 38

National Grid Ref: ST2837

🍴🍺 Quantock Gateway, Malt Shovel

Ash-Wembdon Farm, Hollow Lane, Wembdon, Bridgwater, Somerset, TA5 2BD.
Actual grid ref: ST281381
Enjoy a refreshing and memorable stay at our elegant yet homely farmhouse
Grades: ETC 4 Diamond
Tel: **01278 453097** Mrs Rowe.
Fax no: 01278 445856
D: £20.00-£22.00 **S:** £22.00-£28.00.
Open: All Year (not Xmas)
Beds: 2D 1T
Baths: 2 En 1 Pr
🐾 (5) 🅿 (4) ⅏ 🗙 🛏 🎖 🎹 🔟 ♿

Catcott 39

National Grid Ref: ST3939

🍴🍺 King William, The Crown

Honeysuckle, King William Road, Catcott, Bridgwater, Somerset, TA7 9HV.
Set in award-winning 'Britain in Bloom' village of Catcott, within easy reach mystic Glastonbury
Grades: AA 4 Diamond
Tel: **01278 722890** Mrs Scott.
D: £16.00-£20.00 **S:** £18.00-£25.00.
Open: All Year (not Xmas)
Beds: 1D 1T
Baths: 1 En 1 Sh
🐾 (6) 🅿 (3) ⅏ 🗙 🛏 🎖 🎹 🔟 ⚡ ♿

Greinton 40

National Grid Ref: ST4136

🍴🍺 Pipers Inn

West Town Farm, Greinton, Bridgwater, Somerset, TA7 9BW.
Grades: ETC 3 Diamond
Tel: **01458 210277** Mrs Hunt.
D: £20.00-£24.00 **S:** £25.00-£29.00.
Open: Mar to Sep
Beds: 1D 1T
Baths: 2 En
🐾 (3) 🅿 (2) ⅏ 🛏 🎖 🔟 ♿
A friendly atmosphere, a warm welcome and a high standard of hospitality awaits you at West Town Farm. Ideally situated for visiting Glastonbury, Wells and Bath and discovering the glorious Somerset countryside and coastal resorts

Shapwick 41

National Grid Ref: ST4137

Shapwick House Hotel, Monks Drive, Shapwick, Bridgwater, Somerset, TA7 9NL.
Privately owned C15th historic manor in tranquil countryside setting
Tel: **01458 210321**
Fax no: 01458 210729
D: £27.50 **S:** £32.50.
Open: All Year
Beds: 2F 5D 2T
🐾 🅿 🗙 🛏 🎹 🔟 ⚡ ♿

Street 42

National Grid Ref: ST4836

🍴🍺 Pipers Inn

▲ *Street Youth Hostel, The Chalet, Ivythorn Hill, Street, Somerset, BA16 0TZ.*
Actual grid ref: ST480345
Tel: **01458 442961**
Under 18: £5.65
Adults: £8.35
self-catering facilities, showers, camping available, no smoking
Former holiday home for workers at Clarks' shoemakers, this traditional hostel is a Swiss-style chalet overlooking Glastonbury Tor

Marshalls Elm Farm, Street, Somerset, BA16 0TZ.
400-year-old farmhouse with fine views across the Somerset Levels to Glastonbury Tor
Tel: **01458 442878**
Mrs Tucker.
D: £19.50 **S:** £35.00.
Open: All Year (not Xmas)
Beds: 1T
Baths: 1 En
🐾 🅿 ⅏ 🗙

Glastonbury 43

National Grid Ref: ST5039

🍴🍺 Rose & Portcullis, Who'd A Thought It, The Mitre, Camelot Inn, Pilgrim's Rest, The Lion

Meadow Barn, Middlewick Farm, Wick Lane, Glastonbury, Somerset, BA6 8JW.
Grades: ETC 3 Diamond
Tel: **01458 832351** (also fax no)
Mrs Coles.
D: £19.50-£20.50 **S:** £26.00-£30.00.
Open: All Year (not Xmas)
Beds: 2D 1T
Baths: 3 Pr
🐾 🅿 🗙 🛏 🎖 🎹 🔟 ⚡ ♿
Tastefully converted barn, ground floor ensuite accommodation with olde worlde charm and country-style decor. Set in award-winning cottage gardens, apple orchards and meadows. Beautiful tranquil countryside. Meadow Barn has a luxury indoor heated swimming pool

Blake House, *3 Bove Town, Glastonbury, Somerset, BA6 8JE.*
Actual grid ref: ST503390
Grades: AA 3 Diamond
Tel: **01458 831680** Mrs Hankins.
D: £18.00-£20.00 **S:** £22.50-£25.00.
Open: All Year (not Xmas)
Beds: 1D 1T
Baths: 2 En
P (2) ⌨ 🛏 🗄 📖 V
Lovely welcoming C17th Listed house built of stones from Glastonbury Abbey relaxed atmosphere substantial continental breakfast two minutes to town centre and walking distance of Abbey to Chalice Well and museums easy driving distance to most Somerset attractions

Hillclose, *Street Road, Glastonbury, Somerset, BA6 9EG.*
Warm friendly atmosphere, clean rooms, comfortable beds, full English breakfast
Tel: **01458 831040**
Mr & Mrs Riddle.
D: £16.00-£20.00
S: £25.00-£35.00.
Open: All Year (not Xmas)
Beds: 1F 2D 1T
Baths: 2 Sh
P (4) 🛏 🗄 📖 V ⚡ 🚲

Little Orchard, *Ashwell Lane, Glastonbury, Somerset, BA6 8BG.*
Glastonbury, famous for King Arthur, abbey ruins, alternative centre and panoramic views
Tel: **01458 831620**
Mrs Gifford.
D: £16.00-£19.00 **S:** £17.00-£20.00.
Open: All Year
Beds: 1F 1D 1T 2S
Baths: 5 Sh
🐄 **P** ⌨ 🛏 🐈 🗄 📖 V ⚡ 🚲

191a Wells Road, *Glastonbury, Somerset, BA6 9AW.*
Ground floor detached cottage, 1.5 miles from High Street
Tel: **01458 834733** Mrs Bressey.
D: £15.00-£15.00 **S:** £13.00.
Open: All Year (not Xmas)
Beds: 1T
Baths: 1 Sh
P (1)

Shambhala Healing Centre, *Coursing Batch, Glastonbury, Somerset, BA6 8BH.*
Beautiful house, sacred site on side of the Tor. Healing, massage, great vegetarian food
Grades: AA 2 Diamond
Tel: **01458 833081**
Fax no: 01458 831797
D: £20.00-£30.00 **S:** £20.00-£25.00.
Open: All Year
Beds: 3D 1T 1S
Baths: 3 Sh
🐄 **P** ⌨ 🛏 🗙 🗄 📖 V

Pippin, *4 Ridgeway Gardens, Glastonbury, Somerset, BA6 8ER.*
Comfort, value for money in peaceful home opposite Chalice Hill
Grades: ETC 3 Diamond
Tel: **01458 834262** Mrs Slater.
D: £15.00-£17.50 **S:** £15.00-£17.50.
Open: All Year
Beds: 1D 1T **Baths:** 1 Sh
🐄 **P** (2) 🛏 🐈 🗄 📖 V ⚡ 🚲

All rates are subject
to alteration at the
owners' discretion.

---

1 The Gables, *Street Road, Glastonbury, Somerset, BA6 9EG.*
Tea/coffee all rooms. Shower and toilet separate. 1 minute to town
Tel: **01458 832519** Mrs Stott.
D: £13.00.
Open: Feb to Nov
Beds: 2D 1F 1T
Baths: 1 En 1 Sh
🐄 (8) **P** (4) 🛏 📖 V

Lottisham Manor, *Glastonbury, Somerset, BA6 8PF.*
Actual grid ref: ST574343
C16th manor house. Lovely garden. Hard tennis court. Perfect peace and comfort
Tel: **01458 850205**
Mrs Barker-Harland.
D: £15.00-£17.50 **S:** £17.50-£17.50.
Open: All Year
Beds: 1D 1T 1S
Baths: 2 Sh
🐄 **P** (8) ⌨ 🛏 🗄 📖 V ⚡ 🚲

Wyrrall House, *78 Roman Way, Glastonbury, Somerset, BA6 8AD.*
Luxurious accommodation in beautiful Victorian house. Panoramic views. Private car park. Breakfast menu incl veg
Tel: **01458 835510**
Mr & Mrs West.
Fax no: 0870 0568111
D: £21.00 **S:** £28.00.
Open: All Year (not Xmas)
Beds: 1F 2D 1T
Baths: 1 En 2 Pr 1 Sh
🐄 (10) **P** (8) ⌨ 🛏 🗄 📖 V ⚡

Wells 44

National Grid Ref: ST5445

🍴 🍺 Burcott Inn, City Arms, Fountain Inn, Pheasant Inn, Sheppey Inn, City Arms

The Crown at Wells, *Market Place, Wells, Somerset, BA5 2RP.*
Grades: ETC 3 Diamond
Tel: **01749 673457** Sara Hodges.
Fax no: 01749 679792
D: £27.50-£30.00 **S:** £40.00.
Open: All Year
Beds: 4F 5D 4T 2S
Baths: 15 En
🐄 **P** (10) 🛏 🐈 🗙 🗄 📖 V 🔔
The C15th Crown Inn is situated in the heart of Wells, within a stones throw of Wells Cathedral and moated Bishop's Palace. Delicious meals, snacks and refreshments available all day. We pride ourselves on a warm and friendly service

---

All details shown
are as supplied
by B&B owners in
Autumn 1999.

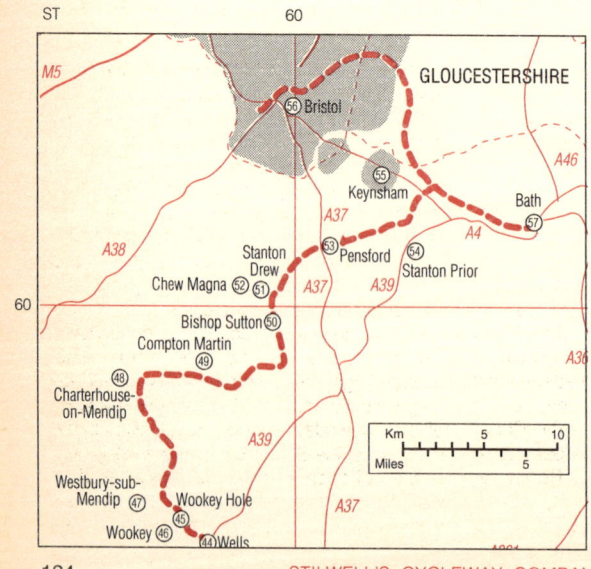

17 Priory Road, *Wells, Somerset,*
BA5 1SU.
Large Victorian house. Homemade
bread and preserves. Few mins'
walk shops, cathedral, bus station
Tel: **01749 677300** Mrs Winter.
D: £17.50-£17.50 **S:** £17.50-£20.00.
Open: All Year (not Xmas)
Beds: 3F 3S **Baths:** 2 Sh
⛟ ₱ (5) ⼻⌷ 👤 🞢 🖾 Ⓥ ⤴🐾

Cadgwith House, *Hawkers Lane,*
Wells, Somerset, BA5 3JH.
Actual grid ref: ST559462
Delightfully-furnished spacious
family house, backing onto field
Grades: ETC 4 Diamond
Tel: **01749 677799** Mrs Pletts.
D: £18.00-£20.00 **S:** £18.00-£25.00.
Open: All Year
Beds: 1F 1D 1T 1S
Baths: 3 En 1 Pr
⛟ ₱ (3) ⌷🐾 👤 🖾 Ⓥ 🛈 ⼻ ⤴🐾

Bekynton House, *7 St Thomas*
Street, Wells, Somerset, BA5 2UU.
Three minutes from cathedral, a
few more to city restaurants
Tel: **01749 672222** (also fax no)
Mr & Mrs Gripper.
D: £23.50-£27.00 **S:** £25.00-£40.00.
Open: All Year (not Xmas)
Beds: 1F 3D 2T
Baths: 4 En 2 Pr
⛟ (7) ₱ (6) ⼻⌷ 👤 🖾 Ⓥ

All cycleways are
popular: you are
well-advised to
book ahead

Infield House, *36 Portway, Wells,*
Somerset, BA5 2BN.
Grades: AA 4 Diamond
Tel: **01749 670989**
D: £21.00-£24.50 **S:** £31.00-£34.50.
Open: All Year
Beds: 2D 1T
Baths: 3 En
⛟ (14) ₱ (4) ⼻⌷🞢🐾🗶👤🖾Ⓥ🛈⼻
Beautifully restored Victorian town
house with period furnishing,
portraits and decor. Backing onto
woodland, just a short walk to city
centre, cathedral and bishop's
palace. Secluded off-street parking,
bountiful breakfasts, traditional
English or vegetarian, touring
centre for Glastonbury, Cheddar,
Bath

Ancient Gate House Hotel, *Sadler*
Street, Wells, Somerset, BA5 2RR.
Situated on the cathedral green,
overlooking West front of cathedral
Grades: ETC 3 Diamond,
AA 1 Star
Tel: **01749 672029** Mr Rossi.
Fax no: 01749 670319
D: £30.00-£35.00 **S:** £45.00-£50.00.
Open: All Year
Beds: 1F 6D 1T 1S
Baths: 7 En 1 Sh
⛟₱⌷🐾🗶👤🖾Ⓥ

Furlong House, *Lorne Place, St*
Thomas Street, Wells, Somerset,
BA5 2XF.
Georgian house, central Wells,
walled gardens, very quiet, ample
parking
Grades: AA 4 Diamond
Tel: **01749 674064**
D: £20.00-£23.00 **S:** £20.00-£42.00.
Open: All Year (not Xmas)
Beds: 2D 1T
Baths: 2 En 1 Sh
⛟₱ (4) ⼻⌷👤🖾Ⓥ⼻🚲⤴🐾

The Limes, *29 Chamberlain Street,*
Wells, Somerset, BA5 2PQ.
Beautifully restored Victorian town
house in the centre of historic Wells
Tel: **01749 675716**
Fax no: 01749 674874
D: £18.00-£20.00.
Open: All Year (not Xmas)
Beds: 1D 1T
⛟₱ (2) ⼻⌷👤🖾Ⓥ🛈⤴🐾

Winsome House, *Portway, Wells,*
Somerset, BA5 2BE.
1930 detached house, 2 mins from
cathedral and city centre
Grades: ETC 3 Diamond
Tel: **01749 679720** (also fax no)
D: £18.00-£20.00 **S:** £20.00-£24.00.
Open: All Year
Beds: 1F 1D 1T
Baths: 1 Sh
₱ (3) ⼻⌷🗶👤🖾Ⓥ🛈⤴🐾

The Old Poor House, *7a St Andrew*
Street, Wells, Somerset,
BA5 2UW.
Close - Cathedral, Bishop's Palace,
Wookey Hole, Bath, cycle route
Tel: **01749 675052** Mrs Wood.
D: £19.00 **S:** £19.00.
Open: All Year (not Xmas)
Beds: 2D 2S
Baths: 1 Sh
🐾👤🖾Ⓥ⼻

All details shown
are as supplied
by B&B owners in
Autumn 1999.

Bristol (see over for Bath)

The rest of the way takes you through the
hilly country of North Somerset to Saltford,
where you join the Bristol and Bath Railway
Path and turn towards **Bristol**, the capital city
of the West Country. A county in its own right
from 1373 until 1974, this status was withdrawn
with the creation of the short-lived County of
Avon, and reinstated in 1996. Before the rapid
industrial development of the Midlands and
North of England during the nineteenth
century, Bristol was England's second city. It
was from here that John Cabot made the first
European voyage to North America, setting
foot on Newfoundland in 1497 - the Cabot
Tower in Brandon Hill Park gives panoramic
views in all directions. St Mary Redcliffe,
Elizabeth I's favourite church, is an
outstanding perpendicular-style edifice with a
famous nineteenth-century spire. In the

seventeenth and eighteenth centuries the city's
shady wealth came from the slave trade, as
the principal port shipping West African
captives to America before this mantle of
shame passed to Liverpool. Bristol is most
notable for the engineering achievements of
Isambard Kingdom Brunel, whose original
railway line from London Paddington still
operates into Temple Meads Station - the
terminus is a surviving Brunel design. Brunel
was also responsible for the SS Great Britain,
the first large iron passenger ship in the world,
which stands in the dry dock; and
outstandingly the Clifton Suspension Bridge,
magnificently spanning the Avon Gorge west
of town. Nowadays the city has a thriving black
community; the St Paul's Carnival in early July
is Bristol's answer to London's Notting
Hill Carnival. The redeveloped quayside has
two Arts Centres, the Watershed and the
Arnolfini.

Bath

From Saltford an alternative route takes you to the small and lovely city of **Bath**, a World Heritage Site which boasts the stately Georgian houses of the Royal Crescent, the fifteenth-century perpendicular Bath Abbey, with its airy stone vault, and the Roman baths, still fed by a hot spring, covered by a Victorian pillared complex. Part of the Roman complex was a temple to Sulis Minerva, a deity combined from the Roman Minerva and Sul, the local Celtic god of the spa.

Wookey Hole 45

National Grid Ref: ST5347

🍴 🍺 Wooley Hole Inn, Ring O' Bells

Broadleys, 21 Wells Road, Wookey Hole, Wells, Somerset, BA5 1DN.
Actual grid ref: ST533470
Grades: ETC 4 Diamond,
AA 4 Diamond
Tel: **01749 674746** (also fax no)
D: £18.50-£20.00. **S:** £18.50-£30.00.
Open: All Year (not Xmas)
Beds: 3D
Baths: 2 En 1 Sh
🛏 (10) 🅿 (4) ⅍ 🗌 🖢 🎹 Ⓥ ⅍ 🚲
Large detached house situated between Wells and Wookey Hole with panoramic countryside views, quality accommodation includes guests' lounge featuring reading material, daily newspapers, videos and satellite television. Friendly well-travelled hosts, excellent parking, quick access to the West Mendip Way

Ganymede, Hurst Batch, Wookey Hole, Wells, Somerset, BA5 1BE.
Comfortable stone cottage, close to Wells, Glastonbury and the Mendips
Tel: **01749 677250**
Mrs Baddeley.
D: £14.00 **S:** £15.00.
Open: Jan to Nov
Beds: 3D
Baths: 1 En 1 Sh
🛏 (8) 🅿 (2) ⅍ 🗌 🖢 🎹 Ⓥ 🛉 ⅌

Whitegate Cottage, Milton Lane, Wookey Hole, Wells, Somerset, BA5 1DG.
Large country cottage overlooking open farmland. Beautiful views near caves
Tel: **01749 675326**
Mr & Mrs Lee.
D: £14.50 **S:** £16.00.
Open: All Year
Beds: 2D 1S
Baths: 1 Pr
🅿 (4) 🗌 🖢 🎹 Ⓥ

Wookey 46

National Grid Ref: ST5145

🍴 🍺 Burcott Inn

Burcott Mill Guest House, Burcott, Wookey, Wells, Somerset, BA5 1NJ.
Actual grid ref: ST522456
Comfortable rooms next to working watermill twixt Mendips and wetlands
Tel: **01749 673118** (also fax no)
Mr & Mrs Grimstead.
D: £17.00 **S:** £20.00.
Open: All Year
Beds: 2F 2D 2T 1S
Baths: 7 Pr
🛏 🅿 (20) 🗌 🖢 🎹 🛉 ⅍ Ⓥ 🛉

Westbury-sub-Mendip 47

National Grid Ref: ST5048

🍴 🍺 Westbury Inn

Box Tree House, Westbury-sub-Mendip, Wells, Somerset, BA5 1HA.
Delightful converted C17th farmhouse
Tel: **01749 870777** Mrs White.
D: £20.00 **S:** £29.00.
Open: All Year
Beds: 1F 1D 1T
Baths: 1 En 2 Pr
🛏 🅿 (4) 🗌 🖢 🎹 Ⓥ

Charterhouse-on-Mendip 48

National Grid Ref: ST5055

🍴 🍺 New Inn

Warren Farm, Charterhouse-on-Mendip, Blagdon, Bristol, BS18 6XR.
1,000 acre sheep farm on the Mendips near Cheddar Gorge
Tel: **01761 462674**
Mrs Small.
D: £17.00-£17.00 **S:** £17.00-£17.00.
Open: Jan to Dec
Beds: 1F 1D 1S
Baths: 1 Sh
🛏 🅿 (20) ⅍ 🗌 🖢 🎹 Ⓥ ⅍ 🚲

Compton Martin 49

National Grid Ref: ST5457

🍴 🍺 Tickled Trout, Queen Adelaide

Herons Green Farm, Compton Martin, Bristol, BS18 6NL.
Farmhouse by lake, oak-beamed dining room, featuring water well
Tel: **01275 333372** Mrs Hasell.
Fax no: 01275 333041
D: £17.50 **S:** £20.00.
Open: Mar to Oct
Beds: 1F 1D **Baths:** 1 Sh
🛏 🅿 (3) ⅍ 🗌 🐾 🖢 🎹 Ⓥ 🛉 ⅌

Bishop Sutton 50

National Grid Ref: ST5859

🍴 🍺 Ring of Bells, Red Lion

Centaur, Ham Lane, Bishop Sutton, Bristol, BS39 5TZ.
Actual grid ref: ST585598
Grades: ETC 3 Diamond
Tel: **01275 332321** Mrs Warden.
D: £17.50-£19.00 **S:** £18.00-£20.00.
Open: Mar to Oct
Beds: 1F 1T
Baths: 1 En 1 Sh
🛏 🅿 (4) 🗌 🖢 🎹 Ⓥ 🛉 ⅌ 🚲
A comfortable family house in the peaceful Chew Valley. Close to Chew Valley Lake for fishing, sailing and bird watching. Within easy reach of Bristol, Bath, Wells and Cheddar. On reaching the village, Ham Lane is opposite the Red Lion

Overbrook, Stowey Bottom, Bishop Sutton, Bristol , BS39 4STN.
Tel: **01275 332648**
Fax no: 0117 935 2052
D: £18.00-£20.00 **S:** £20.00-£20.00.
Open: All Year (not Xmas)
Beds: 2F 1T 1D
Baths: 1 En 1 Pr
🛏 🅿 (5) ⅍ 🗌 🖢 🎹 Ⓥ ⅍ 🚲
Charming house in a lovely garden by a stream, in a quiet and peaceful lane with a little ford by the front gate, half mile from the village. Close to Chew Valley Lake, Bath, Wells, Bristol and Cheddar Gorge within easy reach

Stanton Drew 51

National Grid Ref: ST5963

🍴 🍺 Druids Arms

Auden House, Stanton Drew, Bristol, BS39 4DJ.
Actual grid ref: ST598623
Large modern house in attractive village, stone circles, historic toll house
Tel: **01275 332232** (also fax no)
Mrs Smart.
D: £15.00-£17.50 **S:** £17.50-£17.50.
Open: All Year (not Xmas)
Beds: 2F 1D 1T 1S
Baths: 1 En
🛏 🅿 (6) ⅍ 🗌 🐾 ✕ 🖢 🎹 Ⓥ 🛉 ⅍ 🚲

Bringing children with
you? Always ask for
any special rates.

Valley Farm, Sandy Lane, Stanton
Drew, Bristol, BS18 4EL.
Modern farmhouse, quiet location,
old village with druid stones
Tel: **01275 332723** Mrs Keel.
D: £19.00-£22.00 **S:** £20.00-£24.00.
Open: All Year (not Xmas)
Beds: 1F 2D **Baths:** 3 En
🛏 🅿 (4) 🗲 ⬚ 🏃 ⬚ ⬚ ⬚ 🛏 ⬚ ✦

Chew Magna   52

National Grid Ref: ST5763

🍴 🍺 Queens Arms, Stoke Inn

Woodbarn Farm, Denny Lane,
Chew Magna, Bristol, BS40 8SZ.
Farmhouse B&B near Chew Valley
Lake, Bath, Wells
Tel: **01275 332599** (also fax no)
Mrs Hasell.
D: £18.00 **S:** £20.00.
Open: All Year (not Xmas/
New Year)
Beds: 1F 1D **Baths:** 2 En
🛏 (3) 🅿 (6) 🗲 ⬚ 🏃 ⬚ ⬚ ⬚ 🛏 ⬚

Pensford   53

National Grid Ref: ST6263

🍴 🍺 Carpenters' Arms, Rising Sun, George &
Dragon

The Hollies Guest House,
Pensford Hill, Pensford, Bristol,
BS18 4AA.
Victorian bakery in viaduct village
of Pensford, near Bristol & Bath
Tel: **01761 490456**
Mr & Mrs Jones.
D: £10.00 **S:** £12.00.
Open: All Year
Beds: 1F 1T
Baths: 2 Sh
🛏 🅿 (3) 🗲 ⬚ 🏃 ⬚ ⬚ ⬚ 🛏 ⬚ ✦

Stanton Prior   54

National Grid Ref: ST6762

🍴 🍺 The Wheatsheaf

Poplar Farm, Stanton Prior, Bath,
BA2 9HX.
Spacious C17th farmhouse.
Family-run farm. Idyllic village
setting
Grades: ETC 3 Diamond,
AA 3 Diamond
Tel: **01761 470382** (also fax no)
Mrs Hardwick.
D: £20.00-£27.00 **S:** £20.00-£30.00.
Open: All Year (not Xmas)
Beds: 1F 1D 1T
Baths: 2 En
🛏 (4) 🅿 (6) 🗲 ⬚ ⬚ ⬚ ✦

Keynsham   55

National Grid Ref: ST6568

🍴 🍺 The Talbot

Fiorita, 91 Bath Road, Keynsham,
Bristol, BS31 1SR.
Warm welcome, comfortable
family home midway between
Bristol and Bath
Tel: **0117 986 3738** (also fax no)
Mrs Poulter.
D: £14.50-£16.00 **S:** £16.00-£18.00.
Open: Jan to Dec
Beds: 1D 1T
Baths: 1 En 1 Sh
🛏 🅿 (4) 🗲 ⬚ 🏃 ⬚ ⬚ ⬚ 🛏 ⬚ ✦ 🚲

Bristol   56

National Grid Ref: ST6075

🍴 🍺 Port of Call

▲ **Bristol International Youth
Hostel**, Hayman House, 14 Narrow
Quay, Bristol, BS1 4QA.
Actual grid ref: ST586725
Tel: **0117 922 1659**
Under 18: £8.00 **Adults:** £11.65
evening meal at 6.00-7.30pm,
self-catering facilities, television,
games room, showers, shop,
laundry facilities
*With views over the waterways, this
hostel has been sympathetically
and imaginatively restored to
create a relaxing yet cosmopolitan
atmosphere*

Arches Hotel, 132 Cotham Brow,
Bristol, BS6 6AE.
Actual grid ref: ST588745
Friendly, non-smoking city centre
hotel, close to shops and
restaurants
Grades: ETC 3 Diamond
Tel: **0117 924 7398** (also fax no)
Mr Lambert.
D: £20.50-£25.00 **S:** £23.50-£37.00.
Open: All Year (not Xmas)
Beds: 3F 2D 1T 3S
Baths: 4 En 2 Sh
🛏 (6) 🗲 ⬚ 🏃 ⬚ ⬚ ⬚ 🛏 ⬚ ✦

Downs View Guest House,
38 Upper Belgrave Road, Clifton,
Bristol, BS8 2XN.
Centrally situated. Overlooking
Durdham Down. Near Zoo and
Clifton Suspension Bridge
Tel: **0117 973 7046** Ms Cox.
Fax no: 0117 9738169
D: £20.00-£22.50 **S:** £25.00-£27.50.
Open: All Year (not Xmas)
Beds: 2F 4D 3T 6S
Baths: 7 En 2 Sh
🛏 (2) ⬚ 🏃 ⬚ ⬚ ⬚

Planning a longer
stay? Always ask for
any special rates.

Maison George, 10 Greville Road,
Southville, Bristol, BS3 1LL.
Large Victorian town-house within
walking distance of city centre
Tel: **0117 963 9416** (also fax no)
Mr Evans.
D: £20.00-£30.00 **S:** £20.00-£30.00.
Open: All Year
Beds: 1F 1D 2T 1S
Baths: 2 Sh
🛏 🗲 ⬚ 🏃 ⬚ ⬚ ⬚ 🛏 ⬚

Basca House, 19 Broadway Road,
Bishopston, Bristol, BS7 8ES.
Lovely Victorian home in quiet
residential area. 1 mile city centre
Tel: **0117 942 2182**
Mrs Chawdhary.
D: £19.50 **S:** £20.00.
Open: All Year (not Xmas)
Beds: 2T 2S **Baths:** 2 Sh
🛏 🗲 ⬚ ✕ 🏃 ⬚ ⬚ ⬚ 🛏 ⬚

Norfolk House, 577 Gloucester
Road, Horfield, Bristol, BS7 0BW.
Actual grid ref: ST596774
Pleasant Victorian house
overlooking park
Tel: **0117 951 3191** (also fax no)
Mr Thomas.
D: £18.00 **S:** £20.00.
Open: All Year (not Xmas)
Beds: 2D 1T **Baths:** 1 En 2 Sh
🛏 🗲 ⬚ ✕ 🏃 ⬚ ⬚ ⬚ 🛏 ⬚ 🛏

Bath   57

National Grid Ref: ST7464

🍴 🍺 Royal Oak, The Dolphin, Wheelwrights
Arms, Old Crown, The Huntsman, The George,
Devonshire Arms, The Sportsman, Waldergrave
Arms, The Bear, Park Tavern, Rose & Crown,
Weston Walk, The Boathouse

▲ **Bath Youth Hostel**, Bathwick
Hill, Bath, North East Somerset,
BA2 6JZ.
Actual grid ref: ST766644
Tel: **01225 465674**
Under 18: £6.85 **Adults:** £10.15
evening meal at 5.30-7.30pm,
family bunk rooms, television,
games room, showers, shop,
security lockers
*Handsome Italianate mansion, set
in beautiful, secluded gardens, with
views of historic city and surrounding hills*

Bailbrook Lodge, 35-37 London
Road West, Bath, BA1 7HZ.
Grades: ETC 3 Diamond,
AA 3 Diamond
Tel: **01225 859090** (also fax no)
Mrs Sexton.
D: £29.00-£40.00 **S:** £39.00-£50.00.
Open: All Year
Beds: 4F 4D 4T **Baths:** 12 En
🛏 🅿 (14) 🗲 ⬚ ✕ 🏃 ⬚ ⬚ ⬚ 🛏 ⬚ ✦ 🚲
A warm welcome is assured at
Bailbrooke Lodge, an imposing
Georgian House set it its own
gardens. The elegant period
bedrooms (some four posters) offer
ensuite facilities, TV and
hospitality trays. Situated 1.5 miles
from Bath centre. Close to M4.

Koryu B&B, *7 Pulteney Gardens,
Bath,* BA2 4HG.
Tel: **01225 337642** (also fax no)
Mrs Shimizu.
D: £22.00-£25.00
S: £22.00-£25.00.
Open: All Year
Beds: 1F 2D 2T 2S
Baths: 5 En 2 Sh
🛏 🅿 (2) 🛇✗🖵✗🖳 🎛 Ⅴ ॐ
Completely renovated Victorian
home run by a young Japanese
lady, extremely clean, delicious
breakfasts with wide menu,
beautiful linens; a bright, cheerful
and welcoming house. Abbey and
Roman baths 5 mins, gorgeous
Kennet and Avon canal 2 mins

Kinlet Guest House, *99 Wellsway,
Bath,* BA2 4RA.
Actual grid ref: ST745636
Home from home. Friendly,
comfortable, easy walk into the city
Tel: **01225 420268** (also fax no)
Mrs Bennett.
D: £19.00-£20.00 **S:** £22.00-£27.00.
Open: All Year
Beds: 1F 1D 1S
Baths: 1 Sh
🛏 🛇🖵 ≛ 🖳 Ⅴ 🛢 ॐ

Sarnia, *19 Combe Park, Weston,
Bath,* BA1 3NR.
Actual grid ref: ST730656
Grades: AA 4 Diamond
Tel: **01225 424159**
Mr & Mrs Fradley.
Fax no: 01225 337689
D: £22.50-£30.00 **S:** £25.00-£40.00.
Open: All Year (not Xmas/
New Year)
Beds: 1F 1D 1T
Baths: 2 En 1 Pr
🛏 🅿 (3) 🛇🖵 ≛ 🖳 Ⅴ 🛢 ॐ
Superb bed & breakfast in large
Victorian home, easy reach of town
centre. Spacious bedrooms, private
facilities, newly decorated,
attractively furnished. Breakfast in
sunny dining room, English,
Continental and vegetarian menus,
home made jams, marmalades,
comfortable lounge, secluded
garden, private parking & children
welcome

The Old Red House, *37 Newbridge
Road, Bath,* BA1 3HE.
Grades: AA 3 Diamond
Tel: **01225 330464**
Fax no: 01225 331661
D: £22.00-£33.00
S: £30.00-£45.00.
Open: Mar to Dec
Beds: 1F 4D 1T 1S
Baths: 3 En 1 Pr 1 Sh
🛏 🅿 (4) 🛇🖵 🖈 ≛ 🖳 Ⅴ ॐ
A romantic Victorian gingerbread
house with stained glass windows,
comfortable bedrooms with
canopied or king size beds,
superbly cooked breakfasts around
large family dining table. Sunny
conservatory. Special rates for 3 or
more nights - well-lit car park. No
smoking

14 Raby Place, *Bathwick Hill,
Bath,* BA2 4EH.
Grades: ETC 3 Diamond
Tel: **01225 465120**
Mrs Guy.
Fax no: 01225 465283
D: £22.50-£25.00 **S:** £25.00-£25.00.
Open: All Year
Beds: 1F 2D 1T 1S
Baths: 3 En 2 Pr
🛏 🛇🖵 ≛ 🖳 Ⅴ 🛢 ॐ
Charming Georgian terraced house
with beautiful interior rooms.
Healthy breakfasts, fresh fruit
salads, yoghurts, organic eggs,
granary bread and a selection of
home made jams. We are a no
smoking house

Cedar Lodge, *13 Lambridge
London Road, Bath,* BA1 6BJ.
Come, stay, enjoy. Welcoming,
comfortable lovely, well-placed
period house
Tel: **01225 423468**
Mr & Mrs Beckett.
D: £25.00 **S:** £30.00.
Open: All Year
Beds: 1T 2D
Baths: 2 En 1 Pr
🛏 (10) 🅿 (6) 🛇🖵 ≛ 🖳 Ⅴ 🛢 ॐ

Glan y Dwr, *14 Newbridge Hill,
Bath,* BA1 6PU.
Grades: ETC 3 Diamond
Tel: **01225 317521**
D: £16.00-£24.00 **S:** £18.00-£35.00.
Open: All Year
Beds: 2D 1T 3S
Baths: 1 En 1 Pr 1 Sh
🛏 (11) 🅿 (3) 🛇 🖈 ≛ 🖳 🛢 Ⅴ 🛢 ॐ
We pride ourselves on personal
attention to ensure you have an
comfortable stay in Bath.
Comfortable rooms with a good
selection of breakfasts

Georgian Guest House,
34 Henrietta Street, Bath, BA2 6LR.
Grades: ETC 3 Diamond
Tel: **01225 424103**
Fax no: 01225 425279
D: £28.00-£35.00 **S:** £28.00-£50.00.
Open: All Year (not Xmas)
Beds: 7D 2T 2S
Baths: 7 En 1 Sh
🛏 🛇🖵 ≛ 🖳 Ⅴ ॐ
Grade I Listed town house, situated
just 2 mins walk to city centre in a
peaceful location. Enjoy your
English/continental breakfast in our
sunny dining room overlooking the
garden. Winter breaks available

Wellsway Guest House,
51 Wellsway, Bath, BA2 4RS.
Walking distance to city. Clean,
comfortable
Tel: **01225 423434**
Mrs Strong.
D: £20.00-£20.00 **S:** £20.00-£20.00.
Open: All Year
Beds: 1F 1D 1T 1S
Baths: 4 Sh
🛏 🅿 (4) 🖵 🖈 🖳 ॐ

Dene Villa, *5 Newbridge Hill,
Bath,* BA1 3PW.
Victorian family-run guest house, a
warm welcome is assured
Tel: **01225 427676**
Mrs Surry.
Fax no: 01225 482684
D: £20.00-£22.50 **S:** £19.00-£22.00.
Open: All Year
Beds: 1F 1D 1T 1S
Baths: 3 En
🛏 (3) 🅿 (4) 🖵 ≛ 🖳 Ⅴ ॐ

Joanna House, *5 Pulteney Avenue,
Bath,* BA2 4HH.
City centre Victorian house near
railway, Kennet and Avon canal
Tel: **01225 335246**
Mr House.
D: £16.00-£19.00 **S:** £15.00-£18.00.
Open: All Year
Beds: 1F 1D 1T 1S
🛏 🛇🖵 ≛ 🖳 Ⅴ

The Terrace Guest House,
3 Pulteney Terrace, Bath, BA2 4HJ.
Mid-terrace house, 7 minutes from
city centre and railway station
Tel: **01225 316578**
Mrs Gould.
D: £16.00-£17.50 **S:** £18.00-£20.00.
Open: All Year (not Xmas)
Beds: 1D 1T
Baths: 1 Sh
🛏 (6) 🖵 ≛ 🖳 Ⅴ 🛢 ॐ

Brinsley Sheridan Guest House,
95 Wellsway, Bearflat, Bath,
BA2 4RU.
Lovely friendly guest house only
short walk from city centre
Grades: ETC 4 Diamond
Tel: **01225 429562**
Fax no: 01225 429616
D: £17.50-£25.00
S: £17.50-£30.00.
Open: All Year
Beds: 1F 2D 1T
Baths: 1 En 1 Pr 2 Sh
🛏 🛇🖵 ≛ 🖳 Ⅴ ॐ

Flaxley Villa, *9 Newbridge Hill,
Bath,* BA1 3PW.
Victorian house on west side of
Bath in residential area
Tel: **01225 313237**
Mrs Cooper.
D: £20.00-£25.00
S: £18.00-£36.00.
Open: All Year
Beds: 3D 1T 1S
Baths: 3 En
🛏 🅿 (5) 🖵 ≛ 🖳 Ⅴ ॐ

Cairngorm, *3 Gloucester Road,
Lower Swainswick, Bath,* BA1 7BH.
Charming detached home with
beautiful views over city and
countryside
Grades: AA 2 Diamond
Tel: **01225 429004**
Mrs Biggs.
D: £16.50-£20.00 **S:** £18.00.
Open: All Year (not Xmas)
Beds: 2D 1T
Baths: 3 En
🛏 (2) 🅿 (3) 🛇🖵 ≛ 🖳 🛢 Ⅴ 🛢 ॐ

Westerlea, *87 Greenway Lane, Bath, BA2 4LN.*
Georgian style house, large gardens, friendly, ensuite accommodation, cars garaged
Grades: ETC 4 Diamond
Tel: **01225 311543** (also fax no)
D: £22.50-£30.00
S: £35.00-£50.00.
Open: All Year (not Xmas)
Beds: 2D
Baths: 2 En
ॐ (12) ▣ (2) ⊬◻ﬨ 🖐 ▦ Ⅴ ✂ ⚲

Cheery Tree Villa, *7 Newbridge Hill, Bath, BA1 3PW.*
Small, friendly Victorian home. 1 mile from Bath city centre
Grades: ETC 3 Diamond
Tel: **01225 331617**
D: £16.00-£48.00
S: £18.00-£25.00.
Open: All Year (not Xmas)
Beds: 1D 1T 1S
Baths: 1 Sh
ॐ (4) ▣ (4) ◻ 🖐 ▦ Ⅴ ✂ ⚲

The White Guest House, *23 Pulteney Gardens, Bath, BA2 4HG.*
Ideally situated for all of Bath's famous attractions (great breakfast)
Grades: AA 3 Diamond
Tel: **01225 426075** (also fax no)
Wynne.
D: £22.50-£22.50 **S:** £25.00.
Open: All Year
Beds: 2D 1T
Baths: 3 En
ॐ (3) ⊬◻ 🖐 ▦ Ⅴ ▮

Fyfield, *Ralph Allen Drive, Combe Down, Bath, BA2 5AE.*
Attractive comfortable 1950s house, large garden, 1.5 miles from city centre
Tel: **01225 833561**
Mrs Waterman.
D: £18.00 **S:** £18.00.
Open: All Year (not Xmas)
Beds: 1D 1T 1S
Baths: 1 Sh
ॐ ▣ (4) ◻ 🖐 ▦ Ⅴ

Marisha's Guest House, *68 Newbridge Hill, Bath, BA1 3QA.*
Offering a warm welcome in the relaxed atmosphere of this beautifully restored Victorian house
Tel: **01225 446881** (also fax no)
Mrs Webb.
D: £17.00 **S:** £17.00.
Open: All Year (not Xmas)
Beds: 2F 2T 2D 1S
Baths: 4 En 3 Pr
ॐ (5) ▣ (3) ⊬◻ 🖐 ▦ & Ⅴ ▮ ✂ ⚲

Wentworth House Hotel, *106 Bloomfield Road, Bath, BA2 2AP.*
Imposing Victorian Bath stone mansion (1887) in secluded grounds with stunning views from rear
Tel: **01225 339193** Mrs Kitching.
Fax no: 01225 310460
D: £30.00 **S:** £45.00.
Open: All Year (not Xmas)
Beds: 2F 8D 5T
Baths: 13 En 2 Pr
ॐ (5) ▣ (20) ◻ﬨ 🖐 ▦ Ⅴ ▮

Sustrans White Rose Cycle Route

The **White Rose Cycle Route** is a new section of the developing National Cycle Network, running on traffic-free paths and traffic-calmed roads through 120 miles of the varied landscape of eastern Yorkshire from the Humber to the Tees, skirting the North York Moors National Park towards the northern end. It links three of Yorkshire's major cities – from Hull it takes two alternative routes to York before heading north to Middlesbrough – whilst avoiding the industrial west of the region. At the southern end of the route you can join the **Hull to Harwich Cycle Route**. The route is clearly signposted by blue direction signs with a cycle silhouette and the number 65 in a red rectangle (the northern alternative route from Hull to York is 66).

The route west out of **Hull** skirts the southern end of the gentle limestone Yorkshire Wolds before joining the Trans Pennine Trail at Laxton. This pioneering new project is the first British multi-purpose long distance route, catering for cyclists, walkers, horseriders and people with disabilities; it is also a section of the E8 European Long Distance Path (Kerry to Istanbul). After you have followed the TPT through the market towns of **Howden** and **Selby**, a railway path leads to **York**. The alternative route to York, the National Cycle Network's very own Route 66, crosses the Wolds and visits a chain of picturesque Yorkshire market towns – **Beverley, Market Weighton, Pocklington** and **Stamford Bridge**. A leisurely, level stretch takes you through the Vale of York to **Easingwold**, before you wend your way through the lower-lying hills of the heather-clad North York Moors and the villages of **Coxwold, Kilburn, Sutton-under-Whitestonecliffe** and **Cowesby.** An alternative route from Easingwold leads through the villages of Helperby and Dalton to

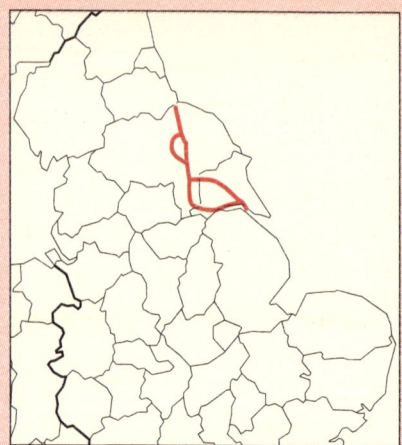

the small market town of **Thirsk**, before rejoining the main route. Now you undertake the somewhat steeper climb over Osmotherley Moor and descent to Cod Beck Reservoir and then **Swainby**. From here it's a more-or-less gentle descent through Hutton Rudby, Maltby and Stainton, and into central **Middlesbrough**.

The indispensable **official route map and guide** for the route is available from Sustrans, 35 King Street, Bristol BS1 4DZ, tel 0117-926 8893, fax 0117-929 4173, @ £5.99 (+ £2.00 p&p).

Maps: Ordnance Survey 1:50,000 Landranger series: 93, 99, 100, 105, 106, 107

Trains: Hull, York, Middlesbrough, Selby and Beverley are all served by main line train services, as are Thirsk and Northallerton, both of which have link routes to the main route.

Hull   1

National Grid Ref: TA0929

🍴 🍺 Hanorth Arms, The Zoological

Marlborough Hotel, 232 Spring Bank, Hull, HU3 1LU.
Family run, near city centre
Tel: **01482 224479** (also fax no)
Mr Norman.
D: £17.00 **S:** £17.00.
Open: All Year
Beds: 2 F 2D 7T 5S
Baths: 3 Sh
🛌 🅿 (10) 🛏 🐾 ✕ 🖾

Beck House , 628 Beverley High Road, Hull, HU6 7LL.
Traditional town house, B&B, fine accommodation, close to university etc
Tel: **01482 445468** Mrs Aylwin.
D: £19.00-£22.00 **S:** £19.00-£22.00.
Open: All Year
Beds: 3S **Baths:** 2 En 5 Pr
🛌 🅿 (4) 🛏 🖂 🖾 Ⓥ 🚲

D = Price range per person sharing in a double room

S = Price range for a single person in a room

The Tree Guest House, 132 Sunny Bank, Spring Bank West, Hull, HU3 1LE.
Close to the city centre and universities
Tel: **01482 448822** (also fax no)
D: £15.00-£18.00 **S:** £16.00-£24.00.
Open: All Year
Beds: 1F 3D 3S **Baths:** 2 En 2 Sh
🛌 🅿 🛏 🐾 🦽 🖾 & Ⓥ

80 Riversdale Road, *Beverley High Road, Hull, HU6 7HB.*
Attractive house built 1932, back lawn facing playing fields; luxury accommodation
Tel: **01482 859750**
Mrs Drake.
D: £15.00-£16.00
S: £16.00-£17.00.
Open: All Year (not Xmas)
Beds: 1D 1S **Baths:** 1 En

Town House, *102 Sunny Bank, Spring Bank West, Hull, HU3 1LF.*
Guest house, quiet location
Tel: **01482 446177** Mr Hogg.
D: £15.00 **S:** £16.00.
Open: All Year
Beds: 1D 2T 4S
Baths: 1 Sh

Admiral Wyndham, *52-54 Sunny Bank, Spring Bank West, Hull, HU3 1LQ.*
A Victorian town house in a tranquil tree-lined avenue. A warm welcome is assured
Tel: **01482 443168**
Fax no: 01482 341889
D: £16.00 **S:** £18.00.
Open: All Year
Beds: 2F 3T 3D 7S
Baths: 2 En 2 Sh

Hessle 2

National Grid Ref: TA0326

 Country Park Inn

Sandford, *79 Ferriby Road, Hessle, E Yorks, HU13 0HU.*
Friendly luxurious Edwardian home quiet location yet close to amenities
Tel: **01482 648655**
D: £19.00-£20.00
S: £26.00-£30.00.
Open: All Year (not Xmas)
Beds: 2F 1T
Baths: 1 En 1 Sh

North Ferriby 3

National Grid Ref: SE9826

B&B at 103, *103 Ferriby High Road, North Ferriby, East Yorks, HU14 3LA.*
Comfortable house, large garden, overlooking river near Humber Bridge and Hull
Grades: ETC 3 Diamond
Tel: **01482 633637** Mrs Simpson.
D: £15.00-£15.00 **S:** £15.00-£15.00.
Open: All Year
Beds: 1D 1T 1S
Baths: 1 Sh

Kingston-upon-Hull is the major port of the Humber (see under *Sustrans Hull to Harwich* for further information).

Howden Minster is a large thirteenth to fifteenth-century church, the tower and nave imposingly intact, the choir and chapter house atmospherically ruined.

Beverley, county town of the East Riding of Yorkshire, is an attractive historic market town with elegant Georgian houses and cobbled streets, most famous for its minster. A cathedral in every respect but the lack of an episcopal seat, this formidable edifice was built over the course of several centuries up to the fifteenth, when it was completed by Hawksmoor's splendid west front, whose twin towers crown the views from miles around.

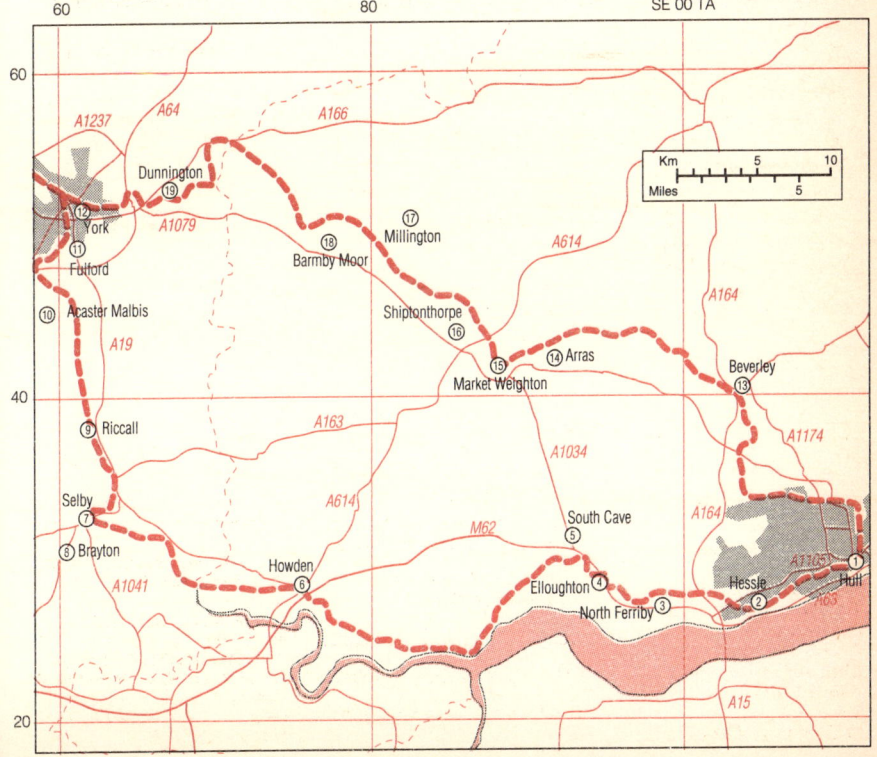

Elloughton 4

National Grid Ref: SE9428

🍴🍺 Half Moon

Chat Moss, 16 Larchmont Close, Elloughton, Brough, E. Yorks, HU15 1AW.
Actual grid ref: SE941275
Large, peaceful, comfortable modern house
Tel: **01482 666514** Mrs Dixon.
D: £16.50-£17.50 S: £16.50-£16.50.
Open: All Year (not Xmas)
Beds: 1D 1T
Baths: 1 Pr
🛏 (9) 🅿 (3) ⅍ 🖵 🛒 📖 Ⓥ ⚡

South Cave 5

National Grid Ref: SE9231

🍴🍺 Fox & Coney

Fairways Farm, Northfield Close, South Cave, Brough, East Yorkshire, HU15 2EW.
Actual grid ref: SE914311
Beautiful bungalow in private location overlooking Cave Castle Golf Course
Tel: **01430 421285** Mrs Jewitt.
D: £20.00 S: £25.00.
Open: All Year (not Xmas)
Beds: 2F 2D
Baths: 4 En
🛏 🅿 (12) 🖵 🖙 🛒 📖 Ⓥ ⚡

Howden 6

National Grid Ref: SE7428

Minster View Country Hotel, 2-3 Cornmarket Hill, Howden, Goole, DN14 7BX.
Actual grid ref: SE747282
Opposite the historic Howden Minster, 500 yards from the marsh
Tel: **01430 430447**
Fax no: 01430 430772
D: £16.00-£16.00 S: £16.00-£18.00.
Open: All Year
Beds: 1F 1D 5T 2S
Baths: 3 Sh
🛏 🅿 (5) ⅍ 🖵 🖙 ✗ 🛒 📖 Ⓥ ⚡ 🚲

Selby 7

National Grid Ref: SE6132

🍴🍺 The Londesborough, Grey Horse

Hazeldene Guest House, 32-34 Brook Street, Selby, N. Yorks, YO8 4AR.
Attractive period house, featuring spacious ensuite rooms, market town location
Grades: ETC 2 Diamond, AA 2 Diamond
Tel: **01757 704809** Mr Leake.
Fax no: 01757 709300
D: £18.00-£22.00 S: £21.00-£30.00.
Open: All Year (not Xmas)
Beds: 3D 3T 2S
Baths: 3 En 2 Sh
🛏 (12) 🅿 (5) ⅍ 🖵 🛒 📖 Ⓥ ⚡ 🚲

Brayton 8

National Grid Ref: SE6030

West Cottage, Mill Lane, Brayton, Selby, N. Yorks, YO8 9LB.
Small family-run B&B set in a delightful cottage garden with grass tennis court
Grades: ETC 4 Diamond
Tel: **01757 213318** (also fax no)
Mrs Fletcher.
D: £20.00 S: £25.00.
Open: All Year
Beds: 1F 1T
Baths: 2 En
🛏 (12) 🅿 (5) ⅍ 🖵 🛒 📖 Ⓥ

Riccall 9

National Grid Ref: SE6237

🍴🍺 Grey Mare, Hare & Hounds, The Drovers

South Newlands Farm, Selby Road, Riccall, York, YO4 6QR.
Friendliness, comfort & home cooking are on offer to our guests
Tel: **01757 248203**
Mrs Swann.
D: £17.00 S: £19.00.
Open: All Year
Beds: 1F 1D 1T
Baths: 2 Pr 1 Sh
🛏 🅿 (4) ⅍ 🖵 ✗ 🛒 📖 Ⓥ 🔒

Villa Nurseries, Riccall, York, YO19 6QG.
Small, friendly C19th guest house seven miles south of historic York
Tel: **01757 248257**
Fax no: 01757 248792
D: £16.50 S: £16.50.
Open: All Year (not Xmas/ New Year)
Beds: 1F 1T
Baths: 2 En 1 Pr
🛏 🅿 (5) 🖵 🖙 🛒 📖 Ⓥ ⚡ 🚲

Pay B&Bs by cash or cheque and be prepared to pay up front.

Acaster Malbis 10

National Grid Ref: SE5845

🍴🍺 Ship Inn

The Manor Country House, Acaster Malbis, York, YO23 2PY.
4.5 miles south of York by River Ouse set in 5 acres of parkland
Tel: **01904 706723** (also fax no)
Viscovich.
D: £25.00 S: £38.00.
Open: All Year (not Xmas/ New Year)
Beds: 2F 2T 5D 1S **Baths:** 10 En

Fulford 11

National Grid Ref: SE6149

🍴🍺 The Saddle, The Plough

Alfreda Guest House, 61 Heslington Lane, Fulford, York, YO10 4HN.
Grades: AA 3 Diamond
Tel: **01904 631698** Mr Bentley.
Fax no: 01904 211215
D: £22.00-£27.00 S: £25.00-£50.00.
Open: All Year (not Xmas)
Beds: 4F 3D 3T **Baths:** 8 En 2 Sh
🛏 🅿 🖵 🖙 🛒 📖 Ⓥ ⚡ 🔒 🚲
Edwardian residence, large grounds. Car park security lighting/camera. Ensuite rooms colour TV, radio, direct dial telephones, tea/coffee, double glazing, gas central heating, close to Fulford Golf. 15 minutes York University

The city of **York** has a rich cultural history dating back through centuries. From the ashes of Roman Eboracum came Anglo-Saxon Eoforwic; but it was Viking Jorvik that gave the city its modern name. At the excellent Jorvik Viking Centre you can take a train back through time and visit a street reconstructed for all the senses, complete with Viking chatter and smells (yes, really). It is striking that the reconstruction is situated immediately next to the specific excavation on which it is based. Among the city's numerous other sights is the National Railway Museum, part heavy-duty array of locomotives, part reconstruction of life on railways past. This includes Queen Victoria's carriage, from which the new-fangled electric lights were stripped out by royal command – but the electric bell for summoning of servants somehow escaped censure. York Minster is the largest European medieval cathedral and the largest Gothic building in Britain. Its superb range of stained glass is impressive for the Big – the Great East Window is the world's largest intact medieval window – and for the Old – dating from as far back as the thirteenth century.

*The Old Registry, 12 Main Street,
Fulford, York, YO10 4PQ.*
Family-run period house. Easy
access to York and University
Grades: ETC 3 Diamond
Tel: **01904 628136** Mr Beckett.
D: £17.00-£25.00 **S:** £17.00-£25.00.
Open: All Year (not Xmas)
Beds: 2D 1T 2S **Baths:** 4 En

York 12

National Grid Ref: SE5951

York Arms, Hole in the Wall, Grange Hotel,
Walnut Tree, Wagon & Horses, Royal Oak, The
Exhibition, The Tankard, The Windmill, Cross
Keys, Shoulder of Mutton, Ye Olde Punch Bowl,
Elliott's, Churchill's, Golden Slipper, Masons'
Arms, The Plough, The Dormouse, The
Gimcrack, The Rubicon, Four Alls

▲ *York International Youth
Hostel, Water End, Clifton, York,
YO3 6LT.*
Actual grid ref: SE589528
Tel: **01904 653147**
Under 18: £10.95 **Adults:** £14.40
evening meal at 5.30-7.30pm,
licensed, self-catering facilities,
television, games room, showers,
laundry facilities
*Comfortable Victorian house with
spacious grounds in a peaceful
location just a walk along the river
from the city*

▲ *York Youth Hotel
(Independent Hostel), 11/13
Bishophill Senior, York, YO1 1EF.*
Actual grid ref: SE600515
Tel: **01904 625904 Adults:** £9.00
self-catering facilities

*The Hazelwood, 24-25 Portland
Street, Gillygate, York, YO3 7EH.*
Grades: ETC 4 Diamond,
AA 4 Diamond, RAC 4 Diamond
Tel: **01904 626548** Mr McNabb.
Fax no: 01904 628032
D: £24.50-£38.50 **S:** £30.00-£48.00.
Open: All Year
Beds: 2F 7D 4T 1S **Baths:** 14 En
Situated in very centre of York only
400 yards from York Minster yet in
extremely quiet location & with its
own car park. An elegant Victorian
town house with individually
designed ensuite bedrooms offering
excellent value. Quality breakfasts
catering for all tastes including
vegetarian. Non-smoking

*City Guest House, 68 Monkgate,
York, YO3 7PF.*
Grades: ETC 4 Diamond,
AA 4 Diamond
Tel: **01904 622483**
Mr & Mrs Robinson.
D: £20.00-£27.00 **S:** £20.00-£27.00.
Open: All Year (not Xmas)
Beds: 1F 4D 1T 1S
Baths: 6 En 1 Pr
Five minutes' walk to Minster, car
park, excellent value

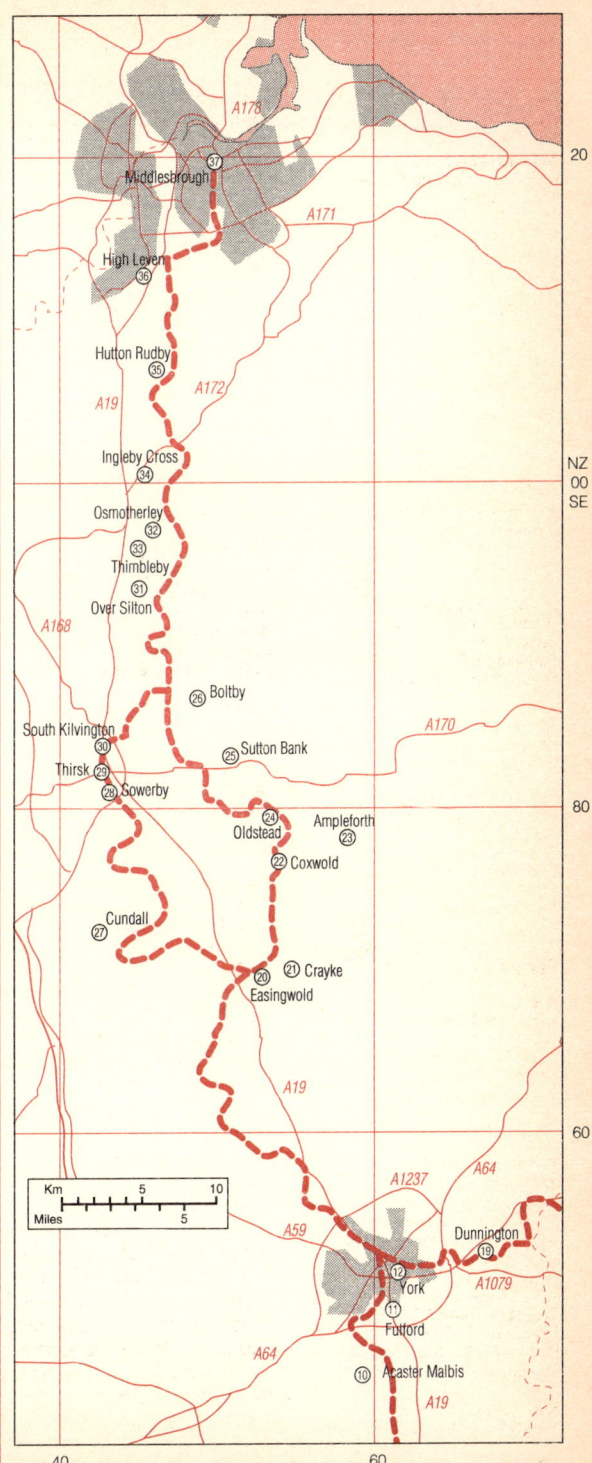

Feversham Lodge International Guest House, Feversham Crescent, York, YO31 8HQ.
Grades: ETC 3 Diamond
Tel: **01904 623882** (also fax no)
Mr & Mrs Lutyens-Humfrey.
D: £20.00-£25.00 **S:** £20.00-£41.00.
Open: All Year
Beds: 2F 5D 2T 1S
Baths: 6 En 1 Pr 2 Sh
♿ ⓟ (9) ⊬ ⊡ 🔥 🏧 🅥
Welcome to our comfortable international house. A former Methodist manse with lovely ensuite rooms. Choice delicious breakfasts. Only 10 minutes walk, York Minster. MInster views, yet ideal for the Yorkshire Moors, Dales. Japanese/Chinese/Italian/French spoken. Winter breaks available

The Beckett, 58 Bootham Crescent, Bootham, York, YO30 7AH.
Large Victorian house in city centre near Minster great breakfast
Grades: ETC 3 Diamond
Tel: **01904 644728** Mrs Brown.
Fax no: 01904 690732
D: £25.00-£27.50 **S:** £23.00-£26.00.
Open: All Year
Beds: 1F 3D 2T 1S
Baths: 5 En 1 Pr 1 Sh
♿ ⓟ ⊬ ⊡ 🔥 🏧 🅥

The Hollies, 141 Fulford Road, York, YO10 4HG.
Grades: ETC 3 Diamond,
AA 3 Diamond
Tel: **01904 634279** Mrs Wise.
Fax no: 01904 625432
D: £18.00-£28.00 **S:** £18.00-£27.00.
Open: All Year
Beds: 1F 3D 1S **Baths:** 3 En 2 Sh
♿ ⓟ (5) ⓟ (5) ⊬ ⊡ 🔥 ⚿ 🏧 🅥 🚲
Distinctive Edwardian residence, recently refurbished to provide quality accommodation and for that special occasion, a luxurious four poster. Close to delightful tree-lined riverside promenade for easy walking into city centre. 'More comfortable and friendly accommodation is hard to find'

Grange Lodge, 52 Bootham Crescent, Bootham, York, YO3 7AH.
Grades: ETC 1 Diamond
Tel: **01904 621137** Mrs Robinson.
D: £16.00-£22.00 **S:** £18.00-£20.00.
Open: All Year
Beds: 2F 3D 1T 1S
Baths: 1 En 5 Pr 2 Sh
♿ ⊡ ✕ 🏧
A fine Victorian town house, 5 or 6 min walk to city centre. Ensuite all with TV and tea and coffee facilities. Open all year round, special winter breaks, evening meals on request, all major credit cards taken

---

D = Price range per person

sharing in a double room

Ascot House, 80 East Parade, Heworth, York, YO31 7YH.
Grades: ETC 3 Diamond,
AA 3 Diamond, RAC 3 Diamond
Tel: **01904 426826** Mrs Wood.
Fax no: 01904 431077
D: £20.00-£24.00 **S:** £20.00-£24.00.
Open: All Year (not Xmas)
Beds: 3F 8D 3T 1S
Baths: 12 En 1 Pr 1 Sh
♿ ⓟ (14) ⊡ 🕯 🔥 🏧 🅥 🚲
A family-run Victorian villa, built in 1869, with rooms of character and many four-poster or canopy beds. Superb English breakfasts. Fifteen minutes' walk to Jorvik Viking Centre, Castle Museum or York Minster. Residential licence, sauna, private enclose carpark

Holly Lodge, 206 Fulford Road, York, YO1 4DD.
Grades: ETC 3 Diamond,
AA 3 Diamond, RAC 3 Diamond
Tel: **01904 646005** Mr Gallagher.
D: £25.00-£30.00 **S:** £40.00-£60.00.
Open: All Year
Beds: 1F 3D 1T
Baths: 5 En 5 Pr
♿ ⓟ (7) ⓟ ⊬ ⊡ 🔥 🏧 🅥 🚲
Ideally located 10 mins' riverside walk from the centre, convenient for all York's amenities. This fine Georgian building, with comfortable rooms, walled garden and car park, offers a warm welcome. Booking recommended. Located on A19, 1.5 miles towards the city from A19/A64 South Junction

Newton Guest House, Neville Street, Haxby Road, York, YO31 8NP.
Grades: ETC 3 Diamond
Tel: **01904 635627** Mrs Tindall.
D: £18.00-£20.00 **S:** £20.00-£25.00.
Open: All Year (not Xmas)
Beds: 1F 2D 1T 1S
Baths: 4 En 1 Pr
♿ ⓟ (5) ⊬ ⊡ 🔥 🏧 🅥 🚲
Non-smoking friendly family-run, only a few minutes walk to York Minster and city centre attractions. Breakfast menu plus vegetarian choice on request. Private off-street parking. Beautiful park opposite. Personal attention. Please ring for details

Nunmill House, 85 Bishopthorpe Road, York, YO23 1NX.
Grades: ETC 4 Diamond,
AA 4 Diamond
Tel: **01904 634047**
Mr & Mrs Whitbourn-Hammond.
Fax no: 01904 655879
D: £25.00-£30.00 **S:** £40.00.
Open: Feb to Nov
Beds: 1F 6D 1T
Baths: 7 En 1 Pr
♿ ⓟ (6) ⊬ ⊡ 🔥 🏧 🅥 ⚡ 🚲
Splendid Victorian house, lovingly furnished & smoke-free, for those looking for comfortable yet affordable accommodation. Easy walk to all attractions. SAE for brochure

Bowen House, 4 Gladstone Street, Huntington Road, York, YO31 8RF.
Grades: ETC 3 Diamond
Tel: **01904 636881** (also fax no)
Mrs Wood.
D: £17.50-£23.00 **S:** £20.00-£25.00.
Open: All Year (not Xmas)
Beds: 1F 2D 1T 1S
Baths: 2 En 1 Sh
♿ ⓟ (4) ⊬ ⊡ 🔥 🏧 🅥
Small, family-run, Victorian guest house with period furnishings throughout. Excellent traditional and vegetarian breakfasts with free-range eggs and home made preserves. Short stroll to York city centre. Private car park. Non smoking in all rooms. Brochure available

Cumbria House, 2 Vyner Street, Haxby Road, York, YO3 7HS.
Beautifully decorated family-run guest house. Private car park. Ideal for city centre & all attractions
Grades: ETC 3 Diamond,
AA 3 Diamond
Tel: **01904 636817** Mrs Curtis.
D: £18.00-£25.00 **S:** £18.00-£25.00.
Open: All Year
Beds: 2F 2D 1S **Baths:** 3 Pr 1 Sh
♿ ⓟ (5) ⊡ 🔥 🏧 🅥

St Raphael Guest House, 44 Queen Annes Road, Bootham, York, YO3 7AF.
Family-run mock Tudor guest house, tastefully decorated
Grades: ETC 2 Diamond,
AA 2 Diamond, RAC 2 Diamond
Tel: **01904 645028** Mrs Foster.
Fax no: 01904 658788
D: £18.00-£25.00 **S:** £17.00.
Open: All Year
Beds: 1F 3D 2T 2S
Baths: 5 En 2 Sh
♿ ⓟ (2) ⊡ 🕯 🔥 🏧 🅥 ∎

Bay Tree Guest House, 92 Bishopthorpe Road, York, YO2 1JS.
Tastefully decorated victorian town house, ten minutes walk from attractions
Grades: ETC 3 Diamond
Tel: **01904 659462** (also fax no)
Mr Ridley.
D: £20.00-£23.00 **S:** £20.00-£22.00.
Open: all year (not Xmas)
Beds: 1F 1D 1T 2S
Baths: 2 En 1 Sh
♿ (1 yr) ⊬ ⊡ 🕯 🔥 🏧 🅥 🚲

Gables Guest House, 50 Bootham Crescent, Bootham, York, YO3 7AH.
Tel: **01904 624381** (also fax no)
D: £18.00-£27.00 **S:** £18.00-£28.00.
Open: All Year
Beds: 1F 2D 2T 1S
Baths: 4 En 2 Sh
♿ ⓟ ⊡ 🕯 ✕ 🔥 🏧 🅥 ∎ ⚡ 🚲
Valerie Lapworth extends a warm welcome to our home & historic city. Friendly comfortable guest house, close to city centre. All rooms with colour TV & tea/ coffee-making facilities, central heating, access to rooms at all times. Easy parking

Northholme Guest House,
114 Shipton Road, York, YO30 5RN.
Grades: ETC 3 Diamond
Tel: 01904 639132
D: £14.50-£19.00
S: £17.00-£24.00.
Open: All Year (not Xmas)
Beds: 1F 1D 2T 1S
Baths: 3 En 1 Sh
♿ P (4) ⏷ ⟋ ☐ ⚲ ▥ Ⓥ ⚡ ⚲
Our family run detached home, in a
semi-rural setting, is convenient for
York city centre and the ring road.
We have comfortable, spacious,
ensuite rooms with colour TV and
welcome tray. Private parking

Midway House Hotel, *145 Fulford
Road, York, YO4 4HG.*
Built in 1897, an elegant detached
late-Victorian villa standing in own
grounds
Grades: ETC 3 Diamond,
AA 3 Diamond
Tel: 01904 659272 (also fax no)
Armitage.
D: £18.00-£27.50 **S:** £18.00-£30.00.
Open: All Year
Beds: 3F 7D 1T 1S
Baths: 10 En 2 Sh
♿ P (14) ⟋ ☐ ⚲ ▥ Ⓥ ⚡ ⚲

Cornmill Lodge, *120 Haxby Road,
York, YO31 8JP.*
Vegetarian/vegan guest house.
15 mins' walk York Minster
Grades: ETC 3 Diamond,
AA 3 Diamond
Tel: 01904 620566
Mrs Williams.
Fax no: 0870 063 6094
D: £20.00-£24.00
S: £20.00-£24.00.
Open: All Year
Beds: 1F 1D 1T 1S
Baths: 3 En 1 Pr
♿ P (4) ⟋ ☐ ⚲ ▥ Ⓥ

Park View Guest House,
*34 Grosvenor Terrace, Bootham,
York, YO3 7AG.*
Family-run 10 mins walk York
centre. Clean, friendly and
comfortable
Grades: ETC 3 Diamond
Tel: 01904 620437 (also fax no)
Mrs Ashton.
D: £22.00-£25.00 **S:** £25.00-£30.00.
Open: All Year (not Xmas)
Beds: 1F 3D 2T 1S
Baths: 5 En 1 Pr
♿ ⟋ ☐ ⚲ ▥ Ⓥ

Georgian Guest House,
35 Bootham, York, YO3 7BT.
Quality city centre accommodation
with car park
Grades: ETC 3 Diamond,
AA 3 Diamond, RAC 3 Diamond
Tel: 01904 622874
Mr Semple.
Fax no: 01904 635379
D: £25.00-£25.00 **S:** £18.00-£35.00.
Open: All Year (not Xmas)
Beds: 2F 7D 1T 5S
Baths: 10 En 3 Sh
♿ (5) P (8) ⟋ ☐ ⚲ ▥ Ⓥ ⚡ ⚲

Dairy Guest House, *3 Scarcroft
Road, York, YO23 1ND.*
Beautiful appointed Victoria house.
Tasteful in many ways!
Grades: ETC 3 Diamond
Tel: 01904 639367
Mr Hunt.
D: £20.00-£25.00 **S:** £30.00-£40.00.
Open: Feb to Dec
Beds: 2F 2D 1T
Baths: 2 Pr 1 Sh
♿ ⟋ ☐ ⚲ ▥ ⚲ Ⓥ

Dalescroft Guest House,
*10 Southlands Road, Bishopthorpe
Road, York, YO2 1NP.*
Warm welcome in family-run guest
house, 10 mins from city & race
course
Tel: 01904 626801
Mrs Blower.
D: £14.00-£22.00 **S:** £15.00-£20.00.
Open: All Year
Beds: 1F 2D 2T 1S
Baths: 2 En 1 Pr
♿ ⟋ ☐ ⚲ ✕ ⚲ ▥ Ⓥ ⚑

York Lodge Guest House,
*64 Bootham Crescent, Bootham,
York, YO3 7AH.*
Comfortable, relaxing
accommodation, friendly service
Tel: 01904 654289
Mr Moore.
D: £20.00-£22.00 **S:** £20.00-£20.00.
Open: All Year
Beds: 2F 3D 2T 1S
Baths: 4 En 2 Sh
♿ ☐ ⚲ ▥ Ⓥ

Bank House, *9 Southlands Road,
York, YO2 1NP.*
Tel: 01904 627803
Mr Farrell.
D: £16.00-£22.00 **S:** £20.00.
Open: All Year
Beds: 7F 2D 2T 3S
Baths: 1 En 7 Pr 7 Sh
♿ ⟋ ☐ ⚲ ✕ ⚲ ▥ Ⓥ ⚲
5 minutes' walk to the city centre.
Comfortable Victorian house.
Non-smoking. Race course nearby.
Riverside nearby (walks). Colour
TV in all rooms. Tea & coffee in all
rooms. All ensuite rooms

Bronte Guesthouse, *22 Grosvenor
Terrace, Bootham, York, YO30 7AG.*
Grades: ETC 4 Diamond,
AA 4 Diamond
Tel: 01904 621066
Fax no: 01904 653434
D: £23.00-£30.00
S: £25.00-£35.00.
Open: All Year (not Xmas)
Beds: 1F 1D 1T 2S
Baths: 5 En
♿ P (1) ☐ ⚲ ▥ Ⓥ ⚲ ⚑
Family-run Victorian guest house,
quietly but conveniently situated
from the historic centre (5-7
minutes' walk). Comfortable
ensuite rooms with facilities to
make your stay enjoyable and
relaxing whether for business or
pleasure. Varied breakfast. Free
car parking

Victoria Villa, *72 Heslington Road,
York, YO10 5AU.*
Tel: 01904 631647
D: £15.00-£20.00 **S:** £16.00-£25.00.
Open: All Year
Beds: 1F 3D 1T 1S
Baths: 2 Sh
♿ P (1) ☐ ⟲ ⚲ ▥ Ⓥ ⚲
The Victorian villa guest house is a
beautiful Victorian town house,
close to York city centre with all its
attractions and only a short stroll to
York University, offering clean and
friendly accommodation. A hearty
English breakfast is our speciality

Foss Bank Guest House, *16
Huntington Road, York, YO31 8RB.*
Small family-run Victorian house,
5 minutes walk from York Minster
Tel: 01904 635548
D: £17.00-£20.00 **S:** £18.50-£22.00.
Open: Feb to Dec
Beds: 3D 1T 2S
Baths: 2 En 2 Sh
♿ P (5) ⟋ ☐ ⚲ ⚲ ▥ Ⓥ ⚡ ⚲

Tower Guest House, *2 Feversham
Crescent, Wiggington Road, York,
YO31 8HQ.*
Grades: ETC 3 Diamond
Tel: 01904 655571
D: £20.00-£25.00 **S:** £22.00-£30.00.
Open: All Year
Beds: 1F 3D 1T 1S
Baths: 6 En
♿ P (6) ⟋ ☐ ✕ ⚲ ▥ Ⓥ ⚡ ⚲
Friendly family-run guest house, 10
mins walk to city centre, full
English breakfast, large Victorian
house with original features, double
glazing, special breaks available,
fire certificate, large rooms,
sky/digital/satellite TV, resident
owners, many return visitors

Mowbray House, *34 Haxby Road,
York, YO31 8JX.*
Clean and comfortable guest rooms
close to the city centre
Grades: ETC 3 Diamond
Tel: 01904 637710 Mrs Dawson.
D: £20.00-£25.00.
Open: All Year (not Xmas)
Beds: 2D 1T
Baths: 3 En
♿ P (3) ⟋ ☐ ⚲ ▥ Ⓥ ⚲

Bootham Park Hotel, *9 Grosvenor
Terrace, Bootham, York, YO30 7AG.*
Listed town house in quiet location
overlooking parkland and York
Minster
Grades: ETC 4 Diamond
Tel: 01904 644262
D: £21.00-£27.00 **S:** £18.00-£24.00.
Open: All Year (not Xmas)
Beds: 2F 4D 1S
Baths: 6 En 1 Pr
♿ (7) P (6) ⟋ ☐ ⚲ ▥ Ⓥ

S = Price range for a single
person in a room

Chelmsford Place Guest House,
85 Fulford Road, York, YO10 4BD.
Victorian house, 300 yards from
river, 5 mins walk to centre
Grades: ETC 3 Diamond
Tel: 01904 624491
D: £17.00-£24.00 **S:** £17.00-£38.00.
Open: All Year
Beds: 2F 3D 2T 1S
Baths: 6 En 1 Sh
⌂ ▣ ❒ 🖚 🕯 🎱 Ⅶ ❖

The Racecourse Centre, Tadcaster
Road, York, YO24.
Superior budget accommodation
for groups only. Minimum of 10
people
Tel: 01904 636553 Mr Patmore.
Fax no: 01904 612815
D: £17.50-£19.50 **S:** £17.50-£24.50.
Open: All Year
Beds: 23F 12T 8S
Baths: 7 Sh
⌂ ▣ (40) ❒ ✗ 🎱 ♿ ⚓ ▪

Warres Guest House, 30 Scarcroft
Road, York, YO23 1NF.
Friendly comfortable Victorian
town house, close to all museums
and attractions
Grades: ETC 3 Diamond
Tel: 01904 643139
D: £21.00-£27.00 **S:** £35.00-£45.00.
Open: Feb to Dec
Beds: 2F 2D 2T
Baths: 6 En
⌂ (1) ▣ (7) ⥅ ❒ 🖚 🕯 🎱 Ⅶ ❖ ⚓

The Bentley Hotel, 25 Grosvenor
Terrrace, Bootham, York, YO30 7AG.
Victorian town house overlooking
York Minster, personal attention
and home from home hospitality
Grades: ETC 3 Diamond
Tel: 01904 644313 (also fax no)
D: £19.00-£26.00
S: £25.00-£30.00.
Open: Feb to Dec
Beds: 3D 1T 2S
Baths: 4 En 1 Sh
⌂ (10) ▣ (1) ⥅ ❒ 🖚 🕯 🎱 Ⅶ ⚓

Vegetarian Guest House, 21 Park
Grove, York, YO31 8LG.
Vegetarian B&B in large Victorian
house, 10 mins walk York centre
Grades: ETC 3 Diamond
Tel: 01904 644790
D: £20.00-£20.00 **S:** £20.00-£20.00.
Open: All Year (not Xmas)
Beds: 1F 1D 1S
Baths: 2 En 1 Sh
⥅ ❒ 🖚 🕯 🎱 Ⅶ ▪ ❖ ⚓

Queen Annes Guest House,
24 Queen Annes Road, Bootham,
York, YO3 7AA.
Clean and comfortable home from
home. Tea/coffee/TV all rooms.
Full English breakfast
Tel: 01904 629389
Mrs West.
D: £16.00 **S:** £16.00.
Open: All Year (not Xmas)
Beds: 4D 1T 1S
Baths: 4 Pr 1 Sh
⌂ (3) ▣ (3) ❒ 🖚 🎱 Ⅶ

Treetops Guest House, 21 St
Marys, Bootham, York, YO3 7DD.
Attractive Victorian terraced town
house five minutes from the
Minster
Tel: 01904 658053 Mr Smith.
D: £20.00 **S:** £22.00.
Open: All Year (not Xmas)
Beds: 7D 1T **Baths:** 8 En
▣ ⥅ ❒ 🖚 🎱 Ⅶ

Kismet Guest House, 147 Haxby
Road, York, YO3 7JW.
Friendly guest house, no restric-
tions. Hearty breakfasts. Lock up
parking
Tel: 01904 621056
D: £18.00 **S:** £20.00.
Open: All Year (not Xmas)
Beds: 1F 2T 3D 2S
Baths: 3 En 1 Sh
⌂ (10) ▣ (7) 🖚 🕯 🎱 ⚓

Avimore House Hotel, 78 Stockton
Lane, York, YO31 1BS.
Edwardian, family-run guest house.
Walking distance to city centre
Tel: 01904 425556 Mrs Lewis.
D: £18.00 **S:** £22.00.
Open: All Year (not Xmas)
Beds: 1F 1D 2T 2S **Baths:** 6 En
⌂ ▣ (5) ❒ 🖚 🕯 ♿ Ⅶ ❖ ⚓

Hobbits Hotel, 9 St Peters Grove,
Clifton, York, YO30 6AQ.
Small & friendly hotel in a quiet
cul-de-sac 10 minutes' walk from
centre
Tel: 01904 624538 Mrs Miller.
Fax no: 01904 651765
D: £25.00 **S:** £27.00.
Open: All Year
Beds: 2F 2D 1T 2S
Baths: 7 En
⌂ ▣ (5) ❒ 🖚 🕯 🎱 Ⅶ

Cornerways Guest House,
16 Murton Way, Osbaldwick, York,
YO1 3UN.
Comfortable detached friendly
guest house, close to 'Park & Ride'
Tel: 01904 645544 Mr White.
D: £24.00 **S:** £18.00.
Open: All Year
Beds: 1F 1D 1S **Baths:** 2 En 1 Pr
⌂ ▣ (4) ⥅ ❒ 🖚 🕯 🎱 Ⅶ

Blakeney Hotel, 180 Stockton
Lane, York, YO31 1ES.
Friendly family-run hotel set in one
of York's finest residential areas
Tel: 01904 422786 (also fax no)
Mr Whiteford.
D: £19.00 **S:** £21.00.
Open: All Year (not Xmas)
Beds: 3F 10D 2T 3S
Baths: 9 En 1 Pr 2 Sh
⌂ ▣ (11) ❒ ✗ 🖚 🎱 Ⅶ ▪ ❖

Riverside Walk Hotel,
9 Earlsborough Terrace, Marygate,
York, YO3 7BQ.
Situated on river's edge. 450 yards
from city wall. Quiet location
Tel: 01904 620769
Fax no: 01904 646249
D: £20.00 **S:** £30.00.
Open: All Year
Beds: 1F 2T 8D 2S **Baths:** 13 En
⌂ ▣ (14) ⥅ ❒ 🖚 🎱 Ⅶ ❖ ⚓

Beverley   13

National Grid Ref: TA0440
🍴 ◁ Rose & Crown, Mokescroft Inn, The
Hayride, Queens Head

▲ **Beverley Friary Youth Hostel,**
The Friary, Friar's Lane, Beverley,
East Yorkshire, HU17 0DF.
Actual grid ref: TA038393
Tel: 01482 881751
Under 18: £5.65 **Adults:** £8.35
evening meal at 7.00pm, self-cater-
ing facilities, showers
Restored Dominican friary men-
tioned in the Canterbury Tales and
next to Beverley Minster

The Eastgate Guest House,
7 Eastgate, Beverley, E. Yorks,
HU17 0DR.
Family-run Victorian guest house
close to Beverley Minster and army
museum
Grades: ETC 3 Diamond
RAC 3 Diamond
Tel: 01482 868464 Ms Anderson.
Fax no: 01482 871899
D: £15.00-£25.00 **S:** £20.00-£35.00.
Open: All Year (not Xmas)
Beds: 7F 3D 3T 5S
Baths: 7 Pr 3 Sh
⌂ ❒ 🖚 🎱

The lovely village of **Coxwold** is most famous as the home
and burial place of Laurence Sterne, author of Tristram Shandy,
a novel whose whose literary self-consciousness seemed merely quirky in the eighteenth century but was later recognised as
a major forerunner of the twentieth-century novel. Shandy Hall,
his home, is now a dedicated museum publicising itself as 'the
Medieval House where the Modern Novel was born'.

Thirsk was made famous as James Herriot's 'Darrowby', the
fictional setting of his Yorkshire veterinary tales. The James
Herriot Visitor Centre will be a must for enthusiasts.

In **Middlesbrough** you can visit the Captain Cook Birthplace
Museum; several other museums and galleries; and Ormesby
Hall, a Georgian mansion notable for its decoration, particularly
the plasterwork.

Number One, 1 Woodlands, Beverley, E. Yorks, HU17 8BT.
Intriguing Victorian house. Walled garden
Tel: **01482 862752** Mrs King.
D: £17.50 **S:** £16.50.
Open: All Year
Beds: 1F 1D 1T 1S
Baths: 1 En 1 Sh
ॐ **P** (2) ⧉ ⛌ ⅏ ✕ 🛆 🏢 **V** 🛉 ⚹

Arras 14

National Grid Ref: SE9241

⒣ ⒤ Light Dragoon

Arras Farmhouse, Arras, Market Weighton, York, E. Yorks, YO43 4RN.
Actual grid ref: SE9242
Friendly family welcome peaceful and comfortable good food working farm
Grades: ETC 3 Diamond
Tel: **01430 872404** (also fax no)
Mrs Stephenson.
D: £17.50-£20.00
S: £20.00-£22.00.
Open: All Year (not Xmas)
Beds: 2D 1T **Baths:** 2 En 1 Sh
ॐ **P** (5) ⧉ 🏢 🛉 ⚹

Market Weighton 15

National Grid Ref: SE8741

⒣ ⒤ Black Horse

The Gables, 38 Londesborough Road, Market Weighton, York, E. Yorks, YO4 3HS.
Actual grid ref: SE877423
Friendly, comfortable, quiet country house
Tel: **01430 872255**
Mr & Mrs Reeson.
D: £16.00 **S:** £16.00.
Open: All Year (not Xmas)
Beds: 1D 1T 1S **Baths:** 1 Sh
ॐ **P** (5) ⧉ ⅏ 🛆 🏢 **V** 🛉 ⚹

Shiptonthorpe 16

National Grid Ref: SE8543

⒣ ⒤ The Crown

Robeanne House Farm & Stables, Driffield Lane, Shiptonthorpe, York, YO4 3LB.
Beautiful house, beautiful rooms. Beautiul countryside, fabulous breakfast
Tel: **01430 873312** (also fax no)
Mrs Wilson.
D: £17.50 **S:** £17.50.
Open: All Year
Beds: 3F 2D 1T
Baths: 6 En
ॐ **P** (10) ⧉ ⅏ ✕ 🛆 🏢 **V** 🛉 ⚹

D = Price range per person
sharing in a double room

Millington 17

National Grid Ref: SE8351

⒣ ⒤ The Gate

Laburnum Cottage, Millington, York, E. Yorks, YO4 2TX.
Actual grid ref: SE831518
Comfortable cottage with beautiful garden, animal lovers, mentally handicapped welcome
Tel: **01759 303055** Mrs Dykes.
D: £18.00-£22.00 **S:** £20.00-£22.00.
Open: Easter to Oct
Beds: 1F 1T
Baths: 1 Sh
ॐ **P** (2) ⧉ ⛌ ⅏ ✕ 🛆 🏢 **V** 🛉 ⚹ 🚲

Barmby Moor 18

National Grid Ref: SE7748

⒣ ⒤ Wellington Oak

Alder Carr House, York Road, Barmby Moor, York, E. Yorks, YO4 5HU.
Tel: **01759 380566** Mrs Steel.
D: £17.00-£20.00 **S:** £20.00-£22.00.
Open: All Year (not Xmas)
Beds: 1F 2D
Baths: 2 En 1 Pr
ॐ **P** (10) ⧉ 🛆 🏢 **V**
Georgian style house set in 10 acres, 7 miles SE of York. Well positioned for historic Beverley and the coast, Moors and Wolds. Within 5 miles:- gliding, riding, golf and National Water Lily Collection. Pleasant 0.5 acre garden for use of guests

Dunnington 19

National Grid Ref: SE6652

⒣ ⒤ Cross Keys

Moonlight Cottage, 8 Greencroft Court, Dunnington, York, YO1 5QJ.
Comfortable and quiet. Convenient to York Moors, dales, castle, Howard Coast
Tel: **01904 489369** (also fax no)
Mrs McNab.
D: £15.00-£17.00.
Open: All Year
Beds: 1D **Baths:** 1 En
ॐ **P** (2) ⛌ ⧉ 🛆 🏢 **V**

Easingwold 20

National Grid Ref: SE5369

⒣ ⒤ Falconberg

Garbutts Ghyll, Thornton Hill, Easingwold, York, North Yorkshire, YO6 3PZ.
A family-run B&B on a working farm in its own valley with panoramic views
Tel: **01347 868644** Mrs Glaister.
Fax no: 01347 868133
D: £20.00-£25.00 **S:** £18.00-£20.00.
Open: Easter to Nov
Beds: 1D 1T **Baths:** 1 En
ॐ **P** ⛌ ⧉ ⅏ 🛆 🏢 **V** ⚹ 🚲

Crayke 21

National Grid Ref: SE5670

⒣ ⒤ Durham Ox

The Hermitage, Crayke, York, YO6 4TB.
Actual grid ref: SE562707
Grades: ETC 3 Diamond
Tel: **01347 821635** Mr Moverley.
D: £26.00-£27.00 **S:** £26.00-£27.00.
Open: All Year
Beds: 1D 2T
Baths: 1 En 1 Sh
ॐ **P** (4) ⧉ 🛆 🏢 **V** ⚹ 🚲
Located on edge of small pretty village, stone-built house set in large garden; quiet setting with magnificent view in Area of Outstanding Natural Beauty, handy for York North York Moors, Wolds and Dales. Two miles from A19

Coxwold 22

National Grid Ref: SE5377

⒣ ⒤ Abbey Inn, Black Swan, Fauconberg Arms

Dale Croft, Main Street, Coxwold, York, YO61 4AB.
Dale Croft is a C17th old worldly cottage; large gardens
Tel: **01347 868356**
Mr & Mrs Richardson.
D: £17.00-£20.00 **S:** £18.50-£20.00.
Open: All Year (not Xmas/New Year)
Beds: 1F 1D 1T
Baths: 1 Sh
ॐ **P** (5) ⧉ ⅏ 🛆 🏢 **V**

Wakendale House, Oldstead Grange, Coxwold, York, YO6 4BJ.
Farmhouse in beautiful Herriot country. Friendly welcome. Comfortable beds
Tel: **01347 868351**
Mrs Banks.
D: £17.00 **S:** £19.00.
Open: Mar to Nov
Beds: 1F 1D 1T
Baths: 1 Sh
ॐ **P** (5) ⛌ ⧉ 🛆 🏢 **V**

Ampleforth 23

National Grid Ref: SE5878

⒣ ⒤ White Horse, Abbey Inn

Carr House Farm, Shallowdale, Ampleforth, York, YO6 4ED.
Idyllic C16th farmhouse, romantic 4 poster bedrooms, internationally recommended, Heartbeat countryside
Grades: ETC 3 Diamond
Tel: **01347 868526**
Mrs Lupton.
D: £17.50 **S:** £17.50.
Open: All Year (not Xmas)
Beds: 3D
Baths: 3 En
ॐ (7) **P** (5) ⛌ ⧉ ✕ 🛆 🏢 **V** ⚹ 🚲

Oldstead 24

National Grid Ref: SE5280

🍴 🍺 Abbey Inn

Oldstead Grange, *Oldstead, York, YO61 4BJ.*
Actual grid ref: SE523793
Grades: ETC 5 Diamond
Tel: **01347 868634** Mrs Banks.
D: £24.00-£27.50 **S:** £28.00-£32.00.
Open: All Year
Beds: 1F 1D 1T
Baths: 3 En
🛇 🅿 (3) ⚡ 🛏 📺 Ⅷ ♦ ⚲ 🚲
Beautiful quiet situation amidst our
fields, woods and valleys.
Traditional C17th features

Sutton Bank 25

National Grid Ref: SE5182

🍴 🍺 Hambleton Inn, Hare Inn

High House Farm, *Sutton Bank, Thirsk, N. Yorks, YO7 2HA.*
Actual grid ref: SE523830
Grades: ETC 3 Diamond
Tel: **01845 597557** Mrs Hope.
D: £20.00-£25.00 **S:** £22.00-£26.00.
Open: Easter to Nov
Beds: 1F 1D
Baths: 1 Sh
🛇 🅿 (6) ⚡ 🛏 ✕ 📺 Ⅷ Ⅵ ♦ ⚲
Family run dairy farm set in open
countryside in a tranquil part of W.
Yorks. Ideal for a quiet, relaxing
holiday. Superb home-made food
and hospitality. Lovely walks on
Moors & Dales. York and East
coast within the hour

Cote Faw, *Hambleton Cottages, Sutton Bank, Thirsk, N. Yorks, YO7 2EZ.*
Actual grid ref: SE522830
Comfortable cottage in National
Park, central for visiting North
Yorkshire
Tel: **01845 597363** Mrs Jeffray.
D: £16.00-£17.00 **S:** £16.00-£17.00.
Open: All Year (not Xmas)
Beds: 1F 1D 1S
Baths: 1 Sh
🛇 🅿 (3) ⚡ 🛏 📺 Ⅷ Ⅵ ♦ ⚲

Boltby 26

National Grid Ref: SE4986

🍴 🍺 Carpenters' Arms, Whitstoncliffe Hotel, Hambleton Inn

Town Pasture Farm, *Boltby, Thirsk, N. Yorks, YO7 2DY.*
Actual grid ref: SE494866
Comfortable farmhouse in
beautiful village, central for
Yorkshire Dales
Grades: ETC 3 Diamond
Tel: **01845 537298** Mrs Fountain.
D: £17.50-£19.50 **S:** £18.50-£20.00.
Open: All Year (not Xmas)
Beds: 1F 1T
Baths: 2 En
🛇 🅿 (3) ⚡ 🛏 ✕ 📺 Ⅷ Ⅵ ♦ ⚲

Willow Tree Cottage, *Boltby, Thirsk, N. Yorkshire, YO7 2DY.*
Actual grid ref: SE492865
Large luxurious room with
kitchenette. Quiet hillside village,
spectacular views
Tel: **01845 537406** Townsend.
Fax no: 01845 537073
D: £22.00-£30.00 **S:** £30.00-£38.00.
Open: All Year (not Xmas)
Beds: 1F
Baths: 1 En
🛇 (5) 🅿 (2) ⚡ 🛏 ✕ 📺 Ⅷ Ⅵ ♦ ⚲

Lower Paradise Farm, *Boltby, Thirsk, N. Yorks, YO7 2HS.*
Actual grid ref: SE502882
Located on edge of moors.
Beautiful views and a warm
welcome
Tel: **01845 537253** Mrs Todd.
D: £17.00 **S:** £20.00.
Open: Apr to Oct
Beds: 1F 1D 1T
Baths: 1 Sh
🛇 (5) 🅿 (6) ⚡ 🛏 ✕ 📺 Ⅷ Ⅵ ♦

Cundall 27

National Grid Ref: SE4272

🍴 🍺 Farmers' Inn

Lodge Farm, *Cundall, York, YO61 2RN.*
Actual grid ref: SE421732
Tel: **01423 360203** (also fax no)
Mrs Barker.
D: £20.00-£25.00 **S:** £30.00-£36.00.
Open: Mar to Nov
Beds: 1D **Baths:** 1 En
🛇 (2) 🅿 (2) ⚡ 🛏 ✕ 📺 Ⅷ Ⅵ ♦ 🚲
A Georgian farmhouse by River
Swale offering accommodation in
own private suite. Panoramic views
of the surrounding countryside and
the White Horse. Ideal location for
visiting the World of James
Herriot, Thirsk, Fountains Abbey,
Studley Royal, York

Sowerby 28

National Grid Ref: SE4281

The Old Manor House, *27 Front Street, Sowerby, Thirsk, N. Yorks, YO7 1JQ.*
Restored C15th manor house.
Guest suites overlooking gardens
or village green
Tel: **01845 526642** Mr Jackson.
Fax no: 01845 526568
D: £20.00 **S:** £35.00.
Open: All Year (not Xmas)
Beds: 1F 1D
Baths: 2 En
🛇 🅿 ⚡ 🛏 📺 Ⅷ Ⅵ ♦

S = Price range for a single
person in a room

All cycleways are
popular: you are
well-advised to
book ahead

Thirsk 29

National Grid Ref: SE4282

🍴 🍺 Hambleton Inn, Hare Inn, Dog & Gun,
Carpenters' Arms, Whitstoncliffe Hotel, Old Oak
Tree, Golden Fleece, Darrowby Inn, Black Swan,
Carpenters' Arms, Sheppards Table, The George

Hambleton House, *78 St James Green, Thirsk, N Yorks, YO7 1AJ.*
Grades: ETC 4 Diamond
Tel: **01845 525532**
Mr & Mrs Boumer.
D: £16.00-£20.00 **S:** £18.00-£25.00.
Open: Easter to Oct
Beds: 2D 1T
Baths: 2 En 1 Pr
🛇 (10) 🅿 ⚡ 🛏 📺 Ⅷ Ⅵ ♦ 🚲
Restored Victorian house (though
parts date back to 1683)
overlooking the green, away from
through traffic, but a mere 3
minutes walk to the market place.
Excellent base for touring the
Moors, Dales and York

Station House, *Station Road, Thirsk, N. Yorks, YO7 4LS.*
Old station master's house retaining
character of railways. Ideal base for
touring Dales & Moors
Tel: **01845 522063** Mrs Jones.
D: £17.00 **S:** £21.00.
Open: Easter to Oct
Beds: 1F 1D
Baths: 2 En
🅿 (6) ⚡ 🛏 📺 Ⅷ Ⅵ ♦ 🚲

Lavender House, *27 Kirkgate, Thirsk, N. Yorks, YO7 1PL.*
Welcoming, comfortable home.
Base for touring Dales and Moors,
next door to James Herriot Centre
Grades: ETC 3 Diamond
Tel: **01845 522224** Mrs Dodds.
D: £17.00-£17.00 **S:** £17.00-£20.00.
Open: All Year (not Xmas)
Beds: 2F 1S
Baths: 2 Sh
🛇 🅿 (3) ⚡ 🛏 📺 Ⅷ Ⅵ

Laburnham House, *31 Topcliff Rd, Thirsk, N. Yorks, YO7 1RX.*
Spacious detached house, tastefully
furnished with antiques and in the
traditional manner
Grades: ETC 4 Diamond
Tel: **01845 524120** Mrs Ogleby.
D: £19.00-£21.00 **S:** £25.00-£35.00.
Open: Easter to Nov
Beds: 1F 1D 1T
Baths: 2 En 1 Pr
🛇 (5) 🅿 (3) ⚡ 🛏 📺 Ⅷ Ⅵ ♦ 🚲

South Kilvington 30

National Grid Ref: SE4284

|O| |€| Old Oak Tree

Thornborough House Farm, South Kilvington, Thirsk, N. Yorks, YO7 2NP.
Actual grid ref: SE426847
A warm welcome awaits you in our comfortable 200 year old farmhouse
Grades: ETC 3 Diamond
Tel: **01845 522103** (also fax no)
Mrs Williamson.
D: £15.00-£19.00 **S:** £15.00-£19.00.
Open: All Year
Beds: 1F 1D 1T
Baths: 2 En 1 Pr
⌂ |P| (4) ⌿ ☐ ♜ ✕ ▲ Ⅲ V ♲ ☙

Over Silton 31

National Grid Ref: SE4593

|O| |€| The Gold Cup

Moorfields Farm, Over Silton, Thirsk, N. Yorks, YO7 2LJ.
Actual grid ref: SE451932
Yorkshire stone farmhouse close to North Yorkshire Moors
Tel: **01609 883351** Mrs Goodwin.
D: £15.00-£15.00 **S:** £15.00-£15.00.
Open: All Year
Beds: 1D 1S
Baths: 1 Sh
⌂ (2) |P| (4) ⌿ ☐ ♜ ✕ ▲ Ⅲ V ♲ ☙

Osmotherley 32

National Grid Ref: SE4597

|O| |€| Golden Lion, Queen Catherine Hotel

▲ *Osmotherley Youth Hostel, Cote Ghyll, Osmotherley, Northallerton, North Yorkshire, DL6 3AH.*
Actual grid ref: SE461981
Tel: **01609 883575**
Under 18: £6.20 **Adults:** £9.15
evening meal at 7.00pm, family bunk rooms, television, games room, showers, shop
Surrounded by woodland, the youth hostel is fully modernised with excellent facilities, right on the edge of the North York Moors National Park

Quintana House, Back Lane, Osmotherley, Northallerton, N. Yorks, DL6 3BJ.
Actual grid ref: SE457974
Detached stone cottage with panoramic view of Black Hambleton Summit
Tel: **01609 883258**
Dr Bainbridge.
D: £18.50.
Open: All Year (not Xmas)
Beds: 1D 1T
Baths: 1 Sh
⌂ (12) |P| (1) ⌿ ☐ ▲ Ⅲ V ♲

Thimbleby 33

National Grid Ref: SE4495

|O| |€| Golden Lion

Stonehaven, Thimbleby, Osmotherly, Northallerton, DL6 3PY.
Comfortable farmhouse, super view, lovely walks, good beds and good food
Tel: **01609 883689** Mrs Shepherd.
D: £18.00-£19.00.
Open: Easter to Nov
Beds: 1D 1T
Baths: 1 Pr
⌂ (1) |P| (3) ⌿ ☐ ▲ Ⅲ V 🛡 ♲ ☙

Ingleby Cross 34

National Grid Ref: NZ4500

|O| |€| Black Horse, Blue Bell Inn

Blue Bell Inn, Ingleby Cross, Northallerton, N. Yorks, DL6 3NF.
Family run, real ales, coal fire, quiet annexed accommodation
Grades: ETC 1 Diamond
Tel: **01609 882272** Mrs Kinsella.
D: £20.00-£20.00 **S:** £20.00-£20.00.
Open: All Year
Beds: 4F 1D 4T
Baths: 5 En
⌂ |P| (20) ☐ ✕ ▲ Ⅲ V 🛡 ♲ ☙

Bringing children with you? Always ask for any special rates.

Hutton Rudby 35

National Grid Ref: NZ4606

|O| |€| Bay Horse

Grenview, 13 Eastside, Hutton Rudby, Yarm, N Yorks, TS15 0DB.
Tel: **01642 701739**
Mrs Ashton.
D: £17.00-£18.00 **S:** £18.00.
Open: All Year
Beds: 1D 1T
Baths: 2 En
⌂ (3) ⌿ ☐ ▲ Ⅲ V ☙
Overlooking the village green at Hutton Rudby, Greenview offers you a delightful stay bordering the National Park in North Yorkshire. Rooms have showers, comfortable beds, with a hearty breakfast. Ideal for Coast to Coast, Cleveland Way and new cycle route

High Leven 36

National Grid Ref: NZ4412

Leven Close Farm, High Leven, Yarm, TS15 9JP.
C17th farmhouse on 250-acre mixed farm
Tel: **01642 750114**
Mrs Simpson.
D: £17.00 **S:** £17.00.
Open: All Year
Beds: 2F 2T
Baths: 1 Sh
⌂ |P| (10) ☐ ♜ ✕ ▲ Ⅲ V

Middlesbrough 37

National Grid Ref: NZ5118

|O| |€| Highfield

White House Hotel, 311 Marton Road, Middlesbrough, TS4 2HG.
Family run, close to centre, good English breakfast, car parking
Tel: **01642 244531**
D: £15.00-£17.50
S: £18.50-£22.00.
Open: All Year
Beds: 2F 2D 6T 5S
Baths: 4 En 3 Sh
⌂ ☐ ♜ ▲ Ⅲ V

Round Berkshire Cycle Route

The **Round Berkshire Cycle Route** is a 140-mile circular route around the county of Berkshire, which has been deliberately routed along minor roads wherever possible. It starts and finishes in Reading, and runs anticlockwise around the whole of the county.

A detailed **guide leaflet** to the route is available free from Bracknell Forest Borough Council, Leisure Services, Edward Elgar House, Skimped Hill Lane, Bracknell, Berkshire RG12 1LR, tel 01344 354107. The route is signposted by blue direction signs with a cycle silhouette on a green outline map of Berkshire.

Maps: Ordnance Survey 1:50,000 Landranger series: 174, 175

Trains: Reading, Maidenhead and Slough (from where there is a connection to Windsor) are on the main line out of London. There are connections to Newbury, Hungerford, Bracknell and many other places on or near the route.

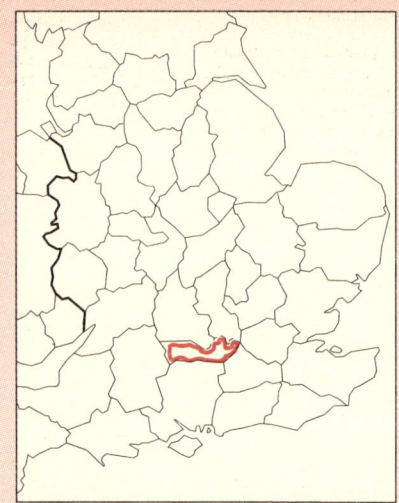

Reading to Tidmarsh

Reading, the county town of Berkshire, lies where the River Kennet joins the Thames, and is economically one of the most important towns of the Thames Valley. It is largely nineteenth-century redbrick, and has a thriving commercial town centre. In medieval times there was a Benedictine abbey, founded in the twelfth century, of which a few ruins remain. The town also has a good museum, which houses the finds from the Roman town at Silchester in Hampshire, and a good theatre, the Hexagon. This is where Oscar Wilde spent two years in prison, after which he wrote the *Ballad of Reading Gaol*. Cycling west from the south bank of the Thames at Caversham Bridge, you leave town after Tilehurst station, and reach the village of **Tidmarsh.** A short detour north at this point leads to the small Thameside town of **Pangbourne**, used by the artist Ernest Shepard as the setting for his illustrations to *The Wind in the Willows*, whose author, Kenneth Grahame, lived here.

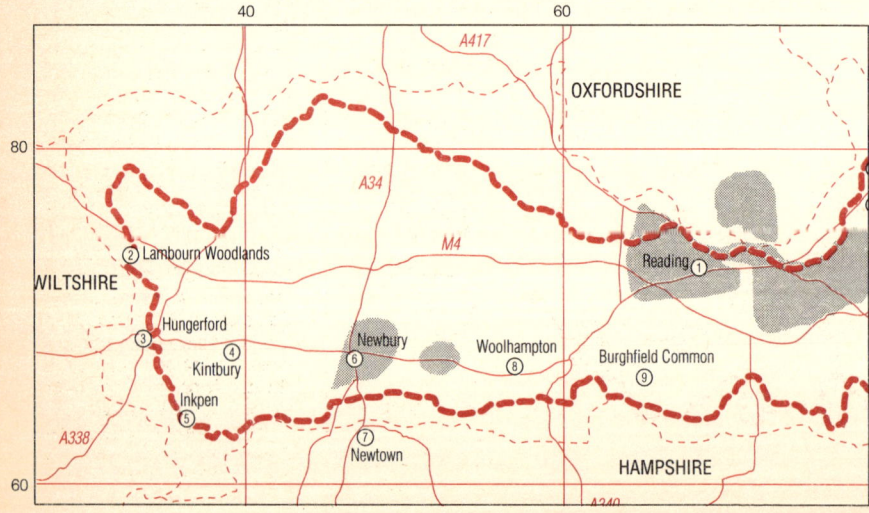

Reading 1

National Grid Ref: SU7173

🍽 🍺 Horse & Jockey, The Unicorn, Red Lion, Grouse & Claret, Rose & Thistle

The Berkeley Guest House,
*32 Berkeley Avenue, Reading,
Berks, RG1 6JE.*
Edwardian family home 10 mins' walk from town. Colour TVs and refrigerators
Tel: **0118 959 5699**
Mr Hubbard.
D: £19.00-£24.00 **S:** £20.00-£27.00.
Open: All Year
Beds: 2F 3T
Baths: 2 Sh
🛏 🅿 (6) 🚭 🍴 🐕 👶 🎍 Ⅲ Ⅵ ♿

Greystoke Guest House,
*10 Greystoke Road, Caversham,
Reading, Berks, RG4 5EL.*
Private home in quiet road, TV & tea/coffee making in lounge
Grades: ETC 3 Diamond
Tel: **0118 947 5784**
Mrs Tyler.
D: £25.00-£30.00.
S: £28.00-£35.00.
Open: All Year (not Xmas)
Beds: 1D 2S
Baths: 1 Sh
🅿 (3) 🚭 🍴 👶 🎍 Ⅲ Ⅵ ♿ 🚲

Dittisham Guest House,
*63 Tilehurst Road, Reading, Berks,
RG30 2JL.*
Quiet central location in a restored Edwardian home. High standards at sensible prices
Tel: **0118 956 9483**
Mr Harding.
D: £19.00-£25.00 **S:** £25.00-£35.00.
Open: All Year
Beds: 2D 1T 2S
Baths: 3 En 2 Sh
🛏 🅿 🚭 🍴 🐕 👶 🎍 Ⅲ Ⅵ ♿ 🚲

St Hilda's, *24 Castle Crescent,
Reading, Berkshire, RG1 6AG.*
Quiet Victorian home near town centre, all rooms have colour TVs & fridges
Tel: **0118 961 0329**
Mr & Mrs Hubbard.
Fax no: 0118 954 2585
D: £19.00-£24.00 **S:** £20.00-£27.00.
Open: All Year
Beds: 3F 2T
Baths: 3 Sh
🛏 (1) 🅿 🚭 🍴 👶 🎍 Ⅲ Ⅵ ♿ 🚲

Lambourn Woodlands 2

National Grid Ref: SU3175

Lodge Down, *Lambourn
Woodlands, Hungerford, Berks,
RG17 7BJ.*
Tel: **01672 540304** (also fax no)
Mrs Cook.
D: £22.50 **S:** £30.00.
Open: All Year
Beds: 1F 2D 2T
Baths: 3 En
🛏 🅿 (6) 🍴 🎍 Ⅲ Ⅵ ♿ ♿
Country house in lovely grounds with luxury accommodation with ensuite bathrooms

Hungerford 3

National Grid Ref: SU3368

🍽 🍺 Just Williams, John O'Gaunt

Wilton House, *33 High Street,
Hungerford, Berks, RG17 0NF.*
Elegant C15th town house in popular antiques centre
Grades: ETC 4 Diamond
Tel: **01488 684228** Mrs Welfare.
Fax no: 01488 685037
D: £25.00-£27.50 **S:** £35.00-£38.00.
Open: All Year (not Xmas)
Beds: 2F 1D 1T **Baths:** 2 En
🛏 (8) 🅿 (3) 🚭 🍴 👶 🎍 Ⅲ Ⅵ ♿

The Honeybones, *33 Bourne Vale,
Hungerford, Berkshire, RG17 0LL.*
Actual grid ref: SU333682
Tel: **01488 683228**
Mr & Mrs Honeybone.
D: £16.00-£17.50 **S:** £17.50-£22.50.
Open: All Year
Beds: 2T 1S
Baths: 1 Pr 1 Sh
🛏 (5) 🅿 (3) 🚭 🍴 👶 🎍 Ⅲ Ⅵ ♿ 🚲
Modern detached family house, southern edge of town, within walking distance town centre, railway and canal. Conservatory breakfast room with panoramic views of local countryside, ideal touring and walking base, 3 miles M4 (J14), guided walks by prior arrangement

Tidmarsh to Hungerford

After Tidmarsh you pass into the **North Wessex Downs** with the villages of Upper Basildon and Aldworth, where you will find the Four Points pub, from where you can head onto an alternative route along **the Ridgeway**, an ancient path along which lie numerous Iron Age forts. Near the point where you join the Ridgeway is the site of the Battle of Ashdown. In 871, the Saxons of Wessex won a resounding victory, under Alfred the Great (then the brother of King Aethelred I), in their campaign against the invasion of England by the Danes – only to be crushed by them at Merton (now in South London) shortly afterwards. After Aldworth you come to Compton, East and West Ilsley and Farnborough, and then down off the downs to the village of **Great Shefford** on the banks of the River Lambourn, which you follow upstream to **Lambourn** town, Berkshire's horseracing centre. After Lambourn it's south until you hit Ermine Street, the lesser of two Roman roads of that name, which runs from Silchester to Gloucester. After a brief stretch you turn right, cross the M4 and head on to **Hungerford**, on the River Kennet. At the Wharf you can view the **Kennet and Avon Canal**, constructed in 1774 and recently restored.

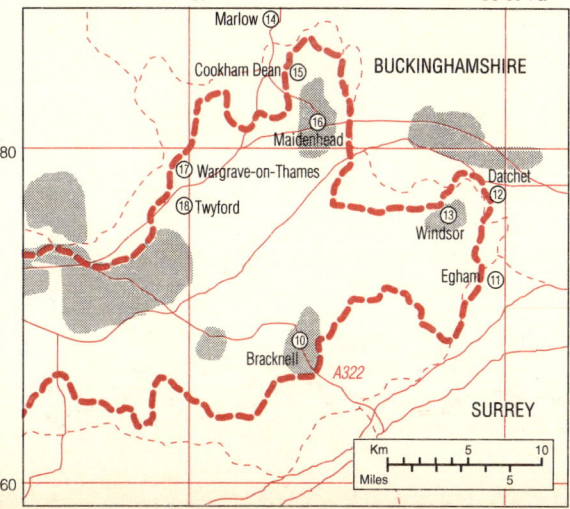

Hungerford to Finchampstead Ridges

Heading across Hungerford Common, the route takes you to the foot of **Walbury Hill**, the highest chalk hill in England. If you fancy a challenge, the view from the top is worth the climb, along quiet lanes. Otherwise, the route takes you around the hill and then eastwards on to **Newbury**, site of two battles in the Civil War, one of which (1643) is commemorated by the Falkland Memorial, close to the route on the way into town. The next stretch takes in two sites of legendary importance to the anti-nuclear movement, **Greenham Common**, just outside Newbury, former site of American Cruise Missiles and the resultant women's peace camp during the 1980s, and **Aldermaston**, site of the Atomic Weapons Research Establishment and of annual CND marches in the 1950s and 60s. Then it's into the coniferous woodland around Mortimer. A short detour over the Hampshire boundary takes you to the site of the Roman town of Calleva Atrebatum, at **Silchester**. This was the capital of the Atrebates tribe in the third and fourth centuries, and the site includes the walls, still upto 13 feet high in places, an amphitheatre, the foundations of a forum and the earliest known Christian church in Britain. After Mortimer it's across the Rivers Loddon and Blackwater near to Swallowfield Park, a seventeenth-century country house, and on to Wellingtonia Avenue, from where you can take a short detour to the viewpoint over the Blackwater Valley at Finchampstead Ridges.

---

15 Sanden Close, *Hungerford, Berks, RG17 0LA.*
Semi-detached bungalow in quiet close. Short walk to shops and station
Tel: **01488 682583** Mrs Hook.
D: £15.00-£16.00 **S:** £17.00-£18.00.
Open: All Year (not Xmas)
Beds: 1D 1S
Baths: 1 Sh
🛇 (5) 🅿 (3) ✡ ☐ 🎹

Brae House, *Salisbury Road, Hungerford, RG17 0LH.*
We warmly welcome you to our family home
Tel: **01488 682747** Mrs Rock.
D: £20.00-£20.00 **S:** £25.00-£35.00.
Open: All Year (not Xmas)
Beds: 1F
Baths: 1 En
🛇 🅿 (2) ✡ ☐ 🎹 🖤 ⚡ 🚲

Wasing, *35 Sanden Close, Hungerford, Berkshire, RG17 0LA.*
Warm welcome to the home of ex farmers. 3 miles M4
Tel: **01488 684127** Mrs Smalley.
D: £15.50-£16.00 **S:** £17.00-£18.00.
Open: All Year (not Xmas)
Beds: 1D 1T 1S
Baths: 1 En 1 Sh
🛇 🅿 ☐ ♨ 🎹 🖤 ⚡ 🚲

Wynbush, *135 Priory Road, Hungerford, Berks, RG17 0AP.*
Detached house, large garden, quiet. 3 miles M4
Tel: **01488 682045** Mrs Simmonds.
D: £15.00 **S:** £17.00.
Open: All Year
Beds: 1D 1S
Baths: 1 Sh
🛇 🅿 (3) ✡ ☐ ♨ 🎹 🖤

D = Price range per person sharing in a double room

S = Price range for a single person in a room

Kintbury   4

National Grid Ref: SU3866

🍴 🍺 Crown & Garter

The Forbury, *Crossways, Kintbury, Hungerford, Berks, RG17 9SU.*
Extended C17th cottage. Lovely position facing south, overlooking own woodlands
Tel: **01488 658377**
Mr Cubitt.
D: £20.00-£25.00 **S:** £20.00-£25.00.
Open: All Year (not Xmas)
Beds: 1F
Baths: 1 Pr 1 Sh
🛇 🅿 (10) ☐ 🐾 ✗ ♨ 🎹 🖤 🛈 ⚡ 🚲

Inkpen   5

National Grid Ref: SU3764

Beacon House, *Bell Lane, Upper Green, Inkpen, Hungerford, Berks, RG17 9QJ.*
Actual grid ref: SU368634
Grades: AA 3 Diamond
Tel: **01488 668640**
Mr & Mrs Cave.
D: £20.00-£20.00 **S:** £20.00-£20.00.
Open: All Year
Beds: 1T 2S
Baths: 2 Sh
🛇 (7) 🅿 (6) ☐ 🐾 ✗ ♨ 🎹 🖤 🛈 ⚡ 🚲
Visit our 1930's country home on Berks/Wilts/Hants border. Maximum four guests ensures our personal attention. Lovely countryside for walking, garden for relaxing, studio for art work. Oxford, Windsor, Winchester, Salisbury one hour by car

Newbury   6

National Grid Ref: SU4767

🍴 🍺 Lord Lyon, Red Lion, Gun Inn

15 Shaw Road, *Newbury, Berks, RG14 1HG.*
Late Georgian terraced house near town centre, rail and canal
Tel: **01635 44962** Mrs Curtis.
D: £17.00-£18.00 **S:** £17.00-£18.00.
Open: All Year
Beds: 1D, 1T **Baths:** 1 Sh
🛇 🅿 ✡ ☐ ♨ 🎹 🖤 🛈 ⚡ 🚲

Laurel House, *157 Andover Road, Newbury, RG14 6NB.*
A warm welcome awaits you in our delightful Georgian house
Tel: **01635 35931**
Mr & Mrs Dixon.
D: £18.00-£18.00.
Open: All Year (not Xmas)
Beds: 1D 1T **Baths:** 1 Sh
🅿 (2) ✡ ☐ ♨ 🎹 🖤 🚲

Newtown   7

National Grid Ref: SU4763

🍴 🍺 Swan Inn, Carpenters Arms

White Cottage, *Newtown, Newbury, Berks, RG20 9AP.*
Delightful semi-rural cottage on the edge of Watership Down
Tel: **01635 43097**
D: £20.00-£25.00 **S:** £25.00-£30.00.
Open: All Year (not Xmas)
Beds: 1D 1T 1S
Baths: 1 Sh
🛇 (3) 🅿 ✡ ☐ 🐾 ♨ 🎹 🖤 🚲

Bringing children with you? Always ask for any special rates.

All rates are subject to alteration at the owners' discretion.

Woolhampton 8

National Grid Ref: SU5766

⛺ 🍺 Rowbarge Inn, Angel Inn

Bridge Cottage, Station Road, Woolhampton, Reading, Berks, RG7 5SF.
Tel: **01189 713138** Mrs Thornely.
Fax no: 01189 714331
D: £26.00-£26.00 **S:** £24.00.
Open: All Year (not Xmas)
Beds: 1D 1T 3S
Baths: 2 En 1 Sh
⛺🅿🚪🔥🐾📺☑✦🚲
Beautiful 300- year- old riverside home with secluded cottage garden, canoes and fishing available here. Conservatory for guest's use with views of canal traffic passing by. Breakfast can be served on terrace w/p. M3, M4, 20 minutes. Heathrow, 45 mins

---

Burghfield Common 9

National Grid Ref: SU6566

⛺ 🍺 Royal Oak

Firlands, Burghfield Common, Reading, Berks, RG7 3JN.
Comfortable Victorian farmhouse in woods on working sheep farm
Tel: **0118 983 2414** Mrs Stuckey.
D: £19.00 **S:** £19.00.
Open: All Year (not Xmas)
Beds: 2D
Baths: 1 Sh
⛺🅿🚪🔥📺☑✦

Bracknell 10

National Grid Ref: SU8668

⛺ 🍺 Downshire Arms

53 Swaledale, Wildridings, Bracknell, Berks, RG12 7ET.
Station near town centre. M3, M4, M5
Tel: **01344 421247** Mrs Webber.
D: £20.00-£20.00 **S:** £20.00-£20.00.
Open: All Year (not Xmas)
Beds: 1T 1S **Baths:** 1 Sh
🅿 (2) 🚪🔥📺

All paths are popular: you are well-advised to book ahead

Egham 11

National Grid Ref: TQ0071

⛺ 🍺 Happy Man, The Beehive

The Old Parsonage, 2 Parsonage Road, Englefield Green, Egham, Surrey, TW20 0JW.
Actual grid ref: SU995709
Georgian parsonage, traditionally furnished, old fashioned gardens. 30 minutes from London
Tel: **01784 436706** (also fax no)
Mr & Mrs Clark.
D: £25.00-£40.00 **S:** £35.00-£55.00.
Open: All Year (not Xmas)
Beds: 1F 2D 2T 1S
Baths: 3 En 1 Sh
⛺🅿 (6) 🚪🔥🐾🍴♨📺☑✦

Beau Villa, 44 Grange Road, Egham, Surrey, TW20 9QP.
Local Heathrow, Gatwick, M25, M4, Thorpe Park, Legoland, London
Tel: **01784 435115** Mrs Wilding.
D: £20.00 **S:** £25.00.
Open: All Year (not Xmas)
Beds: 1D 1T 1S
Baths: 1 En 1 Sh
⛺ (14) 🅿 (4) 🚪🐾♨📺☑

All details shown are as supplied by B&B owners in Autumn 1999.

Datchet 12

National Grid Ref: SU9877

The Chimneys, 55 London Road, Datchet, Windsor, Slough, Berks, SL3 9JY.
Private residence in beautiful surroundings, close to M4, M25 Heathrow and Windsor
Tel: **01753 580401**
Mrs Greenham.
Fax no: 01753 540233
D: £20.00
S: £28.50.
Open: All Year
Beds: 1F 2D 1T
Baths: 2 Pr
⛺🅿🚪🔥♨📺☑✦

Windsor 13

National Grid Ref: SU9676

⛺ 🍺 The Mitre, Bexley Arms, The Trooper, Nags Head, The Queen, Windsor Lad, George Inn, Vansitart Arms

▲ *Windsor Youth Hostel, Edgeworth House, Mill Lane, Windsor, Berkshire, SL4 5JE.*
Actual grid ref: SU955770
Tel: **01753 861710**
Under 18: £6.85
Adults: £10.15
evening meal at 7.00pm, family bunk rooms, games room, showers, shop
Queen Anne residence in the old Clewer village quarter of historic Windsor

---

Finchampstead Ridges to Windsor

Cycling northeast you go around the southern perimeter of Bracknell, via Caesar's Camp, an Iron Age hill fort in Bracknell Forest, and then through woodland and parkland and across the Virginia Water beechlands into **Windsor Great Park**, a large tract of formal parkland replete with grazing deer. The route takes you through the Savill Gardens, and a short detour will bring you to the viewpoint at Snow Hill, by the 'Copper Horse' statue of George III. North of the Great Park you arrive at Old Windsor, from where a short detour east into Surrey will take you to **Runnymede**, the riverside meadow where in 1215 King John relinquished the absolute power of the monarchy with his signature on the Magna Carta. Here also stands the memorial to John F Kennedy. Sticking to the route, you hit the Thames at Datchet, and cycle along the north bank to **Eton**, where you can visit the red-brick Tudor buildings of *that* school, and then cross the river into **Windsor**. This town is dominated by the renowned castle, now restored after the great fire of 1992, whose most notable features are St George's Chapel, one of the most impressive examples of the Perpendicular style in England, and the State Apartments, which house, among other treasures, a large collection of pictures, including a tryptych of Charles I by Van Dyck and works by Canaletto, Holbein, Rubens, Rembrandt, Reynolds and Hogarth, as well as drawings by Leonardo and Michaelangelo.

1 Stovell Road, *Windsor, Berks,*
SL4 5JB.
Actual grid ref: SU958771
Grades: ETC 2 Diamond
Tel: 01753 852055 (also fax no)
Ms Sumner.
D: £22.50-£22.50 **S:** £40.00-£40.00.
Open: All Year
Beds: 1D 1T
Baths: 2 En
🅿 (2) ⊬ 🖵 🕇 🎄 🛋 🕹 Ⓥ 🔋
Quiet comfortable self-contained
ground floor flat comprising 2
ensuite bedrooms which share a
large lounge. 100 yds river and
leisure centre, 7 mins' walk to
castle, town centre and railway
stations, 4 mins to buses

77 Whitehorse Road, *Windsor,*
Berks, SL4 4PG.
Modern, comfortable private house.
Tel: 01753 866803 Mrs Andrews.
D: £18.00-£20.00 **S:** £23.00-£25.00.
Open: All Year (not Xmas)
Beds: 1D 2T
Baths: 2 Sh
🔥 (5) 🅿 (3) ⊬ 🖵 🛋 🚲

Chasela, *30 Convent Road,*
Windsor, Berks, SL4 3RB.
Modern semi-detached near M4,
M40, M25. Castle 1 mile and
Legoland
Grades: ETC 3 Diamond
Tel: 01753 860410 Mrs Williams.
D: £22.00-£24.00 **S:** £22.00-£24.00.
Open: All Year
Beds: 1T 1S **Baths:** 1 Sh
🔥 (12) 🅿 (5) ⊬ 🖵 🛋 Ⓥ

Elansey, *65 Clifton Rise, Windsor,*
Berks, SL4 5SX.
Modern, quiet, comfortable house.
Garden, patio, excellent breakfasts,
highly recommended
Tel: 01753 864438 Mrs Forbutt.
D: £20.00-£20.00 **S:** £20.00-£23.00.
Open: All Year (not Xmas)
Beds: 1D 1T 1S
Baths: 1 En 1 Sh
🅿 (3) 🖵 🛋 Ⓥ

62 Queens Road, *Windsor, Berks,*
SL4 3BH.
Actual grid ref: SU964761
Excellent reputation, quiet, conve-
nient, ground floor rooms. Largest
family room available
Tel: 01753 866036 (also fax no)
Mrs Hughes.
D: £20.00-£25.00 **S:** £30.00-£35.00.
Open: All Year
Beds: 1F 1T 1S **Baths:** 2 Pr
🔥 🅿 (1) ⊬ 🖵 🛋 🕹 🚲

Langton House, *46 Alma Road,*
Windsor, Berks, SL4 3HA.
Victorian house, quiet tree-lined
road, 5 minutes walk to town and
castle
Tel: 01753 858299 Mrs Fogg.
D: £30.00-£32.50 **S:** £27.50.
Open: All Year (not Xmas)
Beds: 2D 1T **Baths:** 2 En 1 Pr
🅿 (2) ⊬ 🖵 🛋 Ⓥ 🚲

Marlow   14

National Grid Ref: SU8586

🍴 Hare & Hounds, Three Horseshoes,
Osbourne Arms, Clayton Arms, Royal Oak

Merrie Hollow, *Seymour Court*
Hill, Marlow, Bucks, SL7 3DE.
Actual grid ref: SU840889
Grades: ETC 3 Diamond
Tel: 01628 485663 Mr Wells.
D: £20.00-£25.00 **S:** £25.00-£30.00.
Open: All Year
Beds: 1D 1T **Baths:** 1 Sh
🔥 🅿 (4) ⊬ 🖵 🕇 🛋 Ⓥ 🚲
Secluded quiet country cottage in
large garden 150 yds off B482
Marlow to Stokenchurch road, easy
access to M4 & M25, 35 mins from
Heathrow & Oxford, private
off-road car parking

Acha Pani, *Bovingdon Green,*
Marlow, Bucks, SL7 2JL.
Actual grid ref: SU836869
Quiet location, easy access Thames
Foothpath, Chilterns, Windsor,
London, Heathrow
Grades: ETC 2 Diamond
Tel: 01628 483435 (also fax no)
Mrs Cowling.
D: £17.00-£18.00 **S:** £17.00-£18.00.
Open: All Year
Beds: 1D 1T 1S
Baths: 1 En 1 Sh
🔥 (10) 🅿 (3) 🖵 🕇 🗶 🛋 Ⓥ 🔋 🚲

Sneppen House, *Henley Road,*
Marlow, Bucks, SL7 2DF.
Within walking distance of town
centre and river. Good breakfast
Grades: ETC 4 Diamond
Tel: 01628 485227 Mr Norris.
D: £22.50-£22.50 **S:** £25.00-£25.00.
Open: All Year
Beds: 1D 1T **Baths:** 1 Sh
🔥 (2) 🅿 (3) 🖵 🛋 Ⓥ 🚲

The Venture, Munday Dean Lane,
Marlow, Bucks, SL7 3BU.
Old World cottage located in
peaceful AONB. Full English
breakfast
Tel: 01628 472195 Mrs Whittle.
D: £17.50 **S:** £25.00.
Open: All Year
Beds: 2D **Baths:** 1 Sh
🔥 (10) 🅿 (4) 🛋 Ⓥ

Cookham Dean   15

National Grid Ref: SU8684

🍴 Checkers

Cartlands Cottage, *King's Lane,*
Cookham Dean, Maidenhead,
Berks, SL6 9AY.
Self-contained guest room in
garden. Rural, very quiet
Grades: ETC 1 Diamond
Tel: 01628 482196
Mr & Mrs Parkes.
D: £22.00-£25.00 **S:** £23.50-£26.00.
Open: All Year
Beds: 1F **Baths:** 1 Pr
🔥 🅿 (2) 🖵 🛋 Ⓥ

Windsor to Reading

At **Maidenhead**, the 128-
foot brick arches - the largest
in the world - of the railway
bridge show that Brunel
could do both kinds of
bridge, Bristol's suspension
bridge at Clifton being his
famous example of the other
kind. **Cookham** was home to
the Artist Stanley Spencer,
whose painting of Cookham
Bridge is in London's Tate
Gallery. The village has a
gallery of his work, as well as
a slightly odd fifteenth-
century church tower with
both a clock and a sundial.
The viewpoint at Winter Hill
yields a panorama onto the
Chilterns in Buckinghamshire.
The final stretch of the route
takes you through some
lovely Thames Valley
countryside, and then by way
of **Wargrave** and **Twyford**
back into Reading.

Maidenhead   16

National Grid Ref: SU8781

🍴 Boulter's Lock Inn, Thames Hotel,
Kingswood Hotel, Windsor Castle, Pond House,
Hare & Hounds

Copperfields Guest House,
54 Bath Road, Maidenhead, Berks,
SL6 4JY.
Comfortable accommodation, near
Windsor, Henley, Reading and M4
to London
Tel: 01628 674941
Mrs Lindsay.
D: £22.50-£25.00
S: £30.00-£33.00.
Open: All Year
Beds: 2T 2S
Baths: 3 Pr
🔥 🅿 (5) 🖵 🛋 🛋 Ⓥ

Sheephouse Manor, *Sheephouse*
Road, Maidenhead, Berks, SL6 8HJ.
Actual grid ref: SU8878
Charming C16th farmhouse, with
health suite and country views
Grades: ETC 3 Diamond
Tel: 01628 776902
Mrs Street.
Fax no: 01628 625138
D: £25.00-£28.00
S: £35.00-£43.00.
Open: All Year (not Xmas)
Beds: 1D 1T 3S
Baths: 5 En
🔥 (3) 🅿 (7) 🖵 🕇 🛋 🛋 Ⓥ 🚲

Laburnham Guest House,
31 Laburnham Road, Maidenhead,
Berks, SL6 4DB.
Actual grid ref: SU881808
Fine Edwardian house, near town
centre, station and M4 motorway
Tel: **01628 676748** (also fax no)
Mrs Stevens.
D: £20.00-£25.00 **S:** £30.00-£40.00.
Open: All Year (not Xmas)
Beds: 1F 2D 1T 1S
Baths: 5 En
⛺ 🅿 (5) ⊁ ☐ 🕯 🍵 🖩 Ⅴ ⮌

Wargrave-on-Thames 17

National Grid Ref: SU7978

🏨 🍺 The Bull

Windy Brow, *204 Victoria Road,*
Wargrave-on-Thames, Reading,
Berks, RG10 8AJ.
Actual grid ref: SU794788
Victorian house overlooking fields.
10 mins M40/M4. Good pubs
nearby
Tel: **0118 940 3336** Mrs Carver.
Fax no: 0118 940 1260
D: £25.00 **S:** £27.50.
Open: All Year
Beds: 2D/T 2S
Baths: 1 Pr 2 Sh
⛺ 🅿 (6) ⊁ ☐ 🕯 🍵 🖩 ⛨ Ⅴ ⮌

Twyford 18

National Grid Ref: SU7975

🏨 🍺 Queen Victoria, La Fontana, Waggon &
Horse, The Bull

Somewhere To Stay, *c/o Loddon*
Acres, Bath Road, Twyford,
Reading, Berks, RG10 9RU.
Grades: ETC 4 Diamond
Tel: **0118 934 5880** (also fax no)
D: £24.50-£27.00
S: £27.50-£27.50.
Beds: 1F 1D 1T 1S
Baths: 3 En 1 Pr
⛺ 🅿 (6) ⊁ ☐ 🕯 🍵 🖩 Ⅴ ⮌
Self-contained, modern, detached
accommodation with kitchenette
and sauna. Situated next to owners
house in beautiful river fronted 2
acre garden, tennis/canoes
available. Rooms ensuite, tastefully
decorated with colour TV, tea/
coffee, easy access to Reading,
Windsor, Maidenhead and
Heathrow

D = Price range per person
sharing in a double room

Pay B&Bs by cash or
cheque and be prepared
to pay up front.

Chesham House, *79 Wargrave*
Road, Twyford, Reading, Berks,
RG10 9PE.
Windsor 20 minutes by car or rail,
to London 30 minutes
Grades: ETC 3 Diamond
Tel: **0118 932 0428**
Mr & Mrs Ferguson.
D: £30.00-£50.00 **S:** £27.50.
Open: Mar to Dec
Beds: 1D 1T **Baths:** 2 En
⛺ (7) 🅿 (3) ☐ 🕯 🖩 Ⅴ

The Hermitage, *63 London Road,*
Twyford, Reading, Berks, RG10 9EJ.
Elegant period house, village cen-
tre, close mainline railway, London
40 mins
Tel: **0118 934 0004** (also fax no)
Mrs Barker.
D: £26.00-£30.00 **S:** £35.00-£48.00.
Open: All Year (not Xmas)
Beds: 2D 3T **Baths:** 3 En 1 Sh
🅿 (6) ⊁ ☐ 🕯 🖩 Ⅴ

Cheshire Cycleway

The 135-mile **Cheshire Cycleway** takes you through the whole range of the county's scenery, from plain and parkland to the edge of the Pennine moors, and also gives a taste of Cheshire's urban landscape: the circular route has the historic towns of Chester and Macclesfield at either pole, and is sprinkled with castles and country houses.

A detailed **guide leaflet** to the cycleway route, which includes a list of cycle repair/hire shops on or near to the route, is available from Cheshire County Council, Tourism and Marketing Unit, 4 Hillyards Court, Chester Business Park, Wrexham Road, Chester CH4 9RD, tel 01244 603107, @ 60p (+20p p&p). The route is signposted by blue Cheshire Cycleway direction signs with a cycle silhouette, only in a clockwise direction as described above.

Maps: Ordnance Survey 1:50,000 Landranger series: 117, 118.

Major **railway** termini along the route are Chester, Crewe, Macclesfield and Wilmslow, north east of Knutsford. Many other places

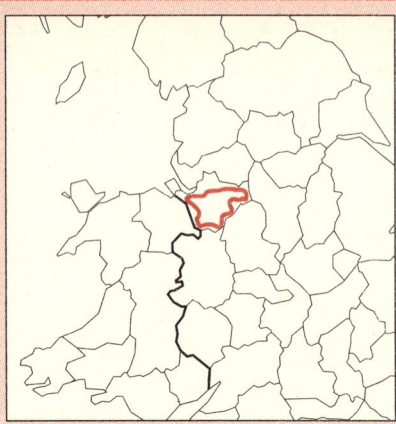

are served by local trains.

If you would like advice or help with planning the cycleway, **Byways Bike Breaks** specialise in cycling holidays in Cheshire. They can be contacted at 25 Mayville Road, Liverpool L18 0HG, tel 0151-722 8050.

Chester

The route begins in **Chester**, the county town with a fortress history. The largest fortified town of Roman Britain, in medieval times it was the centre of the Plantaganets' military campaigns against Wales, and boasts the most complete medieval and Roman city wall in Britain - two miles long with seven gates. Landmarks along the wall include the fifteenth-century King Charles Tower, from which Charles I watched the defeat of the royalist side in the battle of Rowton Moor, and the Water Tower, which contains a display on the city's history. Other features of the city are the cathedral, containing architectural vestiges from the eleventh to the sixteenth centuries, including the intersecting stone arches of the 'crown of stone' and a cloistered garden; and the half-excavated Roman Amphitheatre, the largest in Britain, its estimated capacity of 7000 even greater than that in Caerleon.

Chester   1

National Grid Ref: SJ4066

Bromfield Arms, Faulkner Arms, Spinning Wheel, Chester Bells, The Plough, Red Lion, King's Head, Eversley Hotel, Royal Oak, Swan Inn, Wetherspoons, Cavendish Hotel, Glynne Arms

▲ *Chester Youth Hostel, Hough Green House, 40 Hough Green, Chester, CH4 8HD.*
Actual grid ref: SJ397651
Tel: **01244 680056**
Under 18: £6.85 **Adults:** £10.15 evening meal at 6.00-7.30pm, self-catering facilities, television, games room, showers, shop, security lockers, laundry facilities *Attractive house and mews 1 mile from the city centre, redecorated in keeping with Victorian origins. Comfortable accommodation, a good base for the city, good access to North Wales*

Grosvenor Place Guest House, 2-4 Grosvenor Place, Chester, CH1 2DE.
City centre guest house; proprietor: Alma Wood
Tel: **01244 324455**
Mrs Wood.
Fax no: 01244 400225
D: £17.00-£21.00 **S:** £20.00-£25.00.
Open: All Year (not Xmas)
Beds: 2F 3D 2T 3S
Baths: 4 En 2 Sh

Laurels, 14 Selkirk Road, Curzon Park, Chester, CH4 8AH.
Lovely family home near racecourse; best residential area, very quiet
Tel: **01244 679682** Mrs Roberts.
D: £18.50-£19.50 **S:** £18.50-£19.50.
Open: All Year (not Xmas)
Beds: 1F 2D 1T 1S
Baths: 1 En 1 Pr

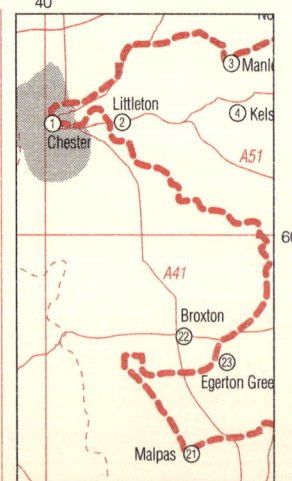

The Georgian House, *131 Boughton, Chester, CH3 5BH.*
Large Georgian town house; most rooms with view over river
Tel: **01244 312186**
Mr Chuter.
D: £18.00-£20.00 **S:** £20.00-£30.00.
Open: All Year (not Xmas)
Beds: 1F 4D 1T 1S
Baths: 4 En 3 Pr
⛅ (7) 🅿 (7) 🗖 🍴 🍖 🎵 Ⅴ

Stone Villa, *3 Stone Place, Hoole, Chester, CH2 3NR.*
A haven of quiet relaxation with individual attention and warm hospitality
Tel: **01244 345014**
Mr Pow.
D: £25.00-£26.00 **S:** £25.00-£32.00.
Open: All Year (not Xmas)
Beds: 1F 6D 2T 1S
Baths: 9 En 1 Pr
⛅ (10) 🗖 🍖 🎵 👶 ⚡ 🚲

Castle House, *23 Castle Street, Chester, CH1 2DS.*
Pre-1580 Tudor house, plus Georgian front (1738)
Tel: **01244 350354**
Mr Marl.
D: £23.00-£23.00
S: £36.00-£36.00.
Open: All Year
Beds: 1F 1D 1T 2S
Baths: 3 En 1 Sh
⛅ 🅿 🗖 🍖 🍴 🎵 Ⅴ ⚡

Devonia, *33-35 Hoole Road, Chester, CH2 3NH.*
Large Victorian family-run guest house. Same owner for 35 years
Tel: **01244 322236**
Fax no: 01244 401511
D: £17.50-£20.00 **S:** £25.00-£30.00.
Open: All Year
Beds: 4F 2D 2T 2S
Baths: 1 En 3 Sh
⛅ 🅿 (20) ✂ 🗖 🍖 🍴 🎵 Ⅴ ⚡

Cavendish Hotel, *42-44 Hough Green, Chester, CH4 8JQ.*
Charming Georgian residence, less than a mile from city centre
Grades: AA 2 Star, RAC 2 Star
Tel: **01244 675100**
Fax no: 01244 678844
D: £27.50-£38.00 **S:** £45.00-£50.00.
Open: All Year
Beds: 1F 13D 3T 2S **Baths:** 19 En
⛅ 🅿 (20) 🗖 🍴 🍖 🎵 Ⅴ 👶 ⚡

Homeleigh, *14 Hough Green, Chester, CH4 8JG.*
Family-run Victorian house, 10 minutes walk from city centre
Tel: **01244 676761**
Mr & Mrs Smith.
Fax no: 01244 679977
D: £18.00-£20.00
S: £20.00-£22.00.
Open: All Year (not Xmas)
Beds: 1F 4D 2T 2S
Baths: 9 En
⛅ 🅿 (10) 🗖 🍖 🍴 🎵 Ⅴ 🚲

Eversley Hotel, *9 Eversley Park, Chester, CH2 2AJ.*
Victorian residential hotel, bar, restaurant
Tel: **01244 373744** Mr Povey.
D: £21.50 **S:** £23.00.
Open: All Year
Beds: 4F 3D 2T 2S
Baths: 9 Pr 2 Sh
⛅ 🅿 (17) 🗖 🍴 🍖 🎵 Ⅴ

Hamilton Court Hotel, *3/7 Hamilton Street, Hoole, Chester, CH2 3JG.*
Family-run hotel, catering for families and business people. 10 minutes' walk from city centre
Tel: **01244 345387**
Mr & Mrs Finan.
Fax no: 01244 317404
D: £26.00 **S:** £35.00.
Open: All Year
Beds: 2F 2D 7T 1S
Baths: 10 En 2 Sh
⛅ 🅿 (8) ✂ 🗖 🍖 🍴 🍖 🎵 Ⅴ

Brookside Hotel, *Brook Lane, Chester, CH2 2AN.*
Privately owned hotel offering comfort and attentive service with friendliness and informality
Tel: **01244 381943** (also fax no)
D: £26.00 **S:** £38.00.
Open: All Year (not Xmas)
Beds: 7F 5D 4T 8S
Baths: 24 En
⛅ 🅿 (16) 🗖 🍖 🍴 🍖 🎵 Ⅴ 👶

Littleton 2

National Grid Ref: SJ4466

¶¶ ⊄ The Plough

Firbank, 64 *Tarvin Road, Littleton, Chester, CH3 7DF.*
Traditional Victorian house, warm welcome, extensive gardens, two miles Chester
Tel: **01244 335644** Mrs Shambler.
Fax no: 01244 332068
D: £20.00-£27.50 **S:** £25.00-£30.00.
Open: All Year (not Xmas)
Beds: 1D 1T
Baths: 2 En
🅿 (2) ☐ ⹁ Ⅲ, Ⅴ

Manley 3

National Grid Ref: SJ5071

¶¶ ⊄ The Goshawk

Rangeway Bank Farm, Manley, Warrington, Cheshire, WA6 9EF.
Actual grid ref: SJ517717
Traditional farmhouse in quiet countryside adjacent to Delamere Forest
Tel: **01928 740236** Challoner.
Fax no: 01928 740703
D: £20.00-£25.00 **S:** £22.00-£25.00.
Open: All Year (not Xmas)
Beds: 1F 1D 1T
Baths: 2 En 1 Sh
🛏 🅿 (6) ⹁ ☐ ⟉ ⹁ Ⅲ, Ⅴ 🛆 ⚡ ⚲

Kelsall 4

National Grid Ref: SJ5268

¶¶ ⊄ Morris Dancer, The Boot

Northwood Hall, Dog Lane, Kelsall, Tarporley, Cheshire, CW6 0RP.
Elegant Victorian farmhouse with cobblestone courtyard. All rooms traditionally appointed
Tel: **01829 752569**
Mr & Mrs Nock.
Fax no: 01829 751157
D: £21.50-£23.50 **S:** £27.50.
Open: All Year (not Xmas)
Beds: 2D
Baths: 2 En
🛏 🅿 (6) ⹁ ☐ ⹁ Ⅲ, Ⅴ 🛆 ⚡ ⚲

Norley 5

National Grid Ref: SJ5672

¶¶ ⊄ Carriers Inn

Wicken Tree Farm, Blakemere Lane, Norley, Warrington, Cheshire, WA6 6NW.
High quality self-contained accommodation and B&B, surrounded by Delamere Forest
Tel: **01928 788355** Mr Appleton.
D: £22.50-£25.00 **S:** £22.50-£31.00.
Open: All Year
Beds: 1F 5D 7T 3S
Baths: 6 En 1 Pr 2 Sh
🛏 🅿 (14) ⹁ ☐ ⟉ ⹁ Ⅲ, ♿ Ⅴ ⚡ ⚲

Cuddington 6

National Grid Ref: SJ6071

¶¶ ⊄ Forest View Inn

Poplar Farm, Cuddington, Northwich, Cheshire, CW8 2S2.
Beautiful oak beamed farmhouse, quiet location on edge of village
Tel: **01606 883985**
Mrs Clarkson.
Fax no: 01606 882212
D: £20.00-£25.00
S: £20.00-£25.00.
Open: All Year (not Xmas)
Beds: 1D 1T
Baths: 1 Pr
🛏 (2) 🅿 (4) ⹁ ☐ ⹁ Ⅲ, Ⅴ ⚲

Acton Bridge 7

National Grid Ref: SJ5975

¶¶ ⊄ The Maypole

Manor Farm, Cliff Road, Acton Bridge, Northwich, Cheshire, CW8 3QP.
Actual grid ref: SJ586766
Grades: ETC 4 Diamond
Tel: **01606 853181**
Mrs Campbell.
D: £20.00-£25.00
S: £20.00-£25.00.
Open: All Year (not Xmas)
Beds: 1F 1T 1S
Baths: 1 En 2 Pr
🛏 (1) 🅿 (10) ⹁ ☐ ⟉ ⹁ Ⅲ, Ⅴ 🛆 ⚡ ⚲
Peaceful, rural, elegantly furnished traditional Georgian-style country house. Secluded location with open views from all rooms, a large garden provides access through woodland into the picturesque valley, in the heart of Cheshire, an ideal location for business or pleasure

Aston-by-Budworth 8

National Grid Ref: SJ6976

¶¶ ⊄ The Red Lion

Clock Cottage, Hield Lane, Aston-by-Budworth, Northwich, Cheshire, CW9 6LP.
Lovely C17th thatched country cottage, beautiful country garden, wooded countryside
Tel: **01606 891271**
Mrs Tanner-Betts.
D: £17.50-£20.00 **S:** £17.50-£20.00.
Open: All Year (not Xmas)
Beds: 1T 2S
Baths: 1 Sh
🛏 (2) 🅿 (4) ⹁ ☐ ⹁ Ⅲ, Ⅴ ⚡ ⚲

Over Tabley 9

National Grid Ref: SJ7280

¶¶ ⊄ The Smoker

The Old Vicarage, Moss Lane, Over Tabley, Knutsford, Cheshire, WA16 0PL.
Set in 2 acres of wooded gardens but close to M6, airport
Grades: AA 4 Diamond
Tel: **01565 652221** Mrs Weston.
Fax no: 01565 755918
D: £29.00-£45.00 **S:** £45.00-£47.00.
Open: All Year (not Xmas)
Beds: 1F 2D 2T
Baths: 5 En
🅿 (20) ⹁ ☐ ✗ ⹁ Ⅲ, Ⅴ 🛆 ⚡ ⚲

Pay B&Bs by cash or cheque and be prepared to pay up front.

Chester to Knutsford

Attractions along the first stretch of the route after Chester include the Mouldsworth Motor Museum, a collection of vintage vehicles which, despite its name, also contains some early bicycles; and Delamere Forest Park, 4000 acres of woodland, with waymarked walks and cycling trails for if you fancy a diversion from the serious business of the cycleway itself. From here you strike out across the Cheshire Plain, and can admire the half-timbered cottages of the village of Great Budworth before reaching the town of **Knutsford**. *Canute's Ford*, where the Danish king crossed the Lily Stream in the early eleventh century, was important in medieval times for its market and coaching inns, but the modern town dates largely from the eighteenth century, and was the model for Elizabeth Gaskell's *Cranford* in the nineteenth. In more recent times, nearby Knutsford Heath was the scene of a memorable confrontation during the 1997 election campaign, between Martin Bell, who became Independent Member of Parliament, and Christine Hamilton, as she leapt heroically but vainly to the defence of her errant husband, Neil, the discredited sitting MP.

Knutsford to Audlem

After Knutsford it's a gradual climb to Alderley Edge, a sandstone ridge inhabited by a legendary wizard, around **Macclesfield**, historically important for its silk production, and towards the edge of the **Peak District National Park**. Attractions along the way include two National Trust properties, a fifteenth-century water mill at Nether Alderley, and Hare Hill Gardens, a Victorian woodland garden and walled garden; and Prestbury, a village notable for its nineteenth-century weaver's cottages. A little way off the route is Tegg's Nose Country Park, where the gritstone hill provides a magnificent panorama in every direction, and then comes the most remote part of the cycleway, as you head towards the village of Wildboarclough inside the White Peak. After this the route takes you back down off the Peak; across the Macclesfield Canal you come to Galsworth Hall, a Tudor house set in beautiful grounds. Past Congleton and Alsager you come to Barthomley, another beautiful Cheshire village with half-timbered cottages and a seventeenth-century pub, the White Lion. The route bypasses Nantwich, famous for its timber-framed Tudor buildings and the fourteenth-century Church of St Mary, after Crewe, famous for its railway junction, and takes you to Audlem, which boasts another fourteenth-century church and stands upon the Shropshire Union Canal, with a succession of locks.

Mobberley   10

National Grid Ref: SJ7879

Laburnum Cottage, *Knutsford Road, Mobberley, Knutsford, Cheshire,* WA16 7PU.
Country house close to Knutsford overlooking Tatton Park, award-winning food
Grades: ETC 4 Diamond
Tel: **01565 872464** (also fax no)
Mr & Mrs Messenger.
D: £22.50-£25.00 **S:** £35.00-£39.00.
Open: All Year
Beds: 1F 1T 1D 1S
Baths: 3 En 1 Sh
🛏 🅿 (10) ✍ 🗖 🌟 ✗ 🔥 🎹 ☑ 🌢 ⚲

Mottram St Andrew   11

National Grid Ref: SJ8778

🍴 🍺 Bull's Head, Legh Arms

Goose Green Farm, *Oak Road, Mottram St Andrew, Macclesfield, Cheshire,* SK10 4RA.
Actual grid ref: SJ876778
Quiet farmhouse with beautiful views. 3 miles off M56
Tel: **01625 828814**
Mrs Hatch.
D: £20.00 **S:** £20.00.
Open: All Year (not Xmas)
Beds: 1D 1T 2S
Baths: 1 En 1 Sh
🛏 (5) 🅿 (10) ✍ 🗖 🔥 🎹 ☑ 🛇 🌢

All rooms full and nowhere else to stay? Ask the owner if there's anywhere nearby

---

S = Price range for a single person in a room

Tytherington   12

National Grid Ref: SJ9175

🍴 🍺 Cock & Pheasant

Moorhayes House Hotel,
27 Manchester Road, Tytherington, Macclesfield, Cheshire, SK10 2JJ.
Warm welcome comfortable home, attractive garden, 0.5 mile from Macclesfield
Grades: ETC 3 Diamond,
AA 3 Diamond, RAC 3 Diamond
Tel: **01625 433228** (also fax no)
Helen Wood.
D: £24.00-£29.00
S: £28.00-£45.00.
Open: All Year (not Xmas)
Beds: 1F 4D 2T 1S
Baths: 7 En 1 Sh
🛏 🅿 (14) 🗖 🔥 🔥 🎹 ☑ 🛇 🌢 ⚲

Wincle   13

National Grid Ref: SJ9566

🍴 🍺 Ship Inn

Hill Top Farm, *Wincle, Macclesfield, Cheshire,* SK11 0QH.
Actual grid ref: SJ959662
Peaceful, comfortable farmhouse accommodation, set in beautiful countryside, lovely walks
Tel: **01260 227257**
Mrs Brocklehurst.
D: £18.00-£20.00
S: £20.00-£22.00.
Open: All Year (not Xmas)
Beds: 2T
Baths: 1 En 1 Pr
🛏 🅿 (4) ✍ 🗖 🌟 ✗ 🔥 🎹 ☑ 🛇 🌢 ⚲

Congleton   14

National Grid Ref: SJ8663

🍴 🍺 Lamb Inn, Bull's Head Hotel, Brown Cow Inn, Edgerton Arms, Brownlow Inn

The Lamb Inn, *3 Blake Street, Congleton, Cheshire,* CW12 4DS.
Central location convenient for Cheshire country houses and attractions
Tel: **01260 272731** Mr Kelly.
D: £16.00-£19.00 **S:** £17.00-£24.00.
Open: All Year
Beds: 1F 2D 2T 1S
Baths: 3 En 3 Sh
🛏 🅿 (40) 🗖 🔥 🔥 🎹 ☑ 🌢

8 Cloud View, *Congleton, Cheshire,* CW11 3TP.
Lovely family home, edge of countryside, good views
Tel: **01260 276048** Mrs Stewart.
D: £18.50-£18.50 **S:** £16.00-£20.00.
Open: All Year (not Xmas)
Beds: 1D 1S **Baths:** 1 En 1 Sh
🛏 🅿 (1) ✍ 🗖 ✗ 🔥 🎹 ☑

Loachbrook Farm, *Sandbach Road, Congleton, Cheshire,* CW12 4TE.
Actual grid ref: SJ833630
C17 working farm close to M6 and many attractions
Tel: **01260 273318** Mrs Dale.
D: £17.50-£19.00 **S:** £18.50-£20.00.
Open: All Year (not Xmas)
Beds: 1D 1T 1S **Baths:** 1 Sh
🛏 (5) 🅿 (4) ✍ 🗖 🔥 🎹 ☑ ⚲

All details shown are as supplied by B&B owners in Autumn 1999.

Audlem to Chester

Two more villages worth a look along the route are Wrenbury and Marbury, before you arrive at **Malpas**, an historic market town with half-timbered buildings, Georgian houses and coaching inns. The town is also the place to sample the range of salty Cheshire cheeses, on sale everywhere. Notable places along the home strait of the cycleway are Stretton Mill, a working water mill that has been restored, and two castles - Peckforton Castle, built in the mid-nineteenth century medievalist revival for Lord Tollemache, and by contrast the ruins of the very genuinely medieval Beeston Castle, dating from the thirteenth century and set romantically against glorious views over the Cheshire Plain. From here you ride parallel to the Shropshire Union Canal back into **Chester**.

Alsager   15

National Grid Ref: SJ7955

🍴 🍺 Wilbraham Arms

The Limes, *32 Sandbach Road South, Alsager, Stoke-on-Trent, Staffs, ST7 2LP.*
Village centre. Elegant detached Victorian private house, surrounded by trees
Tel: **01270 874659** Mrs Morgan.
D: £15.00 **S:** £15.00.
Open: All Year (not Xmas)
Beds: 1T 1S
🅿 (3) 🛏 🖳.

Haslington   16

National Grid Ref: SJ7355

Ferndale House, *Gutterscroft, Haslington, Crewe, Cheshire, CW1 5RJ.*
Tel: **01270 584048** Docherty.
D: £20.00-£23.50 **S:** £20.00-£20.00.
Open: All Year
🛏 🅿 (7) 🛏 🖵 🗙 🏃 🖳 �V 🛡
Large Victorian family home set in a quiet area close to C16th inn. Convenient M6, potteries, Chester, North Wales, Bridgemere. Secure parking, large rooms, kingsize beds, guests' lounge. Excellent food prepared by chef proprietor

Weston   17

National Grid Ref: SJ7352

🍴 🍺 White Lion Inn

Snape Farm, *Snape Lane, Weston, Crewe, Cheshire, CW2 5NB.*
Actual grid ref: SJ743518
Warm comfortable Victorian farmhouse in quiet location near Junction 16 M6
Grades: ETC 3 Diamond
Tel: **01270 820208** (also fax no)
Mrs Williamson.
D: £18.00-£20.00 **S:** £20.00-£28.00.
Open: All Year (not Xmas)
Beds: 3F 1D 2T
Baths: 1 En 1 Pr 1 Sh
🛏 🅿 (6) 🛏 🖵 🏃 🗙 🏃 🖳 V 🖰

Crewe   18

National Grid Ref: SJ7055

🍴 🍺 Hunters Lodge

Hunters Lodge Hotel, *Sydney Road, Sydney, Crewe, Cheshire, CW1 1LU.*
Family-run hotel surrounded by beautiful gardens and Cheshire country
Tel: **01270 583440**
Mr Panayi.
Fax no: 01270 500553
D: £23.50 **S:** £28.00.
Open: All Year
Beds: 2F 33D 4T 10S
Baths: 47 Pr
🛏 🅿 🖵 🗙 🏃 🖳 & V

Shavington   19

National Grid Ref: SJ6951

Oakland House, *252 Newcastle Road, Blakelow, Shavington, Nantwich, Cheshire, CW5 7ET.*
Awarded best B&B in the North West. Superior accommodation. Ideally situated historical Nantwich
Tel: **01270 567134**
Mr & Mrs Wetton.
Fax no: 01270 651752
D: £16.50 **S:** £30.00.
Open: All Year
Beds: 1F 2D 2T **Baths:** 5 Pr
🛏 (14) 🅿 (10) 🛏 🖵 🏃 🖳 & V 🖰

Wybunbury   20

National Grid Ref: SJ6949

Lea Farm, *Wrinehill Road, Wybunbury, Nantwich, Cheshire, CW5 7HS.*
Charming farmhouse set in landscaped gardens where peacocks roam
Grades: AA 3 Diamond
Tel: **01270 841429** (also fax no)
Mrs Callwood.
D: £16.00 **S:** £18.50.
Open: All Year (not Xmas)
Beds: 1F 1D 1T
Baths: 2 Pr 1 Sh
🛏 🅿 (22) 🖵 🏃 🗙 🏃 V 🛡 🖰

Malpas   21

National Grid Ref: SJ4847

Farm Ground Cottage, *Edge, Malpas, Cheshire, SY14 8LE.*
Tel: **01948 820333**
D: £19.50-£21.00 **S:** £20.00-£22.00.
Open: All Year (not Xmas)
Beds: 1D
Baths: 1 Pr
🅿 (2) 🛏 🖵 🏃 🗙 🏃 🖳 V 🛡 🖰 🖰
Relax & enjoy peace & quiet in delightful Victorian cottage in unspoilt rural surroundings, lovely gardens, delicious food. Conservatory for summer. Open fire in winter. Easy reach of Chester Shrewsbury, North Wales, hills and coast. Weekly rates available

Broxton   22

National Grid Ref: SJ4754

🍴 🍺 Frog Manor

Frogg Manor Hotel, *Fullers Moor, Nantwich Road, Broxton, Chester, CH3 9JH.*
Tel: **01829 782629**
D: £45.00-£72.50
S: £60.00-£100.00.
Open: All Year
Beds: 6D
Baths: 6 En
🛏 (4) 🅿 (40) 🛏 🖵 🏃 🗙 🏃 🖳 V 🛡 🖰 🖰
Not far from the madding crowd, a superb Georgian manor house, recently refurbished using traditional decor and period furniture to combine modern comfort with the grace of the Georgian era, an atmosphere that is pure romance, a la carte restaurant

Egerton Green   23

National Grid Ref: SJ5152

🍴 🍺 Cholmondeley Arms

Manor Farm, *Egerton Green, Cholmondeley, Malpas, Cheshire, SY14 8AW.*
A charming farmhouse set in beautiful gardens and peaceful countryside
Tel: **01829 720261**
D: £20.00 **S:** £25.00.
Open: All Year (not Xmas)
Beds: 1F 1T 1D
Baths: 2 En 1 Pr
🛏 (1) 🅿 (6) 🖵 🏃 🖳 V 🛡 🖰 🖰

S = Price range for a single person in a room

STILWELL'S BRITAIN BED & BREAKFAST 2000

The Bed & Breakfast is one of the great British institutions. Like warm beer and the changing of the guard at Buckingham Palace, it's known by people around the world. Of course, you don't have to be a tourist to enjoy this traditional accommodation. Whether you're travelling, on holiday, away on business or just escaping from it all, the B&B is a great value alternative to expensive hotels and a world away from camping and caravanning. And there's no better way of choosing a convenient and desirable B&B than by consulting **Stilwell's Britain: Bed & Breakfast 2000.**

Stilwell's Britain: Bed & Breakfast 2000, the most comprehensive guide of its kind, contains over 7,750 entries - private houses, country halls, farms, cottages, inns, small hotels and guest houses - listed by county and location, in England, Scotland and Wales. Each entry includes room rates, facilities, tourist grades and a brief description of the B&B and its location and surroundings. The average charge per person per night is £18. The listings also provide the names of local pubs and restaurants which serve food in the evening. As with all Stilwell publications, the book has local maps and listings of tourist information offices.

The indispensable guide to great value accommodation: **Stilwell's Britain: Bed and Breakfast 2000**

£9.95 from all good bookstores (ISBN 1-900861-14-3) or £11.95 (inc p&p) from Stilwell Publishing Ltd, 59 Charlotte Road, London EC2A 3QW (020 7739 7179)

Cumbria Cycleway

The **Cumbria Cycleway** is a mammoth 260-mile circular route around the perimeter of the County of Cumbria, from moorland and wooded river valleys inland to a long stretch along the coast, from Morecambe Bay to the Solway Firth. It completely avoids the Lakes (see the *Sustrans Sea to Sea (C2C)* route for a route through the Lake District), and as such takes you to parts of the county not frequented by visitors. The route is clearly waymarked in both directions by brown 'Cumbria' direction signs with a cycle silhouette, and there is no designated start/finish. The description that follows takes the route clockwise from Carlisle.

A detailed **guide leaflet** to the cycleway route, which includes a list of cycle repair/hire shops on or near to the route, is available free from West Cumbria Cycleway Network, Groundwork West Cumbria, Crowgarth House, 48 High Street, Cleator Moor, Cumbria CA25 5AA, tel 01946 813677 and a **guide book**, *The Cumbria Cycleway* by Roy Walker and Ron Jarvis (ISBN 1 852841 06 0) is published by Cicerone Press and available from the publishers at 2 Police Square, Milnthorpe, Cumbria LA7 7PY, tel 01539 562069, @ £6.99 (+75p p&p).

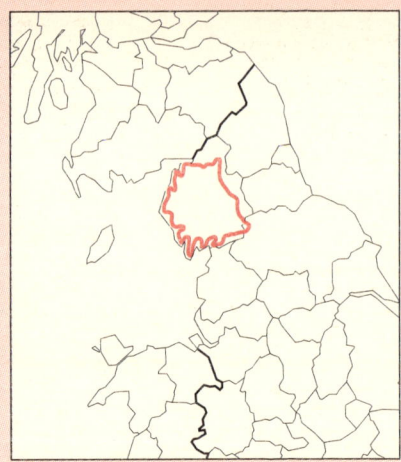

Maps: Ordnance Survey 1:50,000 Landranger series: 85, 86, 89, 90, 91, 96, 97, 98

The major **railway** termini are Carlisle, Oxenholme (near Kendal) and Penrith. There is also the famous scenic Leeds-Settle-Carlisle Railway, which stops at Garsdale, Kirkby Stephen and Appleby-in-Westmorland, and other local services.

Carlisle 1

National Grid Ref: NY3955

🍴 🍺 Metal Bridge Inn, The Beehive, Mary's Pantry, Crown & Thistle, Coach & Horses, Golden Fleece, Black Lion

▲ *Carlisle Youth Hostel, University of Northumbria, The Old Brewery Residences, Bridge Lane, Caldewgate, Carlisle, Cumbria, CA2 5SR.*
Actual grid ref: NY394560
Tel: 01228 597352.
After 6pm: 01228 59486
Under 18: £12.00 **Adults:** £12.00 suitable for disabled people, self-catering facilities, showers, laundry facilities
Accommodation in an award-winning conversion of the former Theakston's brewery. Single study bedrooms with shared kitchen and bathroom in flats for upto 7 people

---

Pay B&Bs by cash or cheque and be prepared to pay up front.

All cycleways are popular: you are well-advised to book ahead

---

Howard Lodge, 90 Warwick Road, Carlisle, Cumbria, CA1 1JU.
Actual grid ref: NY407558
Grades: ETC 4 Diamond, AA 3 Diamond
Tel: 01228 529842
Mr Hendrie.
D: £15.00-£25.00
S: £20.00-£30.00.
Open: All Year
Beds: 2F 1D 2T 1S
Baths: 6 En 1 Sh
🛇 🅿 (6) 🛏 🍽 ✕ 🏊 🎱 Ⓥ 🛡 🐾
Friendly family-run guest house in comfortable Victorian town house in conservation area. Spacious rooms all fully ensuite with satellite TV, welcome tray, hairdryer and clock radio. Large breakfasts. 5 minutes' walk from station and city centre. Evening meals by prior arrangement. Private car park

Craighead, 6 Hartington Place, Carlisle, Cumbria, CA1 1HL.
Actual grid ref: NY405559
Grades: ETC 3 Diamond
Tel: 01228 596767 Mrs Smith.
D: £16.50 **S:** £16.50.
Open: All Year (not Xmas)
Beds: 1F 2D 1T 1S
Baths: 1 En 2 Sh
🛇 🛏 🍽 🏊 🎱 Ⓥ ⚡ 🐾
You will receive a warm welcome at Craighead a grade II Listed spacious Victorian town house with comfortable rooms and original features. CTV tea/coffee tray in all rooms. Minutes' walk to city centre bus and rail stations and all amenities. Friendly personal service

Chatsworth Guest House, 22 Chatsworth Square, Carlisle, Cumbria, CA1 1HF.
City centre Grade II Listed building, close to shops, cathedral, castle, all amenities
Grades: ETC 3 Diamond
Tel: 01228 524023 (also fax no)
Mrs Mackin.
D: £17.00-£22.00 **S:** £20.00-£26.00.
Open: All Year (not Xmas)
Beds: 1F 1D 3T 1S
Baths: 2 En 1 Sh
🛇 (2) 🛏 🏊 🎱 Ⓥ

Angus Hotel & Almonds Bistro,
14 Scotland Road, Stanwix,
Carlisle, Cumbria, CA3 9DG.
Actual grid ref: NY400571
Grades: AA 4 Diamond
Tel: 01228 523546 /
0800 026 2046 Mr Webster.
Fax no: 01228 531895
D: £20.00-£27.00
S: £26.00-£42.00.
Open: All Year
Beds: 4F 3D 4T 3S
Baths: 11 En 3 Sh
♿ P (6) ⚅ ⚃ ✕ 🖥 ⚆ Ⅲ Ⅴ ⚑ ⚙ ♻
Victorian town house, foundations
on Hadrian's Wall. Excellent food,
Les Routiers Awards, local
cheeses, home baked bread.
Genuine warm welcome from
owners. Licensed, draught beer,
lounge, meeting room, internet
cafe, direct dial telephones, secure
garaging

Avondale, *3 St Aidans Road,*
Carlisle, Cumbria, CA1 1LT.
Attractive comfortable Edwardian
house. Quiet central position
convenient M6 J43
Grades: ETC 4 Diamond
RAC 4 Diamond
Tel: 01228 523012 (also fax no)
Mr & Mrs Hayes.
D: £20.00-£20.00
S: £20.00-£40.00.
Open: All Year (not Xmas)
Beds: 1D 2T
Baths: 1 En 1 Pr
♿ P (3) ⚿ ⚃ ✕ 🖥 Ⅲ Ⅴ ⚑ ⚙ ♻

Carlisle

As a border city, **Carlisle**, the county town, was for
centuries the focus of tribal struggles: the original settlement of
Celtic Britons was subdued by the Roman Empire to build an
outpost for the construction of Hadrian's Wall, and later attempts
of Anglo-Saxons, Scots and Danes to prevail ended with the
Norman takeover. However, the Scots never quite gave up, and
captured the town for a brief period during the Jacobite
rebellion of 1745. The notable remains of these struggles are the
eleventh- to twelfth-century city walls and the Castle, built by the
Norman King William Rufus, with many later additions, where
Mary Queen of Scots was kept prisoner by Elizabeth I in 1568,
and Scottish prisoners of war were accommodated after the
crushing of the Jacobite rebellion. Carlisle Cathedral, built in red
sandstone, was begun by the same king, completed by Henry I
and desecrated by Cromwell's men five hundred years later.
Two Romanesque arches remain from the original building, set
against the Gothic East Window; there is also a treasury housing
important objects from the city's ecclesiastical heritage.

All rooms full and
nowhere else to stay?
Ask the owner if
there's anywhere
nearby

Corner House Hotel & Bar,
4 Grey Street, Carlisle, CA1 2JP.
Grades: ETC 3 Diamond
Tel: 01228 533239
Mrs Anderson.
Fax no: 01228 546628
D: £17.50-£21.00
S: £25.00-£30.00.
Open: All Year
Beds: 3F 4D 4T 3S
Baths: 10 En
♿ ⚅ ⚃ ✕ 🖥 ⚆ Ⅲ ♿ Ⅴ ⚑ ⚙ ♻
Small, friendly, licensed hotel. 10
mins to city centre attraction, bar,
large TV, lounge and games room.
Excellent base for golf, walking,
horse-riding, swimming, cycling or
touring by car, bus or train, the
lakes, Roman Wall or border
region

Courtfield Guest House,
169 Warwick Road, Carlisle,
Cumbria, CA1 1LP.
Short walk to historic city centre.
Close to M6, J43
Grades: ETC 4 Diamond
Tel: 01228 522767
Mrs Dawes.
D: £17.50-£20.00 **S:** £20.00.
Open: All Year (not Xmas)
Beds: 1F 2D 2T
Baths: 5 En
♿ P (4) ⚿ ⚃ 🖥 Ⅲ Ⅴ ♻

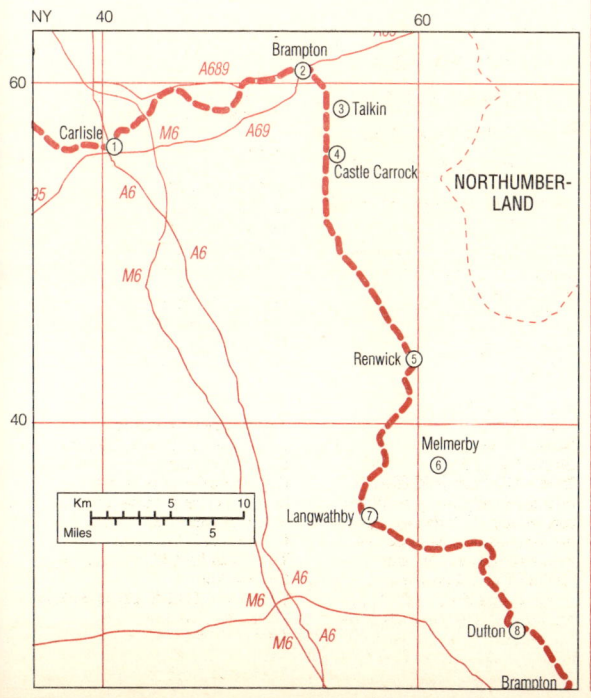

High season,
bank holidays and
special events mean
low availability
everywhere.

East View Guest House,
110 Warwick Road, Carlisle,
Cumbria, CA1 1JU.
Actual grid ref: NY407560
10 minutes' walking distance from
city centre, railway station and
restaurants
Grades: ETC 2 Diamond
Tel: **01228 522112** (also fax no)
Mrs Glease.
D: £18.00-£20.00 **S:** £20.00-£25.00.
Open: All Year (not Xmas)
Beds: 3F 2D 1T 1S
Baths: 7 En

D = Price range per person
sharing in a double room

Cherry Grove, *87 Petteril Street,*
Carlisle, Cumbria, CA1 2AW.
Lovely red brick building close to
golf club and town
Grades: AA 3 Diamond
Tel: **01228 541942**
Mr & Mrs Houghton.
D: £17.50-£20.00 **S:** £20.00-£30.00.
Open: All Year
Beds: 3F 2D **Baths:** 5 En

Cornerways Guest House, *107*
Warwick Road, Carlisle, Cumbria,
CA1 1EA.
Large Victorian town house
Grades: ETC 4 Diamond
Tel: **01228 521733** Mrs Fisher.
D: £14.00-£18.00 **S:** £16.00-£18.00.
Open: All Year (not Xmas)
Beds: 2F 1D 4T 3S
Baths: 2 En 2 Sh

Cambro House, *173 Warwick*
Road, Carlisle, CA1 1LP.
Grades: AA 3 Diamond
Tel: **01228 543094** (also fax no)
Mr & Mrs Mawson.
D: £17.00-£20.00 **S:** £20.00-£25.00.
Open: All Year
Beds: 2D 1T
Baths: 3 En
Guests can expect warm hospitality
and friendly service at this
attractively decorated and well-
maintained guest house. Each
ensuite bedroom includes TV,
clock, radio, hairdryer and
welcome tray. Private off-road
parking available, non-smoking,
close to golf course

Kingstown Hotel, *246 Kingstown*
Road, Carlisle, CA3 0DE.
Grades: AA 3 Diamond
Tel: **01228 515292** (also fax no)
D: £18.50-£22.00 **S:** £29.00-£36.00.
Open: All Year (not Xmas)
Beds: 1F 5D 1T
Baths: 7 En
Situated on the A7, only quarter
mile from M6 (J44), our small
family-run hotel offers weary
travellers comfortable
accommodation and a cosy lounge
bar in which to unwind. An ideal
base to explore historic Carlisle,
Hadrian's Wall and the Lake
District

Whitelea Guest House,
191 Warwick Road, Carlisle,
CA1 1LP.
Good base for lakes and Hadrian's
Wall. Friendly, family run
Tel: **01228 533139**
Croskery.
D: £15.00-£18.00 **S:** £15.00-£18.00.
Open: All Year
Beds: 2F 1T 1S

The Foxgloves, *73 Scotland Road,*
Carlisle, Cumbria, CA3 9HL.
Family-run elegant Victorian town
house, very suitable for Roman
Wall walkers
Tel: **01228 526365** Mrs Apcar.
D: £15.00 **S:** £15.00.
Open: All Year
Beds: 2T 1S

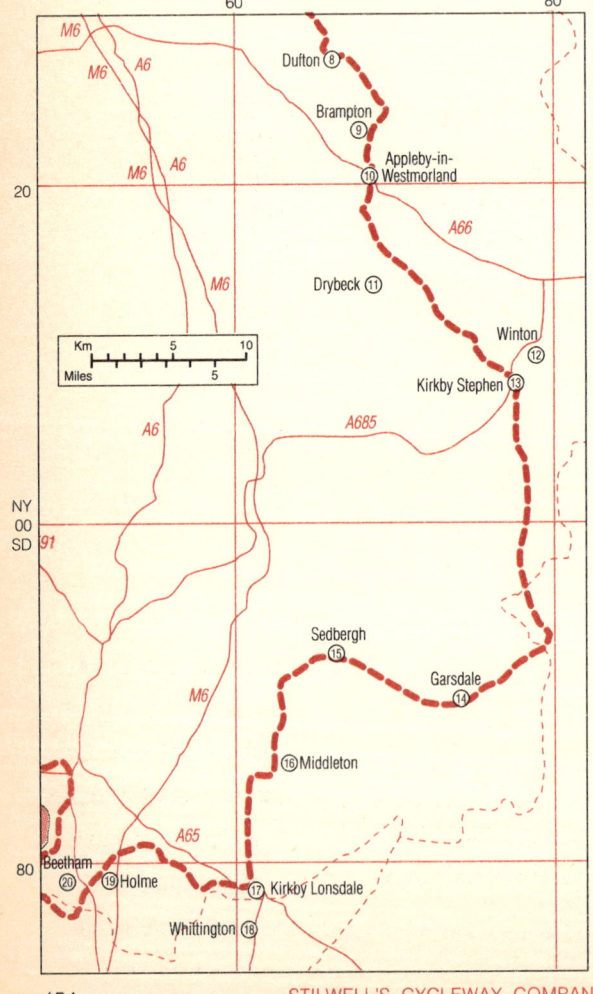

Order your
packed lunches the
evening before you
need them.
Not at breakfast!

Carlisle to the Eden Valley

Out of Carlisle you ride east, via Rickerby Park, to **Brampton**, within reach of a number of buildings of historic interest, including a section of Hadrian's Wall. Then it's south, passing Talkin Tarn Country Park, and down the foothills of the northern Pennines, through a string of villages whose names evidence this region's eclectic ancient history - Celtic (Castle Carrock, Cumrew), Anglo-Saxon (Newbiggin, Croglin), Scandinavian (Glassonby) - into the gentle Eden Valley. Here stand **Long Meg and Her Daughters**, a late neolithic stone circle - Long Meg herself stands 18 feet high and is named from her eerily humanoid profile. A little way off the route is the red sandstone town of **Penrith** and the ruins of Brougham Castle with its Britanno-Roman graveyard. **Appleby-in-Westmorland**, former county town of old Westmorland, has a castle with a Norman keep, a twelfth-century church and an annual gypsy Horse Fair. Crossing the Eden at Appleby, the route heads for **Kirkby Stephen**, where there is a thirteenth-century church. You now follow the Eden to its source on the edge of the **Yorkshire Dales National Park**, briefly leaving Cumbria.

Howard House, 27 Howard Place, Carlisle, Cumbria, *CA1 1HR.*
Actual grid ref: NY407559
Elegant Victorian town house, 5 minutes' walk to city centre
Tel: **01228 529159** Mrs Fisher.
Fax no: 01228 512550
D: £16.00 **S:** £16.00.
Open: All Year
Beds: 2F 3D 3T
Baths: 2 Pr 2 Sh
🛉🖪🗢★✕🕭🔟🖾🗑✇

Brampton (Carlisle)   2

National Grid Ref: NY5360

🍴◀ New Inn, Drove Inn, White Lion

Cracrop Farm, Brampton, Cumbria, *CA8 2BW.*
High standard farmhouse
Grades: ETC 3 Diamond, AA 4 Diamond
Tel: **016977 48245**
Mrs Stobart. Fax no: 016977 48333
D: £25.00-£27.50 **S:** £25.00-£27.50.
Open: All Year
Beds: 2D 1T 1S
Baths: 4 En
🛉🖪(6)⊬🗢🕭🔟🖾🗑✇♻

Please don't camp on *anyone's* land without first obtaining their permission.

Beechwood, Capon Tree Road, Brampton, Cumbria, *CA8 1QL.*
Actual grid ref: NY529599
Detached house in own grounds, golf, fishing, scenery, Hadrian's Wall
Tel: **016977 2239** Mrs Clark.
D: £17.00 **S:** £19.00.
Open: All Year (not Xmas)
Beds: 1D 1T 1S **Baths:** 1 Sh
🛉(2)🖪(10)🗢🕭🔟🔟

Talkin   3

National Grid Ref: NY5457

Blacksmith Arms, Talkin, Brampton, Cumbria, CA8 1LE.
Traditional village inn, central location for Borders, Lakes, Hadrian's Wall
Tel: **016977 3452** Mrs Jackson.
Fax no: 016977 3396
D: £22.50 **S:** £30.00.
Open: All Year (not Xmas)
Beds: 2T 3D **Baths:** 5 En
🛉🖪(20)🗢🕭🔟🔟🖾🗑✇♻

Castle Carrock   4

National Grid Ref: NY5455

🍴◀ The Bluebell

Gelt Hall Farm, Castle Carrock, Carlisle, CA4 9LT.
Near Hadrian's Wall, Scottish border, Gretna Green. Scenic walks all around, looks onto Pennines
Grades: AA 3 Diamond
Tel: **01228 670260** Carrock.
D: £15.00-£16.50 **S:** £16.00-£17.00.
Open: All Year
Beds: 1F 1D 1T **Baths:** 2 Sh
🛉🖪⊬🗢★🕭♻

Renwick   5

National Grid Ref: NY5943

Scalehouse Farm, Scalehouses, Renwick, Penrith, Cumbria, CA10 1JY.
Actual grid ref: NY588451
Tel: **01768 896493** (also fax no)
D: £14.00-£18.00 **S:** £16.00-£20.00.
Open: All Year (not Xmas)
Beds: 2D 1T
Baths: 1 Pr 1 Sh
🛉🖪(6)⊬🗢✕🕭🔟🖾🗑✇♻
Old farmhouse with period features, open fires and beams, tastefully renovated, cosy rooms and period furniture, peaceful setting with wonderful views of the Pennines and Lake District fells, wholesome cooking with produce from our garden in season and home-made bread

Melmerby   6

National Grid Ref: NY6137

🍴 Shepherds Inn

Gale Hall Farm, Melmerby, Penrith, Cumbria, CA10 1HN.
Actual grid ref: NY6236
Large comfortable farmhouse near Pennines and Lake District
Tel: **01768 881254**
Mrs Toppin.
D: £15.00-£15.00 **S:** £15.00-£15.00.
Open: JUN to Nov
Beds: 1F 1T 1S
Baths: 1 Sh
🛉🖪(3)🗢★🗑♻

Langwathby   7

National Grid Ref: NY5733

▲ *Hay Loft B&B Bunkhouse (Independent),* Langwathby Hall, Langwathby, Penrith, Cumbria, *CA10 1PD.*
Actual grid ref: NY568338
Tel: **01768 881771 Adults:** £11.50
evening meals available, showers

The Grid Reference beneath the location heading is for the village or town - *not* for individual houses, which are shown (where supplied) in each entry itself.

Dufton 8

National Grid Ref: NY6825

⭕ 🍺 Stag Inn

▲ **Dufton Youth Hostel,**
Redstones, Dufton, Appleby-in-Westmorland, Cumbria, CA16 6DB.
Actual grid ref: NY688251
Tel: **017683 51236**
Under 18: £5.65 **Adults:** £8.35
evening meal at 7.00pm, family
bunk rooms, showers, shop, no
smoking
*Large stone-built house with log
fire in attractive C18th village
surrounded by fine scenery of the
Eden Valley*

Dufton Hall Farm, *Dufton,
Appleby in Westmorland, Cumbria,*
CA16 6DD.
C18th farmhouse in village centre,
close to pub and shop
Grades: ETC 3 Diamond
Tel: **017683 51573** (also fax no)
Mrs Howe.
D: £20.00-£22.00
S: £20.00-£25.00.
Open: Easter to Nov
Beds: 1F 1D 1T
Baths: 2 En 1 Pr
🛇 🅿 (4) 🖊️🖵 ♨🖩 Ⅴ🛈 ✓ 🚲

Sycamore House, *Dufton, Appleby-in-Westmorland, Cumbria,* CA16 6DB.
Actual grid ref: NY689253
Listed former pub, picturesque
village, cosy living room, open fire
Tel: **017683 51296**
Mrs O'Halloran.
D: £17.00-£20.00
S: £15.00-£20.00.
Open: Easter to Dec
Beds: 2D 1T 1S
Baths: 1 En
🛇 🅿 (2) 🖵 🏵🖨 ♨🖩 Ⅴ🛈 ✓ 🚲

Brampton (Appleby) 9

National Grid Ref: NY6723

⭕ 🍺 New Inn, Drove Inn, White Lion

Sunray, *Brampton, Appleby-in-Westmorland, Cumbria,* CA16 6JS.
Modern bungalow. Guest rooms
overlook Pennines, comfortable,
welcoming, good breakfast
Tel: **017683 52905**
Mrs Tinkler.
D: £15.00-£20.00
S: £18.00-£20.00.
Open: Easter to Oct
Beds: 2D
Baths: 1 En

Pay B&Bs by cash or
cheque and be prepared
to pay up front.

Eden Valley to Ulverston

From here it's through Garsdale to Sedbergh, and along the River Lune to **Kirkby Lonsdale**, where you can find the fourteenth-century stone Devil's Bridge, a thirteenth-century church and the famous view over the Lune Valley painted by Turner and idealised by Ruskin. Now you ride west along a stretch shared with the *Lancashire Cycleway*, to **Hutton Roof**, a hilltop hamlet commanding magnificent views, and then over Farleton Fell, and hit the coast at **Arnside**. You will now be at or near the coast for the rest of the way. Attractions along the next stretch include the Elizabethan Levens Hall, with the world-famous topiary gardens designed by Guillaume Beaumont (1694), a collection of Jacobean furniture and the earliest example of English patchwork. After Grange-over-Sands, **Cartmel** boasts two remainders of a twelfth-century priory which stood here until Henry VIII's Dissolution: St Mary's Church, with its many medieval tombs, and the Priory Gatehouse, now home to an art gallery. The next stage is through woodland via Cark and Greenodd to **Ulverston**, where three important figures from local history are represented in their different ways - the martial Sir John Barrow, secretary of the admiralty, by the Hoad Monument, fashioned after the design of the Eddystone Lighthouse, the pacific George Fox, the Quaker, whose home was Swarthmoor Hall, and the fantastic Stan Laurel, by the Laurel and Hardy Museum, attached to a cinema devoted to L & H's work.

D = Price range per person
sharing in a double room

Appleby-in-Westmorland 10

National Grid Ref: NY6820

⭕ 🍺 Royal Oak, Crown & Cushion

Bongate House, *Appleby-in-Westmorland, Cumbria,* CA16 6UE.
Actual grid ref: NY687202
Grades: ETC 4 Diamond
Tel: **017683 51245**
Mrs Dayson.
Fax no: 017683 51423
D: £18.50-£21.00 **S:** £18.50-£28.00.
Open: Mar to Nov
Beds: 1F 3D 3T 1S
Baths: 5 En
🛇 (5) 🅿 (8) 🖵🏵🍴♨🖩 Ⅴ🛈 ✓ 🚲
*This large Georgian guest house is
in an acre of secluded gardens.
Taste good food in a relaxed
atmosphere, ideal base to tour
Dales, Borders and, of course, the
Settle-to-Carlisle Railway. Make
your holiday one to remember*

Limnerslease, *Bongate, Appleby-in-Westmorland, Cumbria,* CA16 6UE.
Family-run guest house 10 mins
town centre. Lovely golf course &
many walks
Tel: **017683 51578** Mrs Coward.
D: £16.50-£16.50.
Open: All Year (not Xmas)
Beds: 2D 1T **Baths:** 1 Pr 1 Sh
🛇 (13) 🅿 (3) 🖵🏵♨🖩 Ⅴ🛈 ✓ 🚲

Weymyss House, *48 Boroughgate, Appleby-in-Westmorland, Cumbria,* CA16 6XG.
Actual grid ref: NY684203
Georgian house in small country
town
Tel: **017683 51494** Mrs Hirst.
D: £17.00-£17.00 **S:** £17.00-£17.00.
Open: Easter to Oct
Beds: 1D 1T 1S
Baths: 1 Pr 1 Sh
🛇 🅿 (2) 🖵 ♨🖩 Ⅴ🛈 ✓ 🚲

Church View, *Bongate, Appleby-in-Westmorland, Cumbria,* CA16 6UN.
Actual grid ref: NY689198
C18th character house, near old
coaching inn and town facilities
Tel: **017683 51792** (also fax no)
Mrs Kemp.
D: £16.00-£18.00 **S:** £18.00-£20.00.
Open: All Year (not Xmas)
Beds: 1F 1D 1S
Baths: 1 Sh
🛇 (5) 🅿 (4) 🖊️🖵 ♨🖩 ✓ 🚲

Drybeck 11

National Grid Ref: NY6615

East View Farm, *Drybeck, Appleby In Westmorland, Cumbria,* CA16 6TF.
Actual grid ref: NY666153
Comfortable traditional family
farm. Hospitality assured. Bring
your own wine
Tel: **017683 52079** Mrs Simpson.
D: £15.00-£16.00 **S:** £15.00-£16.00.
Open: All Year
Beds: 1D 1T 1S
Baths: 1 Pr 1 Sh
🛇 🅿 🖊️🖵🍴🛈 ✓

Winton 12

National Grid Ref: NY7811

🍴🍺 Bay Horse Inn

South View Farm, *Winton, Kirkby Stephen, Cumbria, CA17 4HS.*
Lovely farmhouse situated in quiet village, easy access to the Lakes and Dales
Tel: **017683 71120**
D: £15.00-£15.00 **S:** £15.00-£15.00.
Open: All Year
Beds: 1F 1D 1S
🛇 🅿 (2) ⛌ ⊬ ✕ 🏃 Ⓥ ⌀ ✦ 🚲

Kirkby Stephen 13

National Grid Ref: NY7708

🍴🍺 The Pennine Hotel, The Old Forge

🔺 **Kirkby Stephen Youth Hostel,**
Fletcher Hill, Market Street, Kirkby Stephen, Cumbria, CA17 7QQ.
Actual grid ref: NY774085
Tel: **017683 71793**
Under 18: £5.65 **Adults:** £8.35
evening meal at 7.00pm, family bunk rooms, showers, central heating, no smoking
Attractive converted chapel, just south of the town square in this interesting old market town in the Upper Eden Valley

---

S = Price range for a single
person in a room

Pay B&Bs by cash or
cheque and be prepared
to pay up front.

Lockholme, *48 South Road, Kirkby Stephen, Cumbria, CA17 4SN.*
Friendly Victorian home with antique furnishings and king sized beds
Tel: **017683 71321** Mrs Graham.
D: £16.00-£18.00 **S:** £16.00-£22.00.
Open: All Year (not Xmas)
Beds: 1F 1T 1D 1S
Baths: 2 En 1 Sh
🛇 🅿 (4) ⊬ ⛌ ⌀ 🏃 Ⓜ Ⓥ ⌀ ✦ 🚲

The Old Coach House, *Faraday Road, Kirkby Stephen, Cumbria, CA17 4QL.*
Quiet comfortable C18th coach house close to town centre
Tel: **017683 71582** Mrs rome.
D: £17.00-£19.00 **S:** £17.00-£22.00.
Open: All Year
Beds: 1D 1T 1S
Baths: 1 En 1 Sh
🛇 (5) ⊬ ⛌ 🏃 Ⓜ Ⓥ ⌀ ✦ 🚲

The Old Court House, *High Street, Kirkby Stephen, Cumbria, CA17 4SH.*
With its roots deep in the past, lovely old house, haven for walkers
Tel: **017683 71061** (also fax no)
Mrs Claxton.
D: £17.50 **S:** £20.00.
Open: All Year
Beds: 1F 1D 1T
Baths: 2 En
🛇 🅿 (2) ⛌ ⌀ 🏃 Ⓜ Ⓥ ✦

Jolly Farmers House, *63 High Street, Kirkby Stephen, Cumbria, CA17 4SH.*
Quality, comfort, right price: something we believe in, so come and relax
Tel: **017683 71063** (also fax no)
Mr Pepper.
D: £18.00 **S:** £18.00.
Open: All Year
Beds: 2F 5T 1S
Baths: 8 En
🛇 🅿 (6) ⛌ ⌀ 🏃 ✕ 🏃 Ⓜ Ⓥ ⌀ ✦

Garsdale 14

National Grid Ref: SD7389

🍴🍺 Dalesman, Red Lion, Bull Hotel

Farfield Country Guest House,
Garsdale Road, Garsdale, Sedbergh, Cumbria, LA10 5JN.
Actual grid ref: SD677919
Tel: **015396 20537**
Mr & Mrs Wilson.
D: £19.00-£24.00 **S:** £20.00-£21.00.
Open: All Year
Beds: 1F 4D 1T 1S
Baths: 4 En 1 Pr 2 Sh
🛇 🅿 (12) ⊬ ⛌ ✕ 🏃 Ⓜ Ⓥ ⌀ ✦ ⚞
Quietly located amongst some of the finest walking country in the Yorkshire Dales

---

Bringing children with
you? Always ask for
any special rates.

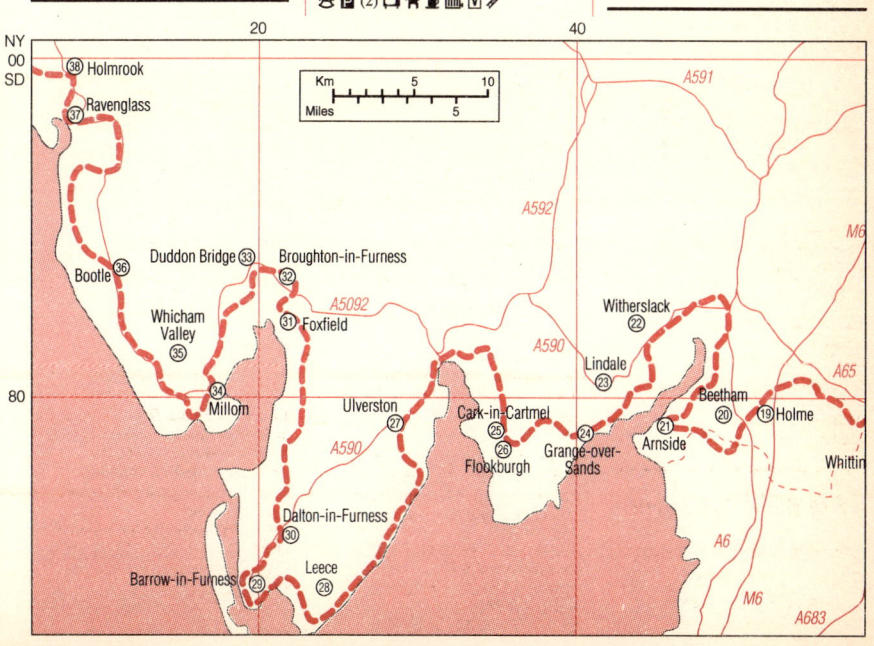

Ulverston to Ravenglass

The road out of Ulverston is largely alongside the beach, overlooking Morecambe Bay, scientifically important for the wading birds it supports. **Barrow-in-Furness** is the biggest town in Cumbria outside Carlisle, and sits at the opposite end of the cycleway and of the county, both in position and in character. This is the Furness Peninsula, the industrial powerhouse of old North Lancashire, the skyline dominated by the cranes of the shipyards. The town was built on the iron industry and is nowadays famous for Trident. The pre-industrial era is represented by Furness Abbey,

the romantic sandstone ruin of a magnificent twelfth-century Cistercian foundation which was accorded the dubious honour of being the first large abbey earmarked for the scrapheap by Henry VIII. The next stage takes you north through several villages called Something-in-Furness and then off the Peninsula at **Duddon Bridge** and back into old Cumberland, as you follow the Duddon Estuary south along the opposite side to **Millom**. Then through a stretch of coast within the Lake District National Park by way of **Bootle** and **Waberthwaite** to **Ravenglass**, where if you wish you can take time out with a trip inland through Eskdale on the old narrow-gauge railway.

Sedbergh 15

National Grid Ref: SD6592

🍴 🍺 Dalesman Inn, Cross Keys, Red Lion, Bull Hotel

Marshall House, Main Street, Sedbergh, Cumbria, LA10 5BL.
Grades: ETC 4 Diamond
Tel: 015396 21053
Mrs Kerry.
D: £22.00-£27.00
S: £35.00-£45.00.
Open: All Year (not Xmas)
Beds: 1D 2T
Baths: 2 En 1 Pr
🛏 (12) 🅿 (5) 🖵 🛋 💻 ♿ 📺 🌴 ⚡ 🚲
Which? recommended Dales town house situated under the magnificent Howgill Fells. Central for the Lakes & Yorkshire Dales. Tastefully furnished rooms: 2 ground floor overlooking our large walled garden with stream running through - oak-pannelled guest lounge with log fire

Stable Antiques, 15 Back Lane, Sedbergh, Cumbria, LA10 5AQ.
Actual grid ref: SD659921
C18th wheelwright's cottage with wonderful views of Howgill Fells
Grades: ETC 2 Diamond
Tel: 015396 20251
Miss Thurlby.
D: £18.00-£19.00
S: £18.00-£19.00.
Open: All Year
Beds: 1D 1T
Baths: 1 Sh
🛏 (10) 🖵 🛏 🛋 💻 📺 ⚡ 🌴

Holmecroft, Station Road, Sedbergh, Cumbria, LA10 5DW.
Actual grid ref: SD650919
Nestling beneath Howgill Fells enjoying lovely views from all aspects
Grades: ETC 3 Diamond
Tel: 015396 20754 (also fax no)
Mrs Sharrocks.
D: £18.50-£18.50
S: £18.50-£18.50.
Open: All Year (not Xmas)
Beds: 1D 1T 1S
Baths: 1 Sh
🛏 🅿 (6) 🌴 🖵 🛋 💻 📺 🔒 ⚡ 🚲

Middleton 16

National Grid Ref: SD6286

🍴 🍺 Swan Inn

Tossbeck Farm, Middleton, Carnforth, LA6 2LZ.
Tel: 015242 76214
D: £16.50-£19.00
S: £22.00-£25.00.
Open: Easter to Oct
Beds: 1F 1D
Baths: 1 En 1Private
🛏 🅿 (2) 🌴 🖵 🛏 🛋 💻 📺 🌴
A friendly welcome awaits you at Tossbeck, mixed farm in unspoilt Lune Valley

---

Kirkby Lonsdale 17

National Grid Ref: SD6178

🍴 🍺 Kings Arms, Sun Inn, Lunesdale Arms

9 Mill Brow House, Kirkby Lonsdale, Carnforth, Lancs, LA6 2AT.
Actual grid ref: SD612786
Wonderful views of river, shops/pubs nearby, holiday apartment available
Tel: 015242 71615 (also fax no)
Mrs Nicholson.
D: £18.00-£21.00
S: £20.00-£25.00.
Open: Easter to Oct
Beds: 1D 1T
Baths: 2 Sh
🛏 🅿 (2) 🌴 🛋 💻 📺 🌴

Please don't camp on *anyone's* land without first obtaining their permission.

Whittington 18

National Grid Ref: SD6076

🍴 🍺 Dragons Head

The Dragon's Head, Main Street, Whittington, Carnforth, LA6 2NY.
Small country pub in Lune valley 2 miles west of Lowesdale
Tel: 015242 72383
D: £20.00-£25.00
S: £20.00-£25.00.
Open: All Year
Beds: 1F 1D 1S
Baths: 1 Sh
🛏 (5) 🅿 (10) 🖵 🛏 ✗ 🛋 💻 📺 🌴

Holme 19

National Grid Ref: SD5279

🍴 🍺 Smithy Inn

Marwin House, Duke Street, Holme, Carnforth, LA6 1PY.
Gateway to Lake District, Yorkshire Dales. M6 (J36) 5 minutes
Grades: ETC 2 Diamond
Tel: 01524 781144 (also fax no)
D: £16.00-£18.00 **S:** £17.00-£19.00.
Open: All Year
Beds: 1F 1T
Baths: 1 Sh
🛏 🅿 (3) 🌴 🖵 🛏 🛋 💻 📺 🔒 ⚡ 🚲

All details shown are as supplied by B&B owners in Autumn 1999.

D = Price range per person sharing in a double room

Beetham · 20

National Grid Ref: SD4979

¶⊲ The Wheatsheaf

Barn Close, Beetham, Milnthorpe,
LA7 7AL.
Peaceful rural setting, large garden,
4 miles (J35) M6
Grades: ETC 3 Diamond
Tel: **015395 63191** (also fax no)
Mrs Robinson.
D: £18.00-£23.00 **S:** £20.00-£30.00.
Open: All Year
Beds: 2T
Baths: 1 En 1 Pr
☎ (9) ☑ (10) ⌇☐🔥🐾🏊🖵Ⅵ🛇≠♿

S = Price range for a single

person in a room

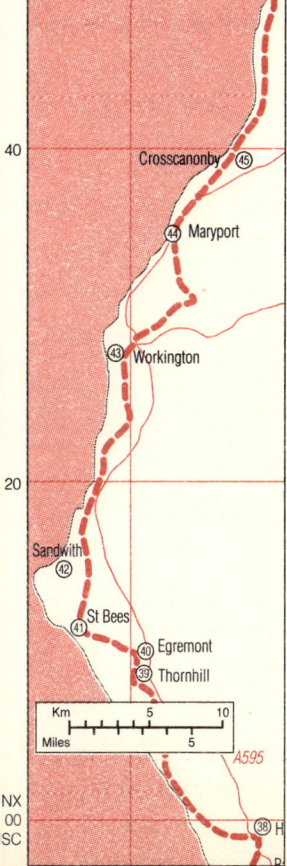

Arnside · 21

National Grid Ref: SD4578

¶⊲ The Albion

▲ *Arnside Youth Hostel,*
Oakfield Lodge, Redhills Road,
Arnside, Carnforth, Lancashire,
LA5 0AT.
Actual grid ref: SD452783
Tel: **01524 761781**
Under 18: £6.20 **Adults:** £9.15
evening meal at 7.00pm, television,
games room, showers, laundry
facilities
A few minutes' walk from the shore
with views across Morecambe Bay
to the Lakeland Fells. A mellow
stone house on the edge of a
coastal village on the Kent estuary.
RSPB reserve nearby

Willowfield Hotel, The
Promenade, Arnside, Carnforth,
Lancs, LA5 0AD.
Actual grid ref: SD455785
Non-smoking family-run hotel in
superb estuary-side location
Grades: ETC 4 Diamond,
AA 4 Diamond, RAC 4 Diamond
Tel: **01524 761354** Mr Kerr.
D: £21.00-£26.00 **S:** £21.00-£36.00.
Open: All Year
Beds: 2F 3D 3T 2S
Baths: 7 En 2 Sh
☎ (8) ⌇☐🔥🐾🖵Ⅵ🛇≠♿

Stonegate, The Promenade,
Arnside, Carnforth, Lancs, LA5 0AA.
Actual grid ref: SD455786
Stonegate offers comfort &
relaxation in AONB overlooking
tidal estuary with panoramic views
Tel: **01524 762560** (also fax no)
D: £19.50-£22.50 **S:** £22.00-£25.00.
Open: All Year
Beds: 2D 1T 1S **Baths:** 2 En 1 Pr
☎ (8) ⌇☐🔥🐾🖵Ⅵ🛇≠♿

Witherslack · 22

National Grid Ref: SD4384

Fernhill Vegetarian Country
House, Witherslack, Grange Over
Sands, Cumbria, LA11 6RX.
Actual grid ref: SD428842
Unwind in the quiet beauty of
Witherslack. Open fires, walking
Tel: **01359 552237**
D: £26.00-£30.00 **S:** £26.00-£30.00.
Open: All Year
Beds: 2D 1S
Baths: 1 En 1 Pr 1 Sh
☑ (20) ⌇🔥🐾✗🏊🖵Ⅵ🛇≠♿

Planning a longer

stay? Always ask for

any special rates.

Lindale · 23

National Grid Ref: SD4180

¶⊲ Lindale Inn

Greenacres Country Guest House,
Lindale, Grange-over-Sands,
Cumbria, LA11 6LP.
Actual grid ref: SD418805
Warm hospitality near lakes, dales
and coast
Grades: ETC 4 Diamond
Tel: **015395 34578** (also fax no)
D: £25.00-£25.00
S: £25.00-£30.00.
Open: All Year (not Xmas)
Beds: 1F 2D 1T 1S
Baths: 5 En
☎ ☑ (5) ⌇☐✗🏊🖵Ⅵ🛇≠

Hill Top, Bell Hill, Lindale,
Grange-over-Sands, Cumbria,
LA11 6LD.
Actual grid ref: SD414804
Pretty village in South Lake
District. Ground floor guest rooms
Tel: **015395 34012** (also fax no)
Mrs Brushett.
D: £20.00-£20.00
S: £20.00-£20.00.
Open: All Year (not Xmas)
Beds: 1T
Baths: 1 Pr
☎ ☑ (1) ⌇🏊🖵&Ⅵ🛇≠♿

Grange-over-Sands · 24

National Grid Ref: SD4077

¶⊲ Lindale Inn, Commodore Hotel, Kents Bank
Hotel, Hard Crag Hotel

The Laurels B&B, Berriedale
Terrace, Lindale Road, Grange-
over-Sands, Cumbria, LA11 6ER.
Actual grid ref: SD416783
Grades: ETC 4 Diamond
Tel: **015395 35919** (also fax no)
D: £20.00-£25.00
S: £25.00-£27.00.
Open: All Year
Beds: 2T 1D
Baths: 3 En
☑ (3) ⌇☐✗🏊🖵Ⅵ🛇≠♿
Relax and enjoy the friendly
atmosphere of our elegant
Victorian villa. Situated on the
Cumbria Cycle Way with
breathtaking views across
Morecambe Bay. Charming rooms,
log fires and home baking. Direct
rail link to Manchester Airport.
Excellent touring base

Cartmel Fell, Hith Tarn Green,
Grange-over-Sands, Cumbria,
LA11 6NE.
Quiet country setting - pets
welcome to use our kennels
Tel: **015395 52314**
D: £16.00-£20.00.
Open: All Year (not Xmas)
Beds: 1F 1D
Baths: 1 En
☎ ☑ ☐ 🔥✗🏊🖵Ⅵ🛇≠

Mayfields, 3 Mayfield Terrace,
Kents Bank Road, Grange-over-
Sands, Cumbria, *LA11 7DW.*
Well-appointed charming
Edwardian town house
Tel: **015395 34730** Mr Thorburn.
D: £20.00 **S:** £18.50.
Open: All Year (not Xmas)
Beds: 1D 1T 1S
Baths: 3 En 1 Sh
🏃 🅿 (3) ⅛ 🗙 🛏 ⛷ 🛒 Ⅶ 🔒

Holme Lea Guest House,
90 Kentsford Road, Kents Bank,
Grange-over-Sands, Cumbria,
LA11 7BB.
Victorian house overlooking bay,
quiet position, gardens, touring,
walking centre
Tel: **015395 32545**
Mrs Barton.
D: £22.00 **S:** £15.00.
Open: Mar to Oct
Beds: 1F 1D 1T
Baths: 3 En
🏃 🅿 (4) 🗙 🛏 🐾 🗙 ⛷ 🛒 Ⅶ ⅛

Cark-in-Cartmel   25

National Grid Ref: SD3676

⒤◀ Engine Inn

Eeabank House, 123 Station Road,
Cark-in-Cartmel, Grange-over-
Sands, Cumbria, *LA11 7NY.*
Tel: **015395 58156** (also fax no)
Mr Reece.
D: £16.50-£24.00 **S:** £16.50-£24.00.
Open: All Year
Beds: 2D 1T
Baths: 2 En 1 Pr
🗙 🐾 🗙 ⛷ 🛒 Ⅶ
C17th coaching house inn, licensed
bar, log fires, Old England is here,
old village pub one-minute walk
away, locals sing, tell old English
jokes. No McDonald's, no fast food
in this area: come and join us for
live music and conversation

Flookburgh   26

National Grid Ref: SD3675

⒤◀ Rose & Crown

The Late Kings Arms, 21 Market
Street, Flookburgh, Grange-over-
Sands, Cumbria, *LA11 7JU.*
Listed former coaching inn.
Excellent home cooking with
renowned breakfasts
Grades: ETC 3 Diamond
Tel: **015395 58991** Whitehead.
D: £17.00-£17.00 **S:** £17.00-£17.00.
Open: All Year
Beds: 1D 1T 1S
Baths: 2 Sh
🏃 ⅛ 🗙 🐾 🗙 ⛷ 🛒 Ⅶ 🔒 ⅛ 🚲

Ulverston   27

National Grid Ref: SD2878

⒤◀ Rose & Crown, Pier Castle, Farmers Arms

Sefton House , Queen Street,
Ulverston, Cumbria, *LA12 7AF.*
Georgian town house in the busy
market town of Ulverston
Tel: **01229 582190** Mrs Glaister.
Fax no: 01229 581773
D: £20.00-£22.50 **S:** £27.50-£30.00.
Open: All Year (not Xmas)
Beds: 2F 1D 1S
Baths: 4 En
🏃 🅿 (15) 🗙 🛏 ⛷ 🛒 Ⅶ 🔒 ⅛ 🚲

Church Walk House, Church
Walk, Ulverston, Cumbria,
LA12 7EW.
Actual grid ref: SD287785
Comfortable and homely Georgian
house, furnished with antiques
Tel: **01229 582211**
Mr Chadderton.
D: £20.00 **S:** £20.00.
Open: All Year (not Xmas)
Beds: 2D 1T 1S
Baths: 2 Pr 1 Sh
🏃 ⅛ 🗙 🐾 🗙 ⛷ 🛒 Ⅶ 🔒

Leece   28

National Grid Ref: SD2469

Winander, Leece, Ulverston,
Cumbria, *LA12 0QP.*
Converted barn in quiet village
location in Lake District Peninsula
Tel: **01229 822353**
D: £18.00-£23.00 **S:** £21.00-£26.00.
Open: All Year (not Xmas)
Beds: 1T 1D
Baths: 1 Pr 1 Sh
🏃 (5) 🅿 (3) ⅛ 🗙 🐾 🗙 ⛷ 🛒 Ⅶ 🔒 ⅛ 🚲

Barrow-in-Furness   29

National Grid Ref: SD1969

⒤◀ Brown Cow

Barrie House, 179 Abbey Road,
Barrow-in-Furness, Cumbria,
LA14 5JP.
Actual grid ref: SD203702
Victorian home among trees and
roses. Nearby lakes and sea
Tel: **01229 825507** (also fax no)
Mrs Maitland.
D: £16.00-£20.00 **S:** £16.00-£20.00.
Open: All Year (not Xmas)
Beds: 1F 1D 4T 5S
Baths: 4 En 3 Sh
🏃 ⅛ 🗙 🐾 ⛷ 🛒 Ⅶ 🔒 ⅛ 🚲

Dalton-in-Furness   30

National Grid Ref: SD2374

⒤◀ Black Dog Inn

Black Dog Inn, Holmes Green,
Broughton Road, Dalton-in-
Furness, Cumbria, *LA15 8JP.*
Actual grid ref: SD233761
Tel: **01229 462561**
Mr Taylor.
Fax no: 01229 468036
D: £15.00-£17.50
S: £12.50-£20.00.
Open: All Year
Beds: 3D 3S
Baths: 3 En 2 Pr 1 Sh
🏃 (1) 🅿 (30) ⅛ 🗙 🐾 🗙 ⛷ 🛒 Ⅶ 🔒 ⅛ 🚲
A cosy, beamed coaching inn with
open fires, a friendly atmosphere,
home-cooked food and local
cask-conditioned ales. Situated in
countryside 1km from Duddon
estuary and South Lakes Wild
Animal Park. Awarded Furness
CAMRA Pub of the Year 1998/99

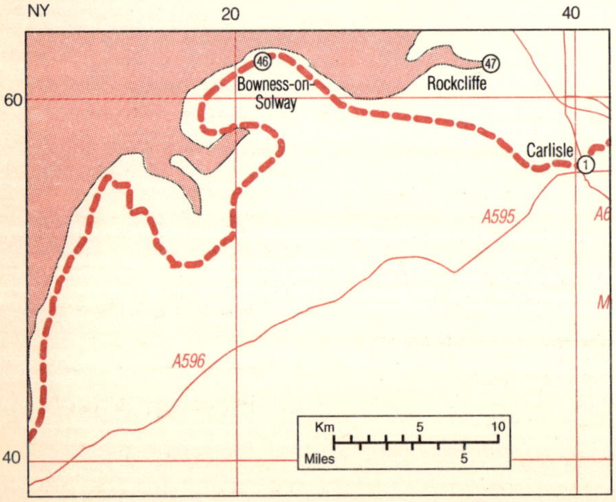

High season,
bank holidays and
special events mean
low availability
everywhere.

Ravenglass to Carlisle

Sellafield will interest anyone on the nuclear trail from Barrow, and after **Egremont**, which offers the ruins of a Norman castle, the route passes **St Bees Head**, with its sandstone cliffs. The final stretch of coast, north-eastwards towards the Solway Firth, takes you through a series of towns reflecting the industrial history of the region: **Whitehaven** has been through a number of incarnations - harbour for St Bees Priory, major tobacco port, during which time the many Georgian buildings went up, and then coal and shipbuilding centre; **Workington** and **Maryport** are major nineteenth-century centres of the iron industry. A different side of Victoriana is reflected in **Silloth**, a planned town and resort. After this there is another Cistercian abbey at **Abbeytown** and then an idyllic section with magnificent views across the **Solway Firth**. Another historic site is the Roman fort at **Burgh-by-Sands**, before you cycle back into Carlisle.

Foxfield   31

National Grid Ref: SD2185

🍴 🍺 Prince of Wales

Woodhouse, Foxfield, Broughton-in-Furness, Cumbria, *LA20 6BT.*
Charming C17th farmhouse, superb views, 3 acres of private grounds
Tel: **01229 716086** Mrs Corkill.
Fax no: 01229 716644
D: £19.00-£22.00 **S:** £30.00-£30.00.
Open: All Year
Beds: 1F 1D
Baths: 2 En
🛇 🅿 🗖 🔭 🗶 🔔 🎟 Ⓥ 🛆 ∥ ♂

All rates are subject to alteration at the owners' discretion.

Please respect a B&B's wishes regarding children, animals & smoking.

Broughton in Furness   32

National Grid Ref: SD2187

🍴 🍺 High Cross Inn, Manor Arms, Newfield Inn, Old Kings Head

The Old Kings Head, Broughton in Furness, Cumbria, *LA20 6HJ.*
Actual grid ref: SD213875
Traditional country inn, excellent food and ales, families and pets welcome
Grades: ETC 3 Diamond
Tel: **01229 716293** (also fax no)
Mrs McClure.
D: £18.00-£36.00 **S:** £18.00-£36.00.
Open: All Year
Beds: 2F 4D 1T
Baths: 2 En 1 Sh
🛇 🅿 (6) 🗖 🔭 🗶 🔔 🎟 Ⓥ 🛆 ∥ ♂

High Cross Inn, Broughton in Furness, Cumbria, *LA20 6ES.*
Hotel with restaurant overlooking the wonderful Duddon Valley
Tel: **01229 716272**
Fax no: 01229 716555
D: £20.00-£24.00
S: £20.00-£24.00.
Open: All Year
Beds: 4D 2T 3S
Baths: 8 En 3 Pr 3 Sh
🛇 🅿 🗖 🔭 🗶 🔔 🎟 Ⓥ 🛆 ∥ ♂ ☕

Manor Arms Hotel, The Square, Broughton in Furness, Cumbria, *LA20 6GHJ.*
Actual grid ref: SD212876
C18th inn, excellent traditional ales. Log fires. Snacks all day. Price quoted for continental breakfast
Tel: **01229 716286**
Mr & Mrs Varty.
D: £20.00 **S:** £25.00.
Open: All Year
Beds: 2D 1T
Baths: 3 En
🛇 (5) 🅿 🗖 🔭 🗶 🔔 🎟 Ⓥ 🛆 ∥

Browside, Seathwaite, Broughton in Furness, Cumbria, *LA20 6EF.*
Actual grid ref: SD237987
Traditional Lakeland former farmhouse, nine miles north of Broughton between Harter and Coniston Fells
Tel: **01229 716612**
D: £14.00 **S:** £14.00.
Open: All Year
Beds: 2D 1S
Baths: 1 Sh
🛇 🅿 (2) 🔭 🔔 Ⓥ

Duddon Bridge   33

National Grid Ref: SD1988

🍴 🍺 High Cross Inn

The Dower House, High Duddon, Duddon Bridge, Broughton in Furness, Cumbria, *LA20 6ET.*
Actual grid ref: SD196882
Grades: ETC 3 Diamond
Tel: **01229 716279** Mrs Nichols.
D: £20.00-£25.00 **S:** £25.00-£27.00.
Open: All Year (not Xmas/New Year)
Beds: 1F 2D 1T 1S
Baths: 1 En 3 Pr
🛇 🅿 (8) 🗖 🗶 🔔 🎟 Ⓥ ∥ ☕
Delightful Victorian country house offering a warm and friendly welcome. Comfortable bedrooms

Millom   34

National Grid Ref: SD1780

Beck Farm, The Knott, Millom, Cumbria, *LA18 5JQ.*
Working farm, rooms self catering or B&B.
Tel: **01229 772753** (also fax no) Tyson.
D: £16.00-£18.00.
🛇 🅿 ⊁ 🗖 🔭 🔔 🎟 🖧 Ⓥ 🛆 ∥ ☕

Whicham Valley   35

National Grid Ref: SD1583

🍴 🍺 Miners Arms

Whicham Old School, WhichaOld School, Whicham Valley, Millom, Cumbria, *LA18 5LS.*
Converted village school, quiet location. Easy access lakes, mountains, sea
Tel: **01229 773945** Mrs Woods.
D: £18.00 **S:** £18.00.
Open: All Year (not Xmas)
Beds: 3D 2T
Baths: 2 En 1 Pr
🛇 🅿 (4) 🗖 🔭 🔔 🎟 Ⓥ 🛆 ∥

Bootle   36

National Grid Ref: SD1188

The Stables, Bootle, Millom, Cumbria, *LA19 5TJ.*
Spacious accommodation, lovely views, two rivers, mountains, fells. Home-cooking
Tel: **01229 718644** Mrs Light.
D: £16.00-£18.50 **S:** £16.00-£22.50.
Open: All Year
Beds: 1F 2D
Baths: 2 En 1 Sh
🛇 🅿 (6) 🗖 🔭 🗶 🔔 🎟 Ⓥ 🛆 ∥ ☕

S = Price range for a single person in a room

D = Price range per person sharing in a double room

Ravenglass 37

National Grid Ref: SD0896

🐾🍺 Ratty Arms, Brown Cow

Muncaster Country Guest House,
Ravenglass, Cumbria, CA18 1RD.
Actual grid ref: SD098967
A very comfortable licensed guest-house with attractive garden adjacent to Muncaster Estate
Tel: **01229 717693** (also fax no)
Mr Putnam.
D: £19.00 **S:** £21.00.
Open: Feb to Dec
Beds: 1F 3D 2T 3S
Baths: 2 En 2 Sh
🛏 🅿 (16) 🗔 🛏 ✕ 🍽 🎥 📷 ✎

Holmrook 38

National Grid Ref: SD0799

🐾🍺 Lulwidge Arms

Hill Farm, Holmrook, Cumbria,
CA19 1UG.
Working farm; beautiful views overlooking River Irt and Wasdale Fells
Tel: **019467 24217**
Mrs Leak.
D: £14.00 **S:** £14.00.
Open: All Year (not Xmas)
Beds: 2F 1D **Baths:** 2 Sh
🛏🅿🗔🛏🐾♨🍽🎥📷🚲

Thornhill 39

National Grid Ref: NY0108

🐾🍺 Royal Oak

The Old Vicarage Guest House,
Thornhill, Egremont, Cumbria,
CA22 2NY.
Grades: ETC 3 Diamond
Tel: **01946 841577**
Mrs Graham.
D: £15.00-£17.00.
S: £15.00-£17.00.
Open: All Year (not Xmas)
Beds: 3F **Baths:** 2 Sh
🛏🅿(6)🗔🛏🐾♨🍽🎥🚲
C19th vicarage of character, within easy reach fells & lakes

All rooms full and nowhere else to stay? Ask the owner if there's anywhere nearby

Egremont 40

National Grid Ref: NY0110

🐾🍺 White Mare

Far Head of Haile, Haile,
Egremont, CA22 2PE.
Actual grid ref: NY042093
Tel: **01946 841205**
Mr Greening.
D: £15.00-£18.50
S: £15.50-£21.00.
Open: All Year
Beds: 1F 2D 5S
Baths: 1 En 3 Sh
🛏🅿(12)✎🗔🛏🍽🎥♨✎🚲
Explore the quieter Western lakes, mountains and coast or visit friends and relatives in West Cumbria. Between Ennerdale and Wastwater, overlooking fells. Quiet, friendly, comfortable, B&B accommodation with large games room and garden. Log fires. Off the beaten track. Large car park. Non smoking

Ghyll Farm Guest House,
Egremont, Cumbria, CA22 2UA.
Tel: **01946 822256**
Mrs Holliday.
D: £14.00-£14.00 **S:** £14.00-£14.00.
Open: All Year (not Xmas)
Beds: 2T 2S
Baths: 2 Sh
🛏🅿(6)🗔🛏♨🍽🎥📷🚲
Comfortable clean friendly farmhouse. Good breakfast, private off road parking. Try a fishing holiday on River Irt at Holmrook and catch salmon and sea trout. Reasonable rates while the men fish, the ladies can visit our beautiful lakes etc.

St Bees 41

National Grid Ref: NX9711

🐾🍺 Queens Head, Manor House, Oddfellows

Fairladies Barn Guest House,
Main Street, St Bees, CA27 0AD.
Large converted barn located in centre of seaside village
Tel: **01946 822718**
Mrs Carr.
D: £16.00-£16.00 **S:** £16.00-£16.00.
Open: All Year
Beds: 2D 1T 1S
Baths: 2 Sh
🛏🅿(10)🗔♨🍽🎥📷🚲

Tomlin Guest House, 1 Tomlin
House, St Bees, Cumbria, CA27 0EN.
Actual grid ref: NX963118
Comfortable Victorian house convenient to beach and St Bees Head
Tel: **01946 822284**
Mrs Whitehead.
Fax no: 01946 824243
D: £15.00-£18.00 **S:** £18.00-£18.00.
Open: All Year (not Xmas)
Beds: 1F 2D 1T
Beds: 2 En 2 Sh
🛏🅿(2)✎🗔🛏♨🍽🎥📷✎🚲

Outrigg House, St Bees, Cumbria,
CA27 0AN.
Georgian guest house of unique character located in village centre
Tel: **01956 822348** (also fax no)
Mrs Moffat.
D: £16.00-£16.00
S: £16.00-£16.00.
Open: All Year (not Xmas)
Beds: 1F 1T 1S
Baths: 1 Sh
🛏🅿(2)✎🗔🍽♨📷✎🚲

Stonehouse Farm, Main Street,
St Bees, Cumbria, CA27 0DE.
Actual grid ref: NX972119
Modern Georgian farmhouse in centre of village, next to railway station
Grades: ETC 2 Diamond
Tel: **01946 822224**
Mrs Smith.
D: £16.00-£20.00 **S:** £20.00-£20.00.
Open: All Year (not Xmas)
Beds: 1F 2D 2T 1S
Baths: 4 En 1 Sh
🛏🅿(20)🗔🛏♨🍽🎥📷✎🚲

Sandwith 42

National Grid Ref: NX9614

🐾🍺 Lowther Arms

▲ *Tarn Flatt YHA Camping*
Barn, Tarnflat Hall, Sandwith,
Whitehaven, Cumbria.
Actual grid ref: NX947146
Adults: £3.35+
Situated on St Bees Head overlooking Scottish coastline and the Isle of Man. RSPB seabird reserve and lighthouse nearby.
ADVANCE BOOKING ESSENTIAL

The Old Granary, Spout Howse,
Sandwith, Whitehaven, Cumbria,
CA28 9UG.
Actual grid ref: NX964147
Tastefully converted barn on C2C route and Coast to Coast path
Tel: **01946 692097**
Mrs Buchanan.
D: £17.00 **S:** £16.00.
Open: All Year
Beds: 1F 1D 1T
Baths: 2 En
🛏🅿(2)🗔🛏♨🍽🎥📷✎🚲

Workington 43

National Grid Ref: NX9927

🐾🍺 Ye Old Sportsman, Traveller's Rest, Miners Arms

Silverdale, 17 Banklands,
Workington, Cumbria, CA14 3EL.
Large Victorian private house. Near start C2C cycleway and lakes
Tel: **01900 61887**
Mrs Hardy.
D: £11.00-£13.50 **S:** £12.50-£15.00.
Open: All Year (not Xmas)
Beds: 2T 2S
Baths: 2 Sh
🛏🗔🛏♨🍽🎥

The Green Dragon Hotel, Portland Square, Workington, Cumbria, CA14 4BJ.
Delightful 1728 coaching house overlooking a Georgian courtyard
Tel: **01900 603803**
Mrs Roberts.
Fax no: 01900 872659
D: £20.00-£25.00 **S:** £25.00-£40.00.
Open: All Year
Beds: 3D 3T 4S
Baths: 8 En 2 Pr
🛏 � 🖵 🏍 ✕ 🦮 Ⅲ. Ⅴ 🛇 ✦ ஃ

Maryport   44

National Grid Ref: NY0336

🍴 ◀ Retreat Hotel

The Retreat Hotel, Birkby, Maryport, Cumbria, CA15 6RG.
Actual grid ref: NY059375
Former Victorian sea captain's residence with large walled garden to rear
Grades: ETC 4 Diamond
Tel: **01900 814056**
D: £23.50-£26.00 **S:** £33.50-£38.50.
Open: All Year (not Xmas)
Beds: 2D 1T
Baths: 3 En
🅿 (12) 🖵 ✕ 🦮 Ⅲ. Ⅴ 🛇 ✦ ஃ

Crosscanonby   45

National Grid Ref: NY0739

🍴 ◀ Stag Inn

East Farm, Crosscanonby, Maryport, Cumbria, CA15 6SJ.
Modernised, comfortable farmhouse; traditional breakfast. Aquaria, leisure centre, beach nearby
Tel: **01900 812153** Mrs Carruthers.
D: £16.00-£17.00 **S:** £17.00-£18.00.
Open: All Year (not Xmas)
Beds: 1F 1D **Baths:** 1 Sh
🛏 (2) 🅿 (2) 🌿 🖵 🦮 Ⅲ. Ⅴ

Bowness-on-Solway   46

National Grid Ref: NY2262

🍴 ◀ Kings Arms

The Old Rectory, Bowness-on-Solway, Carlisle, Cumbria, CA5 5AF.
Actual grid ref: NY224626
Fully ensuite old rectory at end of Hadrian's Wall
Grades: ETC 4 Diamond
Tel: **016973 51055**
Mr & Mrs Knowles Wallsand.
D: £20.00-£25.00 **S:** £20.00-£25.00.
Open: All Year (not Xmas)
Beds: 1F 2D 1S **Baths:** 4 En
🛏 (5) 🅿 (6) 🌿 🖵 🏍 ✕ 🦮 Ⅲ. Ⅴ ✦ ஃ

Maia Lodge, Bowness-on-Solway, Carlisle, Cumbria, CA5 5BH.
Actual grid ref: NY225627
Panoramic views of Solway Firth and Scottish Borders. End of Hadrian's Wall
Grades: ETC 3 Diamond
Tel: **016973 51955** Mrs Chettle.
D: £17.00-£20.00 **S:** £20.00-£20.00.
Open: All Year (not Xmas)
Beds: 1F 1D 1T
Baths: 2 Sh
🛏 (5) 🅿 (4) 🌿 🖵 ✕ 🦮 Ⅲ. Ⅴ 🛇 ஃ

Rockcliffe   47

National Grid Ref: NY3561

🍴 ◀ Metal Bridge Inn

Metal Bridge House, Metal Bridge, Rockcliffe, Carlisle, Cumbria, CA6 4HG.
Actual grid ref: NY356649
In country, close to M6/A74, quality accommodation, friendly welcome
Grades: ETC 3 Diamond
Tel: **01228 674695** Mr Rae.
D: £16.00-£18.00 **S:** £20.00-£22.00.
Open: All Year (not Xmas)
Beds: 1D 2T
Baths: 1 Sh
🛏 🅿 (6) 🌿 🏍 🦮 Ⅲ. Ⅴ ✦ ஃ

Essex Cycle Route

Essex provides good cycling country, as it is relatively flat, whilst offering a gentle agrarian beauty away from its ugly south end, which the cycle route avoids. The **Essex Cycle Route** consists of a large circuit around the interior of the county, with a 'spur' out east to the port of Harwich. Directed along quiet roads and not signposted, it is only a recommended tour, and you can devise your own alternatives at any point. The designated route can be cycled in either direction and you can start anywhere; for no particular reason, the description that follows takes the circuit clockwise from Coggeshall, east of Braintree, and finishes with the section to Harwich.

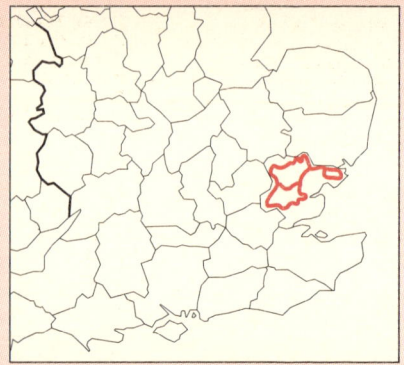

A detailed **guide booklet** to the cycleway route, which includes a list of cycle repair/hire shops on or near to the route, is available from Essex Tourism, Essex County Planning Department, County Hall, Chelmsford, Essex CM1 1LF, tel 01245 437548, @ £1.00 (inc p&p).

Maps: Ordnance Survey 1:50,000 Landranger series: 154, 155, 167, 168, 169

Essex is well-connected by **train** to London and to Eastern and Central England. Major railway termini are Chelmsford, Colchester and Harwich. London also connects to Stansted Airport, Stansted Mountfitchet, Elsenham, Newport and Audley End (for Saffron Walden). There are connections to many other places on or near the route.

Coggeshall to Maldon

Coggeshall is a medieval town on the banks of the Blackwater, one of Essex's major rivers, with the remains of a Cistercian Abbey nearby. In contrast with the Abbey ruins, there are two excellently preserved historic buildings: the Grange Barn is a 120-foot timber-framed barn constructed in 1140 to serve the Abbey, and is the oldest of its kind in Europe. It houses a display of historic farm wagons. Paycocke's is a merchant's house from the turn of the sixteenth century with rich panelling and wood carving, and a display of lace. On to **Cressing**, with more medieval timber-framed barns at nearby 'Cressing Temple', and **Terling**. From here there is an alternative route via **Pleshey**, where

you will find a Norman castle earthwork, and **Great Clanfield**, whose twelfth-century church is a Grade I Listed building with a mural of the Madonna and Child; connecting up to the eastern side of the circuit between Hatfield Broad Oak and Takeley. From Terling proceed to **Maldon**, on the Blackwater Estuary. This ancient town, with an attractive High Street, is famous for a battle fought here in 991, at which Viking invaders defeated the local East Saxons, told of in an early Anglo-Saxon poem, *The Battle of Maldon*. The millennium of the battle was commemorated by the *Maldon Embroidery*, made by local people in 1991. It celebrates the town's history and is on display in the Moot Hall. Also worth a look is the Hythe Quay with its Thames sailing barges.

Coggeshall   1

National Grid Ref: TL8522

🅗 🍴 Woolpack Inn

White Heather Guest House, 19 Colchester Road, Coggeshall, Colchester, Essex, CO6 1RP.
Actual grid ref: TL859228
Modern, family-run guest house, overlooking farmland
Tel: **01376 563004** Mrs Shaw.
D: £22.00-£22.50 **S:** £22.00-£25.00.
Open: All Year (not Xmas)
Beds: 2D 2S
Baths: 2 En 1 Sh
🅿 (8) ⅋ 🖵 🐾 🛏 🕮 Ⓥ

Kelvedon   2

National Grid Ref: TL8518

🅗 🍴 Sun Inn

Highfields Farm, Kelvedon, Colchester, Essex, CO5 9BJ.
Farmhouse in quiet countryside location, convenient for A12 and London
Grades: ETC 3 Diamond
Tel: **01376 570334** (also fax no)
Mrs Bunting.
D: £22.00-£22.00 **S:** £22.00-£24.00.
Open: All Year
Beds: 1D 2T **Baths:** 2 En 1 Pr
🐾 🅿 (4) ⅋ 🖵 🐾 🛏 🕮 Ⓥ ⬥ ⅋ 🐾

Messing   3

National Grid Ref: TL8918

Crispin's, The Street, Messing, Colchester, CO5 9TR.
Candle-lit Elizabethan restaurant with beamed rooms, lounge and secluded garden
Grades: ETC 5 Diamond
Tel: **01621 815868**
D: £24.75-£24.75
S: £30.00-£30.00.
Open: All Year
Beds: 1F 1D
Baths: 2 En

Braintree 4

National Grid Ref: TL7623

The Old House Guesthouse,
*11 Bradford Street, Braintree,
Essex, CM7 9AS.*
Actual grid ref: TL760238
Family-run, C16th guest house
within walking distance town
centre
Tel: **01376 550457**
Mrs Hughes.
Fax no: 01376 343863
D: £19.00-£30.00
S: £23.00-£30.00.
Open: All Year
Beds: 2F 5D 1T
Baths: 6 Pr 2 Sh
🛏 🅿 (10) 🛇 🗖 ✕ 🕮 📷 Ⅴ ♦ ⚲ ⟐

Felsted 5

National Grid Ref: TL6720

🍴 🍺 Flitch of Bacon, The Chequers, The Swan,
Three Horseshoes

Yarrow, *Felsted, Great Dunmow,
Essex, CM6 3HD.*
Actual grid ref: TL668206
Large Edwardian house in historic
village with beautiful countryside
views. No smoking in bedrooms
Tel: **01371 820878** (also fax no)
Mr & Mrs Bellingham Smith.
D: £17.00
S: £18.00.
Open: All Year
Beds: 1D 1T 1S
Baths: 1 En 1 Sh
🛏 🅿 (6) 🛇 🗖 🕮 📷 Ⅴ ♦

Hyfield, *Bannister Green, Felsted,
Great Dunmow, Essex, CM6 3ND.*
C13th Country house. Guest
lounge, large garden. Good pub
300m
Tel: **01371 820372** Mrs Shaw.
D: £18.00 **S:** £18.00.
Open: All Year (not Xmas)
Beds: 2D 2S
Baths: 1 Sh
🛏 🅿 (6) 🛇 🗖 🕮 📷 Ⅴ

Great Dunmow 6

National Grid Ref: TL6221

🍴 🍺 Flitch of Bacon

Homelye Farm, *Homelye Chase,
Braintree Road, Great Dunmow,
Essex, CM6 3AW.*
Actual grid ref: TL6522
Good quality motel-style accom-
modation close to Stansted Airport
Grades: ETC 4 Diamond,
AA 4 Diamond
Tel: **01371 872127** Mrs Pickford.
D: £22.50-£25.00 **S:** £25.00-£30.00.
Open: All Year
Beds: 1F 3D 2T 3S
Baths: 9 En
🛏 🅿 (9) 🛇 🗖 🕮 📷 Ⅴ ⟐

All rates are subject
to alteration at the
owners' discretion.

Margaret Roding 7

National Grid Ref: TL5912

Greys, *Ongar Road, Margaret
Roding, Great Dunmow, Essex,
CM6 1QR.*
Actual grid ref: TL605112
Old beamed cottage, pleasantly
situated amidst our farmland tiny
village
Grades: ETC 3 Diamond
Tel: **01245 231509**
Mrs Matthews.
D: £21.00
S: £22.00.
Open: All Year (not Xmas)
Beds: 2D 1T
Baths: 1 Sh
🛏 (10) 🅿 (3) 🛇 🗖 📷 ♦ ⟐

Hatfield Peverel 8

National Grid Ref: TL7811

🍴 🍺 William Boosey

The Wick, *Terling Hall Road,
Hatfield Peverel, Chelmsford,
Essex, CM3 2EZ.*
Actual grid ref: TL778122
C16th farmhouse. Charming,
comfortable, large garden, duck
pond and stream
Tel: **01245 380705**
Mrs Tritton.
D: £21.50-£23.50
S: £21.50-£23.00.
Open: All Year (not Xmas)
Beds: 2T 1S
Baths: 2 Sh
🛏 (9) 🅿 (4) 🗖 ✕ 🕮 📷 Ⅴ ♦ ⟐

Latchingdon 9

National Grid Ref: TL8800

🍴 🍺 Red Lion, Black Lion

Neptune Cafe Motel, Burnham Road, Latchingdon, Chelmsford, Essex, CM3 6EX.
Grades: ETC 2 Diamond
Tel: 01621 740770 Mr Lloyd.
D: £17.00-£17.00 **S:** £24.00-£24.00.
Open: All Year
Beds: 4F 4D 2T 10S
Baths: 10 En 2 Pr 1 Sh
🛏 🅿 (40) ⚡ 🗹 🛏 🎍 ⅲ ⅲ ⅲ 🛡 ⅲ
Cafe motel, luxury chalets adjoining. Close to boating and fishing areas, golfing and horse riding close by. Lovely rural setting with grand views

Danbury 10

National Grid Ref: TL7705

🍴 🍺 The Bell, Griffin Inn, The Cricketers

Southways, Copt Hill, Danbury, Chelmsford, Essex, CM3 4NN.
House with large attractive garden adjoining National Trust common land **Grades:** ETC 3 Diamond
Tel: **01245 223428** Mrs Deavin.
D: £19.00-£20.00 **S:** £20.00-£20.00.
Open: All Year
Beds: 2T **Baths:** 1 Sh
🛏 🅿 (2) 🗹 🛏 🎍 ⅲ ⅲ

The Cabin, Belhill Wood, Lingwood Common, Danbury, Chelmsford, CM3 4EF.
Self-contained unit surrounded by National Trust woods and commons
Tel: **01245 222956** (also fax no)
Mrs Davies.
D: £15.00-£18.00 **S:** £18.00-£18.00.
Open: Feb to Dec
Beds: 1D **Baths:** 1 Pr
🅿 ⚡ 🗹 🛏 🎍 ⅲ ⅲ ⅲ 🛡 ⅲ ⅲ

3 Millfields, Danbury, Chelmsford, Essex, CM3 4LE.
Good quality, comfortable, quiet, friendly
Tel: **01245 224946** Mrs Law.
D: £25.00 **S:** £25.00.
Open: All Year
Beds: 1D 1T **Baths:** 1 En 1 Sh
🛏 🅿 (3) ⚡ 🗹 🛏 🎍 ⅲ ⅲ

Chelmsford 11

National Grid Ref: TL7006

🍴 🍺 Black Bull

Aarandale, 9 Roxwell Road, Chelmsford, Essex, CM1 2LY.
Large Victorian house close to Chelmsford town centre and park
Tel: **01245 251713** (also fax no)
Mrs Perera.
D: £20.00-£22.00 **S:** £22.00-£32.00.
Open: All Year
Beds: 1F 1T 4S
Baths: 1 En 1 Sh
🅿 (6) 🗹 ✗ 🎍 ⅲ ⅲ ⅲ

Aquila, 11 Daffodil Way, Springfield, Chelmsford, CM1 6XB.
B&B accommodation, quiet family home, English breakfast
Grades: ETC 2 Diamond
Tel: **01245 465274**
D: £19.50-£24.50 **S:** £19.50-£24.50.
Open: All Year
Beds: 1D 1T 1S
🅿 (3) 🗹 🛏 🎍 ⅲ ⅲ

Rettendon Common 12

National Grid Ref: TQ7796

🍴 🍺 The Bell

Crossways, Main Road, Rettendon Common, Chelmsford, Essex, CM3 8DY.
Actual grid ref: TQ764982
Secluded home set well back from A130, dual carriageway
Tel: **01245 400539**
D: £20.00-£20.00 **S:** £20.00-£25.00.
Open: All Year (not Xmas)
Beds: 1T **Baths:** 1 Pr
🅿 (3) ⚡ 🗹 🛏 🎍 ⅲ ⅲ ⅲ 🛡 ⅲ

Billericay 13

National Grid Ref: TQ6794

🍴 🍺 Kings Head, Old Kings Head

Badgers' Rest, 2 Mount View, Billericay, Essex, CM11 1HB.
'Badgers Rest' is a modern detached house in a pleasant, select area of Billericay
Tel: **01277 625384**
Mr & Mrs Parker.
Fax no: 01277 633912
D: £17.50 **S:** £20.00.
Open: All Year
Beds: 1D 3S **Baths:** 1 En 2 Sh
🛏 🅿 (6) ⚡ 🗹 🛏 🎍 ⅲ ⅲ

Blackmore 14

National Grid Ref: TL6001

🍴 🍺 The Bull

Little Lampetts, Hay Green Lane, Blackmore, Ingatestone, Essex, CM4 0QE.
Secluded period house; easy access to M25 mainline stations towns
Tel: **01277 822030** Mrs Porter.
D: £22.50-£25.00 **S:** £25.00-£27.50.
Beds: 2T **Baths:** 1 Pr
🅿 (5) ⚡ 🗹 🛏 ✗ 🎍 ⅲ ⅲ 🛡 ⅲ ⅲ

Kelvedon Hatch 15

National Grid Ref: TQ5799

🍴 🍺 Dog & Partridge

57 Great Fox Meadow, Kelvedon Hatch, Brentwood, Essex, CM15 0AX.
Homely friendly clean comfortable overlooking farmlands. 4 miles from Brentwood and Ongar
Tel: **01277 374659** Mrs Maguire.
D: £15.00-£20.00 **S:** £15.00-£20.00.
Open: All Year (not Xmas)
Beds: 1D 1S **Baths:** 1 Sh
🛏 (3) 🅿 (1) ⚡ 🗹 🛏 🎍 ⅲ ⅲ

Takeley 16

National Grid Ref: TL5520

🍴 🍺 Lion & Lamb

Pippins, Smiths Green, Takeley, Bishop's Stortford, CM22 6NR.
Part of owners detached bungalow, very close to Stansted airport
Grades: ETC 2 Diamond
Tel: **01279 870369** Mrs Matthews.
D: £20.00-£25.00 **S:** £25.00-£30.00.
Open: All Year
Beds: 1D 1T
Baths: 1 Sh
🛏 🅿 (3) ⚡ 🗹 🛏 🎍 ⅲ ⅲ

Henham 17

National Grid Ref: TL5428

🍴 🍺 The Crown, The Cock

Bacons Cottage, Crow Street, Henham, Bishops Stortford, Herts, CM22 6AG.
Thatched cottage in picturesque setting near Stansted Airport, charming village
Tel: **01279 850754** Mrs Philpot.
D: £16.00-£18.00 **S:** £18.00-£22.00.
Open: All Year (not Xmas)
Beds: 1D 1S
Baths: 1 En
🅿 (1) ⚡ 🎍 ⅲ ⅲ

Arkesden 18

National Grid Ref: TL4834

🍴 🍺 Axe & Compass

Parsonage Farm, Arkesden, Saffron Walden, Essex, CB11 4HB.
Victorian farmhouse on arable farm in centre of award-winning village
Tel: **01799 550306** Mrs Forster.
D: £17.50-£25.00 **S:** £25.00-£25.00.
Open: All Year (not Xmas)
Beds: 2D 1T
Baths: 2 En 1 Sh
🛏 🅿 (5) ⚡ 🗹 🛏 🎍 ⅲ ⅲ ⅲ

Saffron Walden 19

National Grid Ref: TL5438

🍴 🍺 The Crown, Eight Bells

▲ *Saffron Walden Youth Hostel, 1 Myddylton Place, Saffron Walden, Essex, CB10 1BB.*
Actual grid ref: TL535386
Tel: **01799 523117**
Under 18: £5.65 **Adults:** £8.35
evening meal at 7.00pm, self-catering facilities, showers, no smoking 500-year-old former maltings with oak beams and uneven floors, and courtyard garden, only 3 minutes' walk from historic town centre

---

S = Price range for a single

person in a room

Maldon to Saffron Walden

From Maldon the route takes you south to **Purleigh**, where George Washington's great-grandfather was the local vicar, and then after East Hanningfield you can take a slight detour to the Royal Horticultural Society's Garden at Hyde Hall, a 24-acre hilltop garden with rose walks and waterfalls, as well as a small plant centre and a cafeteria. Around **Hanningfield Reservoir**, which offers sail-boarding, fishing and a nature trail, it's on to **Ingatestone**, where stands Ingatestone Hall, a redbrick Tudor mansion with 11 acres of grounds including a lake. On to the village of **Greensted**, where the Log Church is the oldest wooden church in the world, and then you turn north, through a string of medieval villages and near to the National Trust-owned **Hatfield Forest**, where there is a nature trail and lake. After this you pass close to **Stansted Airport**, whose magnificent terminal building was designed by Norman Foster. You are now into the relative high ground of the chalk uplands of northwestern Essex. Between **Broxted** and **Thaxted** the route veres out into a loop that takes in the pretty villages of Clavering, Arkesden and Wendens Ambo and the town of **Saffron Walden**. Here you will find an art gallery, a museum, the Sun Inn, embellished with plasterwork decoration, and a maze on the town's common. Nearby stands **Audley End House**. This imposing mansion was built on the foundations of a Benedictine Abbey in the early seventeenth century for Thomas Howard, Lord Treasurer to King James I (who described it as 'too large for a King but might do for a Lord Treasurer'), but the interior was largely remodelled by Robert Adam in the eighteenth century. It has a splendid Renaissance facade and a garden landscaped by 'Capability' Brown.

---

1 Gunters Cottages, Thaxted Road, Saffron Walden, Essex, CB10 2UT.
Quiet comfortable accommodation. Indoor heated swimming pool. Friendly welcome
Grades: ETC 3 Diamond
Tel: 01799 522091 Mrs Goddard.
D: £19.50 **S:** £25.00.
Open: All Year (not Xmas)
Beds: 1D
Baths: 1 Pr
🄿 (4) ⅙ 🞛 🛏 🎞 Ⓥ ♒

Archway Guest House, Church Street, Saffron Walden, Essex, CB10 1JW.
Unique house decorated with antiques, toys and rock & pop memorabilia
Grades: ETC 4 Diamond
Tel: 01799 501500
D: £22.50-£25.00
S: £25.00-£35.00.
Open: All Year
Beds: 1F 2D 2T 1S
Baths: 3 En 1 Pr 1 Sh
♿ 🄿 (3) 🞛 🏠 🛏 🎞 Ⓥ ♒

27 South Road, Saffron Walden, Essex, CB11 3DW.
Pretty, double-fronted Victorian cottage; short walk to town centre
Tel: 01799 525425 Mrs McBride.
D: £18.00 **S:** £18.00.
Open: All Year
Beds: 2T 1S
Baths: 1 Sh
♿ 🞛 🛏 🎞 Ⓥ

Pay B&Bs by cash or cheque and be prepared to pay up front.

D = Price range per person sharing in a double room

Great Chesterford 20

National Grid Ref: TL5042

🍴 🍺 The Plough

White Gates, School Street, Great Chesterford, Saffron Walden, Essex, CB10 1PH.
C18th timber framed cottage in heart of historic village
Grades: ETC 4 Diamond
Tel: 01799 530249 Mrs Mortimer.
D: £18.50-£23.00 **S:** £23.00-£25.00.
Open:
Beds: 1F 1T 1S
Baths: 1 En 1 Sh
♿ 🄿 (3) ⅙ 🞛 🛏 🎞 Ⓥ ♒

Little Walden 21

National Grid Ref: TL5441

🍴 🍺 The Crown

Rowley Hill Lodge, Little Walden Road, Little Walden, Saffron Walden, Essex, CB10 1UZ.
Actual grid ref: TL542407
Tel: 01799 525975
Mr & Mrs Haslam.
Fax no: 01799 516622
D: £22.00 **S:** £25.00.
Open: All Year (not Xmas)
Beds: 1D 1T
Baths: 2 Pr
♿ 🄿 (4) 🞛 🛏 🎞 Ⓥ ♒
C19th farm lodge thoughtfully enlarged. Both bedrooms with baths & power showers

---

Sewards End 22

National Grid Ref: TL5638

🍴 🍺 The Plough

Tipswains, Cole End, Sewards End, Saffron Walden, Essex, CB10 2LJ.
Tel: 01799 523911 Mrs Dighton.
D: £20.00-£25.00 **S:** £25.00-£28.00.
Open: All Year (not Xmas)
Beds: 2D
Baths: 2 Pr
♿ (1) 🄿 (5) ⅙ 🞛 🛏 🎞 Ⓥ 🛆 ♒
Beautiful Listed C17th thatched cottage situated in 1-acre garden surrounded by farmland, two miles from quaint market town of Saffron Walden, with gift shops, historic buildings, tea shops and pubs. Good breakfast

---

Wimbish 23

National Grid Ref: TL5837

🍴 🍺 White Hart

Newdegate House, Howlett End, Wimbish, Saffron Walden, Essex, CB10 2XW.
Grades: ETC 4 Diamond, Silver
Tel: 01799 599748 (also fax no)
Mr & Mrs Haigh.
D: £16.75-£20.00 **S:** £23.00-£29.50.
Open: All Year (not Xmas)
Beds: 1D 1T
Baths: 1 En 1 Pr
♿ (6) 🄿 (10) ⅙ 🞛 🛏 🎞 Ⓥ 🛆 ♒
Warm welcome assured at our comfortable home set in 2 acres of garden; boules pitch and croquet available, conservatory for guests' use. Halfway between the historic towns of Thaxted and Saffron Walden, convenient for Duxford war museum and Cambridge

Debden Green 24

National Grid Ref: TL5732

Wigmores Farm, Debden Green, Saffron Walden, Essex, CB11 3LX. Situated in beautiful open countryside near Thaxted and Saffron Walden
Tel: **01371 830050**
Mr & Mrs Worth.
D: £19.00-£24.00 **S:** £24.00-£24.00.
Open: All Year (not Xmas)
Beds: 1F 2D 1T **Baths:** 2 Sh
🛏 🅿 (10) ⛲ 🐾 ✗ 🖵 💷 ♥ ♿ 🚲

Thaxted 25

National Grid Ref: TL6131

🍴 🍺 Swan Hotel

Crossways Guest House, 32 Town Street, Thaxted, Dunmow, Essex, CM6 2LA.
Elegant C16th town house overlooking 600-year-old guildhall
Grades: ETC 4 Diamond
AA 4 Diamond
Tel: **01371 830348** Mr Millett & Mr Dominguez-Soult.
D: £24.00-£26.00 **S:** £30.00-£35.00.
Open: All Year
Beds: 1D 1T **Baths:** 2 En
🛏 ♥ 🖵 💷 💷 🚲

Great Bardfield 26

National Grid Ref: TL6730

🍴 🍺 The Vine

Bucks House, Vine Street, Great Bardfield, Braintree, Essex, CM7 4SR.
Actual grid ref: TL676305
Beautiful C16th house, great breakfasts, warm welcome. Conservation village centre
Tel: **01371 810519** Mrs Turner.
Fax no: 01371 811175
D: £20.00-£25.00 **S:** £25.00-£25.00.
Open: All Year (not Xmas)
Beds: 2D 1T **Baths:** 3 En 1 Pr
🛏 ♥ 🖵 🐾 🚲 🖳 💷 🛠 ♥ ♿

Toppesfield 27

National Grid Ref: TL7337

🍴 🍺 White Hart

Olivers Farm, Toppesfield, Halstead, Essex, CO9 4LS.
C17th farmhouse peaceful location. Large garden, country views, pretty villages
Tel: **01787 237642**
Mrs Blackie.
Fax no: 01787 237602
D: £25.00-£25.00 **S:** £27.50-£30.00.
Open: All Year (not Xmas)
Beds: 1D 1T
Baths: 1 En 1 Pr
🛏 (10) 🅿 (4) ♥ 🖵 🚲 💷 ♥

Sible Hedingham 28

National Grid Ref: TL7734

🍴 🍺 Bell Castle

Hedingham Antiques, 100 Swan Street, Sible Hedingham, Halstead, Essex, CO9 3HP.
Actual grid ref: TL783341
Victorian house and shop combined in centre of Bustley village
Grades: ETC 3 Diamond
Tel: **01787 460360** (also fax no)
Mrs Patterson.
D: £19.00-£19.00 **S:** £22.00-£22.00.
Open: All Year (not Xmas)
Beds: 1D 1T
Baths: 2 En
🛏 🅿 (4) 🖵 🚲 🖳 💷 🚲

All rooms full and nowhere else to stay? Ask the owner if there's anywhere nearby

---

D = Price range per person sharing in a double room

Castle Hedingham 29

National Grid Ref: TL7835

🍴 🍺 The Bell, White Hart

🔺 *Castle Hedingham Youth Hostel, 7 Falcon Square, Castle Hedingham, Halstead, Essex, CO9 3BU.*
Actual grid ref: TL786355
Tel: **01787 460799**
Under 18: £6.20 **Adults:** £9.15
evening meal at 7.00pm, self-catering facilities, showers
The Norman castle and half-timbered houses of Castle Hedingham add to the atmosphere of this hostel. 16th century building with modern annexe and large lawned garden

Fishers, 36 St James Street, Castle Hedingham, Halstead, Essex, CO9 3EW.
Actual grid ref: TL787355
Peaceful stay overlooking lovely garden. Excellent for touring Essex/Suffolk border
Tel: **01787 460382** (also fax no)
Mrs Hutchings.
D: £20.00-£25.00 **S:** £25.00-£30.00.
Open: All Year (not Xmas)
Beds: 1T
Baths: 1 Pr
🛏 (8) 🅿 (1) ♥ 🖵 🚲 🖳 💷 🚲

Pannells Ash Farm, Castle Hedingham, Halstead, Essex, CO9 3AD.
Period furnished C15th farmhouse
Tel: **01787 460364** Mrs Redgewell.
D: £18.00-£20.00 **S:** £20.00-£22.00.
Open: All Year (not Xmas)
Beds: 1F 1D 1T 1S
Baths: 1 Pr 1 Sh
🛏 🅿 (6) ♥ 🖵 🚲 🖳 💷 ♥

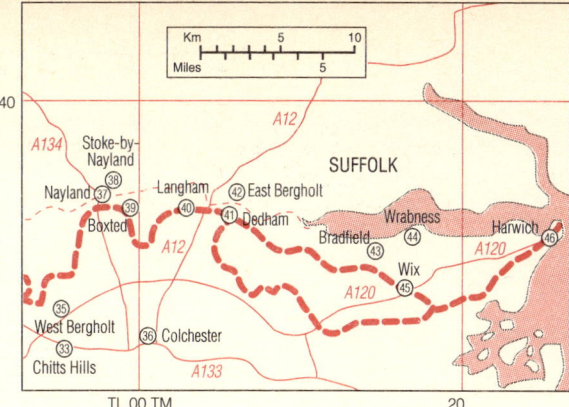

TL 00 TM   20

Saffron Walden to Fordham

Southeast of Saffron Walden you will find an interesting architecturally-eclectic church at **Debden**, before coming to **Thaxted**. Originating in Saxon times, the town has many medieval half-timbered buildings, including the Guildhall, which stands as evidence of the town's prosperity based historically on the cutlery industry. You are now on the long eastwards stretch of the route, which takes you through a series of attractive villages - Great Bardfield, Finchingfield and **Castle Hedingham**, where the well-preserved Norman castle keep is set in grounds with a formal canal and woodland walks. From here you continue east to **Fordham**, from where you can head south, cross the River Colne and proceed to **Coggeshall**; or continue into the eastern 'spur' to **Harwich**. A detour into **Colchester** will enable you to take in some of the rich store of architectural remains on offer in Britain's oldest town. (See under *Sustrans Hull to Harwich*.)

Halstead   30

National Grid Ref: TL8130

The Bull

Mill House, *The Causeway, Halstead, Essex, CO9 1ET.*
Grades: ETC 4 Diamond
Tel: **01787 474451** (also fax no)
Mr & Mrs Stuckey.
D: £24.00-£25.00
S: £30.00-£48.00.
Open: All Year (not Xmas)
Mill House - Listed town house in the market town of Halstead. Adjoining the house is a mill, once owned by Courtaulds, for silk weaving; now an antique centre. Secure private parking, brochure available

The Woodman Inn, *Colchester Road, Halstead, Essex, CO9 2DY.*
Comfortable mock-Tudor public house
Tel: **01787 476218** (also fax no)
Mr Redsell.
D: £18.00-£18.00
S: £18.00-£18.00.
Open: All Year
Beds: 1F 1T 1S
Baths: 1 Sh

Pebmarsh   31

National Grid Ref: TL8433

The Cock

Timbers, *Cross End, Pebmarsh, Halstead, Essex, CO9 2NT.*
Very quiet location only three miles from the Stour Valley
Tel: **01787 269330**
Ms Rice.
D: £17.50 **S:** £17.50.
Open: Mar to Nov
Beds: 1F 1T
Baths: 1 En 1 Pr

Bures   32

National Grid Ref: TL9034

Eight Bells, The Swan

Queens House Guest House, *Church Square, Bures, Suffolk, CO8 5AB.*
Actual grid ref: TL906341
Former C17th coaching inn in beautiful Stour Valley, Constable country
Grades: ETC 3 Diamond
Tel: **01787 227760** Mr Arnold.
Fax no: 01787 227082
D: £24.00-£28.00 **S:** £28.00-£32.00.
Open: All Year (not Xmas)
Beds: 1F 2D 2T **Baths:** 4 En 1 Pr

Swan House, *Bridge Street, Bures, Suffolk, CO8 5AD.*
Actual grid ref: TL905340
Tel: **01787 228098** (also fax no)
Mrs Tweed.
D: £20.00-£22.00 **S:** £22.00-£25.00.
Open: All Year
Beds: 1F 1D 1S
Baths: 2 Pr
A great welcome awaits you at a beautiful, spacious, riverside home in the Stour Valley. All guestrooms overlook garden to water's edge, in the middle of historic village, comfortable bedrooms, each private bathroom and all facilities. English/vegetarian breakfast

Chitts Hills   33

National Grid Ref: TL9525

The Crown

Seven Arches Farm, *Chitts Hills, Lexden, Colchester, Essex, CO3 5SX.*
Farm B&B in northern Essex
Tel: **01206 574896** (also fax no)
Mrs Tod.
D: £18.00-£20.00 **S:** £18.00-£20.00.
Open: All Year
Beds: 1F 2T **Baths:** 2 En 1 Pr

Fordstreet   34

National Grid Ref: TL9226

Coopers Arms, Queen's Head, Shoulder of Mutton

Old House, *Fordstreet, Aldham, Colchester, Essex, CO6 3PH.*
Actual grid ref: TL920270
Fascinating Grade II Listed C14th hall house - oak beams, log fires, large garden
Grades: ETC 3 Diamond
Tel: **01206 240456** (also fax no)
Mrs Mitchell.
D: £20.00-£25.00 **S:** £25.00.
Open: All Year
Beds: 1F 1T 1S **Baths:** 1 En 2 Pr

S = Price range for a single person in a room

West Bergholt   35

National Grid Ref: TL9627

⚑◖ White Hart, Treble Tile

The Old Post House, *10 Colchester Road, West Bergholt, Colchester, Essex, CO6 3JG.*
Actual grid ref: TL9527
Large Victorian private house, warm welcome, quiet secluded garden
Grades: ETC 3 Diamond
Tel: 01206 240379 (also fax no)
Mrs Brown.
D: £20.00-£25.00 **S:** £20.00.
Open: All Year
Beds: 1F 1D 1T **Baths:** 1 En 1 Sh
🛏 (1) 🅿 (3) 🖵 ≟ 🎟 Ⓥ 🛆 ⚡ ♻

Colchester   36

National Grid Ref: TL9925

⚑◖ Forresters, George, Siege House, Red Lion, Roverstye, Peveril Hotel

8 Broadmead Road, Parsons Heath, *Colchester, Essex, CO4 3HB.*
Grades: ETC 3 Diamond
Tel: 01206 861818 (also fax no)
Mr & Mrs Smith.
D: £18.50-£18.50 **S:** £25.00-£25.00.
Open: All Year
Beds: 1D **Baths:** 1 Sh
🅿 ≠ 🖵 ✕ ≟ 🎟 Ⓥ
Friendly family home, quiet residential area. 10 min by bus or car from town centre, bus station, castle, leisure complex, or university. Very convenient for touring Constable country, only 20 min from the sea or zoo

St John's Guest House, *330 Ipswich Road, Colchester, Essex, CO4 4ET.*
Well situated close to town, convenient for A12 and A120 Harwich
Tel: 01206 852288 Mrs Knight.
D: £20.00-£25.00 **S:** £26.00-£45.00.
Open: All Year
Beds: 2F 2D 2T 2S
Baths: 5 En 3 Sh
🛏 🅿 (10) ≠ 🖵 🗪 ≟ 🎟 Ⓥ ♻

Peveril Hotel, *51 North Hill, Colchester, Essex, CO1 1PY.*
Grades: AA 1 Star
Tel: 01206 574001 (also fax no)
D: £27.00-£45.00 **S:** £27.00-£45.00.
Open: All Year (not Xmas)
Beds: 4F 6D 2T 5S
Baths: 6 En 4 Sh
🛏 🅿 (10) 🖵 🗪 ✕ ≟ 🎟 🛆 ♻
Town centre holiday accommodation. Superb food, near castle

Please don't camp on *anyone's* land without first obtaining their permission.

11a Lincoln Way, *Colchester, Essex, CO1 2RL.*
Grades: ETC 3 Diamond
Tel: 01206 867192
Mr & Mrs Edwards.
Fax no: 01206 799993
D: £18.00-£20.00 **S:** £18.00-£22.00.
Open: All Year
Beds: 1T 1S
Baths: 1 Sh
🛏 (4) 🅿 (1) ≠ 🖵 🗪 ✕ ≟ 🎟 Ⓥ 🛆 ♻
Friendly, comfortable modern house in quiet residential area, five minutes walk from town centre, bus station, castle and leisure complex. Close to university and railway station. Convenient for Harwich port and touring Constable country. Colour TVs, washbasins, tea/coffee in bedrooms

Hampton House, *224 Maldon Road, Colchester, Essex, CO3 3BD.*
Friendly family home, tastefully furnished - books - games - on bus route
Tel: 01206 579291 Ms Morgan.
D: £17.00 **S:** £18.00.
Open: All Year
Beds: 1T 2S
Baths: 1 Sh
🖵 ≟ 🎟 Ⓥ ♻

The Old Manse, *15 Roman Road, Colchester, Essex, CO1 1UR.*
Quiet town centre location beside Castle Park. 3 minutes' walk bus station, town, castle
Tel: 01206 545154 Mrs Anderson.
D: £18.00 **S:** £20.00.
Open: All Year (not Xmas)
Beds: 1D 2T
Baths: 1 Pr 2 Sh
🛏 (3) 🅿 (1) ≠ 🖵 ≟ 🎟 Ⓥ

The Red House, *29 Wimpole Road, Colchester, Essex, CO1 2DL.*
Elegant, comfortable Victorian house. Short walk to town centre and stations
Tel: 01206 509005
Mrs Harrington.
Fax no: 01206 795077
D: £18.00 **S:** £20.00.
Open: All Year
Beds: 1T 2D **Baths:** 3 En
🛏 ≠ 🖵 ✕ ≟ 🎟 Ⓥ 🛆

Nayland   37

National Grid Ref: TL9734

⚑◖ The Lion, White Hart

Hill House, *Gravel Hill, Nayland, Colchester, Essex, CO6 4JB.*
Actual grid ref: TL975345
C16th beamed hall house on edge of historic Constable village
Grades: ETC 4 Diamond
Tel: 01206 262782
Mrs Heigham.
D: £20.00-£26.00 **S:** £22.00-£25.00.
Open: All Year (not Xmas)
Beds: 1D 1T 1S
Baths: 1 En 2 Pr
🛏 (8) 🅿 (6) ≠ 🖵 ≟ 🎟 Ⓥ 🛆 ⚡ ♻

Gladwins Farm, *Harpers Hill, Nayland, Colchester, Essex, CO6 4NU.*
Actual grid ref: TL961347
Grades: ETC 4 Diamond
Tel: 01206 262261
Mrs Dossor.
Fax no: 01206 263001
D: £28.00-£30.00
S: £25.00-£25.00.
Open: All Year (not Xmas)
Beds: 2D 1S
Baths: 2 En 1 Pr
🛏 (8) 🅿 (14) ≠ 🖵 ≟ 🎟 Ⓥ 🛆 ⚲ ♻
Traditional Suffolk farmhouse B&B with ensuite rooms, in 22 acres of beautiful rolling Constable country, or choose a self-catering cottage. Heated indoor pool, sauna, aromatherapy suite, hard tennis court, fishing lake, children's playground. Pets welcome. Colour brochure from resident owners

Stoke-by-Nayland   38

National Grid Ref: TL9836

⚑◖ The Angel

Ryegate House, *Stoke-by-Nayland, Colchester, Essex, CO6 4RA.*
Actual grid ref: TL986366
In pleasant village setting. Warm Welcome, Fine Food, Restful Rooms
Grades: ETC 4 Diamond, Silver
Tel: 01206 263679
Mr & Mrs Geater.
D: £20.00-£24.00
S: £28.00-£34.00.
Open: All Year (not Xmas)
Beds: 2D 1T
Baths: 3 En
🛏 (12) 🅿 (5) ≠ 🖵 🗪 ≟ 🎟 Ⓥ

Thorington Hall, *Stoke-by-Nayland, Colchester, Essex, CO6 4SS.*
Warm welcome in beautiful National Trust house
Tel: 01206 337329
Mrs Wollaston.
D: £20.00-£22.00
S: £28.00-£28.00.
Open: Easter to Sep
Beds: 1F 1D 1T 1S
Baths: 1 Sh
🛏 🅿 (4) 🗪 ♻

Order your

packed lunches the

evening before you

need them.

Not at breakfast!

Bringing children with you? Always ask for any special rates.

Boxted   39

National Grid Ref: TL9933

Round Hill House, Parsonage Hill, Boxted, Colchester, Essex, CO4 5ST.
Actual grid ref: TM001334
Stands on a low hill overlooking pastures where cattle graze
Grades: ETC 4 Diamond
Tel: **01206 272392** (also fax no)
D: £22.50-£26.00
S: £30.00-£35.00.
Open: All Year
Beds: 1F 1D 1T
Baths: 2 En 1 Pr
🛏 🅿 (6) ⌨ 🛏 ✕ 🎵 🎤 Ⅲ 🎮 👗 ⚡ 🚴

Langham   40

National Grid Ref: TM0233

🍴 🍺 Shepherd & Dog

Oak Apple Farm, Greyhound Hill, Langham, Colchester, Essex, CO4 5QF.
Actual grid ref: TM023320
Comfortable farmhouse tastefully decorated with large attractive garden
Grades: ETC 4 Diamond
Tel: **01206 272234** Mrs Helliwell.
D: £20.00 **S:** £20.00.
Open: All Year (not Xmas)
Beds: 2T 1S
Baths: 1 Sh
🛏 🅿 (6) ⌨ 🎤 Ⅲ 🎮 ⚡ 🚴

Always telephone to get directions to the B&B - you will save time!

Dedham   41

National Grid Ref: TM0533

🍴 🍺 Marlborough Head

Mays Barn Farm, Mays Lane, Dedham, Colchester, Essex, CO7 6EW.
Actual grid ref: TM0531
Grades: ETC 4 Diamond
Tel: **01206 323191** Mrs Freeman.
D: £20.00-£22.00 **S:** £25.00-£30.00.
Open: All Year (not Xmas)
Beds: 1D 1T
Baths: 1 En 1 Pr
🛏 🅿 (12) 🅿 (3) ⌨ 🎤 🎤 Ⅲ 🎮 🚴
Do you want peace and quiet away from all traffic? Wonderful views of Dedham Vale? A comfortable well-furnished old house and friendly hospitality? Then stay at Mays Barn Farm - ideal for exploring the unspoilt Essex and Suffolk border country

East Bergholt   42

National Grid Ref: TM0735

🍴 🍺 Kings Head

Rosemary, Rectory Hill, East Bergholt, Colchester, Essex, CO7 6TH.
Pleasant family house, surrounded by beautiful garden featured on Gardener's World
Tel: **01206 298241** Mrs Finch.
D: £21.00-£21.00 **S:** £21.00-£21.00.
Open: All Year
Beds: 2T 1S
Baths: 1 Sh
🛏 🅿 (8) 🅿 (3) ⌨ 🎤 Ⅲ 🚴

Bradfield   43

National Grid Ref: TM1430

🍴 🍺 Village Maid

Emsworth House, Ship Hill, Bradfield, Manningtree, Essex, CO11 2UP.
Set in a large beautiful garden with stunning views over the estuary
Tel: **01255 870860**
Mrs Linton.
D: £19.00-£25.00 **S:** £27.00-£36.00.
Open: All Year
Beds: 1F 2D 1T
Baths: 1 En 2 Sh
🛏 🅿 (10) ⌨ 🎤 ✕ 🎤 Ⅲ 🎮 ⚡ 🚴

Wrabness   44

National Grid Ref: TM1731

🍴 🍺 The Wheatsheaf

Dimbols Farm, Station Rd, Wrabness, Manningtree, Essex, CO11 2TH.
Actual grid ref: TM175313
Peaceful Georgian farm house
Grades: ETC 3 Diamond
Tel: **01255 880328** (also fax no)
Mrs Macaulay.
D: £15.50-£16.00 **S:** £21.00-£22.00.
Open: All Year (not Xmas)
Beds: 1F 1D **Baths:** 1 Sh
🛏 🅿 (8) ⌨ 🎤 Ⅲ 🎮 ⚡ 🚴

Wix   45

National Grid Ref: TM1628

🍴 🍺 Village Maid

Dairy House Farm, Bradfield Rd, Wix, Manningtree, Essex, CO11 2SR.
Spacious quality, rural accommodation. A really relaxing place to stay
Grades: ETC 4 Diamond, Gold, AA 4 Diamond
Tel: **01255 870322** Mrs Whitworth.
Fax no: 01255 870186
D: £18.50-£20.00 **S:** £26.00-£26.00.
Open: All Year (not Xmas)
Beds: 1D 2T **Baths:** 2 En 1 Pr
🛏 🅿 (12) 🅿 (4) ⌨ 🎤 Ⅲ 🎮 ⚡ 🚴

New Farm House, Spinnells Lane, Wix, Manningtree, Essex, CO11 2UJ.
Actual grid ref: TM165289
Country guest house in 4 acres of grounds. Residents' licence
Tel: **01255 870365** Mrs Mitchell.
Fax no: 01255 870837
D: £21.00 **S:** £22.00.
Open: All Year
Beds: 5F 1D 3T2S **Baths:** 9 Pr 1 Sh
🛏 🅿 (20) ⌨ 🎤 ✕ 🎤 Ⅲ 🎮 🎮 ⚡

Harwich   46

National Grid Ref: TM2431

🍴 🍺 The Royal Oak

Tudor Rose, 124 Fronks Road, Dovercourt, Harwich, CO12 4EQ.
Harwich international port. Seafront, Railway 5 minutes. London 1 hour
Tel: **01255 552398**
D: £17.50-£17.50 **S:** £20.00-£30.00.
Open: May to Aug
🛏 🅿 (2) ⌨ 🎤 Ⅲ 🎮 ⚡ 🚴

Fordham to Harwich

The village of **Dedham** boasts an immaculate neo-classical row of houses, and a church where one of the pews is decorated in memory of the Apollo 11 moon landing. Just over the border in Suffolk, **Flatford Mill** has become dedicated to the memory of the painter John Constable, whose painting *The Hay Wain* featured the original mill, on the site of which the present Victorian building stands. The route to Harwich runs along two alternative ways - the northern way goes through **Manningtree** and **Mistley**, the southern through **Ardleigh**, where there are a number of buildings of historic interest, and some other villages. The northern way is likely to be the more crowded, particularly during summer. **Harwich** is a major ferry port to the European mainland, and can be used to link the Essex Cycle Route with Continental cycling tours.

Icknield Way

The great prehistoric track that runs from Dorset to The Wash along Southern England's chalk ridgeway is the most ancient road still in use in Europe. Although the name applied historically to the whole section from the Thames to the north coast of Norfolk, the present **Icknield Way** runs from the northern end of the Ridgeway National Trail in Buckinghamshire to the starting point, on Norfolk's southern border, of the Peddars Way, another National Trail. Passing through Buckinghamshire, Bedfordshire, Hertfordshire, Cambridgeshire, Essex and Suffolk, it is now a Regional Recreational Route created, primarily for walkers, by the Countryside Commission on the basis of work done by the Icknield Way Association. A little over 100 miles long, the route is waymarked by a distinctive flint axe emblem. **Note:** Cyclists should follow the route designed for horseriders. This frequently diverges from the walkers' route, which follows many footpaths open only to walkers. Wherever the two are different, follow the waymarks and signposts marked 'Riders' Route'.

Guides: *The Icknield Way Path – A Guide for Horseriders, Cyclists and Others* by Elizabeth Barrett (ISBN 0 951601 12 1), published by Wimpole Books and available from the publishers at Pip's Peace, Kenton, Stowmarket, Suffolk IP14 6JS, tel 01728 860429, @ £4.50 (inc p&p), describes the riders' route, which cyclists should follow. This guide takes the route in reverse from the above description. It finishes at Luton, so you should also get hold of a copy of *The Icknield Way – A Walkers' Guide* (ISBN

0 952181 90 8), published by the Icknield Way Association and available from the Ramblers' Association National Office, 1/5 Wandsworth Road, London SW8 2XX, tel 020-7339 8500, @ £4.50 (+ 70p p&p). This guide has excellent material on the flora and fauna, archaeology and geology of the path.

Maps: Ordnance Survey 1:50,000 Landranger series: 144, 153, 154, 155, 165, 166

Trains: Tring, about 4 miles from Ivinghoe Beacon, is served by trains from London, as is Luton. Letchworth and Baldock are on the line between London and Cambridge. Newmarket is on the line between Cambridge and Ipswich. Thetford, about 6 miles from Knettishall Heath, is on the line between Cambridge and Norwich.

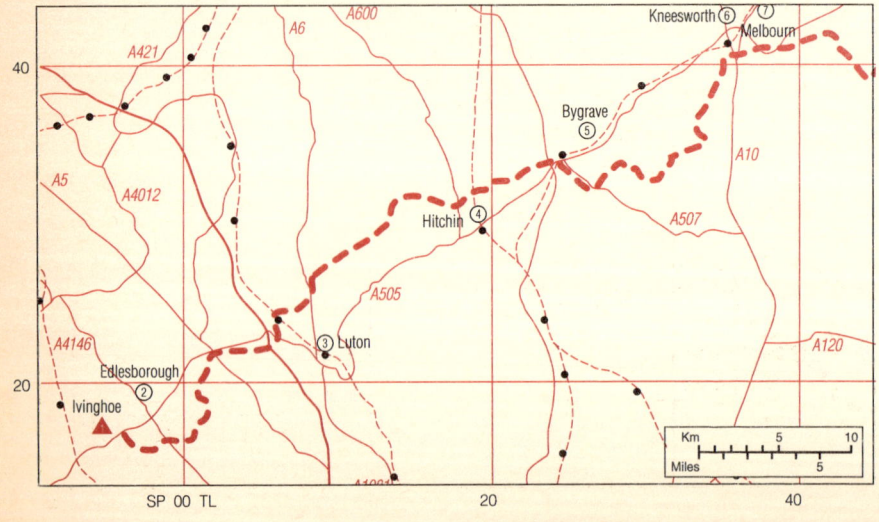

Ivinghoe 1

National Grid Ref: SP9416

▲ *Ivinghoe Youth Hostel, The Old Brewery House, Ivinghoe, Leighton Buzzard, Bedfordshire, LU7 9EP.*
Actual grid ref: SP945161
Tel: **01296 668251**
Under 18: £5.65 **Adults:** £8.35 evening meal at 7.00pm, family bunk rooms, showers, shop *Georgian mansion, once home of a local brewer, next to village church in Chilterns Area of Outstanding Natural Beauty*

All cycleways are popular: you are well-advised to book ahead

---

Pay B&Bs by cash or cheque and be prepared to pay up front.

Edlesborough 2

National Grid Ref: SP9719

🏨 🍺 The Golden Rule

Ridgeway End, 5 Ivinghoe Way, Edlesborough, Dunstable, Beds, LU6 2EL.
Actual grid ref: SP975183
Pretty bungalow in private road, surrounded by fields and views of the Chiltern Hills
Tel: **01525 220405** (also fax no)
Mrs Lloyd.
D: £20.00-£22.00 **S:** £22.00-£24.00.
Open: All Year (not Xmas)
Beds: 1D 1T
Baths: 1 En
🛏 (2) 🅿 (3) ✂ 🖵 🔥 ▥ Ⅴ 🛡 ⚗ ♨

Luton 3

National Grid Ref: TL0921

🏨 🍺 Wigmore Arms

Stockwood Hotel, 41-43 Stockwood Crescent, Luton, Beds, LU1 3SS.
Actual grid ref: TL090206
Tudor-style town centre premises, near M1, airport, golf course
Tel: **01582 721000**
Mr Blanchard.
D: £20.00 **S:** £25.00.
Open: All Year (not Xmas)
Beds: 1F 2D 6T 9S
Baths: 4 Pr 3 Sh
🛏 🅿 (14) 🖵 ✗ ▥

Belzayne, 70 Lalleford Road, Luton, Beds, LU2 9JH.
Modern semi, close to London bus stop. Old fashioned hospitality
Tel: **01582 736591** (also fax no)
Mrs Bell.
D: £12.00-£14.00 **S:** £18.00.
Open: All Year (not Xmas)
Beds: 1F 2T
Baths: 2 Sh
🛏 (7) 🅿 (5) 🔥 ▥ Ⅴ

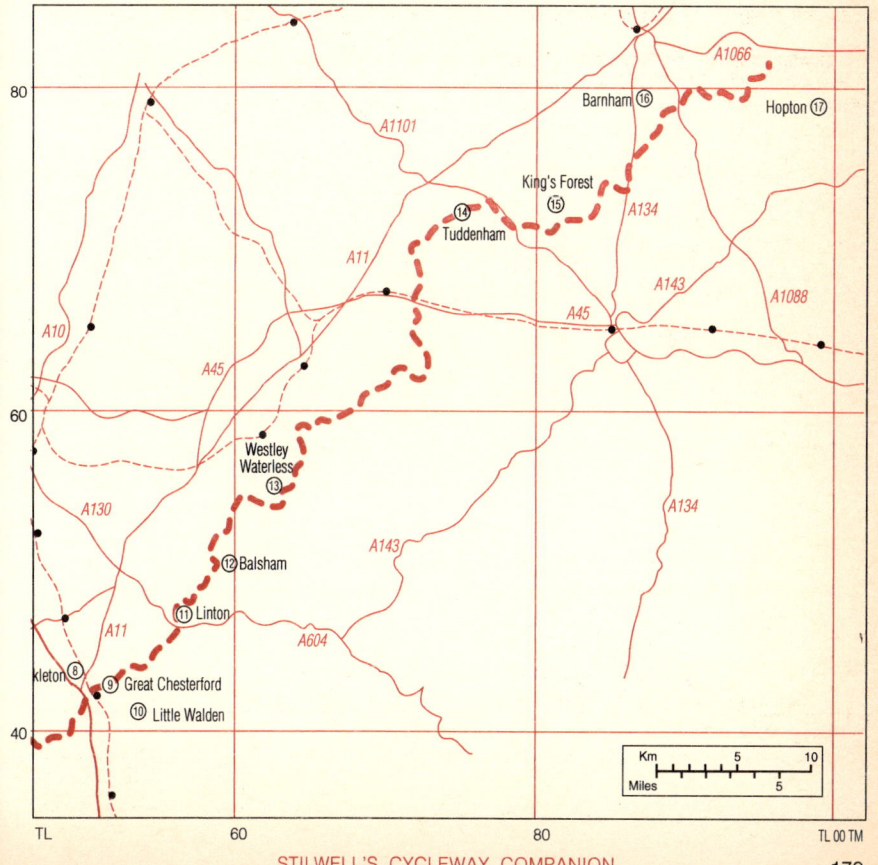

Ivinghoe Beacon to Baldock

The official start of the Icknield Way is at **Ivinghoe Beacon**, a hill with an ancient fort, which yields good views. Close by is Pitstone Windmill, the oldest in England (seventeenth century). Crossing into Bedfordshire, the route passes near **Whipsnade Wild Animal Park**, which you can tour by steam train, as well as on foot; and crosses the **Dustable Downs Country Park**, where there are several Neolithic burial mounds. From here you go through the towns of **Dunstable** and **Luton.** Luton Museum exhibits archaeological finds from the Icknield Way. Into Hertfordshire, and you reach **Telegraph Hill**, one of a series of such hills in a line from London to Great Yarmouth, named from the communication stations, which signalled using a system of shutters on the roof, of the Napoleonic Wars. The views from the hill are excellent. North of Tingley Wood is the Knocking Hoe long barrow, and a nearby National Nature Reserve. You head through the village of **Ickleford**, north of Hitchin, to reach **Letchworth**, an early 'garden city'. From here you pass to the north of **Baldock**, a town important in Iron Age and Roman times and developed by the Knights Templars. There are some fine Georgian buildings.

Hitchin 4

National Grid Ref: TL1828

Firs Hotel, 83 Bedford Road, Hitchin, Herts, SG5 2TY.
Family managed business with relaxed informal atmosphere. Excellent rail and road links
Grades: RAC 2 Star
Tel: **01462 422322** (also fax no)
Girgenti.
D: £23.50-£28.50 **S:** £32.00-£47.00.
Open: All Year
Beds: 3F 3D 8T 16S
Baths: 9 En 3 Sh
🛇 🅿 (30) ⻝🖵🛏✕🌢🏧Ⅲ.Ⅵ🛢♻

Bygrave 5

National Grid Ref: TL2636

🍴 🍺 Bushel & Strike

59 Ashwell Road, Bygrave, Baldock, Hertfordshire, SG7 5DY.
Friendly family home, rural location. Guests' room, use of garden
Tel: **01462 894749**
Mrs Spaul.
D: £22.00-£25.00 **S:** £22.00-£25.00.
Open: All Year (not Xmas)
Beds: 2D 1T 1S
Baths: 1 Sh
🛇 🅿 (3) ⻝🖵🌢Ⅲ.Ⅵ♻

D = Price range per person sharing in a double room

Kneesworth 6

National Grid Ref: TL3444

🍴 🍺 Queen Adelaide

Fairhaven, 102 Old North Road, Kneesworth, Royston, Herts, SG8 5JR.
Actual grid ref: TL347436
Comfortable country home near Cambridge and Duxford Imperial War Museum
Tel: **01763 249471** (also fax no)
Mrs Watson.
D: £20.00-£20.00 **S:** £20.00-£25.00.
Open: All Year
Beds: 1D 1T 1S **Baths:** 1 Sh
🛇 🅿 (3) ⻝🖵🌢Ⅲ.Ⅵ

Melbourn 7

National Grid Ref: TL3844

🍴 🍺 The Star, Black Horse, The Chequers

The Carlings, Melbourn, Royston, SG8 6DX.
Tel: **01763 260686** Mrs Howard.
Fax no: 01763 261988
D: £22.00-£22.00 **S:** £30.00-£35.00.
Open: All Year (not Xmas)
Beds: 1D 1T
Baths: 2 En
🛇 🅿 (3) ⻝🖵🛏🌢Ⅲ.&.Ⅵ♻♻
Luxurious rooms in delightful secluded setting. Separate entrance, conservatory gardens, ideal touring centre for Cambridge, Duxford etc. Many good pubs nearby, friendly welcome guaranteed, non smokers

Ickleton 8

National Grid Ref: TL4843

🍴 🍺 Red Lion

New Inn House, 10 Brookhampton Street, Ickleton, Duxford, Cambs, CB10 1SP.
Tel: **01799 530463** Mrs Fletcher.
Fax no: 01799 531499
D: £15.00-£19.00 **S:** £25.00-£25.00.
Open: All Year (not Xmas)
Beds: 1D 1T
Baths: 1 Sh
🛇 (5) 🅿 (6) ⻝🖵🌢Ⅲ.Ⅵ
Traditional beamed property combining comfortable modern facilities with historic charm. Luxury guest shower room. Good breakfasts. Small rural village, 3 miles Duxford Imperial War Museum, handy for Cambridge and Saffron Walden. 2 miles M11

Great Chesterford 9

National Grid Ref: TL5042

🍴 🍺 The Plough

White Gates, School Street, Great Chesterford, Saffron Walden, Essex, CB10 1PH.
C18th timber framed cottage in heart of historic village
Grades: ETC 4 Diamond
Tel: **01799 530249** Mrs Mortimer.
D: £18.50-£23.00 **S:** £23.00-£25.00.
Open: All Year
Beds: 1F 1T 1S
Baths: 1 En 1 Sh
🛇 🅿 (3) ⻝🖵🌢Ⅲ.Ⅵ♻

Little Walden 10

National Grid Ref: TL5441

🍴 🍺 The Crown

Rowley Hill Lodge, Little Walden Road, Little Walden, Saffron Walden, Essex, CB10 1UZ.
Actual grid ref: TL542407
Tel: **01799 525975**
Mr & Mrs Haslam.
Fax no: 01799 516622
D: £22.00 **S:** £25.00.
Open: All Year (not Xmas)
Beds: 1D 1T
Baths: 2 Pr
🛇 🅿 (4) 🖵🌢Ⅲ.Ⅵ✦
C19th farm lodge thoughtfully enlarged. Both bedrooms with baths & power showers

All rates are subject to alteration at the owners' discretion.

High season, bank holidays and special events mean low availability *everywhere.*

Baldock to Gazeley

After **Ashwell**, an interesting village with a museum on local archaeological finds, the route enters Cambridgeshire and continues along Ashwell Street, a probably Roman road which may well be based on a stretch of the original Icknield Way, to reach **Melbourn**. Here you turn south before continuing eastwards to cross the River Cam into the northwestern corner of Essex, and the village of **Great Chesterford**, which was once a walled Roman town. Back in Cambridgeshire, the village of **Linton** has numerous sixteenth- and seventeenth-century houses, and a garden zoo. At **Balsham**, the county's

highest point, there is a fascinating medieval church, which has a thirteenth-century bell tower, and a three-hundred-year-old musical manuscript on display. Crossing the ancient Fleam Dyke, you cycle up green hedged Fox Lane before wending your way through a string of villages to **Woodditton**, from where there are two routes to **Herringswell** in Suffolk. The northern alternative takes you via **Newmarket**, the famous horseracing centre, where you can visit the National Stud and the National Horseracing Museum, and **Chippenham**, with nearby Chippenham Park. The southern route leads over quieter roads through **Cheveley** and **Gazeley**, with its tower mill.

Linton 11

National Grid Ref: TL5646

🍴 ◀ The Crown, Dog & Duck

Linton Heights, 36 Wheatsheaf Way, Linton, Cambridge, Cambs, CB1 6XB.
Actual grid ref: TL573475
Comfortable, friendly home, sharing lounge, convenient Duxford, Cambridge, Newmarket, Saffron Waldon, Bury
Tel: **01223 892516**
Mr & Mrs Peake.
D: £16.00-£18.00 **S:** £16.00-£18.00.
Open: All Year (not Xmas)
Beds: 1T 1S
Baths: 1 Sh
🛏 (6) 🅿 (2) ⊬ ☐ 🔥 🎆 ♿ 🎥 🛢 ✦

Cantilena, 4 Harefield Rise, Linton, Cambridge, CB1 6LS.
Spacious bungalow, quiet cul-de-sac, edge of historic village. Cambridge, 9 miles
Tel: **01223 892988** (also fax no)
Mr & Mrs Clarkson.
D: £18.00-£20.00 **S:** £18.00-£25.00.
Open: All Year
Beds: 1F 1D 1T
Baths: 1 Sh
🛏 🅿 (3) ⊬ ☐ 🔥 🎆 ♿ 🎥 ✦ ♻

Springfield House, 14-16 Horn Lane, Linton, Cambridge, Cambs, CB1 6HT.
Peaceful, riverside Regency residence with large garden in historic village
Tel: **01223 891383** Mrs Rossiter.
D: £19.00 **S:** £20.00.
Open: All Year
Beds: 2D
Baths: 1 En 1 Pr
🛏 🅿 (4) ⊬ ☐ 🔥 🎆 🎥 🛢 ✦

S = Price range for a single person in a room

Balsham 12

National Grid Ref: TL5849

The Garden End, 10 West Wratting Road, Balsham, Cambridge, CB1 6DX.
Actual grid ref: TL587506
Self-contained ground floor suite - children / pets welcome all year
Tel: **01223 894021** (also fax no)
Mrs Greenaway.
D: £18.00-£18.00 **S:** £20.00.
Open: All Year
Beds: 1F
Baths: 1 En 1 Pr
🛏 🅿 (2) ⊬ ☐ 🔥 🗙 🔥 🎆 ♿ 🎥 🛢 ✦ ♻

Westley Waterless 13

National Grid Ref: TL6256

🍴 ◀ Kings Head

Westley House, Westley Waterless, Newmarket, Suffolk, CB8 0RQ.
Grades: ETC 3 Diamond
Tel: **01638 508112** Mrs Galpin.
Fax no: 01638 508113
D: £22.50-£24.00 **S:** £24.00-£25.00.
Open: All Year
Beds: 2T 2S
Baths: 2 Sh
🛏 (4) 🅿 (6) ☐ 🔥 🗙 🎆 🛢 ✦
C18th Georgian country home in quiet rural area 5 miles from Newmarket

Tuddenham 14

National Grid Ref: TL7371

🍴 ◀ White Hart

Oakdene, Higham Road, Tuddenham, Bury St Edmunds, Suffolk, IP28 6SG.
Very comfortable home from home, ideally situated for Newmarket Races
Tel: **01638 718822** Mrs Titcombe.
D: £17.50 **S:** £18.50.
Open: All Year (not Xmas)
Beds: 2F 1T **Baths:** 1 En 1 Sh
🛏 🅿 (3) ⊬ ☐ 🗙 🔥 🎆 🎥 🛢 ✦

Please respect a B&B's wishes regarding children, animals & smoking.

Gazeley to Knettishall Heath

You are now in the open heath of **the Breckland**. The way through Suffolk leads to **Icklingham**, one of whose two churches is medieval and thatched and whose mill is recorded in the Domesday Book; nearby **West Stow Country Park** has a reconstructed Saxon village, accurately based on excavation work. The route takes you around the west and north of the **King's Forest**, planted from 1935 to celebrate the silver jubilee of George V, to **Euston**, not the London station but a village close to Euston Hall, an attractive eighteenth-century house and grounds with lakes, open to the public on Thursdays. The earlier house was a favourite haunt of the seventeenth-century diarist John Evelyn. From Euston it's on to **Knettishall Heath Country Park**, on the banks of the Little Ouse.

King's Forest 15

National Grid Ref: TL8173

🍴 🍺 Red Lion

North Stow Farm, *King's Forest, Bury St Edmunds, Suffolk, IP28 6UX.*
Listed Georgian farmhouse in middle of Breckland pine forest
Tel: **01842 890356**
Ms Kosviner.
D: £18.00-£18.00 **S:** £18.00-£18.00.
Open: All Year
Beds: 1F 1D 1T
Baths: 1 Pr
🛏 🅿 (10) 🛏 ✕ 🍴 🛏 🎦 🍴 ⌀ ⌀

Barnham 16

National Grid Ref: TL8779

🍴 🍺 Grafton Arms, Dolphin

East Farm, *Barnham, Thetford, Norfolk, IP24 2PB.*
Come & stay in large welcoming farmhouse and enjoy the farm countryside
Grades: ETC 4 Diamond
Tel: **01842 890231** Mrs Heading.
D: £20.00-£22.50 **S:** £23.00-£25.00.
Open: All Year (not Xmas)
Beds: 1D 1T **Baths:** 2 En
🛏 🅿 (6) ⌀ 🛏 🍴 🎦 🍴 ⌀ ⌀

Hopton 17

National Grid Ref: TL9978

🍴 🍺 The Fox

Holly Bank, *High Street, Hopton, Diss, IP22 2QX.*
Tel: **01953 688147** (also fax no)
Mr & Mrs Tomlinson.
D: £17.50-£17.50 **S:** £20.00-£20.00.
Open: All Year
Beds: 2D 1T **Baths:** 1 Sh
🛏 🅿 (8) ⌀ 🛏 🍴 🎦 ⌀ ⌀
Converted 1960s public house, guests' lounge, comfortable bedrooms. Sauna available at extra cost

STILWELL'S NATIONAL TRAIL COMPANION

46 Long Distance Footpaths
Where to Stay • Where to Eat

Other guides may show you where to walk, **Stilwell's National Trail Companion** shows your where to stay and eat. The perfect companion guide for Britain's famous national trails and long distance footpaths, Stilwell's makes pre-planning your accommodation easy. It lists B&Bs, hostels, campsites and pubs – in the order they appear along the routes – and includes such vital information as maps, grid references and distance from the path; Tourist Board ratings; the availability of vehicle pick-up, drying facilities and packed lunches. So whether you walk a trail in stages at weekends or in one continuous journey, you'll never be stuck at the end of the day for a hot meal or a great place to sleep.

Enjoy the beauty and adventure of Britain's – and Ireland's – long distance trails with **Stilwell's National Trail Companion**.

Paths in England
Cleveland Way & Tabular Hills Link • Coast to Coast Path • Cotswold Way • Cumbria Way • Dales Way • Essex Way • Greensand Way • Hadrian's Wall • Heart of England Way • Hereward Way • Icknield Way • Macmillan Way • North Downs Way • Oxfordshire Way • Peddars Way and Norfolk Coast Path • Pennine Way • Ribble Way • The Ridgeway • Shropshire Way • South Downs Way • South West Coast Path • Staffordshire Way • Tarka Trail • Thames Path • Two Moors Way • Vanguard Way • Viking Way • Wayfarer's Walk • Wealdway • Wessex Ridgeway • Wolds Way

Paths in Ireland
Beara Way • Dingle Way • Kerry Way • Ulster Way • Western Way • Wicklow Way

Paths in Scotland
Fife Coastal Walk • Southern Upland Way • Speyside Way • West Highland Way

Paths in Wales
Cambrian Way • Glyndwr's Way • Offa's Dyke Path • Pembrokeshire Coast Path • Wye Valley Walk

£9.95 from all good bookstores (ISBN 1-900861-17-8) or £10.95 (inc p&p) from Stilwell Publishing Ltd, 59 Charlotte Road, London EC2A 3QW (020 7739 7179)

Lancashire Cycleway

At 250 miles, the **Lancashire Cycleway** is one of the longer county cycle routes, and really consists of two circular routes, around the northern and southern halves of the county, together forming a great figure of eight, linking up at the Ribble Valley town of Whalley. The north end of the northern circle links up with the *Cumbria Cycleway* - those with bags of energy and more time can undertake the two cycleways together to make a massive 500-mile tour of the beautiful northwest corner of England. The Lancashire route is signposted with blue cycle silhouette signs with a letter 'N' for the northern circle or 'S' for the southern circle, and can be cycled in either direction, but the County Council recommend cycling clockwise, to beat the prevailing southwesterly wind. The description that follows takes the route clockwise around the northern circle and then clockwise around the southern circle, starting and finishing both sections in Whalley.

A detailed **guide booklet** to the cycleway route is available free from the County Public Relations Officer, PO Box 78, County Hall, Preston PR1 8XJ, tel 01772 263521. In addition, over 200 attractions in the county are list-

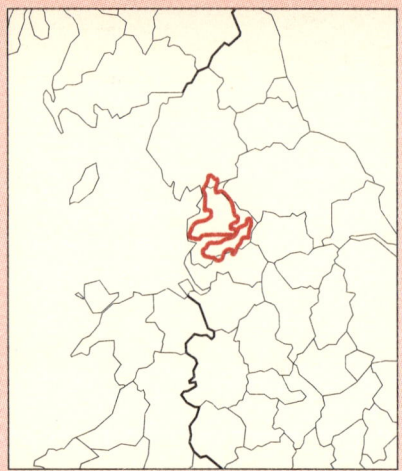

ed in a free leaflet, 'Great Days Out in Lancashire', available from the same address.

Maps: Ordnance Survey 1:50,000 Landranger series: 97, 98, 102, 103, 108, 109

Trains: Whalley is served by trains from Manchester and elsewhere. Numerous places on or near the route are served by the rail network.

Hurst Green   1

National Grid Ref: SD6838

▲ **Hurst Green YHA Camping Barn,** Greengore Farm, Hurst Green, Blackburn, Lancashire.
Actual grid ref: SD674389
Tel: **01200 28366 Adults:** £3.35+ self-catering facilities
Simple barn. Henry VII is reputed to have stayed at the hunting lodge at Greengore Farm. ADVANCE BOOKING ESSENTIAL

Ribchester   2

National Grid Ref: SD6435

▶✚ Hall's Arms, Punch Bowl, Black Bull, White Bull

New House Farm, Preston Road, Ribchester, Preston, Lancs, *PR3 3XL*.
Actual grid ref: SD648354
Old renovated farmhouse, rare breeds
Tel: **01254 878954** Bamber.
D: £18.00-£22.00
S: £22.00-£25.00.
Open: All Year
Beds: 1F 1D 1T
Baths: 3 En
🛏 (4) 🅿 (8) ⌿ 🗖 👤 🛏 🎖 ⅴ ⚡ 🚲

Smithy Farm, Huntingdon Hall Lane, Dutton, Ribchester, Preston, Lancs, *PR3 2ZT*.
Unspoilt countryside 15 mins M6. Friendly hospitality, children half price
Tel: **01254 878250** Jackson.
D: £12.50-£12.50
S: £18.00-£18.00.
Open: Mar to Nov
Beds: 1F 1D 1T
Baths: 1 Sh
🛏 🅿 🗖 👤 🗙 ✕ 🛏 ⅴ ⅰ ⚡ 🚲

Knowle Green   3

National Grid Ref: SD6338

▶✚ New Drop Inn

Oak Lea, Clitheroe Road, Knowle Green, Longridge, Preston, Lancs, *PR3 2YS*.
Ribble Valley Victorian country house, gardens, views, welcoming family atmosphere
Tel: **01254 878486** (also fax no) Mrs Mellor.
D: £18.00-£22.00 **S:** £20.00-£22.00.
Open: All Year (not Xmas)
Beds: 1D 2T 1S
Baths: 2 En 1 Pr
🅿 (4) ⌿ 🗖 👤 🛏 ⅲ ⅴ ⅰ ⚡ 🚲

Longridge   4

National Grid Ref: SD6037

▶✚ Alston Arms

14 Whittingham Road, Longridge, Preston, Lancs, *PR3 2AA*.
Homely, good breakfasts, scenic area, motorways, accessibility sports, shopping, theatres
Tel: **01772 783992** Morley.
D: £18.00-£18.00 **S:** £18.00-£18.00.
Open: All Year
Beds: 1F 1T 1S **Baths:** 1 Sh
🛏 ✚ (4) 🗖 👤 🛏 ⅲ ⅴ

Goosnargh   5

National Grid Ref: SD5536

▶✚ Green Man, The Grapes

Isles Field Barn, Syke House Lane, Goosnargh, Preston, Lancs, *PR3 2EN*.
Actual grid ref: SD561398
Spacious accommodation surrounded by beautiful countryside. Hearty breakfast, friendly welcome
Tel: **01995 640398** Mr McHugh.
D: £19.00-£19.00 **S:** £19.00-£19.00.
Open: All Year
Beds: 1F 1D 1T **Baths:** 3 En
🛏 🅿 (6) 🗖 👤 🛏 ⅲ ⅴ ⚡ 🚲

1 Willow Grove, Goosnargh, Preston, PR3 2DE.
Private house, village location, close to M6, M55, Blackpool, Lancaster
Tel: **01772 865455**
Mrs Dewhurst.
D: £15.00-£15.00
S: £15.00-£15.00.
Open: All Year (not Xmas)
Beds: 1D 1T 1S
Baths: 1 Sh
🛌 ⌦ ☐ 🖳 ▥ Ⓥ ⚡ 🚲

S = Price range for a single person in a room

Bilsborrow 6

National Grid Ref: SD5139

🅙🅐 Roebuck Inn

***Olde Duncombe House,** Garstang Road, Bilsborrow, Preston, Lancs, PR3 0RE.*
Grades: ETC 3 Diamond
Tel: **01995 640336** Mr Bolton.
D: £22.50-£25.00 **S:** £35.00-£39.50.
Open: All Year
Beds: 1F 5D 1T 2S **Baths:** 9 En
🛌 🅟 (2) ☐ 🖰 🐾 🖳 ▥ Ⓥ 🐾
Traditional cottage-style family run bed & breakfast offering a high standard of accommodation. We are situated alongside the tranquil Lancaster canal. Ideal for business people and tourists

---

Barton 7

National Grid Ref: SD5137

🅙🅐 WhiteHorse

***Ratcliffe Farm,** White Horse Lane, Barton, Preston, Lancs, PR3 5AH.*
Friendly welcoming lovely farm house in rural area
Tel: **01995 640536**
Mrs Worden.
D: £15.00
S: £15.00.
Open: All Year (not Xmas)
Beds: 1F 1D 2T 1S
Baths: 1 Sh
🛌 🅟 (4) ☐ 🖳 ▥ Ⓥ

All rooms full and nowhere else to stay? Ask the owner if there's anywhere nearby

---

All rates are subject to alteration at the owners' discretion.

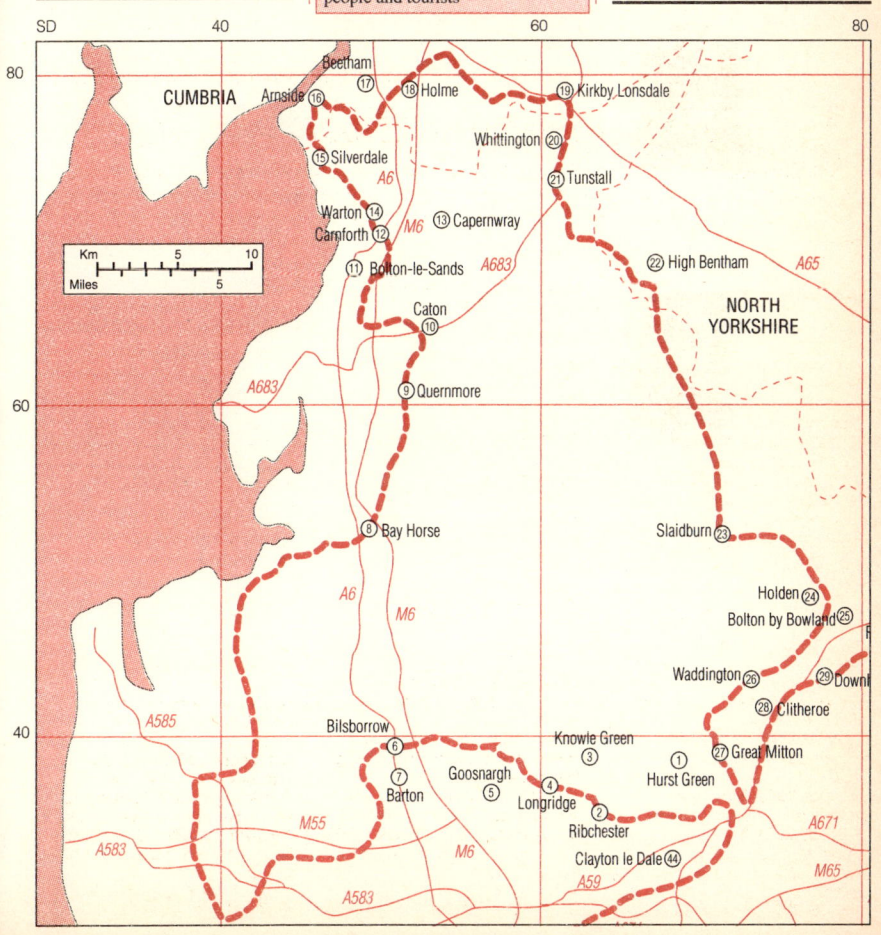

Bay Horse 8

National Grid Ref: SD4953

🏧 🍺 Bay Horse Inn

Saltoke South, Bay Horse, Galgate, Lancaster, *LA2 0HL.*
A beautiful old stone family home set in open countryside
Tel: **01524 752313** Robin.
D: £15.00-£20.00 **S:** £20.00.
Open: All Year (not Xmas)
Beds: 1D 1T **Baths:** 1 Sh
🛬 🅿 (6) 🛏 🍽 📺 ⚲

Quernmore 9

National Grid Ref: SD5160

▲ **Quernmore YHA Camping Barn,** Brow Top Farm, Quernmore, Lancaster.
Actual grid ref: SD528588
Adults: £3.35+
self-catering facilities, parking
Superb remote location on an elevated hilltop with magnificent open views over Morecambe Bay and the Lake District Fells. No electricity: bring a torch. Farm cafe 1m.
ADVANCE BOOKING ESSENTIAL

Caton 10

National Grid Ref: SD5364

14 Brookhouse Road, Caton, Lancaster, *LA2 9QT.*
Friendly welcome set in the Lune Valley. Ideal for walking
Tel: **01524 770271** Miss Beattle.
D: £18.00-£19.50 **S:** £18.00-£20.00.
Open: All Year
Beds: 1F 1D 1T 1S
Baths: 1 En 1 Sh
🛬 🅿 (3) 🛏 ⚲

All cycleways are popular: you are well-advised to book ahead

---

Bolton-le-Sands 11

National Grid Ref: SD4868

🏧 🍺 Robin Hood, Railway Inn

Row-Bar, 4 Whin Grove, Bolton-le-Sands, Carnforth, Lancs, *LA5 8DD.*
Actual grid ref: SD482752
Tel: **01524 735369** Udall.
D: £16.00-£16.00 **S:** £20.00.
Open: Easter to 1
Beds: 2D **Baths:** 2 En
🛬 🛏 📺
Friendly family-run private home close to M6 and Lakes

Carnforth 12

National Grid Ref: SD4970

🏧 🍺 Royal Hotel, County Hotel, Bay Horse, Eagle's Head, Malt Shovel, George Washington

26 Victoria Street, Carnforth, Lancs, *LA5 9ED.*
Small, family-run guest house situated opposite the canal. 6 miles from Lancaster and Morecambe
Tel: **01524 732520** Dickinson.
D: £13.00-£15.00 **S:** £13.00-£15.00.
Open: All Year
Beds: 1F 1D 1T 2S **Baths:** 1 Sh
🅿 (2) 🛏 📺

Capernwray 13

National Grid Ref: SD5371

Capernwray House, Capernwray, Carnforth, Lancs, *LA6 1AE.*
Beautiful country house. Panoramic views. Tastefully decorated throughout. Close Lakes, Dales, Lancaster
Grades: ETC 4 Diamond
Tel: **01524 732363** (also fax no)
Mrs Smith.
D: £21.00-£23.00 **S:** £20.00-£27.50.
Open: All Year (not Xmas)
Beds: 2D 1T 2S
Baths: 3 En 1 Sh
🛬 (5) 🅿 (8) 🛏 ✕ 📺 ⚲

Warton 14

National Grid Ref: SD5072

🏧 🍺 Malt Shovel, George Washington

Cotestone Farm, Sand Lane, Warton, Carnforth, Lancs, *LA5 9NH.*
Near Leighton Moss RSPB Reserve, Lancaster/Morecambe, Lakes & Dales
Tel: **01524 732418** Close.
D: £15.00-£16.00 **S:** £15.00-£16.00.
Open: All Year (not Xmas)
Beds: 1F 1D 1T 1S
Baths: 2 Sh
🛬 🅿 (4) 🛏 📺 ⚲

Whalley to Wrea Green

Whalley nestles in the beautiful Ribble Valley, where wooded lanes form the backdrop to countless picturesque villages. Traces of all aspects of the history of the Red Rose County can be found here - the ruined abbey recalling the Dissolution in the sixteenth century, the railway viaduct a reminder of the county's nineteenth-century history, when it was at the core of the Industrial Revolution. Proceeding west, the route hits the Ribble at **Ribchester**, where the Museum of Roman Antiquities tells of the town's history as a Roman fort, and the many weavers' cottages bear witness to Lancashire's historic textile industry. After the villages of **Inglewhite** and **Bilsborrow** you ride down into **the Fylde**, the plain of Western Lancashire north of the Ribble. Here you pass through the old market town of **Kirkham**, another textile town which made sails for the Royal Navy, and the archetypal picturesque Fylde village of **Wrea Green**.

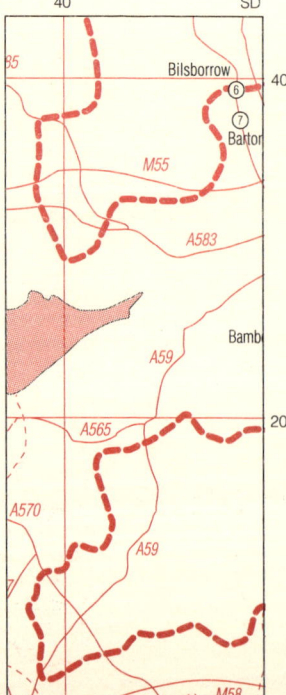

Kiln Croft, 15 Main Street,
Warton, Carnforth, Lancs, LA5 9NR.
Beautiful quiet historic location.
Own organic meat and vegetables
Tel: **01524 735788** Mrs Holmes.
D: £18.50 **S:** £22.50.
Open: All Year
Beds: 3F 1D
Baths: 4 En
⚅ 🅿 (8) 🛏 🗙 🚲 🏠 Ⓥ 🛇 ⚡ ✦

Silverdale   15

National Grid Ref: SD4675

🍴 🍺 The Ship

Havendale, 58 Emesgate Lane,
Silverdale, Carnforth, Lancs,
LA5 0RN.
Family home with good views on
outskirts of village ideal for touring
Lakes, Dales
Tel: **01524 701833** Ms Rushworth.
Fax no: 01524 701884
D: £16.00 **S:** £25.00.
Open: All Year
Beds: 2F **Baths:** 2 En
⚅ 🅿 (4) ✦ 🏠 Ⓥ 🛇 ✦ ⚵

S = Price range for a single

person in a room

Arnside   16

National Grid Ref: SD4578

🍴 🍺 The Albion

▲ *Arnside Youth Hostel,*
Oakfield Lodge, Redhills Road,
Arnside, Carnforth, Lancashire, LA5
0AT.
Actual grid ref: SD452783
Tel: **01524 761781**
Under 18: £6.20 **Adults:** £9.15
evening meal at 7.00pm, television,
games room, showers, laundry
facilities
*A few minutes' walk from the shore
with views across Morecambe Bay
to the Lakeland Fells. A mellow
stone house on the edge of a
coastal village on the Kent estuary.
RSPB reserve nearby*

Willowfield Hotel, The
*Promenade, Arnside, Carnforth,
Lancs,* LA5 0AD.
Actual grid ref: SD455785
Non-smoking family-run hotel in
superb estuary-side location
Grades: ETC 4 Diamond,
AA 4 Diamond, RAC 4 Diamond
Tel: **01524 761354** Mr Kerr.
D: £21.00-£26.00 **S:** £21.00-£36.00.
Open: All Year
Beds: 2F 3D 3T 2S
Baths: 7 En 2 Sh
⚅ 🅿 (8) ✦ 🗙 🚲 🏠 Ⓥ 🛇 ✦ ⚵

Stonegate, The Promenade,
Arnside, Carnforth, Lancs, LA5 0AA.
Actual grid ref: SD455786
Stonegate offers comfort &
relaxation in AONB overlooking
tidal estuary with panoramic
views
Tel: **01524 762560** (also fax no)
D: £19.50-£22.50
S: £22.00-£25.00.
Open: All Year
Beds: 2D 1T 1S
Baths: 2 En 1 Pr
⚅ (8) ✦ 🛏 🚲 🏠 Ⓥ 🛇 ⚡ 🚲

Beetham   17

National Grid Ref: SD4979

🍴 🍺 The Wheatsheaf

Barn Close, Beetham, Milnthorpe,
LA7 7AL.
Peaceful rural setting, large garden,
4 miles (J35) M6
Grades: ETC 3 Diamond
Tel: **015395 63191** (also fax no)
Mrs Robinson.
D: £18.00-£23.00
S: £20.00-£30.00.
Open: All Year
Beds: 2T
Baths: 1 En 1 Pr
⚅ (9) 🅿 (10) ✦ 🛏 🚲 🏠 Ⓥ 🛇 ✦ ⚵

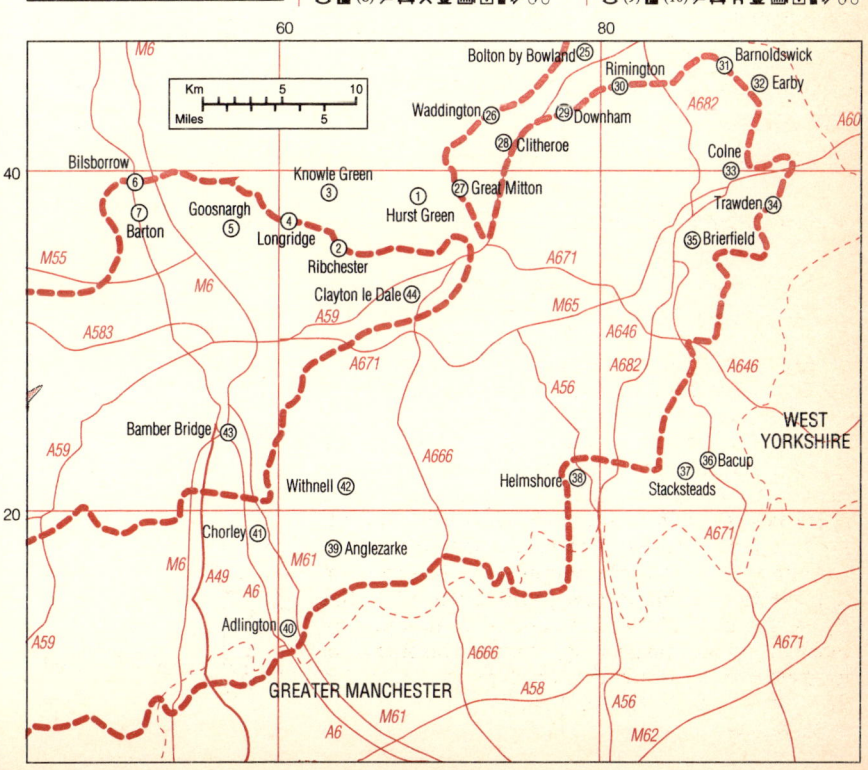

Holme 18

National Grid Ref: SD5279

ᴴⁱ◖ Smithy Inn

Marwin House, *Duke Street, Holme, Carnforth, LA6 1PY.*
Gateway to Lake District, Yorkshire Dales. M6 (J36) 5 minutes
Grades: ETC 2 Diamond
Tel: **01524 781144** (also fax no)
D: £16.00-£18.00.
S: £17.00-£19.00.
Open: All Year
Beds: 1F 1T
Baths: 1 Sh
⛺ ₱ (3) ⅏◻ 🖐 🎋 ▥ Ⓥ ᵭ ⩚ ⚴

Kirkby Lonsdale 19

National Grid Ref: SD6178

ᴴⁱ◖ Kings Arms, Sun Inn, Lunesdale Arms

9 Mill Brow House, *Kirkby Lonsdale, Carnforth, Lancs, LA6 2AT.*
Actual grid ref: SD612786
Wonderful views of river, shops/pubs nearby, holiday apartment available
Tel: **015242 71615** (also fax no)
Mrs Nicholson.
D: £18.00-£21.00 S: £20.00-£25.00.
Open: Easter to Oct
Beds: 1D 1T
Baths: 2 Sh
⛺ ₱ (2) ⅏ 🎋 ▥ Ⓥ ⚴

Whittington 20

National Grid Ref: SD6076

ᴴⁱ◖ Dragons Head

The Dragon's Head, *Main Street, Whittington, Carnforth, LA6 2NY.*
Small country pub in Lune valley 2 miles west of Lowesdale
Tel: **015242 72383**
D: £20.00-£25.00.
S: £20.00-£25.00.
Open: All Year
Beds: 1F 1D 1S
Baths: 1 Sh
⛺ (5) ₱ (10) ◻ 🐓 🗙 🎋 ▥ Ⓥ ⚴

Tunstall 21

National Grid Ref: SD6073

ᴴⁱ◖ Lunesdale Arms

Barnfield Farm, *Tunstall, Kirkby Lonsdale, Carnforth, Lancs, LA6 2QP.*
Actual grid ref: SD607736
1702 family farmhouse on a 200 acre working farm
Tel: **015242 74284**
Mrs Stephenson.
Fax no: 01524 274284
D: £16.00 S: £17.50.
Open: All Year (not Xmas)
Beds: 1F/T 1D
Baths: 2 Sh
⛺ ₱ ⅏◻ 🎋 ▥ Ⓥ ᵭ ⩚ ⚴

High Bentham 22

National Grid Ref: SD6669

ᴴⁱ◖ Punch Bowl

Fowgill Park Farm, *High Bentham, Lancaster, LA2 7AH.*
Beamed farmhouse enjoying panoramic views, close to caves and waterfalls
Grades: ETC 4 Diamond
Tel: **015242 61630** Mrs Metcalfe.
D: £17.00-£20.00.
Open: Easter to Oct
Beds: 1D 1T
Baths: 2 En
⛺ ₱ (4) ⅏◻ 🐓 🗙 🎋 ▥ Ⓥ ᵭ ⚴

Slaidburn 23

National Grid Ref: SD7152

▲ **Slaidburn Youth Hostel,** *King's House, Slaidburn, Clitheroe, Lancashire, BB7 3ER.*
Actual grid ref: SD711523
Tel: **01200 446656. Advance bookings: 015242 41567**
Under 18: £4.65 **Adults:** £6.80
self-catering facilities, showers, shop
Basic village accommodation for walkers and cyclists in the middle of the Forest of Bowland, at the centre of the picturesque village of Slaidburn. C17th former inn: basic facilities with an open fire and central heating

Holden 24

National Grid Ref: SD7749

Baygate Farm, *Holden, Bolton-By-Bowland, Clitheroe, Lancs, BB7 4PQ.*
Actual grid ref: SD758498
Family-run farm in Trough of Bowland
Tel: **01200 447643**
Townson.
D: £14.00 S: £14.00.
Open: All Year (not Xmas)
Beds: 3T
Baths: 1 Sh
⛺ (6) ₱ ◻ 🎋 ᵭ ⩚

Bolton by Bowland 25

National Grid Ref: SD7849

Middle Flass Lodge, *Settle Road, Bolton by Bowland, Clitheroe, Yorkshire, BB7 4NY.*
Idyllic countryside location. Chef prepared cuisine. Cosy rooms. Friendly welcome
Grades: ETC 3 Diamond, AA 4 Diamond
Tel: **01200 447259**
Mrs Simpson.
Fax no: 01200 447300
D: £20.00-£26.00 S: £25.00-£31.00.
Open: All Year
Beds: 1F 2D 2T
Baths: 3 Pr
⛺ ₱ (24) ⅏◻ 🗙 🎋 ▥ Ⓥ ᵭ ⩚ ⚴

Wrea Green to the Lancaster Canal

Cycling north through the Fylde, you cross the River Wyre, and pass by the old marsh village of **Pilling** before crossing the **Lancaster Canal**. A possible detour here takes you to the lovely old port at **Glasson Dock**, from where you may wish to follow the River Lune Path north as an alternative to the designated route of the cycleway, rejoining it north of Lancaster. Either way, the county town is well worth a look. **Lancaster** boasts many elegant Georgian buildings, testament to its shadily prosperous period as a major port in the slave trade; the town's roots go back way beyond then to Roman Britain. Landmarks include Lancaster Castle, whose Norman keep overlooking the Lune presides over a crown court and the county's Shire Hall, the Priory Church of St Mary, a former Benedictine foundation notable for its Saxon doorway, the seventeenth-century Judges' Lodging (now a museum) and the grounds of the Ashton Memorial, sporting a butterfly and palm house.

Spring Head Farm, *Bolton-by-Bowland, Clitheroe, Lancs, BB7 4LU.*
Actual grid ref: SD796505
Comfortable farmhouse in garden setting on outskirts of attractive village
Tel: **01200 447245** Mrs Lund.
D: £15.00-£25.00 S: £10.00-£20.00.
Open: Easter to Dec
Beds: 1D 1T
Baths: 1 Sh
⛺ ₱ (4) ⅏◻ 🗙 🎋 ▥ Ⓥ ⩚ ⚴

Please don't camp
on *anyone's* land
without first obtaining
their permission.

Waddington 26

National Grid Ref: SD7243

🏠🍺 Moorcock Inn, Duke of York

Moorcock Inn, *Slaidburn Road,
Waddington, Clitheroe, Lancs,
BB7 3AA.*
A warm welcome awaits at this
friendly country inn
Grades: ETC 2 Star
Tel: **01200 422333** Fillary.
D: £30.00-£35.00 **S:** £38.00-£42.00.
Open: All Year
Beds: 3D 8T
Baths: 10 Pr 1 Sh
🛇 🅿(15) 🛏🍽🏃🍴🎵📺📋💷✓

Waddington Arms, *Clitheroe Road,
Waddington, Clitheroe, Lancs,
BB7 3HP.*
Traditional country inn, real beer,
real food, real bedrooms
Tel: **01200 423262** Warburton.
D: £25.00-£35.00 **S:** £35.00-£45.00.
Open: All Year
Beds: 4D 2T
Baths: 6 En
🛇 🅿(50) ⚡🛏🍽🏃🍴🎵📺♿📋💷✓🚲

Peter Barn Country House, *Cross
Lane, Waddington, Clitheroe,
Lancs, BB7 3JH.*
Luxurious peaceful, warm. Squashy
sofas, log fires, home-made mar-
malade. Rabbits, birds everywhere
Tel: **01200 428585** Mrs Smith.
D: £19.50 **S:** £25.00.
Open: All Year (not Xmas)
Beds: 2D 1T
Baths: 2 En 1 Pr
🛇 (12) 🅿(6) ⚡🛏🍴🎵📺✓

Great Mitton 27

National Grid Ref: SD7138

Aspinall Arms Hotel, *Great
Mitton, Clitheroe, Lancs, BB7 9PQ.*
Actual grid ref: SD718388
Tel: **01254 826223** Mr Morrell.
D: £22.50-£22.50
S: £30.00-£30.00.
Open: All Year
Beds: 2D 1S
Baths: 3 En
🅿(50) 🛏🎵📺📋💷✓🚲
Originally the ferryman's house, the
Aspinall Arms dates back to coach
and horses times. We
provide good quality home-cooked
meals and a wide range of cask ales
and quality wines. Good
quality bedrooms with en suite
showers. Fishing by arrangement

Planning a longer
stay? Always ask for
any special rates.

Clitheroe 28

National Grid Ref: SD7441

🏠🍺 Swan With Two Necks, Edisford Bridge
Inn, Edisford Inn

Brooklands, *9 Pendle Road,
Clitheroe, Lancs, BB7 1JQ.*
Actual grid ref: SD750414
A warm welcome. Detached com-
fortable Victorian home. Town
centre nearby
Grades: ETC 3 Diamond
Tel: **01200 422797** (also fax no)
Lord.
D: £16.00-£19.50 **S:** £17.00-£22.00.
Open: All Year
Beds: 1D 2T **Baths:** 1 En 1 Sh
🛇 🅿(5) 🛏🏃🎵📺📋💷✓🚲

Selborne House, *Back Commons,
Clitheroe, Lancs, BB7 2DX.*
Detached house on quiet lane
giving peace and tranquillity.
Excellent for walking,
birdwatching, fishing
Grades: ETC 3 Diamond
Tel: **01200 423571** (also fax no)
Barnes.
D: £18.50-£20.00 **S:** £21.00-£22.50.
Open: All Year
Beds: 1F 2D 1T **Baths:** 4 En
🛇 (1) 🅿(4) 🛏🏃🍴🎵📺📋💷✓🚲

Downham 29

National Grid Ref: SD7844

▲ **Downham YHA Camping
Barn**, *Downland Estate, Downham,
Clitheroe, Lancashire.*
Actual grid ref: SD795445
Tel: **01200 28366 Adults:** £3.35+
self-catering facilities
*Simple barn. Near the foot of
Pendle Hill. ADVANCE BOOKING
ESSENTIAL*

Rimington 30

National Grid Ref: SD8045

🏠🍺 Asheton Arms, Moorcock Inn

Wytha Farm, *Rimington, Clitheroe,
Lancs, BB7 4EQ.*
Working farmhouse with fantastic
views, warm welcome, visitors' TV
lounge
Tel: **01200 445295** Oliver.
D: £15.00-£20.00 **S:** £17.50-£20.00.
Open: All Year
Beds: 1F 1D 1S
Baths: 1 Pr
🛇 (1) 🅿(4) ⚡🛏🏃🍴🎵📺📋💷✓🚲

Barnoldswick 31

National Grid Ref: SD8746

🏠🍺 Fosters Arms, Fanny Grey

Monks House, *5 Manchester Road,
Barnoldswick, Colne, Lancs,
BB8 5NZ.*
Georgian house dated 1734,
situated town centre, close to open
countryside. Walks, splendid views
Tel: **01282 814423** (also fax no)
Mrs Robinson.
D: £16.00-£17.00 **S:** £16.00-£17.00.
Open: All Year
Beds: 2T 2S **Baths:** 2 Sh
🛇 (6) 🅿(3) 🛏🍴🎵📺📋💷✓🚲

High season,
bank holidays and
special events mean
low availability
everywhere.

The Lancaster Canal to Whalley

From here you ride north through **Carnforth**, which offers
railway enthusiasts the Steamtown Railway Museum, to the
small coastal village of **Silverdale**, and then over the county
boundary to **Arnside** in Cumbria; the headland between
Silverdale and Arnside, overlooking Morecambe Bay, is a
designated Area of Outstanding Natural Beauty. The next
stretch, as far as Kirkby Lonsdale, is also part of the *Cumbria
Cycleway*, and takes you over Farleton Fell to **Hutton Roof**,
with its panoramic views. **Kirkby Lonsdale** is famous for the
Devil's Bridge, as well as 'Ruskin's View', behind St Mary's
Church. From here it is south through the wooded Lune
Valley, and then the beautiful gritstone moorland of the **Forest
of Bowland**, another designated Area of Outstanding Natural
Beauty which belonged historically to the old rival, Yorkshire.
The village of **Slaidburn** offers welcome refreshment at the
thirteenth-century Hark and Bounty Inn; after this the route
takes you through the old Ribble Valley villages of **Sawley**,
with its twelfth-century abbey ruins, and **Waddington**, back to
Whalley.

Foster's House, 203 Gisburn Road, Barnoldswick, Lancs, BB18 5JU.
A warm welcome awaits at our beautiful home from home
Grades: ETC 2 Diamond
Tel: 01282 850718
Mr & Mrs Walker.
D: £17.50-£20.00
S: £17.50-£25.00.
Open: All Year
Beds: 2D 2T
Baths: 3 En 1 Sh
🛇 🅿 (4) ⏏ 🏠 🎵 🛏 🖥 & ♥ ✦ 🚲

Earby 32

National Grid Ref: SD9046

▲ **Earby Youth Hostel**, Glen Cottage, Birch Hall Lane, Earby, Colne, Lancashire, BB8 6JX.
Actual grid ref: SD915468
Tel: **01282 842349**
Under 18: £5.65
Adults: £8.35
family bunk rooms, showers, central heating, shop, no smoking
Attractive cottage with own picturesque garden and waterfall, on NE outskirts of Earby

---

Please respect a B&B's wishes regarding children, animals & smoking.

Please don't camp on *anyone's* land without first obtaining their permission.

Colne 33

National Grid Ref: SD8940

🍴 🍺 Hare & Hounds, White Bear

Higher Wanless Farm, Red Lane, Colne, Lancs, BB8 7JP.
Beautifully situated, canalside, lovely walking, ideal for business people, Mill, shops etc
Grades: ETC 4 Diamond, AA 4 Diamond
Tel: **01282 865301** Mitson.
Fax no: 01282 865823
D: £20.00-£24.00 **S:** £20.00-£24.00.
Open: Jan to Nov
Beds: 1F 1T 1S **Baths:** 1 En 1 Sh
🛇 (3) 🅿 (4) ⏏ 🛏 🖥 🖥 ♥ ✦ 🚲

Wickets, 148 Keighley Road, Colne, Lancs, BB8 0PJ.
Edwardian family home overlooking open countryside, comfortable and attractive bedrooms
Grades: ETC 4 Diamond
Tel: **01282 862002**
Mrs Etherington.
Fax no: 01282 859675
D: £18.00-£21.00 **S:** £18.00-£22.00.
Open: All Year (not Xmas)
Beds: 1D 1T 1S
Baths: 1 En 1 Pr
🛇 (11) 🅿 (1) ⏏ 🛏 🖥 🖥 ♥ ✦

Trawden 34

National Grid Ref: SD9138

🍴 🍺 Sun Inn

Middle Beardshaw Head Farm, Trawden, Colne, Lancs, BB8 8PP.
Actual grid ref: SD895395
Grades: ETC 3 Diamond
Tel: **01282 865257** Mrs Mann.
D: £18.50-£20.00 **S:** £18.50-£20.00.
Open: All Year (not Xmas)
Beds: 1F 2D 3S
Baths: 1 En 1 Sh
🛇 🅿 (10) ⏏ ✕ 🛏 🖥 🖥 ♥ ✦ 🚲
C18th beamed farmhouse in picturesque setting of woodland, pools and meadows. Furnished in period. Mullion windows, country garden, home-grown fruit and vegetables. Artist in residence with studio facilities; art holidays, walking, historical tours a speciality. French, Italian, Spanish and some Japanese spoken. Green Lantern Award

Brierfield 35

National Grid Ref: SD8436

🍴 🍺 Harper's Inn

179 Reedley Road, Brierfield, Nelson, Lancs, BB9 5ES.
Situated in a quiet residential area offering warm comfortable accommodation
Tel: **01282 616284**
Mrs Leedham.
D: £15.00 **S:** £15.00.
Open: All Year (not Xmas)
Beds: 1T 1S
Baths: 1 Sh
🛇 (8) 🅿 (3) ⏏ 🛏 🖥 🖥 ♥ ✦

The Southern Circle

The northeastern half of the southern circle is a demanding up-and-down ride through the Lancashire Pennines. **Clitheroe** is a busy market town with a twelfth-century Castle keep. From here the route takes you around Pendle Hill; here in 1652 George Fox had the vision that led him to found the Society of Friends. **Downham** is an English village as archetypal as Castle Combe (see the *Wiltshire Cycleway*), but here church, pub, village green and stocks sit astride a hilltop. Now the route takes you to **Barnoldswick**, and around Colne, Nelson and Burnley - you are at the eastern end of Lancashire's central belt of industrial towns. Wycoller Country Park in the **Forest of Trawden** offers welcome respite; Towneley Hall, on the route around Burnley, is a fourteenth century house hosting an art gallery and museum with collections of eighteenth and nineteenth century paintings and decorative arts, and a natural history

centre with an aquarium.

Now it's south, by Rawtenstall, Haslingden and Ramsbottom. The Peel Tower at **Holcombe** commemorates Sir Robert Peel; Turton Tower, by **Chapeltown**, is a medieval tower that was extended over the centuries into a country house: it has a local history museum and nine acres of woodland gardens. The next stretch descends off the West Pennine Moors onto the West Lancashire Plain, skirting the north of Greater Manchester and crossing the Leeds and Liverpool Canal a number of times. The beautiful Lever Park is on the edge of Lower Rivington Reservoir; Beacon Country Park, east of Skelmersdale, affords splendid views in all directions. The route now rounds **Ormskirk** and heads northwards, taking you near the Wildfowl and Wetland Centre at Martin Mere. The final stretch back into **Whalley** takes you south of Leyland and between Preston and Blackburn; attractions along the way include fifteenth-century houses at Rufford and Hoghton.

Bacup 36

National Grid Ref: SD8622

🍺 🍴 Rose & Bowl, The Crown

***Pasture Bottom Farm**, Bacup, Lancs, OL13 0UZ.*
Comfortable farmhouse bed & breakfast in a quiet rural area on a working beef farm
Grades: ETC 3 Diamond
Tel: **01706 873790** (also fax no) Isherwood.
D: £15.00-£16.00 **S:** £15.00-£16.00.
Open: All Year (not Xmas)
Beds: 1D 2T
Baths: 2 En 1 Pr 1 Sh
🛏 🄿 (4) ⟋ 🛏 🗙 ⚓ 🎯 🖤 🖢 ⟋

***Oakenclough Farm**, Oakenclough Road, Bacup, Lancashire, OL13 9ET.*
300-year-old farmhouse on edge of moors. Very peaceful
Tel: **01706 879319** (also fax no) Mr & Mrs Worswick.
D: £17.50-£17.50 **S:** £16.00-£22.50.
Open: All Year
Beds: 1F 1T
Baths: 1 En 1 Pr
🛏 🄿 (3) 🗖 🛏 🗙 ⚓ 🎯 🖤 🖢 ⟋ 🚲

Stacksteads 37

National Grid Ref: SD8421

***Glen Heights**, 190 Booth Road, Stacksteads, Bacup, Lancs, OL13 0TH.*
Comfortable guest house; quiet location, lovely views, near motorway network
Tel: **01706 875459** Graham.
D: £15.00-£16.00 **S:** £18.50-£19.50.
Open: All Year
Beds: 1D 1T 1S
Baths: 1 Sh
🛏 (12) 🄿 (3) 🗖 🛏 🗙 ⚓ 🎯 🖤 ⟋

Helmshore 38

National Grid Ref: SD7821

🍺 🍴 White Horse

***The Willows**, 41 Cherrytree Way, Helmshore, Rossendale, Lancs, BB4 4JZ.*
The Willows - warm welcome awaits, beautiful views, swimming pool
Tel: **01706 212698** Mrs Tod.
D: £18.00-£22.00.
Open: All Year (not Xmas)
Beds: 1D 1T
Baths: 2 En
🛏 🄿 (2) ⟋ 🗖 ⚓ 🎯 🖤 🖢 ⟋ 🚲

Anglezarke 39

National Grid Ref: SD6317

🍺 🍴 Yew Tree

***Jepsons Farm**, Moor Road, Anglezarke, Chorley, Lancs, PR6 9DQ.*
Actual grid ref: SD622169
Beautiful C17th stone farmhouse
Tel: **01257 481691** Hilton.
D: £20.00-£30.00 **S:** £20.00-£30.00.
Open: All Year (not Xmas)
Beds: 1F 1D 1T 1S
Baths: 1 En 1 Sh
🛏 🄿 (10) 🗖 🗙 ⚓ 🎯 🖤 🖢 ⟋ 🚲

Adlington 40

National Grid Ref: SD6013

🍺 🍴 The Millstone

***Briarfield House**, Bolton Road, Anderton, Adlington, Chorley, Lancs, PR6 9HW.*
In own grounds, beautiful views over open countryside. Private parking
Tel: **01257 480105** Mrs Baldwin.
Fax no: 0831 651704
D: £17.50 **S:** £20.00.
Open: All Year
Beds: 1F 2T
Baths: 1 Pr 1 Sh
🛏 ⟋ 🗖 ⚓ 🎯 🖤

Chorley 41

National Grid Ref: SD5817

🍺 🍴 The Hartwood, Seaview Inn

***The Roost**, 81 Pall Mall, Chorley, Lancs, PR7 3LT.*
Late Victorian, homely atmosphere. Five mins' walk market, town centre
Tel: **01257 263856**
Mr & Mrs Edelston.
D: £18.00-£18.00 **S:** £20.00-£20.00.
Open: All Year
Beds: 1T
Baths: 1 Sh
⟋ 🗖 🗙 ⚓ 🎯 🖤 🚲

***Crowtress Cottage Guest House**, 190 Preston Road, Chorley, Lancashire, PR6 7AZ.*
Traditional Lancashire hospitality in a C18th farmers cottage
Grades: ETC 4 Diamond
Tel: **01257 269380**
D: £22.00-£35.00 **S:** £22.00-£28.00.
Open: All Year
Beds: 1D 1T 1S
Baths: 1 En 1 Sh

Withnell 42

National Grid Ref: SD6321

🍺 🍴 Hare & Hounds

***Kerenza Guest House**, Bolton Road, Withnell, Chorley, Lancs, PR6 8BS.*
Pleasant family home in beautiful countryside. Breakfast our speciality
Tel: **01254 830070** Bayliss.
D: £17.50-£17.50 **S:** £17.50-£17.50.
Open: All Year (not Xmas)
Beds: 2D 1T
🛏 🄿 (6) 🗖 ⚓ 🎯 🖤 🖢 ⟋ 🚲

Bamber Bridge 43

National Grid Ref: SD5626

🍺 🍴 Hob Inn

***Anvil Guest House**, 321 Station Road, Bamber Bridge, Preston, Lancs, PR5 6EE.*
Actual grid ref: SD564254
Comfortable, friendly, near M6 J29, M61 J9, central heating, TV lounge
Tel: **01772 339022** Arkwright.
D: £13.50-£13.50 **S:** £15.00-£15.00.
Open: All Year (not Xmas)
Beds: 2F 4D 3T
Baths: 2 Sh
🛏 🗖 ⚓ 🎯 🖤

Clayton Le Dale 44

National Grid Ref: SD6733

🍺 🍴 Royal Oak

***2 Rose Cottage**, Longsight Road (A59), Clayton le Dale, Blackburn, Lancs, BB1 9EX.*
Picturesque cottage, gateway to Ribble Valley. Comfortable, fully equipped rooms
Tel: **01254 813223** Adderley.
Fax no: 01254 813831
D: £19.00 **S:** £23.00.
Open: All Year
Beds: 1F 1D 2T
Baths: 3 En 1 Pr
🛏 🄿 (4) 🗖 🛏 ⚓ 🎯 🖤 🖢 ⟋ 🚲

Pay B&Bs by cash or cheque and be prepared to pay up front.

Leicestershire County Cycle Route

The **Leicestershire County Cycle Route** is a 140-mile circular tour, which goes in an anticlockwise direction around the inside of the perimeter of most of Leicestershire, and through the middle of the County of Rutland, starting and finishing at Rutland Water. It is routed along quiet country lanes and tracks, almost completely avoiding main roads, through gentle terrain without rigorous climbs.

A detailed **guide leaflet** to the route is available from Leicestershire County Council, Environmental Management, Department of Planning & Transportation, County Hall, Glenfield, Leicester, LE3 8RJ, tel 0116-265 7091. Cycle hire is available from Rutland Water Cycling at Whitwell and at Normanton, tel 01780 86705.

Maps: Ordnance Survey 1:50,000 Landranger series: 128, 129, 130, 140, 141

The major **railway** termini are at Oakham, Stamford, Melton Mowbray, Leicester, Loughborough, Hinckley and Market Harborough.

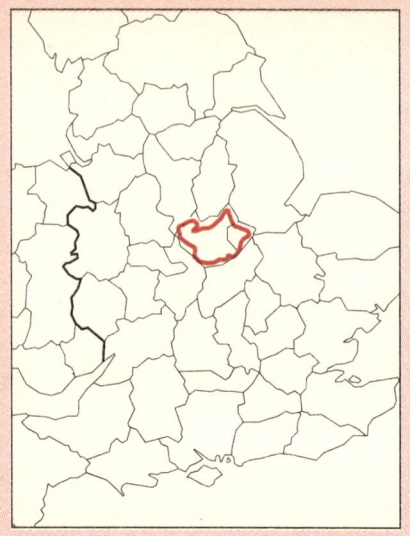

Rutland Water to Belvoir Castle

From Whitwell, on the banks of Rutland Water, you cycle north through the gentle Rutland countryside, and the villages of **Exton**, where the ruins of the early seventeenth-century Old Hall of Exton Park can be seen beyond the village church, Greetham and Thistleton. This stretch runs close to the Viking Way (see Stilwell's *National Trail Companion*), named from the history of this area as part of the Danelaw, ruled by the invaders that the kings of Wessex and England failed to keep at bay.

Through Thistleton Gap, where three counties meet, you take the Bronze Age track called Sewstern Lane into Leicestershire, and follow it north along the border with Lincolnshire before turning west towards **Buckminster**, and then north through a string of old farming villages to **Belvoir Castle**. On the site of a Norman castle, the present extravagant edifice was built in the mid-seventeenth century and rebuilt in 1816. It contains an impressive collection of tapestries and paintings, including Holbein's portrait of Henry VIII, and a garden with seventeenth-century sculptures.

Exton   1
National Grid Ref: SK9211

🍴 ☕ Fox & Hounds

Hall Farm, *Cottesmore Road, Exton, Oakham, Rutland, LE15 8AN.*
Close to Rutland Water and Geoff Barnsdale TV gardens
Tel: **01572 812271**
D: £15.00-£19.50
S: £17.50-£22.00.
Open: All Year (not Xmas)
Beds: 1F 1D 1T
Baths: 1 En 1 Sh
🛇 🅿 (6) ⊬ 🗗 ⊁ ♨ ▥ Ⅴ ∥ ⚲

D = Price range per person sharing in a double room

S = Price range for a single person in a room

Cottesmore   2
National Grid Ref: SK9013

🍴 ☕ Sun Inn

The Tithe Barn, *Clatterpot Lane, Cottesmore, Oakham, Rutland, LE15 7DW.*
Comfortable, spacious, ensuite rooms with a wealth of original features
Grades: ETC 3 Diamond
Tel: **01572 813591**
D: £18.00-£24.00 **S:** £20.00-£35.00.
Open: All Year
Beds: 2F 1D 1T **Baths:** 3 En 1 Pr
🛇 (1) 🅿 (6) ⊬ 🗗 ⊁ ♨ ▥ Ⅴ ▮

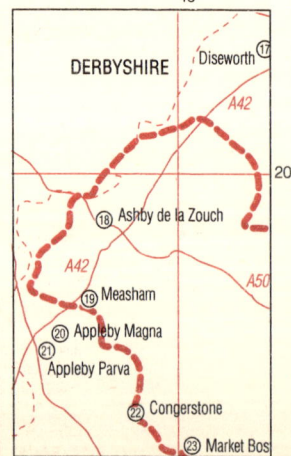

40

DERBYSHIRE   Diseworth 17

A42

20

⑱ Ashby de la Zouch

A42   A50

⑲ Measham

⑳ Appleby Magna

㉑ Appleby Parva

㉒ Congerstone

㉓ Market Bos

Greetham 3

National Grid Ref: SK9214

🍴🍺 The Wheatsheaf

Black Horse Inn, 62 Main Street, *Greetham, Oakham, Rutland,* LE15 7NL.
Actual grid ref: SK924145
Comfortable spacious rooms.
Rutland Water, Creetham Valley
Golf Club nearby
Tel: **01572 812305**
Mrs Harris.
D: £16.00-£16.00 **S:** £20.00-£20.00.
Open: All Year
Beds: 1F 2T **Baths:** 1 Pr 1 Sh
🛇 🅿 (12) 🖊 🗗 🏠 ✗ 🛋 Ⅲ ♦ 🚴

South Witham 4

National Grid Ref: SK9219

🍴🍺 Blue Cow

Rose Cottage, 7 High Street, South *Witham, Grantham, Lincs,* NG33 5QB.
Actual grid ref: SK929192
C18th stone cottage in two acres
midway between
Stamford/Grantham/Rutland Water
Tel: **01572 767757**
Mrs Van Kimmenade.
Fax no: 01572 767199
D: £22.50-£25.00
S: £25.00-£25.00.
Open: All Year
Beds: 1F 1D 1T 2S **Baths:** 3 En
🛇 🅿 (6) 🖊 🗗 🏠 ✗ 🛋 Ⅲ ⑥ 🖩 Ⅴ ♦ 🚴

Pay B&Bs by cash or
cheque and be prepared
to pay up front.

Skillington 5

National Grid Ref: SK8925

🍴🍺 Cross Swords

Sproxton Lodge, Skillington, *Grantham, Lincs,* NG33 5HJ.
Quiet family farm alongside Viking
way. Everyone welcome
Grades: ETC 2 Diamond
Tel: **01476 860307**
Mrs Whatton.
D: £17.00-£18.00
S: £17.00-£18.00.
Open: All Year (not Xmas)
Beds: 1F 1D 1S
Baths: 1 En 1 Sh
🛇 (5) 🅿 (4) 🖊 🗗 ✗ 🛋 Ⅲ 🖩 Ⅴ ♦ 🚴

Croxton Kerrial 6

National Grid Ref: SK8329

The Pottery, Saltby Road, Croxton *Kerrial, Grantham, Lincs,* NG32 1QG.
Actual grid ref: SK837291
2-acre rural site, studio pottery for
quests to view
Tel: **01476 870744** Ms Delamere.
D: £15.00-£15.00 **S:** £17.50-£17.50.
Open: All Year
Beds: 2D **Baths:** 1 Sh
🛇 🅿 (4) 🖊 🗗 ✗ 🛋 Ⅲ 🖩 Ⅴ ♦ 🚴

Redmile 7

National Grid Ref: SK7935

Peacock Farm & Restaurant, & Guest House, Redmile, Vale of *Belvoir, Nottingham,* NG13 0GQ.
Great atmosphere, great food
Tel: **01949 842475** Miss Need.
Fax no: 01949 843127
D: £26.00 **S:** £38.00.
Open: All Year
Beds: 5F 2D 2T 1S
Baths: 6 Pr 1 Sh
🛇 🅿 (20) 🗗 🏠 🛋 Ⅲ Ⅴ

Barkestone-le-Vale 8

National Grid Ref: SK7834

🍴🍺 Windmill Inn

Little Orchard, Chapel Street, *Barkestone-le-Vale, Nottingham,* NG13 0HE.
Picturesque village, 2.5 miles
Belvoir Castle. Convenient Melton
Mowbray, Grantham, Newark,
Nottingham
Tel: **01949 842698** Mrs Fisher.
D: £17.00-£17.00 **S:** £18.00-£18.00.
Open: All Year
Beds: 1F 1D 1T 1S **Baths:** 1 Pr
🛇 (3) 🅿 (4) 🖊 ✗ Ⅲ 🖧 🖩 ♦ 🚴

Please take muddy
boots **off** before
entering premises

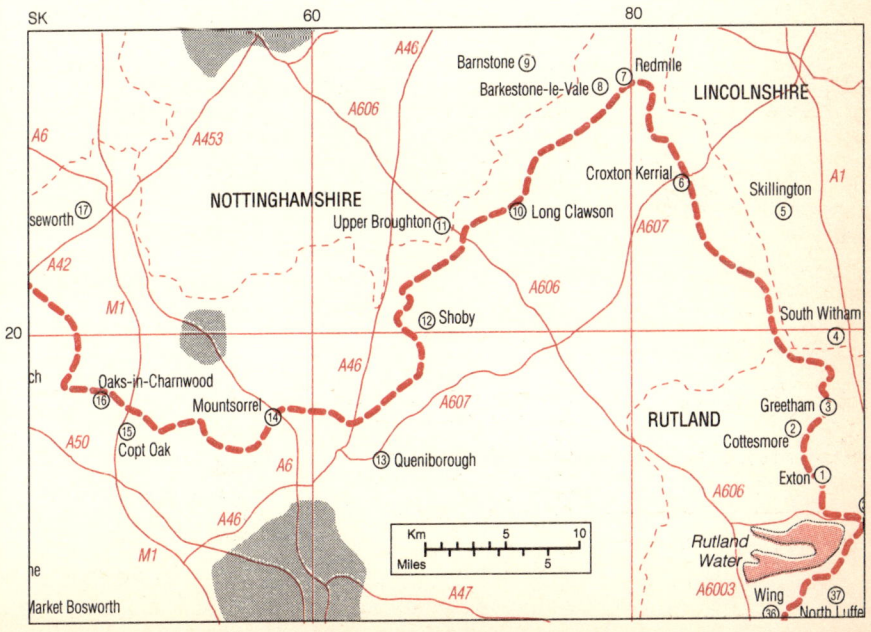

Barnstone 9

National Grid Ref: SK7335

Barnstone Olde House, Barnstone, Nottingham, NG13 9JP.
Central for Newark, Grantham, Nottingham. Landscaped garden, rustic charm, beautiful view
Grades: ETC 3 Diamond
Tel: **01949 860456** (also fax no)
Mrs Maker.
D: £20.00-£25.00
S: £22.50-£30.00.
Open: All Year (not Xmas)
Beds: 2D 1T
Baths: 2 En
ॐ 🅿 (4) 🛏️⛶✗🗕🖳🆚🛡⚡♿

Long Clawson 10

National Grid Ref: SK7227

Elms Farm, 52 East End, Long Clawson, Melton Mowbray, Leics, LE14 4NG.
Warm comfortable old farmhouse village setting in Vale of Belvoir
Tel: **01664 822395**
Mrs Whittard.
Fax no: 01664 823399
D: £17.00-£21.00
S: £18.00-£26.00.
Open: All Year (not Xmas)
Beds: 1F 1D 1S
Baths: 1 En 1 Sh
ॐ 🅿 (4) 🛏️⛶✗🗕🖳🆚🛡⚡♿

Upper Broughton 11

National Grid Ref: SK6826

🔺 *Swan Lodge Bunkhouse Barn (Independent), Station Road, Upper Broughton, Melton Mowbray, Leicestershire, LE14 3BH.*
Actual grid ref: SK677260
Tel: **01664 823686 Adults:** £5.00
self-catering facilities, television, central heating

Shoby 12

National Grid Ref: SK6820

Shoby Lodge Farm, Shoby, Melton Mowbray, Leics, LE14 3PF.
Comfortable spacious farmhouse set in attractive gardens with beautiful views
Tel: **01664 812156** Mrs Lomas.
D: £15.00 **S:** £23.50.
Open: All Year (not Xmas)
Beds: 3D
Baths: 2 En 1 Sh
ॐ (14) 🅿⛶🗕🖳🆚🛡⚡

Please don't camp on *anyone's* land without first obtaining their permission.

Queniborough 13

National Grid Ref: SK6412

🍴🍺 Britannia Horse & Groom

Three Ways Farm, Melton Road, Queniborough, Leicester, Leics, LE7 3FN.
Actual grid ref: SK642129
Welcome to pretty Queniborough. Comfortable quiet bungalow, 0.25 mile A607, links M1
Grades: ETC 3 Diamond
Tel: **0116 260 0472** Mrs Clarke.
D: £20.00-£22.00 **S:** £20.00.
Open: All Year (not Xmas)
Beds: 1F 1T 1S
Baths: 1 Sh
ॐ (5) 🅿 (5) ⛶🗕🖳🆚🛡⚡♿

Mountsorrel 14

National Grid Ref: SK5814

🍴🍺 Quorndon Fox

Barley Loft Guest House, 33a Hawcliffe Road, Mountsorrel, Loughborough, Leics, LE12 7AQ.
Tel: **01509 413514** Mrs Pegg.
D: £17.00-£19.00 **S:** £17.00-£20.00.
Open: All Year
Beds: 2F 1D 1T 2S
Baths: 2 Sh
ॐ 🅿 (12) ⛶🛏️🗕🖳♿♿
Spacious bungalow close to A6 between Leicester and Loughborough. Quiet, rural location, riverside walks, local historical attractions. Comfortable base for working away from home. Guests' fridge, microwave, toaster. Traditional hearty breakfast. Suitable for disabled. Excellent local restaurants, pubs, takeaways

---

Belvoir Castle to Staunton Harold

Shortly after Belvoir, the route turns southwestwards and runs parallel to the Grantham Canal as far as **Long Clawson**, where Stilton cheese is produced. From here you go on to **Old Dalby**, and then south to Hoby and along the River Wreake as far as **Ratcliffe** on the Wreake. From here the route goes through Sileby and crosses the River Soar into **Mountsorrel**. Then on to **Woodhouse Eaves**, a lovely old village built of the local slate. Here you will find Long Close, a 5-acre landscaped garden with wild flowers and shrubs. From here it's a short (if steepish) ride to Beacon Hill, a Bronze Age hill fort which yields magnificent views. You are now in **Charnwood Forest**, where the craggy hills and ferns make a landscape wilder than most of the county. Cycling north out of Charnwood Forest, you come to **Breedon on the Hill**, where there is an iron age hill fort. A detour north from here will take you to the Donington Park motor racing circuit, which stages the British motorcycle Grand Prix every year and hosts an impressive collection of racing cars and motorcycles. Then it's southwest to **Staunton Harold**, with its rare Commonwealth period church.

Copt Oak 15

National Grid Ref: SK4813

▲ *Copt Oak Youth Hostel,*
Whitwick Road, Copt Oak,
Markfield, Leicestershire, LE67 9QB.
Actual grid ref: SK482129
Tel: **01530 242661**
Under 18: £4.65 **Adults:** £6.80
self-catering facilities, showers,
security lockers, no smoking
Converted shoolhouse in the hills
of northwest Leicestershire
providing basic accommodation.
Charnwood Forest is nearby, with
superb countryside for walking and
cycling

Oaks in Charnwood 16

National Grid Ref: SK4716

🕅 🍺 Jolly Farmers

St Josephs, Abbey Road, Oaks in
Charnwood, Coalville, Leics,
LE67 4UA.
Old country house where hosts
welcome you to their home
Tel: **01509 503943** Mrs Havers.
D: £19.00-£19.00 S: £19.00-£19.00.
Open: Apr to Oct
Beds: 2T 1S
Baths: 1 Sh
🛏 🅿 (3) 🍴 🖂 🎵 📖 Ⅴ ⬥ 🚲

All details shown
are as supplied
by B&B owners in
Autumn 1999.

Staunton Harold to Foxton

After a brief foray into Derbyshire, and the village of
Smisby, you pass near to **Ashby-de-la-Zouch**,
which has a striking castle, dating from Norman times to
the fifteenth century and ruined in the Civil War,
featuring an underground passageway for the non-
claustrophobic. From here it's south through
Donisthorpe, parallel to the River Mease through
Measham, and southeastwards along the Ashby Canal
from Shackerstone to **Market Bosworth**. From here it's
on to Sutton Cheney, which is near to the site of the
Battle of Bosworth Field, where the Wars of the Roses
came to an end with the death of Richard III and the fall
of the House of York at the hands of Henry VII, the first
king in the Tudor line. There is a Country Park and Visitor
Centre at the battlefield. Now it's on to Barwell and
through **Burbage Common and Woods**, the remainder
of the medieval Hinckley Forest, and then across the
Fosse Way and east towards the locks on the Grand
Union Canal at **Foxton**.

Diseworth 17

National Grid Ref: SK4524

🕅 🍺 Bull & Swan

Lady Gate Nursery, 47 The Green,
Diseworth, Derby, DE74 2QN.
Close to airport, Donington Park
Racing Circuit, exhibition centre,
M1/M42
Tel: **01332 811565** (also fax no)
Mrs Bebington.
D: £18.00-£25.00 S: £20.00-£25.00.
Open: All Year (not Xmas)
Beds: 1T 1D 1S
Baths: 2 Sh
🛏 (9) 🅿 (5) 🍴 🖂 🎵 📖 Ⅴ ⬥ 🚲

Ashby de la Zouch 18

National Grid Ref: SK3516

🕅 🍺 The Bull & Lion Packington

The Bungalow, 10 Trinity Close,
Ashby de la Zouch, Leicester,
Leics, LE65 2GQ.
Private family home in quiet cul-
de-sac, easy access to motorways
Tel: **01530 560698**
Mrs Chapman.
D: £17.00-£17.00 S: £17.00-£17.00.
Open: All Year
Beds: 1D 1T **Baths:** 1 Sh
🛏 🅿 (3) 🍴 🖂 ✕ 🎵 📖 Ⅴ 🛁

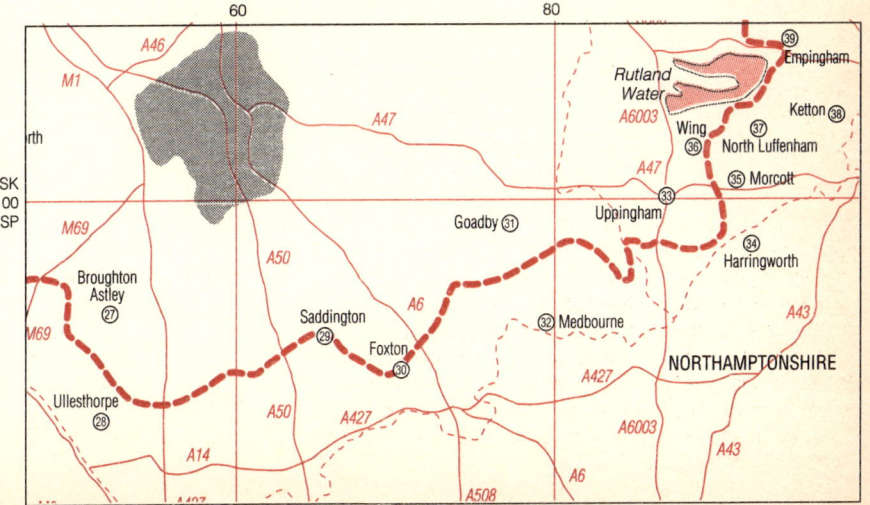

Measham   19

National Grid Ref: SK3312

🛏 🍽 Belper Inn Newton Burgoland

Measham House Farm, Gallows Lane, Measham, Swadlincote, Derbyshire, DE12 7HD.
Actual grid ref: SK348125
Grades: ETC 4 Diamond
Tel: **01530 270465** (also fax no)
D: £21.00-£21.00 **S:** £21.00-£21.00.
Open: All Year (not Xmas)
Beds: 1F 2T
Baths: 3 En 1 Pr
🛏 🖭 (20) ⊬ 🖵 🖈 🔥 🚽 🎟 Ⅵ ✿ ∥ ⚷
Large Georgian farmhouse on 500 acre working farm close to the heart of the National Forest. Warm welcome, spacious garden, country walks, three ensuite bedrooms

Appleby Magna   20

National Grid Ref: SK3110

🛏 🍽 Black Horse Inn

Ferne Cottage, 5 Black House Hill, Appleby Magna, Swadlincote, Derbyshire, DE12 7AQ.
Grades: ETC 3 Diamond
Tel: **01530 271772**
Fax no: 01530 270652
D: £17.00-£25.00 **S:** £17.00-£25.00.
Open: All Year (not Xmas)
Beds: 1F 1D 1T 1S
Baths: 1 En 1 Sh
🛏 🖭 (5) 🖵 🖈 🔥 🚽 🎟 Ⅵ ✿ ∥ ⚷
C18th beamed cottage. Homely, friendly, comfortable accommodation in the quiet historic village of Appleby Magna with off road parking. Half a mile from M42 (J11), 20 mins from NEC, Birmingham and East Midlands Airport. Lace making tuition by arrangement

Appleby Parva   21

National Grid Ref: SK3109

🛏 🍽 Cock Inn Sibson

Elms Farm, Appleby Parva, Swadlincote, DE12 7AG.
Pleasant farmhouse in rural position within 1.5 miles of M42
Grades: ETC 3 Diamond
Tel: **01530 270450**
D: £20.00-£22.00 **S:** £20.00-£22.00.
Open: All Year (not Xmas)
Beds: 1D 1T 1S
Baths: 2 En 1 Pr
🛏 (4) 🖭 (4) 🖵 🚽 🎟 Ⅵ ∥ ⚷

D = Price range per person sharing in a double room

Bringing children with you? Always ask for any special rates.

Congerstone   22

National Grid Ref: SK3605

🛏 🍽 Horse & Jockey, Rising Sun

Church House Farm, Shadows Lane, Congerstone, Nuneaton, Warks, CV13 6NA.
Former farmhouse convenient Bosworth Battlefield, Mallory Park, Twycross Zoo, Motorways
Tel: **01827 880402** Mrs Martin.
D: £20.00-£20.00 **S:** £19.00-£22.00.
Open: All Year (not Xmas)
Beds: 1D 1T 1S
Baths: 1 En 1 Sh
🛏 (12) 🖭 (6) 🖵 🚽 🎟 Ⅵ ⚷

The Old Barn, Shadows Lane, Congerstone, Nuneaton, Warks, CV13 6NF.
Beautiful walled garden in quiet location. Good pub food 300 yds
Tel: **01827 880431** Mrs Savage.
D: £18.00 **S:** £17.00.
Open: All Year (not Xmas)
Beds: 2T 1S
Baths: 1 Pr
🛏 (10) 🖭 (3) ⊬ 🖵 ✗ 🎟 ∥ ⚷

Market Bosworth   23

National Grid Ref: SK4003

Bosworth Firs, Bosworth Road, Market Bosworth, Nuneaton, Warks, CV13 0DW.
Comfortable, clean, friendly. Home cooking, varied menu. Attractive decor, furnishings
Tel: **01455 290727** Mrs Christian.
D: £20.00-£24.00 **S:** £20.00-£30.00.
Open: All Year
Beds: 2D 2T 2S
Baths: 2 En 1 Pr 1 Sh
🛏 🖭 (6) ⊬ 🖵 ✗ 🚽 🎟 & Ⅵ ∥ ✿ ⚷

Dadlington   24

National Grid Ref: SP4098

🛏 🍽 Dog & Hedgehog

Apple Orchard Farm, Fenn Lane, Dadlington, Nuneaton, CV13 6DR.
C17th farmhouse set in heart of Bosworth battlefield site
Tel: **01455 213186**
Fax no: 01455 212500
D: £20.00-£20.00 **S:** £20.00-£20.00.
Open: All Year (not Xmas)
Beds: 1D 1T
Baths: 2 En
🛏 🖭 🖵 🚽 🎟 Ⅵ ∥ ⚷

Foxton to Rutland Water

From here you proceed to **Hallaton**, a typical pretty English village with medieval church, pond and ancient pub on the village green. It is also the site, every Easter, of the centuries-old Hare Pie Scramble and Bottle-Kicking Contest, a permanent home fixture against the nearby village of Medbourne. Then the route takes you through Horninghold and around the **Eye Brook Reservoir**, an important wildfowl site. Back in Rutland, places of interest along the final stretch are the fourteenth-century Bede House at **Lyddington** and the circular maze at **Wing**. **Edith Weston**, on the southern side of Rutland Water, provides access to sailing on England's largest lowland lake. Also available is trout fishing, and many other leisure activities. A detour to the western end of the lake takes you to the nature reserve, and it is not far to **Oakham**, Rutland's county town. **Normanton**, by Edith Weston, has a classical-style church which has now been converted into a museum and juts into the lake.

Stapleton   25

National Grid Ref: SP4399

Woodside Farm Guest House, Ashby Road, Stapleton, Leicester, LE9 8JE.
Quiet family-run guest house set in 16 acres of countryside
Tel: **01455 291929**
Fax no: 01455 292626
D: £20.00 **S:** £27.50.
Open: All Year
Beds: 2F 4D 2T 2S
Baths: 8 En 2 Sh
🛏 🖭 (25) 🖵 🖈 ✗ 🚽 🎟 & Ⅵ ∥ ⚷

S = Price range for a single person in a room

Hinckley 26

National Grid Ref: SP4294

🏠🍺 Holywell Inn, The Milestone, Axe & Compass

The Guest House, 45 Priesthills Road, Hinckley, Leics, LE10 1AQ.
Grades: ETC 3 Diamond
Tel: **01455 619720**
Fax no: 01455 891104
D: £18.00-£18.00 **S:** £22.00-£22.00.
Open: All Year (not Xmas)
Beds: 3T 1S **Baths:** 2 Sh
🛏🔲🛢🏠📺💷
Edwardian period house set in quiet pleasant area of Hinckley. 5 min town centre, train station, convenient M69/A5/M6. Mallory Park race circuit, Stony Cove diving centre, Triumph motor cycle factory, Bosworth Battlefield centre. 30 mins NEC, Birmingham airport

Hollycroft Hotel, 24 Hollycroft, Hinckley, Leics, LE10 0HG.
Small family run hotel. All rooms ensuite, private car park
Tel: **01455 637356** (also fax no)
Mrs Hughes.
D: £25.00-£60.00 **S:** £25.00-£25.00.
Open: All Year
Beds: 2F 2D 1T
Baths: 5 En
🛏🅿(10)🔲🏠✕🛢🛢♿📺💷🚲

Broughton Astley 27

National Grid Ref: SP5292

🏠🍺 White Horse, Bulls Head

The Old Farm House, Old Mill Road, Broughton Astley, Leicester, Leics, LE9 6PQ.
Tel: **01455 282254** Mrs Cornelius.
D: £19.00-£23.00 **S:** £19.00-£23.00.
Open: All Year (not Xmas)
Beds: 1D 2T 1S
Baths: 2 Sh
🅿(6)🔲🛢🏠📺💷
Georgian farmhouse, quietly situated in well-serviced village. Good access M1 (J20/21), M69. We specialise in long-stay business - men or ladies welcome. Home produced eggs, honey and preserves and fruit/vegetables when in season

Ullesthorpe 28

National Grid Ref: SP5087

🏠🍺 The Swan

Forge House, College Street, Ullesthorpe, Lutterworth, Leics, LE17 5BU.
Excellent accommodation with attractive gardens. Ideal for business and pleasure
Tel: **01455 202454** (also fax no)
D: £17.00-£20.00 **S:** £18.00-£25.00.
Open: All Year
Beds: 1D 1T **Baths:** 1 En 1 Sh
🛏(10)🅿(3)🔲✕🛢📺💷

Saddington 29

National Grid Ref: SP6591

🏠🍺 The Queens Head

Breach Farm, Shearsby Road, Saddington, Leicester, Leics, LE8 0QU.
Actual grid ref: SP6491
Modern, comfortable farmhouse.
Panoramic views, breakfast served in large conservatory
Tel: **0116 240 2539** Mrs Thornton.
D: £16.00-£17.00 **S:** £17.00-£18.00.
Open: All Year (not Xmas)
Beds: 2D 1T
Baths: 1 Sh
🛏(1)🅿(4)🔲🛢🏠📺💷🚲

Foxton 30

National Grid Ref: SP7089

🏠🍺 Black Horse

The Old Manse, Swingbridge Street, Foxton, Market Harborough, Leics, LE16 7RH.
Period house in conservation village. Canals, locks, local pubs nearby
Grades: ETC 4 Diamond
Tel: **01858 545456** Mrs Pickering.
D: £22.00-£22.00 **S:** £30.00-£30.00.
Open: All Year (not Xmas)
Beds: 1D 2T
Baths: 2 En 1 Pr
🛏🅿(6)🔲🛢🏠📺💷🚲

Goadby 31

National Grid Ref: SP7598

🏠🍺 Fox & Hounds

The Hollies, Goadby, Leicester, LE7 9EE.
Beautiful Listed house in quiet village in pretty Leicestershire countryside
Grades: ETC 3 Diamond
Tel: **0116 259 8301** Mrs Parr.
Fax no: 0116 259 8491
D: £20.00-£20.00 **S:** £20.00-£20.00.
Open: All Year (not Xmas)
Beds: 1F 1D 1S
Baths: 1 En 1 Sh
🛏(5)🅿(3)🔲🏠🛢🏠📺💷

Medbourne 32

National Grid Ref: SP7993

🏠🍺 Nevill Arms

Medbourne Grange, Nevill Holt, Medbourne, Market Harborough, Leics, LE16 8EF.
Actual grid ref: SP816946
Comfortable farmhouse with breathtaking views; quiet location & heated pool
Tel: **01858 565249** Mrs Beaty.
Fax no: 01858 565257
D: £18.00-£20.00 **S:** £18.00-£20.00.
Open: All Year (not Xmas)
Beds: 2D 1T 1S **Baths:** 2 Sh
🛏🅿(6)🔲✕🛢🏠📺💷🚲

Uppingham 33

National Grid Ref: SP8699

🏠🍺 George & Dragon

8 Main Street, Seaton, Oakham, Rutland, LE15 9HU.
Old cottage in Rutland. Lovely walks, trout fishing, new places of interest
Tel: **01572 747358** Mrs Warburton.
D: £17.00-£17.00 **S:** £17.00-£17.00.
Open: All Year (not Xmas)
Beds: 1D 1S
Baths: 1 Sh
🛏🅿(2)🔲🏠🛢🏠📺💷🚲

Harringworth 34

National Grid Ref: SP9197

🏠🍺 White Swan

The White Swan, Seaton Road, Harringworth, Corby, Northants, NN17 3AF.
C15th Coaching inn. Home cooked food, real ales, close to Rutland Water
Grades: ETC 2 Diamond
Tel: **01572 747543**
Fax no: 01572 747323
D: £19.50-£26.00 **S:** £26.00-£38.50.
Open: All Year (not Xmas)
Beds: 1T 4D 1S
Baths: 6 En
🛏🅿(8)🔲✕🛢🏠📺💷

Morcott 35

National Grid Ref: SK9200

🏠🍺 Boot & Shoe

5 Church Lane, Morcott, Uppingham, Oakham, Rutland, LE15 9DH.
Actual grid ref: SK930001
Grade II Listed building, home from home, warm welcome, quiet village
Tel: **01572 747829** Mrs Martin.
D: £16.00 **S:** £20.00.
Open: All Year
Beds: 1D 1T
Baths: 1 Sh
🛏(2)🅿(2)🔲🏠✕🛢🏠📺💷🚲

The Grid Reference beneath the location heading is for the village or town - *not* for individual houses, which are shown (where supplied) in each entry itself.

Wing   36

National Grid Ref: SK8903

⋈ ⛲ Kings Arms

***The Kings Arms Inn**, Top Street,
Wing, Oakham, Rutland, LE15 8SE.*
Grades: ETC 4 Diamond,
AA 4 Diamond
Tel: **01572 737634** Mr Hornsey.
Fax no: 01572 737255
D: £25.00-£50.00 **S:** £35.00-£70.00.
Beds: 4F 4D 4T 8S
Baths: All En
🛇 🅿 (40) ⅏ ⊡ ✗ 🔥 �🍴 Ⅲ 🆅 🛇 ⚲
A 350-year-old family owned
country inn. Peaceful village,
plenty of character throughout. All
rooms decorated and furnished to
very high standard. Fresh cooked
food, ideal base for
walking/cycling/fishing/sailing.
Rutland Water 2 miles

***4 Westhorpe Close**, Wing,
Oakham, Rutland, LE15 8RJ.*
Detached house, walled garden.
Quiet village location near Rutland
water
Tel: **01572 737508**
Mrs Martin-Pope.
D: £17.50-£17.50 **S:** £17.50-£17.50.
Open: All Year (not Xmas)
Beds: 1D 1T **Baths:** 1 Sh
🛇 (12) 🅿 (3) ⅏ ⊡ 🔥 Ⅲ 🆅 ⚲ ⚲

North Luffenham   37

National Grid Ref: SK9303

***Pinfold House**, 6 Pinfold Lane,
North Luffenham, Oakham,
Rutland, LE15 8LE.*
C18th cottage with large garden,
attractive village near Rutland
Water
Tel: **01780 720175**
Mrs Cook.
D: £15.50 **S:** £17.00.
Open: All Year (not Xmas)
Beds: 2D 1T
Baths: 1 Sh
🛇 🅿 (4) ⅏ ⊡ 🔥 Ⅲ 🆅 🛇 ⚲

Ketton   38

National Grid Ref: SK9704

⋈ ⛲ Northwick Arms

***16 Northwick Road**, Ketton,
Stamford, PE9 3SB.*
Actual grid ref: SK978043
Split-level stone bungalow. Warm
welcome. Between Rutland Water
and Stamford
Tel: **01780 721411** Coyne.
D: £16.50-£16.50 **S:** £16.50-£16.50.
Open: Feb to Nov
Beds: 1T 1S
Baths: 1 Sh
🅿 (1) ⅏ ⊡ Ⅲ ⚲

Empingham   39

National Grid Ref: SK9508

⋈ ⛲ White Horse

***Little Hoo**, Nook Lane,
Empingham, Oakham, Rutland,
LE15 8PT.*
Actual grid ref: SK947085
Tel: **01780 460293** Mr Coxhead.
D: £22.50-£22.50 **S:** £26.00-£26.00.
Open: All Year
Beds: 1F 3T 1S
Baths: 2 Pr
🛇 (2) 🅿 (10) ⅏ ⊡ 🐾 ✗ 🔥 Ⅲ 🆅 🛇 ⚲ ⚲
C16th luxury cottage, 2 minutes
from Rutland Water. Barn for
drying clothes, storage freezer
centre for fishing. Sailing, walking,
cycling, birdwatching, historic
towns etc. Walk to meals nearby.
Great welcome

***

All cycleways are popular: you are well-advised to book ahead

***

STILWELL'S IRELAND BED & BREAKFAST

Think of Ireland and you think of that world famous Irish hospitality. The warmth of the welcome is as much a part of this great island as are the wild and beautiful landscapes, the traditional folk music, the Guinness and the architecture and lifestyle of Dublin and Belfast. Everywhere you go, North or South, you can't escape it. There are few better ways of experiencing this renowned hospitality, when travelling through Ireland, than by staying at one of the country's many Bed and Breakfasts. And there's no better way of choosing a convenient and desirable B&B than by consulting **Stilwell's Ireland: Bed and Breakfast 2000**.

Stilwell's Ireland: Bed and Breakfast 2000 contains over 1,400 entries - private houses, country halls, farms, cottages, inns, small hotels and guest houses - listed by county, in both Northern Ireland and the Republic of Ireland. Each entry includes room rates, facilities, tourist board grades or notices of approval and a brief description of the B&B, its location and surroundings. The average charge per person per night is £17.50. The listings also provide the names of local pubs and restaurants which serve food in the evening. As with all Stilwell B&B guides, **Stilwell's Ireland** has maps, listings of tourist information offices and rail, bus, air and ferry information.

Treat yourself to some Irish hospitality with **Stilwell's Ireland: Bed and Breakfast 2000**.

£6.95 from all good bookstores (ISBN 1-900861-16-X) or £7.95 (inc p&p) from Stilwell Publishing Ltd, 59 Charlotte Road, London EC2A 3QW (020 7739 7179)

Oxfordshire Cycleway

The **Oxfordshire Cycleway** is a circuit of the county, connected to Oxford, where it starts and finishes. It runs mainly along minor country roads and lanes, and takes in the whole range of the varied scenery Oxfordshire has to offer - the Cotswolds in the west, the Chilterns in the southeast and the Vale of the White Horse south of the Thames, where Britain's most ancient hillside carving lies close to the Ridgeway Path, the most ancient road still in use in Europe. The total distance around the circuit and into and out of Oxford is 178 miles, and the route is clearly signposted in both directions by blue Oxfordshire Cycleway direction signs with a cycle silhouette. The description which follows takes the circuit clockwise.

A detailed **guide booklet** to the cycleway route, which includes a list of cycle repair/hire shops on or near to the route, is available from Countryside Service, Department of Leisure and Arts, Oxfordshire County Council, Holton, Oxford OX33 1QQ, tel 01865 810226, @ £3.20 (+ 50p p&p).

Maps: Ordnance Survey 1:50,000 Landranger series: 151, 163, 164, 165, 174, 175

Trains: Oxford, Didcot and Banbury are the main termini, with connections to other places on or near the route. Goring is a stop on the main line out of London.

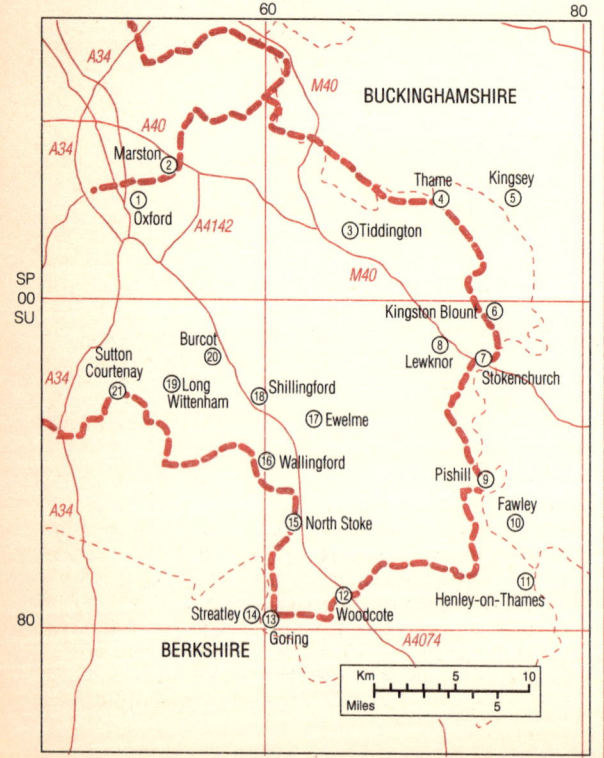

Oxford   1

National Grid Ref: SP5106

🍴 🍺 Carpenters' Arms, The Vine, Bear & Ragged Staff, The Tree, Marsh Harrier, Prince of Wales, Trout Inn, Old Ale House, Radcliffe Arms, Eight Bells, Fox & Hounds

▲ **Oxford Youth Hostel,** *32 Jack Straw's Lane, Oxford,* OX3 0DW.
Actual grid ref: SP533074
Tel: **01865 762997**
Under 18: £6.85
Adults: £10.15
evening meal at 6.00pm, television, games room, showers, shop
Victorian mansion surrounded by trees in the conservation area of this historic university city

Order your

packed lunches the

evening before you

need them.

Not at breakfast!

Green Gables, 326 Abingdon Road, Oxford, OX1 4TE.
Actual grid ref: SP518043
Grades: ETC 3 Diamond,
AA 3 Diamond
Tel: 01865 725870
Mr & Mrs Bhella.
Fax no: 01865 723115
D: £23.50-£28.50
S: £30.00-£47.00.
Open: All Year (not Xmas/
New Year)
Beds: 3F 4D 1T 1S
Baths: 7 En 1 Sh
🛇 ▣ (9) 🗇 🛎 🎟 ₺ ▣
Characterful detached Edwardian house shielded by trees. Bright spacious rooms with TV & beverage facilities. Ensuite rooms. 1.25 miles to city centre, on bus routes. Ample off-street parking. Direct line phones in rooms

Highfield West, 188 Cumnor Hill, Oxford, OX2 9PJ.
Actual grid ref: SP469042
Comfortable home in residential area, heated outdoor pool in season
Grades: ETC 3 Diamond
Tel: 01865 863007
Mr & Mrs Mitchell.
D: £21.25-£25.00
S: £24.00-£26.00.
Open: All Year (not Xmas)
Beds: 1F 1D 1T 2S
Baths: 3 En 1 Sh
🛇 ▣ (5) 🗇 🛎 🎟 ▣

Walton Guest House, 169 Walton Street, Oxford, OX1 2HD.
Most centrally situated guest house in Oxford. 2 mins bus station, 5 to 10 mins from train station
Tel: 01865 52137 Mrs Durrant.
D: £19.00-£25.00
S: £19.00-£35.00.
Open: All Year
Beds: 1F 2D 3T 3S
🛇 🗇 🛎 🎟 ▣ ▮ ✦

Nanford Guest House, Iffley Road, Oxford, OX4 1EJ.
Very economical rates with no loss of welcome. Off road parking
Tel: 01865 244743
Mr Cronin.
Fax no: 01865 249596
D: £17.50-£19.00
S: £23.00-£28.00.
Open: All Year
Beds: 5F 5T 5D 5S
Baths: 20 En
🛇 ▣ 🗇 🛎 🎟 ▣ ✦ ⚬

Arden Lodge, 34 Sunderland Avenue, Oxford, OX2 8DX.
Select spacious modern detached house within easy reach city centre
Tel: 01865 552076
Mr & Mrs Price.
D: £24.00-£25.00
S: £30.00-£35.00.
Open: All Year (not Xmas)
Beds: 1F 1D 1T 1S
Baths: 4 En
🛇 (3) ▣ (7) 🗇 🛎 🎟 ▣ ⚬

Gables Guest House, 6 Cumnor Hill, Oxford, OX2 9HA.
Attractive detached house with beautiful garden, close to city centre, bus and railway stations
Tel: 01865 862153
Mrs Tompkins.
Fax no: 01865 864054
D: £22.00 **S:** £26.00.
Open: All Year (not Xmas)
Beds: 1F 2D 1T 2S
Baths: 5 En 1 Pr
🛇 ▣ (6) 🗇 🛎 🎟 ▣

Bravalla Guest House, 242 Iffley Road, Oxford, OX4 1SE.
Late Victorian home attractively decorated in Sanderson patterns. Close city ring road and river
Grades: ETC 2 Diamond,
AA 2 Diamond, RAC 2 Diamond
Tel: 01865 241326
Ms Downes.
Fax no: 01865 250511
D: £23.00-£25.00
S: £30.00-£40.00.
Open: All Year (not Xmas)
Beds: 1F 3D 2T 1S
Baths: 6 En
🛇 ▣ (4) 🗇 🛎 🎟 ▣

58 St John Street, Oxford, OX1 2QR.
Tall Victorian house central to all colleges, museums and theatres
Tel: 01865 515454 Mrs Old.
D: £18.00-£19.00 **S:** £18.00.
Open: All Year
Beds: 1F 1T 1S
Baths: 1 En
🛇 (1) 🗇 🛎 ▣ ✦ ⚬

Acorn Guest House, 260 Iffley Road, Oxford, OX4 1SE.
Modern comfort in Victorian house convenient for all local amenities
Grades: ETC 2 Diamond,
AA 2 Diamond, RAC 2 Diamond
Tel: 01865 247998 Mrs Lewis.
D: £22.00-£27.00 **S:** £25.00-£27.00.
Open: All Year (not Xmas/
New Year)
Beds: 4F 2D 1T 5S
Baths: 1 En, 4 Sh
🛇 (9) ▣ (11) 🗇 🛎 🎟 ▣ ✦

D = Price range per person sharing in a double room

Oxford

The city of **Oxford** is one of England's architectural treasure houses. The imposing facades, spires and 'quadrangles' (courtyards) of the colleges and other university buildings bear witness to centuries of conspicuous creation. But although the university is a dominant presence, Oxford is also an important commercial city, which has plenty of life of its own away from students and tourists. Of the colleges, Merton is the most beautiful - the Gothic college chapel and the library, which contains centuries-old globes and other trappings of Renaissance scholarship, stand on 'Mob Quad', built in the fourteenth century, which has the eerie atmosphere of a medieval time warp. Magdalen, with its secluded cloisters and the famous tower, is also well worth a visit. Christ Church is big and famous. Also worth a look are Trinity, where the college chapel, the first not built in the Gothic style, was designed by Wren, who also designed the Sheldonian Theatre; and St Catherine's, built in the 1960s in a unique and very distinctive style. Elsewhere, the University Museum is a Pre-Raphaelite gem, its interior constructed around intricate ironwork which plays visually on the dinosaur skeletons, surrounded by statues honouring notable figures of science and philosophy; the adjacent Pitt-Rivers Museum is a fantastic ethnographic collection best known for the shrunken heads from South America. The other major museum is the Ashmolean, the oldest museum in Britain, with a very impressive range of collections; and Christ Church has its own picture gallery, with a collection of Italian art. Away from the university, the city has many interesting pockets, not least the canalside backstreets of Jericho, famous for the Pre-Raphaelite St Barnabas' Church; and don't leave Oxford without trying one or two of its many excellent pubs.

Combermere House, 11 Polstead Road, Oxford, Oxon, OX2 6TW.
Actual grid ref: SP507079
Quiet, tree-lined road, 15 minutes' walk centre and colleges
Tel: **01865 556971** (also fax no)
Mr & Mrs Welding.
D: £20.00 **S:** £24.00.
Open: All Year
Beds: 2F 1D 2T 4S
Baths: 9 En
⌂ ₽ (3) ⌷ ➤ ⚲ ▥ Ⅴ ✦

Pine Castle Hotel, 290 Iffley Road, Oxford, OX4 4AE.
Actual grid ref: SP528048
Close to shops, launderette, post office. Frequent buses. River walks nearby
Grades: ETC 4 Diamond, AA 4 Diamond
Tel: **01865 241497** Mrs Morris.
Fax no: 01685 727230
D: £30.00-£35.00 **S:** £52.00-£58.00.
Open: All Year (not Xmas)
Beds: 1F 5D 2T
Baths: 8 En
⌂ ₽ (4) ⌷ ⚲ ▥ Ⅴ ⌷

S = Price range for a single person in a room

D = Price range per person sharing in a double room

Earlmount Guest House, 322-324 Cowley Road, Oxford, Oxon, OX4 2AF.
Non-smoking modern house, close to colleges, city-centre, major road routes
Grades: ETC 3 Diamond
Tel: **01865 240236**
Fax no: 01865 434903
D: £25.00-£27.50 **S:** £30.00-£45.00.
Open: All Year
Beds: 1F 1T 5D 1S
Baths: 6 En 1 Pr 1 Sh
⌂ (5) ₽ (6) ⌦ ⌷ ⚲ ▥ Ⅴ ⌷ ⚲

Casa Villa Guest House, 388 Banbury Road, Oxford, OX2 7PW.
Modern family run guest house in idyllic city of Oxford
Grades: ETC 2 Diamond, AA 2 Diamond
Tel: **01865 512642** (also fax no)
Mrs Dunbar.
D: £30.00-£32.50 **S:** £45.00-£50.00.
Open: All Year
Beds: 1F 5D 1T 2S
Baths: 1 En 7 Pr 2 Sh
⌂ (6) ₽ (6) ⌦ ⌷ ⚲ ▥ Ⅴ

Oxford to Wallingford

When you've had your fill of **Oxford**, the cycleway commences with a leisurely stretch linking you to the county circuit at **Horton-cum-Studley**, where you turn southeast, to reach **Worminghall** in Buckinghamshire. A short detour from here will bring you to Waterperry Gardens, an 83-acre herbaceous and alpine centre with a Saxon church and a gallery which exhibits and sells paintings, ceramics and textiles. From Worminghall it's not far to the pretty small town of **Thame**. From here you head south and after Sydenham and Kingston Blount up into the beautiful wooded countryside of the **Chiltern Hills**. An attraction along this stretch of the way is Stonor Park. This beautiful house in a picturesque setting was built over centuries and is the ancestral home of a Catholic family and a notable centre of resistance to protestant domination: the martyr Edmund Campion received sanctuary here before being captured and hanged in 1581. There is a fine art collection including paintings by Tintoretto and Caracci. From here it is on to the village of **Bix**. The Fox pub is recommended. From here a detour is possible to **Henley-on-Thames**, famous for rowing, and with a wide Georgian High Street. From Bix it's on to **Goring**, at the southwestern end of the Chiltern range. From here there is an alternative route (best attempted only on an all terrain bicycle) along the ancient **Ridgeway Path**, from which you can link up to the Round Berkshire Cycle Route. From Goring you go north, parallel to the Thames, to Crowmarsh Gifford, where you cross the river into the small town of **Wallingford**.

Milka's Guest House, 379 Iffley Road, Oxford, Oxon, OX4 4DP.
Family run guest house situated close to Iffley village
Grades: ETC 3 Diamond
Tel: **01865 778458**
Fax no: 01865 776477
D: £22.50-£27.50
S: £25.00-£35.00.
Open: All Year
Beds: 2D 1S
Baths: 1 En
⌂ (5) ₽ (5) ⌦ ⌷ ⚲ ▥ Ⅴ ⚲

Vallendiere, 72 Cumnor Hill, Oxford, OX2 9HU.
Country house in acre of garden, 1.5 miles from Oxford
Grades: ETC 3 Diamond
Tel: **01865 863602**
D: £21.00-£24.00
S: £24.00-£30.00.
Open: All Year
Beds: 1D 1T
Baths: 1 En 1 Pr

Athena Guest House, 255 Cowley Road, Oxford, OX4 1XQ.
Close to city centre and university. Car parking, tea and coffee making
Tel: **01865 243124**
Fax no: 01865 241310
D: £21.00 **S:** £22.00.
Open: All Year
Beds: 6F 2D 2T 2S
Baths: 2 En
⌂ (5) ₽ (4) ⌦ ⌷ ⚲ ▥ Ⅴ ⚲

Marston   **2**

National Grid Ref: SP5208

🍽 🍴 Squire Bassett

The Bungalow, Cherwell Farm, Mill Lane, Marston, Oxford, OX3 0QF.
Actual grid ref: SP523098
Modern bungalow in five acres open countryside, no bus route
Grades: ETC 3 Diamond
Tel: **01865 557171**
Burdon.
D: £20.00-£24.00
S: £28.00-£35.00.
Open: Mar to Oct
Beds: 2D 2T
Baths: 2 En 1 Sh
⌂ (7) ₽ (6) ⌦ ⌷ ⚲ ▥ Ⅴ

Tiddington   **3**

National Grid Ref: SP6504

Albury Farm, Draycott, Tiddington, Thame, Oxon, OX9 2LX.
Peaceful open views in quiet location, clean, tidy, friendly. Close to river with private fishing
Tel: **01844 339740** (also fax no)
Mrs Ilbery.
D: £20.00-£20.00
S: £20.00-£20.00.
Open: All Year
Beds: 1D 1T
Baths: 1 Pr 1 Sh
₽ (4) ⌦ ⌷ ✕ ⚲ ▥ Ⅴ ⌷ ✦ ⚲

Thame 4

National Grid Ref: SP7005

🍴🍺 Lion on the Green

Oakfield, Thame Park Road, Thame, Oxon, OX9 3PL.
Grades: ETC 4 Diamond
Tel: **01844 213709**
D: £20.00-£25.00.
Open: All Year (not Xmas)
Beds: 1D 2T
Baths: 1 En 1 Sh
🛏 (8) 🅿 (6) ⅙🗗 🕭📷🕭Ⅲ.♿️Ⅴ✦🚲
We offer a warm welcome to our lovely farmhouse home, set in 25 acres of grounds - part of our larger 400 acre mixed farm. We have good food comfortable beds and a homely atmosphere. Out in the country, but only 10 minutes' walk to town centre

Field Farm, Rycote Lane, Thame, Oxon, OX9 2HQ.
Comfortable bungalow on working farm. Pretty garden, countryside views
Tel: **01844 215428**
Mrs Quartly.
D: £20.00-£20.00 **S:** £25.00-£25.00.
Open: All Year (not Xmas)
Beds: 2D
Baths: 2 En
🅿⅙🗗🕭Ⅲ.Ⅴ

Kingsey 5

National Grid Ref: SP7406

🍴🍺 Three Horseshoes

Foxhill, Kingsey, Aylesbury, Bucks, HP17 8LZ.
Actual grid ref: SU747067
Spacious and comfortable farmhouse with beautiful garden in rural setting
Tel: **01844 291650** (also fax no)
Mr Hooper.
D: £20.00-£23.00 **S:** £23.00-£26.00.
Open: Mar to Nov
Beds: 1D 2T
Baths: 1 Sh
🛏 (8) 🅿 (20) ⅙🗗🕭Ⅲ.Ⅴ

Kingston Blount 6

National Grid Ref: SU7399

Town Farm Cottage, Brook Street, Kingston Blount, Chinnor, Oxon, OX9 4RZ.
Actual grid ref: SU735995
Beautiful beamed comfortable farmhouse in rural quiet location at foot of Chiltern Hills
Tel: **01844 352152**
Mrs Clark.
D: £25.00 **S:** £30.00.
Open: All Year (not Xmas)
Beds: 1T 1D
Baths: 2 En
🅿 (4) ⅙🗗🕭Ⅲ.Ⅴ✦🚲

Stokenchurch 7

National Grid Ref: SU7695

🍴🍺 Blue Flag

Gibbons Farm, Bigmore Lane, Stokenchurch, High Wycombe, Bucks, HP14 3UR.
Tel: **01494 482385**
Mrs McKelvey.
Fax no: 01494 485400
D: £25.00-£30.00
S: £25.00-£30.00.
Open: All Year
Beds: 2F 1D 1T 4S
Baths: 6 En 1 Sh
🛏 (20) 🗗 🕭Ⅲ.♿️Ⅴ✦🚲
Traditional farm offering accommodation in converted barn. Set in courtyard surrounded by open countryside, this family-run B&B offers a warm and friendly welcome with Marlow and Oxford within half-hour drive, situated within 5 mins of M40, London is easily accessible

Lewknor 8

National Grid Ref: SU7197

🍴🍺 Leathern Bottle

Moorcourt Cottage, Weston Road, Lewknor, Oxford, OX9 5RU.
Beautiful C15th cottage, open views, quiet, friendly and comfortable
Tel: **01844 351419** (also fax no)
Mrs Hodgson.
D: £20.00-£22.50
S: £30.00-£30.00.
Beds: 1T 1D
Baths: 1Ensuite 1Private
🅿 (4) 🗗🕭Ⅲ.Ⅴ👜✦🚲

Pishill 9

National Grid Ref: SU7289

🍴🍺 The Crown

Bank Farm, Pishill, Henley-on-Thames, Oxon, RG9 6HJ.
Actual grid ref: SU724898
Quiet comfortable farmhouse, beautiful countryside
Tel: **01491 638601**
Mrs Lakey.
D: £20.00-£20.00
S: £15.00-£20.00.
Open: All Year (not Xmas)
Beds: 1F 1S
Baths: 1 En 1 Sh
🛏 🅿 (5) ⅙🗗🕭🕭Ⅲ.Ⅴ✦🚲

Bringing children with you? Always ask for any special rates.

The Grid Reference beneath the location heading is for the village or town - *not* for individual houses, which are shown (where supplied) in each entry itself.

Orchard House, Pishill, Henley-on-Thames, Oxfordshire, RG9 6HJ.
Tel: **01491 638351** (also fax no)
Mrs Connolly.
D: £20.00-£25.00 **S:** £20.00-£25.00.
Open: All Year
Beds: 2F 1D 1T
Baths: 3 En 1 Pr
🛏 🅿 (6) ⅙🗗🕭🕇✗🕭Ⅲ.Ⅴ✦🚲
Large family house, one acre of garden, on edge of Chilterns, surrounded by woodlands. Quiet area on Oxfordshire Way, close to Ridgeway Paths and Oxfordshire Cycle Way. Henley 6 miles, Oxford 12 miles. Good food available at many local country pubs

Fawley 10

National Grid Ref: SU7586

🍴🍺 Walnut Tree, Golden Ball

Jacksons, Fawley Bottom, Fawley, Henley-on-Thames, Oxon, RG9 6JJ.
Actual grid ref: SU748870
Comfortable farmhouse in rural location, with warm welcome, good food
Tel: **01491 575330** Mrs Brook.
D: £17.50 **S:** £17.50.
Open: All Year (not Xmas)
Beds: 1F 1T **Baths:** 1 Sh
🛏 🅿🗗🕇✗🕭Ⅲ.Ⅴ👜✦

Henley-on-Thames 11

National Grid Ref: SU7682

🍴🍺 Anchor, Bottle & Glass, Golden Ball

Lenwade, 3 Western Road, Henley-on-Thames, Oxon, RG9 1JL.
Beautiful Victorian family home, convenient river, restaurants, public transport
Grades: ETC 5 Diamond, AA 5 Diamond
Tel: **01491 573468** (also fax no)
Mrs Williams.
D: £25.00-£27.50 **S:** £25.00-£27.50.
Open: All Year (not Xmas)
Beds: 2D 1T **Baths:** 2 En 1 Pr
🛏 🅿 (2) ⅙🗗🕭Ⅲ.Ⅴ👜✦🚲

**Always telephone
to get directions to
the B&B - you will
save time!**

New Lodge, Henley Park, Henley-
on-Thames, Oxon, RG9 6HU.
Actual grid ref: SU758847
Victorian cottage, Area of
Outstanding Natural Beauty.
Minimum stay two nights
Grades: ETC 3 Diamond
Tel: **01491 576340** (also fax no)
Mrs Warner.
D: £19.00-£21.00 **S:** £24.00-£27.00.
Open: All Year
Beds: 2D
Baths: 1 En 1 Pr
🛇 🅿 (5) ↙ 🗆 🖢 🎹 ♿ Ⓥ

Alftrudis, 8 Norman Avenue,
Henley-on-Thames, Oxon, RG9 1SG.
Victorian home, quiet cul-de-sac
two minutes town centre station,
river
Grades: ETC 4 Diamond
Tel: **01491 573099** Mrs Lambert.
Fax no: 01491 411747
D: £22.50-£27.50 **S:** £35.00-£50.00.
Open: All Year
Beds: 2D 1T
Baths: 2 En 1 Pr
🛇 (8) 🅿 (2) ↙ 🗆 🖢 🎹 Ⓥ

Ledard, Rotherfield Road, Henley-
on-Thames, Oxon, RG9 INN.
Actual grid ref: SU761814
Elegant Victorian house and garden
within easy reach of Henley
Tel: **01491 575611** Mrs Howard.
D: £20.00-£20.00 **S:** £20.00-£20.00.
Open: All Year (not Xmas)
Beds: 1F 1D 1T
Baths: 2 Pr
🛇 🅿 (4) ↙ 🗆 🖢 🎹 Ⓥ ❢ ⚡

Alexander House, 21 Upton Close,
Henley-on-Thames, Oxon, RG9 1BT.
Clean modern house. Close river
and station. Satellite TV. Parking
Tel: **01491 575331**
Mrs Inglis.
Fax no: 01491 412421
D: £20.00 **S:** £25.00.
Open: All Year
Beds: 1T 1D
Baths: 1 En 1 Pr
🛇 (12) 🅿 (2) 🗆 🖢 🗙 🖢 🎹 Ⓥ

Woodcote   12

National Grid Ref: SU6481

🍴 🍺 Red Lion

Hedges, South Stoke Road,
Woodcote, Reading, Berks, RG8 0PL.
Peaceful, rural situation, historic
Area of Outstanding Natural
Beauty
Grades: ETC 3 Diamond
Tel: **01491 680461**
Mrs Howard-Allen.
D: £17.00-£19.00
S: £17.00-£19.00.
Open: All Year (not Xmas)
Beds: 2T 2S
Baths: 1 Pr 1 Sh
🛇 (2) 🅿 (4) 🗆 🖢 🖢 🎹 Ⓥ ❢ ⚡ 🚲

Goring   13

National Grid Ref: SU6081

🍴 🍺 Catherine Wheel, John Barleycorn, Miller of
Mansfield, Bull Inn, Perch & Pike

The Catherine Wheel, Station
Road, Goring, Reading, Berks,
RG8 9HB.
Accommodation in a Victorian
cottage in riverside village
Tel: **01491 872379**
Mrs Ker.
D: £19.50 **S:** £23.00.
Open: All Year
Beds: 2D 1T
Baths: 2 Sh
🛇 ↙ 🗆 🗙 🖢 🎹 Ⓥ 🚲

14 Mountfield, Wallingford Road,
Goring, Reading, Berks, RG8 0BE.
Modern home in riverside country
village. Pretty garden. Lots of
walks & station
Tel: **01491 872029**
Mrs Ewen.
D: £20.00
S: £23.00.
Open: All Year
Beds: 1D 2T 1S
Baths: 2Sh
🛇 🅿 (4) 🗆 🖢 🗙 🖢 🎹 Ⓥ ❢ ⚡

Streatley   14

National Grid Ref: SU5980

▲ *Streatley-on-Thames Youth
Hostel,* Hill House, Reading Road,
Streatley, Reading, Berkshire,
RG8 9JJ.
Actual grid ref: SU591806
Tel: **01491 872278**
Under 18: £6.85
Adults: £10.15
evening meal at 7.00pm, family
bunk rooms, television, showers,
shop
*Homely Victorian family house,
completely refurbished, in a
beautiful riverside village*

North Stoke   15

National Grid Ref: SU6186

Footpath Cottage, The Street,
North Stoke, Wallingford, Oxon,
OX10 6BJ.
Lovely old cottage, peaceful river
village. Warm welcome, excellent
food
Tel: **01491 839763**
Mrs Tanner.
D: £19.00-£20.00
S: £20.00-£20.00.
Open: All Year
Beds: 2D 1S
Baths: 1 En 1 Sh
🛇 🗆 🖢 🗙 🖢 🎹 Ⓥ ❢ ⚡ 🚲

Wallingford to Lechlade

From here the route takes you west and close to **Didcot**, where there is a railway museum. Between Appelford and Culham you can make a detour to the pretty town of **Abingdon**. There are scant remains of the Benedictine abbey which went the way of all the others under Henry VIII, but there is an impressive Perpendicular church, St Helen's, the seventeenth-century County Hall and many streets with seventeenth- and eighteenth-century houses. Westwards to **Wantage**, birthplace of Alfred the Great, whose statue stands imposingly over the town square. Further westwards, the route passes close to the world-famous prehistoric White Horse

hillside carving. By far the oldest of England's chalk carvings, the figure captures in huge bold lines the movement of a galloping horse. The earthworks of Uffington Castle, a fort from the same era, stand atop the hill. From here, where the Ridgeway alternative rejoins the main route, it's north to **Uffington**, and on to **Faringdon**. A short stretch west to Coleshill and then north to **Buscot** brings you close to Buscot Park, a National Trust property with painted pannels and stained glass by Edward Burne-Jones. Just over the border in Gloucestershire is the village of **Lechlade**, built of Cotswold limestone and boasting a church, St Lawrence's, whose spire is celebrated in a poem by Shelley. The village is the highest navigable point of the Thames.

Please don't camp

on *anyone's* land

without first obtaining

their permission.

Wallingford 16

National Grid Ref: SU6089

🍽 🍺 Shepherds Hut, Six Bells

Little Gables, 166 Crowmarsh Hill,
Wallingford, Oxford, OX10 8BG.
Actual grid ref: SU623889
Delightfully large private house
where a warm welcome awaits you
Grades: ETC 4 Diamond
Tel: **01491 837834** (also fax no)
Mrs Reeves.
D: £25.00-£30.00
S: £30.00-£35.00.
Open: All Year
Beds: 2F 2D 3T 1S
Baths: 2 En 1 Pr
🛏 🄿 ⚲ 🗔 🍽 💻 ♿ 🎗 📷 🐾

North Farm, Shillingford Hill,
Wallingford, Oxon, OX10 8NB.
Actual grid ref: SU586924
Quiet comfortable farmhouse on
working farm, close to River
Thames
Grades: ETC 4 Diamond
Tel: **01865 858406**
Mrs Warburton.
Fax no: 01865 858519
D: £24.00-£28.00
S: £28.00-£38.00.
Open: All Year (not Xmas)
Beds: 2D 1T
Baths: 1 En 2 Pr
🛏 (8) 🄿 (6) ⚲ 🗔 🍽 💻 🎗 📷 ♿ 🐾

Dormer Cottage, High Street,
Ewelme, Wallingford, Oxon,
OX10 6HQ.
Old country cottage in picturesque,
historic village. Homely, relaxed
atmosphere
Tel: **01491 833987**
Mrs Standbridge.
D: £19.00-£19.00
S: £20.00-£20.00.
Open: All Year (not Xmas)
Beds: 1F 1S
Baths: 1 Sh
🛏 (9) 🄿 (2) ⚲ 🗔 🍽 💻 🐾

Munts Mill, Castle Lane,
Wallingford, Oxfordshire, OX10 0BN.
Actual grid ref: SU609895
Near town centre on edge of
Chilterns - advance booking only
Tel: **01491 836654**
Mrs Broster.
S: £20.00-£25.00.
Open: All Year (not Xmas)
Beds: 2S
⚲ 🗔 🍽 💻 🎗

Ewelme 17

National Grid Ref: SU6491

🍽 🍺 Crown, Shepherds Hut

Fords Farm, Ewelme, Wallingford,
Oxon, OX10 6HU.
Picturesque setting in historic
village. Warm, friendly atmos-
phere. Good views
Grades: ETC 4 Diamond
Tel: **01491 839272** Miss Edwards.
D: £22.50-£25.00 **S:** £30.00-£55.00.
Open: All Year
Beds: 1D 2T **Baths:** 1 Pr 1 Sh
🄿 (8) ⚲ 🗔 🍽 💻 🎗 📷

May's Farm, Turner's Court,
Ewelme, Wallingford, Oxon,
OX10 6QF.
Working stock farm. Fabulous
views, quiet location, good walking
Tel: **01491 641294** Mrs Passmore.
Fax no: 01491 641697
D: £19.00-£22.00 **S:** £25.00-£30.00.
Open: All Year
Beds: 1F 1T 1S
Baths: 1 En 1 Sh
🛏 🄿 (4) ⚲ 🗔 🍽 💻 🎗 📷

Planning a longer

stay? Always ask for

any special rates.

Shillingford 18

National Grid Ref: SU5992

🍽 🍺 Six Bells

Marsh House, Court Drive,
Shillingford, Wallingford, Oxon,
OX10 7ER.
Grades: ETC 3 Diamond
Tel: **01865 858496** (also fax no)
Nickson.
D: £20.00-£25.00. **S:** £20.00-£25.00.
Open: All Year (not Xmas)
Beds: 1T 2S **Baths:** 2 En 1 Pr
🛏 (8) 🄿 (4) ⚲ 🗔 🍽 💻 🎗 📷
Spacious house in quiet rural
surroundings, next to the Thames
Path and River Thames. Easy
access to Oxford and London.
Comfortable beds with TV, good
English breakfast, private parking

Long Wittenham 19

National Grid Ref: SU5493

🍽 🍺 Machine Man

Witta's Ham Cottage, High Street,
Long Wittenham, Abingdon, Oxon,
OX14 4QH.
Attractive thatched cottage in beau-
tiful Thameside village. Three pubs
nearby
Tel: **01865 407686** Mrs Mellor.
Fax no: 01865 407469
D: £21.00-£23.00 **S:** £24.00-£30.00.
Open: All Year (not Xmas)
Beds: 1D 1T 1S **Baths:** 1 Sh
🛏 (2) 🄿 (3) ⚲ 🗔 🍽 💻 🎗 📷

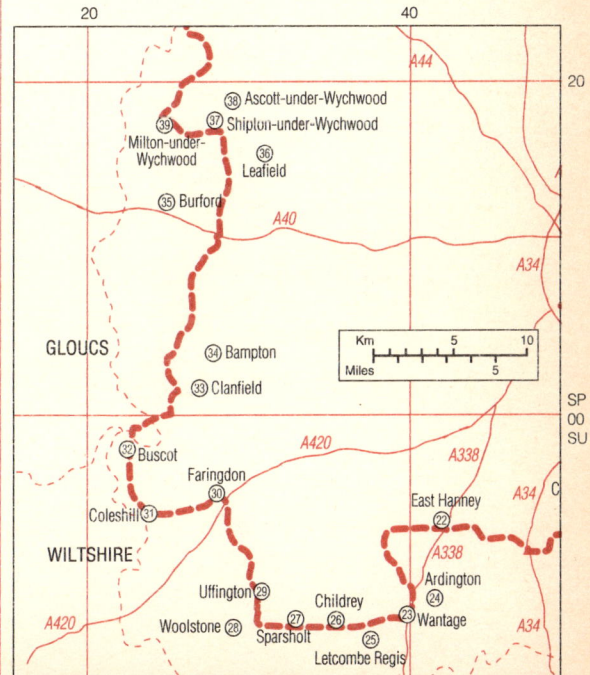

Burcot 20

National Grid Ref: SU5695

Dinckley Court, Burcot, Abingdon, Oxon, OX14 3DP.
Actual grid ref: SU563959
Beautiful riverside coach house, offering luxury ensuite accommodation in 8 acre grounds
Grades: ETC 4 Diamond, AA 4 Diamond
Tel: **01865 407763** Mrs Godfrey.
D: £27.50-£32.50 **S:** £45.00-£55.00.
Open: All Year
Beds: 1D 4T **Baths:** 5 Pr
🛇 🅿 (20) ⅍ ☐ ✕ 👤 🏬 Ⓥ 🔒 ⚡

Sutton Courtenay 21

National Grid Ref: SU5093

🍺 🍽 George & Dragon, The Fish, The Swan

Bekynton House, 7 The Green, Sutton Courtenay, Abingdon, Oxon, OX14 4AE.
Period house on village green near River Thames. Walled garden
Tel: **01235 848630 / 848888**
Ms Cornwall.
Fax no: 01235 848436
D: £25.00 **S:** £25.00.
Open: All Year (not Xmas)
Beds: 1D 1T 1S
Baths: 2 Sh
🛇 🅿 (2) ⅍ ☐ 👤 🏬 Ⓥ 🔒 ⚡

All rooms full and nowhere else to stay? Ask the owner if there's anywhere nearby

---

East Hanney 22

National Grid Ref: SU4192

Bramley House, Mill Orchard, East Hanney, Wantage, Oxon, OX12 0JH.
Close to Berkshire Downs, Cotswolds, Oxford. Pubs, restaurant serve food
Tel: **01235 868314**
D: £19.00-£20.00.
S: £20.00-£22.00.
Open: All Year (not Xmas)
Beds: 2D 1S
Baths: 1 En 1 Sh
🅿 (3) ⅍ ☐ 👤 🏬 Ⓥ

Wantage 23

National Grid Ref: SU4087

The Bell Inn, 38 Market Place, Wantage, Oxon, OX12 8AH.
Tel: **01235 763718** (also fax no)
Mrs Williams.
D: £22.50-£27.50
S: £20.00-£35.00.
Open: All Year
Beds: 2F 5D 4T 7S
Baths: 11 En 2 Sh
🛇 ☐ 🍴 ✕ 👤 🏬 Ⓥ 🔒
C16th market town inn. We serve good beer and home-cooked food in a warm and friendly atmosphere. Comfortable rooms at reasonable rates

Alfred's Lodge, 23 Ormond Road, Wantage, Oxon, OX12 8EG.
Victorian house near town centre. Family run - under new management
Tel: **01235 762409**
Mr & Mrs Wharton.
Fax no: 01235 811652
D: £18.00 **S:** £22.00.
Open: All Year
Beds: 2F 4T 1S
Baths: 3 Pr 2 Sh
🛇 🅿 (8) 👤 🏬 Ⓥ 🔒

All cycleways are popular: you are well-advised to book ahead

---

Ardington 24

National Grid Ref: SU4387

🍺 🍽 Boar's Head, The Hare, Lord Nelson

Orpwood House, Ardington, Wantage, Oxon, OX12 8PN.
Spacious farmhouse in picturesque downland village. Swimming pool in summer
Tel: **01235 833300** Mrs Haigh.
Fax no: 01235 820950
D: £19.50 **S:** £19.50.
Open: All Year (not Xmas)
Beds: 1F 3T 1S **Baths:** 1 Pr 2 Sh
🛇 🅿 (15) ⅍ ☐ ✕ 👤 🏬 Ⓥ 🔒 ⚡

Letcombe Regis 25

National Grid Ref: SU3886

🍺 🍽 The Greyhound

Old Vicarage, Letcombe Regis, Wantage, Oxon, OX12 9JP.
Delightful Victorian home, elegant accommodation, near pub, pretty downland village
Tel: **01235 765827** Mrs Barton.
Fax no: 020 8743 8740
D: £22.00-£25.00 **S:** £22.00-£30.00.
Open: All Year (not Xmas)
Beds: 1D 1T 1S **Baths:** 1 En 1 Sh
🛇 🅿 (2) ⅍ ☐ 🏬 🔒 ⚡ ♺

Quince Cottage, Letcombe Regis, Wantage, Oxon, OX12 9J.
Spacious C18th thatched house in attractive Downland village
Tel: **01235 763652** Mrs Boden.
D: £19.00 **S:** £21.00.
Open: All Year
Beds: 1T 1S **Baths:** 1 Pr
🛇 (1) 🅿 (2) ⅍ ☐ 👤 🏬 Ⓥ 🔒 ⚡

From Lechlade through the Cotswolds

Back in Oxfordshire, **Kelmscott Manor** (open Wednesdays, April-September), a classic Elizabethan manor, was home to the founder of the Arts and Crafts movement, socialist William Morris, for the last twenty-five years of his life. The house sports decor by Morris' friends in the Pre-Raphaelite movement, including Edward Burne-Jones (who worked on Buscot Park whilst staying here) and Dante Gabriel Rossetti, who had an affair with Morris' wife, Jane. From here you ride north; a detour westwards from Shilton will take you to the Cotswold Wildlife Park. On to **Swinbrook**, on the banks of the Windrush, where the church boasts the Tudor and Stuart Fettiplace Monuments. A short detour leads to **Burford,** another beautiful village of Cotswold stone with an impressive sloping High Street lined by fourteenth- to sixteenth-century houses. The most interesting feature of the large parish church is tucked away high up in the rafters - a small statue of a pagan deity by a craftsman hedging his bets for the hereafter. The churchyard was the scene in the seventeenth century of the martyrdom of Levellers in Cromwell's army, members of a radical democratic movement shot for refusing to fight in Ireland. North of Swinbrook you come into the ancient **Wychwood** region. You are now in true Cotswold country, where you remain for most of the remaining distance - this lengthy stretch of the cycleway affords the most picturesque landscape.

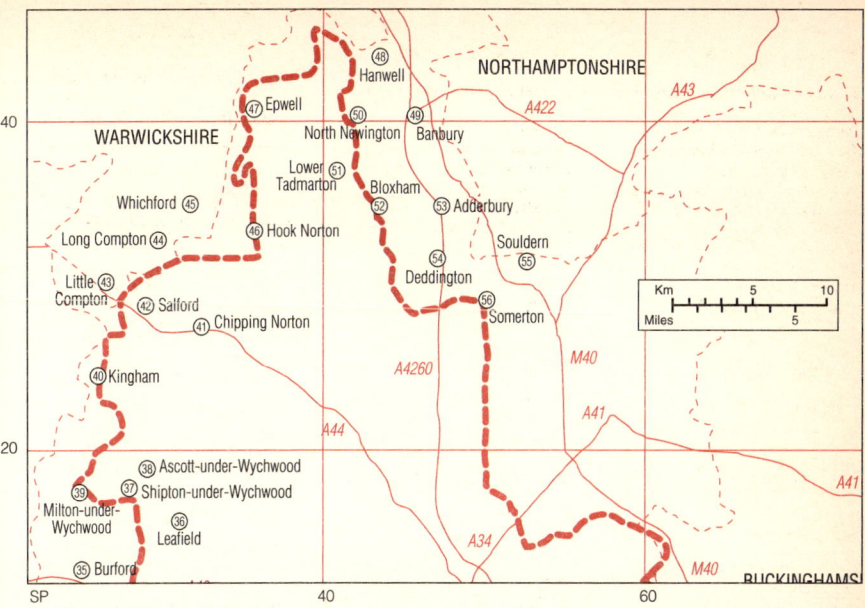

All rates are subject
to alteration at the
owners' discretion.

Childrey   26

National Grid Ref: SU3587

🍴 🍺 The Hatchett

Ridgeway House, *West Street,
Childrey, Wantage, Oxon, OX12 9UL.*
Actual grid ref: SU335873
Grades: ETC 4 Diamond
Tel: **01235 751538** (also fax no)
Mrs Roberts.
D: £20.00-£22.50 **S:** £23.00-£29.00.
Open: All Year
Beds: 1F 1T 1S
Baths: 2 En
🛇 🅿 (5) ⊬ ☐ 📺 Ⅴ ⅋ ♿ ♺
Luxury, countryside home in quiet
Downland village near the
Ridgeway, Oxford, Cotswolds and
Wantage. All rooms ensuite,
tea/coffee, TV, delicious breakfast,
wonderful views, warm welcome
assured

Bringing children with
you? Always ask for
any special rates.

Sparsholt   27

National Grid Ref: SU3487

🍴 🍺 Star Inn

Westcot Lodge, *Westcot, Sparsholt,
Wantage, Oxon, OX12 9QA.*
Actual grid ref: SU338874
Comfortable country house.
Peaceful hamlet, magnificent views
to Ridgeway 1 mile
Tel: **01235 751251** Mrs Upton.
D: £25.00 **S:** £30.00.
Open: All Year (not Xmas)
Beds: 1D 1T 1S
Baths: 1 Sh
🛇 🅿 (2) ⊬ ☐ ✗ 🛌 📺 Ⅴ ⅋ ♿ ♺

Woolstone   28

National Grid Ref: SU2988

🍴 🍺 White Horse

Hickory House, *Woolstone,
Faringdon, Oxon, SN7 7QL.*
Actual grid ref: SU294877
Tel: **01367 820303**
Mr & Mrs Grist.
Fax no: 01367 820958
D: £18.00-£25.00 **S:** £19.00-£23.00.
Open: All Year (not Xmas)
Beds: 2T
Baths: 2 En
🛇 (12) 🅿 (2) ⊬ ☐ 🛌 📺 Ⅴ ⅋ ♺
Situated in a delightful picturesque
village beneath the White Horse
Hill near the Ridgeway, Hickory
House offers comfortable
accommodation in a recently built
self-contained extension. Pub,
serving food, 25m. Oxford, Bath
and the Cotswolds are within easy
driving distance

Uffington   29

National Grid Ref: SU3089

🍴 🍺 Fox & Hounds

Norton House, *Broad Street,
Uffington, Faringdon, Oxon,
SN7 7RA.*
Actual grid ref: SU305895
Friendly C18th family home in
centre of quiet, pretty village
Tel: **01367 820230** (also fax no)
Mrs Oberman.
D: £19.00-£20.00
S: £22.00-£22.00.
Open: All Year (not Xmas)
Beds: 1F 1D 1S
Baths: 2 Pr
🛇 🅿 (3) ⊬ ☐ 🛌 🛌 📺 Ⅴ ⅋ ♿ ♺

Faringdon   30

National Grid Ref: SU2895

🍴 🍺 Fox & Hounds, The Plough

Faringdon Hotel, *1 Market Place,
Faringdon, Oxon, SN7 7HL.*
Situated near C12th parish church,
on site of palace of Alfred the
Great
Grades: ETC 3 Diamond,
AA 2 Star, RAC 2 Star
Tel: **01367 240536**
Fax no: 01367 243250
D: £30.00-£35.00.
S: £45.00-£60.00.
Open: All Year
Beds: 3F 13D 1T 3S
Baths: 20 En
🛇 ☐ 🛌 ✗ 🛌 📺 Ⅴ ♺

From the Cotswolds to Oxford

The northernmost point of the route is **Hornton**, from where you turn southwards and head to **Broughton**, where stands Broughton Castle, an Elizabethan mansion surrounded by a moat. It contains splendid pannelling, fireplaces and plaster ceilings. Inhabited by a Parliamentarian in the Civil War, it was captured by the Royalists after the Battle of Edgehill, a few miles away in Warwickshire. There is a display of Civil War arms and armour. From here you can make a detour to visit **Banbury**, the main town of Northern Oxfordshire. The Victorian market cross stands on the site of a medieval original. After Broughton you head south into the **Cherwell Valley**. A detour from **Upper Heyford** leads to Rousham House, a seventeenth-century mansion which served as a Royalist garrison during the Civil War. It has the only surviving landscape garden by William Kent. From Upper Heyford it's an easy ride to Horton-cum-Studley to complete the county circuit, and you can return to Oxford by the route along which you left.

Portwell House Hotel, *Market Place, Faringdon, Oxon, SN7 7HU.*
Grades: ETC 1 Star
Tel: **01367 240197**
Mr Pakeman.
Fax no: 01367 244330
D: £25.00
S: £40.00.
Open: All Year
Beds: 2F 3D 2T 1S
Baths: 8 En
🛇 (2) 🅿 (4) ⊬ 🗖 ✕ 🔥 🖳 🕭 Ⅵ ⓘ ⅋ ♈
Relax in the ancient market town of Faringdon within reach of the Cotswolds. William Morris Kelmscott Manor & Blenheim Palace half-way between Oxford & Swindon, our C17th house stands in the market place near the Norman parish church

Camden House, *28 Market Place, Faringdon, SN7 7HU.*
Victorian merchant's house; attractive market town, convenient Oxford, Swindon, Cotswolds
Tel: **01367 241121**
D: £15.00-£15.00
S: £15.00-£15.00.
Open: All Year
Baths: 3 Sh
🛇 🅿 🗖 🔥 🔥 🖳 🕭 Ⅵ ⅋ ♈

Gallery Cottage, *21 London Street, Faringdon, SN7 7AG.*
Old world cottage; ideal touring Cotswolds, Oxford, White Horse
Tel: **01367 244853**
D: £17.50-£17.50
S: £25.00-£25.00.
Open: All Year
Beds: 1D 1S
Baths: 1 En 1 Pr
🅿 (2) ⊬ 🗖 🍴 🔥 🖳 Ⅵ

Bowling Green Farm, *Stanford Road, Faringdon, Oxon, SN7 8EZ.*
Attractive C18th period farmhouse, offering C20th comfort
Tel: **01367 240229**
Mr & Mrs Barnard.
Fax no: 01367 242568
D: £20.00 **S:** £28.00.
Open: All Year
Beds: 2F
Baths: 2 En
🛇 🅿 (6) ⊬ 🗖 🔥 🖳 Ⅵ ⓘ

Coleshill 31

National Grid Ref: SU2393

🍴 🍺 Radnor Arms

Ashen Copse Farm, *Coleshill, Highworth, Swindon, Wilts, SN6 7PU.*
Farmhouse in beautiful, peaceful countryside
Grades: ETC 3 Diamond
Tel: **01367 240175**
Ms Hoddinott.
D: £21.00-£24.00 **S:** £21.00-£30.00.
Open: All Year (not Xmas)
Beds: 1F 1T 1S
Baths: 1 Pr 1 Sh
🛇 🅿 (6) ⊬ 🗖 🔥 Ⅵ

Buscot 32

National Grid Ref: SU2397

🍴 🍺 Trout Inn

Apple Tree House, *Buscot, Faringdon, Oxon, SN7 8DA.*
Old property in National Trust village, 5 mins' walk River Thames, one acre garden
Grades: ETC 3 Diamond, AA 3 Diamond, RAC 3 Diamond
Tel: **01367 252592**
Mrs Reay.
D: £18.00-£22.00 **S:** £23.00-£28.00.
Open: All Year (not Xmas)
Beds: 2D 1T
Baths: 1 En 1 Sh
🛇 🅿 (10) ⊬ 🗖 🔥 🖳 Ⅵ ♈

Clanfield 33

National Grid Ref: SP2801

🍴 🍺 Clanfield Tavern

The Granary, *Clanfield, Bampton, Oxon, OX18 2SH.*
Actual grid ref: SP284018
Ground floor twin ensuite, others upstairs. Near Thames, Cotswolds, Oxford
Tel: **01367 810266** Mrs Payne.
D: £17.00 **S:** £17.00.
Open: All Year (not Xmas)
Beds: 1D 1T 1S
Baths: 1 Pr 1 Sh
🅿 (4) ⊬ 🗖 🔥 🖳 Ⅵ ⅋

Bampton 34

National Grid Ref: SP3103

🍴 🍺 Talbot Hotel, Romany Inn

Morar, *Weald Street, Bampton, Oxon, OX18 2HL.*
Actual grid ref: SP312026
Grades: ETC 3 Diamond
Tel: **01993 850162** Ms Rouse.
Fax no: 01993 851738
D: £22.50-£25.00 **S:** £22.50-£25.00.
Open: Mar to Dec
Beds: 2D 1T
Baths: 2 En 1 Pr
🛇 (6) 🅿 (4) ⊬ 🗖 🔥 🖳 Ⅵ ⓘ ⅋ ♈
Wake to the mouthwatering smell of homemade bread baking. Hearty cooked breakfast with homemade jams and marmalades. Peaceful garden, beautiful herbaceous borders. Pet cats, goat, sheep. Bicycles garaged, boots dried, thermos filled free. See our own website: http://www.countryaccom.co.uk/morar/

Elephant & Castle, *Bridge Street, Bampton, Oxon, OX18 2HA.*
Cosy, friendly atmosphere. Lunch time snacks. Real ales. Beer garden
Tel: **01993 850316** Mrs Blackwell.
D: £17.50 **S:** £25.00.
Open: All Year
Beds: 1D 2T
Baths: 3 En
🛇 (12) 🅿 (20) 🗖 🔥 ✕ 🔥 🖳 Ⅵ ⓘ ⅋

Romany Inn, *Bridge Street, Bampton, Oxon, OX18 2HA.*
C19th Georgian building. Chef proprietor. Inn & restaurant, Good Beer Guide, Good Pub Guide
Tel: **01993 850237** Mr Smith.
Fax no: 01993 852133
D: £19.50 **S:** £22.50.
Open: All Year
Beds: 3F 4D 2T 2S
Baths: 10 Pr
🛇 🅿 (7) 🗖 🔥 ✕ 🔥 🖳 🕭 Ⅵ

D = Price range per person sharing in a double room

Burford 35

National Grid Ref: SP2512

⚓ 🍽 Old Bull

The Old Bell Foundry, 45 Witney
Street, Burford, Oxon, *OX18 4RX.*
Grades: ETC 4 Diamond
Tel: **01993 822234** (also fax no)
Ms Barguss.
D: £24.00-£25.00.
Open: All Year (not Xmas)
Beds: 1F
Baths: 1 En
🛌 🅿 (1) 🍴🖵🖥🚲🎥📺 ✦ ♺
Tranquil setting, a short distance
from Burford High Street. One
large double-bedded or family
room which looks down over a
peaceful garden to the River
Windrush. A good base for seeing
the Cotswolds and Oxford

Leafield 36

National Grid Ref: SP3115

⚓ 🍽 The Swan

Langley Farm, Leafield, Witney,
Oxon, *OX8 5QD.*
Lovely Cotswold stone house set in
open country
Tel: **01993 878686**
Mrs Greves.
D: £14.00-£22.00 S: £28.00-£40.00.
Open: May to Oct
Beds: 2D 1T
Baths: 1 Pr 2 Sh
🛌 (8) 🅿 (8) 🖵 🐾 🚲 🎥 📺

Shipton-under-Wychwood 37

National Grid Ref: SP2717

⚓ 🍽 Red Horse, Lamb Inn

6 Courtlands Road, Shipton-under-
Wychwood, Chipping Norton,
Oxon, *OX7 6DF.*
Grades: ETC 4 Diamond
Tel: **01993 830551**
Mr & Mrs Fletcher.
D: £17.50-£22.50 S: £20.00-£25.00.
Open: All Year
Beds: 2D 1T
Baths: 2 En 1 Pr
🅿 (3) 🍴🖵🚲🎥📺🛏 ✦
Friendly, quiet, comfortable
house/garden

Garden Cottage, Fidders Hill,
Shipton-under-Wychwood,
Chipping Norton, Oxon, *OX7 6DR.*
Attractive stone cottage, country
views, quiet, ideal for exploring
Cotswolds
Grades: ETC 3 Diamond
Tel: **01993 830640**
Worker.
D: £15.00-£25.00 S: £25.00-£35.00.
Open: All Year (not Xmas)
Beds: 1D 1T
Baths: 2 En
🛌 (8) 🅿 (2) 🍴🖵🚲🎥📺🛏 ✦

Ascott-under-Wychwood 38

National Grid Ref: SP3018

⚓ 🍽 Shaven Crown

The Mill, Ascott-under-Wychwood,
Chipping Norton, Oxon, *OX7 6AP.*
Actual grid ref: SP309194
Unique tranquil rural location, free
fishing, varied wildlife
Tel: **01993 831282**
Braithwaite.
D: £17.50-£22.00 S: £17.50-£22.00.
Open: All Year
Beds: 1D 1T 1S
Baths: 1 Sh
🛌 🅿 (6) 🖵 🚲 🎥 📺 ✦

Milton-under-Wychwood 39

National Grid Ref: SP2618

⚓ 🍽 Quart Pot, Lamb Inn

Sunset House, Jubilee Lane,
Milton-under-Wychwood, Chipping
Norton, Oxfordshire, *OX7 6EW.*
Tel: **01993 830581**
Mrs Durston.
D: £23.50-£25.00 S: £27.50-£30.00.
Beds: 2D 1T
Baths: 2 En 1 Pr
🛌 (5) 🅿 (3) 🍴🖵🚲🎥📺
Period Cotswold house, charming
bedrooms with ensuite private
facilities, ideal location for touring
this renowned Area of Natural
Beauty. Traditional English
breakfast. Stratford, Oxford and
Cheltenham approx 30 mins. A
wide choice of fine old inns,
restaurants

Hillborough House, Shipton Road,
Milton-under-Wychwood, Chipping
Norton, Oxon, *OX7 6JH.*
Delightful Cotswold village. All
rooms with picture windows
overlooking village green
Tel: **01993 830501**
Mrs Jones.
Fax no: 01993 832005
D: £23.00
S: £28.00.
Open: All Year (not Xmas)
Beds: 1F 3D
Baths: 4 En
🛌 🅿 🖵 🚲 🎥 📺 ✦ ♺

Please respect

a B&B's wishes

regarding children,

animals & smoking.

Kingham 40

National Grid Ref: SP2524

⚓ 🍽 Kings Head

The Old Stores, Foscot, Kingham,
Chipping Norton, Oxon, *OX7 6RH.*
Actual grid ref: SP2522
Tel: **01608 659844** (also fax no)
D: £18.00-£20.00 S: £22.00-£23.00.
Open: Mar to Nov
Beds: 1D
Baths: 1 Pr
🅿 (2) 🍴🖵🚲🎥📺 ✦ ♺
Charming Cotswold stone cottage
in lovely rural location, 1.5 miles
from Kingham and 5 miles from
Stow-on-the-Wold.
Accommodation is private with
own beamed-lounge, home
produce, brochure

Chipping Norton 41

National Grid Ref: SP3126

⚓ 🍽 Blue Boar

The Old Bakehouse, 50 West
Street, Chipping Norton, Oxon,
OX7 5ER.
Family-run 400-year-old
bakehouse; warm & friendly
atmosphere
Tel: **01608 643441**
Mr & Mrs Cashmore.
D: £20.00 S: £30.00.
Open: All Year (not Xmas)
Beds: 1F 1D
Baths: 2 En
🛌 (5) 🅿 (2) 🍴🖵🚲🎥📺 ♺

Salford 42

National Grid Ref: SP2828

⚓ 🍽 Red Lion

1 Lower Barns, Salford, Chipping
Norton, Oxon, *OX7 5YP.*
Barn conversion in quiet Cotswold
village, traditional comfort
Tel: **01608 643276**
Mrs Barnard.
D: £15.00-£16.00 S: £15.00-£16.00.
Open: All Year (not Xmas)
Beds: 1T
Baths: 1 En
🛌 🅿 (2) 🐾 🚲 🎥 📺 ♺

Little Compton 43

National Grid Ref: SP2630

Rigside, Little Compton, Moreton-
in-Marsh, Glos, *GL56 0RR.*
Detached country house, private
parking, midway Moreton-in-
Marsh and Chipping Norton
Grades: AA 4 Diamond
Tel: **01608 674128** (also fax no)
Ms Cox.
D: £20.00-£22.50 S: £20.00-£20.00.
Open: All Year
Beds: 1D 1T 2S
Baths: 1 En 1 Sh
🛌 (9) 🅿 (6) 🚲 🎥 📺 🛏 ✦ ♺

Four Gables, *Little Compton, Moreton-in-Marsh, Glos, GL56 0SQ.*
Attractive village location, ideal base for touring the Cotswolds
Tel: **01608 674233** Mrs Withers.
D: £22.00-£22.50 **S:** £30.00-£40.00.
Open: Mar to Oct
Beds: 1D 1T
Baths: 2 En
🛏 (4) 🅿 (4) ⏚ 🗄 👤 🛒 Ⅳ

Long Compton 44

National Grid Ref: SP2832

Archways, *Crockwell Street, Long Compton, Shipston on Stour, Warks, CV36 5JN.*
Actual grid ref: SP2933
Charming C17th Cotswold cottage midway Oxford Stratford - ideal for Cotswolds
Tel: **01608 684358**
Mrs Cunnington.
D: £16.00-£19.00 **S:** £18.00-£20.00.
Open: All Year (not Xmas)
Beds: 2D 1T
Baths: 2 Sh
🛏 🅿 (4) 🗄 👤 🛒 Ⅳ ⚲ 🚲

Tallet Barn, *Yerdley Farm, Long Compton, Shipston-on-Stour, Warks, CV36 5LH.*
Comfortable annexed rooms, a warm welcome and a quiet village location
Grades: ETC 4 Diamond
Tel: **01608 684248**
Mrs Richardson.
D: £19.00-£20.00 **S:** £25.00-£25.00.
Open: All Year
Beds: 1D 1T
Baths: 2 En
🛏 (6) 🅿 (2) ⏚ 🗄 👤 🛒 Ⅳ ⚲

Whichford 45

National Grid Ref: SP3134

🍴 🍺 The Gate

Ascott House Farm, *Whichford, Long Compton, Shipston on Stour, Warks, CV36 5PP.*
Cotswold farmhouse, area of natural beauty
Tel: **01608 684655** Mrs Haines.
Fax no: 01608 684539
D: £18.00-£20.00 **S:** £20.00-£25.00.
Open: All Year (not Xmas)
Beds: 2D 1T
Baths: 2 En 1 Sh
🛏 🅿 (12) 🗄 🐾 👤 🛒 Ⅳ ⚲

Always telephone
to get directions to
the B&B - you will
save time!

Hook Norton 46

National Grid Ref: SP3533

🍴 🍺 Sun Inn

Symnel, *High St, Hook Norton, Banbury, Oxfordshire, OX15 5NH.*
Victorian house. Ideal Shakespeare country, Cotswolds. Comfortable beds, tempting breakfasts
Tel: **01608 737547**
Mrs Cornelius.
D: £15.00-£15.00 **S:** £15.00-£15.00.
Open: All Year (not Xmas)
Beds: 1D 2T
Baths: 1 Sh
🛏 🅿 ⏚ 🗄 ✕ 👤 🛒 Ⅳ 👤 ⚲ 🚲

Epwell 47

National Grid Ref: SP3441

🍴 🍺 The Bell

Yarnhill Farm, *Shenington Road, Epwell, Banbury, Oxon, OX15 6JA.*
Peaceful farmhouse; ideally situated for Cotswolds, Stratford upon Avon, Oxford
Grades: ETC 3 Diamond
Tel: **01295 780250**
D: £18.00-£25.00 **S:** £18.00-£25.00.
Open: All Year (not Xmas)
Beds: 1D 1T 1S
Baths: 1 Pr 1 Sh
🛏 (8) 🅿 (6) ⏚ 🗄 👤 🛒 Ⅳ ⚲ 🚲

Hanwell 48

National Grid Ref: SP4344

🍴 🍺 The Bell, Shennington

The Coach House, *Hanwell Castle, Hanwell, Banbury, Oxon, OX17 5LJ.*
Part of C15th castle in 20 acres (garden) undergoing restoration
Tel: **01295 730764**
Mrs Taylor.
D: £18.00-£25.00 **S:** £18.00-£25.00.
Open: Apr to Oct
Beds: 1F 1D 1T
Baths: 3 En
🛏 (1) 🅿 (6) 🗄 🐾 👤 🛒 🚹 Ⅳ

Banbury 49

National Grid Ref: SP4540

🍴 🍺 Swan Inn

Belmont Guest House, *34 Crouch Street, Banbury, Oxon, OX16 9PR.*
Large Victorian house (detached). Family-run business, mainly ensuite bedrooms, clean and comfortable
Tel: **01295 262308**
Mr Raby.
Fax no: 01295 275982
D: £20.00 **S:** £25.00.
Open: All Year (not Xmas)
Beds: 1F 2D 3T 2S
Baths: 5 Pr 1 Sh
🛏 (10) 🅿 (6) ⏚ 🗄 👤 🛒 🚹 Ⅳ ⚲

North Newington 50

National Grid Ref: SP4239

🍴 🍺 North Arms

Broughton Grounds Farm, *North Newington, Banbury, Oxon, OX15 6AW.*
Tel: **01295 730315**
Margaret Taylor.
D: £16.00-£18.00 **S:** £16.00-£18.00.
Open: All Year (not Xmas)
Beds: 1D 1T 1S
Baths: 1 Sh
🛏 (2) 🅿 (3) ⏚ 🗄 👤 Ⅳ 🚹 👤 🚲
Enjoy warm hospitality & peaceful surroundings at our C17th stone farmhouse. A working family farm situated on the Broughton Castle estate with beautiful views & walks. Very comfortable spacious accommodation, log fire in dining room, delicious breakfast & cream teas with home produce

Lower Tadmarton 51

National Grid Ref: SP4037

Mill Barn, *Lower Tadmarton, Banbury, Oxon, OX15 5SU.*
Actual grid ref: SP403372
Two spacious ensuite rooms, one downstairs, are available in this comfortable family home
Tel: **01295 780349** Mrs Lee.
D: £20.00 **S:** £25.00.
Open: All Year
Beds: 1F 1D **Baths:** 2 En
🛏 🅿 (2) ⏚ 🗄 👤 🛒 ♿ Ⅳ

Bloxham 52

National Grid Ref: SP4236

🍴 🍺 Red Lion

Brock Cottage, *Little Bridge Road, Bloxham, Banbury, Oxon, OX15 4PU.*
Warm welcome to C17th thatched cottage. Personal management by owner
Tel: **01295 721089**
D: £18.50-£18.50 **S:** £18.50-£18.50.
Open: All Year
Beds: 1D 1T 1S
Baths: 1 En 1 Pr
🅿 (4) ⏚ 🗄 👤 🛒 Ⅳ 👤 🚲

Adderbury 53

National Grid Ref: SP4735

Morgans Orchard Restaurant, *9 Twyford Gardens, Twyford, Adderbury, Banbury, Oxon, OX17 3JA.*
Award-winning French restaurant with quality B&B within rustic village location
Tel: **01295 812047** Mr Morgan.
D: £20.00-£25.00 **S:** £27.50-£40.00.
Open: All Year
Beds: 1D 2T 1S
Baths: 1 En 1 Pr 3 Sh
🛏 🅿 (3) ⏚ 🗄 🐾 ✕ 👤 🛒 Ⅳ 🚹 👤 ⚲ 🚲

Deddington 54

National Grid Ref: SP4631

📍🍴 The Unicorn

Hill Barn, *Milton Gated Road, Deddington, Banbury, Oxon, OX15 0TS.*
Converted barn in open countryside, convenient for Oxford, Cotswolds, Warwick, Stratford
Tel: **01869 338631** Mrs White.
D: £20.00-£24.00 **S:** £25.00-£25.00.
Open: All Year (not Xmas)
Beds: 1F 1D 2T
Baths: 1 En 1 Sh
🛏 🅿 (6) ❑ ✝ 🛉 ▥ V ♿

Stonecrop Guest House, *Hempton Road, Deddington, Banbury, Oxon, OX15 0QH.*
Detached house close to places of interest. A warm welcome
Grades: ETC 2 Diamond
Tel: **01869 338335**
Fax no: 01869 338505
D: £16.00-£19.00 **S:** £16.00-£19.00.
Open: All Year
Beds: 1F 1D 1T 1S
Baths: 2 Sh
🛏 (10) 🅿 (6) ❑ 🛉 ▥ V ⚡ ♿

Souldern 55

National Grid Ref: SP5231

📍🍴 The Fox

The Fox Inn, *Souldern, Bicester, Oxon, OX6 9JN.*
Stone inn, restaurant, beautiful village convenient for Oxford, Woodstock, Stratford and Warwick
Grades: ETC 2 Diamond
Tel: **01869 345284** Mr MacKay.
Fax no: 01869 345667
D: £18.00-£23.00 **S:** £24.00-£30.00.
Open: All Year (not Xmas)
Beds: 3D 1T
Baths: 2 En 1 Sh
🛏 🅿 (6) ❑ ✝ ✗ 🛉 ▥ V

Towerfields, *Tusmore Road, Souldern, Bicester, Oxon, OX6 9HY.*
Ground floor ensuite bedrooms, superb views, quiet, easy access M40
Tel: **01869 346554**
Mrs Hamilton Gould.
Fax no: 01869 345157
D: £24.00 **S:** £24.00.
Open: All Year (not Xmas)
Beds: 1D 1T 1S **Baths:** 3 En
🛏 🅿 (4) ❑ ✝ 🛉 ▥ & V

Somerton 56

National Grid Ref: SP4928

📍🍴 Deddington Arms

Jersey Manor Farmhouse, *Heyford Road, Somerton, Bicester, Oxon, OX6 4LW.*
Charming 400-year-old listed Cotswold stone farmhouse on the edge of the Oxfordshire Cotswolds
Tel: **01869 345414**
Fax no: 01869 345142
D: £18.00 **S:** £20.00.
Open: All Year
Beds: 1F 1T 1D
Baths: 2 Sh
🛏 🅿 ❑ 🛉 ▥ V

All cycleways are
popular: you are
well-advised to
book ahead

Reivers Cycle Route

The **Reivers Route** is a new path through Northumberland and Cumbria (once briefly crossing the Scottish border) from Tynemouth to Whitehaven. Over 180 miles long, it has been developed by the local authorities in conjunction with Sustrans, who designate it a Regional Route, linking in several places to the National Cycle Network. The route is clearly signposted by blue direction signs bearing a cycle silhouette and the legend 'REIVERS' with the number 10 in a rectangle. It can be cycled as a return path with the **Sea to Sea (C2C)**, to form a giant circle through the whole splendid gamut of England's northern scenery between the North Sea and Irish Sea coasts. Passing through the remote grandeur of Northumberland National Park, the Border Forest Park and Kielder Water, you will take in the historic city of Carlisle before skirting the northern Lake District and continuing to the west coast.

The route takes its name from the Border Reivers, outlaw clans who held anarchic sway between the secure hearts of the kingdoms of England and Scotland, feuding, raiding and rustling each other's cattle through most of the fourteenth, fifteenth and sixteenth centuries, after the Anglo-Scottish Wars over rights to the crown of Scotland left this debatable land virtually ungoverned. Many Reiver family names – Armstrong, Graham, Bell, Robson, Nixon (who says there's no criminal gene?) – survive, as well as lasting contributions to the English vocabulary, notably 'blackmail' and 'bereaved'.

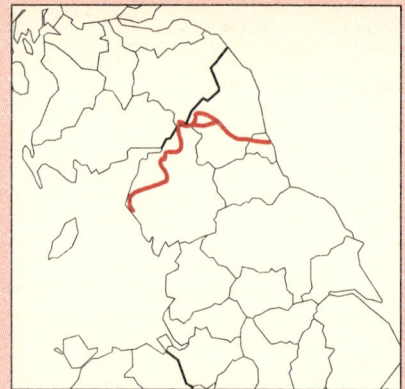

As you experience this wild country, look out for secluded hollows which might have been used to ambush rivals in centuries past.

The indispensable **official route map and guide** for the route is available from Sustrans, 35 King Street, Bristol BS1 4DZ, tel 0117-926 8893, fax 0117-929 4173, @ £4.50 (+ £2.00 p&p).

Maps: Ordnance Survey 1:50,000 Landranger series: 79, 80, 85, 87, 88, 89, 90

Trains: The Intercity west coast main line goes to Carlisle, from where you can connect to Workington or Whitehaven. The Intercity east coast main line goes to Newcastle, from where you can connect to Tynemouth.

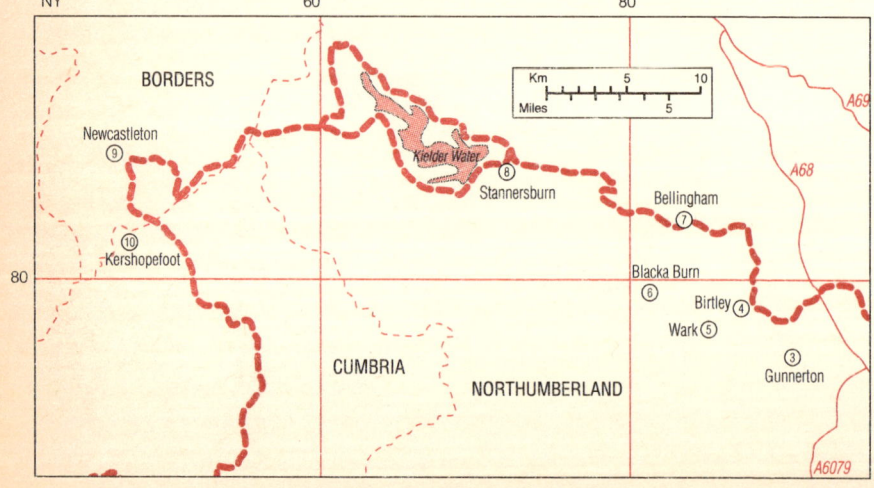

Ponteland 1

National Grid Ref: NZ1673

Blackbird Inn, The Plough

7 Collingwood Cottages, Limestone Lane, Ponteland, Newcastle-upon-Tyne, NE20 0DD.
Actual grid ref: NZ149732
Quiet informal home in countryside. Lovely views from rooms
Tel: **01661 825967**
Mrs Baxter.
D: £17.50-£17.50 **S:** £20.00-£25.00.
Open: All Year (not Xmas)
Beds: 1F 1D
Baths: 1 Sh
🏠 🅿 (4) ⅃⏁📺🏠🛏🖳Ⅴ ⅌

Dalton House, Dalton, Ponteland, Newcastle-upon-Tyne, NE18 0AA.
Elegant Georgian house, quiet village. Easy access to Newcastle Roman Wall
Tel: **01661 886225**
Mrs Trevelyan.
D: £22.00-£22.00 **S:** £22.00-£22.00.
Open: Easter to Oct
Beds: 3T 2S
Baths: 3 Pr
🏠 (14) 🅿 (6) ⅃⏁✗🛏🖳Ⅴ🔒

Stamfordham 2

National Grid Ref: NZ0771

Bay Horse

Church House, Stamfordham, Newcastle-upon-Tyne, NE18 0PB.
Beautiful C17th listed stone house facing green in lovely rural village
Tel: **01661 886736**
Mrs Fitzpatrick.
D: £20.00 **S:** £20.00.
Open: All Year
Beds: 2T
Baths: 1 Sh
🏠 🅿 (4) ⏁🛏🖳Ⅴ🔒 ⅌ ⅌

Tynemouth to Bellingham

The route begins in the urban sprawl around **Newcastle-upon-Tyne** (see under *Sustrans Sea to Sea*), heading through **Tynemouth** and **North Shields** before leaving the industrial wasteland behind and striking out west up the Pont Valley through Reiver country. When you reach the village of Matfen you are only two miles north of **Hadrian's Wall**, the biggest single engineering endeavour of the Roman Empire, built by Emperor Hadrian in the Second Century to keep the Caledonian hordes at bay, and now a World Heritage Site. From the stones that remain atop the bleak Northumberland hills you can trace out the line of the wall in your mind's eye, with the milecastles and turrets from which it was patrolled. At **Bellingham**, the gateway to Northumberland National Park, you will find a mark left by the Reiver era in the shape of Black Middens Bastle House, a sixteenth-century fortified farmhouse where livestock were kept safe from raids on the ground floor, and the family upstairs. St Cuthbert's church has a stone-vaulted roof also built to prevent Reiver raids; the Heritage Centre gives an insight into this period and the rest of the town's social history.

Gunnerton 3

National Grid Ref: NY9075

The Black Horse, Gunnerton, Hexham, Northumberland, NE48 4AU.
Converted C18th inn in heart of Hadrian's wall country
Tel: **01434 681991** (also fax no)
Mr & Mrs Batey.
D: £12.50-£14.00 **S:** £12.50-£14.00.
Open: All Year
Beds: 1D 1T 1S **Baths:** 1 En 1 Sh
🏠 (12) 🅿 (2) ⅃⏁🛏✗🖳Ⅴ🔒 ⅌ ⅌

S = Price range for a single person in a room

Birtley 4

National Grid Ref: NY8778

Barrasford Arms, Tone Inn

Colt Crag Farmhouse, Birtley, Hexham, Northd, NE48 3JD.
Beautiful lakeside farm house; all rooms overlooking garden and lake
Tel: **01434 681419** Mrs Loche.
D: £16.00-£16.00 **S:** £16.00-£16.00.
Open: All Year (not Xmas)
Beds: 1F 1T **Baths:** 1 Sh
🏠 🅿 (10) ⏁🛏✗🖳Ⅴ🔒 ⅌ ⅌

D = Price range per person sharing in a double room

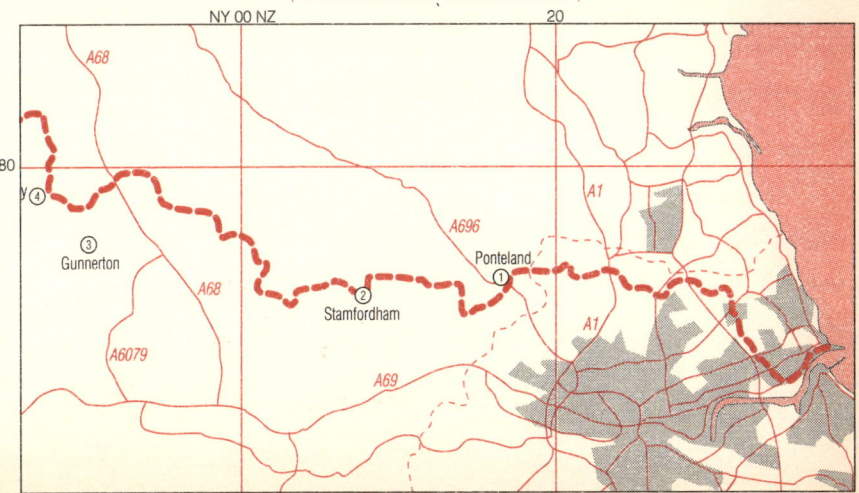

Blacka Burn 5

National Grid Ref: NY8278

🍴 🍺 Battlesteads Hotel

Hetherington Farm, Blacka Burn, Wark, Hexham, Northd, NE48 3DR.
Actual grid ref: NY824782
Traditional farmhouse in lovely countryside. Ideal walking, touring, warm welcome
Tel: **01434 230260**
Mrs Nichol.
D: £18.00-£25.00 **S:** £18.00-£25.00.
Open: Easter to Nov
Beds: 4F 1D 1S
Baths: 1 En 1 Pr 1 Sh
🛏 (10) 🅿 (4) 🔌 🛚 ▼ ⓐ ⌁ 🚲

Wark 6

National Grid Ref: NY8577

Woodpark Farm, Wark, Hexham, Northd, NE48 3PZ.
Listed farmhouse
Tel: **01434 230259**
Mrs Bell.
D: £15.00 **S:** £18.00.
Open: May to Oct
Beds: 1F 1D
Baths: 1 Sh
🅿 (3) ⌀ ⌷ 🔌 ▼ ⓐ ⌁

Battlesteads Hotel, Wark, Hexham, Northd, NE48 3LS.
Converted C17th farm, tastefully modernised
Tel: **01434 230209**
Mr & Mrs Rowland.
Fax no: 01434 230730
D: £21.00 **S:** £25.00.
Open: All Year
Beds: 1F 4D 4T 1S
Baths: 10 En
🛏 🅿 (30) ⌀ ⌷ 🐾 ✕ 🔌 🛚 ▼ ⓐ ⌁

D = Price range per person sharing in a double room

Bellingham 7

National Grid Ref: NY8383

🍴 🍺 Rose & Crown, Cheviot Hotel

▲ *Bellingham Youth Hostel,*
Woodburn Road, Bellingham, Hexham, Northumberland, NE48 2ED.
Actual grid ref: NY843834
Tel: **01434 220313**
Under 18: £4.65 **Adults:** £6.80
self-catering facilities, showers, no smoking
Hostel built of red cedarwood on the Pennine Way, high above the small Borders town of Bellingham. Near Kielder Water (with forest trails and watersports) and Hadrian's Wall

Lyndale Guest House & Holiday Cottage, Bellingham, Hexham, Northd, NE48 2AW.
Grades: ETC 4 Diamond
Tel: **01434 220361** (also fax no)
Mrs Gaskin.
D: £22.50-£25.00 **S:** £22.50.
Open: All Year (not Xmas)
Beds: 1F 2D 1T 1S
Baths: 2 En 1 Pr 1 Sh
🛏 🅿 (5) ⌀ ⌷ ✕ 🐾 🔌 🛚 ⅙ ▼ ⓐ ⌁ 🚲
Tour the Borders, good walking, Hadrian's Wall, Pennine Way, Kielder Water or cycle the Rievers' Route. Enjoy a welcome break. Relax in our walled garden. Sunlounge with panoramic views. Excellent dinners, choice of breakfasts, quality ground floor ensuites. Special discounts

---

Lynn View, Bellingham, Hexham, Northd, NE48 2BL.
Actual grid ref: NY839834
Comfortable friendly accommodation in village
Tel: **01434 220344** Mrs Batey.
D: £17.00 **S:** £20.00.
Open: All Year (not Xmas)
Beds: 2D 1T **Baths:** 1 Sh
🛏 (2) 🅿 (3) 🐾 🔌 🛚 ▼ ⓐ ⌁

Westfield House, Bellingham, Hexham, Northd, NE48 2DP.
Actual grid ref: NY836836
Voted in top 20 by *Which?*. Come and be spoilt
Tel: **01434 220340**
Mr & Mrs Minchin.
Fax no: 01434 220694
D: £25.00 **S:** £30.00.
Open: All Year
Beds: 1F 2D 2T
Baths: 4 En 1 Pr
🛏 🅿 (8) ⌀ ⌷ 🐾 ✕ 🔌 🛚 ▼ ⓐ ⌁

Stannersburn 8

National Grid Ref: NY7287

🍴 🍺 Pheasant Inn

Spring Cottage, Stannersburn, Hexham, NE48 1DD.
1 mile Kielder Water. Warm welcome, good food, beautiful scenery
Grades: ETC 3 Diamond
Tel: **01434 240388**
Mr & Mrs Ormesher.
D: £18.00-£21.00 **S:** £18.00-£21.00.
Open: All Year (not Xmas)
Beds: 1F 1D
Baths: 2 En
🛏 🅿 ⌷ 🔌 🛚 ⅙ ▼ ⓐ ⌁ 🚲

Newcastleton 9

National Grid Ref: NY4887

Woodside Guest House, Newcastleton, Hawick, Roxburghshire, TD9 0RZ.
Actual grid ref: NY485880
Tel: **013873 75431** (also fax no)
Mrs Rabour.
D: £16.00-£18.00 **S:** £16.00-£17.00.
Open: All Year
Beds: 2D 2T 1S
Baths: 2 Sh
🛏 🅿 (6) ⌷ 🐾 ✕ 🔌 🛚 ▼ ⓐ 🚲
Experience Scottish hospitality in a magical land of hills, rivers and forests, ideal for walking, cycling, relaxation. Near border attractions, Hadrians Wall. Spacious old house, H&C all rooms, home/Italian cooking, licensed. Italian and French spoken.

Bellingham to Whitehaven

Kielder Water and Kielder Forest Park are the largest man-made reservoir and forest in Europe. As well as the spectacular scenery, the lake also offers all manner of watersports, and fishing. Close to the Kielder Dam, where the route reaches the lake, the Kielder Water Exhibition at Tower Knowe Visitor Centre documents the development of this remote valley through the ages. At the other end of the lake, **Kielder Castle**, originally an eighteenth-century hunting lodge, is now the Forest Park Centre, with information on the work of the Forestry Commission. Crossing the Scottish border to reach **Newcastleton**, you are now in Liddesdale, heart of the Reiver wildlands, whose story is portrayed in the Liddesdale Trust Museum. Back in England, following a winding route into the Lyne Valley, the approach to **Rockcliffe** at the mouth of the Eden yields views over the Solway Estuary, a renowned wildlife haven, before you come to Carlisle (see under *Cumbria Cycleway*) Heading through the northern Lake District, you pass below the Caldbeck Fells and up the Derwent Valley to reach **Cockermouth**, before striking out west to the coastal towns of **Workington** and **Whitehaven** (see under *Sustrans Sea to Sea (C2C)* for information on these towns).

Bringing children with you? Always ask for any special rates.

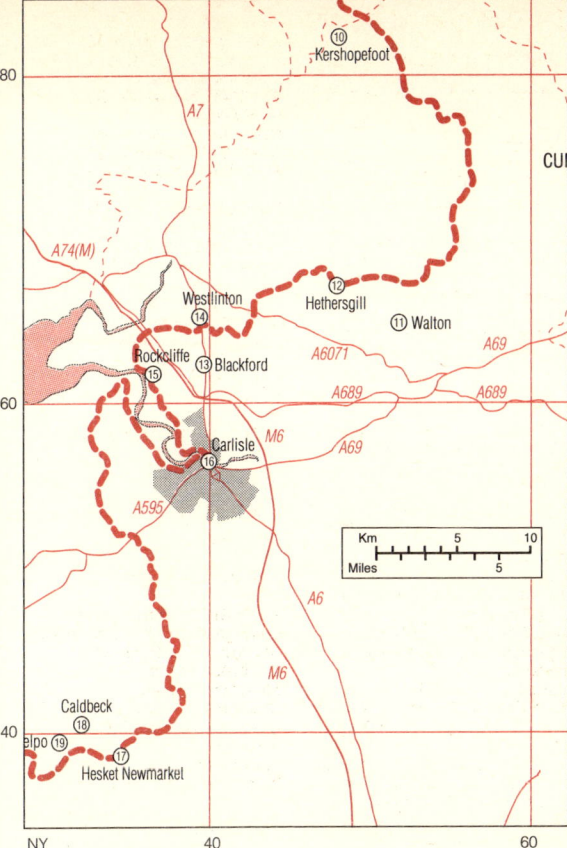

80

A7

CU

A74(M)

Westlinton
14
Hethersgill
12
11 Walton

Rockcliffe
15
13 Blackford
A6071
A69

60
A689
A689

Carlisle
16
M6
A69

A595

Km		5		10
Miles			5	

A6

M6

Caldbeck
18
elpo 19
17
Hesket Newmarket

40

NY   40   60

10
Kershopefoot

The Grid Reference beneath the location heading is for the village or town - *not* for individual houses, which are shown (where supplied) in each entry itself.

Low Rigg Farm, Walton, Brampton, Cumbria, CA8 2DX.
Actual grid ref: NY522651
Comfortable accommodation on a working farm in beautiful Hadrian's Wall country. Excellent home cooking
Grades: ETC 3 Diamond,
AA 3 Diamond, RAC 3 Diamond
Tel: 016977 3233
Mrs Thompson.
D: £15.00-£18.00
S: £18.00-£20.00.
Open: All Year (not Xmas)
Beds: 1F
Baths: 1 Sh

Town Head Farm, Walton, Brampton, Cumbria, CA8 2DJ.
Relax in cosy farmhouse with friendly atmosphere on working beef/sheep farm
Grades: ETC 3 Diamond
Tel: 016977 2730
Ms Armstrong.
D: £15.00-£16.00
S: £15.00-£16.00.
Open: All Year (not Xmas)
Beds: 1F 1D
Baths: 1 Sh

Hethersgill   12

National Grid Ref: NY4767

New Pallyards, Hethersgill, Carlisle, Cumbria, CA6 6HZ.
National gold award winner, close to Carlisle & borders
Grades: ETC 4 Diamond
Tel: 01228 577308 (also fax no)
Mrs Elwen.
D: £21.00-£22.00
S: £22.00-£28.00.
Open: All Year
Beds: 1F 2D 1T
Baths: 4 En

Honey Farm, Newcastleton, Roxburghshire, TD9 0SG.
A warm welcome in spacious and peaceful surroundings. Good home cooking
Grades: STB 4 Star
Tel: 013873 76737
Mrs Stenhouse.
D: £23.00-£25.00 **S:** £23.00-£28.00.
Open: All Year
Beds: 1D 1T
Baths: 1 En 1 Pr

Kershopefoot   10

National Grid Ref: NY4882

North Kershopefoot, Kershopefoot, Newcastleton, TD9 0TJ.
Actual grid ref: NY475829
Half-C17th farmhouse. Gardens, heritage area, castles, walking
Tel: 01387 375734
Mrs Henke.
D: £14.00-£14.00 **S:** £14.00-£14.00.
Open: All Year (not Xmas)
Beds: 1T
Baths: 1 Sh

Walton   11

National Grid Ref: NY5264

The Stag, The Centurion, Lane End Inn, The Centurion

High Rigg Farm, Walton, Brampton, Cumbria, CA8 2AZ.
Grades: ETC 3 Diamond
Tel: 016977 2117 Mrs Mounsey.
D: £16.00-£18.00 **S:** £18.00.
Open: All Year (not Xmas)
Beds: 2F
Baths: 1 Pr 1 Sh

Attractive Listed Georgian farmhouse, warm hospitality, very comfortable. TV and wash basin in bedroom. Spectacular views of Lakeland and Pennines. On roadside but quiet. Excellent parking, easily accessible to explore Scotland, Hadrian's Wall and the Lakes

---

S = Price range for a single person in a room

Always telephone to get directions to the B&B - you will save time!

Blackford 13

National Grid Ref: NY3962

🍴 🍺 Crown & Thistle, Coach & Horses, Golden Fleece

Gill Farm, *Blackford, Carlisle, Cumbria, CA6 4EL.*
Tel: **01228 675326** Mrs Nicholson.
D: £17.50-£18.00 **S:** £18.00-£20.00.
Open: All Year
Beds: 1F 1D 1T
Baths: 2 Sh
🛏 🅿 (7) ⬜ 🖤 ➤ 🌿 🎦 ☑ ✿ 🚲
Large Georgian farmhouse dated 1740 on working beef and sheep farm in peaceful countryside

The Hill Cottage, *Blackford, Carlisle, Cumbria, CA6 4DU.*
Actual grid ref: NY396612
Country house, one minute M6/A74. Spacious modern ground floor rooms
Tel: **01228 674739**
Mr & Mrs Martin.
D: £17.00 **S:** £20.00.
Open: All Year (not Xmas)
Beds: 1F 1D **Baths:** 2 Sh
🛏 (6) 🅿 (4) ⊬⬜ ➤ 🌿 🎦 ☑

Westlinton 14

National Grid Ref: NY3964

Lynebank, *Westlinton, Carlisle, Cumbria, CA6 6AA.*
Family-run, excellent food, ideal stop for England/Scotland journey
Grades: ETC 4 Diamond
Tel: **01228 792820** (also fax no)
Mrs Butler.
D: £18.00-£22.00 **S:** £20.00-£24.00.
Open: All Year
Beds: 2F 3D 1T 3S **Baths:** 9 En
🛏 🅿 (15) ⬜ 🖤 ➤ 🌿 🎦 ☑ ✿ 🚲

Rockcliffe 15

National Grid Ref: NY3561

🍴 🍺 Metal Bridge Inn

Metal Bridge House, *Metal Bridge, Rockcliffe, Carlisle, Cumbria, CA6 4HG.*
Actual grid ref: NY356649
In country, close to M6/A74, quality accommodation, friendly welcome
Grades: ETC 3 Diamond
Tel: **01228 674695** Mr Rae.
D: £16.00-£18.00 **S:** £20.00-£22.00.
Open: All Year (not Xmas)
Beds: 1D 2T **Baths:** 1 Sh
🛏 🅿 (6) ⊬ 🖤 ➤ 🌿 🎦 ☑ ✿ 🚲

Carlisle 16

National Grid Ref: NY3955

🍴 🍺 Metal Bridge Inn, The Beehive, Mary's Pantry, Crown & Thistle, Coach & Horses, Golden Fleece, Black Lion

▲ **Carlisle Youth Hostel**,
University of Northumbria, The Old Brewery Residences, Bridge Lane, Caldewgate, Carlisle, Cumbria, CA2 5SR.
Actual grid ref: NY394560
Tel: 01228 597352.
After 6pm: 01228 59486
Under 18: £12.00 **Adults:** £12.00
suitable for disabled people, self-catering facilities, showers, laundry facilities
Accommodation in an award-winning conversion of the former Theakston's brewery. Single study bedrooms with shared kitchen and bathroom in flats for upto 7 people

Howard Lodge, *90 Warwick Road, Carlisle, Cumbria, CA1 1JU.*
Actual grid ref: NY407558
Grades: ETC 4 Diamond,
AA 3 Diamond
Tel: **01228 529842** Mr Hendrie.
D: £15.00-£25.00 **S:** £20.00-£30.00.
Open: All Year
Beds: 2F 1D 2T 1S
Baths: 6 En 1 Sh
🛏 🅿 (6) ⬜ 🖤 ➤ ✕ 🌿 🎦 ☑ 🛈 🚲
Friendly family-run guest house in comfortable Victorian town house in conservation area. Spacious rooms all fully ensuite with satellite TV, welcome tray, hairdryer and clock radio. Large breakfasts. 5 minutes' walk from station and city centre. Evening meals by prior arrangement. Private car park

Craighead, *6 Hartington Place, Carlisle, Cumbria, CA1 1HL.*
Actual grid ref: NY405559
Grades: ETC 3 Diamond
Tel: **01228 596767** Mrs Smith.
D: £16.50 **S:** £16.50.
Open: All Year (not Xmas)
Beds: 1F 2D 1T 1S
Baths: 1 En 2 Sh
🛏 ⬜ 🖤 ➤ 🌿 🎦 ☑ 🚲
You will receive a warm welcome at Craighead a grade II Listed spacious Victorian town house with comfortable rooms and original features. CTV tea/coffee tray in all rooms. Minutes' walk to city centre bus and rail stations and all amenities. Friendly personal service

All cycleways are popular: you are well-advised to book ahead

All rates are subject to alteration at the owners' discretion.

Angus Hotel & Almonds Bistro,
14 Scotland Road, Stanwix, Carlisle, Cumbria, CA3 9DG.
Actual grid ref: NY400571
Grades: AA 4 Diamond
Tel: **01228 523546/0800 026 2046**
Mr Webster. Fax no: 01228 531895
D: £20.00-£27.00 **S:** £26.00-£42.00.
Open: All Year
Beds: 4F 3D 4T 3S
Baths: 11 En 3 Sh
🛏 🅿 (6) ⬜ 🖤 ✕ ➤ 🌿 🎦 ☑ 🛈 ✿ 🚲
Victorian town house, foundations on Hadrian's Wall. Excellent food, Les Routiers Awards, local cheeses, home baked bread. Genuine warm welcome from owners. Licensed, draught beer, lounge, meeting room, internet cafe, direct dial telephones, secure garaging

Chatsworth Guest House,
22 Chatsworth Square, Carlisle, Cumbria, CA1 1HF.
City centre Grade II Listed building, close to shops, cathedral, castle, all amenities
Grades: ETC 3 Diamond
Tel: **01228 524023** (also fax no)
Mrs Mackin.
D: £17.00-£22.00 **S:** £20.00-£26.00.
Open: All Year (not Xmas)
Beds: 1F 1D 3T 1S
Baths: 2 En 1 Sh
🛏 (2) ⊬ ➤ 🌿 🎦 ☑

Avondale, *3 St Aidans Road, Carlisle, Cumbria, CA1 1LT.*
Attractive comfortable Edwardian house. Quiet central position convenient M6 J43
Grades: ETC 4 Diamond
RAC 4 Diamond
Tel: **01228 523012** (also fax no)
Mr & Mrs Hayes.
D: £20.00-£20.00 **S:** £20.00-£40.00.
Open: All Year (not Xmas)
Beds: 1D 2T **Baths:** 1 En 1 Pr
🛏 🅿 (3) ⊬⬜ ✕ ➤ 🌿 🎦 ☑ 🛈 ✿ 🚲

Corner House Hotel & Bar,
4 Grey Street, Carlisle, CA1 2JP.
Grades: ETC 3 Diamond
Tel: **01228 533239** Mrs Anderson.
Fax no: 01228 546628
D: £17.50-£21.00 **S:** £25.00-£30.00.
Open: All Year
Beds: 3F 4D 4T 3S **Baths:** 10 En
🛏 ⬜ 🖤 ✕ ➤ 🌿 🎦 � 🎦 ☑ 🛈 ✿ 🚲
Small, friendly, licensed hotel. 10 mins to city centre attraction, bar, large TV, lounge and games room. Excellent base for golf, walking, horse-riding, swimming, cycling or touring by car, bus or train, the lakes, Roman wall or border region

Please don't camp on *anyone's* land without first obtaining their permission.

Courtfield Guest House,
169 Warwick Road, Carlisle,
Cumbria, CA1 1LP.
Short walk to historic city centre.
Close to M6, J43
Grades: ETC 4 Diamond
Tel: 01228 522767
Mrs Dawes.
D: £17.50-£20.00
S: £20.00.
Open: All Year (not Xmas)
Beds: 1F 2D 2T
Baths: 5 En
🛏 🅿 (4) 🕭 ⬚ 🎇 Ⅲ Ⅴ ⚲ 🚲

East View Guest House,
110 Warwick Road, Carlisle,
Cumbria, CA1 1JU.
Actual grid ref: NY407560
10 minutes' walking distance from
city centre, railway station and
restaurants
Grades: ETC 2 Diamond
Tel: 01228 522112 (also fax no)
Mrs Glease.
D: £18.00-£20.00
S: £20.00-£25.00.
Open: All Year (not Xmas)
Beds: 3F 2D 1T 1S
Baths: 7 En
🛏 🅿 (4) 🕭 ⬚ 🎇 Ⅲ Ⅴ 🚲

Cherry Grove, *87 Petteril Street,*
Carlisle, Cumbria, CA1 2AW.
Lovely red brick building close to
golf club and town
Grades: AA 3 Diamond
Tel: 01228 541942
Mr & Mrs Houghton.
D: £17.50-£20.00 **S:** £20.00-£30.00.
Open: All Year
Beds: 3F 2D
Baths: 5 En
🛏 🅿 (3) 🕭 ⬚ 🗙 🎇 ⬚ Ⅲ Ⅴ ⚲ 🚲

Cornerways Guest House,
107 Warwick Road, Carlisle,
Cumbria, CA1 1EA.
Large Victorian town house
Grades: ETC 4 Diamond
Tel: 01228 521733
Mrs Fisher.
D: £14.00-£18.00 **S:** £16.00-£18.00.
Open: All Year (not Xmas)
Beds: 2F 1D 4T 3S
Baths: 2 En 2 Sh
🛏 🅿 (4) 🕭 🗙 🎇 ⬚ Ⅲ Ⅴ ⛢ 🚲

Cambro House, *173 Warwick*
Road, Carlisle, CA1 1LP.
Grades: AA 3 Diamond
Tel: 01228 543094 (also fax no)
Mr & Mrs Mawson.
D: £17.00-£20.00 **S:** £20.00-£25.00.
Open: All Year
Beds: 2D 1T
Baths: 3 En
🅿 (2) 🕭 ⬚ 🎇 ⬚ Ⅲ Ⅴ ⛢ ⚲ 🚲
Guests can expect warm hospitality
and friendly service at this
attractively decorated and
well-maintained guest house. Each
ensuite bedroom includes TV,
clock, radio, hairdryer and
welcome tray. Private off-road
parking available, non-smoking,
close to golf course

Kingstown Hotel, *246 Kingstown*
Road, Carlisle, CA3 0DE.
Grades: AA 3 Diamond
Tel: 01228 515292 (also fax no)
D: £18.50-£22.00
S: £29.00-£36.00.
Open: All Year (not Xmas)
Beds: 1F 5D 1T
Baths: 7 En
🛏 🅿 (10) 🕭 🐾 🗙 🎇 ⬚ Ⅲ ⚘ Ⅴ ⚲ 🚲
Situated on the A7, only quarter
mile from M6 (J44), our small
family-run hotel offers weary
travellers comfortable
accommodation and a cosy lounge
bar in which to unwind. An ideal
base to explore historic Carlisle,
Hadrian's Wall and the Lake
District

Whitelea Guest House,
191 Warwick Road, Carlisle,
CA1 1LP.
Good base for lakes and Hadrian's
Wall. Friendly, family run
Tel: 01228 533139
Croskery.
D: £15.00-£18.00
S: £15.00-£18.00.
Open: All Year
Beds: 2F 1T 1S
🛏 🅿 🕭 🗙 🎇 ⬚ Ⅲ Ⅴ ⛢ 🚲

The Foxgloves, *73 Scotland Road,*
Carlisle, Cumbria, CA3 9HL.
Family-run elegant Victorian town
house, very suitable for Roman
Wall walkers
Tel: 01228 526365
Mrs Apcar.
D: £15.00 **S:** £15.00.
Open: All Year
Beds: 2T 1S
🛏 ⬚ 🐾 🎇 ⬚ Ⅲ Ⅴ ⛢

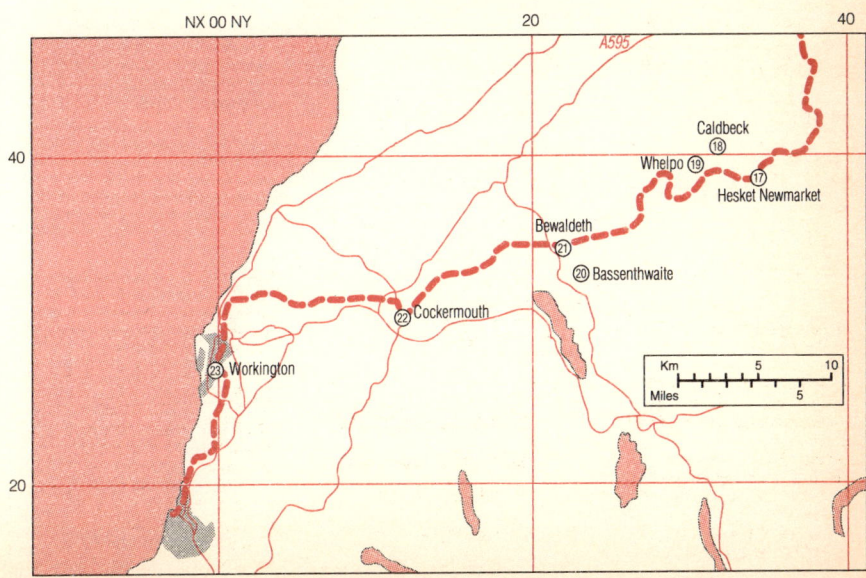

All cycleways are popular: you are well-advised to book ahead

Howard House, 27 Howard Place, Carlisle, Cumbria, *CA1 1HR.*
Actual grid ref: NY407559
Elegant Victorian town house, 5 minutes' walk to city centre
Tel: **01228 529159**
Mrs Fisher.
Fax no: 01228 512550
D: £16.00 **S:** £16.00.
Open: All Year
Beds: 2F 3D 3T
Baths: 2 Pr 2 Sh
🛇🖵🖨🛏🗶🛔🗏🔞🗎⚡

Hesket Newmarket 17

National Grid Ref: NY3338

▲ **Hudscales YHA Camping Barn,** Hudscales, Hesket Newmarket, Caldbeck, Wigton, Cumbria.
Actual grid ref: NY332375
Adults: £3.35+
showers
Part of group of traditional farm buildings situated at 1,000 ft on northernmost edge of Lakeland Fells. ADVANCE BOOKING ESSENTIAL

Newlands Grange, Hesket Newmarket, Caldbeck, Wigton, Cumbria, *CA7 8HP.*
Comfortable, oak beamed farmhouse offering all home cooking. All welcome
Tel: **016974 78676**
Mrs Studholme.
D: £16.50-£19.50
S: £16.50-£19.50.
Open: All Year (not Xmas)
Beds: 1F 1D 1T 1S
Baths: 1 En 1 Sh
🛇🖵🖨🛏🗶🛔🗏🔞🗎⚡🚲

Caldbeck 18

National Grid Ref: NY3239

🝐🍴 Oddfellow Arm

The Briars, Friar Row, Caldbeck, Wigton, Cumbria, *CA7 8DS.*
Actual grid ref: NY3339
In Caldbeck village, right on Cumbria Way. 2 mins' walk pub.
Rooms overlooking Caldbeck Fells
Tel: **016974 78633**
Mrs Coulthard.
D: £18.50-£20.00
S: £18.50-£20.00.
Open: All Year (not Xmas)
Beds: 1D 1T 1S
Baths: 1 En 1 Sh
🖨(4)🛏🖵🛏🛔🗏🔞⚡🚲

Whelpo 19

National Grid Ref: NY3039

Swaledale Watch, Whelpo, Caldbeck, Wigton, Cumbria, *CA7 8HQ.*
Actual grid ref: NY309397
Grades: ETC 4 Diamond, AA 4 Diamond
Tel: **016974 78409** (also fax no)
Mrs Savage.
D: £17.50-£20.50 **S:** £18.50-£25.00.
Open: All Year (not Xmas)
Beds: 2F 2D 1T
Baths: 4 En 1 Pr
🛇🖨(10)🛏🖵🗶🛔🗏🔞🗎⚡🚲
Enjoy great comfort, excellent home cooking, warm friendly farmhouse welcome

Bassenthwaite 20

National Grid Ref: NY2332

🝐🍴 Sun Inn

Willow Cottage, Bassenthwaite, Keswick, Cumbria, *CA12 4QP.*
Peaceful village location, log fires, stencilling, patchwork, beams, flagged floors
Tel: **017687 76440** Mrs Beaty.
D: £20.00-£22.50 **S:** £25.00-£30.00.
Open: All Year (not Xmas)
Beds: 1D 1T
Baths: 2 En
🖨(2)🛏🛔🗏🔞⚡

Bassenthwaite Hall Farm, Bassenthwaite, Keswick, Cumbria, *CA12 4QP.*
Charming, olde worlde, farmhouse - excellent accommodation. By a stream with ducks!
Tel: **017687 76393** (also fax no)
Mrs Trafford.
D: £16.00-£20.00 **S:** £25.00-£30.00.
Open: All Year
Beds: 1D 1T **Baths:** 2 Sh
🛇(10)🖨(4)🛏🖵🛔🗏🔞🗎⚡

Parkergate, Bassenthwaite, Keswick, Cumbria, *CA12 4QG.*
Actual grid ref: NY234303
Wonderful views of mountains and lake. Cosy. Tranquil and relaxing
Tel: **017687 76376**
Fax no: 017687 76911
D: £18.00-£25.00 **S:** £25.00-£30.00.
Open: All year (not Xmas)
Beds: 1F 2D 1T
Baths: 3 En 1 Pr
🛇(5)🖨(4)🛏🖵🛏🗶🛔🗏🔞🗎⚡🚲

Bassenthwaite Hall Farm, Bassenthwaite, Keswick, Cumbria, *CA12 4QP.*
Beautiful village location overlooks riverside at rear and mountain range on front
Tel: **017687 76279** Mrs Mattinson.
D: £16.00-£20.00 **S:** £17.00-£20.00.
Open: Easter to Apr
Beds: 3F 1D 1T 1S
Baths: 1 En 1 Sh
🛇🖨(4)🛏🖵🛔🔞⚡🚲

Dalton Cottage, Bassenthwaite, Keswick, Cumbria, *CA12 4QG.*
Idyllic C17th cottage in remote location. Fantastic views overlooking Bassenthwaite Lake
Tel: **017687 76952** Mrs Mawson.
D: £20.00.
Open: All Year (not Xmas)
Beds: 1D 1T
Baths: 2 En
🛇(4)🖨(2)🛏🖵🛔🗏🔞🗎⚡🚲

Bewaldeth 21

National Grid Ref: NY2034

🝐🍴 Snooty Fox

Riggwood, Bewaldeth, Cockermouth, Cumbria, *CA13 9SX.*
Actual grid ref: NY218343
Lakeland working farm, cattle, sheep, spectacular views, gardens, relaxed atmosphere
Tel: **017687 76692**
Mrs Harrington.
D: £16.00-£22.00 **S:** £18.00-£24.00.
Open: All Year (not Xmas)
Beds: 2F
Baths: 1 Sh
🛇🖨(6)🖵🛏🔞⚡🚲

Cockermouth 22

National Grid Ref: NY1230

🝐🍴 The Bitter End, Shepherds Hotel

▲ **Cockermouth Youth Hostel,** Double Mills, Cockermouth, Cumbria, *CA13 0DS.*
Actual grid ref: NY118298
Tel: **01900 822561**
Under 18: £5.65 **Adults:** £8.35
evening meal at 7.00pm, self-catering facilities, showers, no smoking
Simple accommodation in restored C17th watermill, convenient for northern and western fells and Cumbrian coastline

Shepherds Hotel, Egremont Road, Cockermouth, Cumbria, *CA13 0QX.*
Tel: **01900 822673** (also fax no)
D: £18.75-£20.00 **S:** £37.50-£40.00.
Open: All Year (not Xmas)
Beds: 4D 9T
Baths: 13 En
🛇🖨(99)🛏🖵🗶🛔🗏🔞♿🗎⚡🚲
Modern hotel with views towards Lake District, close to gem town of Cockermouth and bustling Keswick. Excellent hot and cold food available all day. Attached to visitors centre and large gift shop. Ideal for touring on business or pleasure

Bringing children with you? Always ask for any special rates.

Benson Court Cottage, 10 St Helen's Street, Cockermouth, Cumbria, CA13 9HX.
Tel: **01900 822303** Mrs Townley.
D: £15.00-£18.00 **S:** £15.00-£19.00.
Open: All Year
Beds: 1F 1S
☎ (6) ⅍ ⟉ 🖢 Ⅲ. Ⅵ ♦ ⌀ ↝
Homely 1727 cottage in town centre conservation area, log fires. Welcome Host Resident owner. Over 25 eating places within a 5 minute stroll. Tourists and commercial guests equally welcome. Own key. Healthy & hearty breakfasts from 0700 hrs. Room only from £10

The Rook Guest House,
9 Castlegate, Cockermouth, Cumbria, CA13 9EU.
Actual grid ref: NY122307
Cosy C17th town house. Spiral staircase. Convenient for all amenities
Tel: **01900 828496** Mrs Waters.
D: £15.00-£17.50 **S:** £20.00-£20.00.
Open: All Year (not Xmas)
Beds: 2D 1T **Baths:** 1 En 1 Pr 1 Sh
☎ (5) ⅍ ⟉ 🖢 Ⅲ. Ⅵ ♦ ⌀ ↝

Holme Lea, 17 Skiddaw View, Cockermouth, Cumbria, CA13 0DQ.
Friendly accommodation near all amenities on fringe of Northern Lakes
Tel: **01900 828039**
Hewitson.
D: £16.00-£18.00.
Open: All Year (not Xmas)
Beds: 1T 2D
Baths: 2 En 1 Pr
☎ 🄿 (3) ⅍ ⟉ 🖢 Ⅲ. Ⅵ ♦ ⌀ ↝

Workington   23

National Grid Ref: NX9927

🍴 🍺 Ye Old Sportsman, Traveller's Rest, Miners' Arms

Silverdale, 17 Banklands, Workington, Cumbria, CA14 3EL.
Large Victorian private house. Near start C2C cycleway and lakes
Tel: **01900 61887**
Mrs Hardy.
D: £11.00-£13.50 **S:** £12.50-£15.00.
Open: All Year (not Xmas)
Beds: 2T 2S
Baths: 2 Sh
☎ ⟉ 🛏 🖢 Ⅲ. Ⅵ

The Green Dragon Hotel,
Portland Square, Workington, Cumbria, CA14 4BJ.
Delightful 1728 coaching house overlooking a Georgian courtyard
Tel: **01900 603803**
Mrs Roberts.
Fax no: 01900 872659
D: £20.00-£25.00
S: £25.00-£40.00.
Open: All Year
Beds: 3D 3T 4S
Baths: 8 En 2 Pr
☎ ⅍ ⟉ 🛏 ✕ 🖢 Ⅲ. Ⅵ ♦ ⌀ ↝

Order your
packed lunches the
evening before you
need them.
Not at breakfast!

South Downs Way

At 96 miles, this route is shorter than many featured in this book. However, designed as a National Trail for walkers, it is routed mainly along a chalk track, which can get muddy, and involves a considerable amount of climbing, so should only really be undertaken on an all terrain bicycle. It runs west along the ridge of the great chalk escarpment of the South Downs, from Eastbourne in East Sussex to Winchester in Hampshire. The views from the path, southwards out to sea and northwards over the Sussex Weald, are stunning.

The route is waymarked along its whole length by the National Trail acorn symbol, and, by virtue of the fact that these walking routes are long-established by comparison with Britain's still relatively nascent cycleways, is very well served by thoroughgoing **guide books**. You will find everything you need (including mapping) in the *National Trail Guide - South Downs Way* by Paul Millmore (ISBN 1 85410 099 8), published by Aurum Press in association with the Countryside Commission and Ordnance Survey @ £10.99. This book includes a list of cycle repair/hire shops on or near to the route; and a general list of facilities available at locations along the way.

Other guides are *Along the South Downs Way to Winchester* by the Society of Sussex Downsmen, available from the RA's National Office at 1/5 Wandsworth Road, London SW8 2XX, tel 020-7339 8500, @ £5.00 (+£1.00 p&p);

A Guide to the South Downs Way by Miles Jebb (ISBN 09 471170 4), published by Constable & Co Ltd @ £10.95;

and *South Downs Way & The Downs Link* by Kev Reynolds (ISBN 1 85284 023 4), published by Cicerone Press and available from the publishers at 2 Police Square, Milnthorpe, Cumbria LA7 7PY, tel 01539 562069, @ £5.99 (+75p p&p).

Maps: Ordnance Survey 1:50,000 Landranger series: 185, 197, 198, 199

Trains: Services from London go to Eastbourne, Lewes and Brighton (all from Victoria) and to Petersfield and Winchester (from Waterloo). Many other places along or near to the route are covered by local services.

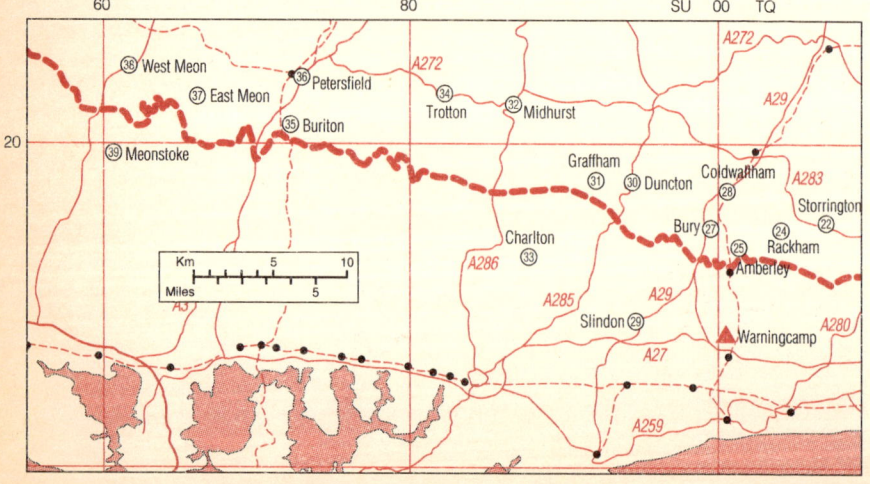

Eastbourne   1

National Grid Ref: TQ5900

🏨 🍴 The Marine, Town House, Castle Inn, Lamb Inn, The Beach, The Waterfront, The Pilot, The Alexander

▲ *Eastbourne Youth Hostel,* East Dean Road, Eastbourne, East Sussex, *BN20 8ES.*
Actual grid ref: TV588990
Tel: **01323 721081**
Under 18: £5.65 **Adults:** £8.35
family bunk rooms, showers, central heating, shop, no smoking
Former golf clubhouse on South Downs, 450ft above sea level with sweeping views across Eastbourne & Pevensey Bay

Heatherdene Hotel, 26-28 Elms Avenue, Eastbourne, E. Sussex, *BN21 3DN.*
Tel: **01323 723598** (also fax no)
Mrs Mockford.
D: £16.00-£41.00
S: £16.00-£25.00.
Open: All Year
Beds: 1F 4D 8T 3S
Baths: 6 En 3 Sh
🛇🗖🏋🗶🎖🎞🔥👁
You will find good food and comfortable rooms at the Heatherdene. This family-run licensed hotel, set in a pleasant avenue, is close to the sea front and town centre. Train and coach stations are nearby, as are the theatres

---

Pay B&Bs by cash or
cheque and be prepared
to pay up front.

Eastbourne to Alfriston

Eastbourne is a typical English seaside resort, with a three-mile seafront and a Victorian pier. One feature worth a mention is the Trower Gallery and Museum, which exhibits contemporary art. The initial stretch of the way skirts Paradise Wood and climbs gently to the top of the Downs, continuing to the village of **Jevington**. (The alternative route over Beachy Head and the Seven Sisters is for walkers only and cannot be cycled.) A little way off the path beyond Jevington, the Lullington Heath National Nature Reserve can be reached by a bridleway. At **Wilmington**, a little way off the route, stands a ruined Benedictine priory and a twelfth-century church, but more renowned is the ancient hillside carving, the Long Man. This massive representation of a figure bearing a staff in each hand had long faded until the Victorian restoration. It is likely they modified the image so as not to offend the sensibilities of the period (compare the Cerne Giant in Dorset), and as such it was not so much a restoration as a desecration, which begs the question, why did they bother restoring it at all? Close by lies the old smuggling village of **Alfriston** with a number of centuries-old inns and an untouched fourteenth-century church known as 'the cathedral of the Downs', and beyond it the noted viewpoint at Firle Beacon.

La Mer Guest House, 7 Marine Road, Eastbourne, E. Sussex, *BN22 7AU.*
Tel: **01323 724926** Mrs Byrne.
D: £18.00-£24.00 **S:** £18.00-£24.00.
Open: May to Sep
Beds: 2D 2T 2S
Baths: 2 En
🛇 (14) 🖳🗖🗶🎖🎞🔥👁🛆
Just 50 yards from Eastbourne's beautiful seafront and beach easy access to South Downs, Beachy Head and Seven Sisters. A few minutes' walk to town centre and all amenities ensuite Rooms with TV available, all to a high standard

Ambleside Private Hotel, 24 Elms Avenue, Eastbourne, E. Sussex, *BN21 3DN.*
Tel: **01323 724991** Mr Pattenden.
D: £18.00-£18.00 **S:** £18.00-£18.00.
Open: All Year
Beds: 4D 4T 2S **Baths:** 2 Sh
🗖🏋🗶🎖🎞👁🔥🚲
Situated on quiet avenue adjacent to seafront, pier, town centre, theatres, convenient for railway and coach stations. Short distance from South Downs Way, Wealdway. Colour TV in bedrooms. Compliant with environmental and fire regulations

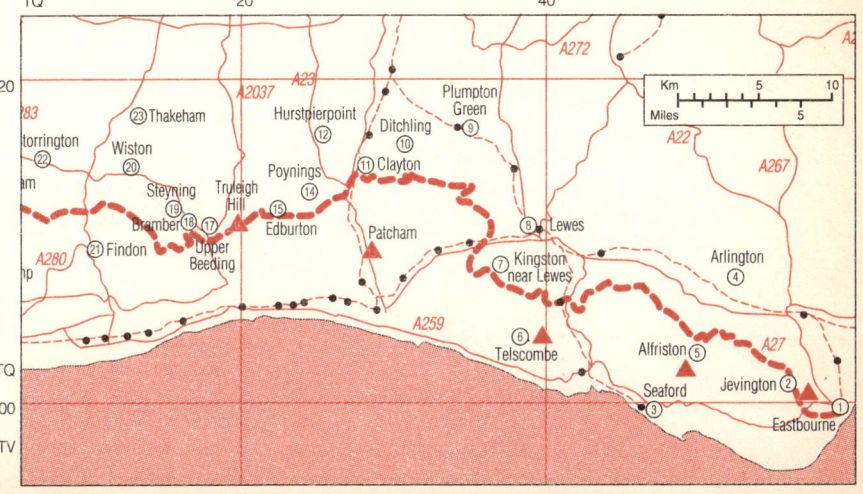

Beachy Rise, *20 Beachy Head Road, Eastbourne, E. Sussex, BN20 7QN.*
Grades: AA 4 Diamond
Tel: 01323 639171
D: £22.00-£28.00
S: £25.00-£29.00.
Open: All Year
Beds: 1F 4D 1T
Baths: 6 En
⏰ (1) 🗐 🛁 Ⓜ Ⓥ 🛈 ⚡ ⚲
In Meads village near Beachy Head and sea and university. Ensuite bedrooms. Very comfortable and homely house, lovely garden. We are known for our excellent English breakfast

Courtlands Hotel, *68 Royal Parade, Eastbourne, E. Sussex, BN22 7AQ.*
Seafront position, business/touring base
Grades: RAC 2 Diamond
Tel: 01323 721068
D: £20.00-£25.00
S: £20.00-£25.00.
Open: All Year
Beds: 3F 2D 1T 2S
Baths: 3 En 1 Pr
⏰ 🅿 (2) 🗐 ✗ 🛁 Ⓥ 🛈 ⚡
Situated in a pleasant avenue close to town centre, sea front and all amenities. Licensed, ensuite, teamaking, colour TV in bedrooms. English breakfast

Camberley Hotel, *27-29 Elms Avenue, Eastbourne, E. Sussex, BN21 3DN.*
Tel: 01323 723789
D: £16.00-£20.00
S: £16.00-£20.00.
Open: Mar to Oct
Beds: 4F 3D 3T 2S
Baths: 7 En 2 Sh
⏰ 🅿 (3) 🗐 ✗ 🛁 Ⓥ 🛈 ⚲
Situated in a pleasant avenue close to town centre, sea front and all amenites. Licensed, ensuite, teamaking, colour TV in bedrooms. English breakfast

The Manse, *7 Dittons Road, Eastbourne, East Sussex, BN21 1DW.*
Tel: **01323 737851** Mrs Walker.
D: £15.00-£20.00 **S:** £20.00-£25.00.
Open: All Year (not Xmas)
Beds: 1F 2T
Baths: 2 En 1 Pr
⏰ (8) 🅿 (1) 🗐 🛁 Ⓜ Ⓥ 🛈 ⚡ ⚲
Originally a Presbyterian manse, this character house is located in a quiet area yet within 5 minutes' walk of the town centre with its shops, restaurants and theatres. Seafront, South Downs, castles and Downland villages nearby

Cherry Tree Hotel, *15 Silverdale Road, Eastbourne, E. Sussex, BN20 7AJ.*
Actual grid ref: TV612982
Non-smoking, family-run hotel, close to sea front, Downlands and theatres
Grades: ETC 4 Diamond
Tel: **01323 722406** Mr Henley.
Fax no: 01323 648838
D: £26.00-£32.00 **S:** £26.00-£32.00.
Open: All Year
Beds: 2F 3D 3T 2S
Baths: 10 En
⏰ (7) ⚘ 🗐 ✗ 🛁 Ⓜ Ⓥ 🛈

Innisfree House, *130a Royal Parade, Eastbourne, East Sussex, BN22 7JY.*
Tel: **01323 646777** (also fax no)
Mrs Petrie.
D: £17.50-£18.75 **S:** £25.00.
Open: All Year (not Xmas)
Beds: 1F 1D 1T
Baths: 3 En
⏰ ⚘ 🗐 🛁 Ⓜ Ⓥ ⚲
Small family run B&B on seafront, close to all amenities, refurbished to high standards. Stay a day or stay a week, your comfort & praise we aim to seek, exclusive location with sea views, easy parking on road outside

Southcroft Hotel, *15 South Cliff Avenue, Eastbourne, E. Sussex, BN20 7AH.*
Actual grid ref: TV609979
Grades: ETC 3 Diamond
Tel: **01323 729071** Mrs Skriczka.
D: £24.00-£26.00 **S:** £24.00-£26.00.
Open: All Year
Beds: 3D 2T 1S
Baths: 6 En
⚘ 🗐 ✗ 🛁 Ⓜ Ⓥ ⚡
Southcroft is a small select private licensed hotel situated in a quiet residential area within easy reach of theatres, Devonshire Park, sea and shopping centre. Unrestricted free parking outside hotel. ETC Member, Welcome Host Award

Channel View Hotel, *57 Royal Parade, Eastbourne, E. Sussex, BN22 7AQ.*
Tel: **01323 736730**
Fax no: 01323 644299
D: £17.00-£22.00 **S:** £22.00-£32.00.
Open: All Year (not Xmas)
Beds: 1F 2D 3T 2S
Baths: 4 En 1 Sh
⏰ 🗐 🐾 ✗ 🛁 Ⓜ Ⓥ
A friendly family-run sea front hotel situated opposite the Redoubt Gardens. Balcony rooms available with sea views. Licensed bar and conservatory, real home cooking, a warm and personalised service given to all our guests. All year round senior citizen discount. Unrestricted street parking

All rates are subject to alteration at the owners' discretion.

Alfriston to Ditchling Beacon

After crossing one of the many English rivers called Ouse into the village of **Southease**, whose church has a circular Saxon tower, a short detour will take you into the pretty town of **Lewes,** site of the 1264 Battle of Lewes between Henry III and Simon de Montfort, and the burning of the Protestant Lewes Martyrs in 1556. Here in the eighteenth century lived the great progressive writer Thomas Paine. Predominantly Georgian, there are older parts including the Norman castle. Several miles after Southease you come to **Ditchling Beacon**, site of an Iron Age fort and close to a Sussex Wildlife Trust nature reserve. A short detour north leads to **Ditchling**, where you will find a house that belonged to Anne of Cleves, who was, for six months in 1540, the fourth wife of Henry VIII, who fell in love with Holbein's portrait of her only to be disappointed with the real thing. I can't imagine she was less disappointed herself, but at least she fared better than Anne Boleyn and Catherine Howard, in that she came out of it with her neck intact (and, indeed, outlived Henry by ten years and Catherine Parr, his last wife, by nine).

Edelweiss Hotel, *10-12 Elms Avenue, Eastbourne, E. Sussex, BN21 3DN.*
Tel: **01323 732071** (also fax no)
Mr & Mrs Butler.
D: £15.00-£20.00 **S:** £15.00-£25.00.
Open: All Year
Beds: 1F 6D 5T 2S
Baths: 3 En 4 Sh
🛇🗆✕🖩🗎☑🛇✦🚲
Set in an attractive avenue 50 yards from the sea a family run hotel with comfortable guests' lounge and bar traditional breakfast and evening meals available. An ideal touring base for the beautiful Sussex countryside the South Downs Way and historic 1066 country

24 Wannock Road, *Eastbourne, E Sussex, BN22 7JU.*
Close to sea, 1 mile town centre. Home from home
Grades: ETC 4 Diamond, AA 4 Diamond, RAC 4 Diamond
Tel: **01323 640670** Mrs Fox.
D: £18.00-£21.00 **S:** £18.00-£21.00.
Open: All Year
Beds: 1T 1S
Baths: 2 En
🛇✦🗆🖰🖩🗎☑✦🚲

Downland Hotel, *37 Lewes Road, Eastbourne, East Sussex, BN21 2BU.*
Grades: ETC 2 Star, AA 2 Star
Tel: **01323 732689**
Fax no: 01323 720321
D: £25.00-£37.50 **S:** £30.00-£40.00.
Open: All Year
Beds: 2F 7D 2T 1S
Baths: 12 En
🅿(9)🗆✕🖰🖩🗎☑✦
Charming small hotel, ideally located for all main amenities and commercial centre. Great base for visiting many local attractions, South Downs Walk and 1066 Country. Substantial breakfast, comfortable lounge, excellent restaurant, cosy bar and own car park

Alfriston Hotel, *16 Lushington Road, Eastbourne, E. Sussex, BN21 4LL.*
Small family-run hotel, close to station, shops, seafront. Level access
Tel: **01323 725640**
D: £18.50 **S:** £18.50.
Open: Mar to Oct
Beds: 2F 3D 1T 4S
Baths: 8 En 1 Sh
🛇🗆✕🖰🖩☑

Tudor House, *5 Marine Road, Eastbourne, E. Sussex, BN22 7AU.*
Just off sea front, close pier, easy reach town centre
Tel: **01323 721796**
D: £18.00 **S:** £16.00.
Open: All Year (not Xmas)
Beds: 2D 2T 2S
Baths: 4 Pr 2 Sh
🗆✕🖰🖩☑

Jevington 2

National Grid Ref: TQ5601

🍴🍺 The Bells, The Tiger, Horse & Groom

Ash Farm, *Filching, Jevington, Polegate, E. Sussex, BN26 5QA.*
Actual grid ref: TQ565029
The welcome, good food, comfortable beds, walks, countryside and the PEACE are something special
Tel: **01323 487335**
Mr & Mrs Steer.
Fax no: 01323 484474
D: £19.50 **S:** £23.00.
Open: All Year
Beds: 1F 1D 1T **Baths:** 2 Pr 1 Sh
🛇🅿(10)✦🗆🖰✕🖩🗎☑✦

Seaford 3

National Grid Ref: TV4898

🍴🍺 White Lion

Holmes Lodge, *72 Claremont Road, Seaford, East Sussex, BN25 2BJ.*
Tel: **01323 898331**
Fax no: 01323 491346
D: £17.00-£25.00 **S:** £18.00-£30.00.
Open: All Year
Beds: 3F 2D 1T 6S
Baths: 1 Pr 2 Sh
🛇🅿(10)✦🗆🖰🖩☑🗎✦🚲
Sherlock Holmes theme. Convenient for Downs, walks/cycling, Cuckmere Haven, 7 sisters, Beachy Head, Newhaven Ferry. Beach/town/trains 300 metres, bus-stop outside, singles/groups welcome all year. Bar/restaurant adjacent. Free tea/coffee room into conservatory, large garden, sea views

Silverdale, *21 Sutton Park Road, Seaford, E. Sussex, BN25 1RH.*
Family run town centre house hotel excellent value for money
Grades: ETC 4 Diamond, AA 4 Diamond
Tel: **01323 491849** Mr Cowdrey.
Fax no: 01323 891131
D: £13.00-£28.00 **S:** £25.00-£45.00.
Open: All Year
Beds: 2F 6D **Baths:** 6 En 2 Sh
🛇🅿(5)🗆🖰✕🖰🖩🗎🛇☑🗎🚲

Arlington 4

National Grid Ref: TQ5407

🍴🍺 Old Oak, Yew Tree

Bates Green, *Arlington, Polegate, E. Sussex, BN26 6SH.*
Actual grid ref: TQ553077
Character farm house, quiet rural position, plantsman's tranquil garden near Glyndebourne
Grades: AA 5 Diamond
Tel: **01323 482039** (also fax no)
Mrs McCutchan.
D: £25.00-£28.00 **S:** £30.00.
Open: All Year (not Xmas)
Beds: 1D 2T **Baths:** 3 En
🅿(4)✦🗆🖰🖩☑✦🚲

Alfriston 5

National Grid Ref: TQ5103

🍴🍺 Wingrove Inn, Ye Olde Smuggler's Inn, The George

▲ **Alfriston Youth Hostel,** *Frog Firle, Alfriston, Polegate, East Sussex, BN26 5TT.*
Actual grid ref: TQ518019
Tel: **01323 870423**
Under 18: £6.20 **Adults:** £9.15
evening meal at 6.30pm, family bunk rooms, television, showers, central heating, shop
A comfortable Sussex country house dating from 1530, set in Cuckmere Valley with views over river and Litlington

Dacres, *Alfriston, Polegate, East Sussex, BN26 5TP.*
Country cottage. Beautiful gardens. Near Glynderbourne, Charleston Farmhouse, Seven Sisters
Tel: **01323 870447** Mrs Embry.
D: £25.00-£25.00 **S:** £25.00-£25.00.
Open: All Year
Beds: 1T
Baths: 1 Pr
🅿(1)✦🗆🖰🖩♿☑🚲

Pleasant Rise Farm, *Alfriston, Polegate, E. Sussex, BN26 5TN.*
Actual grid ref: TQ515027
Very quiet, beautiful house - lovely views & tennis court
Tel: **01323 870545** Mrs Savage.
D: £20.00 **S:** £20.00.
Open: All Year (not Xmas)
Beds: 2D 1T 1S
Baths: 2 Pr
🛇(7)🅿(4)✦🗆🖰🖩☑🗎✦

Telscombe 6

National Grid Ref: TQ4003

▲ **Telscombe Youth Hostel,** *Bank Cottages, Telscombe, Lewes, East Sussex, BN7 3HZ.*
Actual grid ref: TQ405033
Tel: **01273 301357**
Under 18: £5.65
Adults: £8.35
self-catering facilities, family bunk rooms, showers, shop, no smoking
Three 200-year-old cottages combined into one hostel, next to the Norman church in a small unspoilt village in Sussex Downs AONB

All rooms full and
nowhere else to stay?
Ask the owner if
there's anywhere
nearby

Kingston near Lewes   7

National Grid Ref: TQ3908

🚶 🚲 The Juggs

Settlands, *Wellgreen Lane, Kingston near Lewes, Lewes, E Sussex, BN7 3NP.*
Actual grid ref: TQ398082
Tel: **01273 472295** (also fax no)
D: £20.00-£25.00
S: £25.00-£27.50.
Open: All Year (not Xmas)
Beds: 1D 1T
Baths: 1 Pr
🛏 🅿 (3) ⅙ 🖵 👍 🎞 Ⓥ 🎗 ⚡ ♻
Picturesque timber-framed chalet bungalow overlooking the South Downs Way. Downland views from all guest rooms, large lounge with balcony. Convenient for Glyndebourne, ferries and Brighton

Nightingales, *The Avenue, Kingston near Lewes, Lewes, E. Sussex, BN7 3LL.*
Actual grid ref: TQ389083
Marvellous breakfast, lovely garden, quiet. Meet Ben, our black labrador!
Grades: ETC 5 Diamond
Tel: **01273 475673** (also fax no)
Mr Hudson.
D: £25.00-£27.50 **S:** £35.00-£45.00.
Open: All Year (not Xmas)
Beds: 1D 1T
Baths: 2 En
🛏 (9) 🅿 (2) ⅙ 🖵 👍 🎞 🖳 Ⓥ 🎗 ⚡ ♻

Lewes   8

National Grid Ref: TQ4110

🚶 🚲 Royal Oak, Pelham Arms, Cock Inn, Steward's Enquiry, King's Head

Castle Banks Cottage, *Castle Bank, Lewes, E. Sussex, BN7 1UZ.*
Beamed cottage, pretty garden, quiet lane, close to castle, shops, restaurants
Tel: **01273 476291** (also fax no)
Mrs Wigglesworth.
D: £22.50-£22.50 **S:** £22.50-£22.50.
Open: All Year (not Xmas)
Beds: 1T 1S
Baths: 1 Sh
🛏 ⅙ 👍 🎞 Ⓥ ⚡

Crink House, *Barcombe Mills, Lewes, E. Sussex, BN8 5BJ.*
Tel: **01273 400625**
Mrs Gaydon.
D: £25.00-£26.00 **S:** £30.00-£40.00.
Open: All Year (not Xmas)
Beds: 2D 1T
Baths: 3 En
🛏 🅿 (10) ⅙ 🖵 👍 🎞 Ⓥ
Victorian farmhouse with panoramic views. Welcoming rural family home, ideal base for exploring Sussex with its wealth of walks and attractions, castles, country houses, gardens, museums. Within reach Brighton, Eastbourne, Glyndebourne - self catering also available

Normandy, *37 Houndean Rise, Lewes, East Sussex, BN7 1EQ.*
Tel: **01273 473853** (also fax no)
Mrs Kemp.
D: £22.00-£25.00 **S:** £30.00-£35.00.
Open: All Year (not Xmas)
Beds: 1D **Baths:** 1 Pr
🛏 ⅙ 🖵 👍 🎞 Ⓥ 🎗 ♻
Comfortable room in large detached family house, additional bed available, overlooking South Downs and designated Area of Outstanding Natural Beauty. Large garden, easy access South Downs, quiet location near coast Glyndebourne, Brighton, Newhaven and historic Lewes. Easy parking. Non-smoking

Plumpton Green   9

National Grid Ref: TQ3616

🚶 🚲 Winning Post

Farthings, *Station Road, Plumpton Green, Lewes, E. Sussex, BN7 3BY.*
Actual grid ref: TQ365172
Relaxed, friendly atmosphere in village setting under South Downs
Tel: **01273 890415** Mrs Baker.
D: £20.00-£25.00 **S:** £22.00-£30.00.
Open: All Year (not Xmas)
Beds: 2D 1T **Baths:** 1 En 1 Sh
🛏 (11) 🅿 (4) ⅙ 🖵 🎗 🍴 ✕ 👍 🎞 Ⓥ 🛈 ♻

Ditchling   10

National Grid Ref: TQ3215

🚶 🚲 The Bull, White Horse, Blacksmiths' Arms

The White Barn, *Lodge Hill Lane, Ditchling, Hassocks, West Sussex, BN6 8SP.*
Actual grid ref: TQ325153
Comfortable converted barn in pretty garden, down quiet lane, five minutes village & pubs
Tel: **01273 842920** Mrs Blake.
D: £20.00 **S:** £25.00.
Open: All Year
Beds: 1D **Baths:** 1 Pr
🅿 (1) ⅙ 🖵 👍 🎞 Ⓥ 🛈 ♻

Clayton   11

National Grid Ref: TQ3014

🚶 🚲 Jack & Jill

Dower Cottage, *Underhill Lane, Clayton, Hassocks, W. Sussex, BN6 9PL.*
Actual grid ref: TQ309136
Tel: **01273 843363** Mrs Bailey.
Fax no: 01273 846503
D: £22.50-£30.00 **S:** £30.00-£50.00.
Open: All Year (not Xmas)
Beds: 2F 2D 1T 1S
Baths: 2 En 1 Sh
🛏 🅿 (8) ⅙ 🖵 🎞 🛈 ♻
Large country house in beautiful location overlooking the Sussex Weald. Ideal for walking, cycling, riding the South Downs yet only 15 mins from Brighton for nightlife. Library for guest use & colour TVs in all rooms. Peace & quiet away from city stress!

Hurstpierpoint   12

National Grid Ref: TQ2816

🚶 🚲 The Pilgrim, The Goose

Wickham Place, *Wickham Drive, Hurstpierpoint, Hassocks, W. Sussex, BN6 9AP.*
Grades: ETC 4 Diamond
Tel: **01273 832172** Mrs Moore.
D: £22.50-£25.00 **S:** £30.00-£30.00.
Open: All Year (not Xmas)
Beds: 1D 2T **Baths:** 1 Sh
🛏 🅿 (5) ⅙ 🖵 🎗 👍 🎞 Ⓥ
Welcome to Wickham Place - a large house in a lovely village just off the A23. Centrally sited for touring, walking, cycling and especially golf. We love to welcome new guests as well as our regular visitors. Please phone for brochure

Patcham   13

National Grid Ref: TQ3008

▲ **Brighton Youth Hostel**, *Patcham Place, London Road, Patcham, Brighton, East Sussex, BN1 8YD.*
Actual grid ref: TQ300088
Tel: **01273 556196**
Under 18: £6.85 **Adults:** £10.15
evening meal at 7.00pm, family bunk rooms, television, games room, showers, shop, security lockers, parking
Splendid country house with Queen Anne front, on the edge of Brighton and the South Downs

Poynings   14

National Grid Ref: TQ2612

🚶 🚲 Royal Oak

Manor Farm, *Poynings, Brighton, E. Sussex, BN45 7AG.*
Comfortable manor farm house. Paragliding, gliding, golf, riding, walking all nearby
Grades: ETC 4 Diamond
Tel: **01273 857371** (also fax no)
Mrs Revell.
D: £23.00-£25.00 **S:** £30.00.
Open: Apr to Dec
Beds: 1D 2T **Baths:** 3 En
🛏 (8) 🅿 (6) ⅙ 🖵 👍 🎞 Ⓥ 🛈 ♻

Edburton   15

National Grid Ref: TQ2311

Tottington Manor Hotel, *Edburton, Henfield, W. Sussex, BN5 9LJ.*
Actual grid ref: TQ231114
Typical Sussex country manor house in own grounds at foot of South Downs Way
Tel: **01903 815757** Mr Miller.
Fax no: 01903 879331
D: £32.50 **S:** £45.00.
Open: All Year
Beds: 5D 1T **Baths:** 6 Pr
🛏 (5) 🅿 🖵 ✕ 👍 🎞 Ⓥ

Truleigh Hill 16

National Grid Ref: TQ2210

▲ *Truleigh Hill Youth Hostel,*
Tottington Barn, Truleigh Hill,
Shoreham-by-Sea, West Sussex,
BN43 5FB.
Actual grid ref: TQ220105
Tel: **01903 813419**
Under 18: £6.20 **Adults:** £9.15
evening meal at 7.00pm, family bunk
rooms, television, showers, shop
Modern hostel in the Sussex Downs
AONB with conservation project
and old dew pond in grounds

Upper Beeding 17

National Grid Ref: TQ1910

The Rising Sun, Upper Beeding,
Steyning, W. Sussex, BN44 3TQ.
Actual grid ref: TQ197097
Tel: **01903 814424**
Mr & Mrs Taylor-Mason.
D: £17.00-£17.00 **S:** £20.00-£20.00.
Open: All Year (not Xmas)
Beds: 2D 1T 3S **Baths:** 1 Sh
🄿 (20) 🄿 🏠 ✕ 🖳 🕮 Ⓥ ⚡ 🗡
A delightful Georgian country inn,
set amidst the South Downs. Tony
& Sue offer a warm welcome, fine
selection of real ales and traditional
homecooked food lunchtime and
evenings. Comfortable rooms, all
with wash basin. Renowned full
English breakfast

Bramber 18

National Grid Ref: TQ1810

Castle Hotel, The Street, Bramber,
Steyning, W. Sussex, BN44 3WE.
Actual grid ref: TQ189106
Pretty village, spacious characterful
romantic friendly inn
Tel: **01903 812102**
Mr & Mrs Mitchell.
Fax no: 01903 816711
D: £22.00-£30.00 **S:** £35.00-£40.00.
Open: All Year
Beds: 1F 6D 3T **Baths:** 10 En
🄿 (15) 🄿 🏠 ✕ 🖳 🕮 Ⓥ 🗡 ⚡ 🚲

Steyning 19

National Grid Ref: TQ1711

🐾 🍺 The Star

Wapping Thorn Farmhouse,
Horsham Road, Steyning, West
Sussex, BN44 3AA.
Grades: ETC 4 Diamond
Tel: **01903 813236** Mr Shapland.
D: £20.00-£25.00 **S:** £25.00-£35.00.
Open: All Year
Beds: 1F 1T 1D 1S **Baths:** 4 En
🄿 (8) 🄿 🖳 🕮
Traditional farmhouse, recently
refurbished, set in 2 acres of
gardens. Located within our family
operated, 300 acre dairy farm. All
rooms overlook fields and the
South Downs. Good hearty break-
fast. 10 miles Brighton. 8 miles
Worthing. Steyne Village 1 mile

Wiston 20

National Grid Ref: TQ1414

Buncton Manor Farm, Steyning
Road, Wiston, Steyning, W. Sussex,
BN44 3DD.
Actual grid ref: TQ146136
C15th moated farmhouse on
working farm near South Downs
Tel: **01903 812736**
Mrs Rowland.
Fax no: 01903 814838
D: £19.00-£20.00
S: £23.00-£25.00.
Open: All Year
Beds: 1F 1T
Baths: 1 Sh
🄿 🄿 (5) 🄿 ✕ 🖳 🕮 Ⓥ 🗡 ⚡

Findon 21

National Grid Ref: TQ1208

🐾 🍺 Gun Inn

Findon Tower, Cross Lane,
Findon, Worthing, W. Sussex,
BN14 0UG.
Actual grid ref: TQ123083
Elegant Edwardian country house,
walking distance excellent village
pubs/restaurants
Grades: ETC 4 Diamond
Tel: **01903 873870**
Mr & Mrs Smith.
D: £25.00-£30.00
S: £30.00-£40.00.
Open: All Year (not Xmas)
Beds: 2D 1T 1S
Baths: 3 En
🄿 🄿 (10) 🄿 🖳 🕮 Ⓥ 🗡 ⚡ 🚲

Racehorse Cottage, Nepcote,
Findon, Worthing, W Sussex,
BN14 0SN.
Actual grid ref: TQ125082
Cosy, quiet cottage in Downland
village. Homemade bread and
preserves
Tel: **01903 873783**
Mr Lloyd.
D: £17.00
S: £21.00.
Open: All Year (not Xmas)
Beds: 2T
Baths: 1 Sh
🄿 (5) 🄿 (2) 🄿 🏠 🖳 🕮 Ⓥ ⚡

Storrington 22

National Grid Ref: TQ0814

🐾 🍺 New Moon, The Anchor

Willow Tree Cottage, Washington
Road, Storrington, Pulborough,
W. Sussex, RH20 4AF.
Actual grid ref: TQ104134
Tel: **01903 740835**
Mrs Smith.
Fax no: 01903 262277
D: £20.00-£22.50
S: £25.00-£30.00.
Open: All Year (not Xmas)
Beds: 2D 1T
Baths: 3 Pr
🄿 🄿 (10) 🄿 🏠 🖳 🕮 Ⓥ 🗡 ⚡
Welcoming, friendly, quiet. All
rooms ensuite. Colour TV,
tea-making facilities. Situated at
foot of Sussex Downs. Arundel,
Worthing 10 minutes. Children &
dogs welcome

Ditchling Beacon to Buriton

After Ditchling Beacon you cross into West Sussex and
come to **Pyecombe**, before passing Devil's Dyke, a deep valley
formed in the Ice Age with an Iron Age fort, en route to **Upper
Beeding**, with the Saxon Botolphs Church and a ruined
Norman castle at Bramber nearby. A little after this the route
joins the road between Worthing and Steyning and juts north
before leaving the road and passing close to another Iron Age
hill fort, Chanctonbury Ring, which is topped with a coronet of
trees. Past Washington, the route leads to the village of
Amberley, which has a twin-towered castle gatehouse and a
number of attractive pubs, before passing between two chalk
pits. The village hosts the Chalk Pits Museum, including a
narrow-gauge quarry railway. After Amberley and **Houghton**, a
detour along a bridleway is possible to **Bignor**, where there is a
Roman villa with mosaic floors on show. The way now crosses
Stane Street, the Roman route from London to Chichester, and
there are magnificent views southwards to Chichester
Cathedral and the sea. The next stretch is a long wooded
section of the Downs, which takes you to **Cocking**, over **Pen
Hill**, around **Beacon Hill** and on to **Harting Hill**, before
crossing the border into Hampshire. Queen Elizabeth Country
Park, by **Buriton**, is a beautiful woodland area which has an
ancient farm with a reconstruction Iron Age settlement.

Hampers End, *Rock Road, Storrington, Pulborough, W Sussex, RH20 3AF.*
Grades: ETC 4 Diamond
Tel: **01903 742777**
Fax no: 01903 742776
D: £22.50-£27.50.
Open: All Year (not Xmas)
Beds: 1F 2D 1T
Baths: 3 En 1 Pr
⛺ (10) 🅿 (6) 🖵 🛏 🍴 🎹 🔟 Ⓥ ∦ ♿
Mike and Lorna Cheeseman welcome you to their lovely mellowed country house. Quiet location, overlooking secluded gardens. Well equipped bedrooms, colour TV and beverage tray. Full English breakfast - ideal centre for historic stately homes, famous gardens, walking, RSPB reserves, brochure and guide

Thakeham 23

National Grid Ref: TQ1017

🍴 🍺 The Anchor

Oak Field House, *Merrywood Lane, Thakeham, Pulborough, West Sussex, RH20 3HD.*
Actual grid ref: TQ104157
Amidst delightful countryside. Just what you are looking for
Tel: **01903 740843** (also fax no)
Mrs Arter.
D: £22.00-£25.00 **S:** £22.00-£25.00.
Open: All Year (not Xmas)
Beds: 1D 1T 1S **Baths:** 1 Pr
⛺ 🅿 (3) ⚡ 🖵 🛏 🎹 Ⓥ 🔒 ∦ ♿

Rackham 24

National Grid Ref: TQ0413

🍴 🍺 Sportsman

Swan Cottage, *Rackham, Pulborough, W. Sussex, RH20 2EU.*
Mid C17th listed building ground floor room with own entrance
Tel: **01903 746112**
D: £20.00 **S:** £20.00.
Open: All Year (not Xmas)
Beds: 1D **Baths:** 1 En
⛺ 🅿 (2) 🛏 🎹 🔟 Ⓥ 🔒 ∦ ♿

Amberley 25

National Grid Ref: TQ0313

🍴 🍺 The Sportsman, Black Horse

Woodybanks, *Crossgates, Amberley, Arundel, W. Sussex, BN18 9NR.*
Actual grid ref: TQ041136
Tel: **01798 831295**
Mr & Mrs Hardy.
D: £18.00-£18.00 **S:** £20.00-£25.00.
Open: All Year
Beds: 1D 1T
Baths: 1 Sh
⛺ 🅿 (2) ⚡ 🖵 🛏 🎹 ♿ Ⓥ 🔒 ∦ ♿
Magnificent elevated views across the beautiful Wildbrooks, situated in the picturesque and historic village of Amberley beneath the South Downs, excellent for walking. Large guest lounge, garden sitting area with views. Amberley Working Museum, Arundel Castle, Parham House close by

Bacons, *Amberley, Arundel, W. Sussex, BN18 9NJ.*
Pretty old cottage in the heart of the village
Tel: **01798 831234** Mrs Jollands.
D: £18.00 **S:** £18.00.
Open: All Year (not Xmas)
Beds: 2T
Baths: 1 Sh
⛺ 🛏 🎹 ∦ ♿

Warningcamp 26

National Grid Ref: TQ0306

🔺 **Arundel Youth Hostel,** *Warningcamp, Arundel, West Sussex, BN18 9QY.*
Actual grid ref: TQ032076
Tel: **01903 882204**
Under 18: £6.20 **Adults:** £9.15
evening meal at 7.00pm, family bunk rooms, television, games room, showers, shop
Georgian building 1.5 miles from ancient town of Arundel, dominated by its castle & the South Downs

Bury 27

National Grid Ref: TQ0113

🍴 🍺 George & Dragon, The Swan

Harkaway, *8 Houghton Lane, Bury, Pulborough, W. Sussex, RH20 1PD.*
Actual grid ref: TQ012130
Quiet location beneath South Downs. Full English and vegetarian breakfast
Tel: **01798 831843** Mrs Clark.
D: £17.00-£19.00 **S:** £17.00-£19.00.
Open: All Year
Beds: 1D 2T
Baths: 1 En 1 Sh
⛺ (6) 🅿 (3) ⚡ 🖵 🛏 🎹 🔟 Ⓥ 🔒 ∦ ♿

Pulborough Eedes Cottage, *Bignor Park Road, Bury Gate, Bury, Pulborough, W Sussex, RH20 1EZ.*
Actual grid ref: TQ003161
Quiet country house surrounded by farmland, very warm personal welcome
Grades: ETC 4 Diamond
Tel: **01798 831438**
Fax no: 01798 831942
D: £20.00-£22.50 **S:** £25.00-£25.00.
Open: All Year (not Xmas)
Beds: 1D 2T
Baths: 1 En 1 Sh
⛺ 🅿 (10) 🖵 🛏 🎹 🔟 Ⓥ 🔒 ♿

Coldwaltham 28

National Grid Ref: TQ0216

National Grid Ref: TQ0216

Barn Owls, *London Road, Coldwaltham, Pulborough, W. Sussex, RH20 1LR.*
Beautiful Victorian restaurant with ensuite accommodation, in a lovely rural location overlooking South Downs
Tel: **01798 872498** (also fax no)
Mrs Hellenberg.
D: £25.00 **S:** £35.00.
Open: All Year
Beds: 2D 1T
🅿 (17) ⚡ 🖵 🛏 🍴 ✕ 🎹 🔟 Ⓥ 🔒

Slindon 29

National Grid Ref: SU9608

🍴 🍺 Newburgh Arms

🔺 **Gumber Bothy Camping Barn (Independent),** *Gumber Farm, Slindon, Arundel, West Sussex, BN18 0RN.*
Actual grid ref: SU961119
Tel: **01243 814554 (daytime)** / **814484 (evenings)**
Adults: £6.00
suitable for disabled people, self-catering facilities

SU 60

Km 5 10
Miles 5

A34 A33
A34 A32 A325
Winchester 41
Owslebury 40
38 West Meon 36 Petersfield
37 East Meon
35 Buriton
39 Meonstoke

40

20

33

D = Price range per person sharing in a double room

Mill Lane House, *Mill Lane, Slindon, Arundel, W. Sussex, BN18 0RP.*
Actual grid ref: SU964084
In peaceful village on South Downs, views to coast
Grades: ETC 3 Diamond
Tel: **01243 814440** Mrs Fuente.
Fax no: 01243 814436
D: £21.50-£21.50 **S:** £27.50-£27.50.
Open: All Year
Beds: 2F 2D 2T 1S **Baths:** 7 En
⛷ 🅿 (7) 🛇 🛏 ✕ 🚿 ⛁ 🏠 ⚕ Ⓥ 🔒 🌜 🚲

Duncton   30

National Grid Ref: SU9517

🍴 🍺 The Cricketers, The Forresters

Drifters, *Duncton, Petworth, W. Sussex, GU28 0JZ.*
Quiet comfortable country house - TV - tea & coffee making facilities in rooms
Grades: ETC 3 Diamond
Tel: **01798 342706** Mrs Folkes.
D: £19.00-£22.50 **S:** £22.50-£22.50.
Open: All Year (not Xmas)
Beds: 1D 2T 1S
Baths: 1 En 1 Sh
🅿 (3) 🛇 🛏 ✕ 🚿 ⛁ Ⓥ 🔒 ⚕

Graffham   31

National Grid Ref: SU9217

🍴 🍺 The Foresters, White Horse

Brook Barn, *Selham Road, Graffham, Petworth, W Sussex, GU28 0PU.*
Actual grid ref: 19831023
Grades: ETC 4 Diamond, Silver
Tel: **01798 867356**
Mr & Mrs Jollands.
D: £25.00-£25.00 **S:** £30.00-£30.00.
Open: All Year (not Xmas)
Beds: 1D **Baths:** 1 En
⛷ 🅿 (2) 🛇 🛏 ✕ ⛁ 🏠 Ⓥ ⚕ 🌜 🚲
Large double bedroom with ensuite bathroom, leads directly to own conservatory and secluded 2-acre garden. Close to South Downs Way, excellent pubs within walking distance, in quiet rural village in beautiful area of Sussex, ideal for a relaxing break

Midhurst   32

National Grid Ref: SU8821

🍴 🍺 The Wheatsheaf, Half Moon, Bricklayers Arms, The Swan, The Elsted

The Crown Inn, *Edinburgh Square, Midhurst, W. Sussex, GU29 9NL.*
Actual grid ref: SU887215
C16th character inn, real ales, log fires, home-cooked food
Grades: ETC 2 Diamond
Tel: **01730 813462** Mr Stevens.
D: £17.50-£20.00 **S:** £20.00-£25.00.
Open: All Year
Beds: 1D 1T 1S **Baths:** 1 Sh
🛇 🛏 🛏 ✕ 🚿 ⛁ 🏠 Ⓥ ⚕ 🌜 🚲

Oakhurst Cottage, *Carron Lane, Midhurst, W. Sussex, GU29 9LF.*
Close to Midhurst, yet in rural surroundings
Tel: **01730 813523**
Mrs Whitmore Jones.
D: £25.00-£30.00
S: £25.00-£30.00.
Open: All Year
Beds: 1D 1T 1S
Baths: 1 En 1 Sh
⛷ (4) 🅿 (2) 🛇 🛏 🏠 ⚕ 🌜

Carrondune, *Carron Lane, Midhurst, W Sussex, GU29 9LD.*
Comfortable old family country house, quiet location, 5 mins town centre
Grades: ETC 3 Diamond
Tel: **01730 813558**
Mrs Beck.
D: £20.00-£25.00 **S:** £25.00-£30.00.
Open: Feb to Nov
Beds: 1D 1T
Baths: 1 Sh
⛷ (5) 🅿 (4) 🛏 ⛁ 🏠 Ⓥ ⚕ 🚲

Three Elsted, *Midhurst, W Sussex, GU29 0JY.*
Comfortable C16th village house. Excellent pub nearby and very close to South Downs Way
Tel: **01730 825065**
Mrs Hill.
Fax no: 01730 825496
D: £22.50-£25.00 **S:** £22.50-£22.50.
Open: Mar to Nov
Beds: 1D 1T 1S
Baths: 1 Pr 1 Sh

Charlton   33

National Grid Ref: SU8812

The Fox Goes Free, *Charlton, Goodwood, Chichester, W. Sussex, PO18 0HU.*
Beautiful 400-year-old flint freehouse. Offering superb food and ales
Tel: **01243 811461** (also fax no)
Mr Ligertwood.
D: £25.00 **S:** £25.00.
Open: All Year (not Xmas)
Beds: 4D
Baths: 3 En 1 Pr
⛷ 🅿 (8) ✕ 🚿 ⛁ Ⓥ 🔒 🚲

Trotton   34

National Grid Ref: SU8322

🍴 🍺 Keepers' Arms

Mill Farm, *Trotton, Petersfield, Hants, GU31 5EL.*
Welcoming family home in large garden, lovely views. Log fires
Tel: **01730 813080**
Mr & Mrs Field.
Fax no: 01730 815080
D: £17.50-£25.00
S: £20.00-£40.00.
Open: All Year (not Xmas)
Beds: 1F 1T 1D 2S
Baths: 1 En 1 Sh
⛷ 🅿 (8) 🛇 🛏 🛏 ✕ 🚿 ⛁ 🏠 Ⓥ 🔒 ⚕ 🌜

Buriton   35

National Grid Ref: SU7320

Nursted Farm, *Buriton, Petersfield, Hants, GU31 5RW.*
Relax in the atmosphere of our 300 year old farmhouse
Tel: **01730 264278** Mrs Bray.
D: £15.00-£18.00 **S:** £15.00-£18.00.
Open: May to Feb
Beds: 3T
Baths: 1 Pr 1 Sh
⛷ 🅿 🛏 🏠 🔒 ⚕

Pay B&Bs by cash or cheque and be prepared to pay up front.

Buriton to Winchester

The meandering path through Hampshire takes you on from **Butser Hill** to **Old Winchester Hill**, where there is an Iron Age fort, a nature reserve and a viewpoint from which you can see to the Isle of Wight in clear weather. After Exton you climb towards another **Beacon Hill**, with superb views over the Meon Valley. The final stretch leads to **Telegraph Hill** and Chilcomb, with its early Saxon church, and into **Winchester**. The ancient capital of the kingdom of Wessex, the end of Saxon hegemony was confirmed here by the coronation of Norman King William the Conqueror, whose son William Rufus is buried in the cathedral, as is Jane Austen. Built over centuries, the cathedral is a hotch-potch of Norman, Gothic and Perpendicular. The city goes back further, evidenced by the Iron Age fort overlooking it and a remaining part of the Roman town. Other sights include Wolvesey Castle and the City and Westgate Museums.

Petersfield 36

National Grid Ref: SU7423

🍴 🍺 Harrow Inn, Half Moon, Good Intent, Five Bells

Heathside, 36 Heath Road East, Petersfield, Hants, GU31 4HR.
Grades: ETC 2 Diamond
Tel: **01730 262337**
Mrs Cafferata.
D: £20.00-£25.00 **S:** £18.00-£20.00.
Open: All Year (not Xmas)
Beds: 3F 1T 1S
Baths: 1 En 1 Pr 1 Sh
🅿 (3) 🗶 🗖 🖾 🖩 Ⓥ ⬦ ♿
Attractive house overlooking heath. Lovely garden

Heath Farmhouse, Sussex Road, Petersfield, Hants, GU31 4HU.
Actual grid ref: SU7522
Georgian farmhouse, lovely views, large garden, quiet surroundings, near town
Grades: ETC 3 Diamond
Tel: **01730 264709** Mrs Scurfield.
D: £18.00-£20.00 **S:** £20.00-£25.00.
Open: All Year
Beds: 1F 1D 1T
Baths: 1 En 1 Sh
⛺ 🅿 (5) 🗶 🗖 🖾 🖩 Ⓥ ⬦ 🚲

Ridgefield, Station Road, Petersfield, Hants, GU32 3DE.
Actual grid ref: SU743237
Friendly family atmosphere, near town & station; Portsmouth ferries: 20 mins drive
Tel: **01730 261402** Mrs West.
D: £20.00-£20.00 **S:** £25.00-£30.00.
Open: All Year (not Xmas)
Beds: 1D 2T
Baths: 2 Sh
⛺ 🅿 (4) 🗶 🗖 🖩 ♿ ⬦

Beaumont, 22 Stafford Road, Petersfield, Hampshire, GU32 2JG.
Warm welcome, comfortable beds, excellent breakfasts, home-made bread and preserves
Grades: ETC 3 Diamond
Tel: **01730 264744** (also fax no)
Mrs Bewes.
D: £18.00-£18.00
S: £18.00-£25.00.
Open: All Year (not Xmas)
Beds: 2T 1S
Baths: 1 Sh
⛺ (12) 🅿 (2) 🗶 🗖 🖩 ⬦ 🚲

1 The Spain, Petersfield, Hants, GU32 3JZ.
Actual grid ref: SU746232
Architecturally listed building, old house in town centre with lovely walks nearby
Tel: **01730 263261**
Mrs Tarver.
Fax no: 01730 261084
D: £18.00 **S:** £19.00.
Open: All Year
Beds: 1D 1T 1S
Baths: 1 Sh
⛺ 🗶 🗖 🖾 🖩 Ⓥ ⬦

Forge Cottage, Village Street, Sheet, Petersfield, Hants, GU32 2AQ.
C16th cottage with inglenooks and exposed beams on village green
Tel: **01730 268568** Ms Mathiot.
D: £15.00 **S:** £19.50.
Open: All Year (not Xmas)
Beds: 1D 1T **Baths:** 1 Sh
🅿 (2) 🗶 🗖 🖾 🖩 Ⓥ ⬦

East Meon 37

National Grid Ref: SU6822

🍴 🍺 Old George Inn, The Thomas Lord

Coombe Cross House & Stables, Coombe Road, East Meon, Petersfield, Hants, GU32 1HQ.
Actual grid ref: SU667210
Early Georgian House on South Downs, beautiful views, tranquil setting
Tel: **01730 823298** Mrs Bulmer.
Fax no: 01730 823515
D: £25.00 **S:** £30.00.
Open: All Year (not Xmas)
Beds: 2D 2T 1S
Baths: 2 Pr 1 Sh
⛺ (12) 🅿 (10) 🗖 🖾 🖩 Ⓥ ⬦

Drayton Cottage, East Meon, Petersfield, Hants, GU32 1PW.
Actual grid ref: SU669232
Luxury country cottage; antiques and oak beams, overlooking glorious countryside
Grades: ETC 4 Diamond, Silver
Tel: **01730 823472** Mrs Rockett.
D: £20.00-£23.00 **S:** £25.00-£25.00.
Open: All Year
Beds: 1D 1T **Baths:** 1 En 1 Pr
🅿 (3) 🗖 🖾 🖩 Ⓥ ⬦

West Meon 38

National Grid Ref: SU6424

🍴 🍺 The Thomas Lord

Brocklands Farm, West Meon, Petersfield, Hants, GU32 1JN.
Actual grid ref: SU639237
Secluded modern farmhouse in Meon Valley. Traditionally furnished. Outstanding views
Tel: **01730 829228** Mrs Wilson.
D: £19.00-£19.00 **S:** £19.00-£19.00.
Open: All Year (not Xmas)
Beds: 2D 1T **Baths:** 2 Sh
🅿 (6) 🗶 🗖 🖾 🖩 Ⓥ ⬦ ⬦

Meonstoke 39

National Grid Ref: SU6119

🍴 🍺 The Shoe, Buck's Head

Harvestgate Farm, Stocks Lane, Meonstoke, Southampton, SO32 3NQ.
Actual grid ref: SU627201
Modernised farmhouse in beautiful countryside
Tel: **01489 877675** Mrs Allan.
D: £20.00 **S:** £25.00.
Open: Apr to Sep
Beds: 1D 1T **Baths:** 2 En
⛺ (15) 🅿 (5) 🗶 🗖 🖾 🖩 & Ⓥ ⬦ ⬦

Owslebury 40

National Grid Ref: SU5123

🍴 🍺 The Ship

Mays Farmhouse, Longwood Dean, Owslebury, Winchester, Hants, SO21 1JR.
Actual grid ref: SU547241
Lovely C16th farmhouse, beautiful countryside; peaceful with good walks
Tel: **01962 777486** Mrs Ashby.
Fax no: 01962 777747
D: £20.00-£25.00 **S:** £25.00-£30.00.
Open: All Year
Beds: 1F 1D 1T
Baths: 3 Pr
⛺ (7) 🅿 (5) 🗶 🗖 🖾 🖩 & Ⓥ ⬦

Winchester 41

National Grid Ref: SU4829

🍴 🍺 Roebuck Inn, Queen Inn, Bell Inn, Wykeham Arms, White Horse, Stanmore Hotel, Cart Horse, Plough

🔺 *Winchester Youth Hostel, The City Mill, 1 Water Lane, Winchester, Hampshire, SO23 8EJ.*
Actual grid ref: SU486293
Tel: **01962 853723**
Under 18: £6.20 **Adults:** £9.15
evening meal at 7.00pm, family bunk rooms, showers, no smoking
Charming C18th watermill (NT) straddling the River Itchen at East End of King Alfred's capital

5 Ranelagh Road, Winchester, Hants, SO23 9TA.
Actual grid ref: SU476287
Tel: **01962 869555** Mr Farrell.
D: £20.00-£23.00 **S:** £20.00-£40.00.
Open: All Year (not Xmas)
Beds: 1F 1D 1T 1S
Baths: 1 En 1 Pr 2 Sh
⛺ (5) 🗶 🗖 🖾 🖩 Ⓥ ⬦ 🚲
Turn of the century Victorian villa, furnished in that style. We are close to the Cathedral and like to share our love of Winchester with our guests

Shawlands, 46 Kilham Lane, Winchester, Hants, SO22 5QD.
Actual grid ref: SU456289
Grades: ETC 4 Diamond, AA 4 Diamond, RAC 4 Diamond
Tel: **01962 861166** (also fax no)
Mrs Pollock.
D: £19.00-£22.50 **S:** £27.00-£30.00.
Open: All Year
Beds: 2F 1D 2T
Baths: 1 Pr 2 Sh
⛺ (5) 🅿 (4) 🗶 🗖 🖾 🖩 & Ⓥ ⬦ 🚲
Attractive house on edge of Winchester in quietm lane overlooking fields. Bedrooms are clean, bright and attractively decorated. Tea/coffee and colour TV in all bedrooms. Breakfast room overlooks beautiful garden. Excellent English breakfast - home-made bread & preserves

85 Christchurch Road,
Winchester, Hants, SO23 9QY.
Actual grid ref: SU473282
Comfortable detached Victorian
family house, convenient base for
Hampshire sightseeing
Grades: ETC 3 Diamond
Tel: 01962 868661 (also fax no)
Mrs Fetherston-Dilke.
D: £23.00-£24.00 **S:** £23.00-£24.00.
Open: All Year
Beds: 1D 1T 1S
Baths: 2 En 1 Sh
🛏 🅿 (3) ⌔ 🖵 ♨ 🎕 Ⓥ ⚡ ♻

Sycamores, 4 Bereweeke Close,
Winchester, Hants, SO22 6AR.
Actual grid ref: SU472304
Convenient but peaceful location
about 2 km north-west of city
centre
Grades: ETC 3 Diamond
Tel: 01962 867242 Mrs Edwards.
Fax no: 01962 620300
D: £18.00-£20.00.
Open: All Year
Beds: 2D 1T
Baths: 3 Pr
🅿 (3) ⌔ 🖵 ♨ 🎕 Ⓥ ♻

Goldring Hotels Limited, *Giffard
House Hotel, 50 Christchurch
Road, St Cross, Winchester, Hants,
SO23 9SU.*
Tel: **01962 852628**
Fax no: 01962 856722
D: £25.00-£35.00 **S:** £35.00-£45.00.
Open: All Year
Beds: 1F 6D 2T 5S
Baths: 14 En
🛏 🅿 (14) 🖵 ♨ 🎕 Ⓥ
This comfortable Victorian house
within ten minutes' walk of the city
centre has a large garden,
conservatory and lounge all open to
residents. All bedrooms refitted
late 1998 in keeping with the
character of the house

The Lilacs, *1 Harestock Close, off
Andover Road North, Winchester,
Hants, SO22 6NP.*
Attractive, Georgian-style family
home. Comfortable, clean and
excellent cuisine
Tel: **01962 884122** Mrs Pell.
D: £17.50-£18.00 **S:** £22.00-£25.00.
Open: All Year (not Xmas)
Beds: 1D 1T **Baths:** 1 Sh
🛏 🅿 (3) ⌔ 🖵 ♨ 🎕 Ⓥ ⚡ ♻

24 Clifton Road, *Winchester,
SO22 5BU.*
Victorian house, close to city and
station.Quiet, clean and friendly
Tel: **01962 851620**
Mr & Mrs Williams.
D: £17.50-£17.50
S: £25.00-£25.00.
Open: All Year (not Xmas)
Beds: 2D **Baths:** 1 Pr
🅿 (2) ⌔ 🖵 ♨

19 Downside Road, *Winchester,
SO22 5LT.*
Spacious welcoming detached
family home in quiet residential
area
Tel: **01962 861426** (also fax no)
Mrs Quick.
D: £18.00-£19.00 **S:** £20.00-£25.00.
Open: All Year (not Xmas)
Beds: 1D 1T 1S
Baths: 1 Sh
🛏 (8) 🅿 (4) ⌔ 🖵 ♨ 🎕 Ⓥ ⚡ ♻

All cycleways are
popular: you are
well-advised to
book ahead

Order your
packed lunches the
evening before you
need them.
Not at breakfast!

St Margaret's, *3 St Michael's
Road, Winchester, SO23 9JE.*
Comfortable rooms in Victorian
house, close to cathedral and
college
Grades: ETC 2 Diamond
Tel: **01962 861450** Mrs Brett.
D: £20.00-£21.00 **S:** £22.00-£22.00.
Open: All Year (not Xmas)
Beds: 1D 1T 2S
Baths: 2 Sh
🛏 (4) 🅿 (1) ⌔ 🖵 ♨ 🎕 Ⓥ ♻

Littleton   42

National Grid Ref: SU4532

🏨 🍴 Rack & Manger

Downlands, *Kennel Lane,
Littleton, Winchester, Hants,
SO22 6PT.*
Actual grid ref: SU468321
Warm welcome. Easy access
historic Winchester/Salisbury,
Stonehenge, New Forest
Tel: **01962 881969**
Mrs Kane-Smith.
Fax no: 01962 881454
D: £18.00 **S:** £20.00.
Open: All Year (not Xmas)
Beds: 1D 1T 1S
Baths: 1 Pr
🛏 (12) 🅿 (4) ⌔ 🖵 ♨ Ⓥ 🛆 ⚡ ♻

Surrey Cycleway

At 86 miles, the **Surrey Cycleway** is the shortest featured in this book. It is in fact a circular tour of the southeast of the county, over the chalk escarpment that is the North Downs and then through the southern woodlands - steering well clear of London. The route runs anticlockwise and is signposted by brown Surrey Cycleway direction signs with a cycle silhouette; the description that follows starts and finishes at Boxhill and Westhumble Railway Station.

A detailed **guide leaflet** to the cycleway route, which includes a list of cycle repair/hire shops on or near to the route, is available free from the County Cycling Officer, Surrey County Council, Room 314, County Hall, Kingston-upon-Thames KT1 2DY, tel 020-8541 8044.

Maps: Ordnance Survey 1:50,000 Landranger series: 186, 187

Surrey is well-connected by **train** to London and everywhere else in the Southeast. Trains to Boxhill and Westhumble, as well as many other locations, connect to Clapham Junction.

Dorking 1

National Grid Ref: TQ1649

¶ ⊈ King's Arms, Old School House, King William, The Bush

***The Waltons**, 5 Rose Hill, Dorking, Surrey, RH4 2EG.*
Listed house in conservation area. Beautiful views and friendly atmosphere
Tel: **01306 883127** (also fax no)
Mrs Walton.
D: £17.50-£20.00
S: £20.00-£32.50.
Open: All Year
Beds: 1F 1D 1T 1S
Baths: 3 Sh
⯊ ❷ (3) ⊬⌷⼌⋈⽊⬓⍐❖☂⼃

Great Bookham 2

National Grid Ref: TQ1354

¶ ⊈ Windsor Castle

***Selworthy**, 310 Lower Road, Great Bookham, Leatherhead, Surrey, KT23 4DW.*
Attractive location overlooking Green Belt. Convenient, M25, Gatwick and Heathrow airports
Tel: **01372 453952** (also fax no)
Mrs Kent.
D: £18.00-£20.00
S: £20.00-£25.00.
Open: All Year (not Xmas)
Beds: 1D 1T
Baths: 1 Sh
⯊ (10) ❷ (4) ⊬⌷⼌⬓⍐❖

Westcott 3

National Grid Ref: TQ1448

¶ ⊈ The Crown

***The Dene**, Hole Hill, Westcott, Dorking, Surrey, RH4 3LS.*
Actual grid ref: TQ136491
Tel: **01306 885595** Mrs King.
Fax no: 01306 877705
D: £20.00-£25.00 **S:** £25.00-£40.00.
Open: All Year
Beds: 1F 1D 2T
Baths: 1 En 2 Sh
⯊ ❷ (10) ⌷⼌⋈⽊⬓⍐❖☂⼃⽼
Set in 7 acres on the slope of Ranmore Common, this English house has traditional oak beams, and a friendly family atmosphere. There are beautiful views and walks. It is convenient for Gatwick Airport and the M25. Outdoor swimming pool

---

Order your

packed lunches the

***evening before* you**

need them.

Not at breakfast!

D = Price range per person sharing in a double room

Holmbury St Mary 4

National Grid Ref: TQ1144

¶ ⊈ Royal Oak, Parrot Inn, the Volunteer, King's Head

🔺 ***Holmbury St Mary Youth Hostel**, Radnor Lane, Holmbury St Mary, Dorking, Surrey, RH5 6NW.*
Actual grid ref: TQ104450
Tel: **01306 730777**
Under 18: £6.20 **Adults:** £9.15
evening meal at 7.00pm, self-catering facilities, family bunk rooms, grounds available for games, showers, parking, camping available, no smoking
Set in its own 5,000 acres of woodland grounds, this purpose-built hostel offers tranquil beauty among the Surrey Hills

***Bulmer Farm**, Holmbury St Mary, Dorking, Surrey, RH5 6LG.*
Quiet modernised C17th farmhouse/barn, large garden, picturesque village, self-catering
Grades: ETC 4 Diamond
Tel: **01306 730210** Mrs Hill.
D: £21.00-£23.00 **S:** £21.00-£34.00.
Open: All Year
Beds: 3D 5T **Baths:** 5 En 2 Sh
⯊ (12) ❷ (12) ⊬⌷⼌⋈⽊⬓⍐⚿❖☂⼃⽼

Woodhill Cottage, *Holmbury St Mary, Dorking, Surrey,* *RH5 6NL.*
Actual grid ref: TQ108453
Comfortable country family home in lovely rural village
Tel: **01306 730498** Mrs McCann.
D: £18.00 **S:** £21.00.
Open: All Year
Beds: 1F 1D 1T
Baths: 1 En 2 Sh
🛇 🅿 (3) 🌱 🛏 ✗ 🕯 🎪 Ⅶ ⚡

West Horsley 5

National Grid Ref: TQ0752

🍴 🍺 King William IV

Brinford, *Off Shere Road, West Horsley, Leatherhead,* *KT24 6EJ.*
Comfortable modern house in peaceful rural location with panoramic views
Tel: **01483 283636** Mrs Wiltshire.
D: £20.00-£25.00 **S:** £20.00-£25.00.
Open: All Year
Beds: 1D 1T 1S
Baths: 1 En 1 Sh
🅿 (4) 🌱 🖵 🕯 🎪 Ⅶ 🚲

Shere 6

National Grid Ref: TQ0747

🍴 🍺 White Horse, Prince of Wales

Manor Cottage, *Shere, Guildford, Surrey,* *GU5 9JE.*
C16th cottage with old world garden, in centre of beautiful village
Tel: **01483 202979** Mrs James.
D: £20.00-£20.00 **S:** £20.00-£20.00.
Open: May to Sep
Beds: 1D 1S
Baths: 1 Sh
🛇 (5) 🅿 🌱 🕯 Ⅶ ⚡ 🚲

S = Price range for a single person in a room

Westhumble to Bramley

The first part of the route takes you to **Ranmore Common**; nearby stands **Polesden Lacey**, an elegant Regency house with a collection of furniture, silverware, porcelain and paintings amassed in Edwardian times and a country estate with landscaped walks. Cycling around the White Downs and Hackhurst Downs, you come to **Shere**, an old village whose name means 'clear stream', from the brook that runs through it, and then **Wonersh** and **Bramley**. A detour north will take you to **Guildford**, the county town, noted for its cobbled High Street with Georgian architecture, as well as one or two older buildings - the Guildhall dates from Tudor times but has a Restoration facade with a gilded clock dated 1683. Also on the High Street is Guildford House Gallery, a restored seventeenth-century house displaying pictures and craftwork. There is also a small ruined Norman castle, and the red-brick cathedral dating from 1954. Just outside Guildford to the east is Clandon Park, a house dating from c1730 whose grand Palladian exterior contrasts with the Baroque ceiling of the Marble Hall.

All rooms full and nowhere else to stay? Ask the owner if there's anywhere nearby

---

Lockhurst Hatch Farm, *Lockhurst Hatch Lane, Shere, Guildford, Surrey,* *GU5 9JN.*
Actual grid ref: TQ067449
Listed farm house set in secluded valley in surrey hills
Tel: **01483 202689** Mrs Gellatly.
D: £20.00-£24.00 **S:** £23.00-£28.00.
Open: All Year (not Xmas)
Beds: 1F 1T
Baths: 1 En 1 Sh
🛇 🅿 (6) 🌱 🖵 🕯 Ⅶ ⚡ 🚲

Cherry Trees, *Gomshall, Shere, Guildford, Surrey,* *GU5 9HE.*
Actual grid ref: TQ072487
Quiet comfortable home, beautiful garden set in lovely old village
Tel: **01483 202288** Mrs Warren.
D: £20.00 **S:** £20.00.
Open: Jan to Nov
Beds: 1D 2T 1S
Baths: 2 Pr 1 Sh
🛇 🅿 (4) 🌱 🖵 🕯 🎪 Ⅶ 🔒 ⚡

The Chestnuts, *Gomshall Lane, Shere, Guildford, Surrey,* *GU5 9HE.*
Pretty house in olde worlde picturesque village. Surrounded by countryside
Tel: **01483 202541** Mrs Barker.
D: £18.00 **S:** £18.00.
Open: All Year (not Xmas)
Beds: 1T
Baths: 1 Sh
🅿 🕯 🎪 Ⅶ ⚡ 🚲

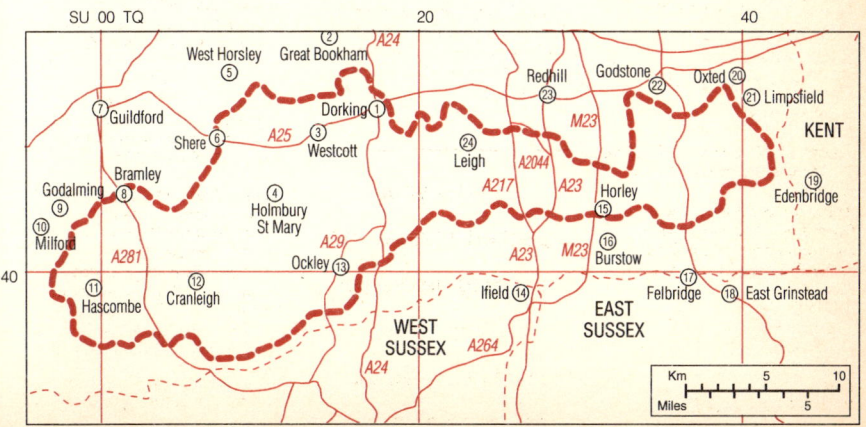

Guildford 7

National Grid Ref: SU9949

🐾 🍺 King's Head, Jolly Farmer, Hare & Hounds, The Fox, White House, George Abbot

Weybrook House, 113 Stoke Road, Guildford, Surrey, GU1 1ET.
Actual grid ref: SU998504
Quiet family B&B. A320 Near town centre/stations. Delicious breakfast
Tel: **01483 302394**
Mr & Mrs Bourne.
D: £19.00-£21.00 **S:** £26.00-£28.00.
Open: All Year (not Xmas)
Beds: 1F 1D 1S
Baths: 2 Sh
🛏🖵🕿🖩Ⓥ🛢⚡🚲

Atkinsons Guest House, 129 Stoke Road, Guildford, Surrey, GU1 1AN.
Small comfortable family-run guest house close to town centre & all local amenities
Tel: **01483 538260** Mrs Atkinson.
D: £19.00-£21.00 **S:** £25.00-£40.00.
Open: All Year
Beds: 1D 1T 2S
Baths: 2 En 1 Sh
🛏(6)🅿(2)🖵🕿🖩Ⓥ⚡🚲

Westbury Cottage, Waterden Road, Guildford, Surrey, GU1 2AN.
Cottage-style house in large secluded garden, 5 mins town centre, 2 mins station
Tel: **01483 822602** (also fax no)
Mrs Smythe.
D: £20.00-£20.00 **S:** £30.00-£30.00.
Open: All Year (not Xmas)
Beds: 1D 2T
Baths: 1 Sh
🛏(6)🅿(3)🚫🖵🕿🖩Ⓥ⚡🚲

Field Villa, Liddington New Road, Guildford, Surrey, GU3 3AH.
Tel: **01483 233961**
Fax no: 01483 234045
D: £19.00-£20.00
S: £19.00-£20.00.
Open: All Year (not Xmas)
Beds: 1D 1T 2S
Baths: 1 Sh
We are a small private B&B in a quiet private road. A friendly welcome awaits you. Very clean, golf courses and sports complex 5 mins away. London Hampton Court, Windsor, Legoland, 30 mins. M25, M3, M4, 15 minutes away

2 Wodeland Avenue, Guildford, GU2 5JX.
Centrally located rooms with panorama. Friendly and modernised family home
Tel: **01483 451142**
Mrs Hay.
Fax no: 01483 572980
D: £20.00-£22.00
S: £20.00-£25.00.
Open: All Year (not Xmas)
Beds: 1D 1T 1S
Baths: 1 Pr 1 Sh
🛏(3)🅿(3)🚫🖵🕿🖩Ⓥ&Ⓥ⚡🚲

Bramley 8

National Grid Ref: TQ0044

🐾 🍺 Jolly Farmer, Grantley Arms

Beevers Farm, Chinthurst Lane, Bramley, Guildford, Surrey, GU5 0DR.
Peaceful surroundings, friendly atmosphere, own preserves, honey, eggs, nearby villages
Grades: ETC 3 Diamond
Tel: **01483 898764** (also fax no)
Mr Cook.
D: £18.00-£25.00 **S:** £30.00.
Open: Easter to Nov
Beds: 1F 2T
Baths: 1 Pr 1 Sh
🛏🅿(10)🚫🖵🕿🖩Ⓥ🛢

Godalming 9

National Grid Ref: SU9643

🐾 🍺 Inn on the Lake

Sherwood, Ashstead Lane, Godalming, Surrey, GU7 1SY.
We have 4 cats and one Dalmatian dog - we welcome animal lovers. Continental breakfast
Tel: **01483 427545** (also fax no)
Mr & Mrs Harrison.
D: £22.00-£22.00 **S:** £22.00-£22.00.
Open: All Year
Beds: 1T 2S
Baths: 1 Sh
🛏(5)🖵🕿🖩Ⓥ⚡🚲

Milford 10

National Grid Ref: SU9442

Coturnix House, Rake Lane, Milford, Godalming, Surrey, GU8 5AB.
Modern house, family atmosphere, countryside position, easy access road/rail
Tel: **01483 416897**
Mrs Bell.
D: £20.00-£20.00 **S:** £20.00-£20.00.
Open: All Year
Beds: 1D 1T 1S
Baths: 1 Pr 1 Sh
🛏(1)🅿(6)🚫🖵🕿🖩Ⓥ🛢⚡🚲

Hascombe 11

National Grid Ref: SU9939

🐾 🍺 White Horse

Hoe Farm, Hoe Lane, Hascombe, Godalming, Surrey, GU8 4JQ.
Actual grid ref: SU997395
Elizabethan farmhouse in tranquil wooded valley, former retreat of Winston Churchill
Tel: **01483 208222**
Mrs Gordon.
Fax no: 01483 208538
D: £25.00-£30.00 **S:** £30.00-£30.00.
Open: All Year
Beds: 1F 3D 3T 1S
Baths: 3 Sh
🛏🅿(8)🚫🖵🕿🗙🖩Ⓥ🛢⚡🚲

Cranleigh 12

National Grid Ref: TQ0638

The White Hart Hotel, Ewhurst Road, Cranleigh, Surrey, GU6 7AE.
Tel: **01483 268647** Mr Silver.
Fax no: 01483 267154
D: £24.00-£26.00 **S:** £38.00-£42.00.
Open: All Year
Beds: 1F 1S **Baths:** 12 En
🛏🖵🕿🗙🔥🖩Ⓥ⚡🚲
The White Hart is situated 8.5 miles South of Guildford. We are a Listed coaching inn with 14 rooms, all with satellite TV, tea/coffee etc. Most rooms are ensuite with a double and single bed in each room

Ockley 13

National Grid Ref: TQ1439

🐾 🍺 Parrot Inn

Hazels, Walliswood, Ockley, Dorking, Surrey, RH5 5PL.
Separate suite. Own entrance. Beautiful gardens. Relaxed & peaceful. Convenient airports
Tel: **01306 627228** Mrs Floud.
D: £20.00-£25.00 **S:** £15.00-£30.00.
Open: All Year
Beds: 1F 1S **Baths:** 1 En 1 Sh
🛏🅿(2)🚫🖵🕿🖩Ⓥ⚡🚲

Ifield 14

National Grid Ref: TQ2537

🐾 🍺 The Plough, Royal Oak, The Gate, The Flight

Waterhall Country House, Prestwood Lane, Ifield Wood, Ifield, Crawley, W Sussex, RH11 0LA.
Grades: ETC 3 Diamond
RAC 3 Diamond
Tel: **01293 520002**
Mr & Mrs Dawson.
Fax no: 01293 539905
D: £22.50-£22.50 **S:** £35.00-£35.00.
Open: All Year (not Xmas)
Beds: 2F 2D 1S **Baths:** 10 En
🛏🅿(25)🚫🖵🕿🖩Ⓥ
Attractive Country house set in 28 acres - ideal for Gatwick bed & breakfast

---

The Grid Reference beneath the location heading is for the village or town - *not* for individual houses, which are shown (where supplied) in each entry itself.

April Cottage, *10 Langley Lane,*
Ifield, Crawley, West Sussex,
RH11 0NA.
Tel: **01293 546222**
Mrs Pedlow.
Fax no: 01293 518712
D: £21.00-£25.00
S: £30.00-£35.00.
Open: All Year
Beds: 1F 1D 1T 1S
Baths: 2 Sh
🛏 (6) ▣ (8) ⊬ ☐ 🛁 🎵 Ⅲ ☑ ▮
Warm & friendly 200-year-old
house in quiet lane, near pubs,
churches, station, shops

The Manor House, *Bonnetts Lane,*
Ifield, Crawley, West Sussex,
RH11 0NY.
100-year-old manor house, rural
courtesy, transport Gatwick,
parking
Grades: ETC 3 Diamond
Tel: **01293 512298**
Jefferies.
Fax no: 01293 518046
D: £21.50-£24.00
S: £28.00-£35.00.
Open: All Year (not Xmas)
Beds: 1F 2D 2T 1S
Baths: 4 En 1 Pr
🛏 ▣ (12) ⊬ ☐ 🛁 Ⅲ ☑ ♿

Horley   15

National Grid Ref: TQ2843

🍴 Foreseters, Ye Olde Six Bells, King's Head

Melville Lodge Guest House,
15 Brighton Road, Gatwick,
Horley, Surrey, RH6 7HH.
Grades: ETC 2 Diamond
RAC 2 Diamond
Tel: **01293 784951**
Mr & Mrs Brooks.
Fax no: 01293 785669
D: £18.00-£22.50
S: £22.00-£30.00.
Open: All Year
Beds: 1F 3D 2T 1S
Baths: 3 En 2 Sh
🛏 (1) ▣ ☐ 🛏 🎵 🛁 Ⅲ ♿ ☑
Welcome to our homely family-run
house, 5 minutes from Gatwick
Airport, TV, tea/coffee in all
rooms, ensuite and ground floor
rooms. Restaurants, pubs, town
centre and trains to
London/Brighton within walking
distance

Logans Guest House, *93 Povey*
Cross Road, Horley, Surrey,
RH6 0AE.
Victorian garden setting, friendly
hosts, holiday parking, really nice
atmosphere
Tel: **01293 783363** (also fax no)
D: £20.00-£30.00
S: £20.00-£30.00.
Open: All Year
Beds: 2F 3D 4T 2S
Baths: 3 En 1 Pr 2 Sh
🛏 ▣ ⊬ ☐ 🛏 🗙 🛁 Ⅲ ♿ ☑ ▮ ⚡ ♿

S = Price range for a single
person in a room

Gorse Cottage, *66 Balcombe Road,*
Horley, Surrey, RH6 9AY.
Gatwick Airport 2 miles, pretty,
detached house in residential area
Tel: **01293 784402** (also fax no)
D: £17.50-£18.00.
Open: All Year (not Xmas)
Beds: 1D 1T
▣ (2) ⊬ 🛏 🛁 Ⅲ ☑

Victoria Lodge Guest House,
161 Victoria Road, Horley, Surrey,
RH6 7AS.
Tel: **01293 432040**
Mr & Mrs Robson.
Fax no: 01293 432042
D: £19.00-£25.00 S: £30.00-£45.00.
Open: All Year
Beds: 2F 2D 2S **Baths:** 2 En 2 Sh
🛏 ▣ (9) ⊬ ☐ 🛁 🎵 Ⅲ ☑ ♿
Well-located for town centre, BR
station, pubs, shops etc. families
welcome

Prinsted Guest House, *Oldfield*
Road, Horley, Surrey, RH6 7EP.
Spacious Victorian house in quiet
situation ideal for Gatwick Airport
Grades: ETC 4 Diamond,
AA 3 Diamond,
RAC 3 Diamond, Sparkling
Tel: **01293 785233** Mrs Kendall.
Fax no: 01293 820624
D: £22.50-£23.50 S: £32.00-£32.00.
Open: All Year (not Xmas)
Beds: 2D 3T 2S **Baths:** 6 En 1 Pr
🛏 ▣ (10) ☐ ♿

Blackberry House, *8 Brighton*
Road, Horley, Surrey, RH6 7ES.
Attractive house on the main A23.
5 mins' drive Gatwick airport
Tel: **01293 772447**
D: £18.00-£20.00 S: £26.00-£30.00.
Open: All Year (not Xmas)
Beds: 1D
▣ (4) ⊬ ☐ 🛁 ☑

Yew Tree, *31 Massetts Road,*
Horley, Surrey, RH6 7DQ.
5 minutes taxi Gatwick Airport,
near town centre & rail station
Tel: **01293 785855** Mr Stroud.
D: £15.00 S: £15.00.
Open: All Year
Beds: 1F 2D 1T 2S **Baths:** 2 Sh
🛏 (1) ▣ (8) ☐ 🛁 Ⅲ ☑

Oakdene Guest House,
32 Massetts Road, Horley, Surrey,
RH6 7DS.
5 mins Gatwick Airport, town
centre. Large car Park. Visa etc
accepted
Tel: **01293 772047** Mrs Ali.
Fax no: 01293 771586
D: £19.00 S: £25.00.
Open: All Year (not Xmas)
Beds: 1F 1D 3S **Baths:** 2 Sh
🛏 ▣ (10) ⊬ ☐ 🛁 Ⅲ ♿ ☑

High season,
bank holidays and
special events mean
low availability
everywhere.

Bramley to Westhumble

From Bramley it's southwest to **Godalming**, and then around
Hydon Heath to **Dunsfold** and east, crossing the Wey and Arun
Canal, to Alfold Crossways and then **Ellen's Green**. Shortly
after here there is a link to Leith Hill, the highest point in
Southeast England. Back on the route and cycling east, you are
now in the lush woodland of the south of the county. Near to
Ockley are nature reserves at Wallis Wood and Vann Lake, and
the Hannah Peschar Sculpture Garden, an open-air gallery
which features annual exhibitions of contemporary sculpture,
both figurative and abstract and in all materials. Then it's east
through a string of villages and small towns whose medieval
names bespeak the era when this whole region was covered by
trees - **Newdigate** ('Gate near a new wood'), **Horley**
('Woodland clearing in a horn of land'), **Lingfield** ('Wood-
dwellers' field') - to the eastern end of the route at **Haxted Mill**,
a working mill with old-world milling machinery, which hosts,
from Easter to mid-September, a museum of the history of
milling. The next stretch takes you via **Bletcingley** to **Outwood**,
with another mill and nearby Outwood Common, and then by
way of Woodhatch, Reigate Heath, Betchworth and Brockham
back into the vicinity of **Box Hill**, which it is worth climbing for
the magnificent view, and to the station at Westhumble.

**All details shown
are as supplied
by B&B owners in
Autumn 1999.**

The Lawn Guest House,
30 Massetts Road, Horley, Surrey,
RH6 7DE.
Luxury Victorian house. Gatwick 5
mins. Horley centre 2 mins. Station
300 yards
Tel: **01293 775751**
Fax no: 01293 821803
D: £22.50 **S:** £40.00.
Open: All Year
Beds: 3F 3T 1D
Baths: 7 En
🛏 🅿 (15) ⅏ ♉ ♠ 🕯 🏛 Ⅶ

Burstow   16

National Grid Ref: TQ3041

📧 🍺 Shipley Bridge

Burstow Park, Antlands Lane,
Burstow, Horley, Surrey, RH6 9TF.
Victorian farmhouse now family
home set in 14 acres
Tel: **01293 785936** Mrs Puttock.
Fax no: 01293 774694
D: £25.00-£25.00 **S:** £25.00-£25.00.
Open: All Year
Beds: 1F 1D
Baths: 2 Sh
🛏 (3) 🅿 (10) ⅏ ♉ ♠ 🕯 🏛 Ⅶ ♽

Felbridge   17

National Grid Ref: TQ3639

📧 🍺 Bat & Ball, The Cricketers, Hare & Hound,
Cherry Tree, Prince of Wales, The Anchor,
Spotted Cow, Hen & Chicken, Jolly Farmer

Toads Croak House, 30 Copthorne
Road, Felbridge, East Grinstead,
W Sussex, RH19 2NS.
Beautiful Sussex cottage-style
house, gardens. Gatwick parking.
16th independent year
Tel: **01342 328524** (also fax no)
D: £18.50-£23.00 **S:** £24.00.
Open: All Year
Beds: 1F 1D 2T 1S
Baths: 2 En 1 Sh
🛏 🅿 (7) ⅏ ♉ 🕯 🏛 Ⅶ ♽

**Always telephone
to get directions to
the B&B - you will
save time!**

East Grinstead   18

National Grid Ref: TQ3938

📧 🍺 Dorset Arms

Brentridge, 24 Portland Road,
East Grinstead, W. Sussex, RH19 4EA.
Beautiful garden, central and quiet.
Close to Gatwick, M25 & south
coast
Tel: **01342 322004**
Mrs Greenwood.
Fax no: 01342 324145
D: £18.00-£25.00
S: £25.00-£25.00.
Open: All Year (not Xmas)
Beds: 2D
Baths: 1 En 1 Sh
🛏 🅿 (1) ⅏ 🏛

Cranston House, Cranston Road,
East Grinstead, W. Sussex,
RH19 3HW.
Actual grid ref: TQ397386
Attractive large detached house in
residential area. Gatwick 15
minutes
Tel: **01342 323609** (also fax no)
Mr Linacre.
D: £20.00-£40.00
S: £28.00-£40.00.
Open: All Year (not Xmas)
Beds: 1F 1D 1T
Baths: 1 En
🛏 (6) 🅿 (4) ⅏ ♉ ♠ 🕯 🏛 Ⅶ ♽ ♽

Edenbridge   19

National Grid Ref: TQ4446

📧 🍺 Four Elms

Knowlands, Four Elms,
Edenbridge, Kent, TN8 6NA.
Actual grid ref: TQ469478
Spacious Edwardian private
country house, non-smoking
Tel: **01732 700314** (also fax no)
Mr & Mrs Haviland.
D: £27.50.
Open: All Year (not Xmas)
Beds: 1D 1T 1S
🅿 (3) ⅏ ♉ 🕯 🏛 Ⅶ 🛉 ♽

Oxted   20

National Grid Ref: TQ3852

📧 🍺 The Oxted, Old Bell, The Crown,
The George, The Gurkha, Royal Oak

Pinehurst Grange Guest House,
East Hill (Part of A25), Oxted,
Surrey, RH8 9AE.
Actual grid ref: TQ393525
Comfortable Victorian ex-
farmhouse with traditional service
and relaxed friendly atmosphere
Tel: **01883 716413**
Mr Rodgers.
D: £21.00-£21.00
S: £26.00-£26.00.
Open: All Year (not Xmas/
New Year)
Beds: 1D 1T 1S
Baths: 1 Sh
🛏 (5) 🅿 (3) ⅏ ♉ 🕯 🏛 Ⅶ 🛉 ♽

**Please don't camp
on *anyone's* land
without first obtaining
their permission.**

Old Forge House, Merle Common,
Oxted, Surrey, RH8 0JB.
Actual grid ref: TQ416493
Welcoming family home in rural
surroundings
Tel: **01883 715969**
Mrs Mills.
D: £18.00-£20.00
S: £18.00-£20.00.
Open: All Year (not Xmas)
Beds: 1D 1T 1S
Baths: 1 Sh
🛏 🅿 (4) ♉ 🕯 🏛 ♽ ♽

Rosehaven, 12 Hoskins Road,
Oxted, Surrey, RH8 9HT.
Centrally situated house in quiet
road. Pubs and restaurants nearby
Tel: **01883 712700** (also fax no)
Mrs Snell.
D: £20.00 **S:** £20.00.
Open: All Year (not Xmas)
Beds: 2T 1S
Baths: 1 Sh
🛏 🅿 (1) ⅏ 🕯 🏛 Ⅶ 🛉 ♽

Limpsfield   21

National Grid Ref: TQ4052

📧 🍺 The George, The Crown, The Gurkha

Arawa, 58 Granville Road,
Limpsfield, Oxted, Surrey, RH8 0BZ.
Actual grid ref: TQ402532
Friendly, comfortable, welcoming.
Lovely garden, excellent breakfast,
good London trains
Grades: ETC 3 Diamond
Tel: **01883 714104** (also fax no)
Gibbs.
D: £18.00-£30.00
S: £18.00-£30.00.
Open: All Year
Beds: 1F 2T
Baths: 1 En 1 Sh
🛏 🅿 (3) ⅏ ♉ ♠ 🕯 🏛 ♿ Ⅶ 🛉 ♽ ♽

**Order your
packed lunches the
evening before you
need them.
Not at breakfast!**

Godstone 22

National Grid Ref: TQ3551

🏨 🍺 Coach House

Godstone Hotel, *The Green, Godstone, Surrey, RH9 8DT.*
C16th coaching house, original timbers, inglenook fireplaces
Tel: **01883 742461** (also fax no)
Mr Howe.
D: £27.50 **S:** £39.00.
Open: All Year
Beds: 6D 2T **Baths:** 8 Pr
🛏 🅿 🖵 🛏 ✕ 🖳 📖 Ⅴ 🛈 ⅍

D = Price range per person
sharing in a double room

Redhill 23

National Grid Ref: TQ2750

🏨 🍺 The Sun

Lynwood Guest House, *50 London Road, Redhill, Surrey, RH1 1LN.*
Actual grid ref: TQ280511
Adjacent to a lovely park, within 6 minutes walking from railway station, town centre
Grades: AA 3 Diamond
Tel: **01737 766894**
Mrs Rao.
Fax no: 01737 778253
D: £25.00-£28.00 **S:** £30.00-£33.00.
Open: All Year (not Xmas)
Beds: 4F 2D 1T 2S
Baths: 3 En 6 Pr 1 Sh
🛏 🅿 (8) 🖵 🖳 📖 Ⅴ ⅍

Leigh 24

National Grid Ref: TQ2246

🏨 🍺 The Plough

Barn Cottage, *Church Road, Leigh, Reigate, Surrey, RH2 8RF.*
Converted C17th barn, gardens with swimming pool, 100 yards from pub, 0.25 hr Gatwick
Tel: **01306 611347** Mrs Comer.
D: £25.00-£30.00 **S:** £35.00-£35.00.
Open: All Year
Beds: 1D 1T **Baths:** 3 Sh
🛏 🅿 (3) ⅍ 🖵 🛏 ✕ 🖳 📖 Ⅴ 🛈 ⅍ 🚲

S = Price range for a single
person in a room

Wiltshire Cycleway

The **Wiltshire Cycleway** is a 160-mile circular tour of the County of Wiltshire, which takes you from rolling hills to the Salisbury Plain, from prehistoric chalk hillside carvings and Stonehenge to old English villages and towns - Salisbury, Marlborough, Malmesbury and close to Bath, across the border in Somerset. It is signposted in both directions by blue Wiltshire Cycleway direction signs with a cycle silhouette, but is designed to be cycled anticlockwise. NB: There are a number of alternative routes, for which the signposts feature coloured spots; for the route featured in this book follow the plain blue signs.

A detailed **guide leaflet** to the cycleway route is available free from the Director of Environmental Services, Wiltshire County Council, County Hall, Trowbridge, Wiltshire BA14 8JD, tel 01225 713349. A separate factsheet on cycle repair/hire shops is also available free from the same address.

Maps: Ordnance Survey 1:50,000 Landranger series: 172, 173, 174, 183, 184

Trains: Bath, Chippenham and Swindon

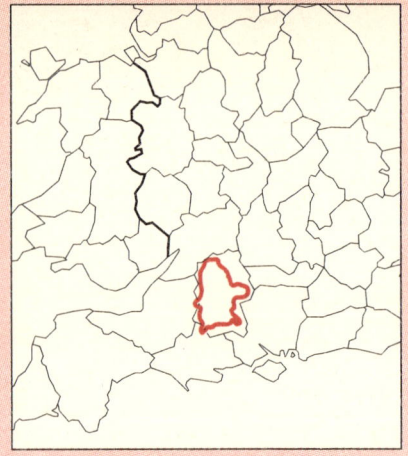

are on the main London (Paddington)-Bristol railway line. Frome, Westbury, Pewsey and Great Bedwyn are on the main London (Paddington)-Penzance line. Salisbury, Tisbury and Gillingham are on the line that runs between London Waterloo and Exeter. Bath, Bradford-on-Avon, Trowbridge, Westbury, Warminster and Salisbury are on the Bristol-Southampton line.

Malmesbury   1

National Grid Ref: ST9387

🏠🍺 Plough Inn, Wheatsheaf Inn, Old Inn, White Horse, Smoking Dog, Whole Hog, Horse & Groom

Bremilham House, Bremilham Road, Malmesbury, Wilts, *SN16 0DQ*.
Grades: ETC 3 Diamond
Tel: **01666 822680** Mrs Ball.
D: £17.00-£17.00
S: £19.50-£19.50.
Open: All Year (not Xmas)
Beds: 2D 1T
Baths: 2 Sh
🛏 🅿 (3) ⚡ 🚪 � 🏇 🎄 📺 ✗ 🚲
Delightful Edwardian cottage set in a mature walled garden in a quiet location on the edge of historic Malmesbury, England's oldest borough. The town, dominated by a stunning Norman Abbey, is central for Bath, Cheltenham, Salisbury and the glorious Cotswolds

---

D = Price range per person sharing in a double room

Whychurch Farm, Malmesbury, Wilts, *SN16 9JL*.
C17th farmhouse, central for Bath/Cotswolds
Tel: **01666 822156**
Mr & Mrs Weaver.
D: £17.50
S: £25.00.
Open: All Year (not Xmas)
Beds: 1D 1T
Baths: 2 En 2 Sh
🛏 🅿 (8) ⚡ 🚪 🐾 🏠 🛁 📺

Castle Combe   2

National Grid Ref: ST8477

🏠🍺 Salution Inn

Alicia Cottage, 3 School Lane, Castle Combe, Chippenham, Wiltshire, *SN14 7HJ*.
300-year-old Cotswold stone cottage. Friendly welcome
Tel: **01249 782110**
Ms Sanders.
D: £22.50-£25.00.
Open: All Year (not Xmas)
Beds: 2D
Baths: 1 En 1 Pr
🅿 (2) ⚡ 🚪 🛁 🏠 📺

Biddestone   3

National Grid Ref: ST8673

🏠🍺 White Horse

Home Farm, Biddestone, Chippenham, Wilts, *SN14 7DQ*.
Listed C17th farmhouse working farm, picturesque village. Stroll to pubs
Grades: ETC 4 Diamond, AA 4 Diamond
Tel: **01249 714475**
Mr & Mrs Smith.
Fax no: 01249 701488
D: £20.00-£22.50 **S:** £25.00-£30.00.
Open: All Year (not Xmas)
Beds: 2F 1D
Baths: 2 En 1 Pr
🛏 🅿 (4) ⚡ 🚪 🛁 🏠 📺 🔒 🚲

Pay B&Bs by cash or cheque and be prepared to pay up front.

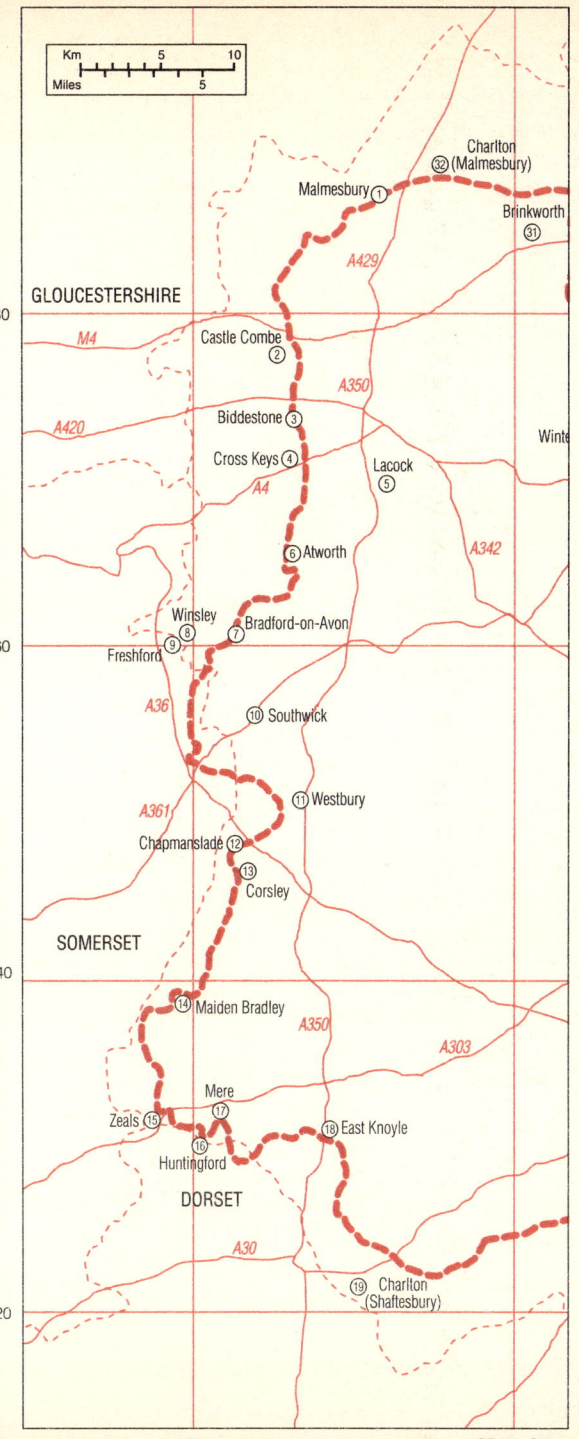

National Grid Ref: ST8671

***Spiders Barn**, Cross Keys, Corsham, Wiltshire, SN13 0DT.*
Extremely well-appointed house. Large comfortable rooms overlooking lovely garden
Tel: **01249 712012**
Ms Thornton-Norris.
D: £20.00-£20.00
S: £25.00-£30.00.
Open: All Year (not Xmas)
Beds: 1D 1T
Baths: 2 En
🅿 (6) ⅍ 🗖 🛋 🎞 Ⓥ ⚡

Malmesbury to Corsham

Malmesbury is a small town which breathes English history. Its partially-ruined Romanesque abbey stands on the site of a seventh-century Benedictine foundation which burned down in the eleventh century; the present Norman structure suffered damage at the Dissolution. In the Dark Ages this county lay at the heart of the domain of the West Saxons, a heritage represented in the abbey by the tomb of King Athelstan, the first Saxon to be acknowledged king of all England and the grandson of Alfred the Great of Wessex. In more recent times, the philosopher Thomas Hobbes was born in Malmesbury in 1588. Cycling south west, slightly off the route but well worth a visit is **Castle Combe**, *the* archetypal English village, where the cottages, church and bridge over the brook are built in the same local stone; it was used as the location for Puddleby-in-the-Marsh in the 1967 film of *Dr Dolittle*. Back on the cycleway and **Corsham** boasts weavers' cottages and the Elizabethan Corsham Court, with Capability Brown gardens and a fine art collection containing pictures from Renaissance masters onwards.

Lacock 5

National Grid Ref: ST9168

🍴 🍺 The George, Red Lion, Carpenters' Arms, The Angel

The Old Rectory, *Lacock, Chippenham, Wilts, SN15 2JZ.*
Grades: ETC 4 Diamond
Tel: **01249 730335** Mrs Sexton.
Fax no: 01249 730166
D: £22.50-£25.00 **S:** £25.00-£27.50.
Open: All Year
Beds: 1F 1D 1T
Baths: 3 En
🛏 🅿 (6) ⊬ 🗆 🛏 ☕ 🎺 🎞 Ⅴ ✦ ♿
Superb Gothic Victorian architecture, set in 8 acres of grounds and gardens, many original features and 4 poster beds. Excellent pubs a stroll away in famous Lacock location for tourists and businessmen, M4 (J17), close by. Bath 12 miles, London 2 hours. Recomm in 'Off the Beaten Track'

Videl, *6A Bewley Lane, Lacock, Chippenham, Wiltshire, SN15 2PG.*
Detached bungalow with annexe. Quiet position, rural location
Grades: ETC 3 Diamond
Tel: **01249 730279** Mrs Joad.
D: £20.00-£22.50 **S:** £25.00-£25.00.
Open: All Year
Beds: 1F 1T
Baths: 1 En 1 Pr
🛏 🅿 (2) ⊬ 🗆 🛏 ☕ 🎞 Ⅴ ♿

Atworth 6

National Grid Ref: ST8665

🍴 🍺 The Golden Fleece

Church Farm, *Atworth, Melksham, Wilts, SN12 8JA.*
Working dairy farm, large garden. Easy access Bath, Lacock, Bradford-on-Avon
Tel: **01225 702215**
Mrs Hole.
D: £17.50-£20.00
S: £20.00-£25.00.
Open: Easter to Oct
Beds: 1F 1D
Baths: 1 Sh
🛏 🅿 (4) 🗆 🎺 ☕ Ⅴ

Bradford-on-Avon 7

National Grid Ref: ST8261

🍴 🍺 Seven Stars, Barge Inn, Cross Guns, King's Arms, Bear Inn, the Beehive, the Plough, Hop Pole, Three Horse Shoes

Great Ashley Farm, *Ashley Lane, Bradford-on-Avon, Wilts, BA15 2PP.*
Actual grid ref: ST813619
Grades: ETC 4 Diamond
Tel: **01225 864563** (also fax no)
Mrs Rawlings.
D: £20.00-£24.00
S: £25.00-£45.00.
Open: All Year (not Xmas)
Beds: 1F 2D
Baths: 3 En
🛏 🅿 ⊬ 🗆 ☕ 🎞 Ⅴ 🛈 ✦ ♿
Come and enjoy our lovely secluded farmhouse set between Bath and Bradford on Avon, offering delightful ensuite rooms, great hospitality and a delicious breakfast. Golf, cycle-hire, Kennet and Avon Canal close by. Convenient for M4, Glastonbury Wells, Stonehenge, Lacock, Castle Combe, making this the ideal touring base. Children welcome, working farm

---

Chard's Barn, *Leigh Grove, Bradford-on-Avon, Wilts, BA15 2RF.*
Tel: **01225 863461**
Mr & Mrs Stickney.
D: £20.00-£23.00 **S:** £20.00-£20.00.
Open: All Year (not Xmas)
Beds: 1D 1T 1S
Baths: 2 En 1 Pr
🛏 🅿 (4) ⊬ 🗆 🛏 ☕ 🎞 & Ⅴ ♿
Quiet C17th barn in unspoilt countryside with lovely gardens, view and walks. All ground floor, individually styled bedrooms, choice of breakfasts. Historic town and golf course, one mile. Close - Bath, Castle Combe, Longleat. Easy for Salisbury Plain and Stonehenge

Great Ashley House, *Ashley Lane, Bradford-on-Avon, Wilts, BA15 2PP.*
A warm welcome to our 200-year-old former family farmhouse
Tel: **01225 863381** (also fax no)
Mrs Rawlings.
D: £17.50-£20.00 **S:** £25.00-£30.00.
Open: All Year (not Xmas)
Beds: 1F 2D
Baths: 1 En 1 Sh
🛏 🅿 (3) ⊬ 🗆 ☕ 🎞 Ⅴ ✦ ♿

The Locks, *265 Trowbridge Road, Bradford-on-Avon, Wilts, BA15 1UA.*
Private house alongside restored canal
Tel: **01225 863358** Mrs Benjamin.
D: £16.00-£19.00 **S:** £20.00-£30.00.
Open: All Year
Beds: 1F 2T **Baths:** 1 En 1 Pr 1 Sh
🛏 (3) 🅿 (6) ⊬ 🗆 ☕ 🎞 Ⅴ 🛈 ✦ ♿

All details shown
are as supplied
by B&B owners in
Autumn 1999.

All paths are
popular: you are
well-advised to
book ahead

Corsham to Salisbury

Bradford on Avon, another quaint English town, centres on an arched stone bridge over the Avon, and also features a tithe barn and the ancient Saxon Church of St Laurence. From here you may wish to take a detour to **Bath**, which is possible to reach by bicycle along the towpath of the Kennet and Avon Canal (see the *Sustrans* West Country Way). South of Bradford-on-Avon you pass the ruins of Farleigh Castle and you can find Iford Manor and its famous landscaped garden with mediterranean plants, by Harold Peto. The next stretch takes in a piece of Wiltshire's famous prehistory, as you pass the renowned Westbury White Horse hillside carving - you are now at the west side of Salisbury Plain.

This pocket of the county contains a clutch of stately piles - **Longleat** boasts the bizarre combination of a splendid renaissance manor and a theme park with only one obvious feature in common with the house: its sheer scale - based on an African safari park, it offers a variety of other attractions including the world's longest maze. **Stourhead**, although built on a comparable scale, is more restrained in every respect. Dating from the eighteenth century, the Palladian mansion is accompanied by a famous landscaped garden, whose carefully-orchestrated classical harmony is mirrored in a lake; also here is King Alfred's Tower, a folly offering impressive views. **Stourton House Gardens**, nearby, have a collection of unusual plants. From here it is a beautiful ride around the West Wiltshire Downs towards Salisbury.

Winsley 8

National Grid Ref: ST7961

📧 🍺 Seven Stars

*3 Corners, Cottles Lane, Winsley,
Bradford-on-Avon, Wilts, BA15 2HJ.*
House in quiet village edge location, attractive rooms and gardens
Tel: **01225 865380** Mrs Cole.
D: £22.50-£25.00 **S:** £26.00-£30.00.
Open: All Year (not Xmas)
Beds: 1F 1D
Baths: 1 En 1 Pr
🛇 🅿 (4) ⅍ ⬜ ✕ 🕭 ⅏ 🎫 ▣ 🔒 ⚡ ⚲

Freshford 9

National Grid Ref: ST7860

📧 🍺 The Inn, Old Coaching Inn

*Tyning House, Freshford, Bath,
BA3 6DR.*
Great hospitality in beautiful surroundings!
Tel: **01225 723288** (also fax no)
Mrs Harward.
D: £16.00 **S:** £21.00.
Open: All Year
Beds: 2D
Baths: 1 Sh
🛇 🅿 (6) ⬜ 🕭 ⅏ ▣

Southwick 10

National Grid Ref: ST8355

📧 🍺 Red Lion, Poplars

*Brooksfield House, Vaggs Hill,
Southwick, Trowbridge, Wilts,
BA14 9NA.*
Delightful converted country barn
Grades: ETC 4 Diamond
Tel: **01373 830615** (also fax no)
Mrs Parry.
D: £20.00-£25.00 **S:** £20.00-£30.00.
Open: All Year (not Xmas)
Beds: 1F 1D 1T
Baths: 1 En 1 Pr 1 Sh
🛇 🅿 (20) ⬜ 🕭 ⅏ ▣ 🔒 ⚡ ⚲

Westbury 11

National Grid Ref: ST8650

📧 🍺 Full Moon

*Brokerswood House,
Brokerswood, Westbury, Wilts,
BA13 4EH.*
Situated in front of 80 acres of woodland, open to the public
Tel: **01373 823428** Mrs Phillips.
D: £15.00-£18.00 **S:** £15.00-£18.00.
Open: All Year (not Xmas)
Beds: 3F 1D 1T 1S
Baths: 1 En 1 Pr 1 Sh
🛇 (1) 🅿 (6) ⅍ ⬜ 🕭 🕭 ⅏ 🔒 ⚡ ⚲

D = Price range per person
sharing in a double room

Chapmanslade 12

National Grid Ref: ST8348

📧 🍺 Three Horseshoes

*Spinney Farm, Thoulstone,
Chapmanslade, Westbury, Wilts,
BA13 4AQ.*
In heart of Wiltshire countryside.
Easy reach of Bath, Longleat
Tel: **01373 832412** Mrs Hoskins.
D: £17.00-£18.00 **S:** £20.00-£20.00.
Open: All Year
Beds: 1F 1D 1T
Baths: 2 Sh
🛇 🅿 (8) ⬜ 🕭 ✕ 🕭 ⅏ ▣ ⅍ ⚲

Corsley 13

National Grid Ref: ST8246

*Sturford Mead Farm, Corsley,
Warminster, Wilts, BA12 7QU.*
Farmhouse in Area of Outstanding
Natural Beauty close to Longleat
Grades: ETC 4 Diamond,
AA 4 Diamond
Tel: **01373 832213** (also fax no)
Mrs Corp.
D: £21.00-£21.00 **S:** £25.00-£28.00.
Open: All Year
Beds: 1D 2T
Baths: 2 En 1 Pr
🛇 🅿 (6) ⅍ ⬜ 🕭 ⅏ ▣ ⚲

Maiden Bradley 14

National Grid Ref: ST7938

📧 🍺 Somerset Arms

*55 The Rank, Maiden Bradley,
Warminster, BA12 7JF.*
Cosy C18th village cottage, close
Stourhead Gardens, Longleat, A303
Tel: **01985 844561** (also fax no)
Mrs Smith.
D: £17.00-£18.00
S: £17.00-£18.00.
Open: Easter to Sep
Beds: 1T 1S
Baths: 1 Pr
🛇 (10) ⅍ ⬜ 🕭 ⅏ ▣ ⚡

Zeals 15

National Grid Ref: ST7731

📧 🍺 White Lion

*Cornerways Cottage, Zeals,
Longcross, Warminster, Wilts,
BA12 6LL.*
Grades: ETC 4 Diamond
Tel: **01747 840477** (also fax no)
Mrs Snook.
D: £18.00-£20.00 **S:** £25.00-£25.00.
Open: All Year
Beds: 2D 1T
Baths: 2 En 1 Pr
🛇 (8) 🅿 (6) ⅍ ⬜ ✕ 🕭 ⅏ ▣ 🔒 ⚡ ⚲
Cornerways is a C18th cottage
offering a high standard of accommodation with a lovely 'cottagey'
feel, complemented by excellent
breakfasts in the old dining room.
Stourhead 2 miles, Longleat 4
miles, Bath/Salisbury 25 miles

Please don't camp
on *anyone's* land
without first obtaining
their permission.

*Stag Cottage, Fantley Lane, Zeals,
Warminster, Wilts, BA12 6NX.*
C17th thatched cottage in AONB.
Tea room, serving homemade
scones, cakes, hot snacks
Tel: **01747 840458** (also fax no)
Mrs Boxall.
D: £18.00 **S:** £18.00.
Open: All Year
Beds: 2D 1T
Baths: 2 En
🛇 🅿 (5) ⅍ ⬜ 🕭 ▣ 🔒 ⚲

Huntingford 16

National Grid Ref: ST8029

📧 🍺 Dolphin Inn

*Huntingford Oak, Huntingford,
Gillingham, Dorset, SP8 5QH.*
Peaceful modern chalet house, rural
surroundings, peaceful atmosphere,
marvellous views
Grades: ETC 4 Diamond
Tel: **01747 860574**
Mrs James.
D: £20.00-£25.00 **S:** £22.00-£27.00.
Open: All Year (not Xmas)
Beds: 1F 1D 1T
Baths: 3 Pr
🛇 🅿 (12) ⬜ 🕭 ⅏ ♿ ▣ 🔒 ⚡

Mere 17

National Grid Ref: ST8132

📧 🍺 Talbot Inn, Butt of Sherry, Old Ship

*Latimer House, Castle Street,
Mere, Warminster, BA12 6JE.*
Georgian town house, walled
garden, Wilts Cycleway, footpaths,
Stourhead 2 miles
Grades: ETC 3 Diamond
Tel: **01747 860894** (also fax no)
Mrs Gale.
D: £20.00-£20.00 **S:** £20.00-£20.00.
Open: All Year
Beds: 1D 1T 1S
Baths: 1 Pr 1 Sh
🛇 (8) ⅍ ⬜ ⅏ ⚡ ⚲

*Norwood House, Mere,
Warminster, Wilts, BA12 6LA.*
Actual grid ref: ST802323
Family house with pleasant outlook
onto large garden. Near Stourhead
Tel: **01747 860992** (also fax no)
Mrs Tillbrook.
D: £16.00 **S:** £20.00.
Open: All Year
Beds: 1F
Baths: 1 En
🛇 🅿 (3) ⬜ 🕭 ⅏ ♿ ▣

Salisbury to Amesbury

Wilton House, just before Salisbury, dates mainly from the seventeenth century, when Inigo Jones rebuilt it after a fire, and includes a fantastic collection of paintings and landscaped parkland with an old English rose garden. **Salisbury** is an historic city most famous for its cathedral, whose 404-foot spire is the tallest in England, and which is also notable for the chapter house, the vaulted cloisters and the library, which contains one of only four existing original copies of the Magna Carta. The secluded Cathedral Close leads into the narrow medieval city streets. Cycling north, **Old Sarum** is the site of an Iron Age fort, and was settled by Romans, Saxons and Normans, and was the original site of the cathedral before it was transferred (including the fabric) to Salisbury. **Amesbury** is where to make the detour to **Stonehenge**, the world-renowned prehistoric enigma at the heart of Salisbury Plain. In fact the remains of several different constructions separated by hundreds of years, the site seems to have been a centre of religious devotion for centuries. The stones of the earlier circle were hewn from a quarry in Wales and transported; the later circle is remarkable for the sheer size of the megaliths, and their construction into sets of two uprights crossed by a lintel.

East Knoyle 18

National Grid Ref: ST8830

|◀| ◀| Fox & Hounds

Moors Farmhouse, *East Knoyle*, *Salisbury, Wilts, SP3 6BU.*
Actual grid ref: ST863301
C17th farmhouse suite of large rooms. Naturally beautiful/ interesting area
Tel: **01747 830385**
Mrs Reading.
D: £25.00-£25.00 **S:** £25.00-£25.00.
Open: All Year (not Xmas)
Beds: 1T
Baths: 1 En
🛏 (8) 🅿 (2) 🖵 🎍 🎖 🎞 Ⓥ ♦ ♿ ♻

Charlton (Shaftesbury) 19

National Grid Ref: ST9022

Charnwood Cottage, *Charlton*, *Shaftesbury, Dorset, SP7 9LZ.*
Actual grid ref: ST902226
C17th thatched cottage with lovely garden. Good base for touring
Tel: **01747 828310**
Mr & Mrs Morgan.
D: £17.00 **S:** £20.00.
Open: All Year (not Xmas)
Beds: 1F 1D
Baths: 1 Sh
🛏 (5) 🅿 (2) 🖵 🎍 🎞

Bringing children with you? Always ask for any special rates.

High season, bank holidays and special events mean low availability *everywhere*.

Coombe Bissett 20

National Grid Ref: SU1026

|◀| ◀| Fox & Goose, Yew Tree Inn, White Hart, Radnor Arms

Swaynes Firs Farm, *Grimsdyke*, *Coombe Bissett, Salisbury, Wilts, SP5 5RF.*
Grades: ETC 3 Diamond
Tel: **01725 519240** Mr Shering.
D: £20.00-£22.00 **S:** £20.00-£25.00.
Open: All Year (not Xmas)
Beds: 1F 2T
Baths: 3 En
🛏 (all) 🅿 (6) 🖵 🎍 🎖 🎞 Ⓥ ♻
Spacious farmhouse on working farm with horses, cattle, poultry, geese & duck ponds

Cross Farm, *Coombe Bissett*, *Salisbury, Wilts, SP5 4LY.*
Modern, comfortable farmhouse on working farm in pretty village
Tel: **01722 718293** (also fax no)
Mrs Kittermaster.
D: £20.00 **S:** £20.00.
Open: All Year
Beds: 1F 1T 1S
Baths: 2 Sh
🛏 🅿 (4) 🖵 🎍 🎖 🎞 Ⓥ ♦ ♻

Salisbury 21

National Grid Ref: SU1430

|◀| ◀| Fox & Goose, White Horse, Avon Brewery, George & Dragon, Bell Inn, Castle Inn, Haunch of Venison, Barford Inn, Yew Tree Inn, White Hart, Radnor Arms, the Ship, Grey Fisher

▲ *Salisbury Youth Hostel*,
Milford Hill House, Milford Hill, Salisbury, Wiltshire, SP1 2QW.
Actual grid ref: SU149299
Tel: **01722 327572**
Under 18: £6.85
Adults: £10.15
evening meal at 5.30-8.00pm, television, laundry facilities, camping available
200-year-old listed building in secluded grounds only a few minutes from the city centre. Enjoy the relaxed atmosphere of the hostel and the well-tended grounds which include a fine old Cedar tree

The Gallery, *36 Wyndham Road, Salisbury, Wilts, SP1 3AB.*
Grades: ETC 4 Diamond
Tel: **01722 324586** (also fax no)
Mrs Musselwhite.
D: £18.00-£20.00 **S:** £30.00-£35.00.
Open: All Year
Beds: 1D 2T
Baths: 3 En
🛏 (12) 🗡 🖵 🎍 🎖 🎞 Ⓥ ♦ ♻
A good base for touring Southern England and only ten minutes' walk from the city centre. Enjoy our warm hospitality, homemade shortbread and preserves and our delicious choices of breakfast. Rina and David look forward to welcoming you

The Old Bakery, *35 Bedwin Street, Salisbury, Wilts, SP1 3UT.*
C15th house, cosy oak-beamed bedrooms, city centre location. Room only rates also available
Grades: ETC 2 Diamond
Tel: **01722 320100**
Mrs Bunce.
D: £19.00-£26.00 **S:** £23.00-£26.00.
Open: All Year (not Xmas)
Beds: 1F 1D 1T 1S
Baths: 2 En 1 Sh
🛏 🖵 🎍 🎖 🎞 Ⓥ ♦ ♻

Websters, *11 Harington Road, Salisbury, Wilts, SP2 7LG.*
Grades: ETC 4 Diamond,
AA 4 Diamond
Tel: **01722 339779** (also fax no)
Mrs Webb.
D: £18.00-£20.00 **S:** £27.00-£30.00.
Open: All Year
Beds: 1D 2T 2S
Baths: 5 En
🛏 (12) 🅿 (5) 🖵 🗡 🎖 🎞 ♿ Ⓥ
Set on the end of a delightfully colourful terrace with sumptuous choices for breakfast, spacious rooms, an easy 15 minutes walk to cathedral and city centre, off-road parking

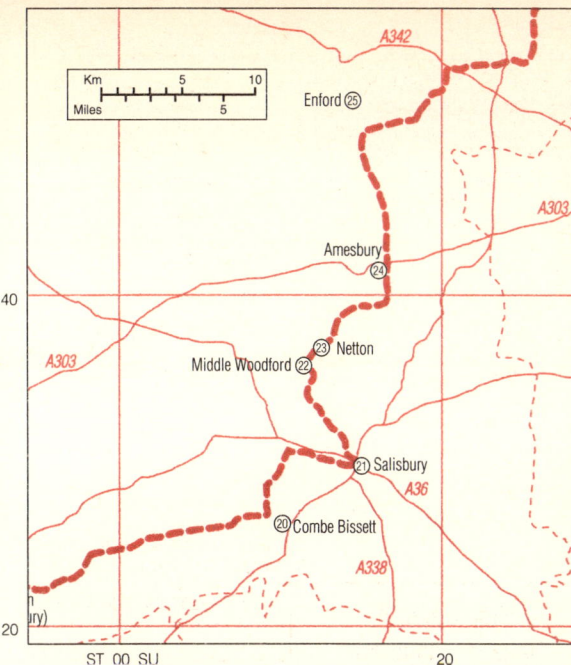

ST 00 SU   20

Castlewood Guest House,
45 Castle Road, Salisbury, Wilts,
SP1 3RH.
Tel: **01722 421494** (also fax no)
Mrs Feltham.
D: £20.00-£22.50 **S:** £20.00-£25.00.
Open: All Year
Beds: 2F 1D 1T 1S
Baths: 2 En 2 Sh
Large Edwardian house tastefully
restored throughout, pleasant 10
minutes riverside walk to city
centre and cathedral, open all year

Leenas Guest House, *50 Castle*
Road, Salisbury, Wilts, SP1 3RL.
Friendly family-run guest house.
Pretty bedrooms and delightful
public areas
Grades: ETC 3 Diamond
Tel: **01722 335419** (also fax no)
Mrs Street.
D: £21.00-£24.00 **S:** £22.00-£36.00.
Open: All Year
Beds: 1F 2D 2T 1S
Baths: 5 En 1 Sh

Farthings, *9 Swaynes Close,*
Wyndham Road, Salisbury, Wilts,
SP1 3AE.
Comfortable old house in quiet
street but near city centre
Grades: ETC 3 Diamond
Tel: **01722 330749** (also fax no)
Mrs Rodwell.
D: £20.00-£23.00 **S:** £20.00.
Open: All Year
Beds: 1D 1T 2S
Baths: 2 En 1 Sh

Gerrans House, *91 Castle Road,*
Salisbury, Wilts, SP1 3RW.
Comfortable detached house,
private facilities and secure parking
Grades: ETC 4 Diamond, Silver
Tel: **01722 334394** Mrs Robins.
Fax no: 01722 332508
D: £20.00-£23.00 **S:** £30.00-£35.00.
Open: Easter to Nov
Beds: 1D 1T
Baths: 2 En

Rokeby Guest House, *3 Wain-A-*
Long Road, Salisbury, Wilts,
SP1 1LJ.
Beautiful, nostalgic Edwardian
guest house quietly situated 10
minutes' walk city/cathedral
Tel: **01722 329800** (also fax no)
Mrs Rogers.
D: £20.00 **S:** £30.00.
Open: All Year
Beds: 5F 1D 3T
Baths: 5 En 2 Pr 2 Sh

Cricket Field House Hotel, *Wilton*
Road, Salisbury, Wilts, SP2 7NS.
Grades: ETC 4 Diamond,
AA 4 Diamond
Tel: **01722 322595** (also fax no)
Mrs James.
D: £25.00-£30.00
S: £35.00-£35.00.
Open: All Year (not Xmas)
Beds: 1F 7D 3T 3S
Baths: 14 En
Situated in a large garden. All
bedrooms are individually
furnished equipped with TV, tea-
making, hair dryers and full private
facilities. Our restaurant , with its
lovely views of the village church
and cricket field, food expertly
cooked and superbly presented by
our in-house chef

48 Wyndham Road, *Salisbury,*
Wilts, SP1 3AB.
Edwardian home, tastefully
restored and furnished with
antiques, close to city centre, quiet
area
Grades: ETC 3 Diamond
Tel: **01722 327757** Mrs Jukes.
D: £17.00-£20.00 **S:** £20.00.
Open: All Year (not Xmas)
Beds: 2D 1T **Baths:** 1 En 1 Sh

Hayburn Wyke Guest House,
72 Castle Road, Salisbury, Wilts,
SP1 3RL.
Grades: AA 3 Diamond,
RAC 3 Diamond
Tel: **01722 412627** Mrs Curnow.
D: £19.00-£24.00 **S:** £28.00-£46.00.
Open: All Year
Beds: 2F 3D 2T **Baths:** 4 En 3 Sh
A family run friendly guest house,
Hayburn Wyke is a fine Victorian
house, situated by Victoria Park,
half a mile riverside walk from
Salisbury Cathedral and city centre.
Many placed to visit locally,
including Stonehenge, Wilton
House and Old Sarum

Weaver's Cottage, *37 Bedwin*
Street, Salisbury, Wilts, SP1 3UT.
C15th city centre cottage, cosy,
oak-beamed, 2 minutes market
square & bus station. Backpackers
especially welcome
Tel: **01722 341812** Mrs Bunce.
D: £15.00-£20.00 **S:** £20.00-£25.00.
Open: All Year (not Xmas)
Beds: 1F 1D **Baths:** 1 Sh

The Winchester Gate,
113-117 Rampart Road, Salisbury,
Wilts, SP1 1JA.
Friendly C17th public house, over-
looking cathedral, near city centre
Tel: **01722 322834** Colman.
D: £15.00-£20.00 **S:** £15.00-£20.00.
Open: All Year
Beds: 1F 1D 1T **Baths:** 1 Sh

D = Price range per person
sharing in a double room

S = Price range for a single
person in a room

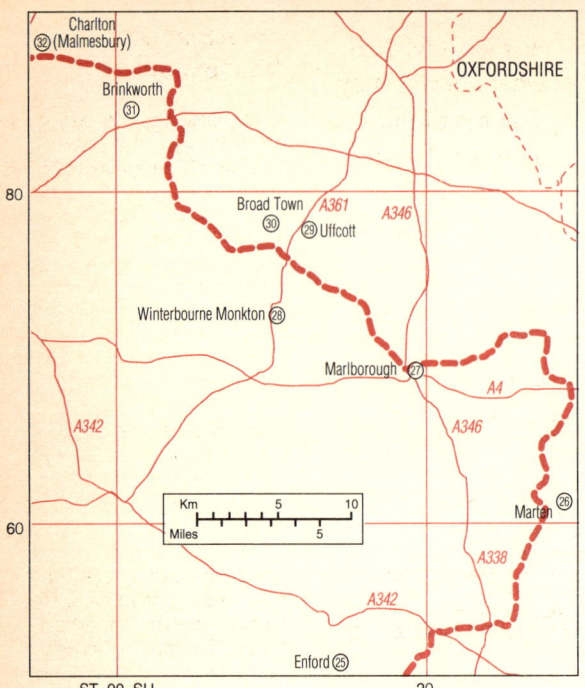

ST 00 SU   20

Hillside, *72 St Marks Avenue, Salisbury, Wilts, SP1 3DW.*
Comfortable home in secluded surroundings. Rooms with tranquil garden views
Tel: **01722 335474**
Mrs Browning.
D: £16.00 **S:** £16.00.
Open: All Year (not Xmas)
Beds: 1D 1T
Baths: 2 Sh
ⓢ (7) 🅿 (4) 🗗 ⛢ 🏛 Ⅵ

The Bell Inn, *Warminster Road, Salisbury, Wilts, SP2 0QD.*
Situated in the picturesque Wylye Valley, 300-year-old village inn, warm welcome
Tel: **01722 743336**
Mrs Phillips & Mr S Cooper.
Fax no: 01722 744202
D: £19.00 **S:** £25.00.
Open: All Year
Beds: 1D 1T 1S
Baths: 3 Pr
ⓢ 🅿 🗗 ⛢ 🏛 Ⅵ

53 Wyndham Road, *Salisbury, Wilts, SP1 3AH.*
Detached family home. Attractive garden, 8 minutes' walk to city centre
Tel: **01722 322955**
Mrs Middleton.
D: £16.00 **S:** £20.00.
Open: All Year
Beds: 1D 1T
Baths: 1 Sh
🅿 (2) ✂ 🗗 ⛢ 🏛 Ⅵ

Middle Woodford   22
National Grid Ref: SU1136

🍴 🍺 The Wheatsheaf

Great Croft, *Middle Woodford, Salisbury, Wilts, SP4 6NR.*
Spacious accommodation in picturesque Woodford Valley overlooking river and water meadows
Tel: **01722 782357**
Mrs Cates.
D: £18.00-£20.00 **S:** £25.00.
Open: All Year (not Xmas)
Beds: 1T **Baths:** 1 En
ⓢ (3) 🅿 (2) 🗗 ⛢ 🏛 Ⅵ

Netton   23
National Grid Ref: SU1336

🍴 🍺 The Bridge, Black Horse

The Old Bakery, *Netton, Salisbury, Wilts, SP4 6AW.*
Actual grid ref: SU128369
Grades: ETC 3 Diamond
Tel: **01722 782351**
Mrs Dunlop.
D: £18.00-£20.00 **S:** £20.00-£25.00.
Open: All Year (not Xmas)
Beds: 1D 1T 1S
Baths: 2 En 1 Pr
ⓢ (5) 🅿 (3) 🗗 ⛢ 🏛 Ⅵ
The Old Bakery is a pleasantly modernised former village bakery in the Woodford Valley situated midway between Salisbury and Stonehenge, overlooking fields and water meadows.

Thorntons, *Netton, Salisbury, Wilts, SP4 6AW.*
Tranquil village convenient for Salisbury and Stonehenge. Home cooking a speciality
Tel: **01722 782535**
Mrs Bridger.
D: £18.00-£20.00 **S:** £20.00-£25.00.
Open: All Year (not Xmas)
Beds: 1F 1D 1S
Baths: 2 Sh
ⓢ (5) 🅿 ✂ 🗗 ✗ ⛢ 🏛 ♿ Ⅵ 🔒 ♦ 🚲

Amesbury   24
National Grid Ref: SU1541

🍴 🍺 New Inn

Catkin Lodge, *93 Countess Road, Amesbury, Salisbury, SP4 7AT.*
The nearest B&B to Stonehenge. Friendly, comfortable and good value
Tel: **01980 624810**
Mr Grace.
D: £19.00-£23.00 **S:** £18.00.
Open: All Year
Beds: 2F 1D 1T
Baths: 1 En 1 Sh
ⓢ (5) 🅿 (5) ✂ 🗗 ⛢ 🏛 Ⅵ 🔒 ♦ 🚲

Enford   25
National Grid Ref: SU1351

🍴 🍺 Swan Inn

Enford House, *Enford, Pewsey, Wilts, SN9 6DJ.*
Salisbury Plain. River village, old rectory, beautiful garden, thatched wall
Grades: ETC 3 Diamond
Tel: **01980 670414**
Mr Campbell.
D: £18.00-£18.00 **S:** £20.00-£20.00.
Open: All Year (not Xmas)
Beds: 1D 2T
Baths: 2 Sh
ⓢ 🅿 (5) ✂ 🗗 ✗ ⛢ 🏛 Ⅵ ♦ 🚲

Marten   26
National Grid Ref: SU2861

The Tipsy Miller, *Marten, Marlborough, SN8 3SH.*
Nestling in the Wiltshire countryside, close to Wilts/Hampshire border
Tel: **01264 731372** (also fax no)
D: £17.50 **S:** £20.00.
Open: All Year
Beds: 1F
Baths: 1 En
🅿 🗗 ✗ ⛢ 🏛 Ⅵ 🔒

All cycleways are popular: you are well-advised to book ahead

---

Marlborough 27

National Grid Ref: SU1869

🍴 🍺 The Bear, The Roebuck

Cartref, *63 George Lane,*
Marlborough, Wilts, SN8 4BY.
Actual grid ref: SU1969
Family home near town centre.
Ideal for Avebury, Savernake,
Wiltshire Downs
Grades: ETC 3 Diamond
Tel: **01672 512771** Mrs Harrison.
D: £18.00-£18.00
S: £20.00-£20.00.
Open: All Year (not Xmas)
Beds: 1F 1D 1T **Baths:** 1 Sh
🛏 (6) 🅿 (2) 🐾 🏢 👜 🖊 🚲

Beam End, *67 George Lane,*
Marlborough, Wilts, SN8 4BY.
Comfortable detached house within
easy walking distance of historic
town
Tel: **01672 515048** (also fax no)
Mrs Drew.
D: £20.00-£27.50
S: £20.00-£20.00.
Open: All Year (not Xmas)
Beds: 1T 2S
Baths: 1 En 1 Sh
🅿 (3) 🖊 ☐ 👜 🏢 👜 🚲

Redlands, *Elcot Lane,*
Marlborough, Wilts, SN8 2BA.
Warm welcome, rural views,
excellent food
Tel: **01672 515477**
Mrs Camm.
Fax no: 01672 516523
D: £17.50 **S:** £25.00.
Open: Easter to Nov
Beds: 2D 1T
Baths: 1 En 1 Sh
🛏 🅿 (4) 🖊 ☐ 👜 🏢 👜

Winterbourne Monkton 28

National Grid Ref: SU1072

The New Inn, *Winterbourne*
Monkton, Swindon, Wilts, SN4 9NW.
Traditional country inn
Tel: **01672 539240**
D: £22.50 **S:** £28.00.
Open: All Year
Beds: 2D 3T
Baths: 5 Pr
🛏 🅿 (25) 🗙 👜 🏢 👜 👜 🖊

🚐 sign means that,
given due notice,
owners will pick you
up from the path
and drop you off
within reason.

All rooms full and
nowhere else to stay?
Ask the owner if
there's anywhere
nearby

Uffcott 29

National Grid Ref: SU1278

🍴 🍺 The Crown

Uffcott House, *Uffcott, Swindon,*
Wilts, SN4 9NB.
Actual grid ref: SU126775
Attractive Georgian farmhouse,
large interesting garden, wonderful
views, near Ridgeway
Tel: **01793 731207** (also fax no)
Mr & Mrs Hussey.
D: £24.00-£24.00.
S: £26.00-£26.00.
Open: All Year (not Xmas)
Beds: 1D 1T
Baths: 1 En 1 Pr
🛏 (8) 🅿 (4) 🖊 ☐ 👜 🏢 👜 🖊 🚲

Broad Town 30

National Grid Ref: SU0977

🍴 🍺 The Crown

Little Cotmarsh Farm, *Broad*
Town, Wootton Bassett, Swindon,
Wilts, SN4 7RA.
Actual grid ref: SU0979
Easy reach of M4 J16. Superb
accommodation in peaceful hamlet
Tel: **01793 731322**
Mrs Richards.
D: £20.00-£22.00.
S: £20.00-£23.00.
Open: All Year (not Xmas)
Beds: 1F 1D 1T
Baths: 2 En 1 Pr
🛏 🅿 (6) 🖊 ☐ 👜 🏢 👜 🖊

Brinkworth 31

National Grid Ref: SU0184

🍴 🍺 Three Crowns

B's B&B, *Bella Pais, Barnes*
Green, Brinkworth, Chippenham,
Wilts, SN15 5AG.
Actual grid ref: SU014843
Comfortable friendly village house
on edge of Cotswolds. 10 mins M4
Tel: **01666 510204**
Mrs Bennett.
Fax no: 01666 510520
D: £17.00
S: £17.00.
Open: All Year (not Xmas)
Beds: 1F 1D 1S
Baths: 1 Sh
🛏 🅿 (4) 🖊 ☐ 🐾 🗙 👜 🏢 👜 👜

Amesbury to Malmesbury

The cycleway now heads
north up the east side of
Salisbury Plain, through the
Vale of Pewsey, back across
the Kennet and Avon Canal
and into the Marlborough
Downs. **Marlborough** has the
widest high street in England,
with a fine display of
Georgian buildings and
half-timbered cottages. Back
up into the Downs, and a
worthwhile detour would be
south along **the Ridgeway**
National Trail to Avebury,
another important prehistoric
site. Here stands a stone
circle far wider than
Stonehenge, though the
stones are much smaller and
not so consummately
finished. Nearby are Silbury
Hill, Europe's largest
man-made prehistoric
mound, and West Kennet
Long Barrow, a burial
complex dating from the
fourth millennium BC. This is
probably best attempted only
on an all terrain bicycle.
Close to the junction of the
cycleway with the Ridgeway
is **Hackpen Hill**, where you
will find another white horse
hillside carving and a
panoramic viewpoint over
Swindon to the Thames
Valley. From here it's off the
Downs into the final stretch to
Malmesbury.

Charlton (Malmesbury) 32

National Grid Ref: ST9588

Stonehill Farm, *Charlton,*
Malmesbury, Wilts, SN16 9DY.
550-year-old farmhouse on dairy
farm, warm welcome, delicious
breakfasts
Tel: **01666 823310** (also fax no)
Mr & Mrs Edwards.
D: £20.00-£25.00
S: £20.00-£25.00.
Open: All Year
Beds: 2D 1T
Baths: 1 En 1 Sh
🛏 🅿 (3) ☐ 🐾 👜 🏢 👜 🖊

Yorkshire Dales Cycleway

The Yorkshire Dales National Park, the heart of the Pennines, is one of England's most beautiful areas, with rolling moors forming the backdrop to gentle river valleys. The **Yorkshire Dales Cycleway** is a 131-mile tour of the Dales, starting and finishing at Skipton. The route is directed along quiet roads, but some sections are very up-and-down, so a reasonably resilient bike (and cyclist!) is necessary. The cycleway is signposted by rectangular blue direction signs with a cycle silhouette.

A detailed **guide** to the cycleway route (6 route cards), which includes a list of cycle repair/hire shops on or near to the route, is available from the Yorkshire Dales National Park Authority, Cragg Hill Road, Horton-in-Ribblesdale, Settle, North Yorkshire BD24 0HN, tel 01729 860481, @ £2.25 (+£2.00 p&p).

Maps: Ordnance Survey 1:50,000 Landranger series: 98, 99, 103, 104

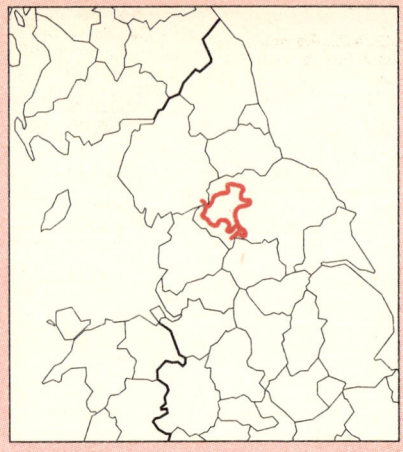

Trains: Skipton, Settle & Dent are served by the famous scenic Leeds-Settle-Carlisle Railway.

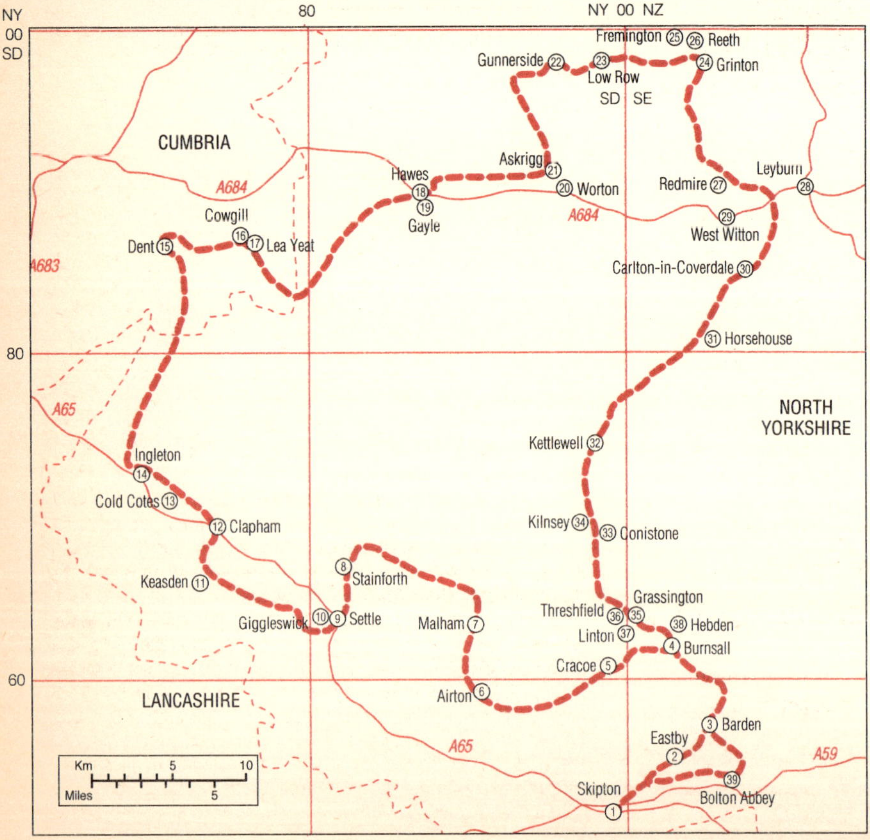

Skipton 1

National Grid Ref: SD9851

🏨🍺 Craven Heifer, The Sailor, The Fleece, Elm Tree, Slaters' Arms

Low Skibeden Farmhouse, *Skibeden Road, Skipton, N. Yorks, BD23 6AB.*
Actual grid ref: SE012524
C16th farmhouse with little luxuries and fireside treats at no extra charge
Grades: AA 3 Diamond
Tel: **01756 793849**
Mrs Simpson.
Fax no: 01756 793804
D: £18.00-£22.00 **S:** £25.00-£38.00.
Open: All Year
Beds: 3F 1D 1T
Baths: 4 En 1 Sh
🛏 (12) 🅿 (5) ⚡🍴🛁🖤📺♿

Dalesgate Lodge, *69 Gargrave Road, Skipton, N. Yorks, BD23 1QN.*
Comfortable cosy rooms, warm friendly welcome. Perfect base touring/walking
Grades: ETC 4 Diamond
Tel: **01756 790672**
Mr & Mrs Mason.
D: £17.50-£20.00 **S:** £20.00-£25.00.
Open: All Year
Beds: 2D/T 2S
Baths: 4 En
🛏 🅿 (2) ⚡🍴🛁🖤📺♿

The Barn, *Main Street, Skipton, BD23 4ND.*
Tel: **01729 840426** Mrs Fleming.
D: £19.00-£21.50 **S:** £22.50-£25.00.
Open: All Year (not Xmas)
Beds: 1F 1D
Baths: 1 En 1 Sh
🛏 🅿 (5) ⚡🍴🛁🖤📺♿
Yorkshire Dales - Long Preston situated on the A65 Keighley to Kendal road. The Barn, converted in 1985, is the family home of Elaine & Michael Fleming. It is within easy access of the Lake District and walking in the Dales

Craven Heifer Inn, *Grassington Road, Skipton, BD23 3LA.*
Country inn set at the gateway to the Yorkshire Dales
Grades: ETC 3 Diamond
Tel: **01756 792521**
Smith.
Fax no: 01756 794442
D: £22.50 **S:** £44.95.
Open: All Year
Beds: 2F 13D 3T 1S
Baths: 16 En 3 Sh
🛏 🅿 (99) ⚡🍴🛁🖤📺♿

Pay B&Bs by cash or cheque and be prepared to pay up front.

Eastby 2

National Grid Ref: SE0154
The Masons Arms, *Eastby, Skipton, N Yorks, BD23 6SN.*
400-year-old Dales pub, real ales and home-cooked food
Tel: **01756 792754**
D: £20.00-£25.00 **S:** £20.00-£25.00.
Open: All Year
Beds: 1D 1T
🛏 🅿 (30) ⚡🍴🛁🖤📺♿

Barden 3

National Grid Ref: SE0557

Little Gate Farm, *Drebley, Barden, Skipton, N Yorks, BD23 6AU.*
Tel: **01756 720200**
D: £19.00-£19.00 **S:** £19.00-£19.00.
Open: Easter to Nov
Beds: 1F 1D 1T
Baths: 1 Pr 1 Sh
🛏 🅿 ⚡🍴🛁🖤📺♿
Beautiful Grade I Listed C15th Dales farmhouse; all rooms look down the valley to the River Wharfe. We are a working sheep-rearing farm, breeding our own collies

---

D = Price range per person sharing in a double room

S = Price range for a single person in a room

Howgill Lodge, *Barden (Skipton), Skipton, N. Yorks, BD23 6DJ.*
Actual grid ref: SE065593
Uninterrupted views over beautiful wharfedale. Once experienced, you will return
Tel: **01756 720655**
Mrs Foster.
D: £27.00-£30.00 **S:** £32.00-£35.00.
Open: All Year (not Xmas)
Beds: 1F 2D 1T
Baths: 4 En
🛏 🅿 (10) 🍴🛁🖤📺♿

Burnsall 4

National Grid Ref: SE0361

🏨🍺 The Fountain

Holly Tree Farm, *Thorpe, Burnsall, Skipton, N. Yorks, BD23 6BJ.*
Actual grid ref: SE014617
Quiet, homely Dales sheep farm
Tel: **01756 720604**
Mrs Hall.
D: £18.00-£20.00 **S:** £18.00-£20.00.
Open: All Year (not Xmas)
Beds: 1D 1S
Baths: 1 Sh
🛏 (5) 🅿 (2) ⚡🍴🛁📺♿

Skipton to Ingleton

Skipton, one of the important market towns of the region, traces its roots to an ancient Anglo-Saxon settlement - its name means 'sheep farm'. Skipton Castle is one of the best-preserved medieval castles in Britain; at the centre stands a single yew tree planted in 1659. Also here are Holy Trinity Church, notable for the fifteenth-century bossed roof, and a museum of Craven, the North Yorkshire district in which the town lies. Out of Skipton the route heads northeast into **Wharfedale**. Here you will find the fifteenth-century Barden Tower, looking out across Barden Moor, before heading on to **Appletreewick** and the picturesque village of **Burnsall**. Then it's west through the beautiful limestone scenery of the Southern Dales into **Malhamdale**, where stand Malham Cove, a breathtaking 300-foot-high limestone natural amphitheatre, and the deep ravine of Gordale Scar. Close by you can find Janet's Foss, a waterfall with overhanging trees. The route passes to the south of **Malham Tarn**, an upland lake with a nature reserve protecting many species of waterfowl, and takes you westwards around the imposing mass of **Fountains Fell** and into **Ribblesdale**. Here you cycle south alongside the famous Leeds-Settle-Carlisle Railway line, through the typically pretty Dales villages of Stainforth and Langcliffe into **Settle**. From here it's northwest to **Clapham**, continuing to Ingleton with **Ingleborough**, one of the so-called Three Peaks, on your right: remains of a Celtic settlement can be found at the gritstone summit by anyone wishing to take time out and make the climb.

Burnsall Manor House Hotel,
Burnsall, Skipton, N. Yorks,
BD23 6BW.
Comfortable, friendly, relaxed.
Good food, ideal base for walking
Tel: **01756 720231** (also fax no)
Mr Lodge.
D: £24.50-£28.50 **S:** £24.50-£28.50.
Open: All Year
Beds: 5D 3T
Baths: 5 En 1 Pr 2 Sh
🛇 🄿 (9) ⚲ 🗆 🕇 ✕ 🎗 🞕 Ⅵ 🛈

Red Lion Hotel, *Burnsall, Skipton,*
N. Yorks, BD23 6BU.
Actual grid ref: SE033612
C16th Ferryman's inn on River
Wharfe overlooking fell & village
green
Tel: **01756 720204**
Mrs Grayshon.
Fax no: 01756 720292
D: £32.00 **S:** £32.00.
Open: All Year
Beds: 2F 4D 4T 1S
Baths: 12 En
🛇 🄿 (40) 🗆 ✕ 🎗 🞕 Ⅵ 🛈 ✦

Cracoe 5

National Grid Ref: SD9860

🍴 🍺 The Devonshire

Langerton Farm, *Cracoe To*
Thorpe Lane, Cracoe, Thorpe,
Skipton, N Yorks, BD23 5HN.
Comfortable accommodation on
working farm. 1 mile from Cracoe
Village
Tel: **01756 730260** Mrs Sutcliffe.
D: £18.00 **S:** £20.00
Open: Easter to Xmas
Beds: 1F 1D 1S
Baths: 1 En
🛇 🄿 🕇 🎗 Ⅵ 🛈 ⚵

Airton 6

National Grid Ref: SD9059

▲ **Airton Quaker Hostel**
(Independent), *Airton, Skipton,*
North Yorkshire, BD23 4AE.
Actual grid ref: SD904592
Tel: **01729 830263**
Adults: £5.00
self-catering facilities

Malham 7

National Grid Ref: SD9062

🍴 🍺 Listers Arms, Buck Hotel

▲ **Malham Youth Hostel,** *John*
Dower Memorial Hostel, Malham,
Skipton, North Yorkshire, BD23 4DE.
Actual grid ref: SD901629
Tel: **01729 830321**
Under 18: £6.85
Adults: £10.15
evening meal at 7.00pm, family
bunk rooms, television, showers,
shop
Superbly located purpose-built
hostel close to centre of pic-
turesque Malham village

Miresfield Farm, *Malham,*
Skipton, N. Yorks, BD23 4DA.
Listed farmhouse in landscaped
garden. Two well-furnished
lounges. Log fires
Tel: **01729 830414** Mrs Sharp.
D: £22.00 **S:** £30.00.
Open: All Year
Beds: 2F 6D 6T 1S
Baths: 12 En 1 Pr
🛇 🄿 🗆 🕇 ✕ 🎗 🞕 ♿ Ⅵ 🛈 ✦

Stainforth 8

National Grid Ref: SD8267

▲ **Stainforth Youth Hostel,**
Taitlands, Stainforth, Settle, North
Yorkshire, BD24 9PA.
Actual grid ref: SD821668
Tel: **01729 823577**
Under 18: £5.65 **Adults:** £8.35
evening meal at 7.00pm, family
bunk rooms, television, showers,
shop
Victorian Listed building with fine
interior, set in extensive grounds
with grazing paddock. Discount
taxi service to/from Horton
available

▲ **Hornby Laithe Bunkhouse**
Barn (Independent), *Husbands*
Barn, Stainforth, Settle, North
Yorkshire, BD24 9PB.
Actual grid ref: SD822674
Tel: **01729 822240 / 825751**
Adults: £7.50
evening meals available, self-cater-
ing facilities

Settle 9

National Grid Ref: SD8163

🍴 🍺 Golden Lion, the Crown

Liverpool House, *Chapel Square,*
Settle, N. Yorks, BD24 9HR.
Actual grid ref: SD822635
Situated in quiet area yet within 3
mins' walk town square
Grades: AA 3 Diamond
Tel: **01729 822247** Mrs Duerden.
D: £18.00-£22.00 **S:** £18.00-£20.00.
Open: All Year
Beds: 4D 1T 2S **Baths:** 2 En 2 Sh
🛇 🄿 (8) ⚲ 🗆 🎗 🞕 Ⅵ 🛈 ✦ ⚵

**The Grid Reference
beneath the location
heading is for the
village or town - *not*
for individual houses,
which are shown
(where supplied) in
each entry itself.**

**Pay B&Bs by
cash or cheque and
be prepared to
pay up front.**

The Oast Guest House, *5*
Penyghent View, Church Street,
Settle, N. Yorks, BD24 9JJ.
Grades: AA 3 Diamond,
RAC 3 Diamond
Tel: **01729 822989** (also fax no)
Mr & Mrs King.
D: £18.50-£23.00 **S:** £15.50-£17.50
Open: All Year
Beds: 1F 2D 2T 1S
Baths: 3 En 3 Sh
🛇 🄿 (4) ⚲ 🗆 ✕ 🎗 🞕 Ⅵ 🛈 ✦
High standards with a Yorkshire
welcome await you. Margaret and
Tony King have been welcoming
people for 11 years, helping to
make their stay as comfortable and
enjoyable as they can

The Knoll, *Settle, BD24 0HD.*
Unique residence, large grounds,
foot of Pen y Ghent, centre of
village
Tel: **01729 860283** (also fax no)
Ireton.
D: £18.00-£20.00.
Open: All Year
Beds: 1F 1D 1T
Baths: 1 Sh
🄿 (6) ⚲ 🗆 🎗 🞕 Ⅵ 🛈 ✦ ⚵

Giggleswick 10

National Grid Ref: SD8164

🍴 🍺 Black Horse, Hart's Head

Yorkshire Dales Field Centre,
Holme Beck, Raines Road,
Giggleswick, Settle, N. Yorks,
BD24 0AQ.
Actual grid ref: SD813641
Excellent cooking - comfortable
well-appointed converted barn
within tasting distance of 2 pubs -
longer stay, groups of 12 plus
people only
Tel: **01729 824180** (also fax no)
Mrs Barbour.
D: £10.50-£10.50 **S:** £10.50-£10.50.
Open: All Year
Beds: 6F 2S **Baths:** 5 Sh
🛇 🄿 (7) ⚲ 🗆 🕇 ✕ 🎗 🞕 Ⅵ 🛈 ✦

Woodlands, *The Mains,*
Giggleswick, Settle, N. Yorks,
BD24 0AX.
Edwardian country house with
superb views. Comfortable and
friendly accommodation
Tel: **01729 822058** (also fax no)
Mr & Mrs Lewton.
D: £16.00 **S:** £18.00.
Open: All Year (not Xmas)
Beds: 1F 1T 2D 2S
Baths: 3 En 3 Pr
🛇 🄿 (8) 🗆 🕇 ✕ 🎗 🞕 ♿ Ⅵ 🛈 ✦ ⚵

Keasden 11

National Grid Ref: SD7266

Lythe Birks, Keasden, Lancaster, LA2 8EZ.
Converted barn in its own grounds overlooking three peaks
Grades: ETC 3 Diamond
Tel: 015242 51688 Mrs Phinn.
D: £19.50-£19.50 **S:** £25.00-£25.00.
Open: All Year
Beds: 2D 1T
⛺ �ⓟ ⊁ 🛏 🐕 ✕ 🛗 🏠 Ⓥ 🌢 ⚡ ⚗ 🚲

Clapham 12

National Grid Ref: SD7469

Flying Horseshoe Hotel, Clapham, Lancaster, LA2 8ES.
Actual grid ref: SD733678
Friendly and family run. Great food and drink. Free fishing
Grades: ETC 2 Diamond
Tel: 015242 51229 (also fax no)
Mr & Mrs Perrow.
D: £20.00-£25.00 **S:** £27.50-£32.50.
Open: All Year
Beds: 3F 3D 1T
⛺ ⓟ (50) 🛏 🐕 🛗 🏠 Ⓥ 🌢

Arbutus House, Riverside, Clapham, Lancaster, LA2 8DS.
Situated in heart of village, overlooking river. Excellent food and parking
Grades: ETC 4 Diamond, AA 4 Diamond
Tel: 015242 51240 (also fax no)
Mrs Cass.
D: £20.00-£24.50 **S:** £20.00-£24.50.
Open: All Year
Beds: 2F 1D 2T 1S
Baths: 5 En 1 Pr
⛺ ⓟ (6) ⊁ 🛏 🐕 ✕ 🛗 🏠 Ⓥ 🌢 ⚡ 🚲

Cold Cotes 13

National Grid Ref: SD7171

📧 ⌨ Gap Inn

Moor View, Cold Cotes, Clapham, Lancaster, LA2 8HS.
Beautiful detached house, peaceful, comfortable, wonderful views and great breakfast
Tel: 015242 42085
Mrs Lupton.
D: £18.00-£20.00 **S:** £20.00-£24.00.
Open: All Year (not Xmas)
Beds: 2D 1T
Baths: 2 En 1 Sh
⛺ (1) ⓟ (3) 🛏 🐕 🛗 🏠 Ⓥ 🌢 ⚗ 🚲

All cycleways are
popular: you are well-
advised to book ahead

Ingleton 14

National Grid Ref: SD6973

📧 ⌨ Bridge Hotel, Craven Heifer, Marton Arms, Wheatsheaf Hotel

▲ *Ingleton Youth Hostel, Greta Tower, Sammy Lane, Ingleton, Carnforth, Lancashire, LA6 3EG.*
Actual grid ref: SD695733
Tel: 015242 41444
Under 18: £5.65 **Adults:** £8.35
evening meal at 7.00pm, self-catering facilities, showers
In a location ideal for families, adjacent to the National Park and with an outdoor swimming pool nearby, the hostel is also popular with walkers and a centre for climbing, caving and exploring the Dales

▲ *Barnstead Bunkhouse Barn (Independent), Stacksteads Farm, Ingleton, Carnforth, Lancashire, LA6 3HS.*
Actual grid ref: SD686724
Tel: 015242 41386 Adults: £8.00
suitable for disabled people, self-catering facilities

D = Price range per person
sharing in a double room

▲ *Timberlodge Bunkhouse (Independent), Pinecroft, Ingleton, Carnforth, Lancashire, LA6 3DP.*
Actual grid ref: SD699719
Tel: 015242 41462 Adults: £7.00
suitable for disabled people, self-catering facilities, showers

Ingleborough View Guest House, Main Street, Ingleton, Carnforth, Lancashire, LA6 3HH.
Lovely Victorian house with picturesque riverside location. excellent accommodation and food
Grades: ETC 3 Diamond
Tel: 015242 41523 Mrs Brown.
D: £19.00-£20.00 **S:** £25.00-£28.00.
Open: All Year (not Xmas)
Beds: 1F 2D 1T **Baths:** 2 En 2 Pr
⛺ ⓟ (6) 🛏 🐕 🛗 🏠 Ⓥ 🌢 🚲

Springfield Hotel, Ingleton, Carnforth, Lancs, LA6 3HJ.
Grades: ETC 3 Diamond, AA 3 Diamond, RAC 3 Diamond, Sparkling
Tel: 015242 41280 (also fax no)
Mr Thornton.
D: £23.00-£23.00 **S:** £23.00-£25.00.
Open: All Year (not Xmas)
Beds: 1F 3D 1T **Baths:** 5 En 1 Pr
⛺ ⓟ (12) ⊁ 🛏 🐕 ✕ 🛗 🏠 Ⓥ 🌢 ⚡ ⚗ 🚲
Detached Victorian villa; large garden at rear running down to river. Great patio, small pond & waterfall. Front garden with fountain & conservatory.

Ingleton to Redmire

From Ingleton you head north through **Kingsdale**, and cross into Cumbria with **Whernside**, another of the Three Peaks, towering to your right and **Gragareth** to the left - you are now in **Deepdale**, one of the most scenic parts of the cycleway. Deepdale leads into **Dentdale**, which shelters the picturesque village of **Dent**, with its cobbled streets. From Dent it's east to **Cowgill** and then across the Leeds-Settle-Carlisle Railway line and back into North Yorkshire. Here you cycle northeast through **Widdale**, with Widdale Fell on the left, to **Hawes**, the main market town of **Wensleydale**, renowned for its eponymous cheese. Worth a visit here is the Dales Countryside Museum, tracing the history of many local industries. There is also a National Park Information Centre. A little to the north of the town is Hardaw Force, the highest above-ground single-drop waterfall in England, and further along the same detour you can find the Buttertubs, a striking group of natural wells. From Hawes you head east through Wensleydale along the banks of the River Ure to **Askrigg**, and then north, climbing steeply across the heather moorland of Askrigg Common, before descending into **Swaledale**, one of the most idyllically beautiful (famous for its distinctive breed of sheep). This rugged landscape, marked by the famous Dales dry stone walls, forms the backdrop for a string of pretty villages before you head south at **Grinton**, climbing over Grinton Moor and then descending back into Wensleydale at the village of **Redmire**. Close to here stands Bolton Castle, dating from 1379, where Mary, Queen of Scots was imprisoned in the late sixteenth century.

Riverside Lodge, *24 Main Street, Ingleton, Carnforth,* LA6 3HJ.
Grades: ETC 3 Diamond, AA 3 Diamond
Tel: 015242 41359
Mr & Mrs Camacho.
D: £20.00-£25.00 **S:** £25.00-£32.00.
Open: All Year (not Xmas)
Beds: 7D 1T
Baths: 8 En
🛇 ⚲ 🗆 🕭 🐾 ♿ 🏢 & Ⅴ ⋕ ⚲ 🚲
A fine Victorian house in large attractive gardens, with private river frontage, fully modernised. All rooms ensuite, wonderful views in all directions. Conservatory, residents' lounge, games room, sauna. An excellent base for touring & walking in the Dales and Lakes

Nutstile Farm, *Ingleton, Carnforth, Lancs,* LA6 3DT.
Rooms with views, dales, lakes, Settle-Carlisle Railway, all easy access
Tel: 015242 41752 Mrs Brennand.
D: £17.00-£19.00 **S:** £17.00.
Open: All Year
Beds: 1F 2D 1T
Baths: 1 En 1 Sh
🛇 🅿 (3) 🗆 🕭 🏢 Ⅴ 🛈

Bridge End Guest House, *Mill Lane, Ingleton, Carnforth, Lancs,* LA6 3EP.
Former mill owner's house, pleasantly situated, adjacent to the waterfalls walk
Grades: ETC 3 Diamond
Tel: 015242 41413
Garner.
D: £19.50-£22.00
S: £23.00-£25.00
Open: All Year
Beds: 1F 1D 1T
Baths: 3 En
🛇 (8) 🅿 (8) 🗆 🗙 🏢 Ⅴ 🛈 ⋕ 🚲

Thorngarth House, *Ingleton, Carnforth,* LA6 3HN.
Country house surrounded by green fields. Wonderful food, open fires
Tel: 015242 41295 (also fax no)
Mr Bradley.
D: £22.00-£35.00
S: £22.00-£35.00.
Open: All Year
Beds: 4D 1T
Baths: 4 En 1 Pr
🅿 (5) ⚲ 🗆 🗙 🏢 Ⅴ 🛈 ⋕ 🚲

All rooms full and nowhere else to stay? Ask the owner if there's anywhere nearby

Always telephone to get directions to the B&B - you will save time!

Langber Country Guest House, *Tattenhorne Road, Ingleton, Carnforth, Lancs,* LA6 3DT.
Detached residence, atop hill - panoramic views. Central Dales, Lakes, coast
Tel: 015242 41587
Mrs Bell.
D: £16.50 **S:** £17.50.
Open: All Year (not Xmas)
Beds: 2F 2D 2T 1S
Baths: 3 Pr 1 Sh
🛇 🅿 (6) 🗆 🕭 🗙 🏢 🛈 ⋕

Dent   15

National Grid Ref: SD7086

🍴 🍺 George & Dragon, Sun Inn, Sportsmans Inn

Rash House, *Dent Foot, Dent, Sedbergh, Cumbria,* LA10 5SU.
Actual grid ref: SD6690
C18th farmhouse situated in picturesque Dentdale
Tel: 015396 20113 (also fax no)
Mrs Hunter.
D: £16.00-£18.00
S: £18.00-£20.00.
Open: All Year (not Xmas)
Beds: 1F 1D
Baths: 1 Sh
🛇 🅿 (2) 🗆 🕭 🗙 🏢 Ⅴ ⋕

Dent Stores, *Dent, Sedbergh, Cumbria,* LA10 5QL.
Village centre, friendly family house. Hearty breakfasts, walking information available
Tel: 015396 25209 Mrs Smith.
D: £17.00-£17.00 **S:** £17.00-£17.00.
Open: All Year (not Xmas)
Beds: 2D 1T 1S
Baths: 1 Sh
🛇 🅿 (2) 🗆 🕭 🏢 Ⅴ 🛈 ⋕ 🚲

Syke Fold, *Dent, Sedbergh, Cumbria,* LA10 5RE.
Actual grid ref: SD726859
Grades: ETC 4 Diamond
Tel: 015396 25486 Mrs Newsham.
D: £21.50-£23.00 **S:** £21.50-£23.00.
Open: Feb to Nov
Beds: 1F 1D
Baths: 2 En
🛇 🅿 (2) ⚲ 🗆 🕭 🐾 🗙 🛈 ⋕ 🚲
Peaceful country hose with stunning views. Quiet location 1.5 miles east of quaint cobbled village of Dent. Spacious, well-appointed ensuite rooms, large elegant lounge with woodburning stove, home-cooked meals using fresh home-grown produce when available

The White House, *Dent, Sedbergh, Cumbria,* LA10 5QR.
House in picturesque Dales village. Quiet location, garden, superb walking
Grades: ETC 3 Diamond
Tel: 015396 25041 Mrs Allen.
D: £17.00-£18.00 **S:** £17.00-£18.00.
Open: Easter to Oct
Beds: 1D 1T 1S
Baths: 2 Sh
🅿 (2) ⚲ 🗆 🕭 🏢 Ⅴ ⋕ 🚲

Smithy Fold, *Whernside Manor, Dent, Sedbergh, Cumbria,* LA10 5RE.
Actual grid ref: SD725859
Small C18th country house
Grades: ETC 3 Diamond
Tel: 015396 25368 Mrs Cheetham.
D: £17.50-£17.50 **S:** £17.50-£17.50.
Open: All Year (not Xmas)
Beds: 1F 1D 1T
Baths: 1 Sh
🛇 (4) 🅿 (6) 🗆 🕭 🗙 🏢 Ⅴ 🛈 ⋕ 🚲

Stone Close Tea Shop, *Main Street, Dent, Sedbergh, Cumbria,* LA10 5QL.
Actual grid ref: SD705868
C17th oak beamed tea shop with log fires
Grades: ETC 3 Diamond
Tel: 015396 25231 Mr Rushton.
D: £17.00-£25.00 **S:** £19.50-£49.00.
Open: Feb to Dec
Beds: 1F 2D 1S
Baths: 1 En 1 Sh
🛇 🅿 (4) ⚲ 🗆 🕭 🐾 🗙 🏢 Ⅴ 🛈 ⋕ 🚲

Little Oak, *Helmside View, Dent, Sedbergh, Cumbria,* LA10 5QY.
Oak-beamed studio for two, warm welcome, pretty, unspoilt village
Tel: 015396 25330
Mr & Mrs Priestley.
D: £18.00-£18.00 **S:** £18.00.
Open: All Year (not Xmas)
Beds: 1D
⚲ 🗆 🕭 Ⅴ 🚲

Cowgill   16

National Grid Ref: SD7587

🍴 🍺 George & Dragon

Scow Cottage, *Cowgill, Dent, Sedbergh, Cumbria,* LA10 5RN.
Actual grid ref: SD774853
Grades: ETC 3 Diamond
Tel: 015396 25445 Mrs Ferguson.
D: £16.00-£17.00 **S:** £19.00-£25.00.
Open: All Year
Beds: 1D 1T
Baths: 1 Sh
🛇 (12) 🅿 (4) 🗙 🕭 🗙 🏢 🛈 ⋕
Attractive and comfortable 250-year-old Dales farmhouse, set in beautiful countryside

D = Price range per person sharing in a double room

Lea Yeat 17

National Grid Ref: SD7686

🅼🄲 Sportsmans Inn

*River View, Lea Yeat, Cowgill,
Sedbergh, Cumbria, LA10 5RF.*
Actual grid ref: SD761869
Converted Quaker meeting house
offering every comfort. Run by
walkers
Tel: **015396 25592**
Mr & Mrs Playfoot.
D: £17.50-£21.00 **S:** £15.00-£21.00.
Open: All Year (not Xmas)
Beds: 1D 1T
Baths: 1 Pr 1 Sh
🅱 (12) 🅿 (2) ⚲☐✗◻🛏♨Ⅵ🅰⚡🚲

Hawes 18

National Grid Ref: SD8789

🅼🄲 White Hart, Herriot's Hotel, Board Hotel,
Fountain Hotel

▲ *Hawes Youth Hostel,*
*Lancaster Terrace, Hawes, North
Yorkshire, DL8 3LQ.*
Actual grid ref: SD867897
Tel: **01969 667368**
Under 18: £6.20 **Adults:** £9.15
evening meal at 7.00pm, family
bunk rooms, television, games
room, showers, shop, no smoking
*Friendly and attractively
refurbished purpose-built hostel
overlooking Hawes and
Wensleydale beyond*

Steppe Haugh Guest House,
Townhead, Hawes, N. Yorks,
DL8 3RH.
Actual grid ref: SD869898
C17th house offering a wealth of
character and atmosphere
Grades: ETC 3 Diamond,
AA 3 Diamond
Tel: **01969 667645** Mrs Grattan.
D: £18.00-£26.00 **S:** £20.00-£23.00.
Open: All Year (not Xmas)
Beds: 3D 1T 1S
Baths: 5 En
🅱 (7) 🅿 (6) ⚲☐🛏♨Ⅵ🅰⚡🚲

*Ebor House, Burtersett Road,
Hawes, N. Yorks, DL8 3NT.*
Actual grid ref: SD876897
Family-run friendly and central.
Off road parking and cycle store
Grades: ETC 3 Diamond
Tel: **01969 667337** (also fax no)
Mrs Clark.
D: £17.00-£20.00 **S:** £19.00-£25.00.
Open: All Year (not Xmas)
Beds: 2D 1T **Baths:** 2 En 1 Sh
🅱 🅿 (5) ⚲☐🛏♨Ⅵ🅰⚡🚲

Redmire to Skipton

From Redmire it's east to **Wensley**, which gave the Dale its name, from where anyone interested can make a detour to see the imposing ruins of Middleham Castle, dating from 1170, for a short time the home of Richard III. At Wensley you cross the Ure and begin the climb southwards through **Coverdale**, the meadows at the bottom giving way to windswept fells. A steep descent to the Park Gill Beck stream leads to the village of **Kettlewell**. From here you cycle south through Upper Wharfedale, below Kilnsey Crag, a great limestone overhang, and through Grass Wood, a swathe of ancient woodland which is now an important conservation area, to **Grassington**, a village with a Georgian cobbled central square, on the site of a seventh-century settlement. Here you will find the Upper Wharfedale Museum. Now it's downdale back to Burnsall, and retracing your tyre-tracks to Appletreewick and Barden Tower you go on to **Bolton Abbey**. Here stand the ruins of Bolton Priory, a twelfth-century Augustinian foundation which fell victim to the Dissolution, one of the sites in the North of England painted by Turner and hyperbolised by Ruskin. From here you return to Skipton.

---

*Tarney Fors, Hawes, N. Yorks,
DL8 3LS.*
Grade II Listed ex-farmhouse, now
a comfortable guest house, in
beautiful setting
Grades: ETC 3 Diamond
Tel: **01969 667475** Mrs Harpley.
D: £25.00-£28.00 **S:** £40.00-£45.00.
Open: Easter to Nov
Beds: 3D **Baths:** 2 En 1 Pr
🅱 (7) 🅿 (8) ⚲☐🛏♨Ⅵ🅰⚡🚲

*The Bungalow, Springbank,
Hawes, N. Yorks, DL8 3NW.*
Large bungalow, excellent views,
quiet, off road parking
Grades: ETC 2 Diamond
Tel: **01969 667209** Mrs Garnett.
D: £17.00-£20.00.
Open: Easter to Mar
Beds: 2D 1T **Baths:** 2 En 1 Sh
🅱 (4) 🅿 🛏♨Ⅵ🅰🚲

*Overdales View, Simonstone,
Hawes, N Yorks, DL8 3LY.*
Friendly welcome. Lovely views,
peaceful surroundings, comfortable
beds good food
Tel: **01969 667186** Mrs Sunter.
D: £15.00-£18.00 **S:** £18.00-£24.00.
Open: Easter to Oct
Beds: 1F 1D 1S
Baths: 1 Sh
🅱 (5) ⚲☐🛏♨Ⅵ⚡

*Pry House, Hawes, N. Yorks,
DL8 3LP.*
Actual grid ref: SD8691
Working farm in Herriot country
Tel: **01969 667241** Mrs Fawcett.
D: £15.00.
Open: Easter to Nov
Beds: 1F 2D **Baths:** 1 Sh
🅱 🅿 (3) ⚲☐🛏♨Ⅵ🅰⚡

Gayle 19

*Gayle Laithe, Gayle, Hawes,
N. Yorks, DL8 3RR.*
Modern, comfortable, converted
barn. Ideal for touring, cycling and
walking
Tel: **01969 667397** Mrs McGregor.
D: £16.00-£17.00 **S:** £16.00-£17.00.
Open: Easter to Nov
Beds: 1D 1T 1S
Baths: 1 Sh
🅱 🅿 (2) ☐🛏♨Ⅵ🅰⚡🚲

Worton 20

National Grid Ref: SD9590

🅼🄲 Kings Arms, the Crown, George & Dragon

*Stoney End, Worton, Leyburn,
N. Yorks, DL8 3ET.*
Actual grid ref: SD956901
C17th Grade II Listed barn convert-
ed to a comfortable family home,
full of character
Tel: **01969 650652** Mrs Hague.
Fax no: 01969 650077
D: £23.50.
Open: All Year (not Xmas)
Beds: 1F 1D
Baths: 1 En 1 Pr
🅱 🅿 (5) ⚲☐🛏♨Ⅵ🅰⚡🚲

Bringing children with
you? Always ask for
any special rates.

All rates are subject
to alteration at the
owners' discretion.

Askrigg 21

National Grid Ref: SD9491

🍴🍺 Kings Arms, Crown Inn, George & Dragon, Rose & Crown

Winville Hotel & Restaurant,
Main Street, Askrigg, Leyburn,
N Yorks, DL8 3HG.
C19th Georgian hotel in centre of Herriot village
Grades: ETC 1 Diamond
Tel: **01969 650515**
Mr Buckle.
Fax no: 01969 650594
D: £24.00-£28.50 **S:** £24.00-£38.50.
Open: All Year
Beds: 4F 4D 2T
Baths: 10 En
🛏🅿(18)🗖🍴✕🐾🖳🍴🔟👤

Milton House, *Askrigg, Leyburn,*
N. Yorks, DL8 3HJ.
Lovely comfortable family home situated in beautiful open countryside. Private parking
Tel: **01969 650217**
Mrs Percival.
D: £19.00-£21.00 **S:** £30.00-£38.00.
Open: All Year (not Xmas)
Beds: 3D
Baths: 3 En
🛏(10)🅿(3)✕🗖🐾🖳🍴🔟👤

Carr End House, *Countersett,*
Askrigg, Leyburn, DL8 3DE.
Charming C17th country house. Idyllic situation, warm, comfortable. Excellent food
Grades: ETC 4 Diamond
Tel: **01969 650346**
Mrs Belward.
D: £20.00-£22.00 **S:** £20.00-£22.00.
Open: All Year (not Xmas)
Beds: 1F 2D
Baths: 2 En 1 Pr
🛏🅿(7)✕🗖🐾🖳🍴🔟👤

Lucys House, *Askrigg, Leyburn,*
N. Yorks, DL8 3HT.
Actual grid ref: SD948910
C17th cottage. Lovely views & garden
Grades: ETC 3 Diamond
Tel: **01969 650586**
Mrs Hartley.
D: £18.00-£20.00 **S:** £18.00-£20.00.
Open: All Year (not Xmas)
Beds: 1T 1S
Baths: 1 Pr
✕🗖🐾🖳🍴🔟👤

Whitfield, *Helm, Askrigg, Leyburn,*
N. Yorks, DL8 3JF.
Actual grid ref: SD934916
Tranquil environment with spectacular views. Footpaths to waterfalls and fells
Tel: **01969 650565** (also fax no)
Mrs Empsall.
D: £19.00 **S:** £19.00.
Open: All Year (not Xmas)
Beds: 2T
Baths: 1 En 1 Sh
🛏🅿(2)✕🗖🐾🖳🍴🔟👤

Gunnerside 22

National Grid Ref: SD9598

🍴🍺 Oxnop Hall

Oxnop Hall, *Low Oxnop,*
Gunnerside, Richmond, N. Yorks,
DL11 6JJ.
Oxnop Hall is in an environmentally sensitive area. Stone walls and barns
Grades: ETC 4 Diamond
Tel: **01748 886253**
Mrs Porter.
D: £24.00-£31.00 **S:** £24.00-£34.00.
Open: All Year (not Xmas)
Beds: 1F 3D 1T 1S
Baths: 6 Pr
🛏(7)🅿(6)✕🗖✕🐾🖳🍴👤

Low Row 23

National Grid Ref: SD9897

🍴🍺 Punch Bowl Inn

▲ ***Low Row YHA Camping Barn,***
Low Whita Farm, Low Row,
Richmond, North Yorkshire.
Actual grid ref: SE003983
Tel: **01629 825850 (Northern Regional Office) Adults:** £3.35+
self-catering facilities, showers
Simple barn. Heart of the fantastic Dales. ADVANCE BOOKING ESSENTIAL

▲ ***Punch Bowl Inn & Bunkhouse***
(Independent), Low Row,
Swaledale, Richmond, North Yorkshire, DL11 6PF.
Actual grid ref: SE003983
Tel: **01748 886233**
Under 18: £4.95
Adults: £6.75
evening meals available,
self-catering facilities, showers

Grinton 24

National Grid Ref: SE0498

▲ ***Grinton Lodge Youth Hostel,***
Grinton, Richmond, North Yorkshire, DL11 6HS.
Actual grid ref: SE048975
Tel: **01748 884206**
Under 18: £5.65
Adults: £8.35
evening meal at 7.00pm, family bunk rooms, television, games room, showers, central heating, shop, parking
Originally built as a shooting lodge, high on the moors above Grinton village, with great views of Swaledale & Arkengarthdale

---

All cycleways are
popular: you are well-
advised to book ahead

Fremington 25

National Grid Ref: SE0499

🍴🍺 Bridge Inn, Kings Arms

Broadlands, *Fremington,*
Richmond, DL11 6AW.
Actual grid ref: SE046989
Peaceful village setting 5 mins from Reeth, spectacular views, comfortable accommodation
Tel: **01748 884297** (also fax no)
Mrs Rudez.
D: £17.00-£19.00 **S:** £23.00-£25.00.
Open: All Year
Beds: 1D 1T 1S **Baths:** 1 Sh
🛏(12)🅿(4)✕🗖🐾🖳♿🍴🔟👤

Reeth 26

National Grid Ref: SE0399

🍴🍺 Kings Arms, Black Bull, Buck Hotel

Elder Peak, *Arkengarthdale Road,*
Reeth, Richmond, N Yorks, DL11 6QX.
Actual grid ref: SE036999
Friendly welcome. Good food. Peaceful, beautiful views. Ideal walking, touring
Grades: ETC 2 Diamond
Tel: **01748 884770** Mrs Peacock.
D: £17.00-£17.00 **S:** £17.00-£20.00.
Open: Easter to Oct
Beds: 1D 1T **Baths:** 1 Sh
🛏(5)🅿(2)🗖🐾🖳🍴🔟👤

The Buck Hotel, *Reeth, Richmond,*
DL11 6SW.
Friendly C18th former coaching inn, ideal walking in Yorkshire Dales
Grades: ETC 3 Diamond,
AA 3 Diamond, RAC 3 Diamond
Tel: **01748 884210** Mrs Stillion.
Fax no: 01748 884802
D: £28.00-£35.00 **S:** £29.00-£56.00.
Open: All Year
Beds: 1F 6D 2T 1S
Baths: 10 En
🛏🗖🐾✕🐾🖳🍴🔟👤

Springfield House, *Quaker Close,*
Reeth, Richmond, N. Yorks, DL11 6UY.
Actual grid ref: SE039993
Stone built, beautiful gardens, superb views. Hearty breakfasts, wonderful walks
Tel: **01748 884634** Mrs Guy.
D: £16.00 **S:** £16.00.
Open: All Year (not Xmas)
Beds: 1D 1T 1S **Baths:** 1 Sh
🛏(9)🅿(5)✕🗖🐾🖳🍴👤

King's Arms Hotel, *Reeth,*
Richmond, N Yorks, DL11 6SY.
C18th hotel with spectacular views down the Swale Valley from the inglenook bar & bedrooms
Tel: **01748 884259**
D: £20.00 **S:** £24.50.
Open: All Year
Beds: 1F 2T 8D 1S
Baths: 13 En 5 Sh
🛏🗖🐾✕🐾🖳🍴🔟👤

Redmire 27

National Grid Ref: SE0491

Bolton Arms

Briar House, *Redmire, Leyburn, North Yorkshire, DL8 4EH.*
Actual grid ref: SE046909
Comfortable C18th farmhouse, 'James Herriot' country. Good walking, cycling, touring
Tel: **01969 622335**
Mr & Mrs Patterson.
D: £16.00-£18.00
S: £20.00-£22.00.
Open: All Year
Beds: 1F 1T 2D
Baths: 3 Sh

Leyburn 28

National Grid Ref: SE1190

Blue Lion, Sandpiper Inn, Golden Lion Hotel, Bolton Arms

Secret Garden House, *Grove Square, Leyburn, N. Yorks, DL8 5AE.*
Acre of walled garden. Private parking
Tel: **01969 623589**
Mr Digges.
D: £22.00-£27.50.
S: £23.00-£28.00.
Open: All Year (not Xmas)
Beds: 2D 1T
Baths: 3 En 1 Sh

Walk Mill , *Off Harmby Road, Leyburn, DL8 5HF.*
Warm welcome in our beautiful disused corn mill. Idyllic setting
Grades: ETC 4 Diamond
Tel: **01969 624829**
Mr & Mrs Millin.
D: £20.00-£25.00.
Open: Mar to Oct
Beds: 1D 1T
Baths: 2 En

Clyde House, *5 Railway Street, Leyburn, N. Yorks, DL8 5AY.*
Listed C18th former coaching inn near market square in Leyburn
Tel: **01969 623941** (also fax no)
Mr & Mrs Morris.
D: £18.00 **S:** £23.00.
Open: All Year
Beds: 3D 2T
Baths: 5 En

Grove Hotel, *Grove Square, Leyburn, N. Yorks, DL8 5AE.*
Friendly 'olde worlde' family-run private hotel. Listed building in one of Leyburn's oldest squares
Tel: **01969 622569**
Mr & Mrs Benson.
D: £24.00 **S:** £34.00.
Open: All Year
Beds: 1F 2T 4D
Baths: 7 En

Mary-Jean's Guest House, *Market Place, Leyburn, N. Yorks, DL8 5BJ.*
A stone-built Victorian guest house with beautiful views of Wensleydale
Tel: **01969 623814** (also fax no)
Mr & Mrs Avery-Smith.
D: £20.00 **S:** £25.00.
Open: All Year (not Xmas)
Beds: 1F 2T 2D
Baths: 5 En

West Witton 29

National Grid Ref: SE0688

Ivy Dene Country House, *West Witton, Leyburn, N. Yorks, DL8 4LP.*
Highly recommended C17th licensed country guest house in beautiful Wensleydale, N Yorks
Tel: **01969 622785**
Mr & Mrs Dickinson.
D: £22.00 **S:** £35.00.
Open: All Year (not Xmas)
Beds: 2F 2D 1T
Baths: 5 Pr

Carlton-in-Coverdale 30

National Grid Ref: SE0684

Abbots Thorn, *Carlton-in-Coverdale, Leyburn, N. Yorks, DL8 4AY.*
Grades: ETC 4 Diamond
Tel: **01969 640620**
Mrs Lashmar.
Fax no: 01969 640304
D: £18.00-£25.00 **S:** £18.00-£23.00.
Open: Jan to Dec
Beds: 1F 1D 1T
Baths: 2 En 1 Pr
Relax and unwind at our comfortable traditional Yorkshire Dales home. Oak-beamed guest lounge with open fire on those chilly evenings. Indulge yourself in our fabulous dinners. Superb scenery, terrific touring, wonderful walking. All bedrooms have beautiful views over glorious Coverdale

Horsehouse 31

National Grid Ref: SE0481

Thwaite Arms

The Thwaite Arms, *Horsehouse, Leyburn, N. Yorks, DL8 4TS.*
Traditional unspoilt dales inn set in beautiful, serene Coverdale
Tel: **01969 640206**
Mrs Powell.
D: £19.00-£19.00
S: £19.00-£38.00.
Open: All Year (not Xmas)
Beds: 1D 1T
Baths: 1 Sh

Kettlewell 32

National Grid Ref: SD9772

Queen's Head, Race Horses, King's Head, The Bluebell

▲ **Kettlewell Youth Hostel,** *Whernside House, Kettlewell, Skipton, North Yorkshire, BD23 5QU.*
Actual grid ref: SD970724
Tel: **01756 760232**
Under 18: £6.20 **Adults:** £9.15 evening meal at 7.00pm, family bunk rooms, television, showers, shop, no smoking
Large house right in the middle of pretty Wharfedale village of Kettlewell, ideal for families and small groups

Lynburn, *Kettlewell, Skipton, N. Yorks, BD23 5RF.*
Ideal area for touring or walking in the Dales
Grades: ETC 3 Diamond
Tel: **01756 760803**
Mrs Thornborrow.
D: £19.00-£20.00 **S:** £25.00-£25.00.
Open: Mar to Oct
Beds: 1D 1T
Baths: 1 Sh

Chestnut Cottage, *Kettlewell, Skipton, N. Yorks, BD23 5RL.*
Delightful country cottage. Beautiful gardens, leading down to village stream
Tel: **01756 760804** Mrs Lofthouse.
D: £18.50 **S:** £18.50.
Open: All Year
Beds: 1D 2T
Baths: 2 Sh

Racehorses Hotel, *Kettlewell, Skipton, N. Yorks, BD23 5QZ.*
Riverside location in popular tourist area. Restaurant and bar food. Winter breaks
Tel: **01756 760233**
Mr Barguss.
D: £25.00 **S:** £30.00.
Open: All Year (not Xmas)
Beds: 10D 1T
Baths: 11 En

Conistone 33

National Grid Ref: SD9867

Tennants' Arms

Ebony House, *Conistone, Skipton, N Yorks, BD23 5HS.*
Picturesque, idyllic hamlet 3 miles Grassington. Peace and tranquillity. Superb walks
Tel: **01756 753139**
Mrs Robinson.
D: £20.00-£24.00 **S:** £25.00.
Open: Easter to Oct
Beds: 2D
Baths: 1 En 1 Pr

Kilnsey 34

National Grid Ref: SD9767

🛏️🍺 Tennant Arms

▲ **Confluence Centre (Independent Bunkhouse Barn)**, *Northcote, Kilnsey, Skipton, North Yorkshire, BD23 5PT.*
Actual grid ref: SD973694
Tel: **01756 760336 Adults:** £8.50
evening meals available,
self-catering facilities

▲ **Skirfare Bridge Dales Bunkhouse Barn (Independent)**, *Northcote, Kilnsey, Skipton, North Yorkshire, BD23 5PT.*
Actual grid ref: SD973688
Tel: **01756 752465 Adults:** £7.00
self-catering facilities, central
heating

Skirfare Bridge Dales Barn, C/o Northcote, Kilnsey, Skipton, N. Yorks, BD23 5PT.
Actual grid ref: SD971689
Tel: **01756 752465** (also fax no)
Mrs Foster.
D: £7.00-£7.00 **S:** £7.00-£7.00.
Open: All Year
Beds: 5F 1T
Baths: 3 Sh
🛏️🅿️ (8) ✗ 🏠 📺 ⅋ 🚲
Converted stone barn in beautiful
limestone countryside of upper
Wharfedale, ideally situated for
outdoor activities. Centrally heated.
25 bunk beds, drying room,
kitchen, common room, all
inclusive. Catering by arrangement.
Individuals or school groups.
Off-road parking. No pets

Grassington 35

National Grid Ref: SE0064

🛏️🍺 Black Horse, The Devonshire, Old Hall, Foresters' Arms

Mayfield Bed & Breakfast, Low Mill Lane, Grassington, Skipton, N. Yorks, BD23 5BX.
Actual grid ref: SE000635
Beautiful Dales longhouse. Guest
rooms overlook fells and river
Tel: **01756 753052**
Mr & Mrs Trewartha.
D: £22.00-£25.00 **S:** £25.00-£25.00.
Open: All Year
Beds: 1F 1D 1T
Baths: 1 En 1 Sh
🛏️🅿️ (5) ⅄ ㅏ 🐕 🏠 📺 🛡️ ⅋ 🚲

Town Head Guest House, 1 Low Lane, Grassington, Skipton, N. Yorks, BD23 5AU.
Actual grid ref: SE040799
Friendly guest house at the head of
the village between cobbled streets
and moors
Tel: **01756 752811** Mrs Lister.
D: £23.00-£25.00 **S:** £30.00.
Open: All Year (not Xmas)
Beds: 3D 1T **Baths:** 4 En
🅿️ (3) ⅄ 🛏️ 🐕 🏠 📺

Lythe End, Wood Lane, Grassington, Skipton, N. Yorks, BD23 5DF.
Actual grid ref: SE000647
Modern stone detached house,
stunning views, quiet village
location
Tel: **01756 753196**
Mrs Colley.
D: £20.00-£20.00 **S:** £30.00-£30.00.
Open: All Year (not Xmas)
Beds: 1F 1D
Baths: 1 En 1 Pr
🛏️ (12) 🅿️ (2) ⅄ 🛏️ 🏠 📺 🛡️ ⅋ 🚲

New Laithe House, Wood Lane, Grassington, Skipton, N. Yorks, BD23 5LU.
Tel: **01756 752764**
Mrs Chaney.
D: £21.00-£24.00 **S:** £25.00-£40.00.
Open: All year (not Xmas)
Beds: 1F 4D 2T
Baths: 4 En 1 Pr
🛏️🅿️ (7) ☐ 🐕 🏠 ♿ 📺 🚲
A converted barn situated in the
picturesque village of Grassington.
The rooms have lovely views of the
surrounding countryside. Ideal
retreat for walking and fishing
holidays or visiting the many
historic towns in North and West
Yorkshire.

Springroyd House, 8a Station Road, Grassington, Skipton, N. Yorks, BD23 5NQ.
Actual grid ref: SD980631
Conveniently situated, friendly
family home
Tel: **01756 752473**
Mrs Robertshaw.
D: £18.00-£20.00 **S:** £20.00-£22.00.
Open: All Year
Beds: 1D 2T
Baths: 1 En 2 Sh
🛏️🅿️ (3) ⅄ ☐ 🐕 🏠 📺 🛡️ ⅋ 🚲

Craiglands, 1 Brooklyn, Grassington, Skipton, BD23 5ER.
Elegant Edwardian house offering
quality accommodation and superb
breakfasts
Grades: ETC 4 Diamond
Tel: **01756 752093**
Mrs Wallace.
D: £21.00-£25.00
S: £20.00-£27.00.
Open: All Year (not Xmas)
Beds: 2D 1T 1S
Baths: 3 En 1 Pr
🅿️ (3) ⅄ ☐ 🐕 🏠 📺 ⅋ 🚲

Station House, Threshfield, Grassington, Skipton, North Yorkshire, BD23 5ES.
Actual grid ref: SD995639
'Old' Station Master's house.
Lovely views, easy access to
Grassington
Tel: **01756 752667** Mrs Huss.
D: £17.00 **S:** £17.50.
Open: All Year (not Xmas)
Beds: 1T
Baths: 1 Pr
🅿️ ☐ 🐕 🐕 🏠 📺 ⅋ 🚲

Threshfield 36

National Grid Ref: SD9863

Bridge End Farm, Threshfield, Skipton, N Yorks, BD23 5NH.
Aga cooking, large garden, fishing,
snooker and music rooms
Tel: **01756 752463** Mrs Thompson.
D: £22.00-£26.00 **S:** £23.00-£27.00.
Open: All Year (not Xmas)
Beds: 1F 1D 1T 4S
Baths: 6 En
🛏️🅿️ (8) ⅄ ✗ 🐕 🏠 📺 🛡️ ⅋ 🚲

Linton 37

National Grid Ref: SD9962

▲ **Linton Youth Hostel**, *The Old Rectory, Linton, Skipton, North Yorkshire, BD23 5HH.*
Actual grid ref: SD998627
Tel: **01756 752400**
Under 18: £6.20 **Adults:** £9.15
evening meal at 7.00pm, family
bunk rooms, showers, parking, no
smoking
*C17th former rectory in own
grounds, across the stream from
the village green, in one of
Wharfedale's most picturesque and
unspoilt villages*

Hebden 38

National Grid Ref: SE0263

Court Croft, Church Lane, Hebden, Skipton, BD23 5DX.
Family farmhouse in quiet village
close to the Dales Way
Grades: ETC 2 Diamond
Tel: **01756 753406** Mrs Kitching.
D: £15.00-£17.50 **S:** £15.00-£17.50.
Open: All Year
Beds: 2T
Baths: 1 Sh
🛏️🅿️ (4) ☐ 🐕 🐕 🏠 📺 🛡️ ⅋ 🚲

Bolton Abbey 39

National Grid Ref: SE0753

🛏️🍺 Devonshire Arms

Hesketh Farm Cottage, Bolton Abbey, Skipton, N. Yorks, BD23 6HA.
Delightful farm cottage, 0.75 mile
from village, Priory and river
Tel: **01756 710332** Mrs Heseltine.
D: £15.00-£18.00 **S:** £15.00-£18.00.
Open: All Year (not Xmas)
Beds: 2D 1S
Baths: 1 En 1 Sh
🛏️🅿️ (3) ⅄ ☐ 🐕 🏠 📺 🛡️ ⅋ 🚲

D = Price range per
person sharing in a
double room